Emerging Trends in Computation Intelligence and Disruptive Technologies

(Volume 3)

Demystifying Emerging Trends in Green Technology

Edited By

Pankaj Kumar Mishra
Hi-Tech Institute of Engineering and Technology
Ghaziabad, UP
India

&

Satya Prakash Yadav
School of Computer Science Engineering and Technology
(SCSET)
Bennett University, Greater Noida
U.P., India

Emerging Trends in Computation Intelligence and Disruptive Technologies

(Volume 3)

Demystifying Emerging Trends in Green Technology

Editor: Pankaj Kumar Mishra and Satya Prakash Yadav

ISBN (Online): 978-981-5324-09-9

ISBN (Print): 978-981-5324-10-5

ISBN (Paperback): 978-981-5324-11-2

©2025, Bentham Books imprint.

Published by Bentham Science Publishers Pte. Ltd. Singapore. All Rights Reserved.

First published in 2025.

need for a court order if at any point you breach any terms of this License Agreement. In no event will any delay or failure by Bentham Science Publishers in enforcing your compliance with this License Agreement constitute a waiver of any of its rights.

3. You acknowledge that you have read this License Agreement, and agree to be bound by its terms and conditions. To the extent that any other terms and conditions presented on any website of Bentham Science Publishers conflict with, or are inconsistent with, the terms and conditions set out in this License Agreement, you acknowledge that the terms and conditions set out in this License Agreement shall prevail.

Bentham Science Publishers Pte. Ltd.
80 Robinson Road #02-00
Singapore 068898
Singapore
Email: subscriptions@benthamscience.net

BENTHAM SCIENCE

CONTENTS

PREFACE

This book titled, Emerging Trends in Computational Intelligence and Disruptive Technologies, is revolutionizing the way we approach the ecological footprint of computer networks. Communication systems, and other IT infrastructures are growing due to high energy consumption and greenhouse gas emissions. Addressing these issues and creating a sustainable environment require new energy models, algorithms, methods, platforms, tools, and systems to support next-generation computing and communication infrastructure.

The chapters within this volume serve as portals to diverse domains where these trends intersect, offering insights, analyses, and projections to innovative ideas. Through these contributions, readers will embark on a journey through cutting-edge developments, envisioning a future where computational intelligence and disruptive technologies intertwine to revolutionize the way we live, work, and interact.

In this book, we explore the role of Disruptive Technologies and Computational Intelligence which aims to bring together leading academic scientists, researchers, and research scientists to exchange and share their experiences and research results in various aspects of green technology and energy science. It also provides a major interdisciplinary platform for researchers, practitioners, and educators to present and discuss the latest innovations, trends, and issues in computational intelligence and disruptive technologies, as well as practical challenges and adopted solutions.

This book is a comprehensive guide for anyone interested in learning about the role of emerging trends in computational intelligence and disruptive technologies in various sectors.

Pankaj Kumar Mishra
Hi-Tech Institute of Engineering and Technology
Ghaziabad, UP
India

&

Satya Prakash Yadav
School of Computer Science Engineering and Technology (SCSET)
Bennett University, Greater Noida
U.P., India

List of Contributors

A.K. Jain — Department Electrical Engineering, Hi-Tech Institute of Engineering & Technology, Ghaziabad, (U.P), India

Anubhav Sharma — Computer Science and Engineering, IMS Engineering College, Ghaziabad, India

Ankit Garg — Management Department, Ajay Kumar Garg Institute of Management, Ghaziabad, Uttar Pradesh, India

Ashish Pandey — School of Computer Science & Application, IIMT University, Meerut, Uttar Pradesh, India

Ashish Diwakar — Depatment of Management Studies, Hi-Tech Institute of Engineering and Technology, Ghaziabad, (U.P.), India

Arunima Jaiswal — Department of Computer Science & Engineering, Indira Gandhi Delhi Technical University For Women, India

Aruna Ippili — Department of Computer Science & Engineering, Indira Gandhi Delhi Technical University For Women, India

Ashutosh Saxena — Department of Computer Science and Engineering, ABES Engineering College, Ghaziabad, India

Aditya Garg — Department of Computer Science and Engineering, ABES Engineering College, Ghaziabad, India

Arun Kumar Singh — Greater Noida Institute of Technology Gr Noida-201306, Uttar Pradesh, India

Akhilesh Kumar Singh — School of Computing and Technology, Galgotias University, Greater Noida 201306, Uttar Pradesh, India

Abhishek Anand — Department of Computer Science Engineering Sharda University, Greater Noida, Uttar Pradesh 201310, India

Abhinav Shrivastav — Department of Computer Science Engineering Sharda University, Greater Noida, Uttar Pradesh 201310, India

Arun Kumar Singh — Department of Computer Science and Engineering, Greater Noida Institute of Technology, Greater Noida, 201310, Uttar Pradesh, India

Adarsh Kumar — Hi-Tech Institute of Engineering and Technology, Ghaziabad, Uttar Pradesh, India

Anupam Singh — Department of ECE, HI-Tech Institute of Engineering and Technology, Gzb, UPTU, India

Anuja Gupta — Department of ECE, HI-Tech Institute of Engineering and Technology, Gzb, UPTU, India

Avinash Kumar Sharma — Department of CSE, ABES Institute of Technology, Ghaziabad, Uttar Pradesh, India

Asjad Moiz Khan — Computer Science & Technology, Sharda University, Greater Noida, (U.P.), India

Ayu Kumar Jain — Department of Applied Science & Humanities, Hi-Tech Institute of Engineering & Technology, Ghaziabad, (U.P), India

Aman Shrivastava — Department Electrical Engineering, Hi-Tech Institute of Engineering & Technology, Ghaziabad, (U.P), India

B. Shajahan — School of Computer Science and Engineering, GB Nagar, Uttar Pradesh, India

Bobbin Preet — CSE Department, UIE, Chandigarh University, Mohali-140413, Punjab, India

Bhaskar Sharma — Department Electrical Engineering, Hi-Tech Institute of Engineering & Technology, Ghaziabad, (U.P), India

Deepanshu Singh — Kiet Group of Institutions, Delhi-Ncr, Ghaziabad, Uttar Pradesh 201206, India

Dhruv Verma — Computer Science and Engineering, Hi-Tech Institute of Engineering & Technology, Ghaziabad, U.P, India

Divya G. — Electrical and Electronics Engineering, CVR College of Engineering, Telangana, Hyderabad, India

Gautam Jaiswal — School of Business Management, NOIDA International University, Gr Noida, Uttar Pradesh, India

Gunjan Aggrawal — Department of Computer Science Engineering Sharda University, Greater Noida, Uttar Pradesh 201310, India

Harsh Dev — Department of Computer Science & Engineering, Pranveer Singh Institute of Technology, Kanpur, Uttar Pradesh, India

Himanshu Monga — ECE Department JLN Government Engineering College Sundar Nagar, Mandi, India

Hoshiyar Singh Kanyal — Depatment of Computer Science & Engg., Hi-Tech Institute of Engineering and Technology, Ghaziabad, (U.P), India

Himanshu Kumar — Depatment of Management Studies, Hi-Tech Institute of Engineering and Technology, Ghaziabad, (U.P.), India

Harsh Panwar — Computer Science and Engineering, Hi-Tech Institute of Engineering & Technology, Ghaziabad, U.P, India

Himanshi Mittal — Hi-Tech Institute of Engineering & Technology, Ghaziabad, (U.P), India

Hoor Fatima — Computer Science & Technology, Sharda University, Greater Noida, (U.P.), India

Istakbal Khan — Department of Applied Science & Humanities, Hi-Tech Institute of Engineering & Technology, Ghaziabad, (U.P), India

Jully — Department of Management, Hi-tech Institute of Engineering & Technology, Ghaziabad, India

Jyoti Rai — Depatment of Applied Science and Humanities R.D. Engineering College, Ghaziabad, (U.P.), India

Khushboo Kem — Department of Computer Science & Engineering, Indira Gandhi Delhi Technical University For Women, India

Laxmi Ahuja — AIIT Amity University Noida, Noida, Uttar Pradesh 201313, India

Lydia Nenghoithem Haokip — Department of Computer Science & Engineering, Indira Gandhi Delhi Technical University For Women, India

Manish Aggarwal	Department of Applied Science & Humanities, Hi-Tech Institute of Engineering & Technology, Ghaziabad, (U.P), India
Manish Kumar	Department of Civil Engineering, Greater Noida Institute of Technology, Greater Noida, U.P., India
Meenu Khurana	Chitkara University Institute of Engineering and Technology Chitkara University, Himachal Pradesh, India
Manu Singh	Department of Computer Science and Engineering, ABES Engineering College, Ghaziabad, India
Mahesh Kumar Singh	Dronacharya Group of Institutions, Greater Noida-201306, Uttar Pradesh, India
Mansi Singhal	Department of Management Studies, Hi-Tech Institute of Engineering and Technology, Ghaziabad, (U.P.), India
Mohd. Naushad Ali	Department of Management, Hi-tech Institute of Engineering & Technology, Ghaziabad, India
Manasvi Agarwal	Computer Science and Engineering, Hi-Tech Institute of Engineering & Technology, Ghaziabad, U.P, India
Mansi Jain	Computer Science and Engineering, Hi-Tech Institute of Engineering & Technology, Ghaziabad, U.P, India
Namrata Dhanda	Department of Computer Science & Engineering, Amity University, Uttar Pradesh, India
Neha Kapur	CSE Department, UIE, Chandigarh University, Mohali-140413, Punjab, India
Nitin Sachdeva	IT Department,, Galgotias College of Engineering, Greater Noida, India
Nitin Vera	Computer Science and Engineering, Hi-Tech Institute of Engineering & Technology, Ghaziabad, U.P, India
Omkar Singh Kardam	Hi-Tech Institute of Engineering and Technology, Ghaziabad, Uttar Pradesh, India
Priyanka	Department of Management Studies, Hi-Tech Institute of Engineering and Technology, Ghaziabad, (U.P.), India
Parul Verma	Depatment of Applied Science and Humanities, Ajay Kumar Garg. Engineering College, Ghaziabad, (U.P.), India
Praveen Chandra Jha	Depatment of Applied Science and Humanities, ITS Engineering College, Greater Noida (U.P.), India
Priyansha Singh	Department of CSE, ABES Institute of Technology, Ghaziabad, Uttar Pradesh, India
Pragya Agarwal	Hi-Tech Institute of Engineering and Technology, Ghaziabad, India
Pushpa Choudhary	Galgotias College of Engineering and Technology, Greater Noida-201306, Uttar Pradesh, India
Pushpendra Singh	SRMIST Delhi NCR Campus Modi Nagar Ghaziabad UP 201204, Uttar Pradesh, India
Piyush Sharma	Computer Science & Technology, Sharda University, Greater Noida, (U.P.), India

Pankaj Kumar Mishra	Department of Mechanical Engineering, HI-Tech Institute of Engineering and Technology, Ghaziabad-201009, India
Praveen Chandra Jha	Department of Applied Science, I.T.S., Greater Noida-201306, India
Pragya Agarwal	Hi-Tech Institute of Engineering & Technology, Ghaziabad, Uttar Pradesh, India
Preeti Dubey	Computer Science & Technology, Sharda University, Greater Noida, (U.P.), India
Pratyush Prashar	Information Technology Sharda University, Plot No. 32-34, Knowledge Park III, Greater Noida, Uttar Pradesh 20131, India
Priyanka Tyagi	Information Technology Sharda University, Plot No. 32-34, Knowledge Park III, Greater Noida, Uttar Pradesh 20131, India
Ramashankar	Department of Civil Engineering, Greater Noida Institute of Technology, GNIOT, Greater Noida, Uttar Pradesh, India
Ranvee Kashyap	School of Computer Science and Engineering, GB Nagar, Uttar Pradesh, India
Rohit Kumar	School of Computer Science and Engineering, GB Nagar, Uttar Pradesh, India
Ramander Singh	Computer Science and Engineering, Amity University, Haryana, Uttar Pradesh, India Depatment of Computer Science and Engineering, IMS Engineering College, Ghaziabad, (U.P.), India
Ritesh Kumar Singhal	Ajay Kumar Garg Institute of Management, Ghaziabad, Uttar Pradesh 201206, India
Riti Rathore	Department of Computer Science and Engineering, Ajay Kumar Garg Engineering College, Ghaziabad-201009, India
Rama Krishna Challa	Chitkara University Institute of Engineering and Technology, Chitkara University Punjab, India
Rashmi Sharma	Department of Information Technology, Ajay Kumar Gag Engineering College, Ghaziabad, UP, India
Ritik Manga	Computer Science and Engineering, Hi-Tech Institute of Engineering & Technology, Ghaziabad, U.P, India
Rishabh Kumar	Computer Science and Engineering, Hi-Tech Institute of Engineering & Technology, Ghaziabad, U.P, India
Ritesh Gautama	Computer Science and Engineering, Hi-Tech Institute of Engineering & Technology, Ghaziabad, U.P, India
Ravi Raman	Department of Civil Engineering, Greater Noida Institute of Technology, GNIOT, Greater Noida, Uttar Pradesh, India
Raj Gopal Mishra	Hi-Tech Institute of Engineering and Technology, Ghaziabad, Uttar Pradesh, India
Ram Kishor Gupta	Department of Mechanical Engineering, HI-Tech Institute of Engineering and Technology, Ghaziabad-201009, India
Sachin	Computer Science ABES Engineering College, Ghaziabad, India

Satpal Singh	Department of Computer Science, Punjabi University, Patiala, India
Subhash Chander	Department of Computer Science, University College Jaito, Jaito, India
Sharda Tiwari	Department of Computer Science & Engineering, Amity University, Uttar Pradesh, India
Satyam Kumar Nikhil	School of Computer Science and Engineering, GB Nagar, Uttar Pradesh, India
Shreyansh Gupta	Computer Science ABES Engineering College, Ghaziabad, India
Sonia Verma	Computer Science ABES Engineering College, Ghaziabad, India
Sachin Kumar	Department of Civil Engineering, Greater Noida Institute of Technology, Greater Noida, U.P., India
Shreeja Kacker	Department of Civil Engineering, Greater Noida Institute of Technology, Greater Noida, U.P., India
Shruti Gupta	ABES Engineering College, Ghaziabad, India
Satish Kumar	Management Department, Ajay Kumar Garg Institute of Management, Ghaziabad, India
Shikha Jain	Kiet Group of Institutions, Delhi-Ncr, Ghaziabad, Uttar Pradesh 201206, India
Swasti Singhal	AIIT Amity University Noida, Noida, Uttar Pradesh 201313, India
Shiva Tyagi	Department of Computer Science and Engineering, Ajay Kumar Garg Engineering College, Ghaziabad-201009, India
Samyak Jain	Department of Computer Science and Engineering, ABES Engineering College, Ghaziabad, India
Shalin Kumar	Department of Applied Science, Greater Noida Institute of Technology, Greater Noida, (U.P), India Hi Tech Institute of Engineering and Technology, Ghaziabad, Uttar Pradesh, India
Surbhi Agarwal	Depatment of Management Studies, Hi-Tech Institute of Engineering and Technology, Ghaziabad, (U.P.), India
Siddhartha Srivastava	Department of Information Technology, Ajay Kumar Gag Engineering College, Ghaziabad, UP, India
Santosh Kumar	Department of Management, Hi-tech Institute of Engineering & Technology, Ghaziabad, India
Shubhangi Singh	Computer Science & Technology, Sharda University, Greater Noida, (U.P.), India
Shivam Raj	Department of Civil Engineering, Greater Noida Institute of Technology, GNIOT, Greater Noida, Uttar Pradesh, India
Sachin Gautam	Department of Civil Engineering, Greater Noida Institute of Technology, GNIOT, Greater Noida, Uttar Pradesh, India
Sumit Kumar	Hi-Tech Institute of Engineering and Technology, Ghaziabad, Uttar Pradesh, India

Somya Goel	Department of ECE, HI-Tech Institute of Engineering and Technology, Ghaziabad, UPTU, India
Shilpa Chaudhary	Hi-Tech Institute of Engineering & Technology, Ghaziabad, (U.P), India
Sheelesh Kumar Sharma	Department of CSE, ABES Institute of Technology, Ghaziabad, Uttar Pradesh, India
Srishti Garg	Department of CSE, ABES Institute of Technology, Ghaziabad, Uttar Pradesh, India
Sujoy Mondol	Computer Science & Technology, Sharda University, Greater Noida, (U.P.), India
Syed Mohammad Moiez Ur Rahman	Computer Science & Technology, Sharda University, Greater Noida, (U.P.), India
Shubham Kumar Mishra	Information Technology Sharda University, Plot No. 32-34, Knowledge Park III, Greater Noida, Uttar Pradesh 20131, India
Surendra Singh	Department of Applied Science & Humanities, Hi-Tech Institute of Engineering & Technology, Ghaziabad, (U.P), India
Somaya Goel	Department Electrical Engineering, Hi-Tech Institute of Engineering & Technology, Ghaziabad, (U.P), India
Tushar	ABES Engineering College, Ghaziabad, India
Tanvi Agarwal	Department of Management, Hi-tech Institute of Engineering & Technology, Ghaziabad, India
Tanu Gupta	Department of ECE, HI-Tech Institute of Engineering and Technology, Gzb, UPTU, India
Uday Tyagi	Computer Science ABES Engineering College, Ghaziabad, India
V.V. Kolomiets	Agriculture University, Kharkov, Ukraine
Varun Upadhayay	ABES Engineering College, Ghaziabad, India
Vartika Srivastava	ABES Engineering College, Ghaziabad, India
Vandana Saini	Chitkara University Institute of Engineering and Technology Chitkara University, Himachal Pradesh, India
Vipul Kumar	Department of Management Studies, Hi-Tech Institute of Engineering and Technology, Ghaziabad, (U.P.), India
Vinay Kumar Agarwal	Department of Management, Hi-tech Institute of Engineering & Technology, Ghaziabad, India
Vipin Kumar Pal	Computer Science and Engineering, Hi-Tech Institute of Engineering & Technology, Ghaziabad, U.P, India
Vipin Kumar Tomer	Hi-Tech Institute of Engineering & Technology, Ghaziabad, (U.P), India
Vijay Kumar	Department of Mechanical Engineering, I.M.T., Greater Noida-201306, India
Vipin Tomer	Hi-Tech Institute of Engineering & Technology, Ghaziabad, Uttar Pradesh, India
Venkata Padmavathi S.	Gitam School of Technology, Gitam Deemed to be University Telangana, Hyderabad, India

Yashaswi   Department of CSE, ABES Institute of Technology, Ghaziabad, Uttar Pradesh, India

Yashraj Mishra   Kiet Group of Institutions, Delhi-Ncr, Ghaziabad, Uttar Pradesh 201206, India

Yash Modi   Kiet Group of Institutions, Delhi-Ncr, Ghaziabad, Uttar Pradesh 201206, India

Trust-Based Neighbor Selection Protocol to Elect Leader in Blockchain using zk-SNARKs Algorithms

Satpal Singh[1,*] and **Subhash Chander**[2]

[1] *Department of Computer Science, Punjabi University, Patiala, India*

[2] *Department of Computer Science, University College Jaito, Jaito, India*

Abstract: Blockchain stores and writes all the transactions because of the unlimited storage capacity. Leader election is the process of electing a node as an overall in-charge of the distributed network. Leader election is a complicated task as we have to choose a leader by giving equal opportunity to all the nodes. We implement all the algorithms of the DONS protocol in order to elect a leader but in our TBNS (Trust Based Neighbor Selection) protocol, we add zk-SNARKs proof to enhance the security of Blockchain. zk-SNARKs (Zero-Knowledge Succinct Non-Interactive Argument of Knowledge) is a type of proof used in cryptography to prove the authenticity of information without revealing any additional information. It allows one party to prove to another that they know a certain piece of information without actually revealing the information itself. In the end, the results of our proposed model are compared with RTT-NS and DONS.

Keywords: Blockchain, TBNS, zk-SNARK.

INTRODUCTION

Blockchain is a distributed ledger that can continuously grow and store a large amount of data. Mining is the process to append a new block onto the chain and this task is completed by the miners. Many nodes in the network compete with each other in order to mine a block and get the reward [1]. We already go through a lot many consensus algorithms *i.e.* PoW, PoS, PoC, *etc.* that help us deduce a miner. However, these algorithms are complex, time-consuming, and waste resources because a lot of resources, energy, time, and efforts are required by the users to find out the validator or miner [2-4].

---

[*] **Corresponding author Satpal Singh:** Department of Computer Science, Punjabi University, Patiala, India;
E-mail: spsingh.mohali@gmail.com

Pankaj Kumar Mishra & Satya Prakash Yadav (Eds.)

In our proposed TBNS model, blockchain stores and writes all transactions because of the unlimited storage capacity. Instead of deducing a miner by implementing complex algorithms like PoW, PoS, PoET, *etc.*, we go for a leader election process. Leader election is the process of electing a node as an overall in-charge of the distributed network [5-8]. Leader election is a complicated task as we have to choose a leader by giving an equal opportunity to all the nodes. We have implemented all eight algorithms of the DONS protocol but with enhanced protection of zk-SNARKs algorithm. It allows one party to prove to another that they know a certain piece of information without actually revealing the information itself [9, 10]. This type of proof is often used in blockchain systems to improve privacy and security. By using zk-SNARKs, a blockchain system can ensure the authenticity of transactions without revealing the details of those transactions to unauthorized parties [11-13].

The contributions of this study are as follows:

1. **Proposal of TBNS Protocol**: The study introduces the Trust-Based Neighbor Selection (TBNS) protocol for leader election in blockchain networks. Unlike traditional consensus mechanisms such as PoW, PoS, and PoET, TBNS focuses on a leader election process that provides an equal opportunity to all nodes, aiming for a more efficient and resource-saving approach.
2. **Integration of zk-SNARKs for Enhanced Security**: The TBNS protocol incorporates zk-SNARKs (Zero-Knowledge Succinct Non-Interactive Argument of Knowledge) to enhance the security of the blockchain network. This cryptographic proof allows for the verification of information authenticity without revealing any additional information, thereby improving privacy and security.
3. **Comparison with Existing Protocols**: The study compares the performance of the TBNS protocol with existing protocols like DONS (Dynamic Optimized Neighbor Selection) and RTT-NS (Round Trip Time Neighbor Selection). The results show that TBNS outperforms these protocols in terms of finalization time, demonstrating its effectiveness and efficiency.
4. **Implementation and Validation**: The algorithms and procedures for leader election using TBNS and zk-SNARKs are implemented in Python, providing a practical validation of the proposed model. This implementation ensures that the theoretical aspects of the protocol are backed by empirical results.
5. **Detailed Protocol Steps and Algorithms**: The study provides a comprehensive set of algorithms (Algorithm 1 to Algorithm 8) that detail the steps involved in the TBNS protocol, including message handling, local record checking, request for confirmation, local network view computation, voting, leader recognition, network topology establishment, and optimized neighbor

selection. This detailed approach ensures that the protocol is transparent and reproducible.

PROPOSED MODEL

Baniata *et al.* proposed DONS (Dynamic Optimized Neighbor Selection) for smart Blockchain, which initially requires the full view of the blockchain network to compute MST. Also, as per network dynamicity, nodes joining and leaving the network must be updated in this view. The network view will be shared with the leader based on which MST derived by the leader in polynomial time will be broadcasted in the network. The network nodes are only able to read their own and neighbor ID's. Therefore, no network node can deduce the miner's private data, also no node has information about the elected leader unless the node itself is a leader.

Problem in Leader election: The Leader node is also a blockchain node with similar characteristics as of other nodes like failure, unavailability, and attacks. So, the Leader election will be performed in the way explained below:

Step I: Network initialization

Initially all the nodes in the network know the identity of their neighbors and expected round trip time (ERT), when communicating with nodes. Also in the beginning, all the node parameters are set to default parameters of the network or protocol as node_status = normal_node.

confirmation_required = equal or higher than the average nodes (50%)

current_Leader = [Null], MST= [], Round_time =T.

Step II: Network view

Once a node or miner fails to join the network *i.e.* network view is fixed then the process for Leader election is initialized. When the process ID is initialized, the default node status as in Step I, is updated to probable leader.

node_status= probable_Leader

Broadcast message to elect the Leader that contains:

Timestamp (t) \\ imported from step I

Votes= Dict{}, nodes_list(NL) = List[]

Message initialized and broadcasted.

Step III: Check node failure

All the nodes that receive the message as in step II will run algorithm I *i.e.* Leader election. The rest normal nodes will run algorithms II, III, and IV.

Step IV: ANV (Anonymous Network View)

Once network nodes receive the required LE_msg with all the conditions as in algorithms II, III, and IV then neighbors act as the witnesses for the node(i) joined or left the network. The protocol then selects one random node with the highest hash value and then LE_msg2 is broadcast to all the neighbors. The message contains node IDs and the content of message 1 and 2. Then ANV can be obtained by running algorithm 4.

Step V: Network Leader Declaration

When any node that is elected as a probable leader receives LE_msg2 then it initializes algorithm 5. This is used to save all node votes and ANV. When,

Current_time − t <= T then

Initialize algorithm 6.

This will compute all the received votes and change the node status to Leader or normal node from probable leader according to the votes.

Step VI: In this step, when a probable leader node receives sufficient votes to be a leader, the network topology is constructed and its MST is computed and broadcasted to nodes as in algorithm 8.

Step VII: All the nodes receive LE_msg3, it verifies whether the message is generated by the leader or not; then every node that receives the MST message as in algorithm 8 will derive its neighbors to share and transmit data.

We implement all the algorithms of the DONS protocol in order to elect a leader but in our TBNS (Trust Based Neighbor Selection) protocol, we add zk-SNARKs proof to enhance the security of Blockchain. zk-SNARKs (Zero-Knowledge Succinct Non-Interactive Argument of Knowledge) is a type of proof used in cryptography to prove the authenticity of information without revealing any additional information. It allows one party to prove to another that they know a certain piece of information without actually revealing the information itself. This type of proof is often used in blockchain systems to improve privacy and security. By using zk-SNARKs, a blockchain system can ensure the authenticity of transactions without revealing the details of those transactions to unauthorized parties [11-13].

Algorithm 1. Message Handler with zk-SNARKs.

	Input: Leader_election_message. Public Key. **zk-SNARKs_proof**
1	*Broadcast: Message to neighbors*
2	*If TBNS and LE_msg [h (i)] ≠ TBNS then*
3	*neighbors = TBNS*
4	*else neighbor = self.neighbor*
5	*End*
6	*for all neighbors in neighbor do*
7	*send (message, neighbor)*
8	*End*
9	*if LE_msg[type] == 'LE_msg3' and LE_msg== [Leader] then run algorithm 8.*
10	*else node_status = normal_node then*
11	*if current_time- LE_msg(t) < T then*
12	*run algorihm 2.*
13	*Broadcast_neighbors (LE_msg)*
14	*End*
15	*End*
16	*if node.staus == probable_Leader then*
17	*if current_time-LE_msg (t) <= T then*
18	*Broadcast_neighbor(LE-msg);*
19	*If LE_ msg[type]=='LE_msg2' then*
20	*run algorithm 5*
21	*else run algorithm 6*
22	*End*
23	*End*
24	*End*

Algorithm 2. Check local records.

1	Receive an LE message (LE_msg).
2	Check if the message's sender ID (h(i)) is in the local records (self.LE_records).
3	If it is, and the message's kth hash (LE_msg[h(mi,k)]) is not in the "Ks" field of the local records, add it to the "Ks" field.
4	If it is not, create a new entry in the local records for the sender ID and add the kth hash to the "Ks" field.
5	Run Algorithm 3 (RFC) on the message to get M_K and RC.
6	Check four conditions: C_1 is true if the kth hash is in M_K, C_2 is true if M_K is in the "Ks" field of the local records, C_3 is true if the size of the "Ks" field is greater than or equal to RC, and C_4 is true if the current node has not yet voted.
7	If all four conditions are true, update the current leader and run Algorithm 4 (Local View Computation). Share the resulting message (LE-2) with neighbors.

Algorithm 3. (RFC) Request for confirmation.

▪	**Input: LE_msg[h(i), h(m$_{i,k}$), t, zk-SNARKs_proof]:**
1	*if verify_zk_snarks_proof(proof, public key) then*
2	*Call_function=Find_neighbor();*
3	*neighbor = [];*
4	*for ∀(row,column) in MST do*
5	*if row [0] = entity and MST [row,column] < ∞*
6	*then append (MST[0] [column]);*
7	*End*
8	***End*** *return neighbor_list //list[]*
9	*End*
10	*if MST ≠ empty then*
11	*list[]= Find_neighbor [h(i)];*
12	***End***
13	*Req_confirmation= length (list []);*
14	*If Req_confirmation == 0 then*
15	*Req_confirmation = DRC (Default Request Confirmation)*
16	***End***
17	*return_list[], Req_confirmation;*

Algorithm 4. Local Network view.

	Input: ANV (Anonymous Network View)
1	*ANV= List[];*
2	*Node_id's= [];*
3	*Weight= [];*
4	*if verify_zk_snarks_proof(proof,public key) then*
5	*for k in mi do*
6	*node_id's.append[h(k)];*
7	*weight.append [ERT(k)/2]; //Expected Round Time*
8	**End** *ANV.append(node_id's);*
9	*ANV.append(weight);*
10	*return ANV;*

Algorithm 5. Voting with zk-SNARKs.

	Input: LE_msg2 [t. h(i). h($m_{i,k}$). List[]. ANV. zk-SNARKs_proof]
1	*if verify_zk_snarks_proof (proof,public key) then*
2	*if ≠ votes [h(i)] then*
3	*vote [h(i)] = timestamp(t), info;*
4	*self.append= status.vote (True);*
5	*else self.append= status.vote(False)*
6	**End**

Algorithm 6. Leader Recognition with zk-SNARKs.

	Input: LE_msg [t, h(i). zk-SNARKS_proof]
1	*if verify_zk_snarks_proof (proof,public key) then*
2	*votes= 0;*
3	*Leader= [Null];*
4	*for Probable_Leader in votes [h(i)] do*
5	*count Probable_Leader = [votes];*
6	*if Probable_Leader > Max_votes then*
7	*Leader = Probable_Leader;*

Algorithm 7. Network Topology with zk-SNARKs.

	Input: h(i). Public Key. zk-SNARKs_proof:
1	*Network topology = [];*
2	*Call_function = add_node();*
3	*if node ≠ network_top then*
4	*Network top[0].append(node)*
5	*Network_top.append ([node]);*
6	*End*
7	*for ANV in self. ANV do*
8	*if ANV [0] = h(i) then*
9	*add_node (ANV[1]);*

10	*End*
11	*End*
12	*for neighbor in ANV[2][0]* **do**
13	*add_node [neighbor] ;*
14	*Node_index_NT= network_top[0][ANV[1]].index*
15	*Neighbor_index_NT=* *network_top[0][neighbor].index*
16	*Neighbor_index_ANV= ANV[2][0][neighbor].index*
17	*Weight= ANV[2][1][neighbor_index_ANV]*
18	*Network_top[neighbor][node_index_NT]=weight*
19	*Network_top[ANV[1]][node_index_NT]=weight*
20	*End*
21	*proof_verified=verify(zk-SNARKs_proof, Public Key)*
22	*if proof_verified*
23	*Self.ANVs.delete(ANV)*
24	**else** *return none;*
25	*End*
26	*if network_top is connected* **then**
27	*return network_top;*
28	**else** *return none;*
29	*End*

Algorithm 8. Optimized Neighbor Selection from MST with zk-SNARKs proof.

	Input: LE_msg3, Public Key, zk-SNARKs_proof
1	*for key in MST do*
2	*append.h(id);* *//Prim's algo.*
3	*Proof_verified=verify(zk-SNARKs_proof, Public Key)*
4	*if proof_verified*
5	*return (MST);*
6	*Broadcast.nodes(MST);*
7	*else return none*
8	*End*
9	*End*

Complexity: The overall complexity of the TBNS protocol is dominated by the MST construction and neighbor selection processes, which are O (N^2). Therefore, the **computational complexity** of the entire TBNS protocol with zk-SNARKs is **O (N^2)**.

The analysis assumes that zk-SNARKs verification and proof generation are efficient, typically O(1) for each proof, but the actual performance may vary based on the specific cryptographic implementation and optimizations used.

RESULTS

We have implemented TBNS in python and compared the outputs of Dynamic Optimized Neighbor Selection (DONS) and Round Trip Time Results (RTT-NS) protocols with our proposed Trust Based Neighbor Selection (TBNS) protocol. Clearly, results produced by Trust Based Leader Election protocol are far better than DONS and RTT-NS in terms of finality time (Fig. **1**).

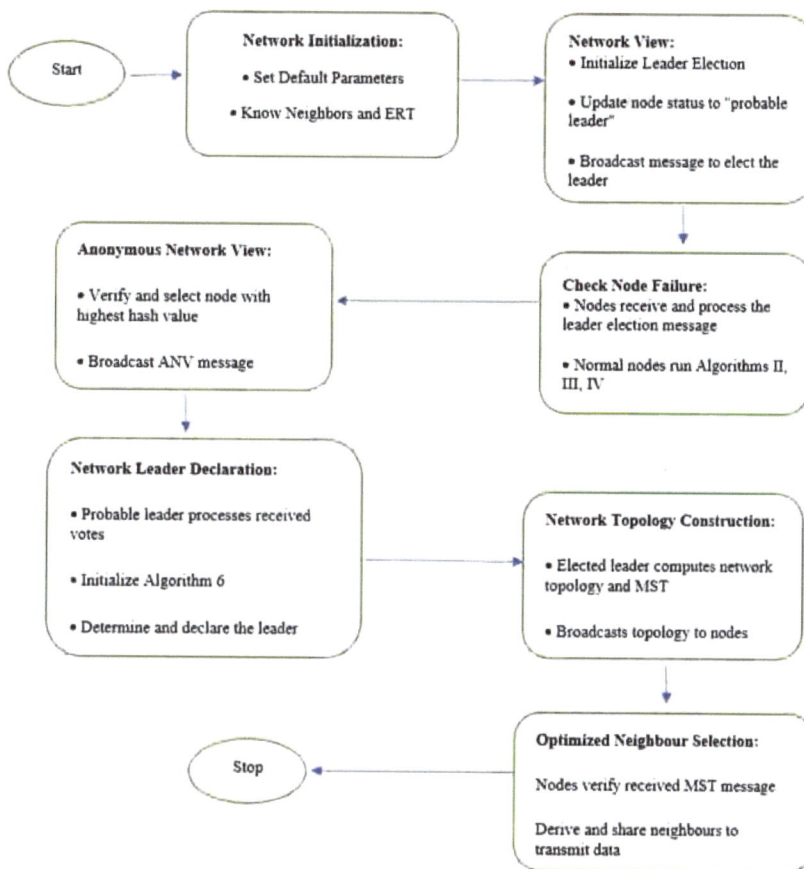

Fig. (1). Flow chart of proposed algorithm.

Finality Time

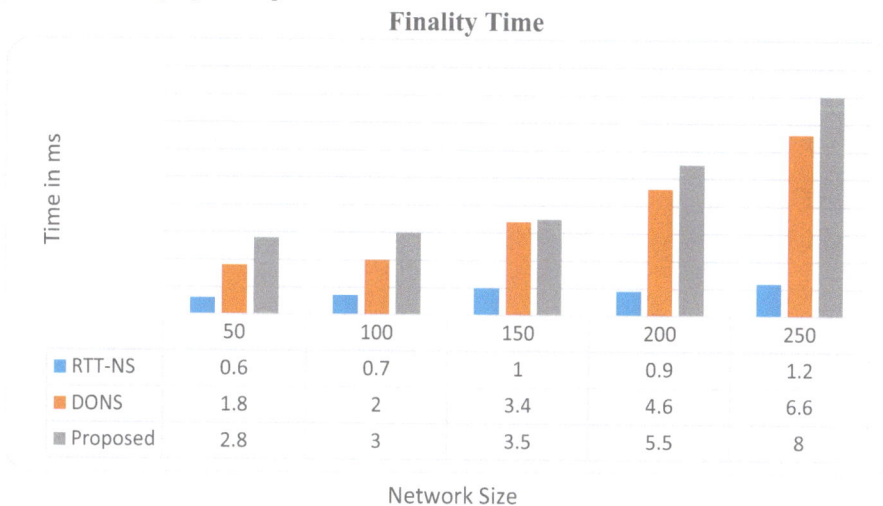

	50	100	150	200	250
■ RTT-NS	0.6	0.7	1	0.9	1.2
■ DONS	1.8	2	3.4	4.6	6.6
■ Proposed	2.8	3	3.5	5.5	8

Network Size

CONCLUSION AND FUTURE SCOPE

Mining is the process to append a new block onto the chain and this task is completed by the miners. Many nodes in the network compete with each other in order to mine a block and get a reward. We already go through a lot many consensus algorithms *i.e.* PoW, PoS, PoC, *etc.* that help us deduce a miner. Instead of deducing a miner by implementing complex algorithms like PoW, PoS, PoET *etc.*, we go for a leader election process. We have implemented all eight algorithms of the DONS protocol but with enhanced protection of the zk-SNARKs algorithm. The results of our Trust Based Leader Election protocol are better than DONS and RTT-NS in terms of finality time.

The proposed TBNS (Trust Based Neighbor Selection) protocol with zk-SNARKs for leader election in blockchain networks opens several avenues for future research and development:

Enhanced Security Mechanisms

- **Quantum-Resistant Algorithms:** As quantum computing evolves, incorporating quantum-resistant cryptographic algorithms to secure zk-SNARKs and overall blockchain protocols becomes crucial.
- **Multi-Factor Authentication:** Integrate multi-factor authentication for nodes participating in leader elections to further enhance security.

Energy Efficiency

- **Energy-Efficient Consensus Algorithms:** New consensus algorithms must be researched and developed,which require less computational power, making the blockchain network more environmentally friendly.
- **Green Blockchain Initiatives:** Renewable energy sources and carbon offset mechanisms must be incorporated to reduce the environmental impact of blockchain operations.

REFERENCES

[1]   T.G. Tan, V. Sharma, and J. Zhou, "Right-of-Stake: Deterministic and Fair Blockchain Leader Election with Hidden Leader", *International Conference on Blockchain and Cryptocurrency (ICBC)*, pp. 1-9, 2020.
[http://dx.doi.org/10.1109/ICBC48266.2020.9169422]

[2]   M.F. Esgin, O. Ersoy, V. Kuchta, J. Loss, A. Sakzad, R. Steinfeld, W. Yang, and R.K. Zhao, (2022), A New Look at Blockchain Leader Election : Simple, Efficient, Sustainable and Post-Quantum. Cryptology ePrint Archive, Paper 2022/993. https://eprint.iacr.org/2022/993

[3]   Zhou Jingjing, Yang Tongyu, Zhang Jilin, Zhang Guohao, Li Xuefeng, and Pan Xiang, "Intrusion Detection Model for Wireless Sensor Networks Based on MC-GRU", *In the preceding of Wireless Communications and Mobile Computing*, p. 1-11, 2022.
[http://dx.doi.org/10.1155/2022/2448010]

[4]   D. Saraswat, A. Verma, P. Bhattacharya, S. Tanwar, G. Sharma, P.N. Bokoro, and R. Sharma, "Blockchain-Based Federated Learning in UAVs Beyond 5G Networks: A Solution Taxonomy and Future Directions", *IEEE Access,* vol. 10, pp. 33154-33182, 2022.
[http://dx.doi.org/10.1109/ACCESS.2022.3161132]

[5]   H. Baniata, A. Anaqreh, and A. Kertesz, "DONS: Dynamic Optimized Neighbor Selection for smart blockchain networks", *Future Gener. Comput. Syst.,* vol. 130, pp. 75-90, 2022.
[http://dx.doi.org/10.1016/j.future.2021.12.010]

[6]   I. Abraham, D. Dolev, and J.Y. Halpern, "Distributed protocols for leader election: A game-theoretic perspective", *International Symposium on Distributed Computing,* pp. 61-75, 2013.
[http://dx.doi.org/10.1007/978-3-642-41527-2_5]

[7]   M. Al Refai, "A new leader election algorithm in hypercube networks", *Symposium Proceedings,* vol. 2, 2006.

[8]   Mohammed Al Refai, "Leader election algorithm in hypercube netwok when the id number is not distinguished", *Inf. Commun. Syst.,* pp. 229-237, 2011.

[9]   A. Biswas, A.K. Maurya, A.K. Tripathi, and S. Aknine, "FRLLE: a failure rate and load-based leader election algorithm for a bidirectional ring in distributed systems", *J. Supercomput.,* vol. 77, no. 1, pp. 751-779, 2021.
[http://dx.doi.org/10.1007/s11227-020-03286-y]

[10]   A.N. Alslaity, and S.A. Alwidian, "A k-neighbor-based, energy aware leader election algorithm (kelea) for mobile ad hoc networks", *Int. J. Comput. Appl.,* vol. 975, p. 8887, 2012.

[11]   D. Yakira, A. Asayag, G. Cohen, I. Grayevsky, M. Leshkowitz, O. Rottenstreich, and R. Tamari, "Helix: A Fair Blockchain Consensus Protocol Resistant to Ordering Manipulation", *IEEE Trans. Netw. Serv. Manag.,* vol. 18, no. 2, pp. 1584-1597, 2021.
[http://dx.doi.org/10.1109/TNSM.2021.3052038]

[12]   D. Yakira, A. Asayag, G. Cohen, I. Grayevsky, M. Leshkowitz, O. Rottenstreich, and R. Tamari, "Helix: A Fair Blockchain Consensus Protocol Resistant to Ordering Manipulation", *IEEE Trans. Netw. Serv. Manag.,* vol. 18, no. 2, pp. 1584-1597, 2021.
[http://dx.doi.org/10.1109/TNSM.2021.3052038]

[13]   Gebrekiros Gebreyesus Gebremariam, "Blockchain-Based Secure Localization against Malicious Nodes in IoT-Based Wireless Sensor Networks Using Federated Learning", *In the preceding of Wireless Communications and Mobile Computing, Hindawi.,* pp. 1530-8669, 2023.
[http://dx.doi.org/10.1155/2023/8068038]

CHAPTER 2

Electronic Healthcare Data Security Using Blockchain

Sharda Tiwari[1,*], Namrata Dhanda[1] and Harsh Dev[2]

[1] *Department of Computer Science & Engineering, Amity University, Uttar Pradesh, India*

[2] *Department of Computer Science & Engineering, Pranveer Singh Institute of Technology, Kanpur, Uttar Pradesh, India*

Abstract: In this paper, a blockchain-based healthcare security system as a solution for preventing data forging is proposed. The proposed model for healthcare data security is based on blockchain and its smart contract execution in a secure way. We proposed a system where users can access the open surveys and participate in these surveys. Moreover, their answers cannot be changed by anonymous or 3rd party people with smart contract control. At the same time, to ensure the confidentiality of the patient's data, we kept the hashed value of the information we collected from the patient's survey data as evidence and the encrypted version so that data can be used for the evaluation, in the relevant storage units of the generated decentralized application.

Keywords: Component, Formatting, Insert (key words), Style, Styling.

INTRODUCTION

Technology is quickly advancing every day. Many tasks were previously completed physically in real life and then shifted to the digital workflow because of this advancement [1-5]. For instance, technology has an impact on finance, trade, multimedia, and advertising. At the same time, another area affected by these technological developments is the health field. Especially with the spread of the internet, the strengthening of computer technologies, and the learning of technology by people working in the field, most health-related data transactions began to be stored in digital areas. During these transitions, databases were used as the first solution for storing health data. As a result of this transition, the amount of data stored electronically has increased day by day. Due to both speed and memory requirements, distributed database structures were established. These

---
* **Corresponding author Sharda Tiwari:** Department of Computer Science & Engineering, Amity University, Uttar Pradesh, India; E-mail: shardatiwari87@gmail.com

Pankaj Kumar Mishra & Satya Prakash Yadav (Eds.)

accomplishments and transitions have been very beneficial for healthcare and many other sectors [6-10]. However, it is an undeniable fact that there are parts of technology that cause difficulties in the field of health, as in every field. The most concerning subject among these challenges is the security of healthcare data. The medical operations and their results may contain sensitive or private data that is not desired to be captured or exposed by others. Therefore, ensuring the security of healthcare data is significantly necessary. Due to the necessity of providing security, many studies have been achieved about e-healthcare data protection, since the beginning of healthcare data processing in digital areas. The solution to the security concerns relies on the fundamentals of cryptography as confidentiality, integrity, and authentication. Many techniques have already been developed to provide these cryptographic fundamentals. These security problems can be eliminated with the combination of cryptographic techniques such as authorization control, encryption, masking, anonymization, *etc.* [11-15].

Research Motivation

The motivation behind the research is the need to revolutionize healthcare systems and improve patient outcomes.

- One of the main motivations is the potential to detect diseases at an early stage. Early disease detection can lower healthcare expenditures and significantly improve treatment outcomes [16-20].
- Another motivation is the ability to remotely monitor and manage patients' health conditions. Remote monitoring allows healthcare providers to track patients' health status in real time, enabling early intervention and personalized care plans. Additionally, IoT Based Disease Prediction systems can contribute to the development of personalized medicine [21-23].
- A further driving force behind research has been the need to solve issues with existing healthcare systems, like excessive wait times, restricted access to care, and underutilization of available resources. IoT Based Disease Prediction systems have the potential to overcome these challenges by providing timely and accurate health monitoring, early detection of diseases, and efficient resource allocation.

Furthermore, research improved population health management. By utilizing IoT devices and predictive models, healthcare providers can gain insights into population health trends, identify high-risk individuals or communities, and implement preventive measures to reduce the prevalence of diseases.

Research Gaps

While there have been significant advancements in the field of IoT-based Disease Prediction and management using Blockchain technology, there are still some research gaps that need to be addressed.

- **Integration of IoT devices and sensors:** Although IoT devices play a crucial role in collecting real-time health data; there is a need for further research on the integration of a wider range of IoT devices and sensors. This integration will allow for more comprehensive and accurate data collection, leading to better disease prediction and management.
- **Standardization and interoperability:** One of the challenges in implementing IoT Based Disease Prediction systems is the absence of common frameworks and protocols for data interchange and interoperability among various IoT platforms and devices. This research gap highlights the need for developing standardized protocols and frameworks that enable seamless interoperability between IoT devices, ensuring effective data sharing and analysis for disease prediction
- **Data security and privacy:** Another research gap in the field of IoT Based Disease Prediction and management using Blockchain is the need for robust data security and privacy mechanisms. The security and privacy of patient data are becoming more and more important as healthcare data becomes more digital. Blockchain technology can help by enabling the decentralized and unchangeable storage of medical records.
- **Integration with Electronic Health Records:** EHR systems play a significant role in healthcare data management. However, there is a research gap in understanding how IoT Based Disease Prediction systems can effectively integrate with existing EHR systems. This integration would allow for seamless data sharing and analysis between IoT devices and EHR systems, leading to more accurate disease prediction and management.
- **Scalability and performance:** The scalability and performance of IoT Based Disease Prediction systems using Blockchain technology are important considerations. Research is needed to explore ways to optimize the performance of Blockchain-based IoT systems, addressing issues such as transaction processing speed and scalability to handle large amounts of data.

CONTRIBUTION

Data preservation and data immutability are the main requirements for electronic health record systems. In this paper, a system has been designed that aims to save the e-health record data and their results as evidence. Since proof immutability is the main requirement of these kinds of systems, an immutable ledger mechanism is an ideal solution for this requirement. Therefore, we have designed a system that can work in sync with the blockchain. The proposed model aims to provide a scalable, fast, and secure healthcare-proof system to users. While designing this model, we used cryptographic algorithms that comply with the standards. In addition, we chose to use parameters according to the specified standards for these algorithms. After this design, we propose an interface and works synchronously with the preferred blockchain structure.

LITERATURE REVIEW

Azaria *et al.* offered a blockchain-based user access control system named MedRec. They used the Ethereum blockchain and its smart contract mechanism. They used nodes with two roles as patient and provider nodes. In MedRec's solution, there are three smart contract designs. The registrar contract ensures the relation between the Ethereum address and the system user. The summary contract provides a record history for each patient, and the patient-provider contract provides access control between patients and related providers. Rajput *et al.* proposed a blockchain-based control management system for the patient healthcare data. In Rajput's system, Hyperledger Fabric was used for the blockchain mechanism. Business logic was implemented with the smart contract such as registering and retrieving data operations. In addition, they used an API connection between the application and the blockchain side. Moreover, they determined access control rules according to the roles of the users in the system for preventing unauthorized user activities on patients, doctors, or staff data. Shahnaz *et al.* developed a pure blockchain system with role-based authorization for ensuring the privacy of healthcare data. In this system, they used Ethereum and its smart contract mechanism Solidity. In their system, there are two types of smart contracts. The first one is the patient record contract, and the other one is for roles. The first one contains all create, read, update and delete (CRUD) functions such as patient record saving, viewing, grant or revoke access controls. The role contract is predefined *via* the Open Zeppelin library. Their user definitions are based on only Ethereum users. Therefore, the blockchain provides interaction between smart contracts and users. Xu *et al.* studied blockchain-based approach to IoT-based healthcare system named Health Chain. They constructed two related chains. The first one is a public blockchain named User chain and the second one is a consortium blockchain named Do chain. The user chain stores the user information data in Unblock. For the confidentiality of the user's IoT data, they have used AES symmetric encryption. In addition, for storing the encryption key and encrypted user's IoT data separately, they have used two different transactions. Doc-chain, on the other hand, stores the diagnostics of the related users in their block named D-block. As a consensus mechanism, the User chain has a PoW mechanism. However, they prefer the PoS-based Byzantine Fault

Tolerance for the Doc chain. Furthermore, the encrypted data are stored on IPFS in storage nodes. Fan *et al.* suggested another blockchain-based electronic medical data-sharing solution named MedBlock. In this solution, they constructed a private blockchain. In parallel, they use a hybrid consensus mechanism for reducing resource wasting and improving the network speed. The data security is provided by a signature-based access control protocol. Accordingly, if the user signature is not among the signature collections in their system, user access is blocked. The studies we have mentioned so far are mostly blockchain studies based on providing access control. Li *et al.* suggested a blockchain-based medical data preservation system with Ethereum. They developed a three-layer application as many solutions have been proposed. These layers are the user layer, the application layer, and the blockchain layer. Briefly, they retrieve the data from the user layer, process, read, or update it at the application layer, and submit the encrypted and hashed data to the blockchain layer. In this process, they used algorithms such as AES and SHA-256 to preserve data confidentiality and integrity. Pavel *et al.* specified the problem as medical data transferring and proposed a blockchain-based solution to their PoS-based blockchain structure. They used signature-based authorization for the image transfer, retrieval, or viewing.

PROPOSED MODEL

The proposed model consists of three main parts. The first part is the web application of the project. The web server provides the connection with the database and constructs all transaction data with the Algorand API in Python. In addition, the survey operations are creation, filling, and consent processed by the web application. During these operations, all requested body data are converted into designed back-end class objects. The other one is the blockchain side. On the blockchain, all types of transaction data are sent by the web server *via* Algorand API. Then the validity of the transactions is checked by the system. In this case, if the sent data is valid then the data is committed to the blockchain. Moreover, on the blockchain side, we use smart contracts and asset technology. The last part is the database module. For each generated survey, we create a new executable decentralized application with a unique ID. With this unique ID, we create a new register in the database and map this register with the smart contract ID. In addition, the survey data such as questions, options, descriptions, *etc.* are stored in the database. Most of the time, the database operations are quicker than backend data operations. However, due to the cryptographic library methods, database encryption is faster than back-end encryption. Hence, we use a database for sending survey data more quickly to the patient side instead of back-end operations. The overview of the general structure is given in Fig. (**1**) below.

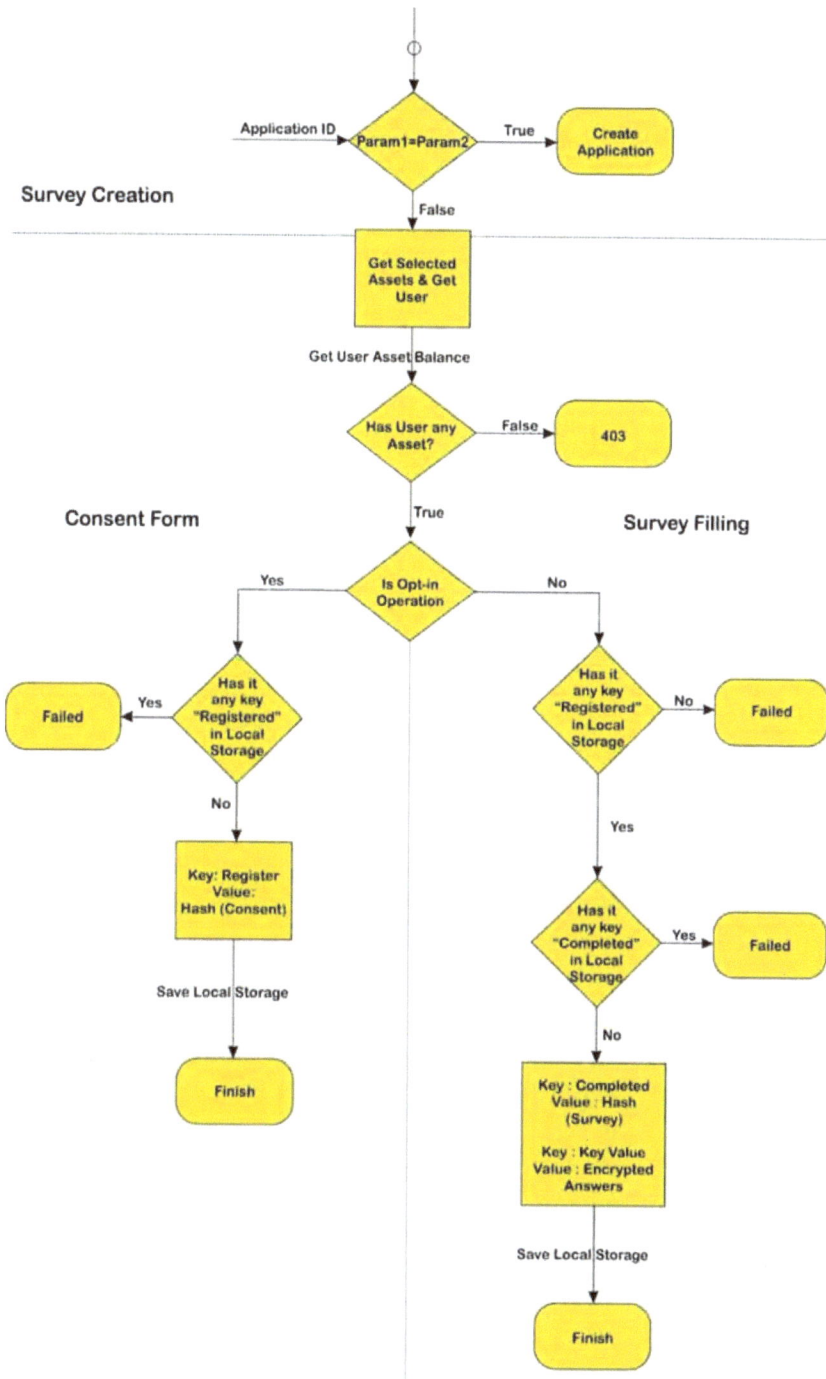

Fig. (1). Mechanism for smart contract execution.

The smart contract initially verifies the kind of application transaction when it is performed by any application transaction. A new application will be produced if the application ID is equal to zero. When creating surveys, this control is utilized. There is already an application if it is not equal to zero. The smart contract then determines if the user has authorization after those controls. The user's MST balance is checked in order to implement this control. If the user's MST balance is more than zero, it is successful. If not, this user's smart contract automatically completes. Both the filling out of permission forms and survey requests use this control. The smart contract has now split into two branches. The permission form approval is handled by this one. The other is used to complete surveys. The smart contract is called when the consent form is filled out. The preceding stages are checked once more. If all requirements are met, the application first looks at the kind of smart contract that was invoked. If it is an opt-in kind, it offers a check to see if the user has already registered. In the event that one is given, the smart contract records the argument sent for the consent form as key-value pairs in the user's local storage. Otherwise, the agreement was broken by the smart contract. The cancellation causes the transaction to fail. When filling out a survey, the smart contract is contacted once again and the attributes are checked again. The smart contract checks two parameters if all requirements are satisfied. The first step is to determine whether or not the user is registered. The presence of previously recorded survey data is examined for the second. If the contract breaches the agreement and discovers any registration-related data that has been saved, the transaction will again fail. In the absence of this, the contract accepts the argument given for the encrypted survey responses and hashed survey data, and saves them as key-value pairs in the user's local smart contract storage as in the consent form procedure.

Survey Creation

Once a survey is created, the blockchain and application sides cooperate. The creation of smart contracts and transforming them into blockchain-compatible agreements are the most important aspects of this stage. Each survey generation activates the new decentralized application with a distinct ID in the blockchain. The doctor is the creator of the survey. Therefore, he prepares the survey and sends it to the application side with his mnemonic key. In this step, the system requires survey data in JSON format. Once the survey data reaches the application, it is adapted to the designed object class for processing. Then, the contract transaction creation process is performed. This transaction is named Application Call Transaction. After validation of the 31 blockchain, if there is not an invalid parameter or operation request, the transaction is committed to the system. And our smart contract is executed in the AVM. Otherwise, the transaction fails. In the successful case, we adapt the survey data to the data transfer object. After that, we save the survey information to our database. During registration in the database, we encrypt the survey data with the AES algorithm with the CBC mode (Fig. **2**).

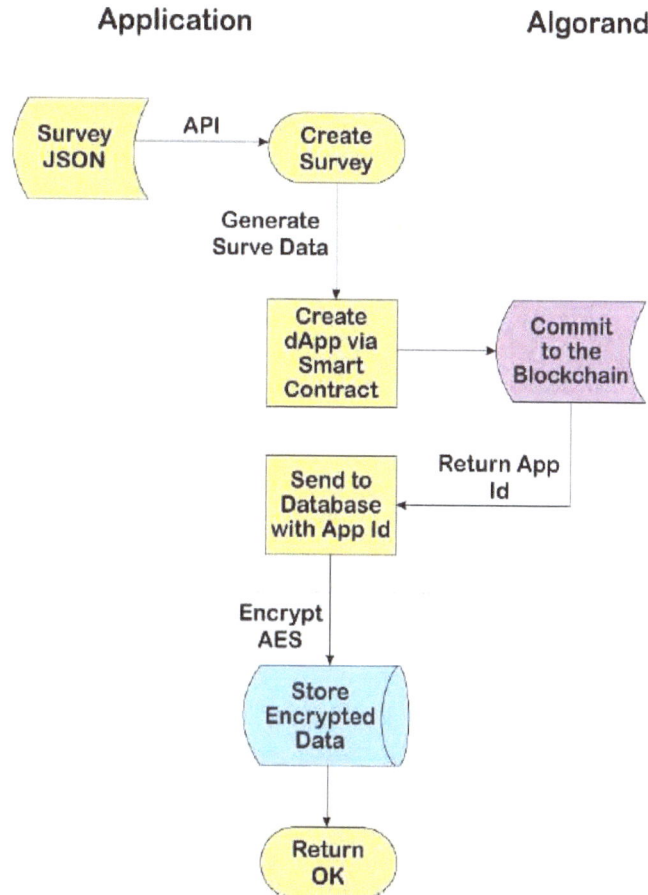

Fig. (2). Mechanism of survey creation.

Consent Form

Medical surveys are widely used in many areas of healthcare. These surveys can be done incrementally, once, continuously, or both before and after some medical operations. The answers or the results of the survey might contain sensitive data. Due to the principle of doctor-patient confidentiality, both doctors and patients avoid the disclosure of this data. Moreover, some tests might have unexpected consequences. Therefore, the consent form is filled out by the patients for the data confidentiality agreements and a disclaimer for unpredictable results. Because of these requirements in the medical surveys, we construct a consent form structure.

Since the consent form is an agreement between the doctor and the patient, we store this consent form on the blockchain side for immutable proof of agreement. Fig. (3) explains the generation of transactions and the execution of the smart contract mechanism for the consent form. Once the participant requests to fill out the determined survey, the consent form first appears to the patients before the survey has been sent. The participant reads the terms and conditions. If the patient declines the terms and conditions, he redirects to the main page, and the survey is canceled until he accepts the consent form. Once he confirms the consent form, the consent data is constructed with the server-side functions and generates the designed object class. Then the hash value of the consent data H(C) is generated *via* the SHA-256 hash function. After this step, the contract transaction generation process begins. The flow chart of consent operation is given in Fig. (3) below.

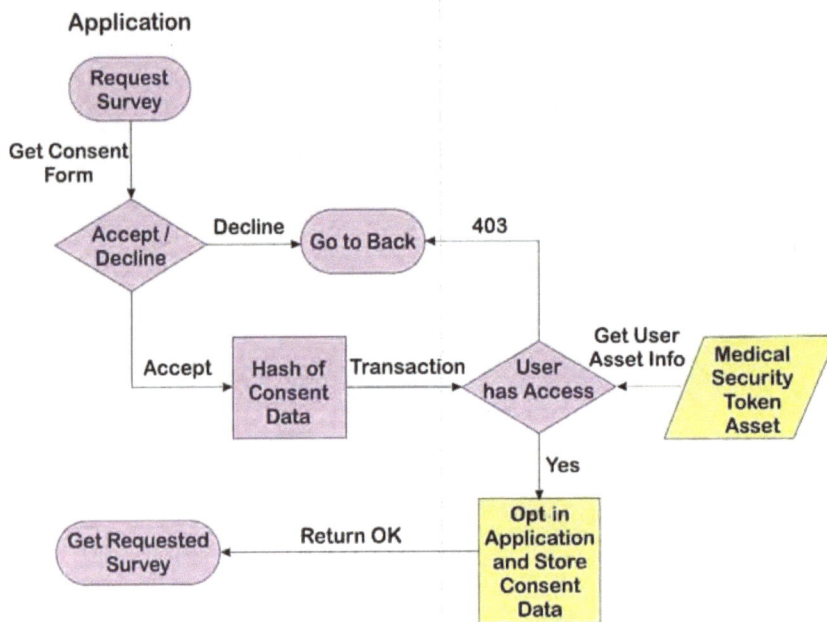

Fig. (3). Consent form mechanism.

Survey Completion

The most important part of our solution is survey completion. The participants who signed the consent form and agreed to the terms and conditions are qualified to respond to the survey's questions. The user must confirm the consent form in the previous step after requesting the survey. Once he has access, he may get the survey and begin filling it out. User responses are used to collect the survey data, which is then prepared into the designated survey object structure. The application is split into two branches at this point. The first step entails using the SHA-256 hash method to calculate the hash value of the survey data. The following sentences describe the objective of this operation:

- It provides unique proof of user's answers.
- It fixes the size of survey data since the size of the survey data depends on the 35 number of questions and options.

In the final step, the smart contract is executed unless there is no violation of the transaction structure. The mechanism of the contract is given as in the following statement:

- It checks user has any MST for the access.
- If he has any MST, then it checks user registry status.
- If it is satisfied then it stores the hash and encrypted data as key-value pair separately. After the smart contract finishes itself, the whole process is completed.

The overview of the survey filling operation is given in Fig. (**4**):

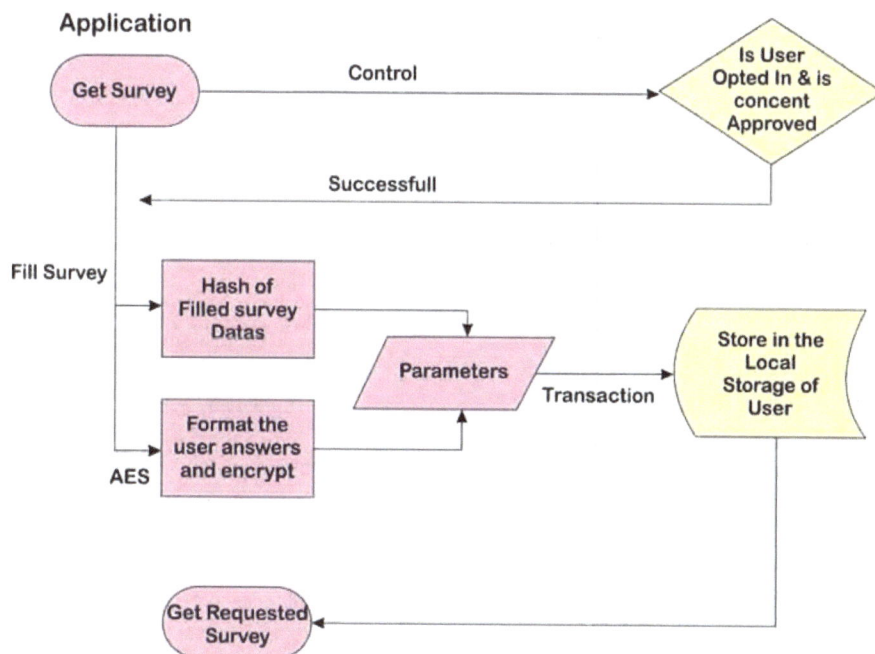

Fig. (4). Survey completion process.

CONCLUSION

The proposed system is efficient in ensuring the healthcare data security. The proposed system tested on sample survey has 10 questions, and each question has 4 options. Therefore, the size of our formatted answer is 39 bytes. Database operations have a fixed size. In this system, average response time of the transaction is 5969 ms with the 319 B memory usage. And their total operation time is between 15 seconds and 18 seconds approximately. Further, the proposed system can be extended with more data along with data learning in future.

REFERENCES

[1]   B. E. Androulaki, A. Barger, V. Bortnikov, C. Cachin, K. Christidis, A. D. Caro, D. Enyeart, C. Ferris, G. Laventman, Y. Manevich, S. Muralidharan, C. Murthy, B. Nguyen, M. Sethi, G. Singh, K. Smith, A. Sorniotti, C. Stathakopoulou, M. Vukolic, S. W. Cocco, and J. Yellick, "Hyperledger fabric: A distributed operating system for permissioned blockchains", *CoRR,* 2018.

[2]   M. Araoz, D. Brener, F. Giordano, S. Palladino, T. Paivinen, A. Gozzi, and F. Zeoli, "ZeppelinOS: An open-source, decentralized platform of tools and services on top of the EVM to develop and manage smart contract applications securely", *Technical Report,* 2017.

[3]   A. Azaria, A. Ekblaw, T. Vieira, and A. Lippman, "Medrec: Using blockchain for medical data access and permission management", *2nd International Conference on Open and Big Data (OBD),* pp. 25-30, 2016.

[4]   D.J. Bernstein, N. Duif, T. Lange, P. Schwabe, and B-Y. Yang, "High-speed high-security signatures", *Journal of Cryptographic Engineering,* vol. 2, no. 2, p. 77-89, 2012.

[5]   D.J. Buterin, "Ethereum white paper", *GitHub repository,* p. 22-23, 2013.

[6]   V. Buterin, "A next-generation smart contract and decentralized application platform", *white paper,* vol. 3, no. 37, 2014.

[7]   K. Celik, "Blockchain based solution for electronic health record integrity", Master of Science, Middle East Technical University, 2022.

[8]   J. Chen, S. Gorbunov, S. Micali, and G. Vlachos, "Algorand agreement: Super fast and partition resilient byzantine agreement", *Cryptology ePrint Archive, Report,* 2018

[9]   J. Chen, and S. Micali, *Algorand.* Algorand Whitepaper, 2016.

[10]   M. Dworkin, E. Barker, J. Nechvatal, J. Foti, L. Bassham, E. Roback, and J. Dray, "Advanced encryption standard", *NES,* 2001.

[11]   K. Fan, S. Wang, Y. Ren, H. Li, and Y. Yang, "Medblock: Efficient and secure medical data sharing *via* blockchain",, *Journal of Medical Systems,* vol. 42, no. 8, p. 136, 2018.

[12]   S. Goldberg, L. Reyzin, D. Papadopoulos, and J. Vcelák, "Verifiable Random ˘ Functions (VRFs), Internet-Draft draft-irtf-cfrg-vrf-13", *Internet Engineering Task Force,* 2022.

[13]   S. Josefsson, and I. Liusvaara, "Edwards-Curve Digital Signature Algorithm (EdDSA)", *Internet-Draft draft-irtf-cfrg-vrf-13,* 2017.

[14]   H. Li, L. Zhu, M. Shen, F. Gao, X. Tao, and S. Liu, "Blockchain-based data preservation system for medical data", *Journal of Medical Systems,* vol. 42, no. 8, p. 141, 2018.

[15]   K. Moriarty, B. Kaliski, and A. Rusch, "PKCS #5: Password-Based Cryptography Specification Version 2.1", *RFC,* 2017.

[16]   S. Nakamoto, *Bitcoin: A peer-to-peer electronic cash system.* Decentralized Business Review, 2008, p.

21260.

[17]   OWASP-CheatSheet-Series-Team, Password Storage Cheat Sheet, August 2021, Accessed on 2022-08-16.

[18]   V. Patel, "A framework for secure and decentralized sharing of medical imaging data *via* blockchain consensus",, *Health Informatics Journal,* vol. 25, no. 4, pp. 1398-1411, 2019.
[PMID: 29692204]

[19]   A.R. Rajput, Q. Li, M. Taleby Ahvanooey, and I. Masood, "Eacms: Emergency access control management system for personal health record based on blockchain", *IEEE Access,* vol. 7, pp. 84304-84317, 2019.
[http://dx.doi.org/10.1109/ACCESS.2019.2917976]

[20]   A. Shahnaz, U. Qamar, and A. Khalid, "Using blockchain for electronic health records", *IEEE Access,* vol. 7, pp. 147782-147795, 2019.
[http://dx.doi.org/10.1109/ACCESS.2019.2946373]

[21]   M. Sonmez, E. Barker, W. Burr, and L. Chen, "Recommendation for Password-Based Key Derivation Part 1: Storage Applications, Special Publication (NIST SP), National Institute of Standards and Technology", *IEEE,* 2010. Gaithersburg, MD, [online], (Accessed November 27, 2024).
[http://dx.doi.org/10.6028/NIST.SP.800-132]

[22]   G. Weiss, "Synchronous networks", *IRE Trans. Automat. Contr.,* vol. 7, no. 2, pp. 45-54, 1962.
[http://dx.doi.org/10.1109/TAC.1962.1105424]

[23]   J. Xu, K. Xue, S. Li, H. Tian, J. Hong, P. Hong, and N. Yu, "Healthchain: A blockchain-based privacy preserving scheme for large-scale health data", *IEEE Internet Things J.,* vol. 6, no. 5, pp. 8770-8781, 2019.
[http://dx.doi.org/10.1109/JIOT.2019.2923525]

CHAPTER 3

E-cops - An Online Crime Reporting System

Ranvee Kashyap[1], Rohit Kumar[1], Satyam Kumar Nikhil[1] and B. Shajahan[1,*]

[1] *School of Computer Science and Engineering, GB Nagar, Uttar Pradesh, India*

Abstract: Transmit information on cutting-edge police and policing tools, create the framework for firms to use in order to obtain incident reports, cut down on employee resources, and enable these enforcement offices to reallocate resources to nearby areas. The E-Cop system is a step toward digitalizing the police station at this time, since everything is going digital. This will bring the public and law enforcement closer together while also enabling communication among all police stations. The E-Cop system allows citizens to report crimes of any kind online to the police station that is closest to them. Every Police Station in this system keeps a general journal, records of crimes and criminal activity, FIRs, and complaints, send the status of complaints, and can view an overview of another police station. Police officers are able to speak with one another. News, notifications, and a plethora of other information are also shown on the system homepage.

Keywords: Criminal, Communication, Digitalizing, Information, Notifications.

INTRODUCTION

"Establishing a data platform that organizations use to receive reports of proximity incidents and provide state-of-the-art police and policing tools [1] will reduce the need for typical assets and enable these authorized offices to reallocate resources to the most desired areas locally." The E-Cop system is a step toward digitalizing the police station at this time since everything is going digital. This will bring the public and law enforcement closer together while also enabling communication among all police stations [2]. The E-Cop system allows citizens to report crimes of any kind online to the police station that is closest to them [3]. Every Police Station in this system keeps a general diary, records of crimes and criminal activity, FIRs, and complaints, sends the status of complaints, and is able to view the general information about another police station [4]. Police officials

*Corresponding author B. Shajahan: School of Computer Science and Engineering, GB Nagar, Uttar Pradesh, India;
E-mail: shajahan@galgotiasuniversity.edu.in

can communicate with each general detail of another police station. Police officers are able to speak with one another [5]. Notifications, news, and a plethora of other information are also displayed on the system's home page [6]. The primary goals of E-Cop are adherence to the Indian Constitution, upholding dignity, compassion, and decency toward citizens, and preserving institutional and personal credibility, [7]. and enforcing law and order equitably and in good faith in order to provide safe and secure protection for all societal segments [8]. Particularly the most vulnerable and defenseless groups are women, youth, the elderly, and minorities [9]. Additionally, we want to maintain racial consistency, recalling popular beliefs based on the majority in our constitution [10], adopting a group-inclusive approach [11]. Human resources enable us to prevent wrongdoings and maintain public control so that we can move forward to assist the public truly.

RELATED WORKS

A more robust online crime reporting system is required due to the rising incidence of crimes involving the Internet [12]. Such an online system, called e-cops, is intended to be a useful tool for reporting any kind of illegal activity. E-cops have potential, but it also has drawbacks [13]. The creation of precise diagnostic models is one of the E-cops' main challenges [14]. These models must enable a smooth user experience and are crucial for assessing the probability of a specific criminal event. One of the primary challenges in creating diagnostic models for E-cops is managing changeable data [15]. Different kinds of data are linked to every type of internet crime [16]. E-cops need to be able to recognize and categorize the data points linked to the reported crime in order to estimate the chance that [17] it will happen again. Additionally, for data to continue being accurate and useful, it must be updated [18]. Secondly, the difficulty of forecasting future criminal activity must be considered while creating diagnostic models for E-cops [19]. Apart from historical trend analysis, more study is required for E-cops models to be effective; advanced techniques for predicting the probability of future events are needed [20]. This calls for an intricate fusion of machine learning data analysis.

OVERVIEW

An online tool for reporting crimes, called E-Cops, was created to make the process of reporting crimes safe and effective. It makes it possible for citizens to swiftly, simply, and safely report criminal incidents online. It gives people a safe place to keep, submit, and retrieve their crime reports. Additionally, it gives the public access to information like the incident's timing and location. In addition, E-Cops acts as a central location for all citizen-submitted crime reports. Law enforcement organizations receive access to all of the data gathered in order to support their criminal investigations. E-cops provide a plethora of features to guarantee safe and convenient crime reporting. These capabilities include real-time case monitoring, user authentication, safe criminal data storage, and customized report layouts. Law enforcement organizations are able to investigate and settle crimes more quickly and effectively thanks to E-Cops, which also helps in improving the reporting of crime situations safely and efficiently.

PROCESS METHODOLOGY

Planning: Setting up the system is the initial phase in the process. In order to do this, requirements must be gathered, goals must be determined, a budget and schedule must be decided upon, and an implementation strategy must be created. Fig. (**1**) shows the Online Crime Reporting System.

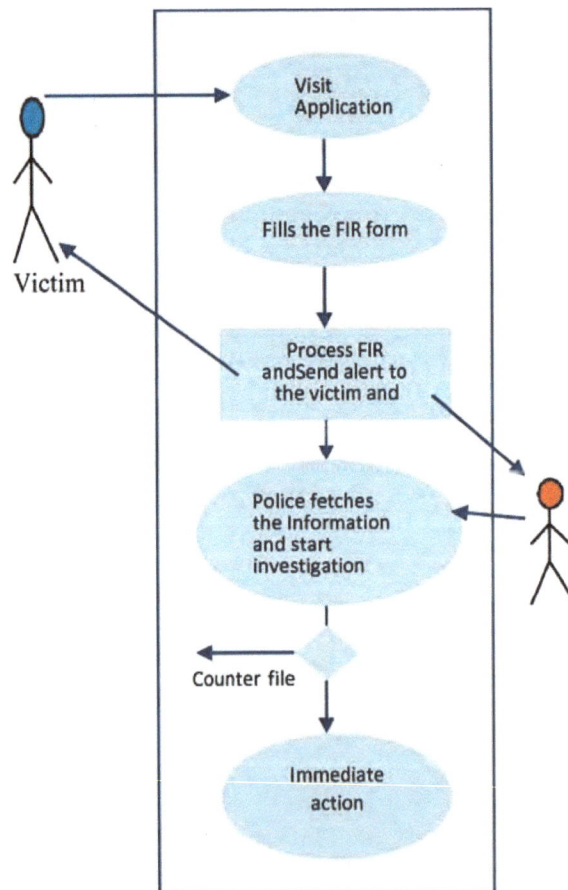

Fig. (1). Shows online crime reporting system.

Design

Following the completion of the planning stage, the design stage starts. Here, the system's architecture, data modelling, and user interface design are all studied in depth.

Development

The system needs to be put into action now. The system must be programmed, tested, and deployed during the development phase.

Data Collection

Data collection aims to provide state-of-the-art law enforcement and policing tools, knowledge platforms that companies can utilize to analyze incident reports, save employee costs, and enable these implementation offices to reallocate resources to areas that are highly anticipated in the local community.

Data Preprocessing

For businesses to operate accessible work without any problems, they require an effective program and the required equipment. As of right now, day one underlying NICs are structurally accessible, meaning that buying them does not cost extra. Our pledge is thus financially feasible.

Data Analysis

Given that it does not affect the different apps that use the framework, this is functionally feasible. Despite this, network traffic is not as negatively impacted. Every frame in the company needs to have it installed.

RESULTS AND ANALYSIS

According to the findings of a study conducted on E-cops, an online crime reporting system, users find the system to be user-friendly and helpful in reporting crimes swiftly and efficiently. Total 31% of users rated the system as very good, while the bulk of users (69%) rated it as great. The consumers also mentioned how simple it was to use the system, how straightforward the user interface was, and how quickly a report could be filed. Users also expressed confidence that their reports would be handled appropriately and swiftly. Fig. (**2**) shows the global geography of cybercrime.

The findings point to the E-cops system being a functional online tool for reporting crimes. Users found it to be speedy, easy to use, and confident in the framework. The findings have ramifications for improving the speed and accuracy of crime reporting as well as for improving efficiency.

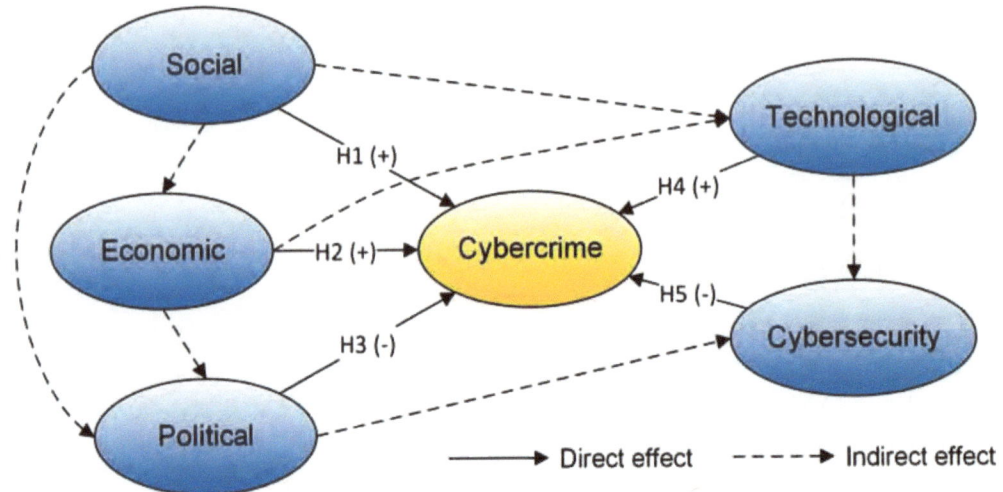

Fig. (2). Shows the global geography of cybercrime.

CONCLUSION

"E-cop" is the name of the internet application business. The program can reveal complaints, missing persons, and web-based infractions in addition to providing the most necessary personal information. Adaptability was considered in the creation of this product. When more modules are needed, they can be added with ease. The product is made using a certain technique. Every module inside the framework has been tested with both legitimate and invalid data, and everything functions as it should. As such, the framework can take the place of the existing framework and meet all of the major objectives. Under the worst possible conditions for the Association's success, the joint venture is essentially finished. The requirements are satisfied and successfully met. The planning of the framework is done as though it were during the planning stage. The mission offers clever suggestions for creating applications that are unquestionable and satisfy client needs. The framework is incredibly flexible and adaptive. Customers will find it easy to use this device because of its easily interpreted screen. Errors are significantly reduced by raised approval checks. A significant redesign of the product is planned. With real-time data, the app tested it out and came out on top. As a result, this product has demonstrated its effectiveness.

REFERENCES

[1]   S.P. Yama, S. Said, C.D.S. Nascimento, V.H.C. de Albuquerque, and S.S. Chauhan, "Analysis and Design of automatically generating for GPS Based Moving Object Tracking System", *International*

Conference on Artificial Intelligence and Smart Communication (AISC), pp. 1-5, 2023. [http://dx.doi.org/10.1109/AISC56616.2023.10085180]

[2]   G. Mahesh, B.G. Kumar, S. Pathak, M. Surekha, K.G. Harsha, and M. Raj, "E-policing and information management system using blockchain technology. In Artificial Intelligence, Blockchain", *Comput. Secur.,* vol. 1, pp. 238-243, 2023.

[3]   S.P. Yadav, and S. Yadav, "Fusion of Medical Images using a Wavelet Methodology: A Survey. In IEIE Transactions on Smart Processing & Computing", *The Institute of Electronics Engineers of Korea,* vol. 8, no. 4, pp. 265-271, 2019. [http://dx.doi.org/10.5573/IEIESPC.2019.8.4.265]

[4]   S. Mehta, K.S. Kumari, P. Jain, H. Raikwar, and S. Gore, "Blockchain driven Evidence Management System", *3rd International conference on Artificial Intelligence and Signal Processing (AISP),* pp. 1-6, 2023. [http://dx.doi.org/10.1109/AISP57993.2023.10134799]

[5]   S.P. Yadav, and S. Yadav, "Fusion of Medical Images in Wavelet Domain: A Discrete Mathematical Model", *Ingeniería Solidaria,* vol. 14, no. 25, pp. 1-11, 2018. [http://dx.doi.org/10.16925/.v14i0.2236]

[6]   M.D. Inavolu, D. Venna, G.V. Kallepalli, and S.S. Surapaneni, "Detection of Missing Persons Using Mobile App", *2nd International Conference for Innovation in Technology (INOCON),* pp. 1-8, 2023. [http://dx.doi.org/10.1109/INOCON57975.2023.10101097]

[7]   S. P. Yadav, and S. Yadav, "Mathematical implementation of fusion of medical images in continuous wavelet domain", *Journal of Advanced Research in dynamical and control system,* vol. 10, no. 10, pp. 45-54, 2019.

[8]   J. Lee, P. Pecorino, and A.C. Souto, "A Comparison of the Female and Male Racial Disparities in Imprisonment", *Journal of Economics, Race, and Policy,* vol. 6, no. 2, pp. 102-125, 2023. [http://dx.doi.org/10.1007/s41996-022-00111-x]

[9]   S.P. Yadav, "Blockchain Security", In: *Blockchain Security in Cloud Computing. EAI/Springer Innovations in Communication and Computing.,* K. Baalamurugan, S.R. Kumar, A. Kumar, V. Kumar, S. Padmanaban, Eds., Springer: Cham, 2022. [http://dx.doi.org/10.1007/978-3-030-70501-5_1]

[10]   R.W. McMahon, *Advancing the Hegemony of Surveillance Capitalism: A Critical Discourse Analysis of Surveillance Representations in Media,* Temple University, 2023.

[11]   X. Xue, R. Shanmugam, S. Palanisamy, O.I. Khalaf, D. Selvaraj, and G.M. Abdulsahib, "A hybrid cross layer with harris-hawk-optimization-based efficient routing for wireless sensor networks", *Symmetry (Basel),* vol. 15, no. 2, p. 438, 2023. [http://dx.doi.org/10.3390/sym15020438]

[12]   P. Dhabe, V. Hatekar, S. Wankhade, I. Kulkarni, R. Chaudhary, and D.D. Patwari, "Video Call-Based Real-Time Crime Reporting System", In: *Designing User Interfaces With a Data Science Approach.,* 2022, pp. 1-20. [http://dx.doi.org/10.4018/978-1-7998-9121-5.ch001]

[13]   K. Suganyadevi, V. Nandhalal, S. Palanisamy, and S. Dhanasekaran, "Data security and safety services using modified timed efficient stream loss-tolerant authentication in diverse models of VANET", *2022 International Conference on Edge Computing and Applications (ICECAA),* pp. 417-422, 2022. [http://dx.doi.org/10.1109/ICECAA55415.2022.9936128]

[14]   S.I.A. Abidi, A.A. Almeida, L.G. Soares, and A. Pansare, "Interactive Map Application For Real-Time Crime Reporting", *International Conference on Advances in Computing, Communication, and Control (ICAC3),* p. 1-8, 2021.

[15]   R. Ramakrishnan, M. A. Mohammed, M. A. Mohammed, V. A. Mohammed, and J. Logeshwaran, "An

innovation prediction of DNA damage of melanoma skin cancer patients using deep learning", *14th International Conference on Computing Communication and Networking Technologies (ICCCNT)*, p. 1-7, 2023.
[http://dx.doi.org/10.1109/ICCCNT56998.2023.10306749]

[16]   I. Hingorani, R. Khara, D. Pomendkar, and N. Raul, "Police complaint management system using blockchain technology", *3rd International Conference on Intelligent Sustainable Systems (ICISS)*, pp. 1214-1219, 2020.
[http://dx.doi.org/10.1109/ICISS49785.2020.9315884]

[17]   M. A. Mohammed, V. A. Mohammed, R. Ramakrishnan, M. A. Mohammed, and J. Logeshwaran, "The three dimensional dosimetry imaging for automated eye cancer classification using transfer learning model", *14th International Conference on Computing Communication and Networking Technologies (ICCCNT)*, pp. 1-6, 2023.
[http://dx.doi.org/10.1109/ICCCNT56998.2023.10307446]

[18]   R.K. Mitra, M.P. Gupta, and G.P. Sahu, "Indian Police E-Government System: A Study of Provincial Police", In: *Handbook of Research on Strategies for Local E-Government Adoption and Implementation: Comparative Studies*, 2009, p. 879-901.

[19]   K.R.K. Yesodha, A. Jagadeesan, and J. Logeshwaran, "IoT applications in Modern Supply Chains: Enhancing Efficiency and Product Quality", *2nd International Conference on Industrial Electronics: Developments & Applications (ICIDeA)*, p. 366-371, 2023.
[http://dx.doi.org/10.1109/ICIDeA59866.2023.10295273]

[20]   A. Manzoor, "Use of social media for policing", *Handbook of research on cultural and economic impacts of the information society.*, pp. 297-326, 2015.
[http://dx.doi.org/10.4018/978-1-4666-8598-7.ch013]

CHAPTER 4

Diabetic Eye Disease Classification by Residual Network based Feature Mapping with Support Vector Machine

Neha Kapur[1,*] and **Bobbin Preet**[1]

[1] *CSE Department, UIE, Chandigarh University, Mohali-140413, Punjab, India*

Abstract: The retinal blood vessels' diameter and tortuosity will alter as a result of diabetic retinopathy. The prediction of differences in retinal blood vessel diameter and new vessel formation is the desired focus of investigation. Segmenting the retinal blood vessels is necessary in order first to observe the alterations. The suggested system improves the quality of the segmentation results over diseased retinal images. A generative and non-generative deep learning model is proposed in this study. The CNN-SVM was separately applied in the experiment. For classification tasks, the CNN-GMM-SVM model that has been suggested does have a sensitivity of 81.0%. When compared to other models, the CNN-GMM-SVM model that has been suggested produces the best outcomes. The CNN-GMM-SVM model increases classification sensitivity by 5.4% when compared to CNN-SVM and CNN-GMM.

Keywords: Classification, Generative deep learning model, Non-generative deep learning model, Prediction, Segmentation.

INTRODUCTION

Classifying diabetic eye illness is a significant issue for the medical community since early identification of the condition might result in effective therapy. Relative networks have proven to be an effective diagnostic tool for a variety of diabetes-related disorders in recent years [1]. This work focuses on automated diabetic eye disease categorization using residual network-based feature mapping and support vector machine (SVM) classification [2]. Residual networks automatically learn picture features, making them effective tools for image processing and feature extraction [3]. The features can be retrieved and mapped into a feature vector either by training the network from scratch or by using the

* Corresponding author Neha Kapur: CSE Department, UIE, Chandigarh University, Mohali-140413, Punjab, India; E-mail: nehakapur1013@gmail.com

Pankaj Kumar Mishra & Satya Prakash Yadav (Eds.)

output layers of pre-trained networks. The study's dataset comprises a collection of photos that were taken from websites about eye issues caused by diabetes [4]. Classes linked to diabetic eye illness, including neovascularization, vitreous section, macula, and retinal blood vessels, were then applied to the photos [5]. For automated diabetic eye disease categorization, a pre-trained residual network was used to build a feature vector from the dataset, which was then fed into an SVM model [6]. Based on the receiver operating characteristic curves on the holdout set, the model's overall accuracy was determined to be good [7]. The findings show that feature mapping is based on the residual network.

RELATED WORKS

Due to the rising incidence of diabetic eye illness, diagnostic models for the classification of the condition have received a lot of attention recently [8]. Millions of patients are impacted by the illness globally, and its manifestations include vitreous pathology, macular edema, and retinopathy [9]. The two most important aspects of managing diabetic eye disease effectively are prevention and prompt therapy [10]. Using machine learning models, such as residual network-based feature mapping using support vector machines (SVM), is one method for accurately diagnosing diabetic eye illness [11]. This method uses convolutional neural networks (CNNs) to identify the most pertinent elements from retinal pictures and blood sugar readings. After that, an SVM integrates these attributes to produce a classification model that may be used to recognize and diagnose diabetic eye illness [12]. Like any device learning model, this method has its challenges [13]. For instance, it depends on the availability of reliable data, which could be hard to come by in underdeveloped or rural nations. Furthermore, the model can only be as strong as the data it has access to; thus, finding high-quality datasets is crucial [14]. Ultimately, the model's effectiveness is determined by the quality of its training; poor training might result in inaccurate predictions and subpar performance. The significance of utilizing sophisticated computational models for the classification of diabetic eye illness has been emphasized by recent research [15]. A technique that is becoming more and more popular utilizes residual network support vector machines (SVM) for feature mapping and deep learning [16]. Utilizing convolutional layers, residual networks are deep learning frameworks that offer a high degree of feature learning capability. It is necessary to learn several layers in order to use these networks; each layer can be adjusted for a different purpose [17], such as picture categorization. The learned features are mapped into a label space using support vector machines (SVM) feature mapping. In the end, classification is done using deep learning models [18]. The use of this kind of model to classify diabetic eye illness has the advantage of being more accurate. Record the connection between the labels and the various aspects. This contributes to improved model interpretability and, consequently, improved classification precision and accuracy [19].

Furthermore, the accuracy of the model is improved by capturing more intricate correlations between characteristics and labels through the use of many convolutional layers [20]. The residual network-based feature mapping combined with the support vector machine deep learning model is a compelling choice for the categorization of diabetic eye illness. It offers the advantages of both shallow and deep learning models and is accurate and efficient.

DIABETIC RETINOPATHY

Diabetes increases the chance of diabetic retinopathy in those who have the disease. Elevated blood sugar levels damage the retina's blood vessels when this happens. They might enlarge and start to leak. Alternatively, they could shut off blood flow by closing. Sometimes abnormal new blood vessels grow on the retina. All of these changes have the power to seize one's view. Diabetes retinopathy does not affect vision until it reaches an advanced stage and is asymptomatic. Diabetic retinopathy is a risk factor for both type 1 (non-proliferative) and type 2 (proliferative) diabetic individuals; hence, screening is necessary.

Diabetic Retinopathy Stages

Non-Proliferative Diabetic Retinopathy (NPDR): This condition represents the early stages of diabetic eye disease. Numerous people have diabetes. In NPDR, tiny blood vessels burst [3], increasing in retinal size. The macula's swelling is known as diabetic macular edema. This is the most common reason why people with diabetes have vision loss. Furthermore, NPDR may cause blood vessels in the retina to collapse. We call it macular ischemia. When that happens, blood cannot reach the macula. Sometimes, tiny particles called exudates form in the retina. Your vision may also be affected by these. Everybody who has NPDR will have a blurry vision. Fig. (**1**) shows the eye with Non-Proliferative DR.

Diabetic Macular Edema

When abnormal blood vessel damage occurs in the surrounding retina, fluid flows into and accumulates in the macula abnormally. This is known as macular edema. Diabetic retinopathy (DR) is a common cause of retinal edema.

Glaucoma

It appears that glaucoma is a condition that can harm the optic nerve, which is found inside the eye. With time, things will only become worse. It frequently results from an increase in intraocular pressure. The fluid inside your eye, called aqueous humor, often escapes *via* a tube that resembles a mesh. The level of that liquid may increase if this channel becomes blocked or if the eye is secreting too much fluid. Changes in blood sugar levels can lead to diabetic retinopathy by weakening and increasing the likelihood of retinal blood vessels rupturing. In due course, this may lead to glaucoma. According to the most widely recognized theory, abnormal blood vessels form in your eye and cause neurovascular glaucoma when the blood vessels in the retina are injured. Such blood vessels have the potential to obstruct the eye's natural drainage system. This can result in an increase in intraocular pressure, which can lead to glaucoma.

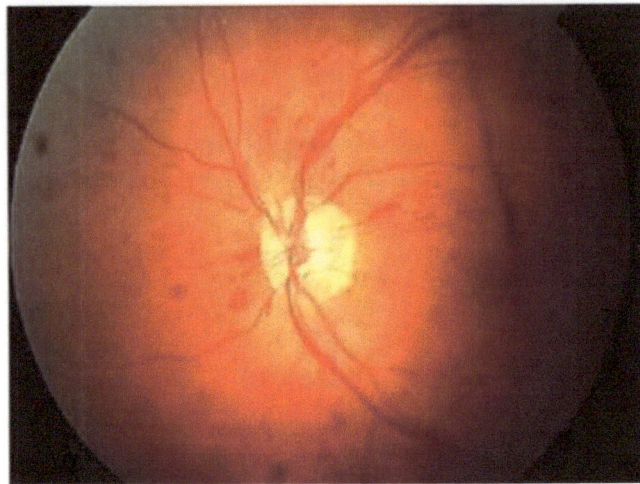

Fig. (1). An eye with non-proliferative DR.

Another explanation for the increased risk of glaucoma associated with diabetic retinopathy directly links elevated blood sugar levels to the condition. Having high blood sugar may actually lead to your eye producing more fibronectin, a particular type of glycoprotein. Increased levels of fibronectin in the eye can obstruct the natural drainage system, leading to glaucoma.

LIMITATIONS OF TRADITIONAL FEATURE EXTRACTION METHODS

Previous advances in computer vision relied on manually designed characteristics. Feature engineering, on the other hand, requires a professional understanding of the problem area and is time-consuming and difficult. A further issue with hand-engineered features, such as Scale Invariant Feature Transform (SIFT), Histogram of Oriented Gradients (HOG), and Speeded-up Robust Feature (SURF), is that their capacity to extract information from images is far too limited. This is because first-order image derivatives are not needed for the majority of computer vision applications, including object detection and picture categorization. Moreover, the application often dictates the features that are selected. More specifically, transfer learning—learning from prior experiences or representations—is hampered by these traits. Additionally, the complexity that Hand-engineered characteristics are limited in what humans can add to them. Deep neural networks and other automatic feature-learning techniques are employed to address each of these issues. For many years, the machine learning classifier combined with hand-crafted features has been an extremely effective technique. Convolutional neural networks, on the other hand, are effective in a wide range of scenarios because they can automatically extract the information required for a given task from the main image. Each layer produces an additional layer of abstraction in a given image. CNN is a feed-forward, neutral network that uses fully connected layers for inference and many convolutional layers for feature extraction. In addition to handling visual translation, scale variations, rotation, and other aspects, CNN generates precise classification results. There is also a chance for other kinds of deformations. These parameters determine how well CNN models perform in classification tasks. Fig. (**2**) shows the Proposed Model- (CNN-GMM).

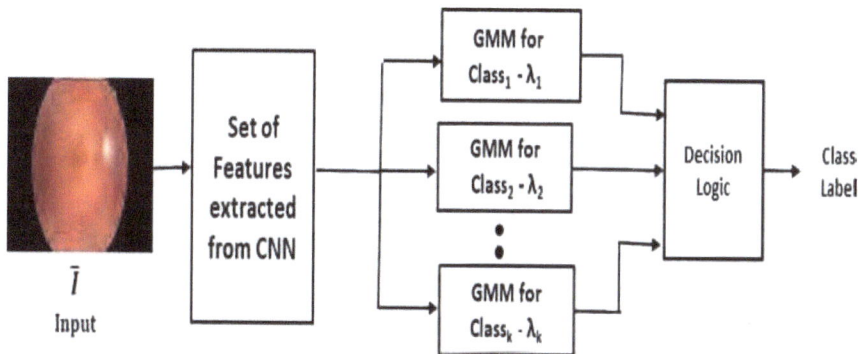

Fig. (2). Proposed Model- (CNN-GMM). 'λ_k' represents the Gaussian mixture model built using examples belonging to Class 'k'.

A very extensive training facility is available. High-speed GPU implementations using the CNN-based feature maps associated with that class, a CNN-GMM, the class-specific Gaussian mixture model is created, as shown in Fig. (**2**). The matching GMM determines the class in which the test feature map has the highest likelihood score, and that class is used for testing. The following decision-making process is used to assign the class label for test feature map X:

Class label for X=argmax c □inin p(cu) □inin p(cu) □inin p(cu) □(1.1) where the class-specific models for C classes are represented by cu, c = 1, 2,... C.

Construction of CNN-SVM

CNN-based feature maps are used to train the SVM classifier in CNN-SVM. We use a one-versus-the-rest approach for classification and grading tasks. A winner-take-all approach is used to classify a sample feature map X using the following decision rule:

Class label for X =argmax k D_k (X) - 1.2

Where the discriminant function of the SVM built for the class "k" is denoted by DC (X).

Construction of CNN-GMM-SVM

The key elements that an improved classification requires can be extracted from an image by a convolutional neural network. In order to extract features from retinal pictures for multi-class classification, we suggest using the CNN architecture. The process of extracting features from convolutional neural networks is essential for creating classifiers that rely on generative models. Table 1 size of feature maps generated by convolutional neural network for classification tasks using E-ophthalmic dataset. Here 'Ml' denotes the model at layer 'l'.

Table 1. Information on the layers and feature maps created from the E-ophthalmic dataset using the CNN architecture.

Model & Layer No.	Type	Maps
M_1	Input Conv1 Pool1	$860 \times 1240 \times 3$ 32 maps of 860×1240 neurons 32 maps of 420×620 neurons
M_2	Conv2 Pool2	32 maps of 640×340 neurons 32 maps of 120×170 neurons
M_3	Conv3 Pool3	32 maps of $221 \times 2\,60$ neurons 32 maps of $110 \times 13\,0$ neurons
M_4	Conv4 Pool4	32 maps of 140×200 neurons 32 maps of 70×100 neurons
M_5	Conv5 Pool5	32 maps of $80 \times 8\,0$ neurons 32 maps of 40×40 neurons
M_6	Conv6 Pool6	32 maps of 30×45 neurons 32 maps of 15×22 neurons
M_7	Conv7 Pool7	32 maps of 10×20 neurons 32 maps of 5×10 neurons

Let the set of "N" photos be the input images. I= {I1, I2, IN}, where 'N' is the overall count of images. Each picture Ii has a dimension of h× w× d, where h, w, and d stand for the retinal images' height, width, and depth, respectively. The CNN is built using f filters with a width of "m". In convolutional network terminology, the second argument—in this case, the function w—is frequently referred to as the kernel, whereas the first argument—in this case, the function (I)—is typically referred to as the input. The map of features is produced as the convolution process's output.

V is equal to (I*W) + B (1.3).

E-ophthalmic Dataset

There are 233 healthy and 148 unhealthy retinal pictures (microaneurysms or microscopic hemorrhages) in the E-naphtha collection. The proposed model is tested on 25% of the total photos in the dataset after being trained on 75% of the images. The training set consists of 286 retinal images, of which 111 are dangerous, and 175 are normal. There are 95 photographs in the test set; 58 of them are in the normal class, and 37 are in the abnormal class. Five times, random selection has been used to choose retinal images for training and testing. Table **2** comparison of the accuracy of the CNN, CNN-GMM, CNN-SVM, and CNN-SVM-GMM classifiers on the E-ophthalmic dataset for classification tasks.

Table 2. Displays the outcomes of the suggested methodology (CNN-GMM-SVM).

Models	\multicolumn{4}{c}{ACCURACY (%)}			
	CNN	CNN-GMM	CNN-SVM	CNN-GMM-SVM(Proposed)
M_1	45	63.1	63.1	62.1
M_2	45	66.3	68.4	69.5
M_3	45	72.6	72.6	74.7
M_4	45	74.7	76.8	78.9
M_5	45	75.8	78.9	83.1
M_6	45	75.8	78.9	85.2
M_7	**45**	**82.1**	**83.1**	**86.3**

This typical GMM-based classifier uses CNN features and traditional CNN for the classification and grading of DR images. All tables share the value of 45 in the standard CNN. Table **2** illustrates that the outcomes obtained from the CNN-GMM and CNN-SVM models exhibit a reasonable degree of correlation. The suggested method produces values for each model that are noticeably better than those obtained using CNN, CNN-GMM, and CNN-SVM separately, as contrasted to using CNN, CNN-SVM, and CNN-GMM, separately. The suggested framework (CNN-GMM-SVM) with trade-off parameter C = 7 (86.3) yields the best results when compared to other models. Compared to the CNN-SVM model, the CNN-GMM-SVM model improves classification accuracy by 3.2%.

The accuracy results utilizing CNN, CNN-GMM, CNN-SVM, and the suggested method (CNN-GMM-SVM) are contrasted in Fig. (**3**). When compared to the other methods, which have the lowest accuracy, the suggested model has the highest accuracy. The accuracy bar graph shows how the suggested model outperforms the current models.

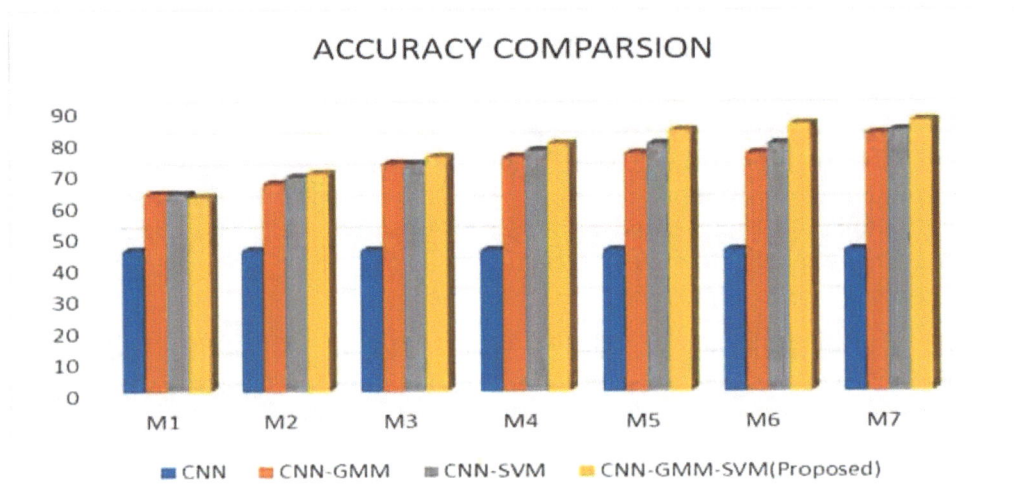

Fig. (3). Comparison of accuracy.

The CNN-GMM and CNN-SVM models' sensitivity results are largely comparable, as Table **3** illustrates. For each model, the CNN-GMM-SVM approach yields results that are clearly better than the CNN, CNN-GMM, and CNN-SVM methods together. The suggested model (CNN-GMM-SVM) does have 81.0% sensitivity for classification tasks, as shown in Table **3**. When compared to other models, the suggested model (CNN-GMM-SVM) produces the best results. By 5.4%, the CNN-GMM-SVM model improves the classification sensitivity compared to CNN-SVM and CNN-GMM.

Table 3. Comparison of the sensitivity of the CNN, CNN-GMM, CNN-SVM, and CNN-SVM-GMM classifiers on the E-ophthalmic dataset for classification tasks.

Sensitivity (in %)			
Models	**CNN-GMM**	**CNN-SVM**	**CNN-GMM-SVM**
M_1	51.3	54	56.7
M_2	56.7	59.4	64.8
M_3	67.5	67.5	72.9
M_4	70.2	72.9	78.3
M_5	72.9	72.9	81
M_6	72.9	70.2	81
M_7	75.6	75.6	81

The sensitivity results for CNN-GMM, CNN-SVM, and the suggested method (CNN-GMM-SVM) are contrasted in Fig. (**4**). In comparison to the other methods, which have the lowest accuracy, the suggested model has the best sensitivity. The suggested model outperforms the current models, as seen by the sensitivity bar graph.

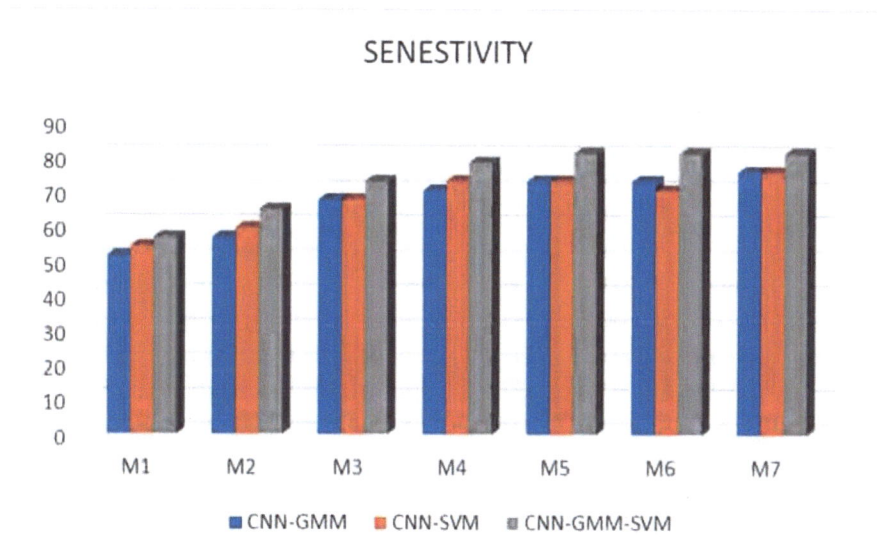

Fig. (4). Comparison of sensitivity.

The specificity outcomes of the CNN-GMM and CNN-SVM models are largely comparable, as Table **4** illustrates. Results for each model generated by the suggested method (CNN-GMM-SVM) are clearly better than those obtained by employing CNN-GMM and CNN-SVM separately. The suggested model (CNN-GMM-SVM) does have 89.6% specificity for classification tasks.

Table 4. Comparison of the specificity of the CNN, CNN-GMM, CNN-SVM, and CNN-SVM-GMM classifiers on the E-ophthalmic dataset for classification tasks.

Specificity (in %)			
Models	**CNN-GMM**	**CNN-SVM**	**CNN-GMM-SVM**
M_1	70.6	68.9	65.5
M_2	72.4	74.1	72.4
M_3	75.8	75.8	75.8
M_4	77.5	79.3	79.3
M_5	77.5	82.7	84.4
M_6	77.5	84.4	87.9
M_7	86.2	87.9	89.6

The results for specificity using CNN, CNN-GMM, CNN-SVM, and the suggested method (CNN-GMM-SVM) are contrasted in Fig. (**5**). In comparison to the other methods, which have the lowest accuracy, the suggested model has the best specificity. The suggested model outperforms the current models, as shown by the specificity bar graph.

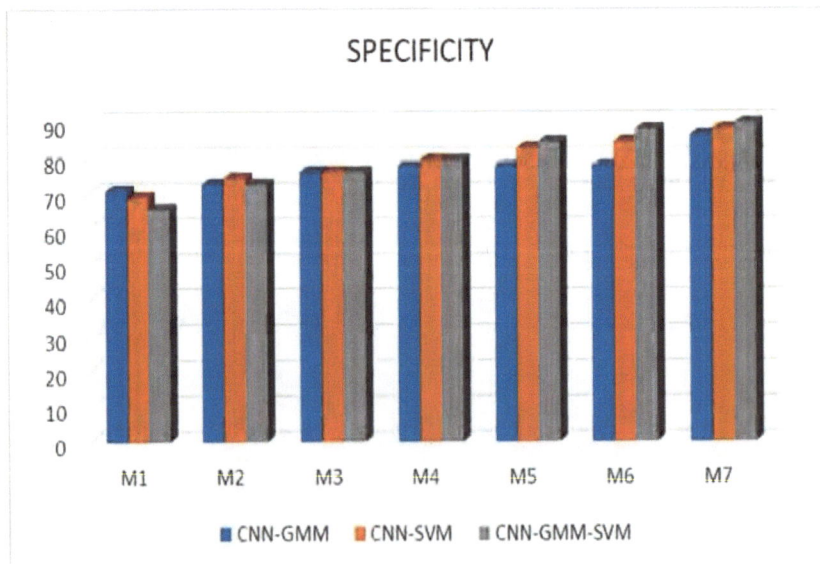

Fig. (5). Comparison of specificity.

CONCLUSION

In this paper, we investigated CNN-GMM-potential SVMs for the purpose of classifying and grading the severity of retinopathy images. Experiments were conducted with the E-ophthalmic. Models such as CNN-SVM, CNN-GMM, and CNN-GMM-SVM were used for evaluation. The experimental data are superior to those from classical CNN and GMM, according to the comparison. The accuracy for the categorization tasks was 86.3%. Results from CNN-GMM-SVM were superior to those from CNN-SVM and CNN-GMM. Moreover, we have conducted additional studies to boost the accuracy even more. Consequently, a feature learning-based approach and an ensemble of classifiers utilizing convolutional networks have been explored and reported in the research for the classification of DR images.

REFERENCES

[1]   S.P. Yadav, S. Zaidi, C.D.S. Nascimento, V.H.C. de Albuquerque, and S.S. Chauhan, "Analysis and Design of automatically generating for GPS Based Moving Object Tracking System", *2023 International Conference on Artificial Intelligence and Smart Communication (AISC)*, pp. 1-5, 2023.
[http://dx.doi.org/10.1109/AISC56616.2023.10085180]

[2]   P. Udayaraju, K.S. Murthy, P. Jeyanthi, B.V.R. Raju, T. Rajasri, and N. Ramadevi, "A combined U-Net and multi-class support vector machine learning models for diabetic retinopathy macula edema segmentation and classification DME", *Soft Comput.*, pp. 1-13, 2023.

[3]   S.P. Yadav, and S. Yadav, "Fusion of Medical Images using a Wavelet Methodology: A Survey", *Transactions on Smart Processing & Computing. The Institute of Electronics Engineers of Korea,* vol. 8, no. 4, pp. 265-271, 2019.
[http://dx.doi.org/10.5573/IEIESPC.2019.8.4.265]

[4]   A. Jain, V. Bhatnagar, A. C. S. Rao, and M. Khari, "Retina disease prediction using modified convolutional neural network based on Inception-ResNet model with support vector machine classifier", *Computational Intelligence,*, pp. 1088-1111, 2023.
[http://dx.doi.org/10.1111/coin.12601]

[5]   S.P. Yadav, and S. Yadav, "Fusion of Medical Images in Wavelet Domain: A Discrete Mathematical Model", *Ingeniería Solidaria*, vol. 14, no. 25, pp. 1-11, 2018.
[http://dx.doi.org/10.16925/.v14i0.2236]

[6]   İ. Kayadibi, and G.E. Güraksın, "An Explainable Fully Dense Fusion Neural Network with Deep Support Vector Machine for Retinal Disease Determination", *International Journal of Computational Intelligence Systems,* vol. 16, no. 1, p. 28, 2023.
[http://dx.doi.org/10.1007/s44196-023-00210-z]

[7]   S. P. Yadav, and S. Yadav, "Mathematical implementation of fusion of medical images in continuous wavelet domain", *Journal of Advanced Research in dynamical and control system,* vol. 10, no. 10, pp. 45-54, 2019.

[8]   P. Jeyanthi, B. V. R. Raju, T. Rajasri, and N. Ramadevi, *A Combined U-Net and Multi-Class Support Vector Machine Learning Models for Diabetic Retinopathy Macula Edema Segmentation and Classification DME.,* 2023.

[9]   S.P. Yadav, "Blockchain Security", In: *Blockchain Security in Cloud Computing. EAI/Springer Innovations in Communication and Computing.,* K. Baalamurugan, S.R. Kumar, A. Kumar, V. Kumar, S. Padmanaban, Eds., Springer: Cham, 2022.
[http://dx.doi.org/10.1007/978-3-030-70501-5_1]

[10] R. Brindha, A. Lakkshmanan, P. Renukadevi, and D. Jeyakumar, "Detection of Retinopathy of Prematurity using ResNet Based Deep Features and Support Vector Machine Classifier", *2023 Second International Conference on Augmented Intelligence and Sustainable Systems (ICAISS),* pp. 1020-1027, 2023.
[http://dx.doi.org/10.1109/ICAISS58487.2023.10250647]

[11] X. Xue, R. Shanmugam, S. Palanisamy, O.I. Khalaf, D. Selvaraj, and G.M. Abdulsahib, "A hybrid cross layer with harris-hawk-optimization-based efficient routing for wireless sensor networks", *Symmetry (Basel),* vol. 15, no. 2, p. 438, 2023.
[http://dx.doi.org/10.3390/sym15020438]

[12] R. Parvathi, and U. Vignesh, "Diabetic Retinopathy Detection Using Transfer Learning", *AI and IoT-Based Technologies for Precision Medicine,* p. 177-204, 2023.
[http://dx.doi.org/10.4018/979-8-3693-0876-9.ch011]

[13] K. Suganyadevi, V. Nandhalal, S. Palanisamy, and S. Dhanasekaran, "Data security and safety services using modified timed efficient stream loss-tolerant authentication in diverse models of VANET", *International Conference on Edge Computing and Applications (ICECAA),* pp. 417-422, 2022.
[http://dx.doi.org/10.1109/ICECAA55415.2022.9936128]

[14] S. Sunkari, A. Sangam, V.S. P, S. M, R. Raman, R. Rajalakshmi, and T. S, "A refined ResNet18 architecture with Swish activation function for Diabetic Retinopathy classification", *Biomed. Signal Process. Control,* vol. 88, p. 105630, 2024.
[http://dx.doi.org/10.1016/j.bspc.2023.105630]

[15] R. Ramakrishnan, M. A. Mohammed, M. A. Mohammed, V. A. Mohammed, and J. Logeshwaran, "An innovation prediction of DNA damage of melanoma skin cancer patients using deep learning", *14th International Conference on Computing Communication and Networking Technologies (ICCCNT),* p. 1-7, 2023.
[http://dx.doi.org/10.1109/ICCCNT56998.2023.10306749]

[16] M. Jian, H. Chen, C. Tao, X. Li, and G. Wang, "Triple-DRNet: A triple-cascade convolution neural network for diabetic retinopathy grading using fundus images", *Comput. Biol. Med.,* vol. 155, p. 106631, 2023.
[http://dx.doi.org/10.1016/j.compbiomed.2023.106631] [PMID: 36805216]

[17] M. A. Mohammed, V. A. Mohammed, R. Ramakrishnan, M. A. Mohammed, and J. Logeshwaran, "The three dimensional dosimetry imaging for automated eye cancer classification using transfer learning model", *14th International Conference on Computing Communication and Networking Technologies (ICCCNT),* p. 1-6, 2023.
[http://dx.doi.org/10.1109/ICCCNT56998.2023.10307446]

[18] M. Nahiduzzaman, M. Robiul Islam, M. Omaer Faruq Goni, M. Shamim Anower, M. Ahsan, J. Haider, and M. Kowalski, "Diabetic retinopathy identification using parallel convolutional neural network based feature extractor and ELM classifier", *Expert Syst. Appl.,* vol. 217, p. 119557, 2023.
[http://dx.doi.org/10.1016/j.eswa.2023.119557]

[19] K.R.K. Yesodha, A. Jagadeesan, and J. Logeshwaran, "IoT applications in Modern Supply Chains: Enhancing Efficiency and Product Quality", *2nd International Conference on Industrial Electronics: Developments & Applications (ICIDeA),* p. 366-371, 2023.
[http://dx.doi.org/10.1109/ICIDeA59866.2023.10295273]

[20] N. Mukherjee, and S. Sengupta, "Application of deep learning approaches for classification of diabetic retinopathy stages from fundus retinal images: a survey", *Multimedia Tools Appl.,* vol. 83, no. 14, pp. 43115-43175, 2023.
[http://dx.doi.org/10.1007/s11042-023-17254-0]

CHAPTER 5

Evaluation of Performance of a Person using Virtual Stock Market

Sachin[1,*]**, Shreyansh Gupta**[1]**, Uday Tyagi**[1] **and Sonia Verma**[1]

[1] *Computer Science ABES Engineering College, Ghaziabad, India*

Abstract: This project's goal was to use research and trading simulations to acquire a fundamental understanding of the stock market. Using suitable investment and technical analysis methodologies along with online simulation tools, investment theory was put into practice. During the simulation, stocks were traded using several tactics. A number of trading techniques' outcomes were analysed and ranked based on profitability. There was also a discussion of each strategy's efficacy. It is obvious that one of the most popular topics these days is the stock market, but what is it really? Sometimes, it needs to be clarified what is intended. The stock market is where? Or is there another possibility? It is an entirely abstract idea for many people. A lot of individuals believe that the stock market and Wall Street are identical to one another. However, Wall Street is the hub of trade and the birthplace of the largest financial market in the world. In actuality, the phrase "stock market" refers to the idea of a system that makes it possible to trade derivatives, other securities, and firm shares. Derivatives are traded on many exchanges, and commodities are exchanged on commodity markets. Most consumers need the resources or financial know-how to trade on stock exchanges. This study aimed to improve people's capacity for learning and their fearlessness. A web-based virtual stock trading system (VST) with integrated financial indicator analysis was created to mimic the stock market. It is anticipated that when students study with objective financial analysis, their mental states will be unaffected by the news, and students who follow market movements can become logical investors.

Keywords: Analysis, Commodities, Identical, Movements, Securities, Tactics.

INTRODUCTION

People are starting to understand the significance of stocks. We may now assist others in developing further in this area [1]. Although more people are becoming aware of investing, some still feel scared [2]. To help alleviate this fear, the

---

* **Corresponding author Sachin:** Computer Science ABES Engineering College, Ghaziabad, India;
E-mail: Sachin.19b121036@gmail.com

Pankaj Kumar Mishra & Satya Prakash Yadav (Eds.)

market offers a service known as paper trading, which helps to establish a virtual environment. Investing in stocks makes fixed money more valuable and helps create profits for both men and women who spend money on it [3]. The majority of people are ignorant investors with no financial need to understand the stock market. Both irrational and rational variables typically have an impact on the stock market [4]. The stock market has been observed to be impacted by the government, well-known individuals, and occasionally external forces as well. Several locations in India were once the source of the stock market, but the Bombay Stock Exchange and the National Stock Exchange are the only two stock exchanges [5]. There are a lot of paper trading platforms available in India, but most of them need to demonstrate how one may advance or how stock market news can help one invest in stocks [6]. They also do not reward users for successful investments and reaching goals. It follows that investors may make poor decisions if they are not led and may find themselves in danger [7]. We have, therefore, devised a fix for this. As a result, regular retail investors must hone their financial research abilities and make prudent investments in potentially lucrative stocks. Regular investors pick things up quickly on their own, but it takes time [8]. Consequently, this platform fosters an extremely conducive environment for stock trading and assists in paving the way for stock market success. The current climate of the stock market is bad; most of them are commercial, and the average individual needs help to understand them. Many individuals invest in it, but they typically provide less feedback [9]. However, for beginners, feedback is crucial. Additionally, these technologies could be more suitable for instruction in financial management. In addition to serving as a tool for instructors to evaluate their students' investments and learning outcomes, the virtual stock trading system presented in this study allows students to analyse the financial parameters of specific stocks in order to help them choose equities that may be successful [10]. We offer instruments for evaluating investment performance that assists you in comprehending the accurate idea of creating a website centered around the virtual stock trading system (VST) in order to draw in students [11]. Acquiring knowledge about stock management and associated topics, as well as utilizing a virtual setting promotes interactive learning and instantaneous stock trading [12]. Implementation tools are used to as models for key figure analysis and performance evaluation of investments [13]. Students would benefit from learning how to make profitable investments. Students should be able to evaluate the financial ratios of certain potential equities before trading once they have grown accustomed to the VST technique [14]. By doing this, you can either profit from your investment or lower the risk [15]. VST systems have shown to be helpful tools for researching individual investors' trading patterns and other financial concerns.

RELATED WORKS

Evaluating an individual's success in the virtual stock market is an extremely difficult assignment [16]. The performance assessment of an individual in the virtual stock market ought to be able to precisely gauge the trading tactics of a user, given the constantly shifting financial landscape [17]. In order to accomplish this, current computational models have been created that can swiftly and correctly calculate an individual's stock market performance. The neural network or backpropagation model is the first one. The foundation of this model is supervised learning [18]. It gradually refines a user's holdings in the virtual stock market and then utilizes what it has learned from the past to forecast the user's stock market performance in the future. For stock market applications, the backpropagation model is a powerful computational tool [19], since it can forecast the future performance of the stock market with greater accuracy than conventional techniques like regression analysis. The random forest model is the second model. In order to categorize a person's stock market positions into one of three groups—progress, stasis, or deterioration—this technique requires building a forest of decision trees [20]. More quickly and precisely than using traditional methods, the random forest model may ascertain an individual's current stock market performance by grouping their positions into these three groups.

LITERATURE REVIEW

Stock Trading Actions

As a result of a lack of knowledge, investors are biased to purchase well-performing equities, more shares of stocks they already hold, and previously owned stocks at discounts to recent sales prices due to psychological factors. To purchase eminent stocks, *etc.*, retail investors can also view their prior investments and draw lessons from past blunders. Investing enthusiasts frequently overlook the risks associated with aggressive stock trading. Those who invest understand that they must purchase at a discount and sell at a premium. The observations above imply that when trading stocks, investors would not be able to make logical selections. Reducing negative emotional impact enables investors to make more logical decisions while trading stocks, which boosts earnings. Digital media are crucial, particularly for individuals. Investors sharing information about stocks and finance affect stock prices and investors' choice of investments. Media outlets, including digital and print ones, typically focus on investors. In the market, individual investors are primarily common. We depend on the most recent news, yet we miss out on important details that could lead to more in-depth research. These uninformed investors frequently make wrong decisions as a result of incomplete or erroneous information or psychological prejudices, which may have detrimental effects and cause a large financial loss.

Online Virtual Stock Trading System

One of the areas where financial services sector excels and completely meets electronic website requirements is online commerce. Virtual stock trading offers a number of benefits, including increased speed, information transparency, a propensity for anticipating previous data, and reduced expenses. However, establishing a trustworthy and risk-free environment is more crucial than generating revenues for users. The virtual market is a complicated, difficult-t--understand system that is full of noise and uncertainty. It is greatly impacted by a wide range of factors, such as corporate financial reporting, government policies, shifting financial regulations, real-time stock price fluctuations, global markets, foreign stock market volatility, and oil prices, among others.

E-Learning

Around the world, e-learning is becoming more and more popular in institutions like colleges and enterprises. The sole explanation is that it makes information easily accessible so that we can learn from it. It provides us with a safe and encouraging learning atmosphere and is affordable for all kinds of organizations, whether they are commercial, business, or educational. It is economical for both companies. The advancement of technologies such as communication and e-learning, which are based on mobile technology, allows students to study in an environment conducive to learning about stock markets and applying what they have learned to the actual stock market. Many subjects, including biology, ecology, history, and nursing education, use e-learning. There is a survey that revealed, regardless of gender, over 80 percent of the general public has expressed a preference for web-based learning as a means of acquiring new knowledge, applying it to real-world situations, and enhancing the quality of learning. There are other helpful approaches as well. For example, telepathology is a helpful method for teaching pathologists to perceive images on the internet that are invisible to the human eye.

DESIGN AND IMPLEMENTATION

Because study is the means by which a researcher hopes to identify and halt the result of a certain issue, the solution aids in the movement's conclusion. "A concerted effort to acquire new knowledge" is how Redman and Mary characterize the investigations.

Research Design

In order to practically integrate compliance with the research's cause with the business organization, the research design combines record testing and series conditions. Lesson planning is actually a conceptual framework for carrying out lessons; it produces green text for data gathering, analysis, and factual evaluation.

Methodology

Prototyping, wind development, waterfall modeling, detailed programming, and numerous other procedures have been the most widely utilized techniques, when developing this gadget, versatile software. Fig. (**1**) shows the use case diagram.

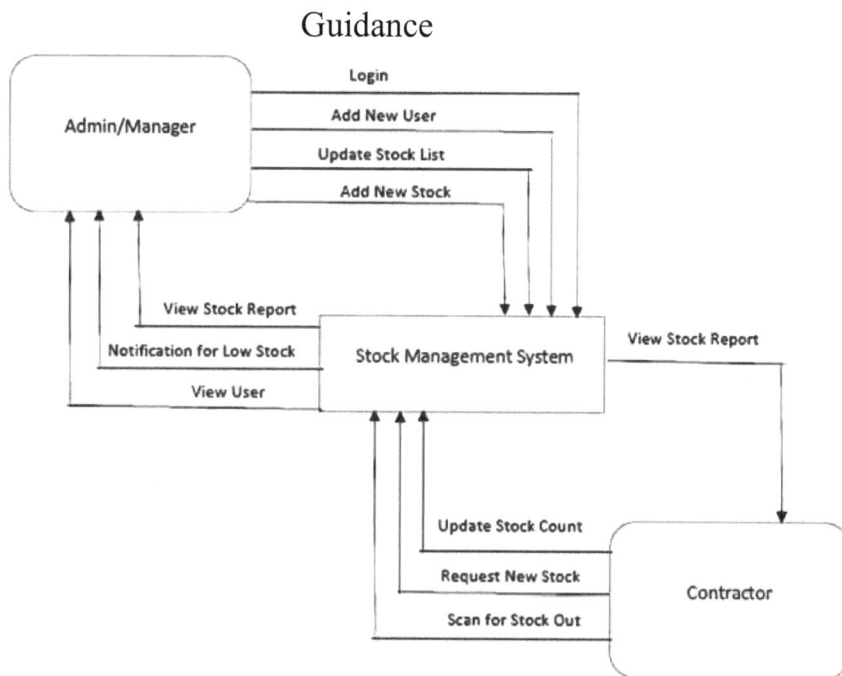

Fig. (1). Use case diagram.

Working of the Project By Diagram

In this case, it will be used to show how the different parts of the project are related. Fig. (**2**) shows the depot Page. Fig. (**3**) shows the Quest Page. Fig. (**4**) shows the Market Page (Table **1**).

Table 1. Features used for the development model approach.

Applications / Features	Stock Controller - inventories	Stock Count (Inventory Scanner)	Smart Inventory System
Registration	Yes	Yes	Yes
Scanner	No	Barcode/QR Code	Barcode/QR Code
Stock Location Info	Yes	No	Yes
Reminder/Notification	Yes	No	No
Database Type	Online/Local	Online/Local	Online/Local
Insert Image Option	Yes	No	Yes
Save/Print data into pdf	Yes	Yes	Yes

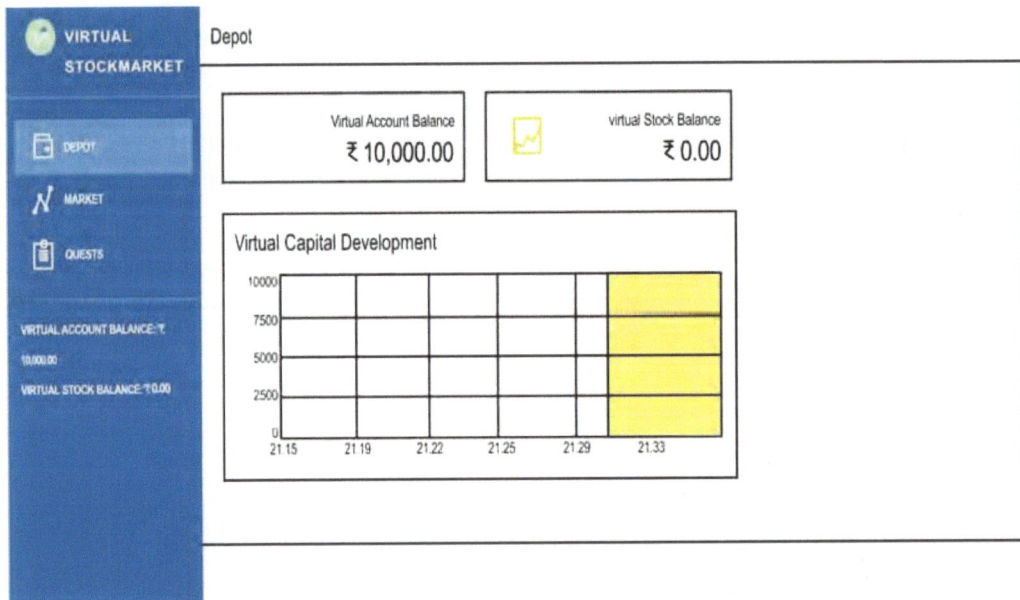

Fig. (2). Depot page.

Fig. (3). Quest page.

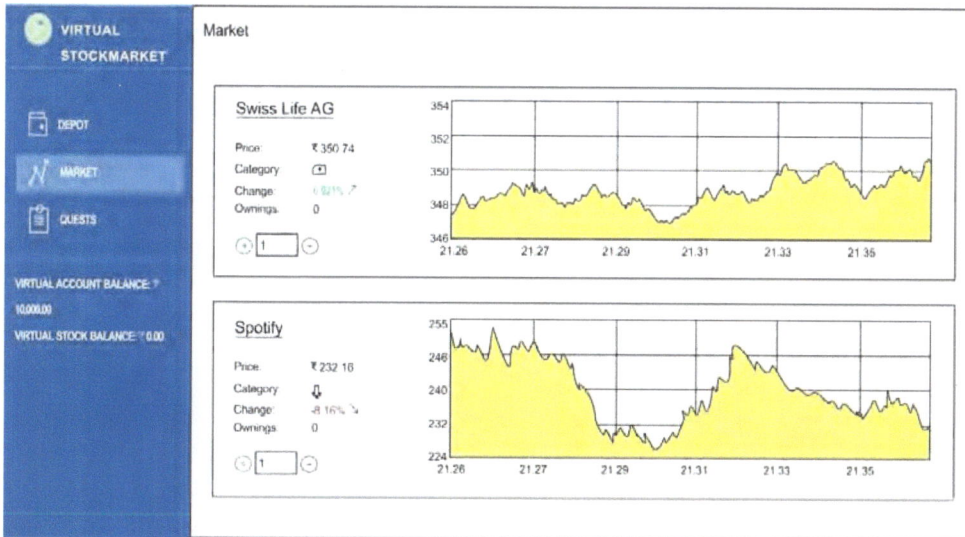

Fig. (4). Market page.

Research Design Used in the Study

Studies usually aim to explain phenomena and give precise descriptions of variables and their connections. Surveys are commonly included in descriptive research designs. Statistical resources for statistics are also available.

 a. Fundamental information.
 b. Back-up documents.

Important statistics: Information gathered from private conversations with approved vendors is used in this procedure.

a. Second facts: The data for the second fact are gathered from yearly reports and statements that contain NOL.

Equipment and analysis techniques: Charts, tables and graph.

FINDINGS OF THE RESEARCH

- The investor can comprehend the usage, buying, and promotion of the product, as well as the risk and partial refund.
- Every investor who aspires to a long-term and immediate investment can reap substantial rewards.
- Projecting a dependable EPS outcome for the future.
- When it comes to computer performance, the investor ought to be the first to know.
- Refrain from searching for stock in a business where the owners are different.
- Customers ought to exhibit leisure activities.

LIMITATIONS

Only tons are taken into account, similar to the stock exchange rate. Only certain companies are included in the testing.

CONCLUSION

Trading habits are ingrained in users' virtual environments to facilitate greater learning. Individuals engage in a lot of money-wasting activities that ultimately fail to teach them how to trade stocks well. As a result, there is a need for improved learning environments that can impart genuine trading skills. In India, it is crucial to learn to stick to trading in a virtual setting since it helps people break free from their fear of taking risks. The psychological and informational theories mentioned above are in favour of active, engaging learning as a more efficient means of developing genuine abilities. It is a great thing that we can start learning stock trading with no money down when we have none at all. According to research, India is a nation that will increase its stock trading investments. Therefore, we need to understand a lot and trade with ease in order to have a more profitable market. Students can participate in trading in the actual share market thanks to this technique. Students who work on real-world issues are more driven to study this.

The following things need to be modified if someone wishes to utilize MIRA Chabot for another use case:

- Adequate information on the use case on the MIRA resource portal.
- New datasets or utilize pre-existing ones to train the DIET architecture.
- A tree with all the steps that the MIRA Chabot needs to take.
- A set of responses that the MIRA Chabot should utilize when responding to customers.

REFERENCES

[1]   S.P. Yadav, S. Zaidi, C.D.S. Nascimento, V.H.C. de Albuquerque, and S.S. Chauhan, "Analysis and Design of automatically generating for GPS Based Moving Object Tracking System", *2023 International Conference on Artificial Intelligence and Smart Communication (AISC)*, pp. 1-5, 2023.
[http://dx.doi.org/10.1109/AISC56616.2023.10085180]

[2]   A. Jarrahi, and L. Safari, "Evaluating the effectiveness of publishers' features in fake news detection on social media", *Multimedia Tools Appl.,* vol. 82, no. 2, pp. 2913-2939, 2023.
[http://dx.doi.org/10.1007/s11042-022-12668-8] [PMID: 35431607]

[3]   S.P. Yadav, and S. Yadav, "Fusion of Medical Images using a Wavelet Methodology: A Survey", *Transactions on Smart Processing & Computing. The Institute of Electronics Engineers of Korea,* vol. 8, no. 4, pp. 265-271, 2019.
[http://dx.doi.org/10.5573/IEIESPC.2019.8.4.265]

[4]   K. Olorunnimbe, and H. Viktor, "Deep learning in the stock market—a systematic survey of practice, backtesting, and applications", *Artif. Intell. Rev.,* vol. 56, no. 3, pp. 2057-2109, 2023.
[http://dx.doi.org/10.1007/s10462-022-10226-0] [PMID: 35791405]

[5]   S.P. Yadav, and S. Yadav, "Fusion of Medical Images in Wavelet Domain: A Discrete Mathematical Model", *Ingeniería Solidaria,* vol. 14, no. 25, pp. 1-11, 2018.
[http://dx.doi.org/10.16925/.v14i0.2236]

[6]   D. Jackson, L. Riebe, S. Meek, M. Ogilvie, A. Kuilboer, L. Murphy, N. Collins, K. Lynch, and M. Brock, "Using an industry-aligned capabilities framework to effectively assess student performance in non-accredited work-integrated learning contexts", *Teach. High. Educ.,* vol. 28, no. 4, pp. 802-821, 2023.
[http://dx.doi.org/10.1080/13562517.2020.1863348]

[7]   S. P. Yadav, and S. Yadav, "Mathematical implementation of fusion of medical images in continuous wavelet domain", *Journal of Advanced Research in dynamical and control system,* vol. 10, no. 10, pp. 45-54, 2019.

[8]   M.N. Ashtiani, and B. Raahemi, "News-based intelligent prediction of financial markets using text mining and machine learning: A systematic literature review", *Expert Syst. Appl.,* vol. 217, p. 119509, 2023.
[http://dx.doi.org/10.1016/j.eswa.2023.119509]

[9]   S.P. Yadav, "Blockchain Security", In: *Blockchain Security in Cloud Computing. EAI/Springer Innovations in Communication and Computing.,* K. Baalamurugan, S.R. Kumar, A. Kumar, V. Kumar, S. Padmanaban, Eds., Springer: Cham, 2022.
[http://dx.doi.org/10.1007/978-3-030-70501-5_1]

[10]   M. Nagy, G. Lăzăroiu, and K. Valaskova, "Machine Intelligence and Autonomous Robotic Technologies in the Corporate Context of SMEs: Deep Learning and Virtual Simulation Algorithms, Cyber-Physical Production Networks, and Industry 4.0-Based Manufacturing Systems", *Appl. Sci. (Basel),* vol. 13, no. 3, p. 1681, 2023.

[http://dx.doi.org/10.3390/app13031681]

[11]   X. Xue, R. Shanmugam, S. Palanisamy, O.I. Khalaf, D. Selvaraj, and G.M. Abdulsahib, "A hybrid cross layer with harris-hawk-optimization-based efficient routing for wireless sensor networks", *Symmetry (Basel),* vol. 15, no. 2, p. 438, 2023.
[http://dx.doi.org/10.3390/sym15020438]

[12]   B. Wu, and W. Chen, "Factors affecting MOOC teacher effectiveness from the perspective of professional capital", *Behav. Inf. Technol.,* vol. 42, no. 5, pp. 498-513, 2023.
[http://dx.doi.org/10.1080/0144929X.2021.2024596]

[13]   K. Suganyadevi, V. Nandhalal, S. Palanisamy, and S. Dhanasekaran, "Data security and safety services using modified timed efficient stream loss-tolerant authentication in diverse models of VANET", *International Conference on Edge Computing and Applications (ICECAA),* pp. 417-422, 2022.
[http://dx.doi.org/10.1109/ICECAA55415.2022.9936128]

[14]   G.G. Jadhav, S.V. Gaikwad, and D. Bapat, "A systematic literature review: digital marketing and its impact on SMEs", *J. Indian Bus. Res.,* vol. 15, no. 1, pp. 76-91, 2023.
[http://dx.doi.org/10.1108/JIBR-05-2022-0129]

[15]   R. Ramakrishnan, M. A. Mohammed, M. A. Mohammed, V. A. Mohammed, and J. Logeshwaran, "An innovation prediction of DNA damage of melanoma skin cancer patients using deep learning", *14th International Conference on Computing Communication and Networking Technologies (ICCCNT),* p. 1-7, 2023.
[http://dx.doi.org/10.1109/ICCCNT56998.2023.10306749]

[16]   K.K. Abdo, H.A.M. Al-Qudah, L.A. Al-Qudah, and M.Z. Qudah, "RETRACTED ARTICLE: The effect of economic variables (workers 'diaries abroad, bank deposits, gross domestic product, and inflation) on stock returns in the Amman Financial Market from 2005/2018", *Journal of Sustainable Finance & Investment,* vol. 13, no. 1, pp. 59-72, 2023.
[http://dx.doi.org/10.1080/20430795.2021.1883384]

[17]   M. A. Mohammed, V. A. Mohammed, R. Ramakrishnan, M. A. Mohammed, and J. Logeshwaran, "The three dimensional dosimetry imaging for automated eye cancer classification using transfer learning model", *14th International Conference on Computing Communication and Networking Technologies (ICCCNT),* p. 1-6, 2023.
[http://dx.doi.org/10.1109/ICCCNT56998.2023.10307446]

[18]   T.T.H. Bui, M. Jambulingam, M. Amin, and N.T. Hung, "RETRACTED ARTICLE: Impact of COVID-19 pandemic on franchise performance from franchisee perspectives: the role of entrepreneurial orientation, market orientation and franchisor support", *Journal of Sustainable Finance & Investment,* vol. 13, no. 1, pp. 264-282, 2023.
[http://dx.doi.org/10.1080/20430795.2021.1891787]

[19]   K.R.K. Yesodha, A. Jagadeesan, and J. Logeshwaran, "IoT applications in Modern Supply Chains: Enhancing Efficiency and Product Quality", *2nd International Conference on Industrial Electronics: Developments & Applications (ICIDeA),* p. 366-371, 2023.
[http://dx.doi.org/10.1109/ICIDeA59866.2023.10295273]

[20]   X. Li, H. Wang, and C. Yang, "Driving mechanism of digital economy based on regulation algorithm for development of low-carbon industries", *Sustain. Energy Technol. Assess.,* vol. 55, p. 102909, 2023.
[http://dx.doi.org/10.1016/j.seta.2022.102909]

CHAPTER 6

GIS Mapping of High Sewage Areas in India and Sustainable Design of Sewage Disposal System

Sachin Kumar[1], Manish Kumar[1] and **Shreeja Kacker[1,*]**

[1] *Department of Civil Engineering, Greater Noida Institute of Technology, Greater Noida, U.P., India*

Abstract: The current study focuses on designing sustainable sewage disposal systems for high-sewage locations in India by using ArcGIS software for GIS mapping. The study maps and examines the spatial distribution of sewage and disposal across the nation using ArcGIS software, which integrates data from multiple GIS sources such as census information, satellite images, and municipal records. The performance of the current sewage disposal systems in high-sewage locations in terms of upholding environmental and public health requirements is examined and evaluated in this article. Of the sewage generated in India, more than 62,000 million liters per day (MLD) are processed, according to the Central Pollution Control Board (CPCB) (2019). Water bodies receive the discharge of untreated sewage and pose a serious risk to human health and water pollution. In high-sewage locations—urban slums and peri-urban areas, for example—where sewage treatment infrastructure is either non-existent or insufficient, the situation is terrible. The study uses GIS mapping techniques to locate high-sewage regions in India using ArcGIS software. Then, it examines the features of these places, including socioeconomic level, housing conditions, and population density. According to the research, places with high sewage levels are primarily found in metropolitan and peril-urban regions that have dense populations and inadequate sanitary infrastructure. In high-sewage locations, the study also shows that the current sewage disposal systems are mostly insufficient and need to be upgraded in order to comply with environmental and public health regulations. The study suggests a sustainable sewage disposal system design for a specific Greater Noida high-sewage area that combines social and technical sewage management. In order to treat sewage at the source and lessen the strain on the centralized treatment plants, the design makes use of decentralized sewage treatment systems, such as septic tanks and anaerobic digesters. The design also places a strong emphasis on the use of affordable and energy-efficient technologies. The study concludes that because the suggested sustainable design incorporates the local community's active engagement in the sewage treatment process, it is both socially and economically acceptable.

Keywords: Affordable, Design, Economic, Infrastructure, Treatment.

---

* **Corresponding author Shreeja Kacker:** Department of Civil Engineering, Greater Noida Institute of Technology, Greater Noida, U.P., India; E-mail: shreeja.ce@gniot.net.in

Pankaj Kumar Mishra & Satya Prakash Yadav (Eds.)

INTRODUCTION

In India, more than 60 million tonnes of waste are generated every day, of which 45 to 50 million tonnes are left untreated. The metros themselves produce ten million tonnes of waste per day. By 2040, it is predicted that metropolitan India alone will generate around 170 million tonnes of waste annually [1 - 3]. Nevertheless, India has one of the poorest sewage systems in the world, despite the country producing enormous amounts of trash. Trash disposal is common on public roadways. In India's rural areas, open defecation still happens because millions of houses lack toilets. Regardless of the harm it does to the environment, spitting and urinating in public are common practices for millions of individuals [4 - 6]. Numerous actions propagate illness, increase squalor, and worsen the country's health. India may become a healthier place to live, lower the rate of illness, and drastically lower the cost of medical care by abstaining from certain behaviours [7].

If we wish to make India clean, we must alter the way we think about cleanliness and instill it in our actions. To achieve this, there is a national campaign called the Swatch Bharat Bahaman. The topic of discussion includes public communication campaigns aimed at increasing public awareness and promoting healthy behaviours. Additionally, it covers the building of alternative infrastructure, including sewage and waste disposal systems, recycling plants, toilets, *etc.*, to eradicate unhealthy activities [8 - 10]. Despite government efforts, India leads the globe in open defecation despite having few toilets in rural areas, according to a UN audit. Urban India produces 1.88 lakh tons of solid waste every day, or 68.8 million tonnes annually, according to official estimates [11]. By 2041, this amount is expected to rise to 16 million tonnes. Thirty percent of garbage in urban areas still needs to be processed. More than two million people, most of them children, die from diseases caused by a lack of access to clean water, inadequate sanitation, and inadequate hygiene every year [12]. People in urban areas discard rubbish and debris on the ground, the sidewalks outside their homes, and the streets instead of using dustbins [13 - 15].

RELATED WORKS

High sewage regions are a significant contributor to environmental pollution in India, endangering public health and compelling governments to implement necessary corrective measures. As a result, these places must be managed properly if sustainable development is to occur. Thus, in order to create a Geographic Information System (GIS) for India's high-sewage areas, a systematic strategy for monitoring and gathering pertinent data is desperately needed [16]. Recent developments in computing technology have made it possible to create computationally complex GIS mapping, which provides precise information about the locations of high sewage areas. High-resolution satellite imagery is the main source of information used in this type of GIS mapping to locate possible contamination sites [17]. High-quality pictures give a thorough picture of the geography, terrain, land cover, population distribution, and other environmental characteristics. Empirical data from earlier research and observations about water contamination are then superimposed on top of this picture [18, 19]. This GIS mapping will enable the development of sustainable and economical strategies for resource identification and allocation, which will significantly lower the number of high-sewage locations in India. For example, the geographic areas could be prioritized such that only particular places are targeted for the installation [20].

LITERATURE REVIEW

According to Scott *et al.*, the majority of developing countries routinely dump untreated urban sewage into open bodies of water. As a result, there may be a negative impact on both public health and the sustainability of agriculture. The amount of rubbish that the Indian city of Hyderabad dumps into the Music River was the subject of research, and between December 2003 and January 2005, a 14-month water quality evaluation was carried out. The survey found that the quality of river water significantly improved with increasing distance from the city. It was recommended that health protection measures be put into place, such as regular anthelmintic medication programs, improvements to the local water supply, and cleanliness. In their paper, Patel *et al.* found that household wastewater contains organic and inorganic particles in suspended, colloidal, and dissolved forms. Wastewater produced in urban areas is a result of industrial and home activities. Illampu is one of the small cities in the Maharashtra area of India that lacks a suitable drainage system. All household wastewater is currently disposed of either in an open sewer or in a public area close to a residence. To aid in future research, this study maps the primary and subsidiary subsurface collection systems using geographic information systems (GIS). The creation of an effective collection system for Illampu town is its aim. The study by Mini *et al.* looks at human health, aquatic toxins, environmental consequences, and sewage disposal methods. Emphasis is placed on the consequences of releasing various pollutants into aquifers and water bodies, which may make the water unsafe for drinking or other domestic or recreational uses. Subramanian *et al.* highlighted that the lithology of the Chennai region, along with rapid horizontal and vertical expansion, is the primary cause of flooding in urban regions, especially during monsoon seasons. Urban storm waterhas an impact on the lifespan of urban facilities.

IMPORTANCE OF THE PRESENT STUDY

According to a UN report, India leads the globe in open defecation in rural areas where there are few toilets. Urban India produces 1.88 lakh tons of solid waste every day, or 68.8 million tons annually, according to official estimates. By 2041, this amount is expected to rise to 16 million tons. Thirty percent of garbage in urban areas still needs to be processed. More than two million people, most of them being children, die from diseases caused by a lack of access to clean water, inadequate sanitation, and inadequate hygiene every year. People in cities discard trash and debris on the ground, the sidewalks outside their homes, and the roads instead of putting them in dustbins, where they eventually accumulate and create massive rubbish. If uncleaned, the smell of the trash quickly draws pathogens harmful to people (Fig. **1**).

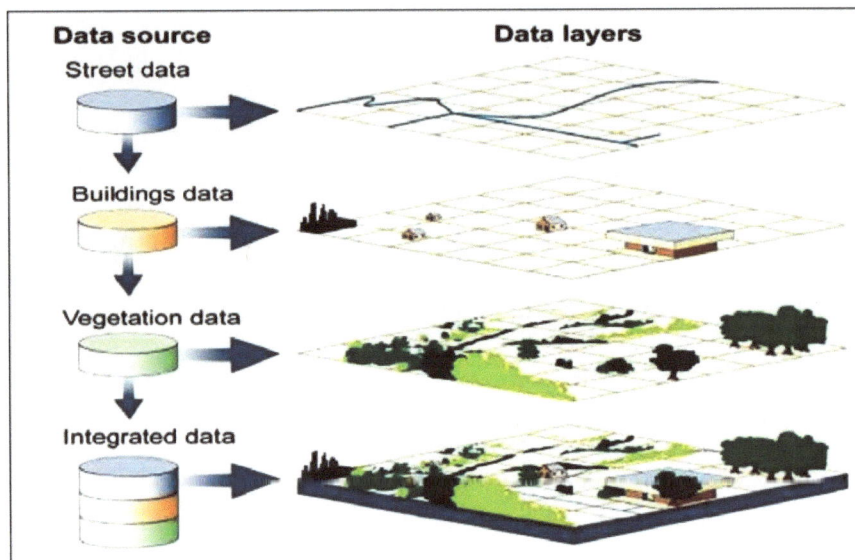

Fig. (1). Working of a GIS software.

Humans come into contact with excrement from public defecation through a number of waterways, contaminating fingers, food, flies, and other objects. A government assessment conducted in May 2017 found that over two lakh communities had abandoned the practice of open defecation (Dash, 2016).

METHODOLOGY

This research study has been carried out in four stages:

Step 1: Using ArcGIS software, map the high sewage zones in India and choose a neighbouring high sewage area.

Step 2: Conduct a site visit to the neighbourhood that made the shortlist and examine its features, such as housing quality, population density, and the current sewage disposal system in place.

Step 3: Make recommendations for sustainable and conventional design approaches for effective sewage disposal in the region.

Step 4: A comparison of the two design approaches.

An information system that uses computers to analyse and digitally depict the physical characteristics and events that take place on Earth's surface is known as a geographic information system or GIS. It can be thought of as a higher-order map that consists of a database system with particular capabilities for geographic reference data and a set of procedures for working with the data. GIS technology combines unique visualization and geographical analytic characteristics with common database operations like query and statistical analysis, making it useful for meaning-making, forecasting outcomes, and planning for a wide range of public and private enterprises. Fig. (**2**) shows the GIS Mapping of High Sewage.

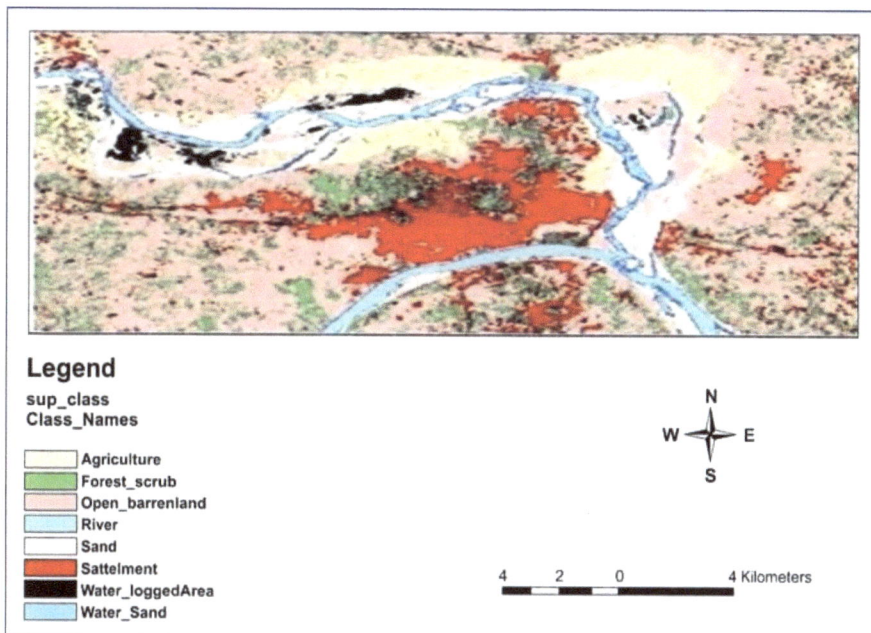

Fig. (2). GIS mapping of high sewage zones in india.

Herein, primary and secondary data are compiled regarding the volume of waste generated from different sources. This helps with wastewater flow estimation and future flow projection. The site's open sewer system was negatively impacting both the environment and people. Sewage needed to be disposed of properly. A neighbouring body of water was contaminated by untreated sewage, which made it even more of a cause of illness for the local populace. At the location, sediments and plastic garbage were in the sewer, making self-cleaning a major problem. The site's circumstances are also readily apparent. Fig. (**3**) shows the site photographs depicting untreated sewage.

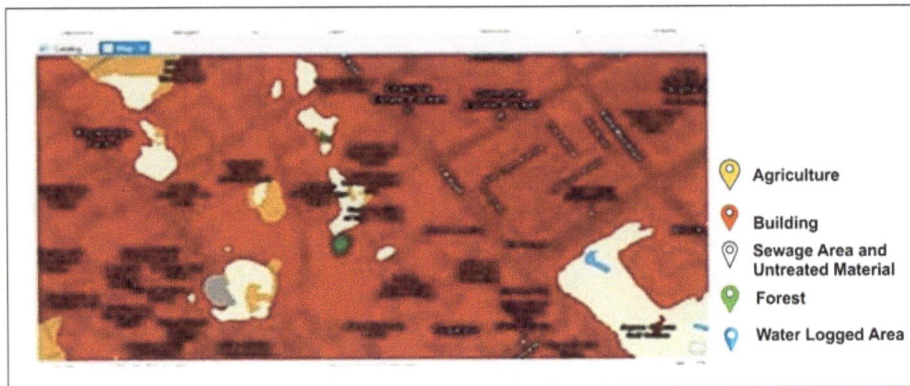

Fig. (3). Site photographs depicting untreated sewage being disposed-off in nearby water body and dumping of plastic waste around the open sewers.

Following the site visit, we calculated the estimated sewage flow rate by taking into account the anticipated user count, the number of restrooms and other fixtures, and the anticipated patterns of water usage. With the current population of 1.12 lakh, population forecasting is done. To design a sewage system with a 30-year design life, the population is projected using a geometric method for the ensuing thirty years.

Assuming that four people are living in each household. A family of four may produce different amounts of sewage on average depending on a number of variables, such as water use patterns, the age of the plumbing system in the house, and the kind of treatment system the local government uses.

SUSTAINABLE DESIGN

- Collection system: A 10-kilometer-long network of PVC pipes will make up the sewage collection system. The anticipated cost of the PVC pipes is $30,000.
- Anaerobic digestion: A 500 cubic meter anaerobic digester will be used to treat the wastewater. Biogas from the digester can be used to create energy. The anaerobic digester is expected to cost $150,000.
- Membrane filtering: A membrane filtration system will be used to treat the anaerobic digester's output further. The system will be made up of 100 square meters of ultra-filtration membranes. The membrane filtration system is projected to cost $50,000. Fig. (4) shows the cost (USD) of the various processes.
- Decreased environmental effects, including greenhouse gas emissions and water pollution;
- Lower long-term running expenses.
- Greater ability to manage large amounts of sewage.
- The potential for anaerobic digestion to recover energy. Fig. (5) shows the Initial & Operating Costs (USD).

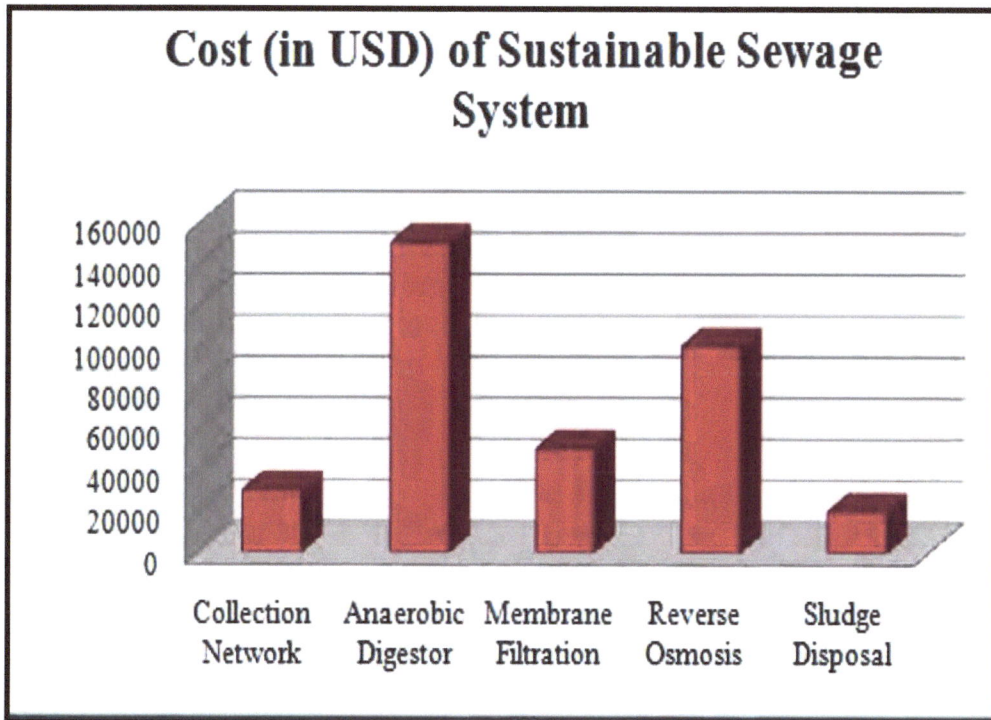

Fig. (4). Post (USD) of the various processes of a sustainable sewage system.

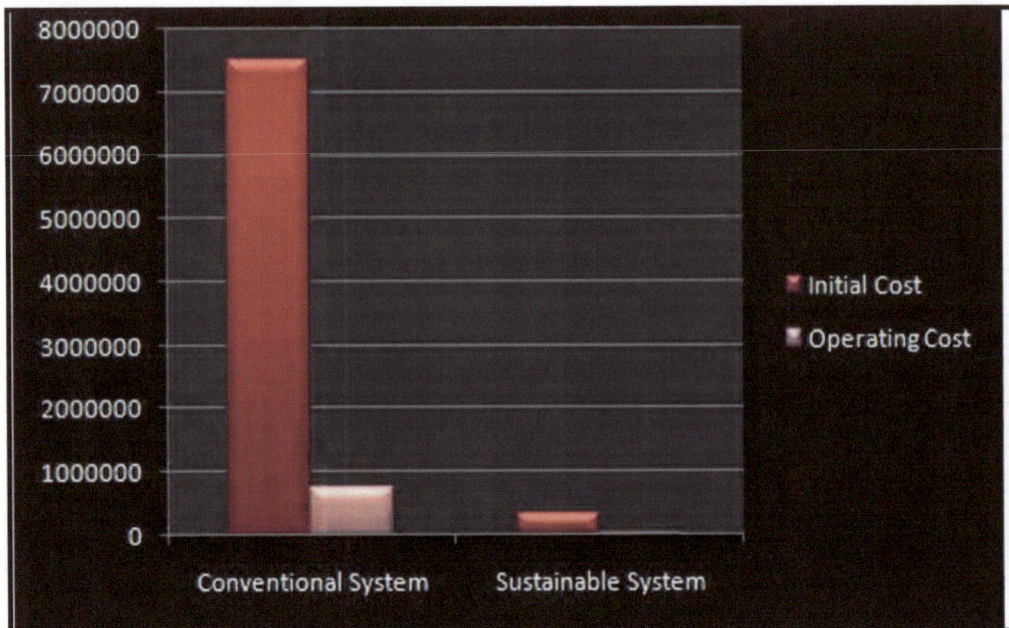

Fig. (5). Comparative Initial & Operating Costs (USD) for conventional & sustainable sewage systems.

CONCLUSION

This study concludes by highlighting the design of sustainable sewage disposal systems for high-sewage locations in India using ArcGIS software for GIS mapping. According to the study, places with high sewage levels are typically found in metropolitan and peril-urban regions that have dense populations and inadequate sanitary infrastructure. To fulfil environmental and public health standards, the sewage disposal systems that are already in place in these locations need to be upgraded as they are mostly insufficient. The suggested environmentally friendly sewage disposal system design for a particular high-sewage location in Greater Noida incorporates both the social and technical facets of sewage management and has the potential to lower the pollutant load from these places greatly. To sum up, this study emphasizes the application of ArcGIS software. Developing sewage disposal systems that can efficiently remove waste while minimizing the impact on the environment requires the use of sustainable design. Sustainable design takes into account a number of variables, including waste reduction, energy efficiency, and water conservation. This study aims to provide a sustainable design for a sewage disposal system in a high-sewage location that may satisfy local needs and lessen environmental effects. Conventional systems have a number of shortcomings despite being efficient in eliminating waste.

To begin with, they use a lot of energy to run the therapy procedures. Second, they can be a big problem because it takes a lot of water to flush the sewage from homes, in areas with limited water resources. Thirdly, a lot of sludge is produced by conventional systems, which needs to be properly disposed of. Finally, because treated wastewater still contains nutrients and pathogens, its release into the environment may still be harmful. In a high-sewage location, a sustainable design for a sewage disposal system is suggested in order to overcome the drawbacks of traditional systems.

REFERENCES

[1] S.P. Yama, S. Zaidi, C.D.S. Nascimento, V.H.C. de Albuquerque, and S.S. Chauhan, "Analysis and Design of automatically generating for GPS Based Moving Object Tracking System", *International Conference on Artificial Intelligence and Smart Communication (AISC),* pp. 1-5, 2023.
[http://dx.doi.org/10.1109/AISC56616.2023.10085180]

[2] K.S. Pillai, M.L. Sneha, S. Aiswarya, A.B. Anand, G. Prasad, and A. Jayadev, "Unlocking Hidden Water Resources: Mapping Groundwater Potential Zones using GIS and Remote Sensing in Kerala, India", *E3S Web of Conferences,* vol. 405, p. 04021, 2023.

[3] S.P. Yadav, and S. Yadav, "Fusion of Medical Images using a Wavelet Methodology: A Survey", *Transactions on Smart Processing & Computing,* vol. 8, no. 4, pp. 265-271, 2019.
[http://dx.doi.org/10.5573/IEIESPC.2019.8.4.265]

[4] N. Al Nasiri, A. Al Fazari, W. Ali, B. Agyekum, and E. Ramadan, "Multi-Criteria Decision-Making Approach for Siting Sewer Treatment Plants in Muscat, Oman", *Urban Science,* vol. 7, no. 3, p. 82, 2023.
[http://dx.doi.org/10.3390/urbansci7030082]

[5] S.P. Yadav, and S. Yadav, "Fusion of Medical Images in Wavelet Domain: A Discrete Mathematical Model", *Ingeniería Solidaria,* vol. 14, no. 25, p. 1-11, 2018.
[http://dx.doi.org/10.16925/.v14i0.2236]

[6] M. Manisha, K. Verma, N. Ramesh, T.P. Anirudha, R.M. Santrupt, "Lakshminarayana Rao, Water, sanitation, and hygiene implications of large-scale recycling of treated municipal wastewater in semi-arid regions", *Science of The Total Environment,* vol. 904, p. 166631, 2023.
[http://dx.doi.org/10.1016/j.scitotenv.2023.166631]

[7] S. P. Yadav, and S. Yadav, "Mathematical implementation of fusion of medical images in continuous wavelet domain", *Journal of Advanced Research in dynamical and control system,* vol. 10, no. 10, pp. 45-54, 2019.

[8] M. Meera, D. Mehta, and U. Yadav, "Citywide inclusive sanitation through scheduled desludging services: emerging experience from India", *Frontiers in Environmental Science,* vol. 7, p. 489278, 2019.

[9] S.P. Yadav, "Blockchain Security", In: *Blockchain Security in Cloud Computing. EAI/Springer Innovations in Communication and Computing.,* K. Baalamurugan, S.R. Kumar, A. Kumar, V. Kumar, S. Padmanaban, Eds., Springer: Cham, 2022.
[http://dx.doi.org/10.1007/978-3-030-70501-5_1]

[10] J. Jiang, X. Hu, Y. Gu, W. Wang, Z. Bi, C. Yao, X. Liang, Q. Wen, M. Luo, Y. Zheng, and X. Xia, "Suitability evaluation of rural sewage treatment facilities in China considering lifcycle environmental impacts and regional differences", *J. Environ. Manage.,* vol. 344, p. 118516, 2023.
[http://dx.doi.org/10.1016/j.jenvman.2023.118516] [PMID: 37413733]

[11] X. Xue, R. Shanmugam, S. Palanisamy, O.I. Khalaf, D. Selvaraj, and G.M. Abdulsahib, "A hybrid cross layer with harris-hawk-optimization-based efficient routing for wireless sensor networks",

Symmetry (Basel), vol. 15, no. 2, p. 438, 2023.
[http://dx.doi.org/10.3390/sym15020438]

[12]   N. Bansal, M. Mukherjee, and A. Gairola, "GIS-based multi-criteria decision analysis for mapping flood-prone areas in Dehradun city, India", *Arab. J. Geosci.,* vol. 16, no. 9, p. 501, 2023.
[http://dx.doi.org/10.1007/s12517-023-11605-9]

[13]   K. Suganyadevi, V. Nandhalal, S. Palanisamy, and S. Dhanasekaran, "Data security and safety services using modified timed efficient stream loss-tolerant authentication in diverse models of VANET", *International Conference on Edge Computing and Applications (ICECAA),* pp. 417-422, 2022.
[http://dx.doi.org/10.1109/ICECAA55415.2022.9936128]

[14]   M. E. Alissa, and M. Ibrahim, "Monitoring of Surface Water Quality in King Talal Dam Using GIS: A Case Study", *The Iraqi Geological Journal.,* p. 36-47, 2023.
[http://dx.doi.org/10.46717/igj.56.2A.3ms-2023-7-12]

[15]   R. Ramakrishnan, M. A. Mohammed, M. A. Mohammed, V. A. Mohammed, and J. Logeshwaran, "An innovation prediction of DNA damage of melanoma skin cancer patients using deep learning", *14th International Conference on Computing Communication and Networking Technologies (ICCCNT),* p. 1-7, 2023.
[http://dx.doi.org/10.1109/ICCCNT56998.2023.10306749]

[16]   I. Elkhrachy, A. Alhamami, and S.H. Alyami, "Landfill Site Selection Using Multi-Criteria Decision Analysis, Remote Sensing Data, and Geographic Information System Tools in Najran City, Saudi Arabia. Remote Sensing, 15(15), 3754.Khan, J., Gupta, G., Singh, N. K., Bhave, V. N., Bhardwaj, V., Upreti, P., ...&Sinha, A. K. (2023). Geophysical and geostatistical assessment of groundwater and soil quality using GIS, VES, and PCA techniques in the Jaipur region of Western India", *Environ. Sci. Pollut. Res. Int.,* pp. 1-16, 2023.

[17]   M. A. Mohammed, V. A. Mohammed, R. Ramakrishnan, M. A. Mohammed, and J. Logeshwaran, "The three dimensional dosimetry imaging for automated eye cancer classification using transfer learning model", *14th International Conference on Computing Communication and Networking Technologies (ICCCNT),* p. 1-6, 2023.
[http://dx.doi.org/10.1109/ICCCNT56998.2023.10307446]

[18]   S. Pande, D. Juizo, E. Mondlane, M. Sivapalan, and M. V. Ramesh, (2023). Districts across India are progressing toward the national JalJeevan Mission goal of piped water supply and 100% Functional Household Tap Connections (FHTC) for all by 2024, While state and national data monitor progress toward tap water connection coverage, the functionality and sustainability of those piped water supplies are less clear. This study presents a Sustainability Planning Framework to assess rural drinking water. Water security and sustainable development in an uncertain world, 137,

[19]   K.R.K. Yesodha, A. Jagadeesan, and J. Logeshwaran, "IoT applications in Modern Supply Chains: Enhancing Efficiency and Product Quality", *2nd International Conference on Industrial Electronics: Developments &Applications (ICIDeA),* p. 366-371, 2023.
[http://dx.doi.org/10.1109/ICIDeA59866.2023.10295273]

[20]   S.C. Vaddiraju, and R. Talari, "Urban flood susceptibility analysis of Saroor Nagar Watershed of India using Geomatics-based multi-criteria analysis framework", *Environ. Sci. Pollut. Res. Int.,* vol. 30, no. 49, pp. 107021-107040, 2022.
[http://dx.doi.org/10.1007/s11356-022-24672-4] [PMID: 36520296]

CHAPTER 7

iGot Garbage

Tushar[1,*], Varun Upadhayay[1], Shruti Gupta[1] and **Vartika Srivastava[1]**

[1] *ABES Engineering College, Ghaziabad, India*

Abstract: The current waste disposal system in India collects unsorted waste from residences; the daily growth in garbage overwhelms the bins placed in public spaces within towns. The process of manually sorting waste is labour-intensive, inefficient, and only sometimes practical because of the volume of waste. Consequently, the concept of "The Smart Waste Management System, an embedded system comprising three smart bins with contemporary sensors, microcontroller, LCD panel, and Wi-Fi modules," is explained in this article. We developed a system that uses a sensor to identify trash, opens the target trash can's lid, determines how much trash is there, and then automatically opens and closes the lid. Upon reaching either the average or maximum level, an alert will be transmitted.

Keywords: Microcontroller, Smart waste management system, Sensors, Unsorted, Waste, Wi-Fi modules.

INTRODUCTION

The UN estimates that by 2025, there will be 8 billion people on the planet, with a 20% increase in population. By 2023 [1], India is expected to have the densest population of any nation, with 1.5 billion people living there by 2030 [2]. There is another issue that arises with this population growth and needs to be handled [3]. One of the main issues facing developing nations is garbage [4]. There are images of trashcans overflowing and garbage shooting out of them everywhere you look [5]. The World Bank has issued data indicating an increase in the rate of garbage generation [6]. Around 1.3 billion tons of solid trash was produced by cities worldwide in 2012. This means that each person produces 1.2 kg of garbage every day. Cities generate an excessive amount of waste as a result [7]. But there is trash in many metropolitan locations. Containers are open for public use [8]. The ecology will, however, continue to deteriorate daily without proper upkeep, which would have grave consequences for humanity [9]. We see images of overflowing trash cans, which is frequently dangerous since it breeds a wide range of insects

---

* **Corresponding author Tushar:** ABES Engineering College, Ghaziabad, India; E-mail: tusharchaudhry1@gmail.com

Pankaj Kumar Mishra & Satya Prakash Yadav (Eds.)

and mosquitoes and causes several diseases. Garbage management must be done correctly to reduce threats to patients' health and safety as well as those of the general public and the environment [10]. This includes managing and disposing of garbage properly, transporting it, and assembling it. Waste must be sorted in order to be valued economically [11]. But as of right now, there needs to be a system in place for separating rubbish. A modern, sustainable waste management system must be put in place to replace the ineffective system in place now [12]. Such a mechanism is suggested in Fig. (**1**). It alters waste segregation systems using the Internet of Things (IoT) as a key instrument to offer affordable, user-friendly, and efficient solutions to some or all of these issues [13].

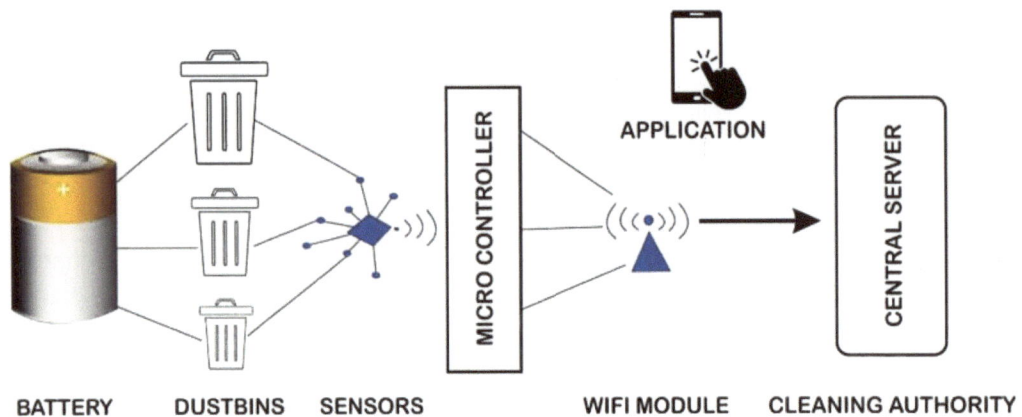

Fig. (1). IoT based SWMS.

Our technology uses smart bins that are internet-connected to collect real-time data. This study offers a really technological solution for maintaining environmental cleanliness [14]. The device keeps an eye on the trash cans, gathers data on the amount of waste there, and finally transmits it to the network for system analysis and necessary decision-making [15]. This will enable us to improve the efficacy of the cleaning systems that are now in use in our nation. One benefit of this activity is that the waste has a great potential for recycling, which lowers the occupational dangers for the people who sort the waste. The goal is to empty the garbage before it gets too full and to overflow it. This study increases the system's capabilities by lowering fuel (energy) usage.

The following lists the sections that make up this paper and how they are used:

• To find pertinent theories, methodologies, and gaps in the literature that can be utilized in a paper, thesis, or dissertation, a literature review entails looking through academic materials that are relevant to a particular subject. It offers a summary of the body of knowledge in the area and can direct further investigation.

- Existing System describes how models and pre-existing systems that have been designed or put into use to achieve the relevant goal operate.
- The output produced by the proposed system is valuable to the user. It serves to showcase our solution for the specified issue as well as our model that that we're going to present.
- The methodology section describes the procedures used to conduct the study. This makes it possible for readers to assess the accuracy and dependability of the process.
- Working outlines the paper's detailed analysis, its operation, and all of the work covered under it for the provided topic.
- A flowchart is a graphic that uses diagrammatic representation to illustrate the movements and actions within a complex system.
- Future scope outlines the improvements and potential solutions we may make to the given situation in the near future.
- A research paper's conclusion is when everything is logically brought together.

RELATED WORKS

Computational models have been employed in the fight against waste management in recent years [16]. The iGot Garbage app, in particular, aims to streamline and improve trash management. The software helps users keep organized and informed about their waste removal efforts [17]. By making it simpler to track the disposal of recyclables and trash, it also aids in the development of more enduring garbage disposal practices. Several computational models are used by the iGotGarbage app. Its most basic feature is predictive analytics, which assists customers in foretelling which materials will be recycled or require disposal [18]. Based on existing waste management practices, these prediction models let consumers plan ahead and determine which things will be recycled [19]. The web-based data dashboard is another feature of the iGotGarbage app, in addition to predictive analytics [20]. Against regional and international standards, users can track and compare their waste disposal practices with the aid of this dashboard. Users can get information on their waste removal activities through the dashboard, including total garbage created, recyclable materials, and compostable products. Users can use this information to gain a better understanding of how their waste management actions affect the environment.

LITERATURE REVIEW

Researchers proposed a waste-collecting strategy in which the residential and industrial sectors of society are included. They used ultrasonic sensors to measure the level of litter bin filling; when a predetermined threshold is achieved, the sensors communicate data to the control room *via* the GSM module. The interface was developed entirely in MATLAB. Slave and master units make up the two units that make up the system. The lid slave unit allows the slave units, which are housed in pods, to receive and send data to the master unit in the control room. The authorities will take an additional action in light of the data they have received. The authors suggest an IoT-enabled platform for the healthcare sector as a workable paradigm for disease self-management. All additional components, including mobile applications that let users access this data, software devices with algorithms and sensor data, and sensor devices that communicate medical patient data, can connect to the platform through a single point. The APIs are composed of these five parts. The 2000 Municipal Solid Wastes (MSW) (Management and Handling) Rules, which made solid waste management a vital duty of urban local bodies, are examined in this study. Users of the health platform can also keep an eye on and take control of their health.

EXISTING SYSTEM

Unsorted waste is collected from habitats and sorted at stations as part of India's current disposal system. Manual labor is used in the process of separation, which is time-consuming, labor-intensive, and requires financial assistance from the workers. The unrestricted dumping has resulted in the development of crowded landfills in the suburbs of cities, which are not only impossible to fill but also have serious negative environmental repercussions such as groundwater pollution and contributions to global warming. Furthermore, there is no signal in the current systems as to whether a bin will overflow. It takes longer and could be more effective. Trucks have to drive and clean the bin, whether it is full or empty, which is a waste of time.

PROPOSED SYSTEM

It is more beneficial to utilize smart dustbins rather than several trash cans. With the use of sensors positioned above the bins, the technology is able to sort garbage and determine trash levels. When the trash level hits the maximum or average level, a Wi-Fi module transmits the bin status to the appropriate authorities. All of the garbage cans that our system manages are readable by our server. Consequently, the suggested approach aids in preventing waste overflow and provides information about the volume of waste in real time. Your actual needs will determine how you use the waste. This procedure is affordable, and supplies are easily available. This system makes cities cleaner and reduces odors, which enhances the quality of the environment. Its proper use saves truck drivers time and energy.

Fig. (**2**) The elements used to implement the proposed waste management system.

METHODOLOGY

The world is currently seeing a significant change in the way humans and machines interact because of the rapid improvements in wireless technology. The latest developments in wireless technology and the resulting modifications are creating new avenues for environmental consequences. Solid waste management is one of the straightforward yet crucial services provided by local governments across the country to maintain clean town centres. However, it is among the basket's least effective products. The poor are marginalized, there needs to be more population coverage, and the institutions need to be updated. Since trash is left lying around a lot, housing conditions need to be cleaned. Solid waste management is a continuous problem that needs to be sufficiently addressed by local laws that control surrounding towns and municipalities. Together with monitoring solid waste, the suggested system would have the ability to control and modify the entire collection process. The technologies included in the suggested system can guarantee that the management, monitoring, and collection of solid waste are appropriate and suitable for a new setting. Integrated Adriano software synchronizes the identification system, machine-controlled lid system, microcontroller, and other components. The garbage can's front is equipped with an infrared sensor. The trash can's lid can open automatically if any employees are known to be within the present range, thanks to a servo motor installed in the upper section. The range of the suggested characteristic system was found to be 30 cm. Garbage should be disposed of in the trash can once the lid has been opened since it will remain open until someone enters the detection range. When an object travels beyond the detection range, the lid will automatically close. The power source for the system may be a +5 V power supply. Fig. (**3**) shows a picture of a closed container to show how to prevent Garbage from being left lying around due to outside influences such as animals and unexpected weather. The trash can's internal infrared sensor continuously measures the amount of waste therein.

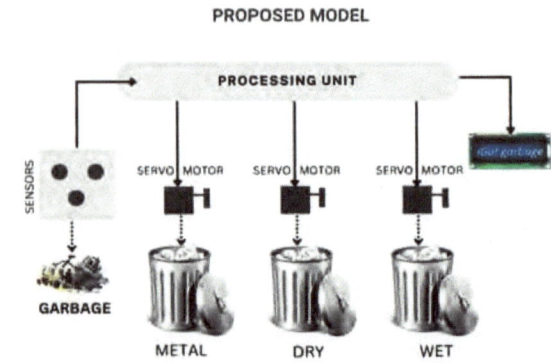

(a) IR Sensor   (b) Servo Motor

(c) Adriano UNO   (d) GPS module

(g) Buck Converter   (h) Wi-Fi module ESP8266

Fig. (2). Components in the system.

a) Three Garbage bins   b) Smart Waste Management System

Fig. (3). Implementation of Project.

WORKING

This IoT-based smart dustbin concept is made up of a Wi-Fi module, a microprocessor, and sensors. The intention is to utilize a sensor to identify the material state of the garbage that is being removed further in addition to its level. Three containers are used by our method to divide waste into three categories: other waste, wet waste, and metal waste. Metal proximity sensors are employed to identify metal waste. In contrast, moisture sensors are used to identify wet waste, such as fruit and flower waste, cooked and raw food, leaf litter, cleaned soil, and other edible materials. This is predicated on a panel having waste detection capabilities. When waste is detected over the inlet section's open and shut mechanism, the bin's lid will open and close.

- IR Sensor: These electrical devices, which measure and detect infrared radiation in their immediate surroundings, are mounted above the garbage cans to monitor the waste level.
- SG90 Servo Motor: This motor is lightweight, compact, and has a high output power. Almost 180 degrees (90 degrees in each direction) of rotation is possible, which is comparable to normal motors but in a smaller form factor. It is used for garbage lid rotation and opening.
- An Uno AdrianotheAdriano Uno is a kind of microcontroller board; the word "Uno" translates to "one" in Italian. It is based on the ATmega328 processor. The Adriano Uno Board 1.0, a microcontroller board, is about to be launched.

FLOW CHART

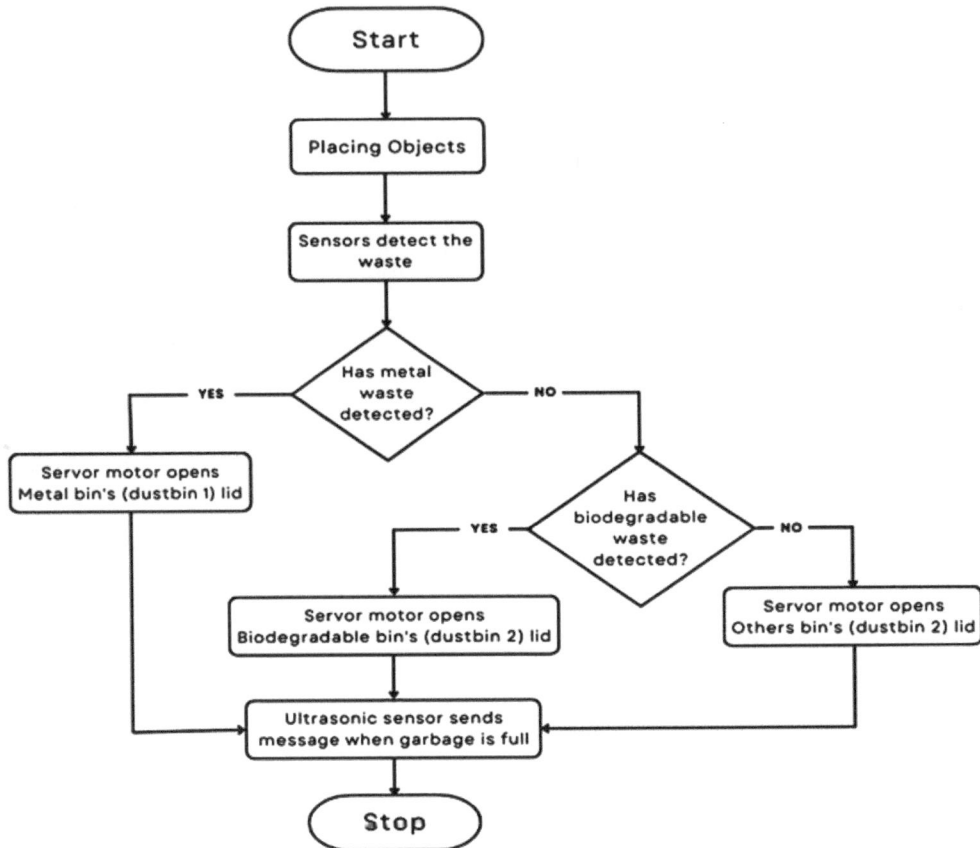

CONCLUSION

The construction of these intelligent dustbins takes several factors into account, such as maintenance requirements, damage prevention, and durability. This garbage management system provides a clean and hygienic environment. When the trash can fills up to the top, a cleaning procedure is initiated. By reducing the number of collection van trips, we can save money and resources by using the appropriate algorithm. Ultimately, it helps maintain the cleanliness of the nation and city. One study claims that if India's waste is recycled properly, the country may avoid needing to invest millions of dollars. This IoT-based garbage management is tremendously advantageous for smart cities in many ways. This makes the idea of an advanced India a reality.

REFERENCES

[1] S.P. Yama, S. Said, C.D.S. Nascimento, V.H.C. de Albuquerque, and S.S. Chauhan, "Analysis and Design of automatically generating for GPS Based Moving Object Tracking System", *International Conference on Artificial Intelligence and Smart Communication (AISC),* pp. 1-5, 2023.
[http://dx.doi.org/10.1109/AISC56616.2023.10085180]

[2] D. Frank, L. Elliott, C.M. Cleland, S.M. Walters, P.J. Joudrey, D.M. Russell, B.E. Meyerson, and A.S. Bennett, ""As safe as possible": a qualitative study of opioid withdrawal and risk behavior among people who use illegal opioids", *Harm Reduct. J.,* vol. 20, no. 1, p. 158, 2023.
[http://dx.doi.org/10.1186/s12954-023-00893-9] [PMID: 37891630]

[3] S.P. Yadav, and S. Yadav, "Fusion of Medical Images using a Wavelet Methodology: A Survey", *Transactions on Smart Processing & Computing,* vol. 8, no. 4, pp. 265-271, 2019.
[http://dx.doi.org/10.5573/IEIESPC.2019.8.4.265]

[4] Kinetic, A., Alexander, G., Natalya, P., Georgy, A., Valentin, A., Leonid, B., & August, L., "Vestnik of saint petersburg university", *Arts. Vestnik,* vol. 13, no. 3, pp. 489-507, 2023.

[5] S.P. Yadav, and S. Yadav, "Fusion of Medical Images in Wavelet Domain: A Discrete Mathematical Model", *Ingeniería Solidaria,* vol. 14, no. 25, pp. 1-11, 2018.
[http://dx.doi.org/10.16925/.v14i0.2236]

[6] A. Plyushteva, and T. Schwanen, "We usually have a bit of flood once a week: conceptualising the infrastructural rhythms of urban floods in Malate, Manila", *Urban Geogr.,* vol. 44, no. 8, pp. 1565-1583, 2023.
[http://dx.doi.org/10.1080/02723638.2022.2105003]

[7] S. P. Yadav, and S. Yadav, "Mathematical implementation of fusion of medical images in continuous wavelet domain", *Journal of Advanced Research in dynamical and control system,* vol. 10, no. 10, pp. 45-54, 2019.

[8] И.Г. Мамонова, "Kinetic Art: The Leningrad Experience, the 1920s–1990s. ВестникСанкт-Петербургскогоуниверситета", *Искусствоведение,* vol. 13, no. 3, pp. 489-507, 2023.

[9] S.P. Yadav, "Blockchain Security", In: *Blockchain Security in Cloud Computing. EAI/Springer Innovations in Communication and Computing.,* K. Baalamurugan, S.R. Kumar, A. Kumar, V. Kumar, S. Padmanaban, Eds., Springer: Cham, 2022.
[http://dx.doi.org/10.1007/978-3-030-70501-5_1]

[10] J. Dickson-Gomez, A. Nyabigambo, A. Rudd, J. Ssentongo, A. Kiconco, and R.W. Mayega, "Water, Sanitation, and Hygiene Challenges in Informal Settlements in Kampala, Uganda: A Qualitative Study", *Int. J. Environ. Res. Public Health,* vol. 20, no. 12, p. 6181, 2023.
[http://dx.doi.org/10.3390/ijerph20126181] [PMID: 37372767]

[11] X. Xue, R. Shanmugam, S. Palanisamy, O.I. Khalaf, D. Selvaraj, and G.M. Abdulsahib, "A hybrid cross layer with harris-hawk-optimization-based efficient routing for wireless sensor networks", *Symmetry (Basel),* vol. 15, no. 2, p. 438, 2023.
[http://dx.doi.org/10.3390/sym15020438]

[12] C. Crome, V. Graf-Drasch, F. Hawlitschek, and D. Zinsbacher, "Circular economy is key! Designing a digital artifact to foster smarter household biowaste sorting", *J. Clean. Prod.,* vol. 423, p. 138613, 2023.
[http://dx.doi.org/10.1016/j.jclepro.2023.138613]

[13] K. Suganyadevi, V. Nandhalal, S. Palanisamy, and S. Dhanasekaran, "Data security and safety services using modified timed efficient stream loss-tolerant authentication in diverse models of VANET", *2022 International Conference on Edge Computing and Applications (ICECAA),* pp. 417-422, 2022.
[http://dx.doi.org/10.1109/ICECAA55415.2022.9936128]

[14] E. Ozturk, and G. Akcay, "Can Environmental Education Supported by Augmented Reality (AR)

Applications Improve the Environmental Awareness of Primary School Students?", *Eurasia Proceedings of Educational and Social Sciences,* vol. 31, pp. 216-229, 2023.
[http://dx.doi.org/10.55549/epess.1381983]

[15]   R. Ramakrishnan, M. A. Mohammed, M. A. Mohammed, V. A. Mohammed, and J. Logeshwaran, "An innovation prediction of DNA damage of melanoma skin cancer patients using deep learning", *14th International Conference on Computing Communication and Networking Technologies (ICCCNT),* pp. 1-7, 2023.
[http://dx.doi.org/10.1109/ICCCNT56998.2023.10306749]

[16]   R.T. Schmidt, "Queering the Brazilian White Patriarchal Home: An Improbable Room/a Deauthorized Voice", *Literatures of the World and the Future of Comparative Literature,* p. 182-193, 2023.

[17]   M. A. Mohammed, V. A. Mohammed, R. Ramakrishnan, M. A. Mohammed, and J. Logeshwaran, "The three dimensional dosimetry imaging for automated eye cancer classification using transfer learning model", *14th International Conference on Computing Communication and Networking Technologies (ICCCNT),* p. 1-6, 2023.
[http://dx.doi.org/10.1109/ICCCNT56998.2023.10307446]

[18]   D. Sarkity, A. Fernando, and N.E.K. Hindrasti, "Designing and Content Validity of Instrument for Measuring Marine Environmental Care Attitude Through Integrated Science Learning", *BIO Web of Conferences,* vol. 70, p. 02011, 2023.
[http://dx.doi.org/10.1051/bioconf/20237002011]

[19]   K.R.K. Yesodha, A. Jagadeesan, and J. Logeshwaran, "IoT applications in Modern Supply Chains: Enhancing Efficiency and Product Quality", *2nd International Conference on Industrial Electronics: Developments & Applications (ICIDeA),* p. 366-371, 2023.
[http://dx.doi.org/10.1109/ICIDeA59866.2023.10295273]

[20]   H.I. Wahyuni, A. Budiman, R. Abidin, and E.T. Yuliandari, "Potential of Fables as Learning Resources for Environmental Education and Its Relevance to the Merdeka Belajar Curriculum", *Jurnal Pendidikan Indonesia Gemilang,* vol. 3, no. 1, pp. 87-96, 2023.
[http://dx.doi.org/10.53889/jpig.v3i1.189]

CHAPTER 8

Examining the Viability of Integrating Blockchain Technology into IoT Devices for the Supply Chain

Anubhav Sharma[1], Ashish Pandey[2], Ramander Singh[3] and Ankit Garg[4,*]

[1] *Computer Science and Engineering, IMS Engineering College, Ghaziabad, India*

[2] *School of Computer Science & Application, IIMT University, Meerut, Uttar Pradesh, India*

[3] *Computer Science and Engineering, Amity University, Haryana, Uttar Pradesh, India*

[4] *Management Department, Ajay Kumar Garg Institute of Management, Ghaziabad, Uttar Pradesh, India*

Abstract: Decentralized solutions with many benefits over centralized systems are something that blockchain and IoT can provide. IoT devices may guarantee the accuracy and dependability of their data by utilizing the blockchain's fault tolerance, security, and data transparency. However, there are difficulties when implementing blockchain in IoT systems, particularly with consensus procedures. Due to their confined computation, connectivity, and battery capacity, IoT devices with limited resources may find it challenging to reach a consensus on the same ledger state.

A recent paper suggests an empirical method for implementing blockchain in supply chain scenarios to overcome these issues. The report also proposes a customized Raft consensus algorithm for use with the Hyperledger permissioned blockchain. Each transaction in this updated protocol is sent to a leader node before being relayed to follower nodes in order to prevent a bottleneck from affecting the system's scalability and throughput. The supply chain context is one where this strategy can be especially useful.

Overall, the paper addresses some of the issues related to consensus protocols while highlighting the potential advantages of combining blockchain and IoT in supply chain contexts. By assuring data integrity and eliminating fraudulent actions, this technique can make managing supply chain data more secure, transparent, and effective.

Keywords: Blockchain technology, IoT devices, mRAFT, Supply chain, Transaction execution flow.

---

* **Corresponding author Ankit Garg:** Management Department, Ajay Kumar Garg Institute of Management, Ghaziabad, Uttar Pradesh, India; E-mail: drankitgarg108@gmail.com

Pankaj Kumar Mishra & Satya Prakash Yadav (Eds.)

INTRODUCTION

The daily lives of people and corporate activities are changing as a result of the Internet of Things (IoT), a rapidly developing technology [1]. IoT systems are evolving from automatic to autonomous, where intelligent devices can learn from their environment and make decisions on their own, as intelligent computing units continue to spread. A new era of intelligent systems that are altering the digital world is being brought about by this change [2].

IoT devices are now commonplace and employed for a variety of purposes, including supply chains, healthcare, smart grids, and transportation systems [3]. Making wise decisions depends on the precision and purity of the data these devices produce [4].

The typical IoT network architecture, which employs a centralised client-server strategy and a cloud backbone network, has a number of drawbacks, though. This architecture is ineffective for managing and controlling a large number of IoT devices because it involves a significant amount of overhead to manage the varied range of heterogeneous devices that must interact in a delay-critical way. The centralised architecture's single point of failure renders it susceptible to system failure, hampers communication amongst IoT devices, and makes it expensive to operate and maintain [5].

For IoT network infrastructure control, a decentralised, fault-tolerant, secure, and highly scalable approach is needed to get over these limitations. Blockchain technology provides a system that is highly fault-tolerant, secure, transparent, traceable, and scalable and gives all of these benefits [6]. There is no need for a central authority because existing nodes in a peer-to-peer network confirm transactions.

In conclusion, IoT devices and their data can be effectively and dependably controlled using blockchain technology. This technology circumvents the drawbacks of traditional centralised IoT network design by offering a decentralised, fault-tolerant, secure, and scalable approach for controlling IoT network infrastructure [7].

RESEARCH REVIEW

In this essay, the limits of the current IoT device networks are examined in relation to the promise of blockchain technology. It starts with a thorough analysis of earlier studies in this area, highlighting the advantages and disadvantages of various blockchain-based consensus methods for IoT. The second section introduces mRAFT, a new consensus technique that makes use of idle follower nodes to speed up throughput and cut latency in blockchains that support the Internet of Things. The effectiveness of the algorithm is demonstrated through a case study of supply chain management employing blockchain technology [8-10].

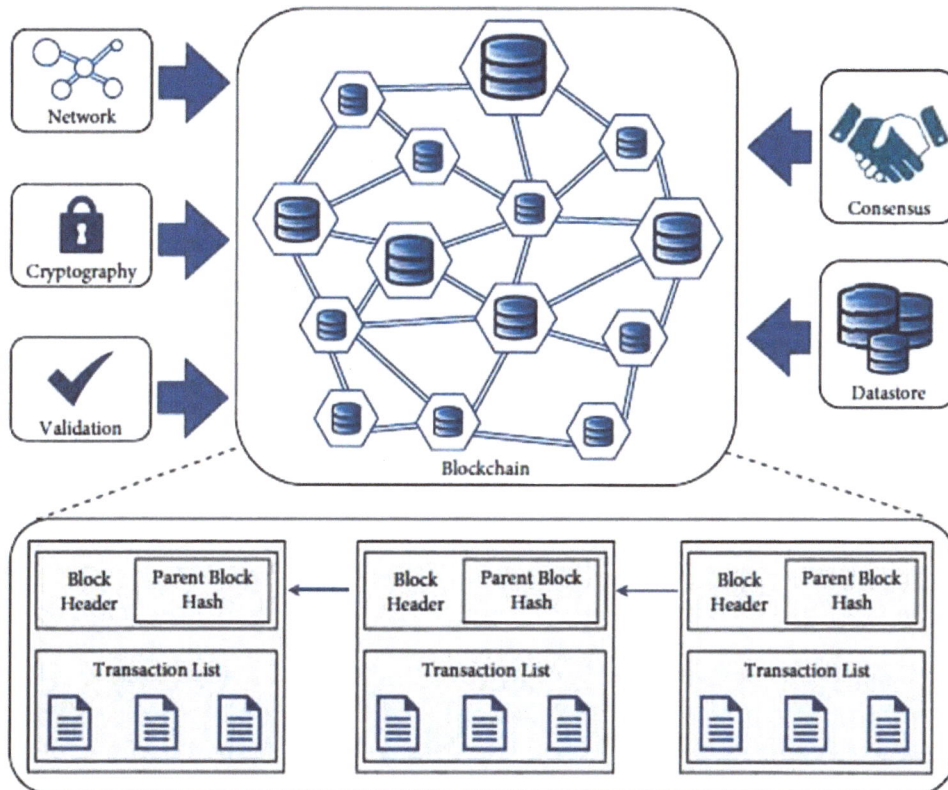

Fig. (1). Basic components of a blockchain architecture.

The essay also emphasizes the need for additional study to overcome performance snags and other problems with blockchain-enabled IoT [11-15]. The necessity for all nodes to execute smart contracts, the execution of non-deterministic smart contracts, and rigid consensus procedures are only a few of the restrictions of current permissioned blockchain frameworks that are explored (Fig. **1**). The use of gas to control nondeterminism in smart contracts on open blockchains is also explored in the paper [16, 17].

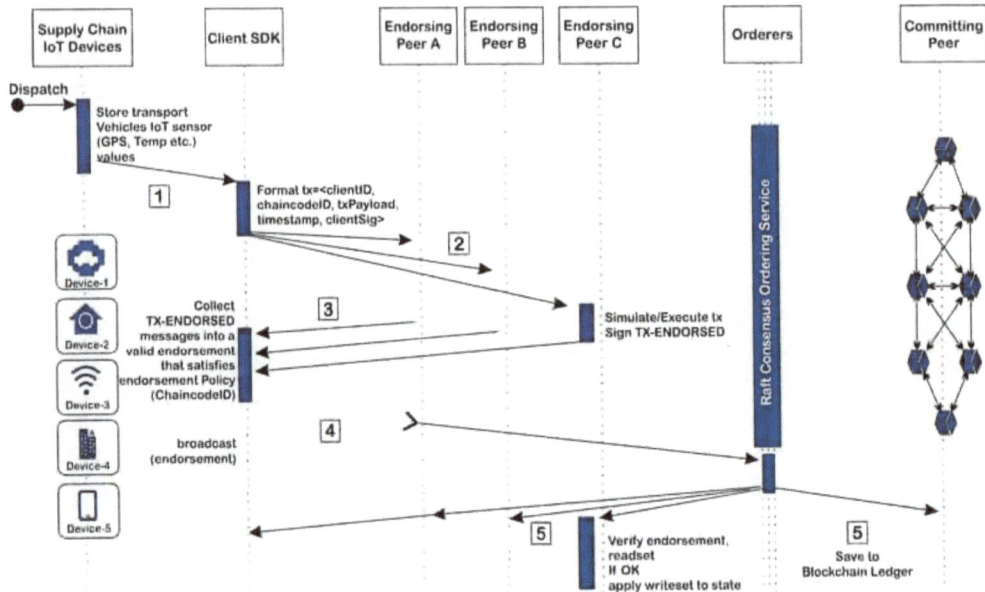

Fig. (2). Transaction execution flow.

The article describes how the Practical Byzantine Fault Tolerance (PBFT) consensus process used in Bitcoin was converted to suit Ethereum's permissioned network. The permissioned blockchain of Ethereum streamlines the validation process into a single step through the use of Smart Contracts. The essay concludes by contrasting popular permissioned blockchain frameworks, such as Fabric, Corda, and Quorum, based on a variety of factors, including modularity, language support, privacy, transactions per second, currency support, and flexibility. Fabric's high ranking for adaptability is a result of its modular design and pluggable ordering system (Fig. **2**).

Several articles go through the use of blockchain technology in various fields, including permissioned blockchain frameworks, IoT networks, and supply chain management. Different permissioned blockchain frameworks are compared in terms of their scalability, performance, privacy, adoption, and consensus methods by Ban *et al.* and Polge *et al.* The use of blockchain in IoT networks and supply chain management is investigated by Christidis and Devetsikiotis and Cao *et al.*, with an emphasis on consensus techniques that are appropriate for IoT devices with minimal resources. A supply chain system design for IoT with blockchain is additionally put out, using integrated sensors to monitor and manage the delivery of diverse goods in a secure, open, and reliable manner. These articles offer researchers and professionals insight into the benefits and constraints of blockchain technology as well as how it may be used in various use cases.

Authors	Year	Approach	Contribution	Limitations
Li *et al.*	2021	Practical byzantine fault tolerance (PBFT).	Proposed PBFT consensus mechanism based on punishment and rewards.	RS erasure code made storage an efficient compute-intensive solution.
Wang *et al.*	2021	Routing in unmanned aircraft systems (UAS).	Proposed lightweight proof of traffic (PoT) consensus mechanism.	Security vulnerabilities of PoT are not discussed significantly.
Raghav *et al.*	2020	Probabilistic consensus approach.	Proposed proof of elapsed work and luck (PoEWAL).	Lacks in-depth analysis of security resistance against cyberattacks.
Biswas *et al.*	2020	Enterprise grade business blockchain.	Proposed lightweight proof of block and trade (POBT) consensus mechanism.	The proposed mechanism is not addressed for a public blockchain.
Khalid *et al.*	2020	Authentication mechanism based on fog computing.	Efficient as compared to traditional blockchain authentication techniques.	Authentication mechanisms in private blockchain are not discussed.
Huang *et al.*	2019	Directed Acyclic Graph (DAG) based blockchain.	Proposed credit-based consensus mechanism.	Security threats due to the asynchronous nature of the consensus mechanism.
Dorri *et al.*	2017	Smart homes with HPC miners	Lightweight and efficient consensus eliminating PoW.	Vulnerable due to PoW exclusion.
Christidis and Devetsikiotis	2016	Consensus *via* the white-list scheme	Proposed lightweight consensus mechanism.	Security concerns due to preselected consensus nodes.

The Hyperledger Fabric network was built and tested using the Raft and mRAFT consensus protocols, and the system build environment was created and tested using the Linux virtual machine services. The environmental parameters for both software and hardware are shown. On a virtual server housed on a laptop with constrained processing power and capabilities, experimental evaluation and testing of the prototype solution were carried out. Although the performance at scale may change when the blockchain nodes are installed on server machines with more processing power in a production setting, the underlying logic and rationale will remain the same.

Software & Hardware Environment	Version
Server Machine (PC).	Intel Core™ i5-6500 Processor, 8gb Memory, 512gb Hard Disk
Operating System.	Ubuntu 17.05
Hyperledger Fabric.	2.2

(Table) cont.....

Software & Hardware Environment	Version
Docker Engine.	17.09.0
Hyperledger Caliper.	0.5.0

RESULTS AND DISCUSSION

Until 11 nodes, the distribution of request messages through follower nodes has no effect on the speed of the mRAFT and Raft consensus algorithms in the leader selection phase. The Raft consensus mechanism, however, experiences an increase in leader selection time when there are more than 12 nodes because of a bottleneck in the dissemination of vote request messages to follower nodes. Through experiments, the effectiveness of the mRAFT consensus protocol is assessed, with a focus on metrics like network latency, throughput, and leader selection time (Fig. **3**).

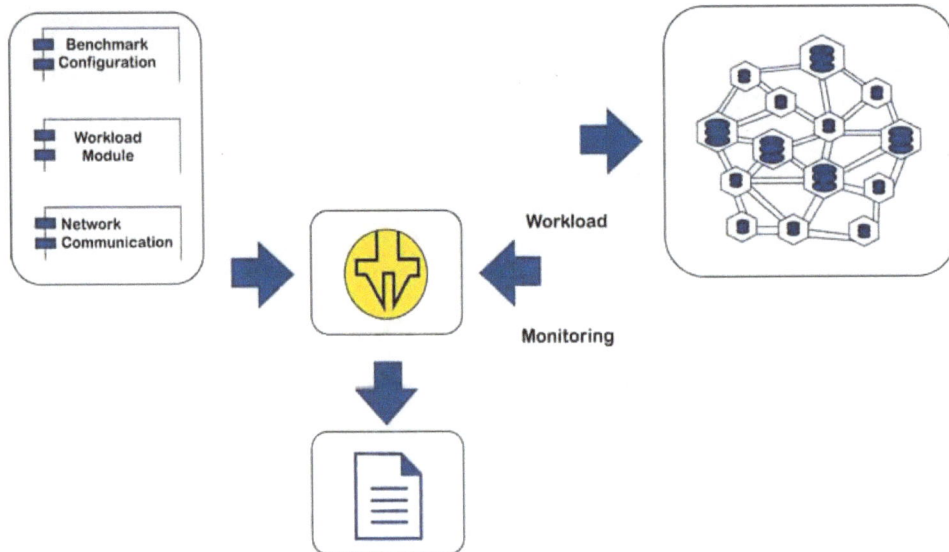

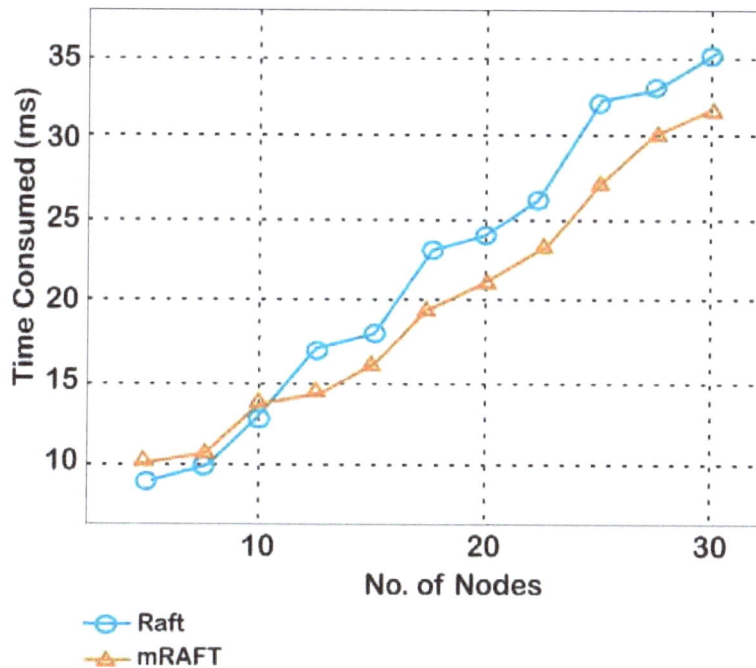

Fig. (3). Leader selection time on varying numbers of nodes

CONCLUSION AND FUTURE WORK

In order to address difficulties with scalability, transparency, and fault tolerance, a thorough analysis of the literature on the use of blockchain technology in enterprise IoT networks was first carried out. This literature analysis gave readers a thorough overview of the core ideas behind blockchain and the Internet of Things (IoT) as well as how those ideas compare to conventional technologies in terms of delivering digital solutions. Additionally, the technical characteristics of various blockchain-based consensus algorithms were researched to find the best one for resource-constrained IoT device networks.

The literature research also examined how various blockchain consensus mechanisms could be applied to IoT in order to discover the most effective consensus mechanism for IoT given the restricted storage and power consumption limitations of IoT devices. The evaluation also looked at the idea of adding high-performance computing capabilities to crowded smart homes' resource-constrained IoT devices in order to supply extra computing power for lightweight IoT device consensus. The invention of credit-based consensus mechanisms, which increase the computational workload for dishonest nodes while decreasing it for honest ones, resulted from the examination of incentives as a technique for enhancing consensus algorithms.

The study examined consensus algorithms, taking into account their technological characteristics, which would be appropriate for blockchain frameworks based on IoT. The study concentrated on permissioned blockchain consensus algorithms and proposed mRAFT consensus as a development of the Hyperledger Fabric-based Raft consensus algorithm that would be suitable for IoT device networks. By lowering latency and boosting throughput, the suggested improvements aimed to make blockchain adoption simpler for IoT devices with constrained resources.

If the leader node manages all operations, becoming a bottleneck point and leaves followers idle, the workload of peers will be uneven in the IoT-based supply chain scenario. Utilizing follower nodes to distribute vote request messages, append entries messages, and replicate log messages substantially minimizes the workload on the leader node in the proposed improvements to the Hyperledger Fabric Raft consensus mechanism. The leader node then distributes messages for vote requests and log replication *via* idle follower nodes.

To demonstrate the merits of the Raft consensus protocol improvements, an experimental investigation was carried out. The outcomes showed that the suggested improvements considerably increased throughput, latency, and leader selection time. To obtain consensus across a wider number of nodes, the follower nodes inadvertently inundated vote request packets. Furthermore, mRAFT consensus surpassed the original Raft consensus in terms of network throughput for a node count greater than 13.

The study used trials to assess how well the mRAFT consensus algorithm handled transaction requests in IoT device networks with limited resources. The experiment demonstrated that the algorithm had a higher throughput when handling several concurrent transaction requests, however the dispersion of transaction requests over follower nodes increased the delay for individual transactions. Consequently, mRAFT is the perfect consensus method for Internet of Things (IoT) devices that need high transaction throughput.

The study recommended using quorum nodes in read or write transactions, which are more dependable than the leader, to further optimise the Raft consensus technique for Hyperledger Fabric. However, the consensus process' applicability in real-world situations is constrained by the lack of Byzantine faults.

REFERENCES

[1] O. Pal, B. Alam, V. Thakur, and S. Singh, "Key Management for Block chain Technology", *ICT Express,* vol. 7, no. 1, pp. 76-80, 2019.

[2] S. Suzuki, and J. Murai, "Blockchain as an audit-able com-munication channel", *Proceedings of the 2017 IEEE 41st Annual Computer Software and ApplicationsConference(COMPSAC),* vol. 2, pp. 516-522, 2017.

[http://dx.doi.org/10.1109/COMPSAC.2017.72]

[3]   S. Zhang, and J.H. Lee, "Analysis of the main consensus protocols of blockchain", *ICT Express,* vol. 6, no. 2, pp. 93-97, 2020.
[http://dx.doi.org/10.1016/j.icte.2019.08.001]

[4]   M. Muzammal, Q. Qu, and B.Nasrulin, "Renovatingblockchainwithdistributeddatabases:anopensource system", *Future Generation Computer Systems,* vol. 90, pp. 105-117, 2016.

[5]   Z. Zheng, S. Xie, H. Dai, X. Chen, and H. Wang, "An overviewof blockchain technology: architecture, consensus, and futuretrends", In: *In Proceedings of the 2017 IEEE International congresson Big Data (Big Data congress) IEEE,* Honolulu, HI, USA, 2017, pp. 557-564.

[6]   M. Ertzand E´Boily, "The rise of the digital economy: thoughts on blockchain technology and cryptocurrencies for the col-laborativeeconomy", *InternationalJournalofInnovationStudies,* vol. 3, no. 4, pp. 84-93, 2019.

[7]   S. Pinna, Ibba, G. Baralla, R. Tonelli, and M.Marchesi, "Amassive analysis of ethereum smart contracts empirical studyandcodemetrics,", *IEEE Access,* vol. 7, pp. 78194-78213, 2019.
[http://dx.doi.org/10.1109/ACCESS.2019.2921936]

[8]   T.T.A. Dinh, R. Liu, M. Zhang, G. Chen, B.C. Ooi, and J. Wang, "Untangling blockchain: a data processing view ofblockchain systems", In: *Transactions on Knowledge and Data Engineering* vol. 30. , 2018, no. 7, pp. 1366-1385.

[9]   A. Garg, and D.S. Kumar, "Consumer Panic Buying and Consumer Behaviour during Pandemic Years for Innovative Sanitization Good: A Study of Buying Behaviour to Sanitization Durable Goods. Manager", *Br. J. Adm. Manag.,* vol. 58, no. 154, pp. 1-11, 2022.

[10]   A. Garg, and R.K. Singhal, "Study of Online Shopping In Ghaziabad and Noida Region – A Customer Perspective", *Int. J. Adv. Innov. Res.,* vol. 4, no. 5, p. 48, 2015.

[11]   A. Garg, and D. S. Kumar, "The Relevance of Engel-Blackwell-Miniard Model of Consumer Behavior during Covid-19: A Contemporary Consumer Behavior Survey on FMCG Products in Urban Demography in Uttar Pradesh", *ANVESAK,* vol. 51, no. 2, pp. 1-17, 2021.

[12]   R.K. Singhal, A. Garg, S. Das, and M. Gaur, "Marketing Intelligence Recent Research Trends: Systematic Literature Review Approach", *Neuroquantology,* vol. 20, no. 7, pp. 1464-1479, 2022.

[13]   A. Garg, R.K. Singhal, S. Das, and T. Pandey, "Health Care Management using Block Chain Technology A conceptual framework", *Neuroquantology,* vol. 20, no. 7, pp. 452-1463, 2022.

[14]   R. Taparia, A. Chatterjee, A. Garg, and T.G. Pandey, "A Study Of The Impact Of Risk Avoidance And Financial Welfare On The Intent To Invest In The Equity Market", *Neuroquantology,* vol. 58, no. 9, pp. 1-14, 2022.

[15]   A. Garg, S. Tripathi, S. Agarwal, D. Tomar, and V. Kumar, "Consumer Attitude towards Counterfeit Products: An Extension of Theory of Planned Behaviour", *Empirical Economics Letters,* vol. 22, no. 2, pp. 76-91, 2023.

[16]   A. Garg, P. Agarwal, and S. Singh, "A Study of Different Aspects of Consumer Behavior for Online Buying in Delhi NCR for Fmcd Products. PRANJANA the Journal of Management Awareness A Bi-Annual Peer-Reviewed", *Refereed Ejournal,* vol. 22, no. 2, p. 76, 2023.

[17]   A. Garg, and R. Singhal, "Impact of Office Ergonomics on Business Performance – (In Special Reference to Noida Region)", *Int. J. Adv. Innov. Res.,* vol. 5, no. 4, p. 888, 2016.

CHAPTER 9

Blockchain-Based Secure Storage for IoT Management with Edge Computing

Ramander Singh[1], Anubhav Sharma[2], Ashish Pandey[3], Satish Kumar[4] and Ankit Garg[4,*]

[1] *Amity University, Haryana, Uttar Pradesh, India*

[2] *IMS Engineering College, Ghaziabad, India*

[3] *School of Computer Science & Application, IIMT University, Meerut, Uttar Pradesh, India*

[4] *Management Department, Ajay Kumar Garg Institute of Management, Ghaziabad, India*

Abstract: As blockchain is used in applications like smart grids and healthcare systems, its significance as a management tool for decentralised systems is becoming clearer. However, its application on mobile devices with constrained resources is restricted because of its high resource requirements and poor scalability with frequent, intense transactions. To get around this restriction, mobile devices can use edge computing to outsource their mining operations to the cloud, which offers scalable and secure transactions with reliable access, dispersed computing, and unaltered storage. Key issues including security, scalability, and resource management must be solved to successfully combine blockchain with edge computing. Flexibility, anonymity, and integrity issues still need to be investigated for the development of a useful and secure decentralized data storage system, even if researchers have explored the relevant architectural criteria and included several specific applications.

Keywords: Blockchain, Edge computing, IoT, Peer-to-peer, Security.

INTRODUCTION

Blockchain has recently attracted a lot of interest as a platform that makes use of community validation to synchronize the data in many users' replica ledgers (Conoscenti, Vetro, & De Martin (2016)) [1-5]. Blockchain surpasses alternatives built on centralised digital ledgers as a decentralised ledger that verifies and records transactions. Blockchain technology stores data records as blocks, with logical links listed as a linked list of chained-together blocks (Feng, He, Zeadally, Khan, & Kumar (2018)). In order to create a tamper-proof platform for data storage and exchange, the consensus process replicates changes to data blocks

---

* **Corresponding author Ankit Garg:** Management Department, Ajay Kumar Garg Institute of Management, Ghaziabad; E-mail: drankitgarg108@gmail.com

Pankaj Kumar Mishra & Satya Prakash Yadav (Eds.)

across the network (Garg, Agarwal, & Singh (2023)). Blockchain-based automatic data transfer decreases the requirement for outside involvement by facilitating a paradigm shift from centralised to decentralised administration. Its applications have grown to include smart grid, medical, delivery, and logistics systems, despite being primarily developed to address Bitcoin's double-spending difficulties (Garg & Kumar (2021)). However, its two biggest drawbacks are its low capacity for expansion and acceptance of occupations with high frequency (Garg & Kumar (2022)) [6-10].

For platforms like the Internet of Things (IoT), which connects countless physical things to the Internet, the security properties of blockchain may make it simpler to design privacy-preserving apps. The Internet of Things (IoT) is a huge network of linked devices that can exchange data *via* the Internet, generate enormous amounts of data, including sensitive data, and speak with one another [6]. Peer-t--peer (P2P) privacy may be preserved in these networks thanks to block blockchain's decentralised nature without compromising the security of shared data. However, it is difficult to use blockchain directly in IoT and other mobile applications due to the significant resource consumption during the mining and consensus procedures and the limited resources of IoT nodes (Feng, He, Zeadally, Khan, & Kumar (2018)) [11-15].

According to the hypothesis, mobile edge computing enhances the integration of blockchain into IoT systems and offers an alternate approach to problems with proof-of-work (PoW). In order to deliver resources and services, edge computing is a cutting-edge technology that makes use of both the network edge and the cloud (Garg, Singhal, Das, & Gaur (2022)). Through a variety of access points, users have access to features similar to those found in the cloud, such as greater processing power, application space, and storage. This makes it possible for mobile devices with limited resources to increase their processing power by delegating mining and storing operations to edge servers. A decentralised ecosystem for outsourced computation and safe storage for scalable and secure transactions is created by combining blockchain with edge computing. The biggest barriers to implementing this combination, however, continue to be security worries and edge computing's distributed management (Garg & Singhal (2015)).

Similar Works

Using safe cryptographic methods, the blockchain is a secure system that generates a decentralised electronic record made up of a number of chronologically related transaction blocks (Garg & Singhal (2016), Garg, Tripathi, Agarwal, Tomar, & Kumar (2023)). Blockchain guarantees that authorized transactions are transferred and preserved tamper-proof by requiring nodes in a P2P network to keep immutable and publicly verifiable records (Garg, Agarwal, & Singh (2023)). Using a predetermined consensus method, network participants must concur on a transaction in the same order that it is validated before it can be added to the blockchain (Garg & Singhal (2016)). A network architecture known as the Internet of Things (IoT) enables data to be exchanged between data centres and actual physical objects like actuators, sensors, cars, and other intelligent devices (Xiong, Zhang, Niyato, Wang, & Han (2018)). IoT makes it possible for various pieces of hardware and software to communicate with one another by promoting a heterogeneous environment. Smart grids, smart healthcare, and smart transportation are just a few of the applications that can benefit from the Internet of Things (IoT) devices that are continually being integrated into their surroundings and implanted with inexpensive sensors. According to the term's definition, mobile edge computing (MEC) offers an IT service environment and cloud computing capabilities near mobile users at the edge of the mobile network, inside the Radio Access Network (RAN), and close to the mobile network. This new paradigm has emerged as a result of the quick development of technology, which has led to the "edge" of the mobile network serving as the new location for previously cloud-based services and applications (Garg & Singhal (2015)). Traditional centralised cloud computing is no longer able to offer many applications the required quality of service (QoS) due to the growing use of mobile devices.

Current Research Work

Blockchain can offer secure storage and verified transactions for IoT devices, according to a study by (Vukolić (2015)). Finding an appropriate hosting environment, however, is the biggest obstacle to integrating blockchain with IoT devices. According to the authors, cloud computing may offer more deployment benefits than fog computing. A prototype for integrating blockchain technology into low-resource mobile devices *via* edge computing was shown by (Kim & Jeong (2018)) in a different study. Their findings demonstrated that when additional miners join the network, this integration could benefit both service providers and miners. (Kubendiran, Singh, & Sangaiah (2019)) suggested a resource allocation method based on edge computing to make it simpler to integrate blockchain into transcoding video streaming systems. To ease the burden of transcoding operations in an edge computing environment, they developed a system of incentives and tried two different approaches. Through resource dumping and adaptive allocation tactics, simulation results have shown that the approach could maximize average revenue.

Situational Statement

There are a number of issues with data integrity, confidentiality, and flexibility that are raised by the adoption of blockchain technology in IoT applications and have not yet been fully addressed. The security of the data that is stored is still in jeopardy despite continual efforts. Although blockchain offers pseudonymity, maintaining data integrity requires a large number of reliable miners, and scalability is impacted by PoW's complexity. Research is required to provide solutions that guarantee adaptive data integrity and provide stronger anonymity than pseudonymity in order to overcome these issues.

In this section, we investigate the idea of fusing edge computing with blockchain technology to meet the Internet of Things (IoT) processing and storage requirements. This system's layered architecture enables the separation of IoT devices with limited resources from resource-intensive blockchain operations. We go into further detail about the functions of each layer in the framework. The topic of network traffic management, computation offloading, and external data storage are three basic IoT requirements that are also discussed. Along with a description of service deployment, the framework's solutions for anonymity, integrity, and adaptability are illustrated visually. The IoT framework built on the blockchain with edge computing is shown in Fig. (**1**).

Design of the Proposed Framework's Prototype

In order to address the processing and storage requirements of the Internet of Things, the authors' proposed framework for merging edge computing and blockchain technology is described in this part along with its experimental design and prototype implementation. The edge computing server for the prototype was a potent workstation, while the IoT end nodes were Android-compatible cell phones. For development, deployment, and testing, a number of cloud service providers were employed, including IBM BlueMix, Amazon S3, Digital Ocean, and Microsoft Azure. To increase the processing and storage capabilities of edge computing servers, the authors used IoT end nodes as miner nodes and Microsoft Azure cloud services. They used the Ethereum JavaScript API web3, TestRPC, Truffle, and MetaMask to create a decentralised application (DApp) for data storage. Before being made available to the broader public, smart contracts were tested locally using TestRPC, an Ethereum client. Solidity-based Ethereum-based smart contracts were developed using the Truffle toolkit, and npm was used to access them. The authors also go over using the project tree to host smart contracts, control deployment files, and store test files; the framework is shown in Fig. (**2**).

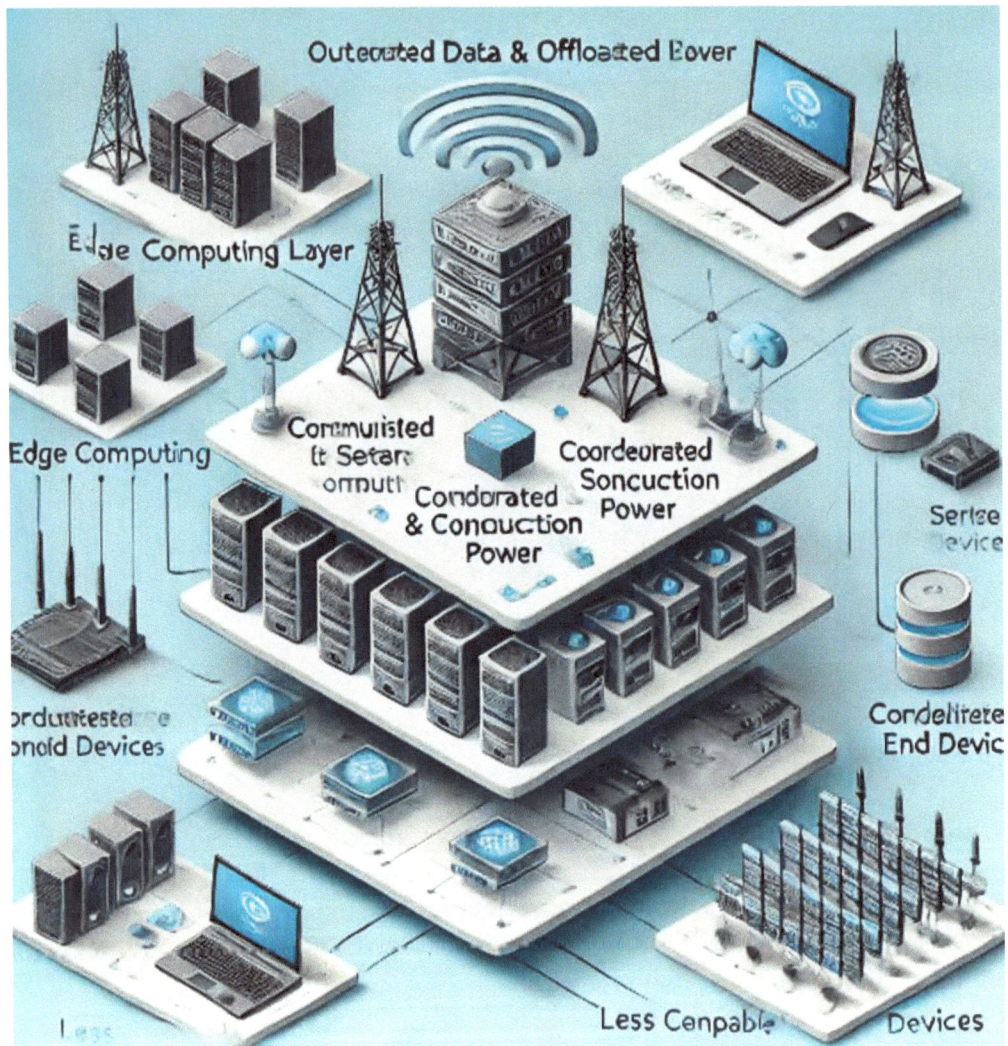

Fig. (1). Actions performed by IoT device layer operations.

In this section, we go over how to put our suggested framework into practice using a decentralised application (DApp) that communicates with the Ethereum network using the Ethereum JavaScript API web3. To expose the web3 API to the DApp and enable the DApp's operation on the Ethereum network, we used MetaMask, a lightnode Ethereum client. Through the Chrome extension, MetaMask can connect with many Ethereum networks, including the main network, specific internet test networks, and the local network on TestRPC.

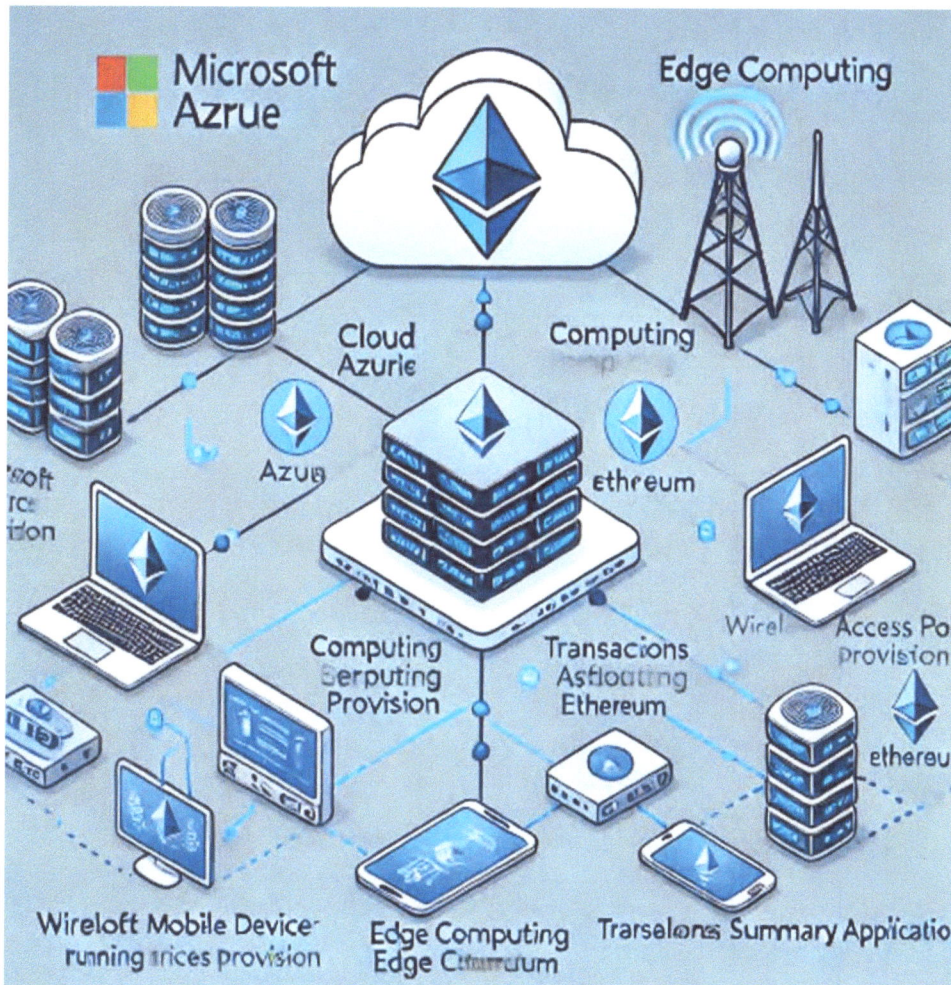

Fig. (2). Prototype implementation setup.

In order to improve anonymity, we updated our DApp with the Zerocash project. Scalable and quick transactions were carried out using the Raiden network, an extension of the Ethereum network. The mined transaction blocks were accessed and distributed using the Ethereum smart contracts built for the DApp's data integrity service. The mobile devices served as miners and connected to the edge server wirelessly using an AP in order to carry out mining activities using the integrated DApp. The miners were assisted by the Ethereum network to ask the edge server for the required processing and storage resources. Framework for data integrity using blockchain is shown in Fig. (**3**).

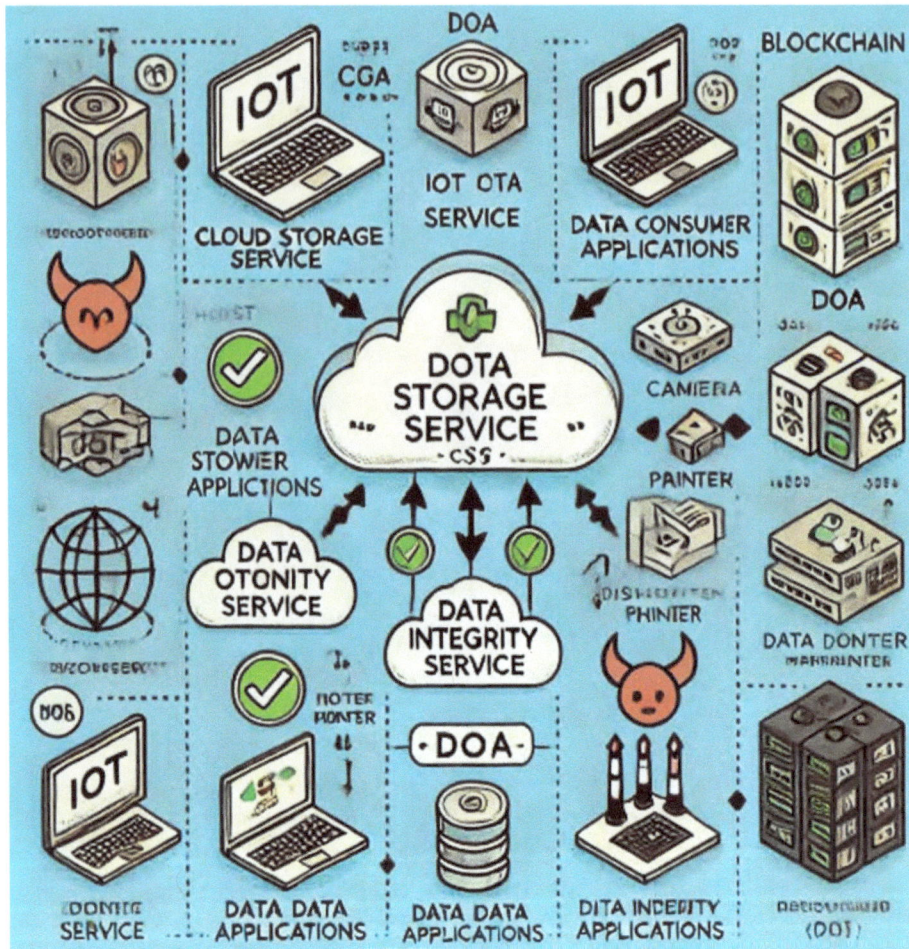

Fig. (3). Framework for data integrity using blockchain.

We present the testing procedure used to gauge the effectiveness of our framework in this section. To replicate the Ethereum network, we used our built-in DApp, smart contracts, and TestRPC. The test was started by using Node.js to generate 5000 simple blocks. Then, using three, four, or five pieces of mining hardware in each case, we installed mobile nodes to mine blocks on top of the primary blockchain. The "difficulty" objectives for the Proof of Work (PoW) tasks were changed using smart contracts. The number of transactions to be included in each block was also decided. To determine the most effective block mining strategy for each circumstance, the edge server's CPU use was tracked. At this point, our main objective was to assess the computing service demands caused by diverse miner populations and their unique requirements. We discovered that the demand for the service was inversely connected with the possibility of successfully mining the blocks. As part of our research plan, we also extensively used incentive-driven outsourced storage with improved offloading models to study energy and memory usage.

Evaluation and Discussion of Concepts

In order to accomplish our design objectives of anonymity, integrity, and adaptability in our framework, our research centered on blockchain technology. We combined all the solutions into a single decentralised application on the blockchain network to produce an efficient solution. Scaling and interoperability challenges were brought on by the variety of IoT devices and the various protocols utilised in the edge computing environment. We added a layered design to the blockchain system to address these problems, List of tools, equipment, and technologies for prototype development and testing is shown below:

List of tools, equipment and technologies for prototype development and testing.

Serial	Item Name	Item Description
1	Android Mobile Devices.	End nodes on which IoT applications run.
2	Edge Computing Server.	A powerful server to host offloaded tasks.
3	Wireless Access Point.	A network hub to provide connectivity between devices.
4	Microsoft Azure Cloud.	Provision of cloud services.
5	TestRPC.	Simulation of Ethereum blockchain.
6	Truffle.	Framework for development of smart contracts.
7	MetaMask.	Ethereum client for web browser.
8	web3 API.	Ethereum JavaScript API.
9	npm.	JavaScript's Node Package Manager.
10	Node.js.	JavaScript's run-time environment.
11	Data integrity service.	Smart contracts-based framework for data integrity.
12	Raiden network.	Ethereum extension to provide off-chain scaling.
13	Linkable ring signatures.	A digital signature scheme to verify anonymous message signer.
14	Zerocash.	A cryptocurrency to enable selective transparency of transactions.

We separated the blockchain deployment into multiple tiers and isolated it from the application layer in order to make sure that even less capable IoT devices could store the portion of the blockchain required for their own transactions. The activities and interactions of various entities at each level were specified in our suggested framework.

In order to allow specific blockchain features, we also built off-chain state channels. With this strategy, processes that strongly rely on blockchain can be divided into different layers. IoT devices can manage complicated transactions and significant volumes of data storage by utilising system peers and off-chain resources at the edge layer. The design provides tremendous processing and storing capabilities, enabling blockchain to adapt to IoT applications by combining enormous processing and storing capacity in a P2P network.

Off-chain outsourcing of labor-intensive operations could lead to an IoT system that is more effective and secure and can adapt to environmental changes, user growth, and increasing transaction volume, the prototype is shown below in Fig. (**4**).

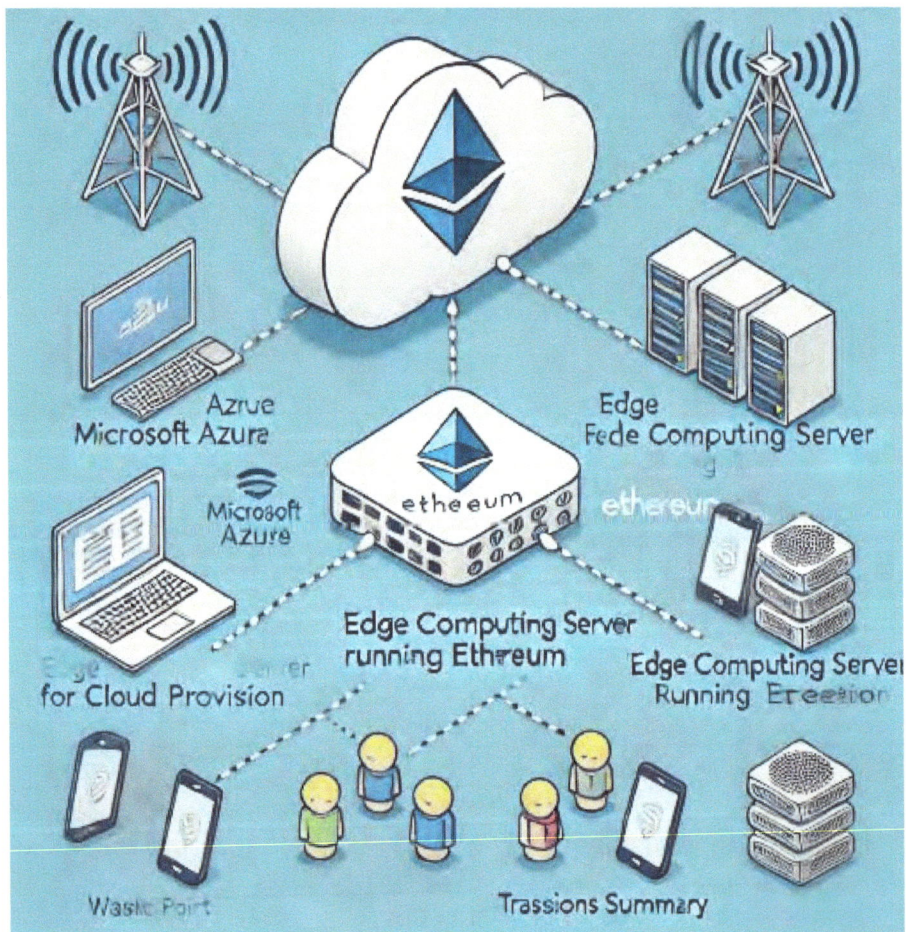

Fig. (4). Prototype implementation setup.

Blockchain pseudonyms are insufficient in decentralised systems to provide anonymity because distributed computation, secure data storage, and authenticated transactions are also necessary. A mix of cryptographic algorithms is required to achieve total anonymity. Linkable ring signatures are one example of a technology that can be used to conceal the sender's identity while still enabling secure network connections. The best options for obscuring transactional information are provided by Zerocoin and Zerocash, which employ non-interactive zero-knowledge proof. These protocols make it difficult for attackers to decipher even the most minute transactional details by converting transaction data bits into random, meaningless bit sequences that cannot be linked back to the original data.

A possible option for guaranteeing data integrity is provided by smart contracts with proof-of-space functionality and Ethereum-based data integrity services. To fulfil their various data and storage needs, these strategies bring together data owners and users. Smart contracts include reward and punishment systems to entice new miners to join the network and commit their storage space while punishing those who fail to keep an eye on their activities, preserving the integrity and validity of the data. We were successful in completing the objective requirements of our integrated system by utilising a variety of tools and cryptographic techniques.

We developed a system prototype and used the answers we found to establish a secure IoT device blockchain storage system in order to put our concept into practise. We built a decentralised application using the Ethereum JavaScript API and tested it on the TestRPC Ethereum simulated network.

Recommendations and Next Steps

By fusing the blockchain with edge computing technologies, our research intended to provide a reliable and effective IoT architecture for data storage. We created a P2P network-based integrated IoT architecture that made use of the edge computing and blockchain's significant storage capacity and security capabilities. For the integrity, flexibility, and anonymity concerns of our concept, we looked into cutting-edge technologies that can manage the crucial security and performance needs of fusing blockchain with edge computing.

We chose a Proof-of-Space-based solution for a smart contract-based data integrity service that checks recorded transactions in order to guarantee data integrity without relying on a central authority. We separated the blockchain from the application layer and added rapid and scalable transactions to Ethereum using the raiden network to increase scalability. To further strengthen anonymity and mask user names and transaction details, our system prototype also made use of linkable ring signatures and zerocash.

Our research resulted in the development of a functioning system prototype that combined edge computing and blockchain for safe and distributed data storage. The integration was powerful and effective enough, according to our conceptual analysis, to handle enormous amounts of data exchanged across numerous IoT devices.

Upcoming Works

In order to assess the system's performance and optimise its many components, the major aim of this article is to give a conceptual framework for a system prototype and a quick analysis of the selected alternatives. Using the decentralised software created to evaluate the success of the proposed plan, our research intends to enhance its performance. We will first look at some fundamental patterns in the CPU, memory, and power usage of the edge server before assessing the system's performance. Then, in order to enhance throughput and speed up system response, we will move on with a thorough rollout across all levels and create effective models for outsourcing and offloading. The effectiveness of bandwidth use and network delay will then be assessed for all pertinent aspects. Our objective is to enhance the system's functionality and produce the finest results feasible for our suggested design.

CONCLUSION

The chapter explores the many facets of algorithms and data structures, with a particular emphasis on node management and specialized trees. The chapter emphasizes how crucial it is to comprehend the various node kinds and how they fit into different kinds of structures, like binary trees, AVL trees, and B-trees. The chapter emphasizes the importance of these ideas in streamlining data processing and boosting algorithmic effectiveness by examining operations such as geometrical length and other computational strategies. The goal of this chapter is to give readers a thorough knowledge of the contributions these data structures make to the larger fields of software development and computer science through these discussions. Professionals and students who are eager to grasp the intricacies of algorithmic design and data management must possess this understanding.

REFERENCES

[1]   M. Conoscenti, A. Vetro, and J.C. De Martin, "Blockchain for the Internet of Things: A systematic literature review", *Proceedings of the 2016 IEEE/ACS 13th International Conference of Computer Systems and Applications (AICCSA)*, 2016.
      [http://dx.doi.org/10.1109/AICCSA.2016.7945805]

[2]   Q. Feng, D. He, S. Zeadally, M.K. Khan, and N. Kumar, "A survey on privacy protection in blockchain systems", *J. Netw. Comput. Appl.,* vol. 13, pp. 45-58, 2018.

[3]   A. Garg, P. Agarwal, and S. Singh, "A study of different aspects of consumer behavior for online buying in Delhi NCR for FMCD products", *Pranjana: The Journal of Management Awareness,* vol. 22, no. 2, p. 76, 2023.

[4]   A. Garg, and D. S. Kumar, "The relevance of Engel-Blackwell-Miniard model of consumer behavior during COVID-19: A contemporary consumer behavior survey on FMCG products in urban demography in Uttar Pradesh", *Anvesak,* vol. 51, no. 2, no. 1, p. 17, 2021.

[5]   A. Garg, and D.S. Kumar, "Consumer panic buying and consumer behaviour during pandemic years for innovative sanitization goods: A study of buying behaviour for sanitization durable goods. Manager -", *Br. J. Adm. Manag.,* vol. 58, no. 154, pp. 1-11, 2022.

[6]   A. Garg, R.K. Singhal, S. Das, and T. Pandey, "Health care management using blockchain technology: A conceptual framework", *Neuroquantology,* vol. 20, no. 7, pp. 452-1463, 2022.

[7]   A. Garg, R.K. Singhal, S. Das, and M. Gaur, "Marketing intelligence recent research trends: Systematic literature review approach", *Neuroquantology,* vol. 20, no. 7, pp. 1464-1479, 2022.

[8]   A. Garg, and R.K. Singhal, "Study of online shopping in Ghaziabad and Noida region – A customer perspective", *Int. J. Adv. Innov. Res.,* vol. 4, no. 5, p. 48, 2015.

[9]   A. Garg, and R. Singhal, "Impact of office ergonomics on business performance – (In special reference to Noida region)", *Int. J. Adv. Innov. Res.,* vol. 5, no. 4, p. 888, 2016.

[10]   A. Garg, S. Tripathi, S. Agarwal, D. Tomar, and V. Kumar, "Consumer attitude towards counterfeit products: An extension of Theory of Planned Behaviour", *Empirical Economics Letters,* vol. 22, no. 2, pp. 76-91, 2023.

[11]   H. W. Kim, and Y. S. Jeong, "Secure authentication-management human-centric scheme for trusting personal resource information on mobile cloud computing with blockchain", *Human-centric Computing and Information Sciences,* vol. 8, no. 11, 2018.

[12]   M. Kubendiran, S. Singh, and A.K. Sangaiah, "Enhanced security framework for e-health systems using blockchain", *Journal of Information Processing Systems,* vol. 15, pp. 239-250, 2019.

[13]   R. Taparia, A. Chatterjee, A. Garg, and T.G. Pandey, "A study of the impact of risk avoidance and financial welfare on the intent to invest in the equity market", *Neuroquantology,* vol. 58, no. 9, pp. 1-14, 2022.

[14]   M. Vukolić, "The quest for scalable blockchain fabric: Proof-of-work vs. BFT replication", *International Workshop on Open Problems in Network Security,* 2015.

[15]   Z. Xiong, Y. Zhang, D. Niyato, P. Wang, and Z. Han, "When mobile blockchain meets edge computing", *IEEE Commun. Mag.,* vol. 56, no. 8, pp. 33-39, 2018. [http://dx.doi.org/10.1109/MCOM.2018.1701095]

CHAPTER 10

A Review of Applications Combining Blockchain Technology with Artificial Intelligence

Ashish Pandey[1], Ramander Singh[2], Anubhav Sharma[3], Pragya Agarwal[4] and Ankit Garg[5,*]

[1] *School of Computer Science & Application, IIMT University, Meerut, Uttar Pradesh, India*

[2] *Amity University, Haryana, Uttar Pradesh, India*

[3] *IMS Engineering College, Ghaziabad, India*

[4] *Hi-Tech Institute of Engineering and Technology, Ghaziabad, India*

[5] *Management Department, Ajay Kumar Garg Institute of Management, Ghaziabad, India*

Abstract: The adoption of AI and blockchain paradigms is moving very quickly in the market. Although each has its own advantages, there are differences in the complexity and the level of innovation. Automated payments in the digital age are possible thanks to blockchain technology, which also ensures the secure, decentralized transmission of information, documents, and personal data. At the moment, blockchain and artificial intelligence are the two technologies that are most frequently discussed. Blockchain can automate Bitcoin transactions, providing users with decentralized, trustworthy, and secure access to a shared ledger of transactions, records, and data. Smart contracts on the blockchain can also control user behaviour without the need for centralized administration. AI, on the other hand, gives robots intelligence, cognition, and decision-making capabilities similar to those of humans.

This insight has led to a thorough analysis of the blockchain and AI advancements that have occurred between 2012 and 2022. A review of 121 articles from the past ten years that evaluate the present status of blockchain and AI technology and support its use in a variety of sectors has been done. This study's main objective is to examine how these two technologies have been integrated. Additionally, the focus has been shifted to examining the shortcomings, gaps, and problems of this combination through literature research in the field.

Keywords: Artificial intelligence, AI applications, Blockchain technology, Critical analysis.

---

[*] **Corresponding author Ankit Garg:** Management Department, Ajay Kumar Garg Institute of Management, Ghaziabad, India; E-mail: drankitgarg108@gmail.com

Pankaj Kumar Mishra & Satya Prakash Yadav (Eds.)

INTRODUCTION

A well-liked decentralized ledger system with many uses is the blockchain. It has been regarded as a potentially revolutionary idea since its creation in the 1920s, with the potential to alter how people communicate, automate payments, monitor markets, and record transactions. Each mining node cryptographically hashes and verifies every transaction on the blockchain, which could eliminate the need for a central authority to oversee and verify transactions between various parties [1, 2]. As a result, time-stamped records are created, which are secure, permanent, and open to the public.

Another area of interest that is expanding quickly is artificial intelligence (AI). According to recent estimates, the AI sector might be worth USD 13 trillion by 2030 [3]. This is not the case yet, despite the fact that a number of competing technologies aim to make data in smart homes attack-proof. One of the most promising strategies for defending the home network from command and control attacks on encrypted data and offering a secure connecting point for all networked devices is the development of blockchain technology [4].

It is challenging to carry out a control attack on data that is being kept or sent across a single exchange because the nodes in a blockchain come to an agreement to ensure that every transaction is permanently documented. Combining these two technological developments, the idea of decentralised AI has gained popularity recently [5]. Decentralised AI offers a solid framework for safeguarding the vast volumes of data necessary for AI to operate, enabling distributed, intermediary-free execution and archiving of trustworthy, precisely labelled, and shareable data on the blockchain [6].

A blockchain can be used to construct smart contracts, which let trusted third parties manage who can access and share user data. After being exposed to an autonomous system, machine, and varied settings, they can adapt and learn, resulting in decision-making outputs that are accurate and dependable that are recognized by all blockchain mining nodes [7]. Everyone with a stake in the outcome can rely on and support such judgements. To determine the optimal methods for enhancing security and confidence in data interchange and decision results, independent operators can take part in, organise, and vote on future decisions [8].

RESEARCH TECHNIQUES

The research questions are:

1. What is the current state of science?

2. Which sectors stand to benefit from the convergence of blockchain and AI technology?

3. What uses do AI and blockchain have?

4. What challenges are presented by blockchain and AI technology?

RESEARCH APPROACH

A broad viewpoint was required to perform a thorough analysis of the literature. To assure the accuracy of the data shown here, sources from Scopus were examined frequently, and pertinent databases underwent thorough analysis. For a variety of reasons, not all well-known literary works were included in the search parameters, necessitating a thorough literature assessment. A total of 353 Scopus results were examined; 121 of them stood out as being especially pertinent. The search phrase was created with the specific research topics and study domain in mind, and suitable results were found by searching for "Artificial intelligence" or "AI" AND "blockchain" [9, 10].

SELECTION RESULTS

A total of 353 artefacts were discovered throughout the search, and this critical evaluation closely analyzed 232 of them. The final selection consists of 121 articles mentioned below, along with a summary of the most important conclusions from the classification. To assure the accuracy and relevance of the material offered here, a thorough study of the literature was conducted. For a variety of reasons, several well-known literary works were left out of the search parameters, and the study domain and research topics had an impact on how the search string was put together. Searching for "Artificial intelligence" or "AI" AND "blockchain" produced the most pertinent results [11] (Figs. **1** and **2**).

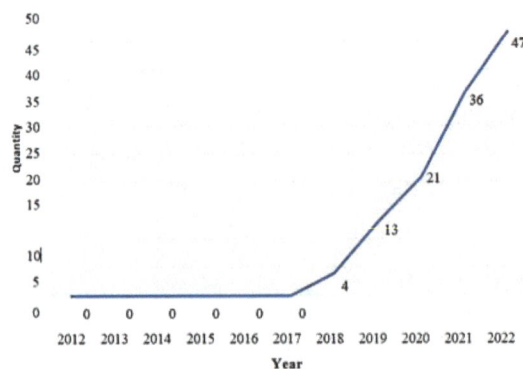

Fig. (1). The Number of annual publications between 2012 and 2022.

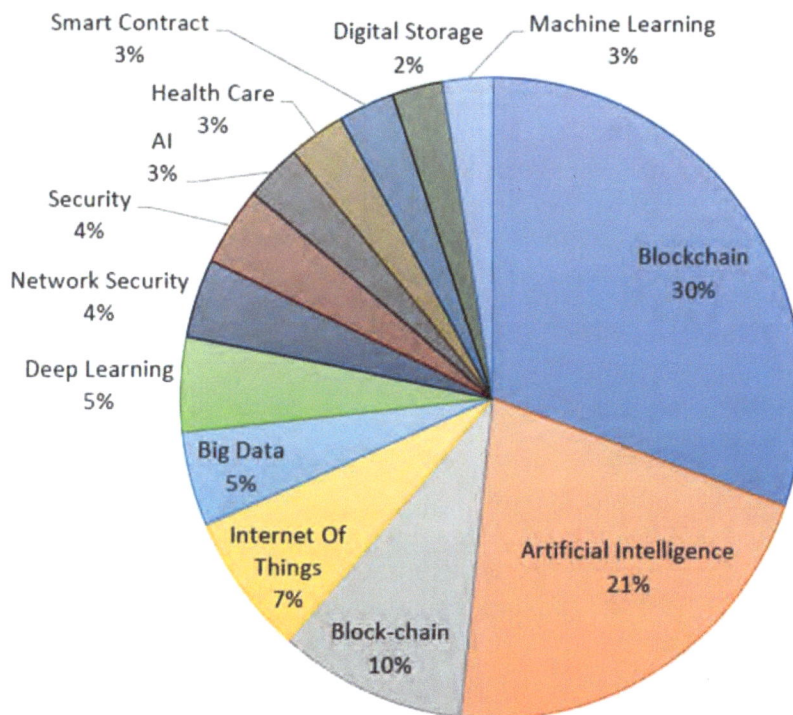

Fig. (2). The articles' primary keywords.

THE BENEFITS OF AUTOMATION USING BLOCKCHAIN AND AI

The goal of the study by Rajagopal *et al*. [35] was to look into how blockchain and AI technology can affect automated services. The researchers employed a secondary data collection strategy to compile pertinent data and information. To speed up the data analysis process, they also used quantitative analysis. The study's conclusions show how AI can efficiently handle automated jobs and give readers insightful information about the subject.

AUGMENTATION

According to the architecture proposed by Lopes *et al*. [36], oracles or outside parties would preserve the data while blockchain technology served as a ledger for robotic control. This architecture takes advantage of blockchain's better control over model sharing, access to enormous volumes of data from both inside and outside the firm, and a more accurate and transparent data market, as well as AI's capacity to quickly scan, analyse, and correlate data. Businesses may improve their operations with the help of this sophisticated technology that combines blockchain and AI.

AUTHENTICITY

By using blockchain technology, it is possible to get more understanding of the inner workings of the AI and the data it consumes, which is one way to deal with the problem of explainable AI. This may boost confidence in the AI's output. Additionally, especially when paired with AI, blockchain can improve data security. The proposal of Li *et al.* [37], for instance, called for a blockchain-based data security solution for AI in 6G networks. Data security can be enhanced by using blockchain to share and store AI models.

AI AND BLOCKCHAIN USE CASES

Chain of Supply

Supply chain operations in a variety of industries are being transformed by the combination of AI and blockchain technologies, which allows for transaction automation and intelligence, dependable and secure data sharing, and the digitization of paper-based processes. By tracking emissions data at the product level, this change is enabling manufacturing organisations to acquire more accurate measurements of carbon emissions data and deeper insight into their decarburization operations [12].

Monetary Services

With the aid of AI and blockchain, the financial services industry is undergoing a revolutionary upheaval. By enabling quicker transaction times, lowering friction in multi-party transactions, and fostering trust, they are advancing business. The procedure for applying for loans is one area where they are making a big adjustment. Applicants can go through automated application screening by granting blockchain access to their data, speeding up the process and improving customer satisfaction [13].

Health Sciences

By utilizing AI and blockchain technology, the pharmaceutical sector can significantly raise the success rates of clinical studies and improve transparency and traceability throughout the prescription supply chain. It is possible to guarantee data integrity, automate trial participation and data collecting, monitor patients, control permissions, and boost data transparency by integrating accurate data analysis with a decentralized clinical trial infrastructure [14].

Healthcare

The use of AI and blockchain technology has the potential to significantly improve many different facets of healthcare, including but not limited to discovering new scientific discoveries, speeding up patient response times, and gaining insightful knowledge from pattern recognition and patient data. Additionally, blockchain offers a safe way for healthcare professionals to exchange electronic health records (EHR) and other private patient data [15].

Analysis of social networks

According to a study, the social networking potential of blockchain technology has not yet been completely realized. Psychological tests have been used in several studies to identify personality traits. Based on the results, various models have been created to help us better understand the relationships between personality, career success, mental illnesses, and interpersonal interactions. Social networks present a strange opportunity to perform personality research on particular groups due to their massive user bases and richness of data.

Table 1. The citation rate indicates that the combination of AI and blockchains is significant and progressing.

Objective	Year	Cited By
An in-depth analysis of the COVID-19 pandemic and its management impact using 5G, blockchain, Al, drones, and IoT (Internet of Things).	2020	540
Blockchain for Al: Look at it and come up with a new research problem.	2019	349
Decentralizing and accelerating biomedical research and healthcare *via* the convergence of blockchain and next-generation AI.	2018	234
Block loT Intelligence: Bringing Al to the IoT with blockchain.	2020	180
Al and blockchain coming together in an loT network to create a sustainable smart city.	2020	165
Knowledge trading in edge-Al powered IoT: a consortium-based incentive and effective approach.	2019	104
The convergence of blockchain, Al, and 3D printing has the potential to revolutionize how humanitarian supply chains are run.	2020	80
Problems, strategies, and future trends of energy cloud management with blockchain and AI.	2020	67
Business transformation *via* digital innovations: use of cloud, data analytics, blockchain, Al, and other technologies.	2022	58
How Al powered by many sensors and blockchain might change the cyclic economy of plastic waste from garbage to cash?	2020	42

Why Combine Blockchain and AI

Blockchain and AI are anticipated to gain substantial traction in the corporate sector and custom software development services over the next five to ten years. Tech-savvy business executives are becoming more and more aware of the enormous possibilities of merging AI with blockchain. Investigating the many applications of these technologies in the workplace is worthwhile.

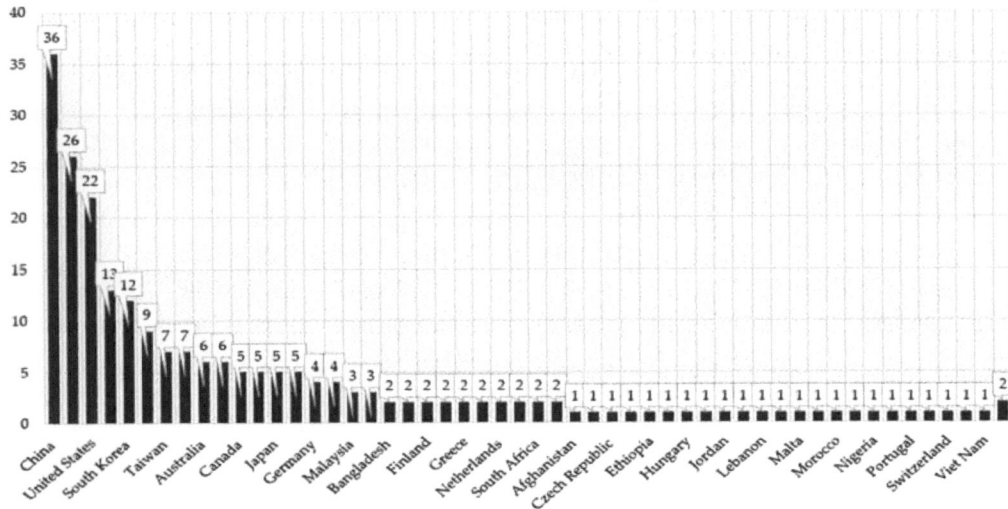

Fig. (3). Distribution of authors by country

Understanding AI Thought Processes

Due to the complexity of computer behaviour, AI is not intended to totally replace human judgement and may not be well received by the general public. However, people are more inclined to believe and embrace AI decision-making processes if they are transparent and understandable.

Safety Enhancement

A secure method for storing private and sensitive data is a blockchain because the technology comes with built-in encryption. In particular, blockchain storage can protect professional advice and medical information. The need for substantial and ongoing data makes having a trustworthy source essential for AI. The creation of AI systems that can safely decode encrypted data is currently a top priority.

Gaining Access to and Control over the Data Sector

Additional security measures must be put in place in order to securely store massive amounts of encrypted data on a decentralized ledger and enable quick AI analysis. New use cases are made possible by this.

Intelligent Contract Improvement

As recently shown, the blockchain technology has a few flaws that could leave it open to attacks from bad actors. When certain circumstances are met, smart contracts, which are still in their early phases, automatically release and transfer funds, subject to agreement among the blockchain community.

Increased Energy Efficiency

Data mining can be time-consuming, especially for businesses. But machine learning has proven that it can solve this problem. For instance, Google's DeepMind AI was able to use past information from a data center's hundreds of sensors to cut the amount of energy needed to maintain a comfortable temperature by 40%.

AI Applications Powered by Blockchain

A study exploring the possible advantages of combining blockchain and AI to enhance data and algorithm management is available in the literature. How blockchain and AI can be used to improve the management and upkeep of data and algorithms is the major goal of the project. In the report, many use cases of these two technologies combined are highlighted, including secure data exchange, increased data accuracy, decreased data breaches, increased data transparency, and streamlined business procedures.

Modern Grid

The shift of smart grids from centrally managed to decentralised power may be considerably aided by the distributed nature of the blockchain. Smart grids, which are a part of the energy internet, allow everyone to contribute to the energy supply, and distributed energy trading is used. However, the centralization of traditional networks is incompatible with this strategy (Fig. **4**).

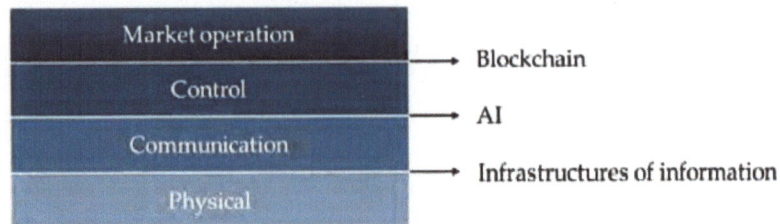

Fig. (4). Block chain Infrastructure Information.

Farming-related aspects

Understanding the effects of blockchain technology on the agrifood sector is the goal of the PPP project "Blockchain for Agrifood". The project looks at the unique aspects of supply chain management and the demand for blockchain adoption in agri-food systems. Markets & Markets predicts that the worldwide blockchain market for the agriculture and food supply chain will reach an estimated value of USD 429.7 million in 2019 and expand at a CAGR of 47.8% by 2023. Using blockchain-based data management, the agricultural supply chain may better incorporate resources.

Medical Aspect

AI has the ability to process enormous volumes of patient data rapidly and effectively in the healthcare industry. Nevertheless, some healthcare professionals are still cautious to use AI in decision-making that could have an impact on a patient's health despite its excellent capabilities. However, the combination of blockchain and AI offers a wide range of opportunities to enhance the delivery of healthcare, including ensuring data integrity, automating trial participation and data collection, patient monitoring, permission management, and improving transparency and traceability throughout the medication supply chain (Fig. **5**).

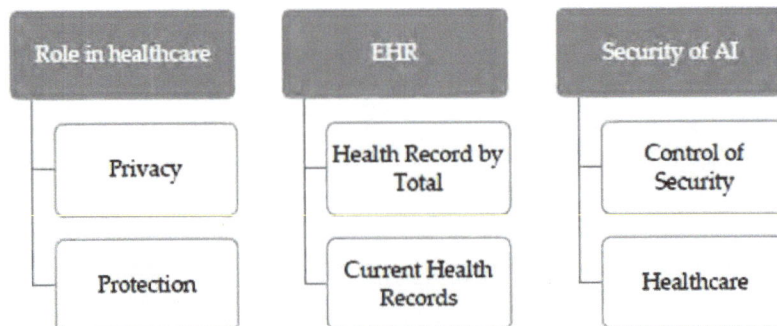

Fig. (5). Medical applications of AI and blockchains.

CONCLUSION

It is impossible to ignore the explosive growth of blockchain and AI technologies. Both paradigms provide something distinctive, yet there are considerable differences in their novelty and complexity. Due to the extensive usage of digital currency in contemporary society, blockchain technology has the ability to automate payments and securely disseminate sensitive data, information, and transaction records. Meanwhile, AI is quick enough to analyze healthcare data and has the processing power to manage enormous amounts of patient data.

Although each of these technologies is cutting edge on its own, when used together, they have the potential to revolutionize the market and streamline and speed up procedures. As a result, there has been a lot of research on the combination of blockchain and AI, with 121 different publications being taken into consideration between 2012 and 2022.

The study focuses on the advantages of merging blockchain and AI, with applications in supply chains, banking, healthcare, life sciences, smart grids, agriculture, and the Internet of Things. Also taken into consideration were the reliability of oracles, the security of smart contracts, the results of their deterministic execution, scalability, privacy, and security.

Users have access to a shared database of transactions, documents, and data thanks to the integration of blockchain technology with AI, making it possible to automate decentralized, reliable, and secure Bitcoin payments. The administration of decentralized user interaction may be made possible by the adoption of smart contracts in blockchain technology. Even though some robots currently think and act like people, merging these two technologies could have a significant market impact.

Overall, blockchain and AI have bright prospects, and their combination can be quite advantageous. This study explores the current state of blockchain and AI collaborations, their uses, and the ground-breaking implications of their distinct features.

REFERENCES

[1]   Z. Baynham-Herd, "Enlist blockchain to boost conservation", *Nature,* vol. 548, no. 7669, p. 523, 2017. [http://dx.doi.org/10.1038/548523c] [PMID: 28858318]

[2]   A. Maxmen, "AI researcher sembrace Bitcoin technology to share medical data", *Nature,* vol. 555, no. 293, p. 295, 2018.

[3]   Nakamoto, S. Bitcoin, "A Peer-to-Peer ElectronicCashSystem; 2009", https://bitcoin.org/bitcoin.pdf (accessedon1October2022)

[4]   Taherdoost, H, "An Overview of Trends in Information Systems: Emerging Technologies that

Transform the Information Technology Industry", *Cloud Computing and Data Science,* vol. 4, pp. 1-16, 2022.
[http://dx.doi.org/10.37256/ccds.4120231653]

[5]   N. Moosavi, and H. Taherdoost, "Blockchain and Internet of Things (IoT): A Disruptive Integration", *Proceedings of the 2nd International Conference on Emerging Technologies and Intelligent Systems (ICETIS 2022),* 2022.

[6]   M. Swan, "Blockchain: Blue print for a New Economy", In: *O'Reilly Media, Inc.* Sebastopol, CA, USA, 2015.

[7]   A. Garg, and D.S. Kumar, "Consumer Panic Buying and Consumer Behaviour during Pandemic Years for Innovative Sanitization Good: A Study of Buying Behaviour to Sanitization Durable Goods. Manager –", *Br. J. Adm. Manag.,* vol. 58, no. 154, pp. 1-11, 2022.

[8]   A. Garg, and R.K. Singhal, "Study of Online Shopping In Ghaziabad and Noida Region – A Customer Perspective", *Int. J. Adv. Innov. Res.,* vol. 4, no. 5, p. 48, 2015.

[9]   A. Garg, and D. S. Kumar, *The Relevance of Engel-Blackwell-Miniard Model of Consumer Behavior during Covid-19: A Contemporary Consumer Behavior Survey on FMCG Products in Urban Demography in Uttar Pradesh.,* 2021.

[10]   R.K. Singhal, A. Garg, S. Das, and M. Gaur, "Marketing Intelligence Recent Research Trends: Systematic Literature Review Approach", *Neuroquantology,* vol. 20, no. 7, pp. 1464-1479, 2022.

[11]   A. Garg, R.K. Singhal, S. Das, and T. Pandey, "Health Care Management using Block Chain Technology A conceptual framework", *Neuroquantology,* vol. 20, no. 7, pp. 452-1463, 2022.

[12]   R. Taparia, A. Chatterjee, A. Garg, and T.G. Pandey, "A Study of the Impact of Risk Avoidance and Financial Welfare on the Intent to Invest In the Equity Market", *Neuroquantology,* vol. 58, no. 9, pp. 1-14, 2022.

[13]   A. Garg, S. Tripathi, S. Agarwal, D. Tomar, and V. Kumar, "Consumer Attitude towards Counterfeit Products: An Extension of Theory of Planned Behaviour", *Empirical Economics Letters,* vol. 22, no. 2, pp. 76-91, 2023.

[14]   A. Garg, P. Agarwal, and S. Singh, "A Study of Different Aspects of Consumer Behavior for Online Buying in Delhi NCR for Fmcd Products. PRANJANA the Journal of Management Awareness A Bi-Annual Peer-Reviewed", *Refereed Ejournal,* vol. 22, no. 2, p. 76, 2023.

[15]   A. Garg, and R. Singhal, "Impact of Office Ergonomics on Business Performance – (In Special Reference to Noida Region)", *Int. J. Adv. Innov. Res.,* vol. 5, no. 4, p. 888, 2016.

CHAPTER 11

Decentralized Application for Fundraising in Healthcare Using Blockchain Technology

Shikha Jain[1,*], **Deepanshu Singh**[1], **Yashraj Mishra**[1] and **Yash Modi**[1]

[1] *Kiet Group of Institutions, Delhi-Ncr, Ghaziabad, Uttar Pradesh 201206, India*

Abstract: The advancement of contemporary technologies has provided individuals and organizations with the means to gather financial resources in order to meet their health-related requirements. The finance framework for addressing health-related requirements is centralized, with a single governing body making choices on behalf of everyone. However, this centralized approach often results in inefficiencies and trust concerns. Tracing the entire system is crucial in order to address the trust issue, which has a negative impact on the process. In this study, we implement a mechanism that empowers each individual to independently collect funds and carry out their operations, thereby eliminating the control exerted by the inefficient central institution. This facilitates fundraising in the health industry with more transparency, providing donors with exact visibility into how funds flow from the donor to the beneficiary. This utilization of the public and unchangeable characteristics of blockchain enhances efficiency.

Keywords: Advancement, Independently, Inefficient, Mechanism, Organizations, Technologies.

INTRODUCTION

Evidently, there has been a decline in public confidence in fundraising efforts for the health-related needs of individuals or organizations. Data reveals that the percentage of donations made by Americans in these areas has decreased from 66% in 2000 to 53% in 2016. We have come to recognize the considerable authority vested in a central institution, enabling them to exercise unrestricted control. It undermines the purpose of fundraising in the healthcare sector. Blockchain provides an alternate means for individuals to have control over the monitoring of the entire process. It empowers individuals at lower levels of the hierarchical structure by granting them greater authority and autonomy. It enables

---

* **Corresponding author Shikha Jain:** Kiet Group of Institutions, Delhi-Ncr, Ghaziabad, Uttar Pradesh 201206, India; E-mail: shikha.jain.cse@kiet.edu

Pankaj Kumar Mishra & Satya Prakash Yadav (Eds.)

them to seek funds for healthcare needs actively. Decentralization is a powerful mechanism that ensures equality for all individuals, eliminating the need to depend on a single dominant entity that may unfairly receive the majority of support, even if it may not be the most beneficial option. It is feasible to employ a mechanism to eradicate biases that may exist in the centralized domain. It provides a greater number of individuals with the chance to secure the necessary finances to treat their health-related ailments. This will result in human advancement and will continue to expand at an accelerated pace. It highlights the necessity for a traceability program that utilizes modern technology to enhance transparency in the fundraising process for healthcare. The study introduces a novel approach to healthcare fundraising, utilizing decentralization as a means to achieve the desired goal. Fundraising is gaining popularity as a means to generate finances. The government is providing support for these efforts as well. The removal of the banking system from the entire process simplifies the operation. It is efficient. It is an effective method to contribute to the well-being of individuals. The platform is indifferent to caste or gender. The program reduces search and transaction costs, hence enhancing people's engagement in healthcare campaigns. Public misuse can occur due to the absence of a regulatory authority. Money laundering or fraud might occur due to the absence of a centralized authority. Transparency and accountability can be attained. The primary objective is to ensure that the funds are delivered directly to the intended destination without the intervention of intermediaries. Documentation is essential to prevent the misuse of funds. Blockchain technology is utilized for digital transactions due to its immutable ledger properties (see picture Fig. **(1)**.

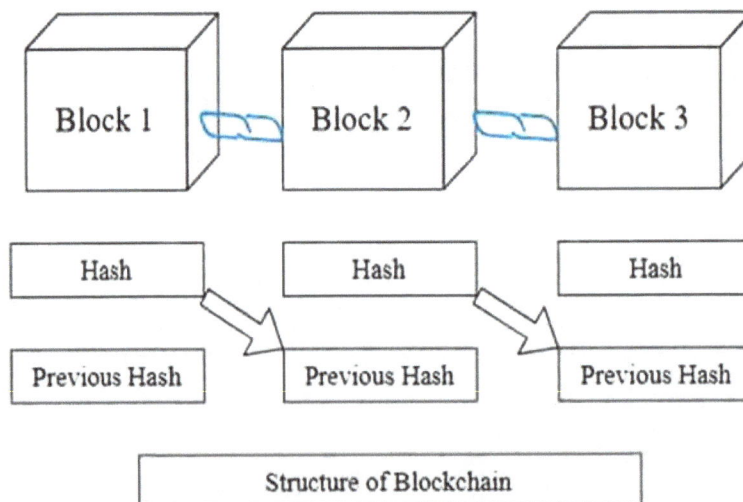

Fig. (1). Structure of blockchain

LITERATURE REVIEW

Irma Latif Atul Laily, Oman Kamrudin, Suci Fadhilah, and Ade Azurat utilized Information Technology to enhance the efficiency of the charity organization in 2018. It was carried out for the Indonesian population. The charity organizations were either small or unregistered and needed more resources. Information systems can significantly cut expenses. Their objective is to develop innovative methods for leveraging information technology to enhance the value provided by charitable organizations [1].

Shang Gao, Daniel Macrinici, and CristianCarto are individuals. In the year 2018, smart contracts provide a high level of customizability to transactions. This characteristic has been applied in various domains, such as banking, healthcare, voting, and energy resources. Smart Contracts continue to provide hurdles for developers, users, and organizations. Essentially, they have discussed the issue and its respective resolution concerning smart contracts [2].

Shweta Jain and Rahul Simha (2018) proposed the implementation of a distributed ledger application to enhance social welfare by incorporating attributes such as adaptability, transparency, and accountability. Here, the donors stipulate a condition for their donation. It is intended for recipients who have expressed interest. It is accomplished by distributed consensus. Subsequently, there is a retrograde movement that returns to the donor, providing information on how their funds are allocated. It fosters responsibility and openness [3].

The authors of the publication (2019) are Aiste Rugeviciute and Afshin Mehrpouya. The study aimed to gain a comprehensive grasp of blockchain in order to ascertain the true capabilities of this technology. The study primarily relies on reports and discussions. Improving the transparency of cash flow in the finance sector has been discovered to decrease administrative expenses [4].

In 2019, HadiSaleh, Azamat Dzhonov, and Sergey Avdoshin suggested a "Platform for Tracking Donations of Charitable Foundations Based on Blockchain Technology." They highlighted the need for more transparency in how donors' funds are utilized, leading to trust concerns. The primary objective is to consolidate the fundraising organization, centralizing all information pertaining to the entire fundraising process in one location and facilitating easy report generation. Implementing this measure will enhance the level of transparency and foster trust among the donors [5].

In 2020, Ashutosh Ashish Khanolkar, Ashish Rajendra Gokhale, Ambrish, and Vinayak A. Bharadi proposed the concept of "Blockchain-based Trusted Charity Fundraising." This decentralized application aims to fully utilize the capabilities of Blockchain technology to create a transparent, accountable, and trustworthy system. The objective is to streamline the procedure of charitable donations and alleviate any concerns regarding trust among the contributors. The charity system transitioned from a centralized structure to a decentralized structure. The objective was to facilitate the transfer of funds from donors to the beneficiary while enhancing the donors' confidence in the donation process [6, 7].

In their 2020 publication titled "Developing a Reliable Service System of Charity Donation during the Covid-19 Outbreak," Hanyang Wu and Xianchen Zhu asserted that the Covid 19 pandemic has significantly impacted the entire process of charity donations. The implementation of blockchain technology will enhance data security, promote transparency in the donation system, and improve overall efficiency. The user's text is " [8, 9]".

In their 2020 study titled "Research on Charity System Based on Blockchain," Baokun Hu and He Li discovered that the charity system in China lacks transparency, which hinders Chinese contributors from effectively participating in the giving process. Blockchain has the potential to enhance transparency and bolster data security. Blockchain facilitates the comprehensive documentation of transactional data, ensuring transparency, security, and efficiency [10, 11].

AbinSojan, Akruty Bang, AmalShaji, Er. Anna Ann Alexander and Feno Sony (2021) show that donors will have the ability to monitor their funds, hence fostering trust and transparency in the charitable system. Eliminating administrative participation will result in a decrease in costs. Ensuring transparency in the allocation of donor funds and providing them with information about how their money will be utilized instills confidence in the charitable system [12, 13]

AdalbertoRangone and Luca Busolli [2021] examine the efficacy of blockchain technology in revolutionizing the charity system during the Covid-19 outbreak. It is accomplished by utilizing data obtained from the philanthropic database. A multitude of unique solutions were derived. We gain an understanding of how blockchain technology might enhance the charity system and mitigate instances of fraud within it. The user's text is " [14, 15]".

Nor *et al.* established a technique to solicit funds from a large number of people. This platform enables individuals to transfer funds to areas affected by disasters efficiently. The utilization of the Ethereum Smart Contract within the system effectively addressed concerns pertaining to fraud, transaction costs, transaction delay, and lack of accountability [16, 17].

Hu *et al.* developed a system with the objective of facilitating charitable activities. The solution utilizes Ethereum smart contracts and leverages blockchain technology to enhance transparency in the charity sector. It led to an augmentation in public trust [18, 19].

Hai-Ying YU, Pei-wu DONG, and Tao MA Yang Qilin conducted experiments on a model that successfully established confidence in online charity systems. According to the model, trust is contingent upon the structural quality of information and the knowledge of the information source [20].

PROPOSED SYSTEM

The application will resolve the transparency issue. Due to the multitude of transactions involved in the fundraising process, it is imperative to carry out the relevant legal documents and handle them accordingly. The smart contract facilitates the execution of identical actions. A transaction protocol is responsible for overseeing, carrying out, and recording transactions in accordance with the agreement between the funder and the individual or organization initiating the campaign.

The web application is centralized, meaning that a single body governs all activities. The health campaign information, contributions, and finances in a Decentralized application are maintained on a blockchain network that is decentralized and accessible to all individuals. The entire concept is referred to as Distributed Ledger technology.

The content is universally available on the network. POS, or Point of Sale, is utilized in transactions for its rapidity and high level of security. Proof of Stake (POS) obviates the need for intricate computations. Therefore, there is a reduction in the complexity of the calculation. Therefore, proof of stake is characterized by its energy efficiency.

The transactional record is unchangeable. The transaction method is recorded once using a shared ledger, which eliminates the need for duplicate efforts while recording the transaction. Once registered on the shared ledger, the transaction becomes unmodifiable. In the event of any error in the transaction record, it is necessary to initiate a new transaction in order to correct it. However, all transactions will remain accessible. Nodes can hold funds and transactions, limiting the information that needs to be stored on a centralized entity.

Ensuring the protection of money allocated for health welfare is crucial to prevent their misallocation, which could fail to achieve the objectives of the health campaign. The utilization of blockchain technology facilitates the fulfillment of our objectives.

METHODOLOGY

The methodologies used are as follows:

Blockchain

Blockchain is a decentralized form of data storage. Data in blockchain is stored in a digital format. Blockchain serves as a decentralized ledger that securely records and stores transactional data. It possesses robust security measures and operates in a decentralized manner. Blockchain ensures the security and openness of data, fostering trust and eliminating the need for third-party involvement in the process. Blockchain is a decentralized database that organizes data into blocks, which are interconnected by cryptographic techniques. When new data is received, it is stored in a newly allocated block. Once the block is filled, it will be linked to the preceding block. Blockchain operates without a central authority, granting control to each participant on the network. They cannot be changed. Once the data is inputted, it becomes immutable. The transactions are recorded and permanently accessible for public viewing. The primary objective of Blockchain is to securely store information in a decentralized manner, ensuring its accessibility to all participants while preventing any unauthorized modifications. The ledger is immutable, ensuring that all transactions are impervious to alteration, deletion, or destruction. Consequently, the Blockchain is classified as a Distributed Ledger Technology (DLT).

Polygon

Polygon is a layer-two scaling platform designed to address the challenges encountered by Ethereum-based applications. The first issue is the low throughput problem, indicating that Ethereum is capable of processing only 30 transactions per second. The processing speed is significantly slow. Due to their increased processing capacity, numerous alternatives can handle a significantly higher number of transactions within a given period. As an illustration, the Cardano blockchain achieves a throughput of approximately 257 transactions per second. Polkadot has a maximum capacity of 1000, but Solana can handle up to 65000 transactions. The second issue pertains to the need for more user-friendliness in the Ethereum network. The Ethereum blockchain imposes constraints on developers, restricting their choices. Polygon is an alternative that utilizes Ethereum's technology, providing increased throughput, significantly reduced transaction fees, and improved possibilities. The main objective is to enhance the adoption of DeFi tools and apps by effectively establishing interconnections between blockchains.

The EVM, short for Ethereum Virtual Machine, is the executable code that is executed by computers worldwide to implement the smart contracts of the Blockchain. Polygon indeed possesses an Ethereum Virtual Machine (EVM). All of them employ the primary Ethereum code, and as they essentially execute the same code, they are functionally identical. The ease with which developers can migrate their projects to a different network, with minimal modifications, is understandable.

Polygon is a blockchain that operates as a side chain to Ethereum, employing a Proof of Stake consensus process. Polygon encompasses a collection of blockchains that serve the purpose of scaling Ethereum rather than being limited to a single Proof of Stake chain. Once these developers accomplish this, they can effortlessly generate other scaling options for Ethereum, such as entirely distinct chains (as seen in Fig. **2**).

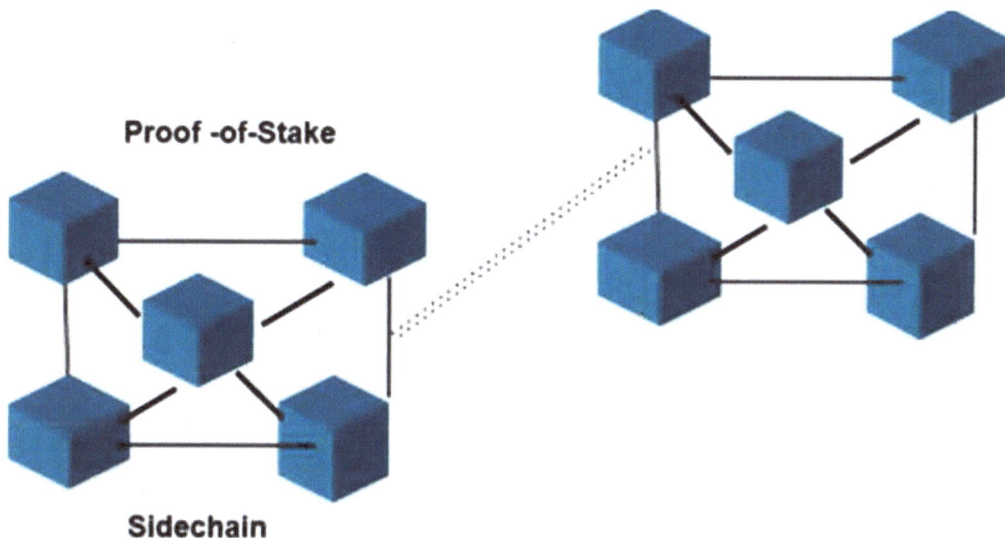

Fig. (2). Proof of stake.

Solidity

Solidity is a statically typed programming language primarily utilized for the creation of smart contracts on the Ethereum network. Solidity incorporates object-oriented programming features, including inheritance, polymorphism, and abstraction. It functions as a tool for generating machine-level code and compiling it on the Ethereum Virtual Machine.

Module Details

The application has been divided into two modules: one for creating a health campaign and another for contributing to the health campaign.

Initiating the health campaign can be accomplished with great ease. The smart contract monitors the data and ensures its integrity by preventing any unauthorized alterations. The necessary information for the campaign, such as the campaign title, the campaign's story, the required quantity of funds, and the campaign poster, should be provided (Fig. **3**). Prior to commencing the campaign (Table **1**), the wallet must be linked. If the user lacks a wallet and has not connected their wallet *via* MetaMask, they will be unable to establish the health campaign.

Fig. (3). Create health campaign.

Table 1. Metamask test accounts.

Metamask Account	Metamask Account Address	Balance(MATIC)
Creator A	0x78f740c2C69961a9D9ff844190E311d45412835D	0.3974
Donor B	0x9971a76Df12e9FdC3cb71A3cf721165ABC94911C	0.4789
Donor C	0x5CbE66e1159663436f1832366B0Eea44938821c1	0.7654
Beneficiary D	0xBedb4f3F3B4Bb1DDCe1C50D47A158840feE8c5C2	0

Any individual can contribute to the health campaign established (see Fig. **4**). Upon selecting the "Go to Campaign" option from the available campaigns, the user will be brought to the information page where they can donate to the health campaign (Table **2**).

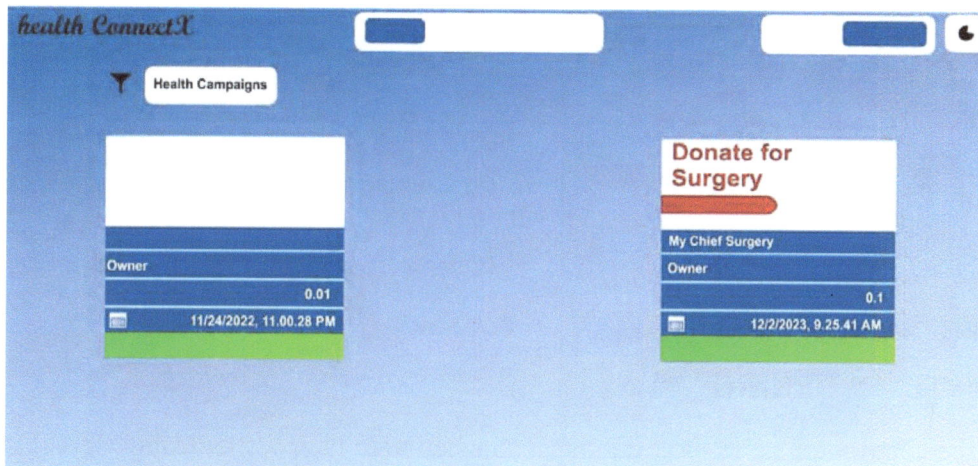

Fig. (4). List of health campaigns.

Table 2. Fundraising chest healthcare project.

Attributes	Values
Creator.	Creator A.
Health Campaign Details.	Need funds for curing my Chest related health issue.
Required Amount.	50 MATIC.
Donor.	Donor C.
Receiver.	Beneficiary D.

In that page, the details of the recent donations are also available (Fig. **5**). A particular past donation is also available. The required amount for the health campaign and the received amount for the campaign are also present on the page.

The previous contribution is also accessible. The page displays both the specified funding amount for the health campaign and the actual money received for the campaign.

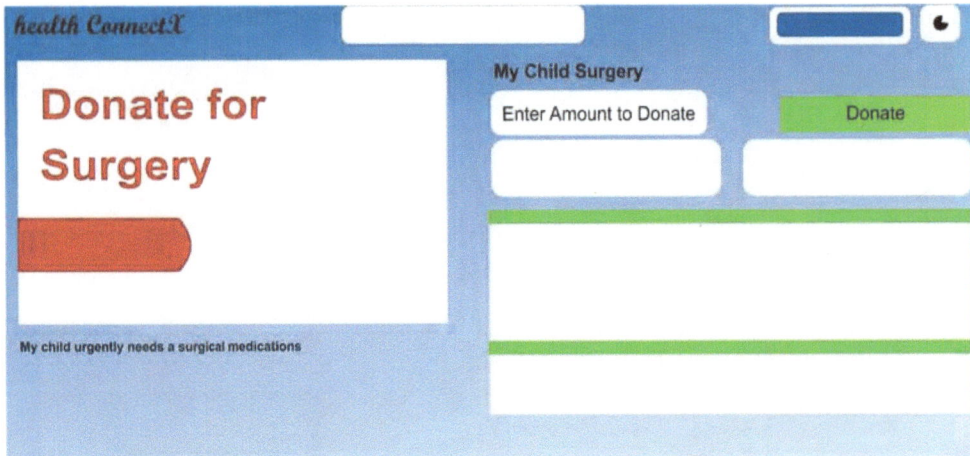

Fig. (5). Donation page of health campaign.

SYSTEM WORKING

If the contributor has yet to establish a connection to their wallet using MetaMask, they will be unable to contribute to the health campaign. The contributions will be transferred to the designated campaign address, ensuring transparency and security throughout the entire process.

The system is functioning well.

Users can either initiate the health campaign or make contributions towards it. To initiate a health campaign, the user must provide:

• The narrative for the campaign.
• The necessary funding for the campaign.
• Relevant visuals that align with the campaign's objectives.

Users can make contributions to the existing roster of health campaigns. The user's contribution to the health campaign is only accepted if the amount provided by the user is below the specified threshold in Table **3**. Once the transaction is completed, the user can monitor the progress of their donation. It enhances the level of transparency within the system, as depicted in Fig. (**6**).

Table 3. Fundraising chest healthcare project donation tests.

Donor	Amount(MATIC)	Status	Remarks
Donor B	52	Failed	Amount more than the Required Amount.
Donor B	49	Success	-

(Table 3) cont.....

Donor	Amount(MATIC)	Status	Remarks
Donor C	12	Failed	Beneficiary Metalmark Address does not exist.

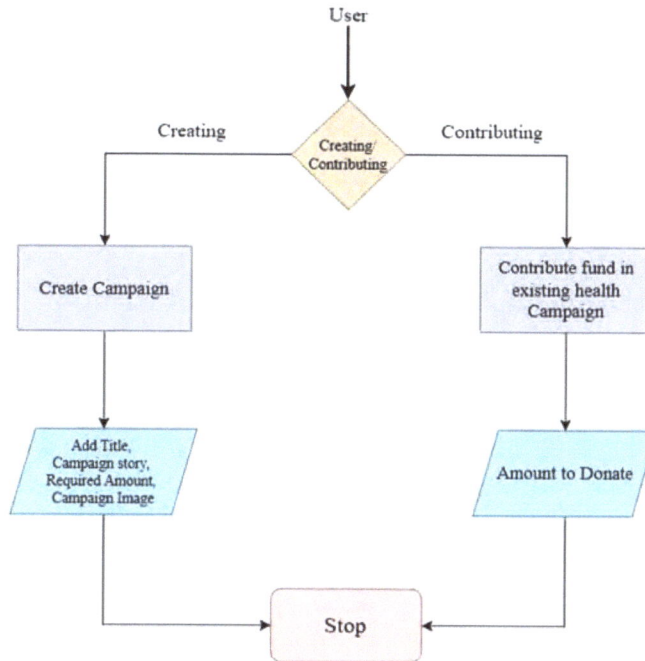

Fig. (6). The working flow of the user creating the new health campaign or the contributor's contribution to the existing health campaign.

Create and Donate *Via* Blockchain

Creating a Health Campaign

To initiate a health campaign, an organization or individual can invoke the create campaign function. The function possesses four parameters: The title of the campaign is essential. The requested information includes the Campaign Amount, imgURI, category, and storyURI. The "Title" field is mandatory and should contain the title of the health campaign. The Campaign Amount refers to the exact funding required for addressing a particular health-related issue. The imgURI is used for uploading posters that are associated with the health campaign. The story is used to provide information about the health issue that the campaign aims to address. Once the health campaign is established, it undergoes a thorough verification process to ensure its authenticity. This process leads to the creation of a transaction, which is then added to a block. As a result, the health campaign becomes accessible to the public, allowing anyone to make donations towards it.

Donating to health campaigns

Upon the establishment of the health campaign, the specific health campaigns are eligible to receive the allocated funding. We are now acquiring funds in MATIC. Every health campaign has a predetermined campaign amount, which represents the specific quantity of resources required to address the health issue at hand effectively. The donate option will facilitate the reception of contributions for health programs.

CONCLUSION

Utilizing decentralized fundraising platforms is secure. Conventional methods of fundraising exhibit numerous irregularities, thus necessitating the implementation of an anti-fraudulent, safe, and decentralized system. The entire fundraising process in healthcare is implemented through the utilization of blockchain technology, ensuring transparency and decentralization. The system provides both security and authenticity as necessary criteria. It enhances transparency in the fundraising process and instills trust in donors. This will additionally eradicate the intermediary in the fundraising process. It enhances efficiency and decreases the cost of the fundraising process by eliminating the need for third-party engagement.

REFERENCES

[1]   H. Yadav, S. Singh, K.K. Mishra, S. Srivastava, M.S. Naruka, and S.P. Yadav, "Brain Tumor Detection with MRI Images", *International Conference on Computational Intelligence and Sustainable Engineering Solutions (CISES),* pp. 519-527, 2022.
[http://dx.doi.org/10.1109/CISES54857.2022.9844387]

[2]   P. Rani, S. Verma, S.P. Yadav, B.K. Rai, M.S. Naruka, and D. Kumar, "Simulation of the Lightweight Blockchain Technique Based on Privacy and Security for Healthcare Data for the Cloud System", *International Journal of E-Health and Medical Communications,* vol. 13, no. 4, pp. 1-15, 2022.
[http://dx.doi.org/10.4018/IJEHMC.309436]

[3]   F. Al-Turjman, S.P. Yadav, M. Kumar, V. Yadav, T. Stephan, Ed., *Transforming Management with AI, Big-Data, and IoT.* Springer International Publishing, 2022.
[http://dx.doi.org/10.1007/978-3-030-86749-2]

[4]   J. Bhardwaj, A. Nayak, C.S. Yadav, and S.P. Yadav, "A Review in Wavelet Transforms Based Medical Image Fusion", In: *Evolving Role of AI and IoMT in the Healthcare Market.,* F. Al-Turjman, M. Kumar, T. Stephan, A. Bhardwaj, Eds., Springer: Cham, 2021.
[http://dx.doi.org/10.1007/978-3-030-82079-4_9]

[5]   J. Jasmine, N. Yuvaraj, and J. Logeshwaran, "DSQLR-A distributed scheduling and QoS localized routing scheme for wireless sensor network", *Recent trends in information technology and communication for industry 4.0,* vol. 1, p. 47-60, 2022.

[6]   M. Ramkumar, J. Logeshwaran, and T. Husna, "CEA: Certification based encryption algorithm for enhanced data protection in social networks", *Fundamentals of Applied Mathematics and Soft Computing,* vol. 1, p. 161-170, 2022.

[7]   J. Logeshwaran, "The control and communication management for ultra dense cloud system using fast Fourier algorithm", *ICTACT Journal on Data Science and Machine Learning,* vol. 3, no. 2, pp. 281-

284, 2022.

[8] V. Bibhu, L. Das, A. Rana, S. Sharma, and S. Salagrama, "AI Model for Blockchain Based Industrial Application in Healthcare IoT", In: *AI Models for Blockchain-Based Intelligent Networks in IoT Systems: Concepts, Methodologies, Tools, and Applications.* Springer International Publishing: Cham, 2023, pp. 163-184.
[http://dx.doi.org/10.1007/978-3-031-31952-5_8]

[9] S. Salagrama, Y.S. Boyapati, and V. Bibhu, "Security and Privacy of Critical Data in Ad Hoc Network Deployed Over Running Vehicles", *3rd International Conference on Intelligent Engineering and Management (ICIEM),* pp. 411-414, 2022.
[http://dx.doi.org/10.1109/ICIEM54221.2022.9853172]

[10] K. Zhu, "Blockchain Technology: Applications, Opportunities, Challenges, and Countermeasures", *International Conference on Finance, Trade and Business Management (FTBM 2023),* pp. 460-468, 2023.
[http://dx.doi.org/10.2991/978-94-6463-298-9_50]

[11] R. Parkavi, S. Vigneshwaran, N. Sambath, and P. Sanjai, "Charity Management Using Blockchain Technology", *Handbook of Research on Data Science and Cybersecurity Innovations in Industry 4.0 Technologies,* pp. 291-314, 2023.
[http://dx.doi.org/10.4018/978-1-6684-8145-5.ch015]

[12] M. Pandey, M. Velmurugan, G. Sathi, A.R. Abbas, N. Zebo, and T. Sathish, "Blockchain Technology: Applications and Challenges in Computer Science", *E3S Web of Conferences,* p. 04035, 2023.

[13] J. Swati, and P. Nitin, "CryptoScholarChain: Revolutionizing Scholarship Management Framework with Blockchain Technology", *Int. J. Adv. Comput. Sci. Appl.,* vol. 14, no. 8, 2023.
[http://dx.doi.org/10.14569/IJACSA.2023.0140872]

[14] S. Dong, K. Abbas, M. Li, and J. Kamruzzaman, "Blockchain technology and application: an overview", *PeerJ Comput. Sci.,* vol. 9, p. e1705, 2023.
[http://dx.doi.org/10.7717/peerj-cs.1705] [PMID: 38077532]

[15] A.K. Tyagi, "Decentralized everything: Practical use of blockchain technology in future applications", In: *Distributed Computing to Blockchain.* Academic Press, 2023, pp. 19-38.
[http://dx.doi.org/10.1016/B978-0-323-96146-2.00010-3]

[16] M. Verma, "Blockchain and AI Convergence: A New Era of Possibilities", *Published in International Journal of Trend in Scientific Research and Development (ijtsrd),* vol. 7, no. 5, pp. 130-138, 2023.

[17] V. Tiwari, S. Goundar, K.B.R. Teja, B. Agarwal, and P. Harjule, "A Transparent, Distributed, and Secure Crowdfunding Platform Based on Blockchain", In: *Integrating Blockchain and Artificial Intelligence for Industry 4.0 Innovations.* Springer International Publishing: Cham, 2023, pp. 185-199.

[18] I. Iswahyudi, D. Hindarto, and R. E. Indrajit, "Digital Transformation in University: Enterprise Architecture and Blockchain Technology", *Sinkron: jurnaldanpenelitianteknikinformatika,* vol. 8, no. 4, pp. 2501-2512, 2023.

[19] K. Ulrich, "Blockchain technology-based crypto assets: new insights into the evolution of the understanding of digital entrepreneurship", *Manage. Decis.,* 2023.

[20] N. Kshetri, K. Miller, G. Banerjee, and B.R. Upreti, "FinChain: Adaptation of Blockchain Technology in Finance and Business - An Ethical Analysis of Applications, Challenges, Issues and Solutions", *International Journal of Emerging and Disruptive Innovation in Education : VISIONARIUM,* vol. 1, no. 1, p. 4, 2023.
[http://dx.doi.org/10.62608/2831-3550.1010]

CHAPTER 12

Investigating Technology Adoption and Consumer Behaviour in Digital Age

Ritesh Kumar Singhal[1,*], **Ankit Garg**[1], **Pragya Agarwal**[2] and **Gautam Jaiswal**[3]

[1] *Ajay Kumar Garg Institute of Management, Ghaziabad, Uttar Pradesh 201206, India*

[2] *Hi-Tech Institute of Engineering & Technology, Ghaziabad, Uttar Pradesh 201206, India*

[3] *School of Business Management, NOIDA International University, Gr Noida, Uttar Pradesh, India*

Abstract: The rapid advancements of equipment and technology, economic globalization, and other external factors are causing a shift in consumer behavior. Researchers have employed theories from various allied disciplines, such as psychology, sociology, economics, behavioral economics, and anthropology, to examine and understand consumer behavior.

The advent of information and telecommunications technology has greatly enhanced the efficiency and timeliness of communication, facilitating the seamless exchange of information within and outside organizations. Nevertheless, the use of these technologies presents challenges for both businesses and society, potentially detrimentally impacting consumer behavior.

Research on consumer behavior in electronic environments indicates that information technologies generate distinct and dynamic patterns of behavior, which differ from the typical interactions and transactions observed in traditional marketplaces. The study identified idiosyncrasies in behavior that were caused by information and communications technologies.

Keywords: Anthropology, Consumer behavior, Equipment, Economic globalization, Sociology, Technology.

INTRODUCTION

In the future, civilizations will prioritize the accumulation and advancement of knowledge, transforming it into innovative and practical solutions, thereby recognizing knowledge as a vital resource. Knowledge workers are highly esteemed as important contributors to the labor force in contemporary culture that

---

* **Corresponding Ritesh Kumar Singhal:** Ajay Kumar Garg Institute of Management, Ghaziabad, Uttar Pradesh, India; E-mail: spsingh.mohali@gmail.com

Pankaj Kumar Mishra & Satya Prakash Yadav (Eds.)

relies on knowledge and information. The Information Society is the main benchmark for information-based societies in the American and European Union, and it sets the essential approach for achieving this knowledge society. The objective is to augment Internet accessibility while concurrently generating knowledge that enriches the scientific and cultural legacy of emerging economies. Consumer behavior is a complex and ever-changing process that encompasses individuals' emotions, cognitions, and actions, as well as broader societal influences. Multiple factors, such as personality, lifestyle, psychographics, and motivation, influence it. The adoption of information technology has caused a shift in consumer behavior both in India and globally. While the initial acceptance of these technologies may be slow, once customers start utilizing them, they often continue to do so indefinitely. India had a total of 560 million internet users in 2018, making it the second-largest market for digital consumers and experiencing rapid growth, second only to China. Mobile data in India: On average, users consume 8.3 gigabits (GB) of data each month. In comparison, mobile users in China consume 5.5 GB of data, while in South Korea, a country with a highly advanced digital economy, the consumption ranges between 8.0 and 8.5 GB. In 2018, the number of app downloads in India exceeded 12 billion, while the country had a total of 1.2 billion active mobile phone subscribers. India is leading the way in digitalization among 17 major and developing economies, with the exception of Indonesia. Moreover, there is ample room for further growth, as only a little over 40% of the population currently has internet access. Consequently, businesses are unable to apply the same criteria to online transactions as they do to traditional ones.

Objective

The study aims to examine atypical conduct resulting from the utilization of information and telecommunication technology by analyzing consumer behavior in a digital setting.

Research Methodology

The researcher employs established quantitative and qualitative research methodologies, including categorization, analysis, statistical techniques, and so on.

Theoretical and Methodological Foundation

The foundation of this research is built upon statistical data obtained from legal institutions, information collected by the author during the survey, and publications from the media and professional literature.

Theoretical Framework

Computers and electronic communication networks have become essential instruments in the computer age and information society due to the increasing significance of information handling and processing. They provide the fastest data transfer and storage, as well as being more precise and cost-efficient compared to human labor. The ability of an organization to exchange information efficiently and generate profit is essential for its success in this scenario.

A multitude of global experts and researchers have conducted studies on two pivotal dimensions: organizations and individuals—in order to comprehend the mechanisms and motivations behind the adoption of new technologies. The Technology Acceptance Model, Motivation Model, Theory of Planned Behaviour, and Innovation Diffusion Theory are notable models commonly used for this objective [1, 2].

The Davis Technology Acceptance Model, developed by Davis in 1989, forecasts the acceptance and utilization of information technology. According to this paradigm, the perceived utility and usability of a technology influence a user's willingness to employ it. Originally designed to investigate the reception of technology in professional environments, this model has recently expanded its scope to analyze the reception of consumer services such as e-commerce and internet services.

The Technology Acceptance Model provides a dependable framework for identifying obstacles that may impede users' acceptance of technological solutions. In addition, Davis and Venkatesh have shown how the model may be enhanced beyond its original application of assessing consumer acceptance of existing products to evaluating future product concepts, such as prototypes [3]. It implies that, in alignment with the human-centered design approach, the Technology Acceptance Model could be employed to assess the effectiveness of proposed solutions in technology development initiatives (Fig. 1).

In today's world, computers and electronic communication networks are indispensable for the management and processing of information due to their precision, cost-effectiveness, and ability to facilitate rapid storage and exchange of information. In the digital age, the smooth transmission of information is vital for the prosperity of businesses. Due to the adoption of new technology by both organizations and individuals, much research is conducted to understand the methods and motivations behind this phenomenon [4].

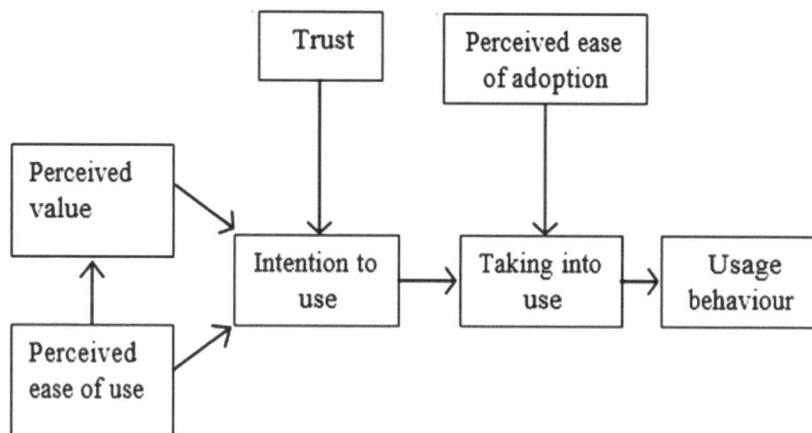

Fig. (1). Technology Acceptance Model for Mobile Services (Kaasinen,2005).

The Technology Acceptance Model is a prominent framework used to understand the adoption of technology. It predicts the acceptance and utilization of information technology based on the user's perception of its utility and simplicity of use. The Motivation paradigm is a framework that explains behavior based on both internal and extrinsic motivation. The inclusion of the construct of perceived behavioral control in the Theory of Planned Behaviour, an extension of the Theory of Reasoned Action, aims to enhance the comprehension of human behavior.

The Innovation Diffusion Theory is a well-known concept that identifies five key factors—compatibility, complexity, observability, relative benefit, and trial ability—that impact the adoption of innovative technology. Seven constructs were developed to measure individual acceptability of technology, taking into account variables such as voluntariness of usage, relative advantage, and convenience of use, among others [5].

Various elements, such as organizational and technological infrastructure, social influence, and expectations for performance and effort, impact consumer behavior and the adoption of information technology. The author aims to analyze the impact of information technologies on consumer behavior, namely the acceptance of new technologies, and provide guidance to businesses on the development and promotion of technologies such as web and portals, along with recommendations for user adoption. Consequently, firms will enhance their capacity to cater to their clients and maintain a competitive edge in terms of technology.

Organizations heavily depend on information and communications technology to enhance internal and external communication, exchange information, and stay competitive in the current corporate landscape. In order to accomplish this, they create a range of digital platforms such as websites, portals, forums, and e-commerce sites. Enterprises that employ information technologies benefit from reduced expenses, enhanced competitiveness, rapid and uncomplicated information exchange, and continuous access to up-to-date information and additional services. The adoption of new technology by customers is hindered by factors such as changes in processes, uncertain return on investment, unstable data networks, and government regulations [6].

These challenges could be addressed by applying current ways of adopting new technology to model web technologies and e-commerce. These models encompass all aspects of client behavior and highlight certain traits that organizations should consider. The characteristics encompass perceived utility and ease of use, compatibility, complexity, relative benefit, demonstrability, visibility, and voluntariness of use. Organizations can develop strategies for implementing new technologies, analyze and oversee the associated processes, derive insights from failures, simulate consumer behavior, and devise methodologies and techniques based on these simulations. Gaining insight into the factors that influence client behavior can enable organizations to enhance their advertising strategies and innovate new technologies, thereby gaining a competitive edge. The user's text is " [7]".

Consumer Information Behavior

Organizations must consider that human information-seeking behavior is contingent upon an individual's characteristics, expertise, knowledge, and motivation, as well as the impact of external factors when designing their websites or other communication channels with customers. Having this knowledge will allow the organization to develop a strategy for implementing the system and execute the plan. The adoption of information systems is significantly influenced by human information behavior [8].

Human information behavior refers to the examination of individuals' interactions with information, encompassing their processes of seeking, utilizing, adapting, disseminating, accumulating, and disregarding it. When we engage in information behavior management, we deliberately strive to enhance the overall effectiveness of the information environment within an organization. Today, it is particularly imperative as people seek information, compare prices, and secure the most advantageous deals for themselves. Data indicates that the main activities conducted on the Internet are information sharing and information retrieval.

T. Wilson's 1999 information behavior model illustrates the correlation between information about a user's sense of a need and their subsequent information-seeking behavior. To address this requirement, the user submits inquiries to formal or informal sources of information or services, achieving varied levels of success in finding relevant data. If the individual successfully finds the data, their perceived requirement may be partially fulfilled. If they cannot find the necessary data, they may need to attempt their search again [9].

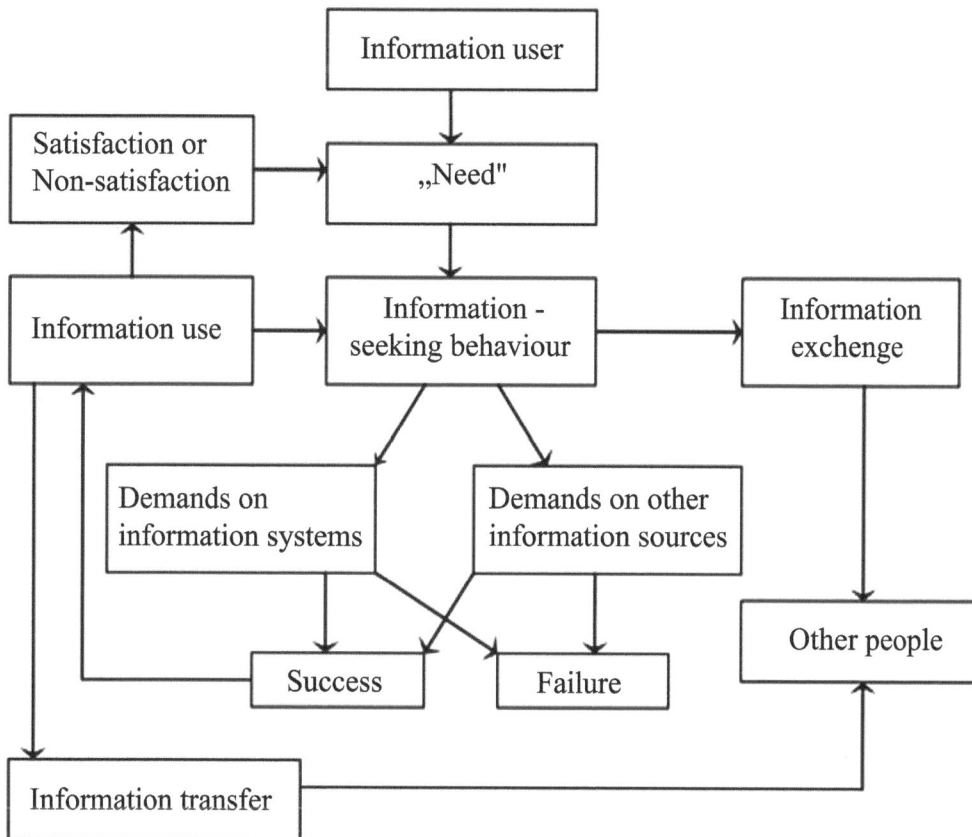

Fig. (2). Wilson's information behavior model (Wilson,1999).

The model also highlights the role of information-seeking behavior in facilitating information flow among individuals and the potential for shared knowledge to be exploited by individuals. This underscores the communal nature of information-seeking behavior and underscores the need to understand how individuals engage with information to improve the effectiveness of an organization's information ecosystem.

The elusive concept of information demand complicates the understanding of information-seeking behavior. In 1981, Wilson argued that an individual's need for information is a personal and subjective phenomenon that is limited to their consciousness and cannot be directly observed by others. Consequently, determining the appropriate time and manner to address someone's request for information can take time and effort. In order to identify a person's information demands, researchers must depend on their behavior or their self-reports [10] (Fig. **2**).

The concept of necessity is also rooted in psychology as it pertains to emotions and the underlying motivations that drive individuals to articulate their requirements. A significant amount of research has been conducted to understand the subjective nature of need and its impact on behavior. Acquiring this knowledge is essential for developing strategies to provide effective information services that meet the needs of both individuals and organizations.

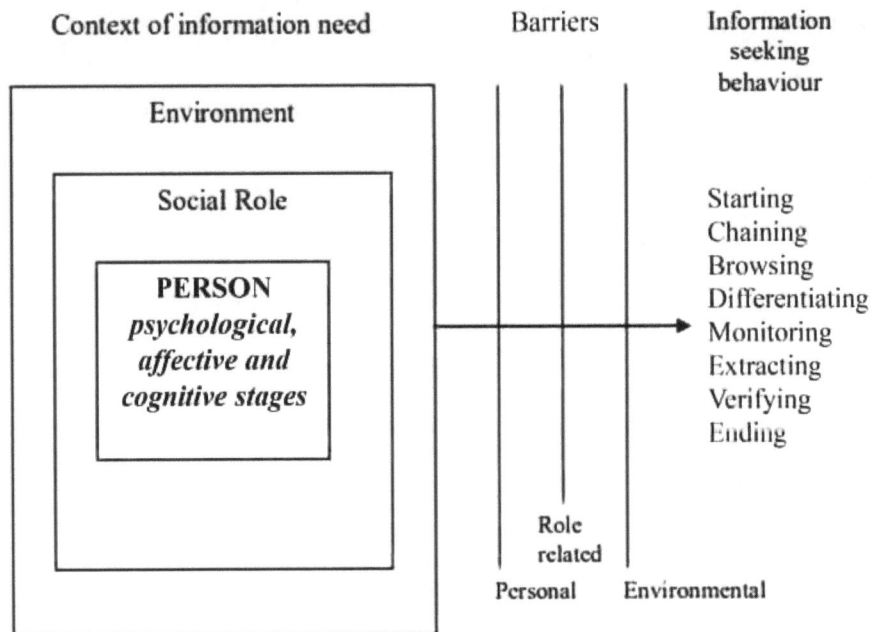

Fig. (3). Model of information-seeking behavior(Wilson,2002).

Analysis

The author conducted a study on individuals aged 18 to 25 to analyze the differences in consumer behavior motivations in both physical and online marketplaces. This particular demographic was selected based on the fact that, according to the statistical data, 96% of individuals within the age bracket of 16 to

25 were active Internet users in the year 2023. The survey was carried out during January and February of 2023. A total of 172 replies were received from individuals of both genders. The questionnaire consisted of six distinct sets of questions, each targeting a different set of variables. The survey's summary is provided below [11] (Fig. **3**).

  i. According to the survey, the respondents use the internet tools for:

 ii. This survey prescribes the benefits of internet usage and e-commerce for the target group that are follows (Fig. **4**):

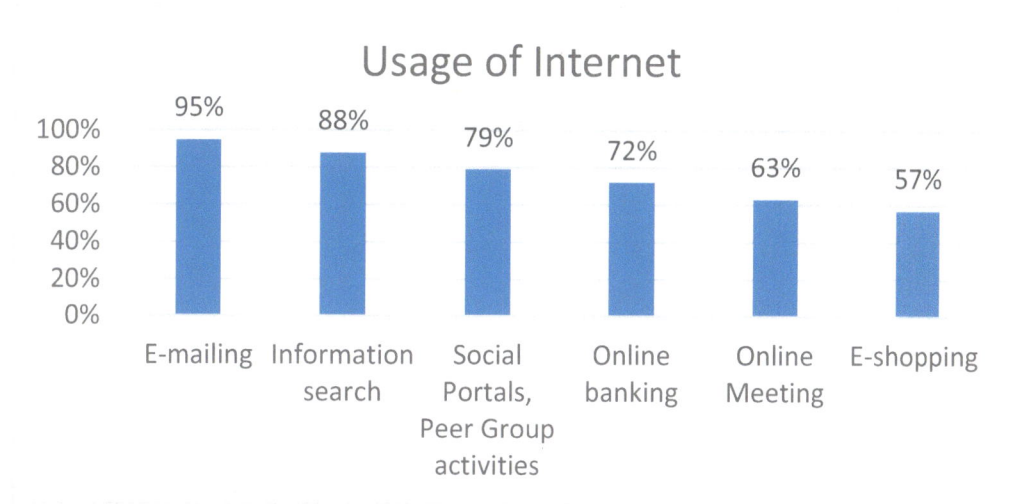

Fig. (4). Use of Internet Tools by Respondents.

S.No.	Item	Percentage
1.	Speed.	93%
2.	Saves time.	91%
3.	Help to facilitate many processes.	86%
4.	Finding detailed information.	84%
5.	Ease of access.	76%
6.	24x7 Availability.	64%
7.	Ease of use.	63%
8.	Latest Information.	59%
9.	Conveniences in general.	56%
10.	Convenient opportunity to compare prices and products.	54%
11.	Accuracy and timeliness.	49%

(Table) cont.....

S.No.	Item	Percentage
12.	Availability of goods in one place.	45%
13.	Discount & offers.	48%
14.	Order execution.	36%
15.	Eco-friendly (less paper & brochures *etc*).	32%

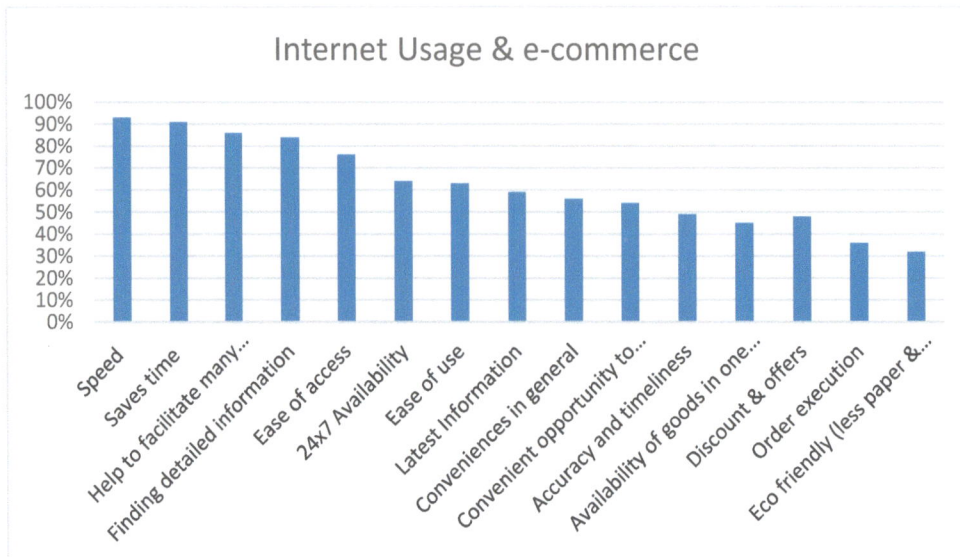

Fig. (5). Internet Usage and E-commerce.

The results of this study, as well as prior studies conducted by other companies, suggest that email is a crucial e-commerce medium utilized by 93% of internet users. The results indicate the target audience's interests and their awareness of e-shopping as an upcoming leisure activity. Hence, it is crucial to anticipate the potential transformations that e-shopping might undergo in the upcoming period, as well as to analyze the rationales, advantages, and disadvantages of e-shopping for this specific demographic [12] (Fig. **5**).

The survey's results clearly demonstrate that the target population highly prioritizes convenience, up-to-date information, efficiency, and time efficiency. According to the authors, the survey's results provide evidence that new technologies, including the Internet and e-commerce, are influencing consumer behavior. Contemporary consumer values encompass autonomy, expeditious decision-making, convenience, and resource optimization [13].

One can offer recommendations to a business wanting to compete in the market through a new Internet communication channel by integrating principles from three fundamental theories: technology adoption, information-seeking behavior, and evolving consumer behavior. In order to achieve success, this business must captivate consumers and differentiate itself in the competitive electronic marketplace [14 - 17].

In order to effectively penetrate the electronic market and differentiate itself from competitors, a corporation must consider three key concepts: technology adoption, information-seeking behavior, and altering consumer behavior. The author recommends utilizing the table above as a point of reference [18].

i. Mix of factors what should be taken into account for development of new e-channel

Creating models for the development and adoption of new e-commerce technologies is possible by combining theoretical breakthroughs and real-world experience through the process of synthesis. An exhaustive examination of all factors influencing customer behavior could result in the development of a strategic plan by establishing connections with real-life illustrations [19, 20]. The given input is a list containing the numbers 13 and 15.

CONCLUSION

The study provides valuable insights into the factors that influence customer behavior in the digital realm. Novel procedures and approaches ought to be developed to assess e-consumer behavior, and further investigation is necessary to grasp its intricacies completely.

The findings suggest that integrating many theoretical perspectives can lead to a more comprehensive understanding of e-consumer behavior. However, this study is but a small addition to the numerous unresolved challenges in e-consumer behavior research, given the vast scope of the field.

REFERENCES

[1]   X. Xue, S. Palanisamy, M. A, D. Selvaraj, O.I. Khalaf, and G.M. Abdulsahib, "A Novel partial sequence technique based Chaotic biogeography optimization for PAPR reduction in generalized frequency division multiplexing waveform", *Heliyon,* vol. 9, no. 9, p. e19451, 2023. [http://dx.doi.org/10.1016/j.heliyon.2023.e19451] [PMID: 37681146]

[2]   G. Muttashar Abdulsahib, D. Sekaran Selvaraj, A. Manikandan, S. Palanisamy, M. Uddin, O. Ibrahim Khalaf, M. Abdelhaq, and R. Alsaqour, "Reverse polarity optical Orthogonal frequency Division Multiplexing for High-Speed visible light communications system", *Egyptian Informatics Journal,* vol. 24, no. 4, p. 100407, 2023. [http://dx.doi.org/10.1016/j.eij.2023.100407]

[3]   V.A. Mohammed, M.A. Mohammed, M.A. Mohammed, J. Logeshwaran, and N. Jiwani, "Machine Learning-based Evaluation of Heart Rate Variability Response in Children with Autism Spectrum Disorder", *2023 Third International Conference on Artificial Intelligence and Smart Energy (ICAIS),* pp. 1022-1028, 2023.
[http://dx.doi.org/10.1109/ICAIS56108.2023.10073898]

[4]   G. Ramesh, J. Logeshwaran, and V. Aravindarajan, "A Secured Database Monitoring Method to Improve Data Backup and Recovery Operations in Cloud Computing", *BOHR International Journal of Computer Science,* vol. 2, no. 1, pp. 1-7, 2023.
[http://dx.doi.org/10.54646/bijcs.019]

[5]   AvinashKhatri, K.C., Krishna Bikram Shah, Logeshwaran, J., & AshishShrestha (2023), "Genetic algorithm based techno-economic optimization of an isolated hybrid energy system", *ICTACT Journal on microelectronics,* vol. 8, no. 4, pp. 1447-1450, 2023.

[6]   P. Rani, S. Verma, S.P. Yadav, B.K. Rai, M.S. Naruka, and D. Kumar, "Simulation of the Lightweight Blockchain Technique Based on Privacy and Security for Healthcare Data for the Cloud System", In: *International Journal of E-Health and Medical Communications (IJEHMC)* vol. 13. , 2022, no. 4, pp. 1-15.
[http://dx.doi.org/10.4018/IJEHMC.309436]

[7]   F. Al-Turjman, S.P. Yadav, M. Kumar, V. Yadav, T. Stephan, Ed., *Transforming Management with AI, Big-Data, and IoT.,* Springer International Publishing, 2022.
[http://dx.doi.org/10.1007/978-3-030-86749-2]

[8]   J. Bhardwaj, A. Nayak, C.S. Yadav, and S.P. Yadav, "A Review in Wavelet Transforms Based Medical Image Fusion", *Evolving Role of AI and IoMT in the Healthcare Market.,* Springer: Cham, 2021.
[http://dx.doi.org/10.1007/978-3-030-82079-4_9]

[9]   R.M. Pujahari, S.P. Yadav, and R. Khan, "Intelligent farming system through weather forecast support and crop production", In: *Application of Machine Learning in Agriculture.* Elsevier, 2022, pp. 113-130.
[http://dx.doi.org/10.1016/B978-0-323-90550-3.00009-6]

[10]   V. Chaurasia, and S. Pal, "A novel approach for breast cancer detection using data mining techniques", *International journal of innovative research in computer and communication engineering (An ISO 3297: 2007 Certified Organization) ,* vol. 2, 2017.

[11]   S. Abbas, Z. Jalil, A.R. Javed, I. Batool, M.Z. Khan, A. Noorwali, T.R. Gadekallu, and A. Akbar, "BCD-WERT: a novel approach for breast cancer detection using whale optimization based efficient features and extremely randomized tree algorithm", *PeerJ Comput. Sci.,* vol. 7, p. e390, 2021.
[http://dx.doi.org/10.7717/peerj-cs.390] [PMID: 33817036]

[12]   R.M. Mann, R. Hooley, R.G. Barr, and L. Moy, "Novel approaches to screening for breast cancer", *Radiology,* vol. 297, no. 2, pp. 266-285, 2020.
[http://dx.doi.org/10.1148/radiol.2020200172] [PMID: 32897163]

[13]   J. Pereira-Carrillo, D. Suntaxi-Dominguez, O. Guarnizo-Cabezas, G. Villalba-Meneses, A. Tirado-Espín, and D. Almeida-Galárraga, "Comparison between two novel approaches in automatic breast cancer detection and diagnosis and its contribution in military defense. In Developments and Advances in Defense and Security", *Proceedings of MICRADS,* vol. 2021, pp. 189-201, 2022. [Springer Singapore].

[14]   G.G.N. Geweid, and M.A. Abdallah, "A novel approach for breast cancer investigation and recognition using M-level set-based optimization functions", *IEEE Access,* vol. 7, pp. 136343-136357, 2019.
[http://dx.doi.org/10.1109/ACCESS.2019.2941990]

[15]   U.M. Pal, M. Saxena, G.K. Anil Vishnu, D. Parsana, B.S.R. Sarvani, M. Varma, M. Jayachandra, V. Kurpad, D. Baruah, G. Gogoi, J.S. Vaidya, and H.J. Pandya, "Optical spectroscopy-based imaging

techniques for the diagnosis of breast cancer: A novel approach", *Appl. Spectrosc. Rev.,* vol. 55, no. 8, pp. 778-804, 2020.
[http://dx.doi.org/10.1080/05704928.2020.1749651]

[16] Heng-Da Cheng, R.I. Freimanis, and R.I. Freimanis, "A novel approach to microcalcification detection using fuzzy logic technique", *IEEE Trans. Med. Imaging,* vol. 17, no. 3, pp. 442-450, 1998.
[http://dx.doi.org/10.1109/42.712133] [PMID: 9735907]

[17] E. Malar, A. Kandaswamy, D. Chakravarthy, and A. Giri Dharan, "A novel approach for detection and classification of mammographic microcalcifications using wavelet analysis and extreme learning machine", *Comput. Biol. Med.,* vol. 42, no. 9, pp. 898-905, 2012.
[http://dx.doi.org/10.1016/j.compbiomed.2012.07.001] [PMID: 22871899]

[18] S. Abirami, P. Chitra, "Energy-efficient edge based real-time healthcare support system", *Advances in Computers,* vol. 117, Elsevier, no. 1, pp. 339-368, 2020.

[19] K. Gupta, N. Jiwani, G. Pau, and M. Alibakhshikenari, "A Machine Learning Approach Using Statistical Models for Early Detection of Cardiac Arrest in Newborn Babies in the Cardiac Intensive Care Unit", *IEEE Access,* vol. 11, pp. 60516-60538, 2023.
[http://dx.doi.org/10.1109/ACCESS.2023.3286346]

[20] M.C. Elish, "The stakes of uncertainty: developing and integrating machine learning in clinical care", *Ethnographic Praxis in Industry Conference Proceedings,* vol. 2018, 2018 no. 1, pp. 364-380
[http://dx.doi.org/10.1111/1559-8918.2018.01213]

CHAPTER 13

Comprehensive Life Cycle Methodology for the Development of Product Metrics

Swasti Singhal[1,*], **Laxmi Ahuja**[1] and **Himanshu Monga**[2]

[1] *AIIT Amity University Noida, Noida, Uttar Pradesh 201313, India*

[2] *ECE Department JLN Government Engineering College Sundar Nagar, Mandi, India*

Abstract: This study proposes an approach that encompasses the entire product life cycle, aimed at offering comprehensive product metrics for sustainable manufacturing. The metrics are designed to consider the three dimensions of sustainability, namely environmental, economic, and social factors. This paper centers on life cycle assessment and categorizes it into five stages of a product's life cycle, namely: the product's inception and design phase, the manufacturing phase, the transportation phase, the user experience phase, and the post-use and end-of-life cycle phases. This study centers on the metrics of the product and the challenges associated with creating a sustainable product, in addition to examining its life cycle. These provide an opportunity to establish a system of stratification for the metrics, based on the presence of distinct metrics throughout various stages of the life cycle. The generic metrics that were developed have been categorized into distinct metric clusters, which presents an opportunity to establish a metric levelling framework.

Keywords: Product life cycle, Product metrics, Sustainable manufacturing, Sustainable products.

INTRODUCTION

Sustainable products are products that are designed, manufactured, and distributed in a way that minimizes their environmental impact and ensures social and economic responsibility. These products are typically made with eco-friendly materials, are energy-efficient, and have a minimal carbon footprint throughout their lifecycle; for example, clothing made from sustainable materials such as organic cotton, bamboo, or recycled polyester. Solar panels, wind turbines, and other renewable energy systems that reduce reliance on non-renewable energy sources come under renewable energy systems. Sustainable products are becoming increasingly popular as consumers become more aware of the environ-

---

* **Corresponding author Swasti Singhal:** AIIT Amity University Noida, Noida, Uttar Pradesh 201313, India; E-mail: swasti.singhal@gmail.com

Pankaj Kumar Mishra & Satya Prakash Yadav (Eds.)

mental and social impact of the products they buy [1, 2]. By choosing sustainable products, consumers can help reduce their environmental footprint, support ethical and responsible manufacturing practices, and create a more sustainable future for all [3].

Sustainable manufacturing refers to the production of goods in a way that minimizes the environmental impact [4-6], reduces resource consumption, and ensures the well-being of workers and surrounding communities. It involves incorporating sustainable practices and technologies throughout the entire manufacturing process, from raw material sourcing to product design, manufacturing, packaging, distribution, and disposal. Some of the sustainable manufacturing practices include energy-efficient manufacturing processes that use renewable energy sources and optimizing production processes to minimize energy consumption and carbon emissions [8, 9]. Also, ensuring that raw materials are sourced from sustainable and ethical sources that prioritize environmental and social responsibility [10].

The development of product-based sustainable metrics [11, 12] involves identifying and measuring the environmental and social impacts of a product throughout its entire lifecycle, from raw material extraction to end-of-life disposal. These metrics can help companies evaluate the sustainability of their products, identify areas for improvement, and track progress over time. Some common product-based sustainable metrics include carbon footprint, the total amount of greenhouse gases (GHGs) emitted during the production, transportation, use, and disposal of a product. Water footprint is the amount of water used during the production and use of a product, including both direct and indirect water use. Materials footprint is the number of natural resources used to manufacture a product, including raw materials, energy, and water. Waste footprint is the amount of waste generated during the production, use, and disposal of a product, including both solid waste and hazardous waste. Social impact is the impact of a product on workers, communities, and society as a whole, including labor practices, human rights, and community engagement.

To develop product-based sustainable metrics, companies need to collect data on their products' lifecycle and analyze it to identify areas of improvement. They can then use this information to set sustainability goals, implement sustainable practices, and track progress over time. The development of sustainable product metrics requires collaboration across all stages of the product lifecycle, including designers, manufacturers, suppliers, and customers, to ensure that sustainability is integrated into every aspect of the product's development and use. The triple bottom line (TBL) is a framework for sustainability that takes into account three key dimensions of a company's performance: economic, social, and environmental. It is often referred to as "people, planet, and profit." The economic dimension refers to the financial performance of a company and its impact on the economy, including factors such as revenue, profits, and return on investment. The social dimension refers to a company's impact on society, including factors such as labour practices, employee relations, community involvement, and customer satisfaction. The environmental dimension refers to a company's impact on the natural environment, including factors such as resource use, waste generation, pollution, and greenhouse gas emissions.

The TBL framework recognizes that a company's success depends not only on its financial performance, but also on its ability to create value for society and minimize its impact on the environment. By considering all three dimensions of sustainability, companies can take a more holistic approach to business and ensure that they are creating value for all stakeholders, not just shareholders. The TBL has become an important tool for companies, investors, and policymakers seeking to promote sustainable development and responsible business practices. It provides a comprehensive framework for evaluating the sustainability of companies and identifying areas for improvement, and it can help companies enhance their reputation, reduce risk, and create long-term value for all stakeholders. Defining and containing the system boundaries while attempting to define the interrelationships between metrics across the triple bottom line is difficult. A complete life-cycle-based approach aids in overcoming this obstacle by developing metrics within the five life-cycle stages of a product [13 - 15].

LIFE CYCLE ASSESSMENT

LCA stands for Life Cycle Assessment, which is a methodology used to evaluate the environmental impact of a product, process or service throughout its entire life cycle, from the extraction of raw materials to the disposal or recycling of the product. LCA is a comprehensive approach that considers all the stages of a product's life cycle, including raw material extraction, transportation, manufacturing, distribution, use, and end-of-life disposal. The goal of LCA is to quantify the environmental impact of a product and identify areas for improvement in order to reduce the product's overall environmental footprint. It is highly important to consider the entire the entire product life cycle when assessing the environmental impacts of food products and the potential for reducing these impacts through sustainable production and packaging practices. It can be used to inform decision-making by companies and policymakers seeking to promote sustainable food production and reduce the environmental impact of food products. In this paper, the authors propose several optimization strategies to reduce the environmental impact of polycarbonate production, including the use of renewable energy sources, the optimization of production processes, and the use of alternative raw materials. The study provides valuable insights into the environmental impacts of polycarbonate production and identifies potential strategies for reducing these impacts. The study also highlights the importance of considering the entire product life cycle when assessing the environmental impacts of products, as well as the need for ongoing research and innovation to develop more sustainable production practices and materials. LCA is widely used by companies, governments, and NGOs to evaluate the environmental impact of products and processes and identify opportunities for sustainable design and development. LCA involves four main stages:

- Goal and scope definition: This stage involves defining the goals and boundaries of the LCA study, including the purpose of the study, the system boundaries, and the functional unit being analysed.
- Inventory analysis: This stage involves compiling a detailed inventory of all the inputs and outputs of the product system being studied, including raw materials, energy use, emissions, and waste.
- Impact assessment: This stage involves evaluating the potential environmental impacts associated with the product system being studied, such as greenhouse gas emissions, resource depletion, and ecosystem damage.
- Interpretation: This stage involves synthesizing the results of the inventory analysis and impact assessment to draw conclusions about the environmental performance of the product system being studied and identify opportunities for improvement.

TOTAL LIFE CYCLE CONSIDERATION TOWARD PRODUCT METRICS DEVELOPMENT

The duration of the entire life cycle pertaining to the development of product metrics may differ based on the particular product and industry. The development of product metrics is significantly influenced by the total life cycle. The present research endeavors to establish indicators and metrics for product sustainability by employing a comprehensive life-cycle methodology. This paper examines the five discrete stages that comprise the life cycle of a manufactured product in a closed-loop system. These stages include the product's inception and design phase, manufacturing phase, transportation phase, user experience phase, and post-use and end-of-life cycle phase. The concise definition of each phase of the life cycle aims to enhance the understanding of its extent of influence. The importance of this lies in the categorization of different indicators/metrics based on specific life-cycle phases, as defined earlier.

Step 1: PID Phase

The initial phase involves establishing the aims and objectives of the product, along with the metrics that will be employed to assess its efficacy. The process may entail the collection of feedback from various stakeholders, including customers, investors, and internal teams. After establishing the objectives, the subsequent phase involves the identification of crucial metrics for the design process that will be utilized to gauge the advancement towards the aforementioned objectives. The metrics utilized ought to be precise, quantifiable, and pertinent to the objectives. It is imperative to ascertain the requisite data for evaluating the identified metrics. The process may entail the acquisition of data from internal systems, third-party sources, or direct customer feedback.

Step 2: Manufacturing Phase

Upon identification of the data sources, it is imperative to establish protocols for the collection and storage of said data. This could potentially entail the integration of novel software applications, recruitment of supplementary personnel, or formulation of innovative protocols. The analysis and reporting of the gathered data are imperative to inform and update pertinent stakeholders. The task at hand may encompass the creation of dashboards, reports, or other forms of visual representations that offer valuable insights into the primary metrics.

Step 3: Transportation Phase

The transportation phase plays an important role in the product life cycle, and sustainable transportation practices are essential for promoting a more sustainable and responsible approach to product design and production. Efforts to reduce the environmental impact of transportation in the product life cycle include the use of more efficient transportation modes, such as rail and sea transport, and the adoption of alternative fuels and low-carbon technologies. Supply chain optimization and more sustainable packaging design can also help to reduce the environmental impact of transportation by reducing the amount of space and energy required for transport.

Step 4: User Experience Phase

The user experience phase in the product life cycle refers to the stage where a product is used or consumed by the end-user or customer. This phase is critical because it determines whether the product meets the customer's needs, expectations, and satisfaction. The user experience phase includes product use, maintenance, repair, and end-of-life disposal. Efforts to promote a sustainable user experience include the design of products that are durable, repairable, and recyclable at the end of their life cycle. Companies may also provide repair and maintenance services to extend the product's lifespan and reduce the need for replacement. By promoting a positive and sustainable user experience, companies can enhance the product's value, reduce waste, and promote a more responsible approach to product design and consumption.

Step 5: Post-use and End-of-Life Cycle Phase

The end-of-cycle phase typically includes disposal, such as landfilling or incineration, and recycling or reusing the product's materials and components. The choice of the end-of-cycle phase depends on the product's material composition, the availability of recycling and disposal options, and the environmental and social impacts of each option. Efforts to promote sustainable end-of-cycle practices include designing products that are recyclable or biodegradable, minimizing the use of hazardous materials, and encouraging the recovery and reuse of materials and components. Companies may also participate in take-back programs or extended producer responsibility initiatives to ensure the proper disposal and recycling of their products (Fig. **1**).

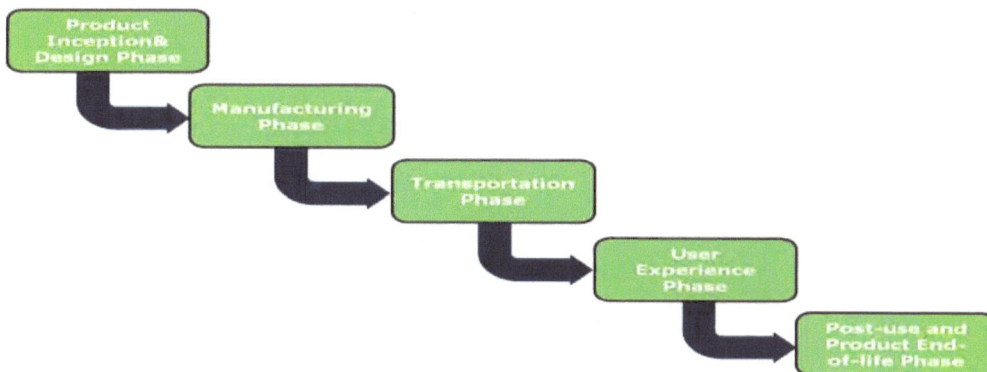

Fig. (1). Total life cycle towards product development.

RECENT REVIEWS ON PRODUCT SUSTAINABILITY

Sheng, X., and Chen, L. (2023) review highlights that sustainability evaluations promote environmentally and socially responsible product design and development. The author initially addresses horizontal and Vertical-axis wind turbine generators and their technological and economic pros and cons. Life cycle evaluation to evaluate the environmental implications of each wind turbine generator type is discussed in this paper. Each generator type and its environmental implications are assessed during production, transit, operation, and disposal. Horizontal-axis wind turbines had a lower environmental impact than vertical-axis turbines in all impact categories. The paper emphasizes the necessity for considering the local context and conditions when choosing a wind turbine generator type, as this can affect the product's environmental and social sustainability. Sustainability evaluations promote environmentally and socially responsible product design and development. Life cycle assessment may evaluate product sustainability and inform product design and development decisions, as shown in the wind turbine generator case study.

According to Omodara, L (2023), circular economy and its potential to lessen the environmental implications of linear production and consumption models cover the problems of product packaging, manufacture, and end-of-life disposal into the LCA framework, including the necessity for standardized metrics and the difficulty of considering circular economy concepts throughout a product's life cycle. The author shows that circular economy indicators can considerably impact the sustainability assessment of the two items. Reusable packaging reduces the environmental impact of product creation and disposal, according to the data.

Gallo (2023) first examines the sustainability evaluation problems in bio-based products, such as the lack of standardized methods and indicators, the complexity of life cycle assessment, and stakeholder's involvement. The integrated assessment method evaluates bio-based products' environmental, economic, and social implications throughout their life cycles. The multi-criteria analysis tool evaluates sustainability using quantitative and qualitative indicators. The author discussed the outcomes of the case study of an integrated evaluation tool's bio-based product. The results show the tool's capacity to identify the product's sustainability, strengths, and flaws and offer improvements. The study emphasizes the necessity of a comprehensive approach to assessing a bio-based product's sustainability and the possibilities of an integrated evaluation tool. The tool can help governments, companies, and other stakeholders design and create bio-based products more sustainably and responsibly.

The paper "Holistic approach in the evaluation of the sustainability of bio-based products: An Integrated Assessment Tool" reviews various tools and methodologies that can be used for sustainable product design and development, including life cycle assessment, eco-design, design for sustainability, and sustainable manufacturing. It also discusses the application of these tools in various industries, including electronics, automotive, and construction. The author also highlights the importance of stakeholder engagement in sustainable product design and development and discusses the role of consumers, regulators, and other stakeholders in driving sustainable product design and development practices. Finally, the author outlines several research prospects related to sustainable product design and development, including the development of sustainable materials, the integration of renewable energy sources in manufacturing processes, and the use of artificial intelligence and machine learning to optimize sustainable product design and development.

Ahmad (2018) emphasizes the importance of considering environmental, economic, and social factors across the entire life cycle of a product to promote sustainable and responsible product design and development. The proposed framework can provide valuable insights to the policymakers, companies, and other stakeholders to promoting sustainable and responsible product design and development. The framework includes sustainability measures, a life cycle assessment technique, and a sustainability index. The triple bottom line approach's sustainability measurements cover environmental, economic, and social sustainability throughout a product's life cycle. The sustainability index uses sustainability metrics and the life cycle assessment results to quantify a product's overall sustainability.

Happuwatte (2022) claims life cycle thinking improves sustainable production. Life cycle thinking considers a product's environmental impact from raw materials through disposal. According to the author, life cycle thinking can reduce a product's environmental impact and promote sustainable design and development. This paper presents a case study of institutional theory and life cycle thinking in sustainable automobile production. The case study creates an eco-design tool utilizing life cycle thinking and institutional pressures to promote sustainable design and development. Eco-design assesses product sustainability over its life cycle utilizing environmental, economic, and social aspects. The paper claims that sustainable manufacturing involves institutional theory and life cycle thinking. The framework can help policymakers, industry, and stakeholders to promote sustainable manufacturing and a sustainable future.

METRICS CLUSTERS AND PRODUCT METRICS

The term "metrics cluster" refers to a group of metrics that are used together to measure and assess the sustainability of a product or system. Metrics clusters typically consist of a set of environmental, social, and economic indicators that are used to evaluate the sustainability of a product or system across its entire life cycle. Environmental metrics in a metrics cluster might include indicators such as greenhouse gas emissions, water consumption, and waste generation. Social metrics might include indicators such as labor standards, human rights, and community engagement. Economic metrics might include indicators such as cost-effectiveness, resource efficiency, and profitability. Metrics clusters are useful in promoting sustainable development because they provide a comprehensive and integrated approach to measuring and assessing sustainability. By using a set of metrics that are designed to measure different aspects of sustainability, metrics clusters can provide a more complete picture of the sustainability of a product or system. This, in turn, can help policymakers, companies, and other stakeholders make more informed decisions about product design, development, and management, and can help promote sustainable practices and behaviors.

The structure of the metrics is displayed in Fig. (**2**). The product's inception and design phase, the manufacturing phase, the transportation phase, the user experience phase, and the post-use and end-of-life cycle phases are each represented by one of the five circles in this illustration of the product's life cycle. The following are some examples of metrics (environmental, sociological, and economic), as well as the interaction among these measures. A metric cluster has been formed by these five circles.

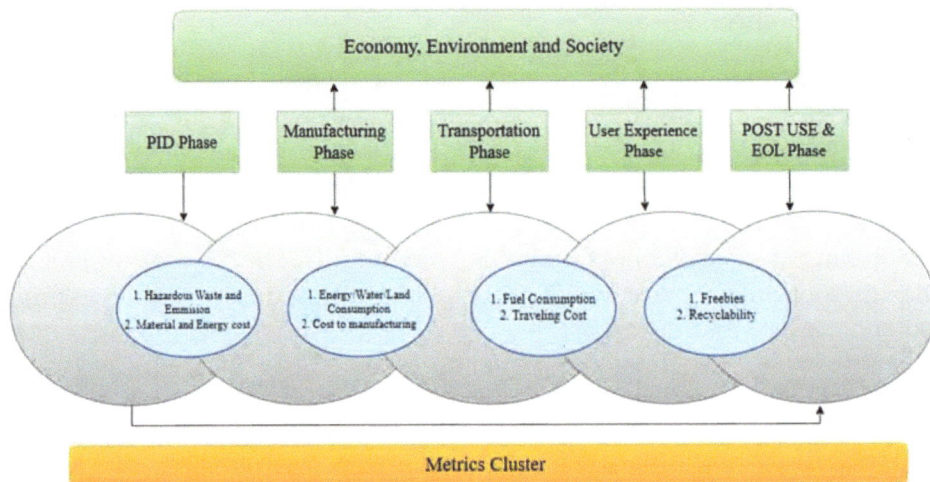

Fig. (2). Examples of metrics across total life-cycle phases.

The total number of metric clusters is 13, and the metric cluster known as the 'post-use and end-of-life phase' is the one that is most frequently seen among the triple bottom line. Several different measures have been uncovered and characterized within their respective clusters. The following are some instances of metrics and the clusters that they belong to, displayed in Table **1**. In order to acquire an all-encompassing knowledge of the influence of each given metric, metrics are organized in accordance with the numerous stages that make up a product's life cycle.

Table 1. Metric Cluster.

TRIPLE BOTTOM LINE			
METRICS CLUSTER	Waste materials	Funding	Education
	Renewable Energy	Development	Customer Satisfaction
	Post use and End-of-Life.	Post use and End-of-Life.	Post use and End-of-Life.
	Management	Management	Management
	Utilization of Recourses.	Quality	Safety and Societal Well-being.
	Utilization of Water Recourse.	-	-

CHALLENGES IN SUSTAINABLE PRODUCT TO CREATE PRODUCT METRICS

There are several challenges associated with product sustainability and product metrics, some of which are as follows:

1. Data availability and quality: Obtaining accurate and reliable data throughout the product life cycle can be a challenge, particularly for products that have complex supply chains or are manufactured in different regions of the world. Data gaps and inconsistencies can affect the accuracy of sustainability assessments and metrics.

2. Lack of standardized methodologies: There is a lack of standardized methodologies for assessing sustainability across different products, industries, and regions. This can lead to inconsistencies in the measurement and comparison of sustainability metrics.

3. Limited stakeholder engagement: Engaging stakeholders throughout the product life cycle, including suppliers, consumers, and regulators, is critical to promoting sustainable practices. However, stakeholders may not always be engaged or may have differing priorities and perspectives on sustainability.

4. Complexity of sustainability: Sustainability is a complex concept that encompasses environmental, social, and economic considerations. Balancing these different factors can be challenging, particularly when they may conflict with each other.

5. Limited regulatory frameworks: There are limited regulatory frameworks for promoting product sustainability, particularly at the global level. This can make it difficult for companies to prioritize sustainability and invest in sustainable practices.

6. Costs and benefits: The costs and benefits associated with sustainable product development and implementation can be difficult to quantify, particularly over the long term. This can make it challenging for companies to make informed decisions about sustainability investments and prioritize sustainability initiatives.

CONCLUSION

This paper proposes sustainable manufacturing metrics for product life cycle methodology including a triple bottom line that is environmental, economic, and society. Life cycle evaluation covers product inception and design, manufacturing, transportation, user experience, and post-use and end-of-life cycles. In this study, we investigate issues pertaining to product metrics, life cycle, and sustainability. These give rise to the possibility of classifying indicators in accordance with the stages at which they appear in the life cycle. The general metrics were grouped together, which made it possible to develop a framework for metric leveling.

REFERENCES

[1]   J. Ding, Y. Li, J. Liu, G. Qi, Q. Liu, and L. Dong, "Life cycle assessment of environmental impacts of cold and hot break tomato paste packaged in steel drums and exported from Xinjiang, China", *Environ. Impact Assess. Rev.,* vol. 98, p. 106939, 2023.
[http://dx.doi.org/10.1016/j.eiar.2022.106939]

[2]   X. Zhou, Y. Zhai, K. Ren, Z. Cheng, X. Shen, T. Zhang, Y. Bai, Y. Jia, and J. Hong, "Life cycle assessment of polycarbonate production: Proposed optimization toward sustainability", *Resour. Conserv. Recycling,* vol. 189, p. 106765, 2023.
[http://dx.doi.org/10.1016/j.resconrec.2022.106765]

[3]   M. Rusch, J.P. Schöggl, and R.J. Baumgartner, "Application of digital technologies for sustainable product management in a circular economy: A review", *Bus. Strategy Environ.,* vol. 32, no. 3, pp. 1159-1174, 2023.
[http://dx.doi.org/10.1002/bse.3099]

[4]   X. Sheng, L. Chen, X. Yuan, Y. Tang, Q. Yuan, R. Chen, Q. Wang, Q. Ma, J. Zuo, and H. Liu, "Green supply chain management for a more sustainable manufacturing industry in China: a critical review", *Environ. Dev. Sustain.,* vol. 25, no. 2, pp. 1151-1183, 2023.
[http://dx.doi.org/10.1007/s10668-022-02109-9]

[5]   L. Omodara, P. Saavalainen, S. Pitkäaho, E. Pongrácz, and R.L. Keiski, "Sustainability assessment of products - Case study of wind turbine generator types", *Environ. Impact Assess. Rev.,* vol. 98, p. 106943, 2023.
[http://dx.doi.org/10.1016/j.eiar.2022.106943]

[6]   F. Gallo, A. Manzardo, D. Camana, A. Fedele, and A. Scipioni, "Integration of a circular economy metric with life cycle assessment: methodological proposal of compared agri-food products", *Int. J. Life Cycle Assess.,* 2023.
[http://dx.doi.org/10.1007/s11367-022-02130-0]

[7]   L. Ladu, and P. Morone, "Holistic approach in the evaluation of the sustainability of bio-based products: An Integrated Assessment Tool. Sustainable Production and Consumption", *Sustainable Production and Consumption,* vol. 28, 2021pp. 911-924e6.
[http://dx.doi.org/10.1016/j.spc.2021.07.006]

[8]   S. Ahmad, K.Y. Wong, M.L. Tseng, and W.P. Wong, "Sustainable product design and development: A review of tools, applications and research prospects", *Resour. Conserv. Recycling,* vol. 132, pp. 49-61, 2018.
[http://dx.doi.org/10.1016/j.resconrec.2018.01.020]

[9]   B.M. Hapuwatte, K.D. Seevers, and I.S. Jawahir, "Metrics-based dynamic product sustainability performance evaluation for advancing the circular economy", *J. Manuf. Syst.,* vol. 64, pp. 275-287, 2022.
[http://dx.doi.org/10.1016/j.jmsy.2022.06.013]

[10]   S. Mohammad Ebrahimi, and L. Koh, "Manufacturing sustainability: Institutional theory and life cycle thinking", *J. Clean. Prod.,* vol. 298, p. 126787, 2021.
[http://dx.doi.org/10.1016/j.jclepro.2021.126787]

[11]   C.E. Cortés-Estrada, C. Ramírez-Márquez, J.M. Ponce-Ortega, J.G. Segovia-Hernández, and M. Martín, "Optimization and sensitivity analysis of a multi-product solar grade silicon refinery: Considering environmental and economic metrics", *Chem. Eng. Process.,* vol. 183, p. 109237, 2023.
[http://dx.doi.org/10.1016/j.cep.2022.109237]

[12]   Y. Chen, L. Kotamarthy, A. Dan, C. Sampat, P. Bhalode, R. Singh, B.J. Glasser, R. Ramachandran, and M. Ierapetritou, "Optimization of key energy and performance metrics for drug product manufacturing", *Int. J. Pharm.,* vol. 631, p. 122487, 2023.
[http://dx.doi.org/10.1016/j.ijpharm.2022.122487] [PMID: 36521636]

[13]   M. Breth-Petersen, K. Bell, K. Pickles, F. McGain, S. McAlister, and A. Barratt, "Health, financial and environmental impacts of unnecessary vitamin D testing: a triple bottom line assessment adapted for healthcare", *BMJ Open,* vol. 12, no. 8, p. e056997, 2022.
[http://dx.doi.org/10.1136/bmjopen-2021-056997] [PMID: 35998953]

[14]   A. Liute, and M.R. De Giacomo, "The environmental performance of UK☐based B Corp companies: An analysis based on the triple bottom line approach", *Bus. Strategy Environ.,* vol. 31, no. 3, pp. 810-827, 2022.
[http://dx.doi.org/10.1002/bse.2919]

[15]   L. Jum'a, D. Zimon, M. Ikram, and P. Madzík, "Towards a sustainability paradigm; the nexus between lean green practices, sustainability-oriented innovation and Triple Bottom Line", *Int. J. Prod. Econ.,* vol. 245, p. 108393, 2022.
[http://dx.doi.org/10.1016/j.ijpe.2021.108393]

CHAPTER 14

Detailed Overview of the Internet of Things and Its Amalgamation with Artificial Intelligence

Shiva Tyagi[1,*] and **Riti Rathore**[1]

[1] *Department of Computer Science and Engineering, Ajay Kumar Garg Engineering College, Ghaziabad-201009, India*

Abstract: Recommender systems can guide users towards engaging content from a diverse array of options. They serve fundamental functions in information retrieval and e-commerce by providing suggestions that narrow down extensive information spaces and guide consumers toward the goods that most effectively meet their needs and preferences. Recommender systems are computer programs that assist us in narrowing down our choices and providing optimal recommendations depending on our preferences. The recommendation algorithm autonomously filters options based on the user's preferences, making it effortless for users to locate appropriate rental properties. This research uses the cosine similarity measure to analyze its effectiveness and potential enhancements for our rental property dataset.

Keywords: Amalgamation, Algorithm, Domain, Integration, Recommender systems.

INTRODUCTION

In the contemporary period, the internet has become an integral aspect of every individual's existence. It has emerged as one of the most influential instruments worldwide. Due to significant technological advancements, the Internet now serves various purposes, one of which is the Internet of Things [1]. It facilitates the operation of different gadgets, allowing them to carry out tasks and minimize human exertion. The Internet of Things (Iota) encompasses various characteristics, including artificial intelligence, connectivity, and compact gadgets [2].

Iota employs technologies like edge computing, cloud computing, and machine learning, which utilize algorithms to enable real-time decision-making in smart

---

* **Corresponding author Shiva Tyagi:** Department of Computer Science and Engineering, Ajay Kumar Garg Engineering College, Ghaziabad-201009, India; E-mail: tyagishiva1@gmail.com

Pankaj Kumar Mishra & Satya Prakash Yadav (Eds.)

devices [3, 4]. The Internet of Things (Iota) enhances individuals' lives and productivity by enabling them to operate more intelligently and efficiently with minimal exertion. It offers insight into the operational mechanics of the business field [5]. The Internet of Things (Iota) offers advantages in various sectors. In agriculture, it utilizes analytical tools to monitor, survey, and map fields. In smart cities, Iota devices connected to sensors collect data about the city [6]. In the health sector, sensors are used to track equipment like oxygen pumps and other medical appliances. In the Industrial Internet of Things (Eliot), intelligent sensors are deployed throughout the manufacturing process to detect product production [7]. In smart homes, Iota technology is employed for various purposes. The Internet of Things (Iota) is highly beneficial for the automation of households, particularly in the context of contemporary society where nuclear families are prevalent. The adoption of home automation has experienced significant growth, facilitated by the utilization of Internet of Things (Iota) sensors [8]. This technology enables the implementation of many automated features such as digital door locks, automatic fans, LED lighting, smart switches, televisions, gardens, and kitchens (Fig. **1**).

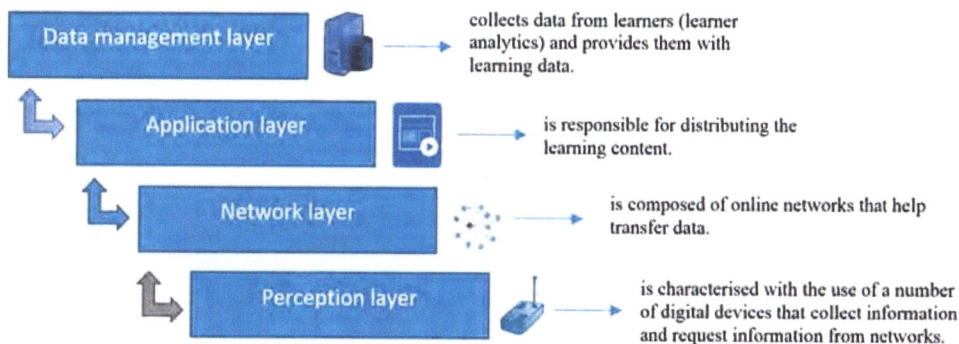

Fig. (1). IoT layers.

Sensors

It is a device utilized for the conversion of physical signals into electrical signals. Sensors are extensively utilized in Iota devices, as they are embedded within the devices to enable their functionality. There are a variety of sensors available, including temperature, light, and industrial sensors [9]. Sensors are utilized in smart homes for several purposes, like:

• Light sensors are capable of automatically deactivating the lights in the event that they are left on inadvertently. Alternatively, they can be operated manually through the use of remote controls. Additionally, it is advantageous as it conserves a significant amount of energy.

- Windows and doors - Sensors create a warning if a door or window is left open, providing valuable assistance.
- Video doorbells provide a means of detecting and visually identifying those who approach our doors, safeguarding us against potential fraudulent activities. By utilizing these sensors, we can refrain from granting access to unfamiliar individuals.

IoT for Smart Homes

A smart home is a living environment equipped with technology that enables remote control of household devices, such as appliances, through the internet. Home automation exemplifies the Internet of Things (Iota) exceptionally well [10]. In a smart house, all electronic devices can be remotely controlled *via* the internet. It allows the user to control electronic gadgets that are equipped with sensors remotely [11]. For instance, by utilizing Apple's Home Kit, consumers may effectively control and manage their household equipment through an application. However, their operation must fulfill a universal security need. There are an excessive number of issues observed in the Smart Home system. The intruder can easily compromise the security of digital locks and other related systems. Another potential issue is connectivity [12 - 14]. The sensors exhibit intermittent responsiveness. Fig. (2) shows the smart home technologies.

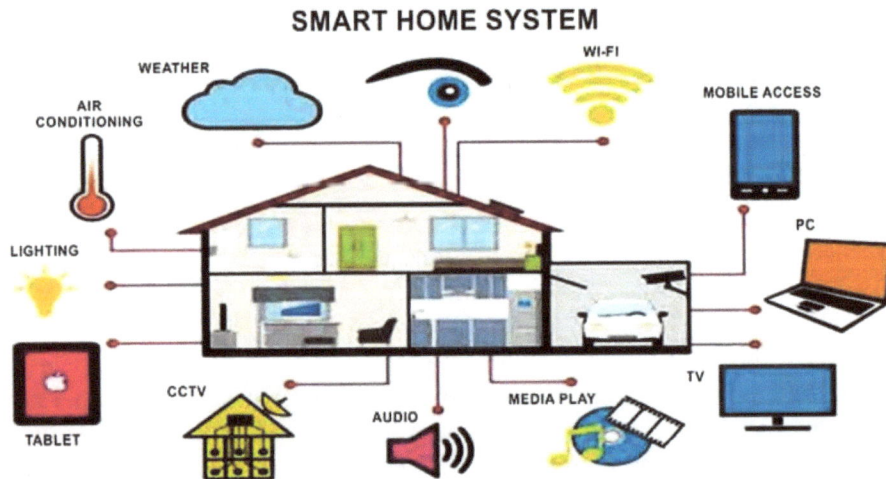

Fig. (2). Smart Home Technologies.

Benefits of IoT in Home Automation

Iota enhances home processing by gathering and analysing data to provide valuable insights and control over various aspects. Controlling the operations of our homes from outside has become significantly more convenient. It is achievable through the utilization of Internet of Things (Iota) sensors [15]. Convenience: The primary motivation for individuals to transition to Iota is the enhanced convenience it provides.

Disadvantages of IoT in Smart Home Technology

Expense: Internet of Things (Iota) devices typically have a high cost. One of the primary considerations when buying smart gadgets for your house is whether professional installation is necessary, depending on the specific products you are interested in [16].

RELATED WORKS

The Internet of Factors (IoT) is a tremendous generation that has revolutionized the way humans engage with machines and gadgets. It connects physical gadgets to the net, enabling them to share information with customers. With the help of IoT, gadgets may be operated remotely and monitored for facts and data. These statistics can be used to optimize tactics, enhance performance, and provide insights to customers [17]. In recent years, the IoT has emerged as increasingly intertwined with artificial Intelligence (AI). AI-enabled gadgets have become a bit common in houses and workplaces. AI-connected gadgets are getting better as they are fed greater facts, allowing them to analyze from their beyond studies and understand patterns. It allows them to interpret information highly and make better selections that can be used to enhance the performance of IoT. AI can assist the IoT in accommodating new technology, developing new and optimizing present methods [18]. AI can help the IoT to be extra resilient to cyberattacks. AI can be used to locate and save unauthorized intrusions into connected devices. AI can also be used to learn personal conduct and put it to use for personalizing experiences. AI, and the IoT are being utilized in numerous approaches, including the healthcare industry. AI-enabled devices can discover fitness traits and notify medical professionals and caregivers. It can help save you from viable emergencies and provide more green remedies. AI and the IoT are also being used in the production industry to improve automation and performance. AI-connected structures can display manufacturing methods in real-time, which could optimize them and improve ordinary overall performance. The IoT is being used in retail for personalized hints and focused advertising and marketing. AI-enabled structures can examine patron possibilities and habits, allowing retailers to create tailored buying studies. They can also use the facts to chain operations and create extra efficient tactics. In the end, Artificial Intelligence and the Internet of Factors can extensively grow efficiency and productivity [19]. They're becoming increasingly intertwined and feature a plethora of applications. AI can provide the

IoT with the capability to come across records and learn from them. It may assist in optimizing processes, enhance performance, and provide insights to customers. AI and the IoT are the present and the future of the sector. The Internet of Factors (IoT) is all about connecting actual global gadgets *via* the net. This connection permits the one item to speak with every different, exchange data, and allow customers to get entry to and have an interaction with them at any time and from anywhere. The concept of the "Internet of Things" refers to the capacity for normal items to be related to the Internet on the way to generate, save, and exchange records. It now only opens up a variety of new approaches to controlling items [20]. Still, it also enables effective analytics and insights that can be used to improve any activity or enterprise. The amalgamation of IoT and synthetic Intelligence (AI) can bring about a revolution within the manner corporations operate. AI can provide smarter automation, singularity, and cognitive analytics, which can enhance substantial volumes of useful statistics that might be accrued through the IoT. However, the combination of IoT and AI is not without its issues.

LITERATURE REVIEW

The topic of Iota (Internet of Things) is has garnered considerable attention in both industry and academia [5]. Presented below is a comprehensive literature analysis encompassing significant studies conducted on the subject of the Internet of Things (Iota).

- In their 2013 publication, Gobi *et al.* put up an all-encompassing framework for the Internet of Things (Iota), comprising layers dedicated to hardware, software, networks, and services. The writers analyse the difficulties and possibilities in the Internet of Things (Iota) and propose that Iota possesses the capability to revolutionize diverse industries.
- Al-Fuqua *et al.* (2015) surveyed the utilization, structures, and communication methods of Internet of Things (Iota) applications. The authors delineate the primary realms of Iota applications, encompassing smart homes, smart cities, and industrial Iota. In addition, they analyse the diverse Iota designs and protocols employed in different Iota applications.
- Atmore *et al.* (2010) introduced a classification system for Internet of Things (Iota) applications and examined the difficulties and possibilities associated with Iota. The authors categorize Iota applications into six distinct domains: healthcare, environmental monitoring, assisted living, transportation, smart homes, and industrial Iota.
- Canella *et al.* (2014) examined the structure of the Internet of Things (Iota) and its constituent parts, which encompass sensors, networks, cloud computing, and

data analytics. The authors emphasize the significance of data analytics in the Internet of Things (Iota) and analyse the obstacles and prospects in this domain.

- In 2017, Haddadpajouh *et al.* did a comprehensive analysis of the security and privacy concerns related to the Internet of Things (Iota). The authors analyse the primary security and privacy risks associated with Iota and suggest measures to alleviate these risks. In addition, they address the significance of establishing standards and norms for ensuring the security and privacy of Iota.
- Am *et al.* (2014) introduced an Internet of Things (Iota) smart home automation system that utilizes a fusion of wireless sensor networks and cloud computing. The authors analyse the structure, execution, and assessment of their system, encompassing diverse smart home applications such as security, energy management, and healthcare.

Collectively, these studies emphasize the significance of the Internet of Things (Iota) across multiple industries and delve into the obstacles and possibilities within this domain. The studies also offer valuable insights into various Iota designs, protocols, and applications. Furthermore, they emphasize the significance of security and privacy in Iota and suggest measures to alleviate the risks.

CHALLENGES

Limitations of Iota devices remain a major obstacle to implementing a deep learning model, hindering efficiency. Efficient memory use and time optimization are critical challenges when implementing deep learning in practical Iota systems. Although it is possible to develop complicated learning models autonomously, effectively expressing them remains a challenge. The power of a profound learning model lies in the utilization of a substantial number of nonlinear and layered neurons in its architecture. Deep learning models make decisions by analysing raw data that the neurons within them have processed. The constant problem in applications with constrained resources is the need to decrease the storage and processing requirements for executing deep learning models. The advancement of deep learning technology has led to the emergence of several innovative designs that surpass the current state-of-the-art performance. However, a significant portion of devices were not expressly designed for the Internet of Things (Iota) framework. Undoubtedly, the results of ongoing research will be enhanced by effectively adapting these algorithms to an Internet of Things (Iota) situation.

Adaptive: Deep learning must possess the ability to adjust in sync with the continuous evolution of devices and applications inside the Iota ecosystem. Zero-day attacks are unavoidable in an actual network [6]. Subsequently, supplementary functionalities are incorporated into the Internet of Things (Iota) system. Moreover, the allocation of network traffic or signal frequency is likely to vary as more devices connect to the network. Another variable that changes throughout time is the final interest of users. As a result of these improvements, deep learning applications in the Internet of Things (Iota) now face additional obstacles.

Diverse Data: Internet of Things (Iota) devices produce a significant volume of data with different characteristics, including signal recurrence and organization traffic data. Although this data originates from the same device, it will have unique formats [7]. Indeed, even comparable categories of data, such as the quantity of packages and bytes, may exhibit variations in magnitude. Although they exhibit unexpected scaling, they are strongly connected with network utility. Discovering a technique to handle these varied information collections effectively is an ongoing challenge. If there are other factors to examine, the algorithm is unable to determine the appropriate response to an IoAT event.

Consequently, there is no requirement to program any Internet of Things (IoT) applications due to the existence of artificial intelligence (AI) and machine learning software. The IoAT program employs simulations of human emotions to gather extensive information for AI inference. It is imperative to prioritize and thoroughly investigate the future implications of the convergence of Iota and AI. Fig. (**3**) shows the challenges.

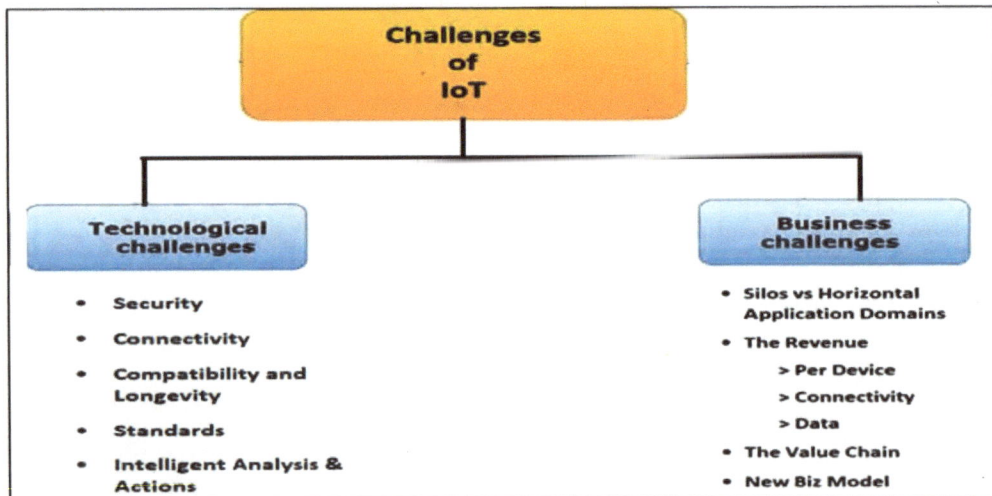

Fig. (3). Challenges.

EXPERIMENT

Combining IOT and AI

The Iota and Ioat technology have the potential to revolutionize daily life, ranging from basic applications like fitness monitoring to a wide array of possibilities [9]. The potential for businesses and urban planning may bring us closer to a more intelligent future than we currently anticipate. In order to increase production, certain logistical challenges need to be addressed and managed. In the future, algorithms and artificial intelligence (AI) will be employed in the Internet of Things (Iota) operations to automate, optimize, and provide valuable insights to improve decision-making (Fig. **4**). Ioat (Internet of Autonomous Things) receives and interprets signals from real-world events and generates the corresponding response that is essential for every Ioat application that uses software to generate a response to a triggering event, as it plays a critical role in the process. AI is direct and uncomplicated. Fig. (**5**) depicts the integration of the Internet of Things (Iota) and Artificial Intelligence (AI). Fig. (**5**) shows the IoT and AI.

Table 1. Growth in IoT in various places.

Places	No of Users	POI	Categories	Density
Beijing	795	1329	106	0.194
Shanghai	1290	2975	2976	0.176
New York	741	1802	234	0.174
Tokyo	1690	2559	210	0.142

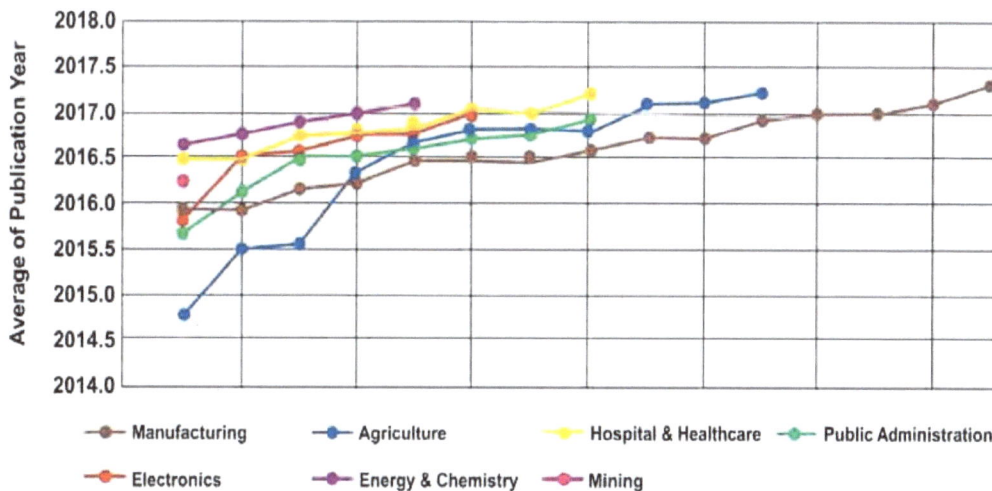

Fig. (4). Growth in IoT.

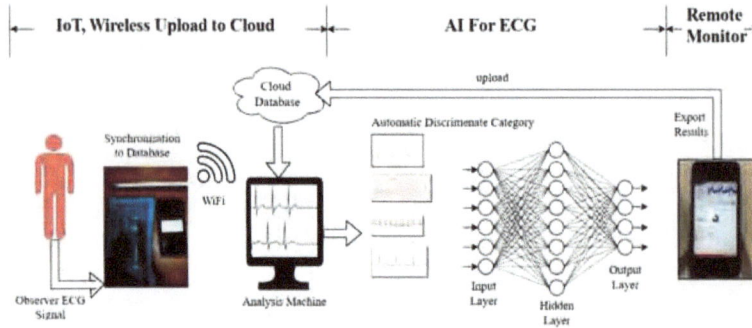

Fig. (5). IoT and AI.

Technology Used in Smart Homes

Ensuring security is the primary focus of our existence. Smart houses utilize a range of technologies, including digital doors and windows. Several methods, including PIR-based security and laser security, are utilized.

PIR Sensor

The PIR sensor is utilized for detecting the presence of humans. These sensors are commonly employed in digitally secured doors. When an individual approaches the door, the sensor detects their presence. It promptly sends a message or initiates a call to the registered mobile number of the owner using GSM technology. Fig. (**6**) shows the circuit diagram.

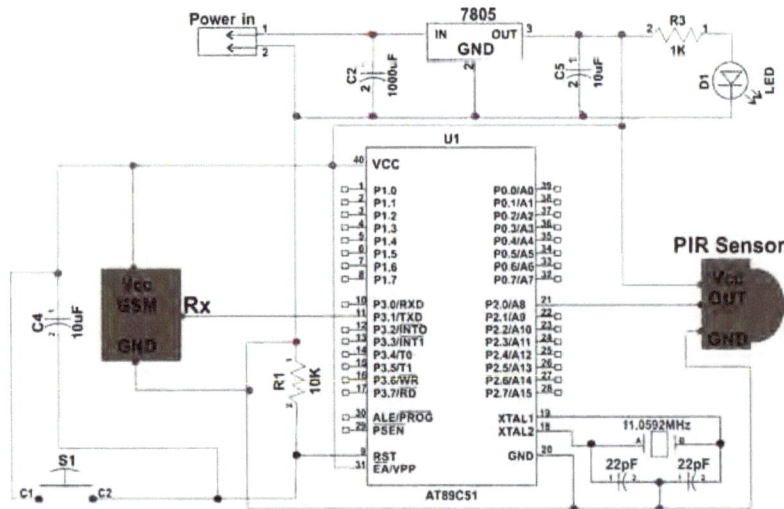

Fig. (6). Circuit diagram.

```
#include<reg51.h>

Sit PIR=P2^0;

Void delay (int n)

{

int a, j;

for (a=0; a<n; a++)

For (j=0; j<1275; j++);

}

Void begins ()

{

TMOD=0x20;

SCON=0x50;

TH1=0xfd;

TR1=1;

}

Void writes (char at)

{

SBUF=at;

While (! TI);

TI=0;

}

Void printing (char *p)

{

while(*p)
```

```
{

write(*p);

p++;

}

write(0x0d);

}

Void main ()

{

//P2=0x00;

Begin ();

Printing ("ATE0");

Delay (50);

While (1)

{

If (PIR)

{

Printing ("ATD+919821757249 ;");

Delay (1000);

// lcdcmd (192);

// lcdprint ("Message Sending.");

Printing ("AT+CMGF=1");

Delay (50);

Printing ("AT+CMGS=\"+919821757249\"");

Delay (50);
```

Printing ("Someone is Enter in your Place.");

Delay (50);

Write (26);

}

}

}

CONCLUSION

The interaction between various network nodes in the Internet of Things provides us with ideas [10]. Within the same vicinity, it becomes more apparent how various categories of nodes are interconnected. In this study, we introduce the RFUPT recommendation framework to address the disparity between the user selection method and the conventional two-step recommendation strategy in POI recommendation. UPPM aims to map user preferences onto potential targets, whereas PFPM maps points of interest onto possible targets. SCM calculates ranking scores for all user-POI combinations based on the potential targets of the users and provides a list of suggestions. Our RFUPT implementation is designed to be direct and uncomplicated, utilizing linear layers and embedding vectors as its fundamental components. It is user-friendly but efficient. We generate training samples for the model parameters by employing a time-aware sampling strategy that considers user behaviour in situations, including point of interest (POI) recommendations. The results indicate that RFUPT outperforms the most sophisticated algorithms in recommending Points of Interest (POIs).

FUTURE SCOPE OF IOT

The future potential of Iota (Internet of Things), AI (Artificial Intelligence), and smart homes is immense and filled with excitement. Below are a few prospective advancements and patterns that may manifest in the future:

- The growing awareness of the advantages of smart homes will likely lead to a rise in the rate of adoption. Smart homes provide users with ease, enhanced energy efficiency, and heightened security.
- Voice assistants, such as Amazon Alexi and Google Assistant, are already incorporated into numerous smart home products. We anticipate a greater level of integration in the future, facilitating customers to manage their intelligent residences solely by spoken commands effortlessly.

- Personalization: AI algorithms will possess the capability to acquire user preferences and customize their smart home experience according to their requirements. As an illustration, the lights might autonomously adapt to the user's desired level of luminosity, while the thermostat could regulate itself to the user's preferred temperature.
- Smart cities encompass the utilization of Internet of Things (Iota) devices and artificial intelligence (AI) to enhance the efficiency and liability of urban areas. Examples of such advancements encompass traffic management systems, intelligent lighting solutions, and enhanced waste management techniques.
- Enhanced security: With the growing number of internet-connected devices, the significance of security will escalate. Artificial intelligence algorithms will possess the capability to identify and avert cyber assaults, thereby guaranteeing the safety and protection of smart homes.

Collectively, the prospects for the future of the Internet of Things (Iota), Artificial Intelligence (AI), and smart homes are brimming with immense possibilities. We anticipate a persistent progression of innovation in this domain as novel technology and applications arise gradually.

REFERENCES

[1]   V. Bibhu, L. Das, A. Rana, S. Sharma, and S. Salagrama, "AI Model for Blockchain Based Industrial Application in Healthcare IoT", In: *AI Models for Blockchain-Based Intelligent Networks in IoT Systems: Concepts, Methodologies, Tools, and Applications.* Springer International Publishing: Cham, 2023, pp. 163-184.
[http://dx.doi.org/10.1007/978-3-031-31952-5_8]

[2]   K.K. Ezhilarasi, and M.J. Rex, "Reliable and energy-saving forwarding technique for wireless sensor networks using multipath routing", *SSRG International Journal of Computer Science and Engineering,* vol. 1, no. 9, pp. 11-15, 2014.

[3]   V.A.K. Gorantla, S.K. Sriramulugari, A.H. Mewada, and J. Logeshwaran, "An intelligent optimization framework to predict the vulnerable range of tumor cells using Internet of things", *2023 IEEE 2nd International Conference on Industrial Electronics: Developments & Applications (ICIDeA),,* pp. 359-365, 2023.Imphal, India,
[http://dx.doi.org/10.1109/ICIDeA59866.2023.10295269]

[4]   G. Ramesh, J. Logeshwaran, T. Kiruthiga, and J. Lloret, "Prediction of Energy Production Level in Large PV Plants through AUTO-Encoder Based Neural-Network (AUTO-NN) with Restricted Boltzmann Feature Extraction", *Future Internet,* vol. 15, no. 2, p. 46, 2023.
[http://dx.doi.org/10.3390/fi15020046]

[5]   J. Logeshwaran, N. Shanmugasundaram, and J. Lloret, "L-RUBI: An efficient load-based resource utilization algorithm for bi-partite scatternet in wireless personal area networks", *Int. J. Commun. Syst.,* vol. 36, no. 6, p. e5439, 2023.
[http://dx.doi.org/10.1002/dac.5439]

[6]   J. Kaur, J. Saxena, and J. Shah, "Fahad and S. P. Yadav, "Facial Emotion Recognition", *2022 International Conference on Computational Intelligence and Sustainable Engineering Solutions (CISES),* pp. 528-533, 2022.
[http://dx.doi.org/10.1109/CISES54857.2022.9844366]

[7]   H. Yadav, S. Singh, K.K. Mishra, S. Srivastava, M.S. Naruka, and S.P. Yadav, "Brain Tumor

Detection with MRI Images", *2022 International Conference on Computational Intelligence and Sustainable Engineering Solutions (CISES)*, pp. 519-527, 2022.
[http://dx.doi.org/10.1109/CISES54857.2022.9844387]

[8]　S.P. Yadav, S. Zaidi, C.D.S. Nascimento, V.H.C. de Albuquerque, and S.S. Chauhan, "Analysis and Design of automatically generating for GPS Based Moving Object Tracking System", *2023 International Conference on Artificial Intelligence and Smart Communication (AISC)*, pp. 1-5, 2023.
[http://dx.doi.org/10.1109/AISC56616.2023.10085180]

[9]　R. Salama, F. Al-Turjman, D. Bordoloi, and S.P. Yadav, "Wireless Sensor Networks and Green Networking for 6G communication- An Overview", *2023 International Conference on Computational Intelligence, Communication Technology and Networking (CICTN)*, pp. 830-834, 2023.
[http://dx.doi.org/10.1109/CICTN57981.2023.10141262]

[10]　C. Tomazzoli, S. Scannapieco, and M. Cristani, "Internet of Things and artificial intelligence enable energy efficiency", *J. Ambient Intell. Humaniz. Comput.*, vol. 14, no. 5, pp. 4933-4954, 2023.
[http://dx.doi.org/10.1007/s12652-020-02151-3]

[11]　A.K. Abed, and A. Anupam, "Review of security issues in Internet of Things and artificial intelligence-driven solutions", *Secur. Priv.*, vol. 6, no. 3, p. e285, 2023.
[http://dx.doi.org/10.1002/spy2.285]

[12]　S.D. Shelare, P.N. Belkhode, K.C. Nikam, L.D. Jathar, K. Shahapurkar, M.E.M. Soudagar, I. Veza, T.M.Y. Khan, M.A. Kalam, A-S. Nizami, and M. Rehan, "Biofuels for a sustainable future: Examining the role of nano-additives, economics, policy, internet of things, artificial intelligence and machine learning technology in biodiesel production", *Energy*, vol. 282, p. 128874, 2023.
[http://dx.doi.org/10.1016/j.energy.2023.128874]

[13]　S.E. Bibri, and S.K. Jagatheesaperumal, "Harnessing the potential of the metaverse and artificial intelligence for the internet of city things: cost-effective XReality and synergistic AIoT technologies", *Smart Cities*, vol. 6, no. 5, pp. 2397-2429, 2023.
[http://dx.doi.org/10.3390/smartcities6050109]

[14]　H. Dadhaneeya, P.K. Nema, and V.K. Arora, "Internet of Things in food processing and its potential in Industry 4.0 era: A review", *Trends Food Sci. Technol.*, vol. 139, p. 104109, 2023.
[http://dx.doi.org/10.1016/j.tifs.2023.07.006]

[15]　N. Rane, "Integrating Building Information Modelling (BIM) and Artificial Intelligence (AI) for Smart Construction Schedule, Cost, Quality, and Safety Management: Challenges and Opportunities", *Cost, Quality, and Safety Management: Challenges and Opportunities.*, 20232023. Available from: https://ssrn.com/abstract=4616055
[http://dx.doi.org/10.2139/ssrn.4616055]

[16]　P. Bothra, R. Karmakar, S. Bhattacharya, and S. De, "How can applications of blockchain and artificial intelligence improve performance of Internet of Things? – A survey", *Comput. Netw.*, vol. 224, p. 109634, 2023.
[http://dx.doi.org/10.1016/j.comnet.2023.109634]

[17]　D. Thakur, J.K. Saini, and S. Srinivasan, "DeepThink IoT: The Strength of Deep Learning in Internet of Things", *Artif. Intell. Rev.*, vol. 56, no. 12, pp. 14663-14730, 2023.
[http://dx.doi.org/10.1007/s10462-023-10513-4]

[18]　K. Kasture, and P. Shende, "Amalgamation of Artificial Intelligence with Nanoscience for Biomedical Applications", *Arch. Comput. Methods Eng.*, vol. 30, no. 8, pp. 4667-4685, 2023.
[http://dx.doi.org/10.1007/s11831-023-09948-3]

[19]　S. Garse, K.S. Turabi, J. Aich, A. Ranjan, S. Nagar, S. Basu, and S. Devarajan, "Cancer Diagnosis Using Artificial Intelligence (AI) and Internet of Things (IoT)", *Revolutionizing Healthcare Through Artificial Intelligence and Internet of Things Applications* , pp. 50-71, 2023.

[20]   E. S. Bibri, J. Krogstie, A. Kaboli, and A. Alahi, *Smarter eco-cities and their leading-edge artificial intelligence of things solutions for environmental sustainability: A comprehensive systematic review.*, 2023.

CHAPTER 15

A Dual Transfer Learning Based Model for Mammogram Images Enhancement and Classification

Vandana Saini[1,*], **Meenu Khurana**[2] and **Rama Krishna Challa**[2]

[1] *Chitkara University Institute of Engineering and Technology Chitkara University, Himachal Pradesh, India*

[2] *Chitkara University Institute of Engineering and Technology, Chitkara University Punjab, India*

Abstract: Accurate and timely detection of breast cancer is very important to save a patient's life. Therefore, designing an accurate computer-aided diagnosis (CAD) for mammogram cancer detection is quite important for providing an interpretation to radiologists. In this paper, a CAD-based model has been proposed based on double transfer learning. The CAD system is trained to detect various abnormalities or cancers from the input mammogram images. In this study, the MIAS mammogram dataset is used to evaluate the proposed work. The original images in the dataset are also enhanced in this paper using a pre-trained VGG-16 network. The pre-processing of images has shown a better peak signal-to-noise (PSNR) value. The proposed network has shown a promising PSNR of more than 70 and classification accuracy of more than 99% with lesser system training complexity.

Keywords: Cancer, CAD, Mammogram, Transfer-learning, VGG-16.

INTRODUCTION

Breast cancer is one of the major diseases that affect around 5% of the women population in the world. Breast cancer is divided into three categories microcalcification, masses calcification, and normal. The calcium deposits around the breast region may cause breast cancer. So, the accurate and timely detection of the cancer from the beginning stage is very crucial as a patient's life is associated with the outcome. The radiologists sometimes may fail to diagnose the beginning stage, so they use a computer-based diagnosis that assists a radiologist before the final report. The rapid development in the field of machine learning and deep learning also helps revolutionize medical CAD systems. Breast cancer is one of

---

[*] **Corresponding author Vandana Saini:** Chitkara University Institute of Engineering and Technology Chitkara University, Himachal Pradesh, India; E-mail: vandana.s@chitkara.edu.in

Pankaj Kumar Mishra & Satya Prakash Yadav (Eds.)

the most common and progressive diseases majorly found in women after the age of 50. During the early stages of cancer, sometimes even a doctor cannot diagnose the calcifications as cancerous or non-cancerous. So, an automatic CAD system is used to assist a doctor for a better diagnosis. Nowadays most CAD systems are based on deep neural network learning due to higher accuracy. Transfer learning is one of the most used methods to classify mammogram images after network training as they are pre-trained networks. Also, these networks are easy to train rather than developing a model and train it from starch. In this work, a multistage model is proposed for mammogram image classification into micro or mass calcification. The rapid development in the field of deep learning also helps to revolutionize medical CAD systems [1].

LITERATURE REVIEW

Contrast enhancement helps in enhancing the mammogram images for better cancer detection [2]. The author proposed an enhancement method based on CLAHE and LCM for mammogram image contrast improvement. The used method is quite adaptive in terms of pixel distribution and replacement during the preprocessing stages. The work done showed a significant improvement in the mammogram images in terms of PSNR (Peak Signal to Noise Ration).

Automated breast ultrasound can be an adjacent technique for mammography to detect breast cancer during early stages [3]. The author compared three major clinical techniques used for breast cancer detection. Tomo-synthesis and ABU can provide a close accuracy for cancer detection in contrast with existing mammogram-based methods. The study was performed to evaluate the accuracy and consistency of 3-D imagining for breast cancer detection.

The advancement in the field of machine learning helps in improving the computer-aided diagnosis system (CAD) accuracy [4]. In this work, a review of various existing methods and the latest tools was provided by the author to help other authors make CAD systems more advanced and robust. There are many available methods to improve the accuracy of mammogram images using machine learning, but now many machine learning techniques are outdated, and researchers are relying more on deep neural networks.

Breast cancer detection during early stages is very important as every year worldwide many women die due to breast cancer [5]. In this paper, the author proposed a novel method for mammogram image enhancement, so that it can help a radiologist or doctor to detect breast cancer during early stages. The implemented system can classify the images into further mass and micro calcifications.

Breast calcification is one of the common problems among women after the age of 50. Calcifications are deposition of calcium at some places in the breast, which are further classified as micro and masses calcification [6]. These calcification deposits may cause cancer, so it becomes very important to detect them in the early stages and cure it as per the doctor's advice. Micro calcification signifies small, tiny dots like calcium deposits whereas, in masses, classification is for big visible calcium deposits.

A convolutional neural network can improve breast cancer detection as it helps in accurately classifying the images as micro or mass calcification. In his work, the author used the concept of transfer learning. A pre-trained RESNET-16 network is used, which is pre-trained for a specific task. It is better to use transfer learning and a pre-trained learning network instead of training a complete network from starch [7, 8]. These networks are also easy to train and can classify the images accurately with fewer computations and training time.

PROPOSED MODEL

Image Acquisition and Pre-processing

In this step, a benchmark dataset will be acquired as input for the proposed CAD-based system. In this paper, the MIAS dataset is used. Most of the datasets including all the images were exposed to various types of images like impulse, Gaussian, *etc.* This noise may degrade the performance of classification, so a VGG-16 network is used in this work to denoise the dataset. The VGG-16 network is transformed into an adaptive denoising network by defining its fully connected as depicted in Fig. (**1**). The adaptive behavior helps the network to learn at a dynamic rate *i.e.*, the value of the learning factor (**α**) keeps on changing. This helps in improving the network learning rate and will return better PSNR.

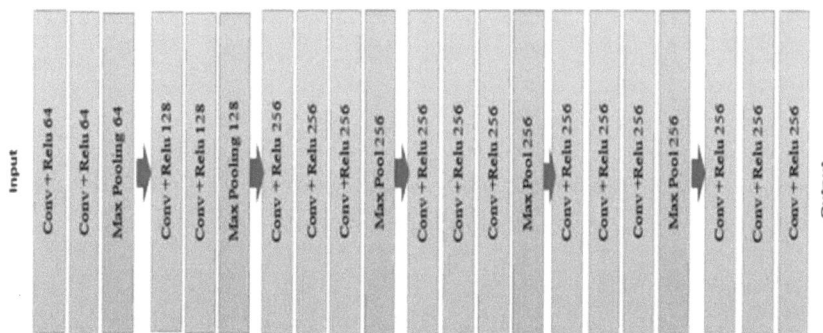

Fig. (1). VGG-16 Network Architecture.

Further, the data augmentation is performed over the dataset before the final enhancement to overcome the problem of data imbalance and overfitting.

Algorithm I: Input: Dataset (MIAS)

- Rotation of the images at a random angle ranging between 45 to 315 degrees.
- Crop the ROI using the pixel localization method.
- Perform the operations of changing the brightness and contrast of the images randomly.
- Perform the morphological operation of erosion that helps in shrinking the objects in the image that is defined in equation (1) as below:

$$A\Theta B = \{ z \in E \mid Bz \subseteq A\} \tag{1}$$

- Then the dilation is performed on the images that will increase the object area in the image.
- Segmentation of ROI using Otsu thresholding with Morphology Feature Extraction as depicted in Fig. (2).

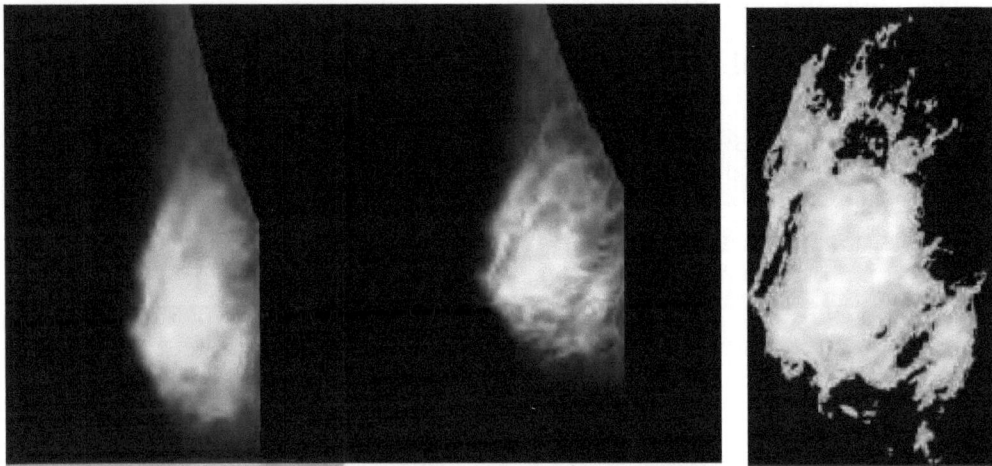

Fig. (2). Orignal image enhanced image segmented image.

The PSNR value of the proposed network outperformed in contrast with various existing methods [6, 8, 10] as shown in Table **1**.

Table 1. PSNR value of different images in dataset.

MIAS Dataset	PSNR (Adaptive VGG-16)
mdb01.pgm	71.08

(Table 1) cont.....

MIAS Dataset	PSNR (Adaptive VGG-16)
mdb02.pgm	70.90
mdb11.pgm	71.10
mdb18.pgm	71.16
mdb27.pgm	69.90

Learning Networking Training and Testing

In this paper, a double transfer learning (DTL) is proposed, where a TL helps in fine-tuning the CN model.

Algorithm 2 (DTL): Input: MIAS (Preprocessed)

- Load: ResNet-50, import architecture and standard parameters defined for ImageNet. //Fully connected layer (fc) operational.
- while: training epochs do TL function computation.
- Input (images + ground truth) //VGG-16 enhanced images.
- Compute and predict the output of forward propagation function p (y | x) //do compute o/p y given x in each round..
- Repeat step (iv): compute back propagation output.
- Update network and compute loss each round as:

$$N\ (x, y, \lambda) = -L_{(x,y)}(\log P\ (y|x; \lambda))$$

Update λ by λ_{TL} = min arg (N(dataset , λ ImageNet)) // λ defines

weights and biases parameters for hidden layer

- While training == True, initiate dual training.
- Input W_x, W_y, weights of TL model in the previous step.
- for $\forall$ inputs, repeat.

Compute forward and back propagation till TL = true

$$\text{Calculate J} \ (x, y, \lambda) = \frac{1}{N} \sum_1^n x\ log\ \frac{1}{1+ e{-}(\lambda** xi + yj)} + (1 - y)$$

- $log\ \dfrac{e**(xi + yj)}{1+ e{-}(\lambda** xi + yj)}$

Update, λ by, λ_{DTL}

- Calculate → fc_1024-layer output of the DTL model with features.
- Return: DTL (Features, acc, sensitivity, spec).

As shown in Table **2**, the accuracy of the proposed system outperforms in contrast with other existing models.

Table 2. Accuracy of Various Exiting Architecture and proposed.

Method	Architecture	Accuracy
[3]	Transfer Learning	96.10%
[5]	Transfer Learning Based Method	92.50%
[6]	RESNET	92%
[8]	RESNET-50	79%
[9]	VGG-16	96%
[10]	CNN and SVM	90%
[11]	VGG-RESNET	93%
[12]	Dense-NET	98%
[13]	Google-NET	88%
Proposed	DTL	99.10%

CONCLUSION AND FUTURE WORK

Effective screening of mammogram cancer can extend the survival rate for women. Mammography is the recommended imaging test for breast cancer identification because it can recognize breast cancer cells many years in advance before physical indicators appear. However, many suspicious findings on a mammogram are benign tumors that eventually require a patient to undergo unnecessary biopsies, consequently causing anxiety to patients and increasing the cost of diagnosis.

In this paper, an efficient CAD system for mammogram analysis has been proposed. The proposed network utilizes the existing pre-trained classification model, rather than training a CNN model from scratch. As it is very time-consuming, the training cost is also high. In the preprocessing phase, a VGG-1--based denoising network is used for image enhancement. The classification phase uses a pre-trained model ResNet-50 that has been dually trained in this work. This double-trained model parallelly performs forward and backward propagation of the weights processed by the model in the first round. This results in delivering a promising accuracy of classification and detection. The proposed model achieved an accuracy of 99.10%.

REFERENCES

[1]   L. Shen, L.R. Margolies, J.H. Rothstein, E. Fluder, R. McBride, and W. Sieh, "Deep Learning to Improve Breast Cancer Detection on Screening Mammography", *Sci. Rep.,* vol. 9, no. 1, p. 12495,

2019.
[http://dx.doi.org/10.1038/s41598-019-48995-4] [PMID: 31467326]

[2]   M.R. Shelda Mohan, "Optimized Histogram Based Contrast Limited Enhancement for Mammogram Images", *ACEEE Int. J. Inf. Technol.,* vol. 3, no. 1, pp. 66-71, 2013.

[3]   L.M.B. Hashem, R.H.M. Ali, M.H. Helal, E.E.L.E.L. Gemeae, and A.F.I. Moustafa, "Characterization of breast masses: a comparative study between automated breast ultrasound (ABUS) and digital breast tomosynthesis (DBT)", *Egypt. J. Radiol. Nucl. Med.,* vol. 51, no. 1, p. 47, 2020.
[http://dx.doi.org/10.1186/s43055-020-00161-x]

[4]   S.J.S. Gardezi, A. Elazab, B. Lei, and T. Wang, "Breast cancer detection and diagnosis using mammographic data: Systematic review", *J. Med. Internet Res.,* vol. 21, no. 7, p. e14464, 2019.
[http://dx.doi.org/10.2196/14464] [PMID: 31350843]

[5]   W.A. Yousef, "Method and System for Image Analysis to Detect Cancer", *arXiv,* vol. 26, no. 19, pp. 1-21, 2019.

[6]   S.G. Komen, "Breast calcifications", *American Cancer Society,* 2020.

[7]   F. Jiang, and H. Liu, "Breast Mass Lesion Classification in Mammograms by Transfer Learning", *ICBCB '17 Hong Kong,* 2017.
[http://dx.doi.org/10.1145/3035012.3035022]

[8]   L.G. Falconí, and M. Pérez, "Transfer Learning in Breast Mammogram Abnormalities Classification With Mobilenet and Nasnet", *IEEE Access,* vol. 19, no. 7, pp. 109-114, 2019.

[9]   D.F. Santos-bustos, B. Minh, and H. Eduardo, "International Journal Towards automated eye cancer classification *via* VGG and ResNet networks using transfer learning", *Eng. Sci. Technol. an Int. J,* p. 101214, 2022.
[http://dx.doi.org/10.1016/j.jestch.2022.101214]

[10]   A. Altameem, C. Mahanty, R. C. Poonia, A. Khader, J. Saudagar, and R. Kumar, "Breast Cancer Detection in Mammography Images Using Deep Convolutional Neural Networks and Fuzzy Ensemble Modeling Techniques", *Diagnostics,* vol. 12, no. 8, p. 1812, 2022.
[http://dx.doi.org/10.3390/diagnostics12081812]

[11]   A. Baccouche, B. Garcia-Zapirain, and A.S. Elmaghraby, "An integrated framework for breast mass classification and diagnosis using stacked ensemble of residual neural networks", *Sci. Rep.,* vol. 12, no. 1, p. 12259, 2022.
[http://dx.doi.org/10.1038/s41598-022-15632-6] [PMID: 35851592]

[12]   A. Vulli, P.N. Srinivasu, M.S.K. Sashank, J. Shafi, J. Choi, and M.F. Ijaz, "Fine-Tuned DenseNet-169 for Breast Cancer Metastasis Prediction Using FastAI and 1-Cycle Policy", *Sensors (Basel),* vol. 22, no. 8, p. 2988, 2022.
[http://dx.doi.org/10.3390/s22082988] [PMID: 35458972]

[13]   J. Zhu, J. Geng, W. Shan, B. Zhang, and L. Cheng, *Development and validation of a deep learning model for breast lesion segmentation and characterization in multiparametric MRI,* 2022.
[http://dx.doi.org/10.3389/fonc.2022.946580]

CHAPTER 16

Empirical Analysis of Face Mask Detection Using Deep Learning

Arunima Jaiswal[1,*], Khushboo Kem[1], Aruna Ippili[1], Lydia Nenghoithem Haokip[1] and Nitin Sachdeva[2]

[1] *Department of Computer Science & Engineering, Indira Gandhi Delhi Technical University For Women, India*

[2] *IT Department , Galgotias College of Engineering , Greater Noida , India*

Abstract: Covid-19 has been highly destructive to human health across the globe. Ever since it was discovered in 2019, the pandemic has continued to take the lives of millions. Global efforts like wearing a face mask in public areas have led to the decline of infection, which has given rise to many face mask detection models to ensure that individuals are wearing their masks properly. In this paper, we aim to compare five deep learning models for face mask detection on two different datasets namely the face mask detection dataset (DS1) and the face mask 12k images dataset (DS2). The different models that we have implemented are YOLOV3, YOLOV5, ResNet 50, MobileNet V2, and VGG-16 . The results are evaluated on the grounds of precision, recall, mean average precision (mAP), and accuracy.

Keywords: Deep learning models, Empirical analysis, Face Mask Detection, Object detection techniques, Pandemic.

INTRODUCTION

The ongoing COVID-19 pandemic has severely hit the world with the novel coronavirus also known as COVID-19 [1], which is caused by severe acute respiratory syndrome coronavirus2 (SARS-CoV-2) [2]. The unprecedented rise of the coronavirus killed around 6 million people worldwide and governments have since focused on preventing and curing the disease. As the virus is highly communicable, it can be transferred to anyone who comes in close contact with a patient who at the time of exposure may or may not show the signs and symptoms of the disease. Governments have made it mandatory for masks to be worn [3] in public spaces, which gives rise to the need to monitor individuals to ensure that they are wearing their masks properly. To make this tedious job easier, many deep

---

* **Corresponding author Arunima Jaiswal:** Department of Computer Science & Engineering, Indira Gandhi Delhi Technical University For Women, India; E-mail: arunimajaiswal@igdtuw.ac.in

Pankaj Kumar Mishra & Satya Prakash Yadav (Eds.)

networking models [4] are used to incorporate safe monitoring like face mask detection [5] and social distance [6].

To ensure safety measures in public, various combined and unified objects are being used like social distance trackers and face mask detectors [6]. The main concept following these is to discover the bounding boxes belonging to the class of the training dataset. Face mask detection [7] is an important area of pattern recognition, which is carried out through deep learning models [8], which is a highly sophisticated subset of machine learning based on artificial neural networks that facilitate a computer to understand and act like the human brain [9]. The models can detect target objects like masks on the human face [10] and when they are integrated with existing technology they give rise to surveillance technology [11], which allows accurate monitoring. These automated finding and management systems are a simple, efficient, and cost-effective method for controlling COVID-19 transmission in public spaces.

This paper mainly compares the five models namely, YOLOV3 [12],YOLO V5 [13], ResNet50 [14], using TensorFlow, MobileNet V2 [15], and VGG-16 [3] for face mask detection based on two datasets namely face mask detection dataset (DS1) and face mask 12k images dataset (DS2). The datasets have been divided into training, testing, and validation datasets. The performance parameters taken into account in this paper are accuracy [16], precision, recall [17], and mean average precision [18]. The paper has been divided as follows. Section 2 provides a brief background on the key concepts of the work. Section 3 explains the system architecture. Section 4 refers to the result of the analysis and section 5 confers the conclusion and future scope of this work.

RELATED WORK

Object Detection proves to be one of the best and impactful studies in terms of computer vision, which is a great boon in such life-threatening times of COVID-19. Deep networking models have given promising results in many fields with good values of accuracy, which increases human trust in these Artificial Intelligence technologies. Researchers [3, 4, 8, 15] have used different datasets for drawing the comparisons by working on different techniques like YOLOv3 [6], YOLOv5 [5], and MobileNetV2 [15] and measured the results through parameters like precision, recall, accuracy, and F1 score. While studying the background of object detection history, we came across that some research papers involved working on the FMD dataset using YOLOv5 [11] whereas some approached the details by creating their dataset with the collection of images using CNN [19] as the main architecture and MobileNet as the backbone [20].

This section digs into the history of work done on face mask detection especially using the ones that used deep learning models. Object detection algorithms come into play for detecting multiple objects in images or videos as per the data given in the datasets [21]. Deep neural models are used in a study [13, 16] to detect whether the person is wearing a face mask or not.

Table **1** below explains the details of research papers that have been analysed to draw a conclusion on which of the techniques and parameters should be considered to achieve maximum accuracy results.

Table 1. Research papers analysis

S. No	Author	Techniques	Dataset	Performance Parameters	Result
1	Ullah *et al.* [1] 2022	DeepMaskNet model and compare with 9 different models.	MDMFR	Accuracy, Precision, Recall, F1 Score.	Accuracy = 100%
2	Kumar *et al.* [2] 2022	ETL-YOLOv4, Tiny YOLOv4.	Face mask detection dataset.	Precision, Recall, Average Precision, mean average precision (mAP).	mAP (ETL-YOLOv4) = 67.64%, mAP (Tiny YOLOv4) = 57.71%.
3	Saravanan *et al.* [3] 2022	Pretrained CNN *i.e* - Vgg16.	Two face mask datasets with different concentrations.	Accuracy	face mask dataset 1 = 96.50%, face mask dataset 2 = 91%.
4	Kaur *et al.* [5] 2022	CNN.	Face dataset (with/without mask).	-	-
5	Ottakath *et al.* [4] 2022	Mask RCNN, YOLOv4, YOLOv5 , YOLOR.	MOXA3K, ViDMASK dataset.	Precision, Recall, Average Precision, mean average precision (mAP).	Precision, Recall, Average Precision, mean average precision (mAP).
6	Prasad *et al.* [6] 2022	CNN. YOLOv3, LBPH.	COCO	Accuracy	Acc = 95.77%

(Table 1) cont.....

S. No	Author	Techniques	Dataset	Performance Parameters	Result
7	Han *et al.* [7] 2022	SMD-YOLOv4	public face mask detection.	Precision, Recall, Average Precision, mean average precision (mAP).	mAP is increased from 62.45% to 67.01%.
8	Gupta *et al.* [8] 2022	Ex Mask R CNN	ICVL, KTH, SGSITS.	-	-
9	Yuan *et al.* [11] 2022	YOLOv5 R6.1	Based on open datasets.	Precision, mAP, Recall.	Precision = 94.1%, mAP = 92.9%, recall = 88.5%.
10	Tabassum *et al.* [10] 2022	DWT (Discrete Wavelet Transform) LDA, CNN.	-	Accuracy	accuracy of recognition rate in worst case it is 89.56% and 93.34% for best case.
11	Durga *et al.* [9] 2022	2D ResNet CNN	Public dataset JAFFE.	Accuracy, recall, F1-Score, Sensitivity.	Accuracy = 99.3%
12	Youssry *et al.* [12] 2022	YOLOv5	face mask detection dataset.	precision, mAP	precision = 95.9%, mAP = 84.8%.
13	Bhole *et al.* [13] 2022	YoloV5	AIZOO	mAP	95.20%
14	Xu *et al.* [14] 2022	open CV	Self dataset of 4000 images.	Precision, Recall, f1 score, support.	99.99%
15	Sethi *et al.* [15] 2021	Models used for feature extraction- Mobile-Netv2,RESNET50,AlexNet.	MAFA converted into unbiased dataset.	Precision, Recall	Accuracy-98.2%
16	Leamsaaed *et al.* [16] 2021	comparative model with different epochs.	-	Accuracy	accuracy = 96.5%

(Table 1) cont.....

S. No	Author	Techniques	Dataset	Performance Parameters	Result
17	Loey *et al.* [17] 2021	Two components used 1). for feature extraction- RESNET50, 2)classical machine learning techniques like decision trees, SVM, *etc.*	Three Datasets used- RMFD,SMFD,LFW.	Recall, precision, f1 score, accuracy validation0	SVM classifier achieved 99.64% in RMFD, 99.49% IN SMFD, 100% IN LFW.
18	Militante *et al.* [18] 2021	CNN with Raspberry-pi	Own created dataset.	Recall, precision, f1 score, accuracy validation.	96% of accuracy score.
19	Prasad *et al.* [19] 2021	Transfer Learning with mobile-Net and resnet for comparison with backbone as CNN,Using HAAR cascade Algorithm for mask detection.	Dataset collected from individuals.	Training loss, validation loss, training accuracy , validation accuracy.	-
20	Suganthalakshmi *et al.* [20] 2021	OpenCV, tensor flow,.keras,.python,MobileNet as backbone, and CNN model as main architecture.	Collection of the images for creating a dataset.	Accuracy	-
21	Singh *et al.* [21] 2021	YOLOv3 and faster R-CNN.	Custom manual dataset.	Average precision and Inference time.	Yolov3 is better than F- RCNN.
22	Loey *et al.* [22] 2021	Yolov2 with ResNet-50 using with adam optimizer.	MMD and FMD.	Precision, recall.	Avg. precision equal to 81%.
23	Mbunge *et al.* [23] 2021	Different AI models eg- Hybrid deep transfer learning, SRCNet, Yolov3, Yolov2 with ResNet-50.	Different datasets for every models *eg.-* FMD,CelebA,RMFD, SMFD *etc.*	Accuracy	The highest accuracy for 99.9% for Inception v3 CNN.
24	Chavda *et al.* [24] 2021	Two-stage CNN architecture is used.	RWMFD	Accuracy, precision, recall, f1- score, loss.	NASNetMobile has better performance than other models.
25	Mandal *et al.* [25] 2021	Transfer Learning with ResNet-50.	RMFRD	Precision, recall,f1 score, accuracy.	Accuracy of 89.7016% with a loss of 0.4698.

(Table 1) cont.....

S. No	Author	Techniques	Dataset	Performance Parameters	Result
26	Alguzo *et al.* [26] 2021	Deep Learning with MGCN.	RWMFD	Precision, recall, accuracy, f1 score.	Accuracy of 97.9% by performing the different models.
27	Zhao *et al.* [27] 2021	YoloV5	MAFA	Recall, loss-function, precision.	70.03%
28	Degasawala *et al.* [28] 2021	YoloV4	wider face and MAFA.	Precision, recall, f1 score , support	79%%
29	Kaur *et al.* [29] 2021	CNN	Face Dataset	percentage score of whether mask is detected or not shown.	99.00%
30	Arora *et al.* [30] 2021	mobileNetV2	self-created	Recall, precision, f1 score, support.	96%
31	Shanmughapriya *et al.* [31] 2020	YOLOv3	Face mask detection-Kaggle.	LOSS function	99%
32	Sachdeva *et al.* [32] 2020	open CV	Dataset created by Prajna Bhandary.	Precision, f1 score, recall, support.	99%
33	Gupta *et al.* [33] 2020	CNN	Self dataset of 1238 images.	Ttraining loss, variation loss, training accuracy, validation accuracy.	95%
34	Bhadani *et al.* [34] 2020	MobileNetV2, CNN	Self dataset where 800 were masked face and 750 unmasked.	Recall,f1 score, precision, support	97.00%
35	Ruifang *et al.* [35] 2020	lightweight face detection approach based on YOLO algorithm.	WIDER face dataset	Accuracy	A lightweight approach gives better results as compared to the original one.

(Table 1) cont.....

S. No	Author	Techniques	Dataset	Performance Parameters	Result
36	Sammy *et al.* [36] 2020	VGG16	Own collected dataset with 25k images.	Accuracy	96%

SYSTEM ARCHITECTURE

Data Collection

The initial step is to collect the datasets that were collected from Kaggle. Collected datasets are the Face mask detection dataset [12] known as DS1 and the Face mask 12k images dataset known as DS2. Both of the datasets were publically available and were downloaded from kaggle. DS1 in total has 853 images which comprise both single and grouped images along with images where the subject(s) are simultaneously wearing a mask and not wearing a mask. The images can be broadly classified into two categories: masked and unmasked. In DS2, there are 12,000 single-face images with and without masks. Both the datasets were then further distributed for training, testing, and validation process in their respective folders (Fig. **1**).

This study considers that the datasets were created artificially without the real-world environment, which in the end affects the precision [22] and accuracy [23]. The main purpose here is to get a bounding box around the object (in our case, the face mask) because such a box will focus on the subject's face and make it easy for the model to recognise the needed presence or absence of a mask. The detection process of a face is a difficult task for a model but certain libraries like dlib make the process much easier for the model to identify the face [24]. After preprocessing, choosing a model is a crucial stage, where this paper works with YOLOv3 [21], YOLOv5 [12], ResNet50 [21], MobileNetv2 [16], and Vgg16 [3]. Then by training and testing the data, the desired comparisons and graphs are achieved (Table **2**).

Models Used

Table 2. Details of the use of Deep Learning Model.

Techniques	Description
YOLOV3	Yolov3 "You Only Look Once" [23] is an object detection technique and also the fastest one. It employs a single CNN on a complete image to divide the image into different regions and predict the bounding box making it more efficient to find the accuracy [25] because you can make multiple predictions at the same time. YOLOv3 [26] uses an algorithm to return a correctly output image that contains a bounding box drawn for all patches in the image that are most likely detectable objects. This is a faster process than traditional sliding window algorithms, which look for objects thoroughly.
YOLOV5	Yolo V5 [27] is the 5th version of the, You Only Look Once model, where there are changes in the architecture as well as in some of its parameters. It is a single-stage detector comprising the following three main components: • Backbone • Neck • Head Backbone's main feature is to extract the features that are prone to give higher accuracy from our input image and mainly uses CSPNet for feature extraction. Model neck is the part where feature bounding boxes as well as the correctness score and class probabilities scaling are done. The model head is the last part where object detection is done by predicting the class of the image. Yolov5 [27] uses .yaml files for configuration [28].
ResNet 50	ResNet [23] is an abbreviation for Residual Network, and is a type of convolutional neural network CNN [29]. ResNet-50 [25] is a CNN that is 50 layers deep. The bottleneck design is used for the building block in the 50-layer ResNet [25]. A bottleneck residual block employs 11 convolutions to reduce the number of parameters and matrix multiplications. This allows for a much faster training layer. It employs a three-layer stack rather than two layers.
MobileNet V2	MobileNetV2 [30] is a CNN structure designed for Android gadgets. The MobileNetV2 deep learning [31] architecture initially involves a 32 filter convolutional layer, and subsequently has a layer of 19 residual bottleneck layers. MobileNetV2 works faster than MobileNetV1 resulting in better accuracy and precision [32].
VGG-16	VGG-16 [3] is a 16-layer deep convolutional neural network [33, 34]. It is a popular image classification algorithm that works well with transfer learning. VGG16 [3] has a convolutional layer, a max pooling layer, and a dense layer that include 13, 5, and 3 layers making a total of 21 layers. Once a set of images is loaded, it can identify 1000 different categories of images like chair, table, and others. It is a network that has learned the basic feature representation for different categories which in our case is face mask detection.

Library Used

Dlib [23], numpy, shutil, random, cv2 [30], TensorFlow, and Keras are a few very commonly built-in libraries that were used in the implementation of the models.

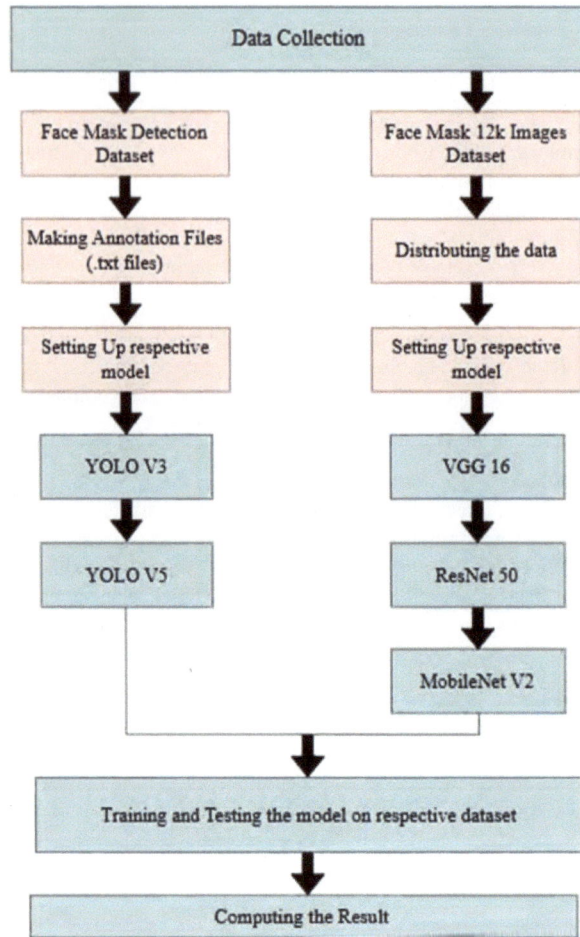

Fig. (1). Implementation Framework.

Training and Testing

DS1 and DS2 are used to train the model by feeding it with samples of the data it will encounter when it is run later. Usually, a major percentage of the data is sent for training so that the model or algorithm can become fit. The model learns the behaviour of the data and is then able to fit itself in alignment with the expected output. Validation [33] data acts as the first test for the model against unseen data as it contains a different set of data the model has not seen during its training. Validation data helps to reinforce what the model has learned during its training [33]. The test data provides a final check to see how the model will perform in the real world and the test accuracy is used as a parameter of how well the model has performed.

RESULTS AND DISCUSSION

The main performance parameters that have been used to compare the deep learning model are precision, recall [34], mAP (mean average precision), accuracy [35], and val_accuracy (validation_accuracy). The following Table **3** and Table **4** exhibit the results of applying the 5 deep learning techniques on the two datasets, respectively.

Table 3. Final result on DS1.

Parameters	YOLOV3	YOLOV5
Precision	95%	93.5%
Recall	78%	87.8%
mAP (mean average precision).	83%	92.4%

Table 4. Final result on DS2.

Parameters	VGG-16	ResNet50	MobileNetV2
Accuracy	99.9%	94.5%	95.4%
val_accuracy	99.6%	93%	-

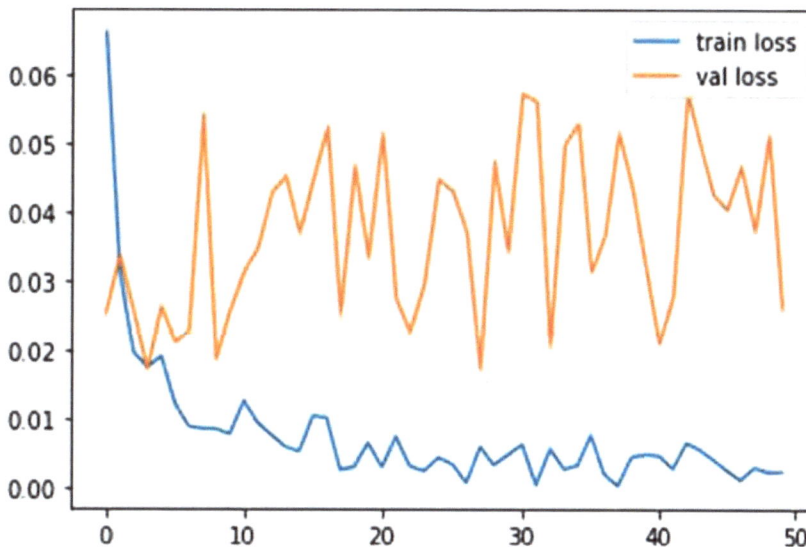

Graph 1. Loss Graph of Vgg16 on DS2.

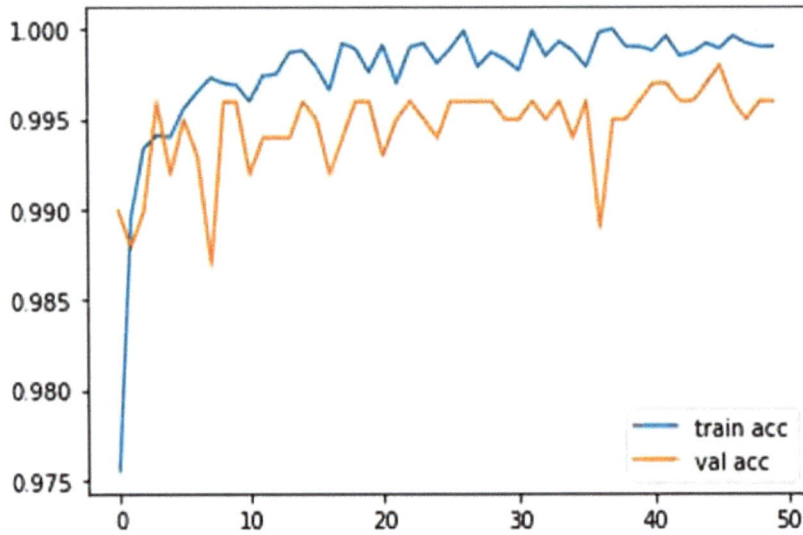

Graph 2. Accuracy Graph of Vgg 16 on DS2.

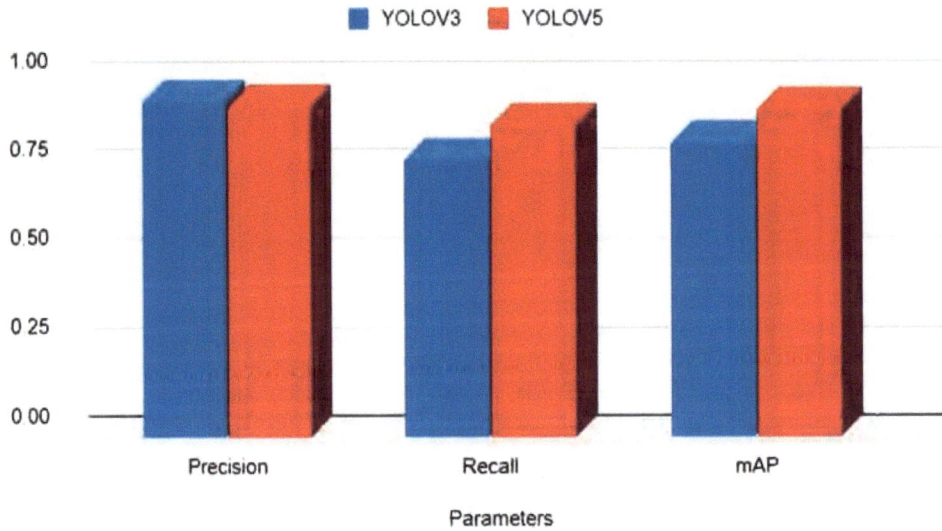

Graph 3. Result on DS1.

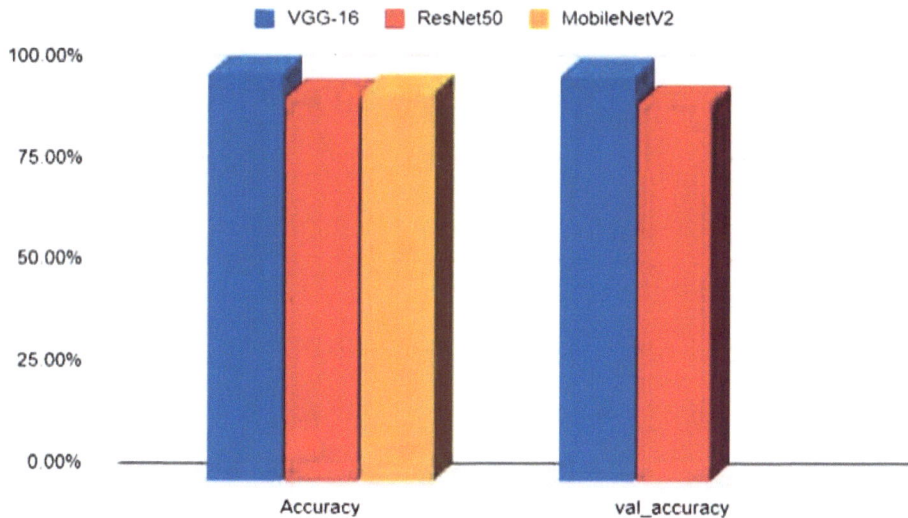

Graph 4. Result on DS2.

CONCLUSION AND FUTURE SCOPE

This paper empirically compares the results of models performed on DS1 and DS2. DS1 has single as well as crowded images, for this purpose, YOLOv3 [27] has shown the best results compared to YOLOv3 and YOLOv5. In comparison to yolov5, it was able to detect the face with and without the mask more correctly and precisely but for training it took more time (approx an hour) to execute as in DS1 [22]. On the other hand, we implemented the three other deep learning models on DS2, which consisted of 12k images of single-face only. It was observed that out of three models, VGG16 [36] outperformed with an unmatched accuracy result of 99.9%.

Along with humanity's leap into a more technologically advanced future along with growing populations, it is becoming more arduous to keep a check on large populations at all times to which technologies such as these models on machine learning, as discussed in this paper, can become useful when integrated with existing technologies such as surveillances, applications, websites, *etc.* This allows them to be used to monitor large groups of people at the individual level even remotely in real time. Alert Systems to detect when one is not wearing a mask can also be implemented using deep neural networks [35]. Moreover, Face mask detection technology can be implemented in public spaces like schools, offices, transportation stations, *etc.*

REFERENCES

[1]   N. Ullah, A. Javed, M. A. Ghazanfar, A. Alsufyani, and S. Bourouis, "A novel DeepMaskNet model for face mask detection and masked facial recognition", *Journal of King Saud University- Computer*

and Information Sciences, 2022.

[2]   A. Kumar, A. Kalia, and A. Kalia, "ETL-YOLO v4: A face mask detection algorithm in era of COVID-19 pandemic", *Optik (Stuttg.),* vol. 259, p. 169051, 2022.
[http://dx.doi.org/10.1016/j.ijleo.2022.169051] [PMID: 35411120]

[3]   T.M. Saravanan, K. Karthiha, R. Kavinkumar, S. Gokul, and J.P. Mishra, "A novel machine learning scheme for face mask detection using pretrained convolutional neural network", *Mater. Today Proc.,* vol. 58, pp. 150-156, 2022.
[http://dx.doi.org/10.1016/j.matpr.2022.01.165] [PMID: 35079578]

[4]   N. Ottakath, O. Elharrouss, N. Almaadeed, S. Al-Maadeed, A. Mohamed, T. Khattab, and K. Abualsaud, "ViDMASK dataset for face mask detection with social distance measurement", *Displays,* vol. 73, p. 102235, 2022.
[http://dx.doi.org/10.1016/j.displa.2022.102235] [PMID: 35574253]

[5]   G. Kaur, R. Sinha, P. K. Tiwari, S. K. Yadav, P. Pandey, R. Raj, and M. Rakhra, "Face mask recognition system using CNN model", *Neuroscience Informatics,* p. 100035, 2021.

[6]   J. Prasad, A. Jain, D. Velho, and S. Kumar K S, "COVID vision: An integrated face mask detector and social distancing tracker", *International Journal of Cognitive Computing in Engineering,* vol. 3, pp. 106-113, 2022.
[http://dx.doi.org/10.1016/j.ijcce.2022.05.001]

[7]   Z. Han, H. Huang, Q. Fan, Y. Li, Y. Li, and X. Chen, "SMD-YOLO: An efficient and lightweight detection method for mask wearing status during the COVID-19 pandemic", *Comput. Methods Programs Biomed.,* vol. 221, p. 106888, 2022.
[http://dx.doi.org/10.1016/j.cmpb.2022.106888] [PMID: 35598435]

[8]   P. Gupta, V. Sharma, and S. Varma, "A novel algorithm for mask detection and recognizing actions of human", *Expert Syst. Appl.,* vol. 198, p. 116823, 2022.
[http://dx.doi.org/10.1016/j.eswa.2022.116823] [PMID: 35280934]

[9]   B.K. Durga, and V. Rajesh, "A ResNet deep learning based facial recognition design for future multimedia applications", *Comput. Electr. Eng.,* vol. 104, p. 108384, 2022.
[http://dx.doi.org/10.1016/j.compeleceng.2022.108384]

[10]   F. Tabassum, M. I. Islam, R. T. Khan, and M. R. Amin, "Human face recognition with combination of DWT and machine learning", *Journal of King Saud University-Computer and Information Sciences,* 2020.

[11]   Shenghai Yuan, Yudong Wang, Tiancai Liang, Wenchao Jiang, Sui Lin, Zhiming Zhao, "Real-time recognition and warning of mask wearing based on improved YOLOv5 R6.1,", *International journal of intelligent system,* 2022.

[12]   N. Youssry, and A. Khattab, "Accurate Real-Time Face Mask Detection Framework Using YOLOv5", *International Conference on Design & Test of Integrated Micro & Nano- Systems (DTS),* p. 1-6, 2022.
[http://dx.doi.org/10.1109/DTS55284.2022.9809855]

[13]   S. Xu, Z. Guo, Y. Liu, J. Fan, and X. Liu, "An improved lightweight yolov5 model based on attention mechanism for face mask detection", *International Conference on Artificial Neural Networks,* pp. 531-543, 2022.
[http://dx.doi.org/10.1007/978-3-031-15934-3_44]

[14]   B. Varsha, S. Tiwari, V. Chaudhari, and V. Patil, "Face Mask Detection with alert system using Tensorflow, Keras and Open CV", *International Journal of Engineering and Applied Physics,* vol. 2, no. 1, pp. 339-345, 2022.

[15]   S. Sethi, M. Kathuria, and T. Kaushik, "Face mask detection using deep learning: An approach to reduce risk of Coronavirus spread", *J. Biomed. Inform.,* vol. 120, p. 103848, 2021.
[http://dx.doi.org/10.1016/j.jbi.2021.103848] [PMID: 34171485]

[16]   leamsaard, J., Charoensook, S. N., & Yammen, S., "(2021, March). Deep learning-based face mask

detection using yolov5", *In 2021 9th International Electrical Engineering Congress (iEECON),,* pp. 428-431, 2021.

[17] M. Loey, G. Manogaran, M.H.N. Taha, and N.E.M. Khalifa, "A hybrid deep transfer learning model with machine learning methods for face mask detection in the era of the COVID-19 pandemic", *Measurement,* vol. 167, p. 108288, 2021.
[http://dx.doi.org/10.1016/j.measurement.2020.108288] [PMID: 32834324]

[18] S.V. Militante, and N.V. Dionisio, "Real-time facemask recognition with alarm system using deep learning", *11th IEEE Control and System Graduate Research Colloquium (ICSGRC),* p. 106-110, 2020.
[http://dx.doi.org/10.1109/ICSGRC49013.2020.9232610]

[19] S. Hebbale, and V. Vani, "Real time COVID-19 facemask detection using deep learning", *learning,* vol. 6, no. S4, pp. 1446-1462, 2022.

[20] R. Suganthalakshmi, A. Hafeeza, P. Abinaya, and A. G. Devi, "Covid-19 facemask detection with deep learning and computer vision", *Int. J. Eng. Res. Tech. (IJERT) ICRADL,* 2021.

[21] S. Singh, U. Ahuja, M. Kumar, K. Kumar, and M. Sachdeva, "Face mask detection using YOLOv3 and faster R-CNN models: COVID-19 environment", *Multimedia Tools Appl.,* vol. 80, no. 13, pp. 19753-19768, 2021.
[http://dx.doi.org/10.1007/s11042-021-10711-8] [PMID: 33679209]

[22] M. Loey, G. Manogaran, M.H.N. Taha, and N.E.M. Khalifa, "Fighting against COVID-19: A novel deep learning model based on YOLO-v2 with ResNet-50 for medical face mask detection", *Sustain Cities Soc.,* vol. 65, p. 102600, 2021.
[http://dx.doi.org/10.1016/j.scs.2020.102600] [PMID: 33200063]

[23] E. Mbunge, S. Simelane, S.G. Fashoto, B. Akinnuwesi, and A.S. Metfula, "Application of deep learning and machine learning models to detect COVID-19 face masks - A review", *Sustainable Operations and Computers,* vol. 2, pp. 235-245, 2021.
[http://dx.doi.org/10.1016/j.susoc.2021.08.001]

[24] A. Chavda, J. Dsouza, S. Badgujar, and A. Damani, "Multi-stage CNN architecture for face mask detection", *6th International Conference for Convergence in Technology (i2ct),* p. 1-6, 2021.
[http://dx.doi.org/10.1109/I2CT51068.2021.9418207]

[25] B. Mandal, A. Okeukwu, and Y. Theis, "Masked face recognition using resnet-50", *arXiv preprint arXiv:2104.08997,* 2021.

[26] A. Alguzo, A. Alzu'bi, and F. Albalas, "Masked face detection using multi-graph convolutional networks", *12th International Conference on Information and Communication Systems (ICICS),* p. 385-391, 2021.
[http://dx.doi.org/10.1109/ICICS52457.2021.9464553]

[27] Y. Zhao, and S. Geng, "Face occlusion detection algorithm based on yolov5", *J. Phys. Conf. Ser.,* vol. 2031, no. 1, p. 012053, 2021.
[http://dx.doi.org/10.1088/1742-6596/2031/1/012053]

[28] S. Degadwala, D. Vyas, U. Chakraborty, A.R. Dider, and H. Biswas, "Yolo-v4 deep learning model for medical face mask detection", *International Conference on Artificial Intelligence and Smart Systems (ICAIS),* pp. 209pp. 209-213-213, 2021.
[http://dx.doi.org/10.1109/ICAIS50930.2021.9395857]

[29] G. Kaur, R. Sinha, P. K. Tiwari, S. K. Yadav, P. Pandey, R. Raj, and M. Rakhra, "Face mask recognition system using CNN model", *Neuroscience Informatics,* p. 100035, 2021.

[30] M. Arora, S. Garg, and S. A, "Face mask detection system using Mobilenetv2", *Int. J. Eng. Adv. Technol.,* vol. 10, no. 4, pp. 127-129, 2021.
[http://dx.doi.org/10.35940/ijeat.D2404.0410421]

[31] M. Shanmughapriya, J.R. Fenitha, and R. Sanchana, "Proper Face Mask Detection Using Deep

Learning", *Elementary Education Online,* vol. 19, no. 2, pp. 2158-2158, 2022.

[32]   R. Sachdeva, "Face Mask Detection System", *SSRN,* p. 3755508, 2020.

[33]   Gupta, and Chhaya, "A novel finetuned YOLOv8 model for real-time underwater trash detection", *Journal of Real-Time Image Processing,* vol. 21, no. 2, p. 48, 2024.

[34]   A. K. Bhadani, and A. Sinha, "Coronamask: a face mask detector for real-time data", *Int. J. Adv. Trends Comput. Sci. Eng.,* 2020.

[35]   Z. Ruifang, J. Tianyi, and D. Feng, "Lightweight face detection network improved based on YOLO target detection algorithm", *Proceedings of the 2020 2nd International Conference on Big Data and Artificial Intelligence,* pp. 415-420, 2020.
[http://dx.doi.org/10.1145/3436286.3436429]

[36]   S.V. Militante, and N.V. Dionisio, "Real-time facemask recognition with alarm system using deep learning", *11th IEEE Control and System Graduate Research Colloquium (ICSGRC),* p. 106-110, 2020.
[http://dx.doi.org/10.1109/ICSGRC49013.2020.9232610]

CHAPTER 17

Estimation of the Price of Used Cars Using Machine Learning

Ramander Singh[1,*]

[1] *Department of Computer Science and Engineering, IMS Engineering College, Ghaziabad, (U.P.), India*

Abstract: The manufacturer sets the price of new vehicles in the market, and taxes are an additional expense imposed by the government. Consumers can confidently purchase a new car, expecting a favourable return on their investment. However, with the rising cost of new automobiles, there is a growing trend worldwide for people to opt for purchasing pre-owned vehicles. As a result, there is an increasing need for a proficient and comprehensive system that can accurately predict the prices of pre-owned vehicles based on several features. This article demonstrates the predictive capability for older cars by using linear lasso regression, a machine-learning technique. This approach ensures a prediction accuracy of 83%, making it the most precise among three distinct algorithms. The data includes information on the model year, car model, engine type, and price. Over the past decade, one of the most significant advancements in technology has been machine learning, which has had a crucial impact on precise forecasting and reliability.

Keywords: Automobiles, Advancements, Crucial, Forecasting, Precision, Worldwide.

INTRODUCTION

According to the data, predicting car behaviour is a significant and intriguing issue. Forecasts on the pricing of vintage automobiles will prove beneficial to the majority of individuals. Anticipating the costs of vehicles is an essential and noteworthy method, especially for older, non-new vehicles [1]. An increasing number of car buyers are seeking alternatives to buying new automobiles directly, as there has been a surge in demand for used cars and a decrease of up to nine percent in demand for new cars in 2014 [2]. Leasing is a more prevalent option compared to purchasing an automobile, as it entails a legally binding agreement between the customer and seller. The seller group encompasses direct sellers, third-party entities, enterprises, and insurance providers [3]. Through a lease

---

[*] **Corresponding author Ramander Singh:** Department of Computer Science and Engineering, IMS Engineering College, Ghaziabad, (U.P.), India; E-mail: ramendera@gmail.com

Pankaj Kumar Mishra & Satya Prakash Yadav (Eds.)

arrangement, the buyers make periodic payments for the item over a predetermined duration. Vendors are interested in understanding the lease payments as the anticipated expense of the car determines them. Precise automotive price prediction requires specialized expertise, as the price of a car typically relies on a variety of unique characteristics and factors [4]. The primary factors of importance are often the brand, age, mileage, horsepower, and model [5]. The price of a car is significantly affected by the type of petrol used and the amount of fuel consumed each mile due to the regular changes in petroleum prices [6]. The price of an automobile is influenced by factors such as the number of doors, exterior colour, gearbox type, presence of air conditioning, size, GPS capability, safety features, and interior design [7]. This study focused on exploring a range of methods and approaches to enhance the precision of predicting the prices of pre-owned vehicles. In addition to ensuring the accuracy of information, Machine Learning approaches primarily aim to enhance the predictive capabilities of software programs without the need for explicit programming [8]. Machine learning primarily utilizes pre-existing data to forecast output values. "Machine Learning (ML) has proven its utility by offering solutions to problems at a velocity and magnitude surpassing the capabilities of the human intellect." Machines can be trained to identify patterns and correlations in incoming data by linking the significant processing power of a single activity or multiple distinct tasks [9]. It enables machines to perform mundane activities autonomously. This study aims to assess the extent to which machine learning enhances prediction outcomes in terms of accuracy and data diversity. Fig. (**1**) illustrates the process flowchart:

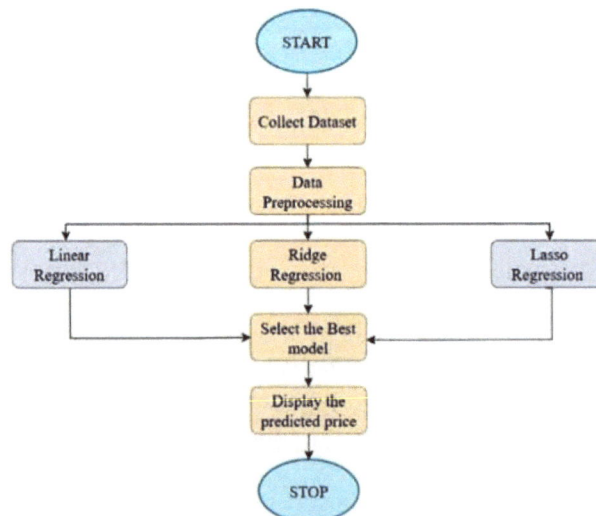

Fig. (1). Flow Chart.

In this research, linear and lasso regression are utilized to enhance the accuracy of the prediction. These algorithms outperform other machine learning algorithms in terms of accuracy [10]. After the user has acquired a prediction rate for the car, they can subsequently execute numerous other functions with high accuracy. In the proposed System, depicted in Fig. (**1**), we have endeavored to tackle the issues present in the current System. We have developed a graphical user interface (GUI). In order to improve the precision and reliability of our output forecasts, we have included three separate machine learning algorithms - lasso regression, linear regression, and ridge regression - in our company.

Lasso Regression

Lasso regression is primarily built around the principle of regularization. Regression techniques are utilized to improve the precision of forecasts. This approach integrates the concept of reduction [11]. The term "LASSO" is an abbreviation for "Least Absolute Shrinkage and Selection Operator." To achieve improved balance, we use lasso regression. Regression methods are preferred when the goal is to obtain a more accurate estimate.This concept is more efficient when it is scaled down [12]. Shrinkage is the term used to describe the phenomena when the values in a dataset approach the average. The lasso method facilitates the creation of concise models with little intricacy. This form of regression is advantageous in situations when there is a notable presence of multicollinearity in a model or when there is a need to streamline the model selection process by automating tasks such as variable selection and parameter removal [13]. In this scenario, the price of the car is regarded as the dependent variable, while all other factors are regarded as independent variables. Used cars have extensive input dimensions [14]. The multitude of characteristics and factors that influence the pricing of an automobile results in a significant amount of data that is inherently difficult to analyze. The objective of the research is to develop a model that can efficiently handle high degrees of complexity and produce precise outcomes, irrespective of the extent of data collection [15].

Software Requirement Properties

Python 3.6.0, an agile and object-oriented programming language, is well-suited for many software development projects. It may be obtained quickly within a few days, has substantial existing libraries, and offers strong support for integrating various languages and technologies [16]. A significant number of Python programmers assert that their efficiency has greatly increased and that the language facilitates the development of superior, more organized code. The Jupyter Notebook: The Jupyter Notebook App is a software that operates as a server-client system, capable of being installed on a computer and accessed using a web browser. It enables the modification and execution of notebook documents. The Jupyter Notebook App can be utilized offline on a computer and can also be accessed remotely on an internet-connected server. The Jupyter Notebook App, as described in this paper, enables the visualization, editing, and execution of notebook documents [17]. Furthermore, it has a "Dashboard" (sometimes referred to as the Notebook Dashboard) and a "control panel" that enables users to access local files and provides the option to inspect notebook documents or terminate a notebook engine. Fig. (**2**) shows the Lasso Regression Graph [18].

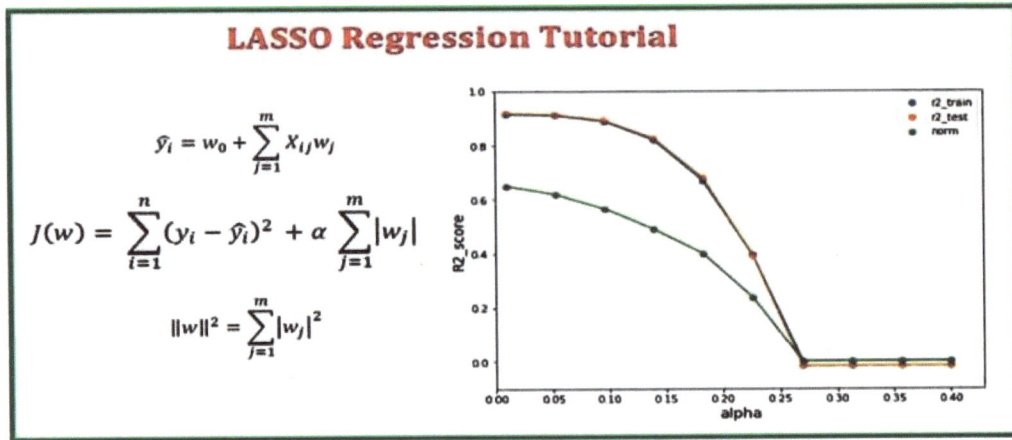

LASSO Regression Tutorial

$$\hat{y}_i = w_0 + \sum_{j=1}^{m} x_{ij} w_j$$

$$J(w) = \sum_{i=1}^{n} (y_i - \hat{y}_i)^2 + \alpha \sum_{j=1}^{m} |w_j|$$

$$\|w\|^2 = \sum_{j=1}^{m} |w_j|^2$$

Fig. (2). Lasso Regression Graph.

RELATED WORKS

Machine learning is a powerful tool for predicting the prices of used vehicles. Machine learning algorithms can consider a variety of factors to estimate a car's value, including its make and model, mileage, and service history. By analysing a wide range of data points, machine learning provides buyers and sellers with a more accurate estimate of a vehicle's true worth.

The first step in using machine learning to estimate the price of used vehicles is to gather all the necessary data to feed into the algorithm. Examples of statistical factors used to price a vehicle include the model year, mileage, condition, estimated repair costs, and local sales data. This information can be collected by analysing various automotive websites and calculating estimates based on the available data.

Once the data is collected, the next step is to apply a machine learning algorithm to generate an estimate. Machine learning algorithms, such as regression models, tree-based models, and deep learning networks, can be used to help produce an accurate price estimate [19].

Through education, the set of rules on a large sample of information, it may learn to expect the pricing of a car. Once the model is educated, it can be used to expect the pricing of new cars. Through growing a system and learning a set of rules to help estimate the pricing of used motors, automobile buyers and sellers will have better information about what's a truthful charge for an automobile. Machine learning algorithms can offer an extra correct estimate of pricing than conventional techniques, making it an effective tool for buyers and sellers. The primary difficulty with the use of system learning to estimate the price of used cars is the substantial amount of information generated. In addition, exclusive elements of the u. s. a. has specific pricing requirements, meaning that country-wide averages may not be accurate [20]. Finally, gadget-mastering algorithms can be susceptible to mistakes, mainly due to erroneous predictions.

METHODOLOGY

This section outlines the approach employed in developing the module, encompassing the algorithms utilized and the dataset employed for training purposes. The dataset utilized comprises 92386 records and underwent processing to exclude extraneous data. The valuation of a vehicle is contingent upon several aspects, including mileage, car brand, registration year, fuel type, car model, financial stability, and gear type. In order to address this regression problem, a total of five distinct methodologies were employed, encompassing K-Nearest Neighbors (KNN) Regression, Random Forest Regression, Linear Regression, Decision Tree Regression, and XG Boost Regression. The themes in this section are organized hierarchically, with the paper title serving as the main heading and the subsequent topics as subheadings. Fig. (**3**) shows the proposed methodology blueprint.

Dataset Collection

It involves gathering data from the source to develop an evaluation. The Old Car data set, formatted in CSV, was collected *via* the Kaggle website. The study examines 14 variables, including unknown serial number, name, location, kilometres, engine gearbox, new price, petrol type, distance traveled, proprietor type, year, power, chairs, and price.

Data Preparation

This stage is crucial in supervised machine learning. It contains:

i. Separating the non-numerical elements from the numerical aspects. This stage excludes non-numerical terms from attributes like power, engines, and mileage.

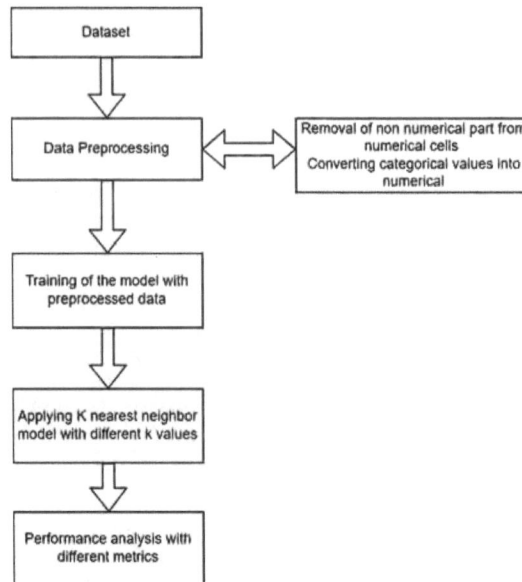

Fig. (3). Proposed methodology blueprint.

Step 1: In this step, we convert the data frame into a list.

Step 2: Segregate the list based on a delimiter.

Step 3: Reincorporate the necessary information into the data frame.

i. Transformation of category values into numerical values. In this instance, category data such as Name, Address, Fuel Type, Location, and owner type have been changed to numerical values. This conversion enables machine learning algorithms to analyze them efficiently, as machines easily understand numerical values. This task can be achieved by utilizing the Label Encoder Python module.

Step 1: Categorical values should be chosen according to the data type.

In **Step 2**, the category values are converted into numerical values using Python's Label Encoder API.

In this scenario, it is important to differentiate between the intended characteristic and the forecast. The Optimal factor in this scenario is the price.

Step 1: The variable "y" is assigned the value of the target variable price.

Step 2: With the exception of the target variable, the processed data set is allocated to the variable "X."

After finishing all preparation procedures, the data was displayed.

Algorithms KNN

Regression

We utilised the K-Nearest Neighbour (KNN) algorithm with a range of 1 to 100 neighbours. By plotting the mean squared error against the number of neighbours, we found that the highest accuracy, as indicated by reference [12], was achieved with 6 neighbours. In this study, our objective was to develop a model using the KNN method to predict the cost of used vehicles. Machine learning algorithms can be easily implemented when utilising the K-Nearest Neighbours (KNN) method. It is a nonparametric approach that is employed for both classification and regression tasks. It employs a similarity metric to ascertain the anticipated quantity of goals. Calculating the mean of the number objective of the K nearest neighbours is a simple implementation of the K-nearest neighbours algorithm.

Random Forest Regression

To assess the effectiveness of the Gradient Boost method using a bagging methodology, we take into consideration the vast number of attributes in the data files.

Linear Regression

Linear regression is a fundamental and widely employed technique in machine learning. It is a statistical strategy used to do predictive research based on evidence. Linear regression can be utilized to make predictions for variables that possess continuous, real, or quantitative attributes. Examples of such factors encompass revenue, salary, age, and product pricing.

XG Boost Regression

To improve performance in comparison to standard Gradient Boosting, we incorporate parallel processing, regularisation, and second-order gradients.

Decision Tree Regression

Decision trees, characterized by their tree-like structure, are employed for constructing regression models. The dataset is partitioned into progressively narrower subsets based on the information gain value of each unique characteristic. This process gradually forms an associated decision tree. The result is a tree structure consisting of decision nodes and leaf nodes (Table **1** and **2**).

Table 1. Dataset example before data cleansing.

Sr.No	Car_Name	Year	Present Price	Selling Price	K/M Driven	FuelType	SellerType	Transmission	Owner
1	**i10**	2013	5.539	3.539	2700	Petrol	Owner	Auto	1
2	Brio	2011	6.524	2.524	41000	Diesel	Owner	Manual	0
3	Ciaz	2023	19.65	5.65	6700	Petrol	Dealer	Auto	3
4	Kwid	2015	14.75	9.75	2300	Diesel	Dealer	Manual	0
5	Vitara	2016	16.87	8.87	33450	Petrol	Owner	Auto	2

Table 2. Dataset example before data cleansing.

Sr.]No	CarName	Year	PresentPrice	SellingPrice	KmsDriven	SellerType	SellerType	Transference	Owner
1	i10	2014	5.59	3.59	28000	0	0	0	0
2	Brio	2013	9.54	4.54	43000	0	1	0	0
3	Ciaz	2017	7.25	9.85	6900	0	0	0	0
4	Kwid	2011	2.85	4.15	5200	0	0	0	0
5	Vitara	2014	4.60	6.87	42450	1	0	0	0

FUTURE SCOPE

Potential integration of this computer model with diverse web pages capable of providing real-time data for price forecasting is feasible. Incorporating a substantial amount of historical data on automotive prices could greatly enhance the accuracy of the machine-learning system. You can construct an Android application that functions as the interface for interacting with individuals and employ it. Our strategy involves meticulously designing intricate deep-learning network architectures, implementing adaptable learning rates, and conducting training on subsets of data instead of the entire dataset. In addition, we can employ sophisticated machine learning methods such as ensemble learning and random forests. These techniques build many decision/regression trees and effectively mitigate overfitting, resulting in more precise models.

CONCLUSION

Anticipating automotive expenses can be challenging due to a plethora of variables that must be considered. The acquisition and analysis of data are essential stages in creating a prediction. This study employed PHP to develop programs for data normalization, data standardization, and data purification. The goal of these programs was to eliminate unwanted noise from machine learning approaches. Data cleansing is a method that can be used to improve the accuracy of predictions. However, for intricate datasets such as the ones utilized in this work, further measures are necessary. The authenticity of the data acquired utilizing a single computer tool was less than 50%. Consequently, a multitude of machine-learning techniques have been introduced. The precision of this particular assemblage of machine learning methodologies is 92.38%. Employing a distinctive machine learning methodology is much less efficient in comparison to this substantial enhancement. The proposed strategy has the disadvantage of requiring significantly more computer resources in comparison to a single machine learning algorithm.

REFERENCES

[1] R.O. Lasisi, "Cybersecurity Workforce Readiness Recommender System Using NLP", *Proceedings of the Future Technologies Conference,* vol. 2, 2023 pp. 597-610 Cham
[http://dx.doi.org/10.1007/978-3-031-47451-4_43]

[2] S.P. Yadav, S. Zaidi, C.D.S. Nascimento, V.H.C. de Albuquerque, and S.S. Chauhan, "Analysis and Design of automatically generating for GPS Based Moving Object Tracking System", *2023 International Conference on Artificial Intelligence and Smart Communication (AISC),* 2023 pp. 1-5 Greater Noida, India
[http://dx.doi.org/10.1109/AISC56616.2023.10085180]

[3] T. Thamaraimanalan, M. Mohankumar, S. Dhanasekaran, and H. Anandakumar, "Experimental analysis of intelligent vehicle monitoring system using Internet of Things (IoT)", *EAI Endorsed Transactions on Energy Web,* vol. 8, no. 36, 2021.

[4] S.P. Yadav, and S. Yadav, "Fusion of Medical Images using a Wavelet Methodology: A Survey", *IEIE Transactions on Smart Processing & Computing,* vol. 8, no. 4, pp. 265-271, 2019.
[http://dx.doi.org/10.5573/IEIESPC.2019.8.4.265]

[5] X. Xue, R. Shanmugam, S. Palanisamy, O.I. Khalaf, D. Selvaraj, and G.M. Abdulsahib, "A hybrid cross layer with harris-hawk-optimization-based efficient routing for wireless sensor networks", *Symmetry (Basel),* vol. 15, no. 2, p. 438, 2023.
[http://dx.doi.org/10.3390/sym15020438]

[6] S.P. Yadav, and S. Yadav, "Fusion of Medical Images in Wavelet Domain: A Discrete Mathematical Modeling", In: *Solidar* vol. 14. , 2018, no. 25, pp. 1-11.
[http://dx.doi.org/10.16925/.v14i0.2236]

[7] V. Kumar, A.K. Gupta, R.R. Garg, N. Kumar, and R. Kumar, "The ultimate recommendation system: proposed Pranik System", *Multimedia Tools Appl.,* vol. 83, no. 14, pp. 43177-43198, 2023.
[http://dx.doi.org/10.1007/s11042-023-17370-x]

[8] S. P. Yadav, and S. Yadav, "Mathematical implementation of fusion of medical images in continuous wavelet domain", *Journal of Advanced Research in dynamical and control system,* vol. 10, no. 10, pp. 45-54, 2018.

[9] C.Z. Tsai, H. Huang, C.J. Wei, and M.C. Chiu, "Apply Deep Learning to Build a Personalized Attraction Recommendation System in a Smart Product Service System", In: *Leveraging Transdisciplinary Engineering in a Changing and Connected World.* IOS Press, 2023, pp. 151-160.
[http://dx.doi.org/10.3233/ATDE230607]

[10] R. Ramakrishnan, M. A. Mohammed, M. A. Mohammed, V. A. Mohammed, and J. Logeshwaran, "An

innovation prediction of DNA damage of melanoma skin cancer patients using deep learning", *2023 14th International Conference on Computing Communication and Networking Technologies (ICCCNT),* pp. 1-7, 2023.Delhi, India
[http://dx.doi.org/10.1109/ICCCNT56998.2023.10306749]

[11]   V. Sethi, R. Kumar, S. Mehla, A.B. Gandhi, S. Nagpal, and S. Rana, "LCNA-LSTM CNN based attention model for recommendation system to improve marketing strategies on e-commerce", *Journal of Autonomous Intelligence,* vol. 7, no. 1, 2023.
[http://dx.doi.org/10.32629/jai.v7i1.972]

[12]   M. A. Mohammed, V. A. Mohammed, R. Ramakrishnan, M. A. Mohammed, and J. Logeshwaran, "The three dimensional dosimetry imaging for automated eye cancer classification using transfer learning model", *2023 14th International Conference on Computing Communication and Networking Technologies (ICCCNT),* Delhi, India, pp. 1-6, 2023.
[http://dx.doi.org/10.1109/ICCCNT56998.2023.10307446]

[13]   C.M. Tang, Y.G. Zhao, and X. Yu, "Intelligent stock recommendation system based on generalized financial knowledge graph", *Third International Conference on Intelligent Computing and Human-Computer Interaction (ICHCI 2022),* vol. 12509, 2023 pp. 332-338
[http://dx.doi.org/10.1117/12.2655851]

[14]   K.R.K. Yesodha, A. Jagadeesan, and J. Logeshwaran, "IoT applications in Modern Supply Chains: Enhancing Efficiency and Product Quality", *2023 IEEE 2nd International Conference on Industrial Electronics: Developments & Applications (ICIDeA),* 2023 pp. 366-371 Imphal, India
[http://dx.doi.org/10.1109/ICIDeA59866.2023.10295273]

[15]   J. Lee, E. Na, K. Han, and D. Na, "Recommending K-Wave Items Tailored for Small-Sized Exporters by Incorporating Dense and Sparse Vectors", *Sustainability (Basel),* vol. 15, no. 22, p. 16098, 2023.
[http://dx.doi.org/10.3390/su152216098]

[16]   V.A.K. Gorantla, S.K. Sriramulugari, A.H. Mewada, and J. Logeshwaran, "An intelligent optimization framework to predict the vulnerable range of tumor cells using Internet of things", *2023 IEEE 2nd International Conference on Industrial Electronics: Developments & Applications (ICIDeA),* 2023 pp. 359-365 Imphal, India
[http://dx.doi.org/10.1109/ICIDeA59866.2023.10295269]

[17]   N. Wijerathne, J. Samarathunge, K. Rathnayake, S. Jayasinghe, S. Ahangama, and I. Perera, "Deep Learning Based Personalized Stock Recommender System", *International Conference on Neural Information Processing,* 2023 pp. 362-374 Singapore

[18]   S. Salagrama, "An Effective Design of Model for Information Security Requirement Assessment", *Int. J. Adv. Comput. Sci. Appl.,* vol. 12, no. 10, 2021.
[http://dx.doi.org/10.14569/IJACSA.2021.0121001]

[19]   S. Salagrama, Y.S. Boyapati, and V. Bibhu, "Security and Privacy of Critical Data in Ad Hoc Network Deployed Over Running Vehicles", *In 2022 3rd International Conference on Intelligent Engineering and Management (ICIEM),* 2022 pp. 411-414
[http://dx.doi.org/10.1109/ICIEM54221.2022.9853172]

[20]   Available from: https://www.kaggle.com/datasets/shree1992/housedata

CHAPTER 18

Crop Recommendation System

Samyak Jain[1,*], **Ashutosh Saxena**[1], **Aditya Garg**[1] and **Manu Singh**[1]

[1] *Department of Computer Science and Engineering, ABES Engineering College, Ghaziabad, India*

Abstract: Agriculture serves as a prominent source of employment for Indian farmers. A prevalent issue among Indian farmers is their inability to make informed decisions regarding crop selection based on soil type. It has a profound impact on productivity. Precision agriculture provides a solution to this issue. This strategy is characterized by the utilization of a soil database that is based on farms, the provision of crops by agricultural experts, and the satisfaction of specific requirements, such as soil quality, through the use of a dataset obtained from a soil testing laboratory. The soil-testing lab offers data derived from the system of recommendations. Subsequently, it will be employed to collect data and construct a band model by employing a technique of determining the outcome according to the preference of the majority. The researchers utilize an Artificial Neural Network (ANN) in conjunction with a Support Vector Machine (SVM) to provide precise recommendations for crop selection based on site-specific conditions and efficacy.

Keywords: ANN, Band model, Data, Majority vote process, Support vector machines.

INTRODUCTION

India is a prominent force in global agriculture. Approximately 60% of India's populace depends on agriculture as their primary source of livelihood. In FY 2021-22, the agriculture industry accounted for 18.8% of the total Gross value added. In 2019, the average monthly income per farming household in the country was INR 10,218. Based on the 2011 census, approximately 2000 farmers ceased agricultural activities on a daily basis [1, 2]. Approximately 1100 farmers in India took their own lives, representing 7% of the overall suicide rate in the country. The farmers utilize outdated and conventional techniques for farming and crop selection. The non-scientific methods of crop selection lead to the following issues: diminished profitability, reduced production, and declining soil quality [3 - 5]. Consequently, this leads to a decline in the number of farmers engaged in agri-

---

[*] **Corresponding author Samyak Jain:** Department of Computer Science and Engineering, ABES Engineering College, Ghaziabad, India; E-mail: samyakjain3305@gmail.com

Pankaj Kumar Mishra & Satya Prakash Yadav (Eds.)

culture, an increased rate of migration towards urban areas, and elevated levels of suicide. In order to address this issue and foster self-sufficiency among Indian farmers, we suggest implementing the following system: To facilitate the process of choosing crops, it is important to take into account soil parameters such as the ratio of nitrogen, potassium, and phosphorus, as well as the pH value [6, 7]. Additionally, environmental elements such as relative humidity, rainfall, and temperature should also be considered. The system is constructed utilizing machine learning techniques, enabling autonomous updates and continuous improvement. The suggested approach provides recommendations for both native and alien crops that are suitable for the specific soil and environmental conditions at a given time [8, 9].

Definition

Accurate crop production forecast is of utmost importance for federal and provincial decision-makers to facilitate prompt decision-making. Predictive models can assist farmers in determining optimal development and manufacturing timelines. There exist various methods for predicting agricultural crop yields [10].

Scope

The objective of the project is to ascertain the agricultural productivity of a location by graphically representing a dataset containing key factors such as temperature, humidity, rainfall, and crop yield. Regression models are employed for the purpose of forecasting a continuous variable [11].

RELATED WORKS

Agriculture is a primary source of income for Indians. Nevertheless, Indian ranchers diligently work in their fields, yet natural factors compromise their productivity. It is an indisputable fact that natural variables are unpredictable. Hence, the most efficient approach is to eliminate the majority of them from the equation while disregarding the organic factors. Soil degradation is a significant problem that can be prevented by cultivating the most suitable crops for the region [12]. Regardless of the rancher's choice of crop, the appropriate application of fertilizers would be beneficial. Another significant concern is insect infestation, which may be effectively addressed by using suitable pesticides. It will benefit cattle farmers. The government conducts many soil tests in India to examine the properties of the soil, but farmers need to gain knowledge on how to interpret the results of these tests [13]. Therefore, the Crop Recommendation System leverages all the benefits of the test and aids farmers with crop recommendations.

LITERATURE REVIEW

Agriculture is a major source of employment in India, and Indian farmers dedicate their utmost effort to provide sustenance to the population. Ranchers primarily oversee the cultivation and fertilization of crops. The Harvest proposal framework aims to support Indian farmers by utilizing the yield components. The topic of crop recommendation has been extensively researched. However, the various systems vary based on the parameters handled in the machine learning model. Many ML models employ random forests. Some use decision trees, while others utilize ensemble methods such as majority voting [14]. The primary explanation can be attributed to fragmented information. However, the Harvest proposal framework aggregated data from several sources and organized it to create a well-structured dataset. A word reference-based arrangement is implemented in the Harvest recommendation system. The yield proposal framework incorporates ISO 9001 and ISO 14001 standards [15]. The following is the analysis of many examination papers about the services offered by the Harvest recommendation system. The citation provided is from Rajak *et al.* on pages 951-952. The research examines crop predictions using several algorithms such as Support Vector Machines (SVM), Naive Bayes, Multi-layer Perceptron (ANN), and Random Forests. The parameters employed for crop prediction include pH, depth, water retention capacity, drainage, and erosion. The diagram below depicts the suggested recommendation framework. The pH level is slightly alkaline. The depth is greater than 90. The water holding capacity is low. The drainage is moderate [16]. If erosion is low, then it is suitable for growing paddy. (Dighe *et al.* 476-480) In other words, the study examined CHAID, KNN, Kimplies, Choice Tree, Brain Organisation, Innocent Bayes, C4.5, Fellow, IBK, and SVM algorithms and generated rules for the suggested framework. Various criteria, such as soil pH level, duration of growth, local climate, temperature, soil type, and others, were taken into consideration to determine the optimal crops for the estate. A study was conducted on area identification, information analysis, and storage, as well as comparative location detection and suggestion generation by Mokarrama and Arefin. The final Harvest was obtained using the physiographic information base, Warm zone data set, Harvest developing period data set, crop creation rate data set, and occasional yield data set [17]. The work by Gandge and Sandhya explores the topics of characteristic choice, numerous direct relapses, and choice trees using various algorithms such as ID3, SVM, brain organisations, C4.5, K-means, and K-nearest neighbors (KNN). The proposed framework consists of two main steps: firstly, the identification of a specific horticultural field, and secondly, the selection of a recently planted harvest [18]. The framework takes input from the client, pre-processes it, and then performs characteristic determination in the backend. A calculation of information characterization follows it, and finally, the framework suggests the yield. (Mishra *et al.*) In their study, the paper employed J48, Fellow Tree, LWL, and IBK algorithms for calculation. The primary tool used was WEKA [19]. The results revealed that the Chap tree had the lowest accuracy, although the errors could be reduced by pruning the tree. On the other hand, the IBK algorithm demonstrated high precision [20].

PROPOSED METHODOLOGY

Our suggested model incorporates both soil quality and environmental parameters. The soil factors considered are as follows:

- Nitrogen ratio.
- Phosphorus ratio.
- Potassium ratio.
- pH level.

The environmental factors considered are as follows:

- Temperature (in degrees Celsius).
- Rainfall (in millimeters).
- Percentage of relative humidity.

Both soil and environmental elements are considered as they can independently influence the suitability of a crop in a certain location. Soil conditions can be favorable for a crop, while the environmental conditions may not be, and vice versa. The user is required to input soil parameters, such as the nitrogen ratio and phosphorus ratio.

- The current sectors utilize costly IoT devices to evaluate soil health indicators such as nitrogen, phosphorus, potassium value, pH, *etc.*, which renders it impractical.
- The utilization of costly IoT devices for data collection poses a challenge in scaling the strategy to a wider audience. Our model suggests employing soil health cards as a solution to address this issue. The Government of India initiated the Soil Health Card program in 2015, which has resulted in the issuance of over 10 crore soil health cards to Indian farmers. A soil health card provides information on the nutrient composition of a farmer's property. It displays the soil's nutritional condition in relation to 12 criteria.
- The proportion of nitrogen, phosphorus, and potassium.
- Levels of sulphur.
- The values of zinc, iron, copper, manganese, and boron.

• The pH, EC, and OC (Physical Parameters).

Our approach utilizes the ratio of nitrogen, phosphorus, and potassium values, as well as the soil's pH, among these parameters. Our model utilizes a meteorological API to gather data on the environmental elements of rainfall, temperature, and humidity. Our approach incorporates supply and demand data as the third element. Based on the demand statistics of various crop commodities such as rice, wheat, maize, cereals, pulses, food grains, oilseeds, and sugarcane over five years, we will meet the demand in the next years. Fig. (**1**) shows the flowchart.

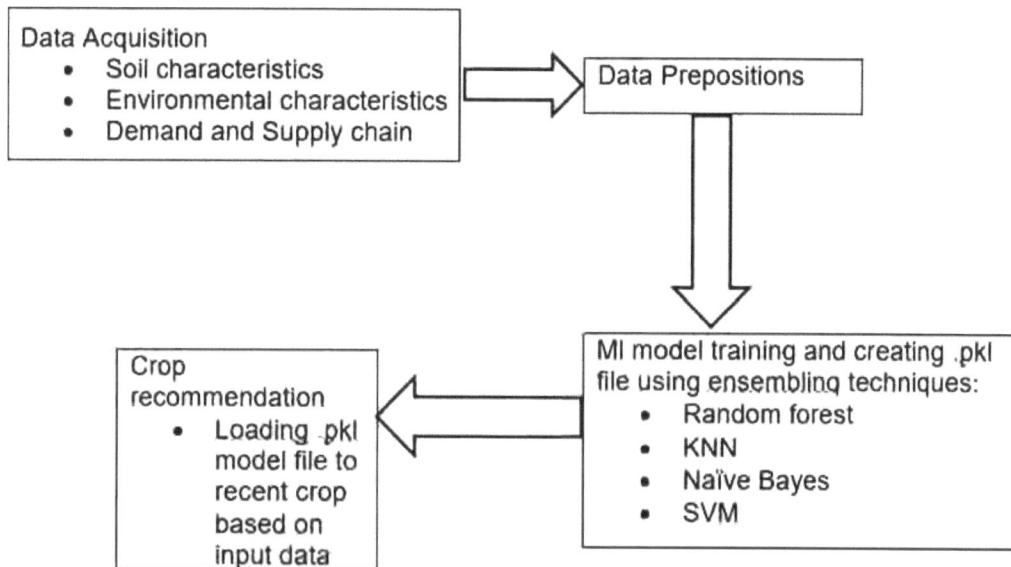

Fig. (1). Flowchart.

The subsequent section examines the implementation of the "Crop Recommendation System". The implementation of the Crop Recommendation system can be carried out in four distinct processes, which are outlined below:

Data Acquisition

The dataset can be obtained *via* Kaggle.

Values Input

Users are required to provide the site-specific characteristics, including N, P, and K (expressed as percentages), temperature (measured in °C), relative humidity (expressed as a percentage), rainfall (measured in millimeters), and pH.

ML Model Training and Creating .pkl File

The recommendation system utilizes an ensemble model employing a majority voting technique. The models that make up the constituents are:

- Support Vector Machine (SVM).
- Random Forest.
- Naive Bayes.
- k-Nearest Neighbours (kNN) upon completion of the training process, a .pkl file is generated.

Crop Recommendation

The .pkl file is loaded to provide crop recommendations depending on the input. Fig. (**2**) shows the methodology for crop recommendation.

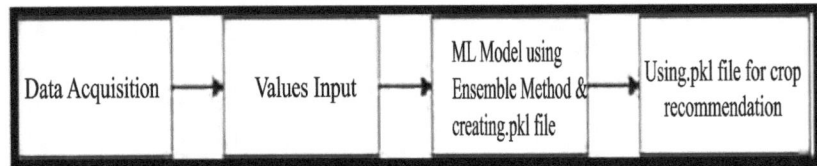

Fig. (2). Methodology for crop recommendation.

CONCLUSION AND RESULTS

The "Crop Recommendation System" can be determined from several perspectives. The precision score is used to evaluate the effectiveness of the arrangement in predicting the most suitable yield based on site-specific constraints using the ML model. A majority voting approach was employed in the gathering model. The pupils are Credulous Bayes, kNN, SVM, and Irregular Timberland. The precision score was determined to be 96.44%. The desired level of precision was set at 90%. However, the machine learning model was able to achieve a remarkable accuracy of 96.44%, making it highly estimable. The presentation metric focuses on the accuracy of preparation and approval, as well as the loss incurred during these processes. Our concept advocates for Indian farmers to cultivate crops that are compatible with their geographical and soil conditions. Our methodology assists farmers in making more informed crop choices by taking into account elements that are typically overlooked in traditional methodologies.

- This leads to reduced reliance on the importation of specialized crops.
- This contributes to the augmentation of farmers' revenue and fosters India's self-reliance.
- The diagram in Fig. (**1**) illustrates the operational process of our crop recommendation system.
- The diagram presented in Fig. (**3**) illustrates the methods employed in our crop recommendation system.
- Fig. (**3**) illustrates the comparative accuracy of various models throughout different epochs. An epoch is a precise moment in time that serves as a reference for a given period.
- Fig. (**4**) displays the precision of various models.

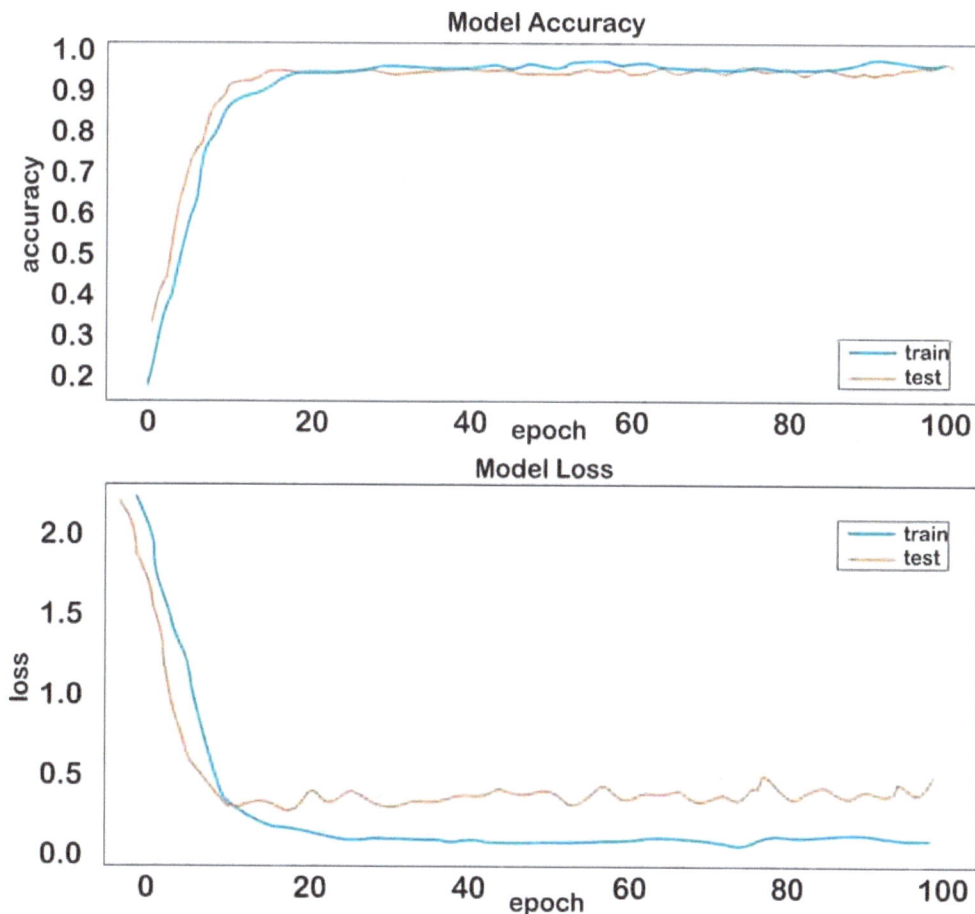

Fig. (3). Model Accuracy *vs* Epochs.

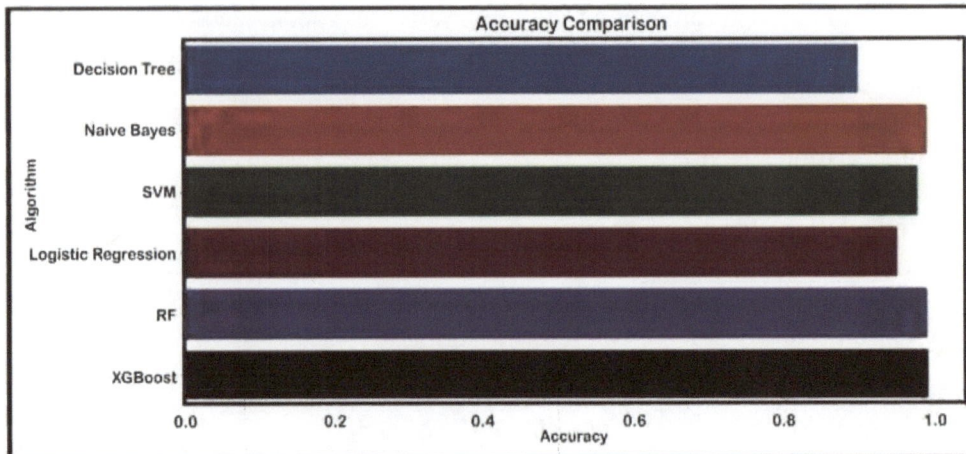

Fig. (4). Accuracy comparison of different models.

The accuracy and loss values in training and validation are presented in Table **1** above. Gap analysis are presented in Table **2**.

Table 1. Accuracy data.

-	Accuracy	Loss
Training	0.9699	0.0712
Validation	0.9520	0.4681

Table 2. Gap analysis.

S.No.	Name of Researcher, Year of Publication.	Paper Title	Parameters Used/Database Used.	Methodology Adopted/Modules Used.
1.	Rajak *et al.*,2017	Crop Recommendation System to Maximize Crop Yield Using Machine Learning Technique.	pH, depth, water holding capacity, drainage, erosion.	SVM is used as a classifier, naïve Bayes, Multilayer perceptron (ANN) and Random Forest.
2.	Dighe *et al*, 2018	Crop Recommendation System for Precision Agriculture.	The pH level of the soil, the month of cultivation, the weather in the region, temperature, type of soil.	CHAID, KNN, K-means, Decision Tree, NeuralNetwork, Naïve Bayes, C4.5, LAD, IBK And SVM

(Table 2) cont.....

S.No.	Name of Researcher, Year of Publication.	Paper Title	Parameters Used/Database Used.	Methodology Adopted/Modules Used.
3.	Mokarrama and Arefin, 2017.	RSF: A Recommendation System for Farmers.	Physiographic database, Thermal zone database, Crop growing period database, crop production rate database and seasonal crop database.	Location Detection, Data analysis and storage, Similar location detection and Recommendation generation.
4.	Gandge and Sandhya , 2017	A study on various data mining techniques for crop yield prediction.	Agricultural field, Crop previously planted.	Attribute selection, Multiple Linear Regression, and Decision Tree using ID3.

REFERENCES

[1] V. Vashisht, A.K. Pandey, and S.P. Yadav, "Speech Recognition using Machine Learning", *Transactions on Smart Processing & Computing,* vol. 10, no. 3, pp. 233-239, 2021.
[http://dx.doi.org/10.5573/IEIESPC.2021.10.3.233]

[2] S.P. Yadav, B.S. Bhati, D.P. Mahato, and S. Kumar, "Federated Learning for IoT Applications. EAI/Springer Innovations in Communication and Computing", *Springer International Publishing,* p. 85559-8, 2022.
[http://dx.doi.org/10.1007/978-3-030-85559-8]

[3] J. Kaur, J. Saxena, and J. Shah, "Facial Emotion Recognition. In 2022 International Conference on Computational Intelligence and Sustainable Engineering Solutions (CISES)", *International Conference on Computational Intelligence and Sustainable Engineering Solutions (CISES),* 2022.
[http://dx.doi.org/10.1109/CISES54857.2022.9844366]

[4] H. Yadav, S. Singh, K.K. Mishra, S. Srivastava, M.S. Naruka, and S.P. Yadav, "Brain Tumor Detection with MRI Images", *2022 International Conference on Computational Intelligence and Sustainable Engineering Solutions (CISES),* 2022.
[http://dx.doi.org/10.1109/CISES54857.2022.9844387]

[5] G. Ramesh, J. Logeshwaran, and K. Rajkumar, "The smart construction for image preprocessing of mobile robotic systems using neuro fuzzy logical system approach", *Neuroquantology,* vol. 20, no. 10, pp. 6354-6367, 2022.

[6] S. Raja, J. Logeshwaran, S. Venkatasubramanian, M. Jayalakshmi, N. Rajeswari, N.G. Olaiya, and W.D. Mammo, "OCHSA: Designing Energy-Efficient Lifetime-Aware Leisure Degree Adaptive Routing Protocol with Optimal Cluster Head Selection for 5G Communication Network Disaster Management", *Sci. Program.,* vol. 2022, pp. 1-11, 2022.
[http://dx.doi.org/10.1155/2022/5424356]

[7] B. Gopi, J. Logeshwaran, J. Gowri, and T. Kiruthiga, "The moment probability and impacts monitoring for electron cloud behavior of electronic computers by using quantum deep learning model", *Neuroquantology,* vol. 20, no. 8, pp. 6088-6100, 2022.

[8] P.S. Kumar, S. Boopathy, S. Dhanasekaran, and K.G. Anand, "Optimization of multi-band antenna for wireless communication systems using genetic algorithm", *2021 International Conference on Advancements in Electrical, Electronics, Communication, Computing and Automation (ICAECA),* pp. 1-6, 2021.
[http://dx.doi.org/10.1109/ICAECA52838.2021.9675686]

[9] S. Dhanasekaran, and J. Ramesh, "Channel estimation using spatial partitioning with coalitional game

theory (SPCGT) in wireless communication", *Wirel. Netw.,* vol. 27, no. 3, pp. 1887-1899, 2021.
[http://dx.doi.org/10.1007/s11276-020-02528-4]

[10] A. Bagwari, and G.S. Tomar, "Improved spectrum sensing technique using multiple energy detectors for cognitive radio networks", *Int. J. Comput. Appl.,* vol. 62, no. 4, pp. 11-21, 2013.
[http://dx.doi.org/10.5120/10067-4666]

[11] P. Whig, K. Gupta, and N. Jiwani, "Real-Time Detection of Cardiac Arrest Using Deep Learning", *AI-Enabled Multiple-Criteria Decision-Making Approaches for Healthcare Management* , p. 1-25, 2022.
[http://dx.doi.org/10.4018/978-1-6684-4405-4.ch001]

[12] K. Gulati, R.S. Kumar Boddu, D. Kapila, S.L. Bangare, N. Chandnani, and G. Saravanan, "A review paper on wireless sensor network techniques in Internet of Things (IoT)", *Mater. Today Proc.,* vol. 51, pp. 161-165, 2022.
[http://dx.doi.org/10.1016/j.matpr.2021.05.067]

[13] J. Wang, Y. Gao, W. Liu, A.K. Sangaiah, and H.J. Kim, "An intelligent data gathering schema with data fusion supported for mobile sink in wireless sensor networks", *Int. J. Distrib. Sens. Netw.,* vol. 15, no. 3, 2019.
[http://dx.doi.org/10.1177/1550147719839581]

[14] A. Ghosal, S. Halder, and S.K. Das, "Distributed on-demand clustering algorithm for lifetime optimization in wireless sensor networks", *J. Parallel Distrib. Comput.,* vol. 141, pp. 129-142, 2020.
[http://dx.doi.org/10.1016/j.jpdc.2020.03.014]

[15] B.M. Sahoo, R.K. Rout, S. Umer, and H.M. Pandey, "ANT colony optimization based optimal path selection and data gathering in WSN", *International Conference on Computation, Automation and Knowledge Management (ICCAKM),* pp. 113-119, 2020.
[http://dx.doi.org/10.1109/ICCAKM46823.2020.9051538]

[16] X. Wang, H. Chen, and S. Li, "A reinforcement learning-based sleep scheduling algorithm for compressive data gathering in wireless sensor networks", *EURASIP J. Wirel. Commun. Netw.,* vol. 2023, no. 1, p. 28, 2023.
[http://dx.doi.org/10.1186/s13638-023-02237-4]

[17] P.V.P. Raj, A.M. Khedr, and Z.A. Aghbari, "Data gathering *via* mobile sink in WSNs using game theory and enhanced ant colony optimization", *Wirel. Netw.,* vol. 26, no. 4, pp. 2983-2998, 2020.
[http://dx.doi.org/10.1007/s11276-020-02254-x]

[18] G.M. Abdulsahib, and O.I. Khalaf, "Accurate and effective data collection with minimum energy path selection in wireless sensor networks using mobile sinks", *J. Inf. Technol. Manage.,* vol. 13, no. 2, pp. 139-153, 2021.

[19] X. Du, Z. Zhou, Y. Zhang, and T. Rahman, "Energy-efficient sensory data gathering based on compressed sensing in IoT networks", *J. Cloud Comput. (Heidelb.),* vol. 9, no. 1, p. 19, 2020.
[http://dx.doi.org/10.1186/s13677-020-00166-x]

[20] O. Diallo, J.J.P.C. Rodrigues, M. Sene, and J. Lloret, "Distributed database management techniques for wireless sensor networks", *IEEE Trans. Parallel Distrib. Syst.,* vol. 26, no. 2, pp. 604-620, 2015.
[http://dx.doi.org/10.1109/TPDS.2013.207]

CHAPTER 19

A Smart System for Tracking and Analyzing Human Hand Movements using MediaPipe Technology and TensorFlow

Mahesh Kumar Singh[1,*], Arun Kumar Singh[2], Pushpa Choudhary[3], Pushpendra Singh[4] and Akhilesh Kumar Singh[5]

[1] *Dronacharya Group of Institutions, Greater Noida-201306, Uttar Pradesh, India*

[2] *Greater Noida Institute of Technology Gr Noida-201306, Uttar Pradesh, India*

[3] *Galgotias College of Engineering and Technology, Greater Noida-201306,Uttar Pradesh, India*

[4] *SRMIST Delhi NCR Campus Modi Nagar Ghaziabad UP 201204, Uttar Pradesh, India*

[5] *School of Computing and Technology, Galgotias University, Greater Noida 201306, Uttar Pradesh, India*

Abstract: Gesture recognition is the latest and the most popular technology nowadays. The main aim of this technology is to recognize human body parts using mathematical algorithms MediaPipe and TensorFlow. The hand is a very important part of the human body for performing any activity. The detection and analysis of body language have recently gained a lot of attention. In this paper, we look at the skeleton poses of a person. It is easy to grasp and have images with low dimensionality statistics. Underfed interpretations generalize a person's appearance and background, allowing them to be identified. This paper describes a real human chasing channel capable of anticipating the structure of both hands and the location of the fingers, focusing on motion recognition, and creating virtual hand brushes that can be very beneficial and easing activities like the selection of colors and paintings in combination with paint art. This paper, which uses hand gesture detection and has a 95% confidence accuracy rate, was built using MediaPipe, a deep learning framework, in addition to assessing numerous static or dynamic hand motion detection methods.

Keywords: Artificial intelligence, Deep hand gesture recognizer, Extensible calculators, HMMs, Hand tracking, MediaPipe, Machine learning, Paintbrush.

INTRODUCTION

According to a survey by Ipsos for the World Economic Forum, nearly 60% of individuals believe that AI-powered services and products will significantly

---

[*] **Corresponding author Mahesh Kumar Singh:** Dronacharya Group of Institutions, Greater Noida-201306, Uttar Pradesh, India; E-mail: maheshkrsg@gmail.com

Pankaj Kumar Mishra & Satya Prakash Yadav (Eds.)

impact daily life activities [1]. Artificial intelligence (AI) stands for imitating humanoid intelligence using robots, which are skilled in acting as well as thinking as persons. This expression may also be related to an appliance that exhibits capabilities like humans or persons such as knowledge gaining as well as the ability to solve complex problems. This type of intelligence has one of the strongest features, its power to investigate appropriate actions proven by showcasing the best possibility for attaining a particular goal. Artificial education is an application of intelligent retrieval, which corresponds to the concept of processor software learning in addition to the adaptation of changing information deprived of the assistance of humans. Artificial neural networks enable self-learning by consuming enormous amounts of raw data such as literature, images, and film. Machine learning has mostly played a significant role in today's modern civilization, as technology advances and simplifies all our daily tasks. At the same time, this is becoming more prominent because of recent advancements in the disciplines of artificial intelligence and machine learning. Any aspect of human life and society that has not been influenced by AI is nearly impossible to envisage or idealize. It always influences many aspects of our lives to help us become more productive with our time.

In today's innovative world, where technology is progressing as well as simplifying all our day-to-day tasks, artificial intelligence has always been playing a very prominent role. It has always been constantly influencing every facet of our lives to help us become more time-efficient [2]. Artificial intelligence now penetrates every aspect of our online lives, both personal and professional. Global communication and connectivity in business is a topic that is becoming increasingly important. Artificial intelligence and information science must be used, and their growth potential is limitless. Artificial intelligence is becoming increasingly important in a range of industries, including [3]:

- Medical science.
- Transportation.
- Banks and Financial Institutions.
- Entertainment and Gaming.

Our dependence on cell phones and virtualized assistants such as Alexa as well as Cortana, which respond to our inquiries, is an obvious and classic example of AI affecting our daily lives. As a result, current social media sites such as Facebook, Instagram, and Twitter account for a large portion of almost everyone's lives. Furthermore, the volume of data produced by humans and machines is much more numerous than our ability to absorb, analyze, evaluate, and make complex as well as correct decisions based just on computed data. Some recent statistics that have been recorded are given below:

- According to Statista [4], the worldwide Artificial Intelligence (AI) technology industry is expected to reach 126 billion USD by 2025.
- As per Gartner [5], 37% of companies have implemented AI in some manner. The number of organizations utilizing AI has increased by 270 percent in the previous four years.
- According to Servion Global Solutions [6], AI will power 95 percent of customer communications by 2025.
- The worldwide AI software business is expected to grow 54 percent annualized in 2020, reaching an estimated value of USD 22.6 billion, as per Statista's latest prediction [7].

AI is the foundation of all computer learning, and AI seems to be the future of all intelligent decision-making. Artificial Intelligence seems to have the power to accelerate our operations and procedures while retaining high precision and reliability, which is critical in today's environment. The capacity to be blunder-free, accurate, and fast at the same time is what distinguishes a useful and crucial tool [8].

RELATED WORK

The human hand is an essential tool for communication when people interact with one another and their environment in daily life. The identification of hand gestures and human actions is directly related to the postures and orientations of human hands. Because of this, accurately identifying human hands from single-color images or videos taken with conventional image sensors is essential in several computer vision applications [9, 10], such as human-computer interface, estimation of human hand posture, gesture recognition, activity analysis, and so forth. Hand tracking [11] is the method by which a computer detects a hand from an input image using computer vision and maintains focus on the hand's movement and position. Hand tracking allows you to create a variety of applications that use hand movement and orientation as input. Many computer vision tasks related to the human hand, such as hand pose estimation [12], hand gesture identification [13], and human activity analysis [14], have previously been a processing approach .

Gesture recognition is a popular issue in the field of Human-Computer Interaction [15, 16]. There are several data scientists and academicians, who have successfully used hand-gesture detection and identification including blind interpreters, wearable technology, and hand-controlled robotics [17] in recent decades; "A motion of a part of the human, such as hand or perhaps the forehead, that is meant to communicate a concept or a message," says the dictionary. Hand gestures were the first step in the evolution of communication in human history, according to evolutionary research, even newborn babies use hand gestures to communicate their wants before they can talk. Gestures may be used to interact with machines to convey or conduct actions. Hand gestures may be used to control virtual environments [18, 19], translate sign languages, control robots, and compose music, among other things. One of the most practical and popular solutions for increasing human-computer interaction is hand gesture recognition. Its use in gaming devices like the Xbox and PlayStation 4, as well as other devices such as computers and smartphones, has made it extremely popular in recent years. Hand identification is utilized in many areas.

In various technical fields and applications, hand shape and motion recognition can help improve the user experience. It can decode sign language, control hand gestures, and even overlay digital data and materials onto the real world in augmented reality. Reliable, instantaneous hand recognition is a difficult challenge for computer vision because palms are regularly separated (*e.g.*, due to finger/palm constraints and hand motion) and palms do not lack high dynamic range patterns. MediaPipe tackles this challenge with targeted recognition. MediaPipe is a slightly elevated hand and finger-tracking device [20]. Machine learning extracts 3D markers (ML) of 21 points of a hand from one image. While previous state-of-the-art systems relied on complex desktop environments for inference, our solution delivers real-time performance on mobile phones and can even scale to large numbers of users. MediaPipe Hands [21] has a deep learning pipeline. MediaPipe may be used to design a perception pipeline just as a graph that is directed and has modular parts called calculators. On a variety of devices and platforms, MediaPipe provides a collection of extensible calculators that can be used to perform activities like model interpretation, media data processing, and data conversions.

Gesture recognition in the past required the usage of extra hardware controllers or linked gloves that might register your user's intention through hand and arm motions. Microsoft's Kinect [22], which debuted in November 2010 and achieved a Guinness Book of World Records for the highest consumer item, is among the most well-known examples of such hardware gadgets. Today's technique, on the other hand, is mainly reliant upon Deep Learning Algorithms and Computer Vision technologies, with no hardware devices. This entire method is called as Air Gesture technology [23] since it needs not to look at the screen or your keyboard to interact with the computers. Recognition of hand shape and motion can assist in enhancing the experience of users all over a wide variety of technical areas and platforms. We show how to anticipate a hand movements from a snapshot by using a true on-device hand tracking approach. There is only one RGB camera. It is accomplished with MediaPipe, a cross-platform supervised learning application framework.

The raised MediaPipe Hand is a hand and finger-tracking gadget. It offers customized Python solutions that are ready to use. It establishes the foundation for understanding sign language and manipulating the hand's movements, as well as overlaying digital data and content over the physical environment in augmented reality. Because of the prevalence of handshakes and the lack of high-contrast patterns, humans have difficulty identifying hands in real time. Machine learning was used to extract 21 3D features of one hand (ML) [24, 25]. From a slice image region defined by the palm, the hand feature model generates meaningful 3D hand points. The pipeline is written as a MediaPipe structure that takes the hand-stop tracking subgraph from the hand-stops module and renders it using a special hand-rendered subgraph as shown in Fig. (**1**).

There are several approaches to gesture recognition, discussed here. Feature representation uses neural network models, HMMs, fuzzy C-means grouping, and orientation histograms. Figs. (**1a, 1b, 1c,** and **1d**) represent some collections of different gestures that can be used to implement specific actions in MediaPipe.

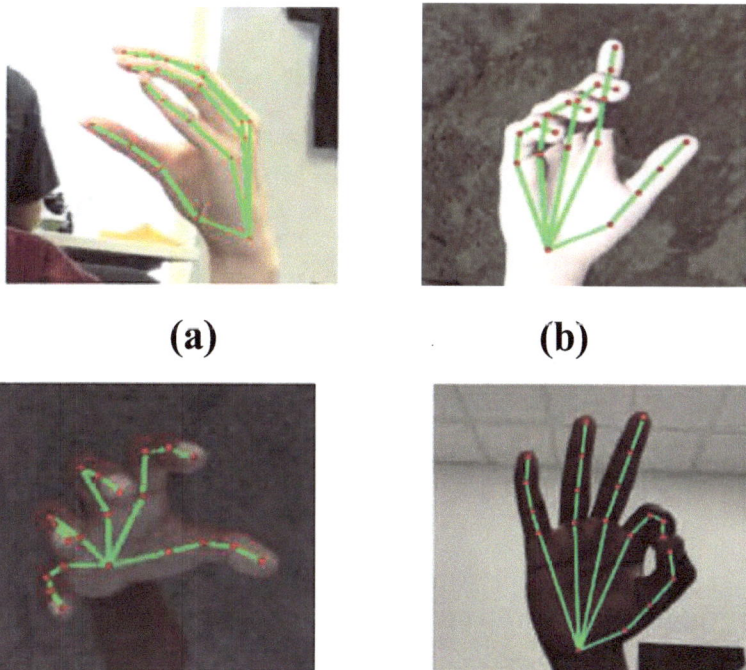

(a)   **(b)**

Fig. (1). Hands motion and shape detection.

Even feature extraction for capturing the shape of the hand requires multiple methodologies and algorithms. The gestures system's application areas are listed below. A full examination of contemporary recognition systems is also included, as well as an understanding of gesture recognition issues. The paper "Real-time Hand Gesture Recognition and Segmentation Using Convolutional Neural Networks" was presented by Okan Kop, Ahmet Gunduz, Neslihan Kose, and Gerhard Rigoll [26]. A unique two-model hierarchical design for authentic gesture recognition systems is described. The given architecture provides resource productivity, early detection methods, and point-in-time activation, all of which are essential in real-time action recognition applications.

In the paper titled "Virtual Vision-Based Hand Gesture Recognition: An Engineering Survey" [27], the researcher focused on developing a robust framework that could handle the most common challenges with less inconvenience and produce accurate and consistent hand motion detection results. Hand gesture recognition overcomes a shortcoming in the interactive system. Hand movements are more natural, simpler, more adaptable, and less expensive, without having to overcome difficulties caused by hardware devices. The hand gesture recognition method combines a hand-like algorithm, effective area ratio, and efficient edge computation [28]. When images of hands are twisted, stretched, and scaled, and also when multiple hand types are used, the most popular gesture-based algorithms proposed show low recognition rates. We present a new feature-based hand gesture recognition method that combines an efficient hand-like algorithm with an effective area ratio. After the samples were divided into groups according to the palm shape of the participants, training was performed using self-collected data. In this paper, we built a deep Hand Gesture Recognizer using the MediaPipe technology and TensorFlow in OpenCV. It is implemented in Python programming language.

WORKING OF THE PROPOSED MODEL

The MediaPipe graph for hand tracking using the object detection method is shown in Fig. (**2**). The graph is split into two sections; one is for human hand detection [29] and another for landmark computation. The palm sensor is an essential characteristic of MediaPipe to save significant processing time. This is done by extracting the palm placement in the actual video frame from the computed hand features inside the previous frame, eliminating the need to employ the palm sensor on each frame. For further robustness, the hand-tracking model generates an extra variable that represents the probability of palm positioning in the input crop. Whenever the probability falls below the minimum threshold, then the hands classification method is implemented in the next frame.

The hand gesture recognition [30] method incorporates a deep learning system that uses a variety of models, including a hand direction bounding box turned back by an active palm, and full image animation from the palm finder - cropped image area. The hand marker model provides higher 3D hand function points. There are 21 arc palm markers in total, which provide information about x, y, and comparison depth.

When the hand landmark model is supplied with a precisely cropped hand image, the demand for data preprocessing (*e.g.* rotations, translations, and scaling) is considerably decreased; allowing the networks to focus on coordinates prediction accuracy instead. Crops could also be built in our pipeline based on hand landmarks detected in the previous film, with the use of palm detection once the marker model can no longer detect hand presence.

The palm detection model [31] aims to recognize the initial hand position, and we designed a unique detection model optimized for real-time mobile applications, similar to the recognition method face in MediaPipe Face Mesh. Hands are difficult to recognize with our lightweight, full-featured models, as they must detect obscured palms as well as self-closing palms and work on a wide range of hand sizes with large proportions (> 20x) compared to the frame of the picture. The faces displayed significantly contrasting patterns around the eyes and mouth, but not the hands, making it even more difficult to recognize people based on their visual parts alone. Instead, providing other information, such as arm, body, or human features, helps determine the correct hand position. To address these challenges, our plan combines multiple approaches.

Landmark Model by Hand

Subsequent to palm recognition across the entire image, the following hand landmarks algorithm utilizes regress for precisely localizing 21 three-dimensional hand-knuckle coordinates within the recognized hand sections. This model produces a consistent interior hand posture representation with even faintly visible hands. The method comprises three outputs, as shown in the diagram:

Step 1. There are 21 x, and y, as well as relative depth hand landmarks.

Step 2. A hand flag indicates the existence of a palm in the input image.

Step 3. The binary classification of handedness is left or right hand.

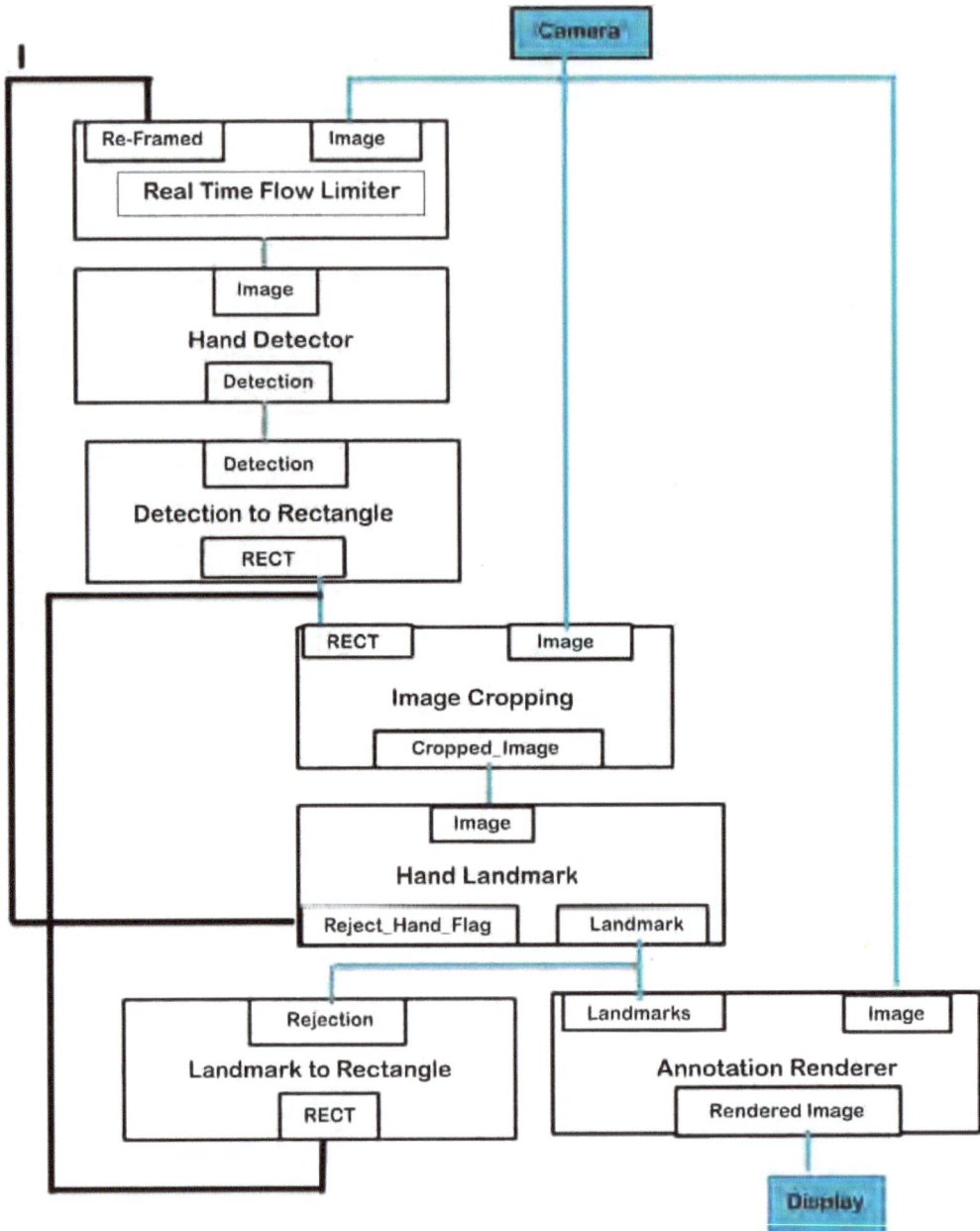

Fig. (2). Object detection workflow.

2D locations are learned from different datasets, with both the relative thickness w.r.t. a wrist point learned only from synthetic photos, as previously stated. We created a fresh model output, identical to the one that generates the chance that a correctly oriented hand is found in the given crop, for recovery from tracking failure. If the score goes below a certain level, the detector is triggered, and tracking is restarted. Consequently, a binary classifier head (see Fig. **3**) was constructed to detect whether the input hand was left or right.

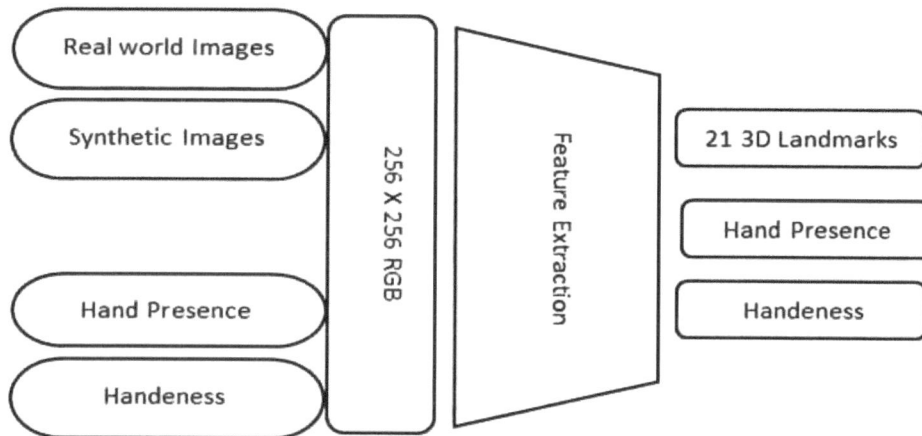

Fig. (3). Feature extraction.

Experimental Work

To obtain ground truth information for multiple aspects of the problem, we created the following datasets: This dataset contains 6K photographs of a variety of themes, including geographic diversity, lighting conditions, and hand appearance. The absence of complex hand articulation in this dataset is a disadvantage. An in-house collection of gestures contains ten thousand images depicting all physically possible hand gestures from various angles. The dataset's flaw is that it was assembled from only 30 people with minimal diversity in their backgrounds. The in-the-wild as well as in datasets work well together to boost robustness.

To further cover all probable hand locations and provide extra depth monitoring, we generate an elevated artificial hand model over several backgrounds and transfer it to the appropriate 3D coordinates. To control the thicknesses of the fingers plus palm, we use a commercial digital hand model featuring 24 bones as well as 36 blend shapes. There are five different skin tones as well as textures included with the figurine. We sampled 100K pictures from the movies and created a video sequence of hand position shifting. Three different lenses as well as a random high-dynamic-range illumination situation were used to produce each position see Fig. (**4**).

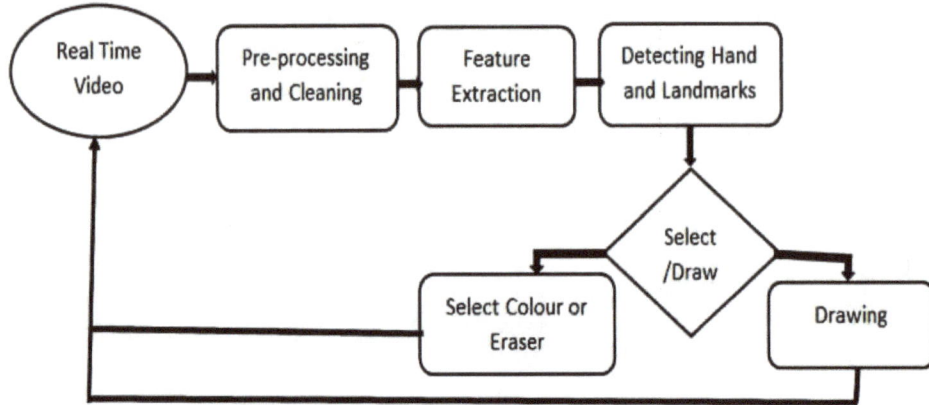

Fig. (4). Work flow of the proposed model.

Procedure

First, we capture the image of a hand, and then two types of features are extracted namely, local and global features. The local features are extracted using geometric central moments in two different moments X_{00} and X_{11} using Equation **1**.

$$X_{pp} = \sum_{x}\sum_{y}(x - X_x)^p(y - X_y)^p f(x,y) \tag{1}$$

$$X_{pp}^k = \sum_{y}\sum_{x}(x^k - X_x^k)^p(y^k - X_y^k)^p . f(x^k, y^k) \tag{2}$$

$$\forall k \in \{1,2,3 \ldots \ldots \ldots 88 \ \& \ \forall p \in \{0,1\}$$

Where X_x and X_y are the mean values of the input feature area of x, and y coordinates and the input image is represented by 88*2 features as shown in Equation **2**. The global features for both the first and second moments are computed for the whole hand area. The primary concept is to identify the hand and other necessary features. There are two modes one is selection and the other is drawing. If the user selects the selection mode, the user has two options either to choose the paint color brush or choose an Eraser. While, in the drawing mode, the user has just one option to draw the desired image or to create art. The index finger and middle finger are used for drawing and selection purposes, and Equation **3** is used to identify upward and downward fingers.

$$self.ImsList[self.tipIds[0]][1]$$
$$< self.ImsList[self.tipIds[0] - 1][1]$$

(3)

A hand landmark model is used to generate high-fidelity 3D hand key points from a clipped picture area. We know that the index and middle fingers are the most used fingers, therefore we chose to employ these fingers to simplify the procedure since they are user-friendly and simple to learn and apply. Therefore, we know that the most utilized node markers for effective tool usage are the top nodes of each finger. To employ the model, these crucial points are saved in an array as follows: [4, 8, 12, 16, 20,]. For sketching and selection purposes, indicator finger and the middle finger are used, respectively. To determine the upward and the downward finger motion, Equation **4** is used.

$$self.ImsList[self].tipIds[0][1]$$
$$\geq [self.tipds[0] - 1].self.ImsList[1]$$

(4)

From a clipped image region, a hand landmark model is employed to produce high-fidelity 3D hand key points.

Table **1** and Fig. (**5**) depict the suggested nomenclature for fingers referring to this model for easy universal understanding. It shows the real-time human-hand comparable node position with the node number stating the most used fingers along with their most used nodes.

Table 1. Finger points nomenclature.

Points	Nomenclature	Points	Nomenclature
0	Wrist	11	Middle_Finger_DIP
1	Thumb_CMC	12	Middle_Finger_TIP
2	Thumb_MCP	13	Ring_Finger_MCP
3	Thumb_IP	14	Ring_Finger_PIP
4	Thumb_TIP	15	Ring_Finger_DIP
5	Index_Finger_MCP	16	Ring_Finger_TIP
6	Index_Finger_PIP	17	Pinky_MCP
7	Index_Finger_DIP	18	Pinky_PIP
8	Index_Finger_TIP	19	Pinky_DIP
9	Middle_Finger_MCP	20	Pinky_TIP
10	Middle_Finger_PIP	-	-

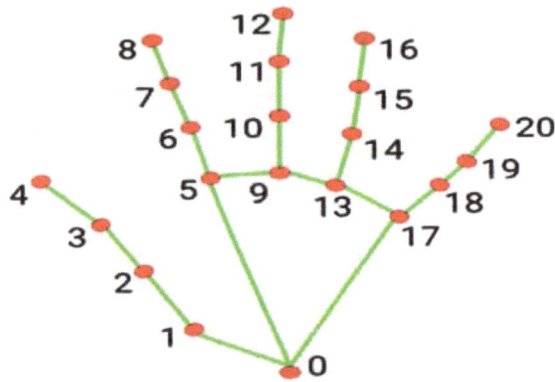

Fig. (5). Node position of the hand.

Algorithm of the Model

The frame dimensions are 720, and 1280, where: 1280 is the frame's horizontal length and 720 is the frame's vertical depth.

Steps for Thumb:

Step 1: Determine whether self.lmList[self] exists .tipIds[0]] [1] [self.tipIds[0] - 1 [1]] self.lmList

Step 2: If it is true, then go to step 3; else, go to step 4.

Step 3: the fingers.append(1)

Step 4: Finally, the fingers.append(0)

Steps for Fingers:

Step-1: While id is within the acceptable range (1, 5)

Step-2: Verify self.lmList[self.tipIds[id]] [2] is true. 2 [2]: self.lmList[self.tipIds[id]

Step-3: If it is true, go to step 4; else, go to step 5.

Step-4: fingers.append(1)

Step-5: fingers.append(0)

Steps in the Selection Mode:

Step-1: If finger [1] and [2] are equal,

Step-2: Set xp and yp to 0.

Step-3: Determine whether y1 is greater than 125:

Step-4: Verify that 250 x 1 = 450:

Step-5: If it is true, go to step 6; else go to step 8.

Step-6: overlayList[0] = header

Step-7: drawColor = (255, 0, 255)

Step-8: If 550 x 1= 750, then

Step-9: If it is true, go to step 10; else go to step 12.

Step-10: header = overlayList [1]

Step-11: drawColor = (255, 0, 0)

Step-12: Otherwise, if 800 x 1 950:

Step-13: If it is true, go to step 14; else, go to step 17.

Step-14: header = overlayList [2]

Step-15: drawColor = (0, 255,0)

Step-16: Else if 1050 < x1 < 1200

Step-17: If it is true, then go to step 18

Step-18: header = overlayList [3]

Step-19: drawColor = (0, 0, 0)

Steps in the Drawing Mode:

Step-1:Check if fingers [1] and not fingers [2]

Step-2: then cv2.circle(img, (x1, y1), 15, draw Color, cv2.FILLED)

Step-3: if xp == 0 and yp == 0

Step-4: If it is true, then go to Step 5 otherwise to Step 7

Step-5: xp = x1

Step-6: yp = y1

Step-7: Check if drawColor == (0, 0, 0):

Step-8: If it is true, then go to step 9 otherwise to step 11

Step-9: cv2.line(img, (xp, yp), (x1, y1), drawColor, eraserThickness)

Step 10: cv2.line(imgCanvas, (xp, yp), (x1, y1), drawColor, eraserThickness)

Step 11:else goto step 12

Step 12: cv2.line(img, (xp, yp), (x1, y1), drawColor, brushThickness)

Step 13: cv2.line(imgCanvas, (xp, yp), (x1, y1), drawColor, brushThickness)

Step 14: Stop

Whenever we speak about detection, whether it is of an item, a person, an animal, or, in our case, hands, the first step is to establish the model with proper parameters. This is true regardless of whether we're using Mediapipe or Yolo, but initializing the model is crucial.

Code-breakdown

- In the first phase, we used the Mediapipe library's process function to save the hand landmarks detection results in a variable, as well as convert the picture from BGR to RGB.
- Before moving on to the next phase, we will check for some validation, such as if the points were detected or not, and whether the variable included any results.
- If affirmative, we will loop over all of the identified locations in the picture that include the hand's landmarks points.
- We can see that there are just two iterations in the other loop since we only want to show two hand landmarks.
- Finally, we will print out all of the landmark points that have been discovered and filtered according to the criteria.

We used regression to precisely pinpoint 21 3-dimensional hand-knuckle locations inside the recognized hand portions after performing palm recognition over the entire image. The model depicts a continuous internal palm posture with weakly visible hands and self-occlusions. The palm detection model aims to recognize initial hand positions, so we designed a unique detection model optimized for mobile applications in real-time, similar to the face recognition as shown above. We manually labeled 30,000 real-world photos with 21 3D locations to provide database truth (where we took the Z value of corresponding image depth map if it exists according to the required corresponding coordinates). We also created a second high-quality prosthetic hand model with multiple backgrounds and converted it into the necessary 3D coordinates to cover all accessible hand positions and provide additional monitoring of this type of hand.

RESULTS AND DESCRIPTION

With the assistance of Artificial Intelligence and Machine Learning, we have designed an application, wherein, the interested user can virtually design the desired art or picture and idealize their thoughts to shape the art with the support of various accessible color variants. This achieves real-time performance on multiple platforms. The model detects the hand motion at the front of the lens and draws on the screen in response to it. This is achieved through the beautifully designed user interface, which is easily approachable and user-friendly. Once reached there, one can easily sketch his or her desired art or write down notes or anything using the three-color palettes showcased using three brushes, along with an eraser to reduce error. Also, a user is provided with the advantage of brush thickness. According to the preferences, the user can pick up the desired brush thickness and go ahead with creative exploration.

We first established a new model, then read the picture to check the source images, and scaled down the landmark's points for pre-processing; however, those points were not significant to the user, so we restored this to the original state, and last, we painted the landmark points on the image. Media Pipe's solutions are straightforward. The efficient interpersonal relationships has been aided by such sign language recognition technology. The use of hand gesture recognition has shown a lot of promise in the technology industry. This paper, which uses hand gesture detection and has a 95% confidence accuracy rate, was built using Media Pipe, a deep learning framework. In addition to assessing numerous static or dynamic hand motion detection methods, we wish to enhance our system by interacting with other devices and human body parts. Using a big fake dataset reduces visible jitter between frames, in addition to boosting quality. As more than just a consequence of this finding, we feel that real-world databases should be expanded to increase generality. Overall, it is a nice, quickly growing collection with promising results. The bulk of challenges that happen while working on such a deep learning project are eliminated by using MediaPipe in projects. There is no need to be concerned about synchronization or difficult settings. This allows you to focus on the actual development process.

The prediction quality of hand movements is analyzed using three different criteria; Tracking pipeline (baseline), Pipeline without re-crops, and Pipeline with re-crops in Mean error per hand (MEH) parameter. From Fig. (**6**), it can be seen that hand tracking prediction with re-crop is much better than the other two criteria.

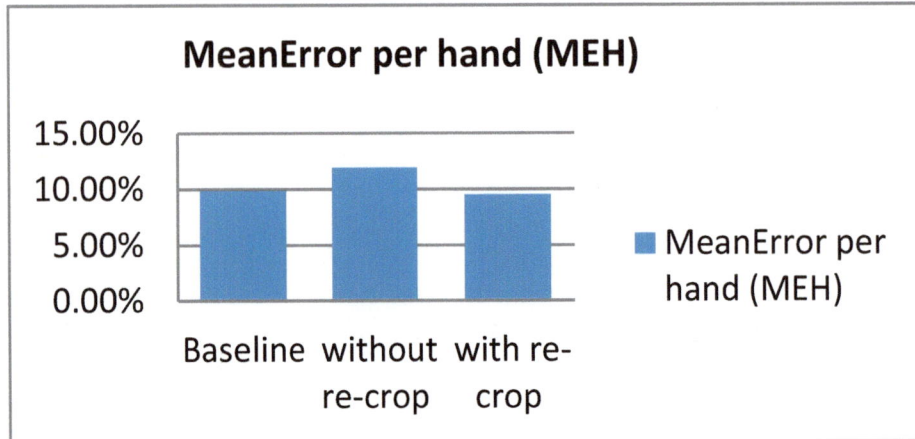

Fig. (6). Hand recognition quality graph.

CONCLUSION AND FUTURE SCOPE

This paper has discussed the concept of a hand gesture recognition system using Media Pipes to build efficient human-machine interaction. There is a wide range of technologies in this field, but Media Pipe as a framework using machine learning plays a vital role in improving the performance of the system with 95% confidence accuracy. The quality of the model is measured in terms of mean error per hand parameter and compared with various baseline methods with and without re-corp. We will extend our model to develop collaboration with other AI devices and other parts of the human body in a static and dynamic nature.

REFERENCES

[1]   Availble from: https://www.weforum.org/agenda/2021/11/what-worries-the-world-ipsos-survey/

[2]   I.H. Sarker, "AI-Based Modeling: Techniques, Applications and Research Issues Towards Automation, Intelligent and Smart Systems", *SN Computer Science,* vol. 3, no. 2, p. 158, 2022. [http://dx.doi.org/10.1007/s42979-022-01043-x] [PMID: 35194580]

[3]   T. Davenport, A. Guha, D. Grewal, and T. Bressgott, "How artificial intelligence will change the future of marketing", *J. Acad. Mark. Sci.,* vol. 48, no. 1, pp. 24-42, 2020. [http://dx.doi.org/10.1007/s11747-019-00696-0]

[4]   https://www.statista.com/statistics/607716/worldwide-artificial-intelligence-market-revenues/

[5]   Availble from: https://marketbusinessnews.com/ai-gartner-survey/194856/

[6]   Availble from: https://aibusiness.com/document.asp?doc_id=760184

[7]   Availble from: https://www.statista.com/statistics/607960/worldwide-artificial-intelligence-market-growth/

[8]   M. Darrell, and R. West John, "Report how artificial intelligence is transforming the world", 2018.

[9]   M.K. Singh, and O.P. Rishi, "Dynamic Knowledge-based Recommendation System for E-commerce using Deep Neural Network", *Mathematics in Engineering, Science, and Aerospace (MESA)*, vol. 12, no. 4, pp. 1023-1036, 2021.

[10]   N. Shahdadpuri, "Real Image of Computer Vision Application and its Impact: Future and Challenges", *Wesleyan Theol. J.*, vol. 13, no. 62, 2020.

[11]   Z. Chen, "Real-Time Hand Gesture Recognition Using Finger Segmentation", *The Scientific World Journal*, vol. 2014, p. 9, 2014.

[12]   S. Saremi, S. Mirjalili, and A. Lewis, "Vision-based hand posture estimation using a new hand model made of simple components", *Optik (Stuttg.)*, vol. 167, pp. 15-24, 2018.
[http://dx.doi.org/10.1016/j.ijleo.2018.02.069]

[13]   R. Zaman Khan, and N.A. Ibraheem, "Hand Gesture Recognition: A Literature Review", *International Journal of Artificial Intelligence & Applications*, vol. 3, no. 4, pp. 161-174, 2012. [IJAIA].
[http://dx.doi.org/10.5121/ijaia.2012.3412]

[14]   J-H. Sun, T-T. Ji, and S-B. Zhang, J. -K. Yang a G. -R. Ji, "Research on the Hand Gesture Recognition Based on Deep Learning", *12th International Symposium on Antennas, Propagation and EM Theory (ISAPE)*, pp. 1-4, 2018.

[15]   M.K. Singh, "O. P. Rishi."Knowledge-Based Recommendation System for Online Business Using Web Usage Mining", In: *Rising Threats in Expert Applications and Solutions.*, V.S. Rathore, N. Dey, V. Piuri, R. Babo, Z. Polkowski, J.M.R.S. Tavares, Eds., vol. 1187. Advances in Intelligent Systems and Computing, 2021, pp. 293-300.
[http://dx.doi.org/10.1007/978-981-15-6014-9_34]

[16]   M.A. Rady, S.M. Youssef, and S.F. Fayed, "Smart Gesture-based Control in Human-Computer Interaction Applications for Special-need People", *Novel Intelligent and Leading Emerging Sciences Conference (NILES)*, pp. 244-248, 2019.
[http://dx.doi.org/10.1109/NILES.2019.8909324]

[17]   J.S. Raheja, R. Rajsekhar, and A. Prasad, "Real-Time Robotic Hand Control Using Hand Gestures. Robotic Systems - Applications", *Control and Programming*, vol. 2012, pp. 413-428, 2012.

[18]   A. Alnuaim, M. Zakariah, W.A. Hatamleh, H. Tarazi, V. Tripathi, and E.T. Amoatey, "Human-Computer Interaction with Hand Gesture Recognition Using ResNet and MobileNet", *Comput. Intell. Neurosci.*, vol. 2022, no. 16, pp. 1-16, 2022.
[http://dx.doi.org/10.1155/2022/8777355] [PMID: 35378817]

[19]   Ö. Çelik, "A Research on Machine Learning Methods and Its Applications", *Journal of Educational Technology and Online Learning*, vol. 1, no. 3, pp. 25-40, 2018.

[20]   F. Zhang, V. Bazarevsky, A. Vakunov, A. Tkachenka, G. Sung, C. L. Chang, M. rundmann, "MediaPipe Hands: On-device Real-time Hand Tracking", *ArXiv*, pp. 1-5, 2018.

[21]   G.S. Sung, K. Uboweja, E. Bazarevsky, V. Baccash, J. Bazavan, and E. Chang, *Chuo-Ling & Grundmann, Matthias.*, On-device Real-time Hand Gesture Recognition, pp. 1-5, 2021.

[22]   L. Cruz, D. Lucio, and L. Velho, "Kinect and RGBD Images: Challenges and Applications", *2012 25th SIBGRAPI Conference on Graphics, Patterns and Images Tutorials, Ouro Preto, Brazil*, pp. 36-49, 2012.
[http://dx.doi.org/10.1109/SIBGRAPI-T.2012.13]

[23]   X. Dang, Y. Liu, Z. Hao, X. Tang, and C. Shao, "Air Gesture Recognition Using WLAN Physical Layer Information", *Wirel. Commun. Mob. Comput.*, vol. 2020, pp. 1-14, 2020.
[http://dx.doi.org/10.1155/2020/8546237]

[24]   I.H. Sarker, "Machine Learning: Algorithms, Real-World Applications and Research Directions", *SN Computer Science*, vol. 2, no. 3, pp. 160-181, 2021.

[http://dx.doi.org/10.1007/s42979-021-00592-x] [PMID: 33778771]

[25]   M.K. Singh, and O.P. Rishi, "Event Driven Recommendation for E-commerce using Knowledge-based Collaborative Filtering Technique", *Scalable Computing: Practice and Experience,* vol. 21, no. 6, pp. 369-378, 2020.
[http://dx.doi.org/10.12694/scpe.v21i3.1709]

[26]   O. Köpüklü, A. Gunduz, N. Kose, and G. Rigoll, "Real-time Hand Gesture Detection and Classification Using Convolutional Neural Networks", *Published at IEEE International Conference on Automatic Face and Gesture Recognition,* p. 1-8, 2019.
[http://dx.doi.org/10.1109/FG.2019.8756576]

[27]   P. Shah, K. Pandya, H. Shah, and J. Gandhi, "Survey on Vision based Hand Gesture Recognition", *Int. J. Comput. Sci. Eng.,* vol. 7, no. 5, pp. 281-288, 2019.
[http://dx.doi.org/10.26438/ijcse/v7i5.281288]

[28]   X. Wang, J. Jiang, Y. Wei, L. Kang, and Y. Gao, "Research on Gesture Recognition Method Based on Computer Vision", *MATEC Web of Conferences,* 2018.
[http://dx.doi.org/10.1051/matecconf/201823203042]

[29]   R. Sutoyo, B. Prayoga, D.S. Fifilia, and M. Shodiq, "The Implementation of Hand Detection and Recognition to Help Presentation Processes", *Procedia Computer Science,* vol. 59, pp. 550-558, 2015.
[http://dx.doi.org/10.1016/j.procs.2015.07.539]

[30]   M. Yasen, and S. Jusoh, "A systematic review on hand gesture recognition techniques, challenges and applications", *PeerJ Comput. Sci.,* vol. 5, p. e218, 2019.
[http://dx.doi.org/10.7717/peerj-cs.218] [PMID: 33816871]

[31]   I. Bonet, F. Caraffini, A. Peña, A. Puerta, and M. Gongora, "Oil Palm Detection *via* Deep Transfer Learning", *2020 IEEE Congress on Evolutionary Computation (CEC),* pp. 1-8, 2020.
[http://dx.doi.org/10.1109/CEC48606.2020.9185838]

CHAPTER 20

Initiatives for Challenges Faced By Developed Countries and India on Green Growth and Sustainable Development in the World

Shalin Kumar[1,*], Parul Verma[2], Hoshiyar Singh Kanyal[3], Praveen Chandra Jha[4] and Jyoti Rai[5]

[1] *Department of Applied Science, Greater Noida Institute of Technology, Greater Noida, (U.P), India*

[2] *Depatment of Applied Science and Humanities, Ajay Kumar Garg. Engineering College, Ghaziabad, (U.P.), India*

[3] *Depatment of Computer Science & Engg., Hi-Tech Institute of Engineering and Technology, Ghaziabad, (U.P), India*

[4] *Depatment of Applied Science and Humanities, ITS Engineering College, Greater Noida (U.P.), India*

[5] *Depatment of Applied Science and Humanities R.D. Engineering College, Ghaziabad, (U.P.), India*

Abstract: Most of the countries are facing challenges in green growth and sustainable development, which affects the world's economy and raises issues related to the environment and eco-system. In this manuscript, we studied and analyzed data on green growth indicators that influence the ecosystem, environment, land resources, biodiversity, and the lifestyle of human beings. Initiatives and strategies that are outlined in this manuscript provide concrete recommendations and measurement tools to support countries to overcome the issues related to air pollution, carbon productivity, land resources, climate change, and water and energy sectors in green growth and sustainable development.

Keywords: Air-pollution, Biodiversity, Carbon productivity, Climate change, Energy, Green growth, Land resources, Water.

* **Corresponding author Shalin Kumar:** Department of Applied Science, Greater Noida Institute of Technology, Greater Noida, (U.P), India; E-mail: shalinkumar@rediffmail.com

INTRODUCTION

Green growth refers to the promotion and efficient utilization of natural resources in order to mitigate the environmental dangers that constitute a threat to all life forms on Earth [1]. According to the union budget for 2023-24, Green growth and sustainable development are among the seven main priorities (SAPTRISHI) for promoting the green industrial and economic transition, environmentally friendly agriculture, and sustainable energy in the country [2]. The National Action Plan on Climate Change (NAPCC), in alignment with the State Action Plan on environmental protection, is a significant achievement in integrating green growth and sustainable development [3]. The concept of green growth extends beyond climate change and adaptation, focusing on the sustainable development of the country [4]. The MOEFCC (Ministry of Environment, Forest and Climate Change) aims to identify the fundamental factors contributing to the elimination of poverty, while also promoting environmentally sustainable economic development. The Finance Commission of India and the Central Government are collaborating to reassess policies about green growth and their effects on the environment, ecosystem, and natural resources that are accessible to impoverished and vulnerable populations [5]. In addition, the Indian Government has implemented the smart city mission, which seeks to foster communities that offer a high standard of living to their residents in various aspects, including infrastructure, cleanliness, sustainability, and a pollution-free environment. Environmental performance has a positive correlation with the economic growth of countries.

RELATIVE WORKS

By examining both perspectives on this matter, the effort aims to ascertain methods through which both nations might collaborate in order to establish more environmentally friendly policies that are advantageous to all [6]. The program focuses on addressing difficulties arising from environmental, economic, and social considerations and offers customized solutions that cater to the unique needs and capacities of each country [7]. In addition, the program aims to investigate how collaborations between developed countries and India might narrow the divide between them and foster enhanced environmentally friendly economic growth and sustainable development for both nations [8]. Recently, the world has encountered an unparalleled obstacle in achieving sustainable development and promoting environmentally friendly economic growth [9]. Developed nations, specifically, have faced mounting demands to decrease carbon emissions and achieve energy efficiency goals [10]. As a result, there has been a rise in the development of advanced computational models that are designed to address and overcome this challenge effectively [11]. Two highly effective models implemented by the EU are the Clean Energy Package and the Eco-Innovation framework. These models have played a significant role in advancing secure and environmentally friendly energy efforts in various sectors [12]. The Ministry of Environment [13], Forest and Climate Change (MoEFCC) in India is leading the country's efforts towards sustainable development and environmentally friendly growth [14]. This is being achieved through the implementation of initiatives like the National Mission on Sustainable Development (NMSD) and the National Action Plan on Climate Change (NAPCC). These programs align with multiple research endeavors that aim to promote the utilization of data-driven and evidence-based computational models to create practical solutions for issues related to the Sustainable Development Goals (SDGs) [15]. The Government of India has recently created several country-specific computational models to address challenges connected to the Sustainable Development Goals (SDGs) [16]. These models focus on issues such as ensuring access to water and sanitation, combating air pollution, addressing extreme weather occurrences, and enhancing energy access. Sustainable development and green growth have been the focal points of global infrastructure progress for an extended period. Developed nations have effectively implemented steps to promote green growth, whereas countries like India still need to establish appropriate models for this complex process fully [17]. This essay examines the hurdles encountered by industrialized countries and India in achieving green growth and sustainable development [18]. It emphasizes the crucial role of using suitable diagnostic models to solve these difficulties. Given the increasing importance of sustainability and green growth as indicators of development, it is evident that the monitoring models for these processes need to be meticulously crafted [19]. Diagnostic models are particularly crucial in the context of green growth and sustainable development since they assist in identifying the specific locations where problems arise. These models enable governments and policymakers to pinpoint the obstacles preventing countries from achieving their sustainable goals. A significant obstacle encountered by both industrialized and developing nations in their pursuit of sustainable growth is the substantial financial burden involved [20]. Although policymakers can employ sophisticated diagnostic models, the implementation of these initiatives incurs significant financial expenses. Several countries, especially those in the developing world, still need more financial resources to establish and implement such models.

CHALLENGES IN GREEN GROWTH AND SUSTAINABLE DEVELOPMENT

According to the World Bank report, India is expected to be the world's fastest-expanding economy. However, its economic growth is forecast to decrease to 6.9% in the financial year 2023 and 6.6% in the financial year 2024, down from

8.7% in 2021-22. Green growth has the potential to not only address the budget deficit in the economy but also enhance living standards through the implementation of LiFE (lifestyle for the environment). The Prime Minister of India has declared Operation Life, which aims to prioritize individual behaviors in the global climate action narrative with the objective of improving the living standards of impoverished individuals. This paper presents the important indices of green growth in India and selected nations, focusing on air pollution, carbon productivity, land resources, climate change, biodiversity, water, and energy consumption.

Air-Pollution

Air pollution poses significant environmental and health risks globally. It has been noted that the concentrations of pollutants, as measured, indicate that the proportion of people living in locations with high levels of pollutants exceeds the International/national ambient air quality requirements. According to the OECD (Organization for Economic Co-operation and Development), the percentage of individuals residing in regions where the yearly levels of particulate matter measuring 2.5 microns (PM 2.5) surpass 10 micrograms per cubic meter. Rahman *et al.* have observed in their research that hazardous emissions have a greater impact on economic growth. The data shown in Table **1** demonstrates the correlation between population growth and the escalation of pollution levels in the environment.

Table 1. Comparison study of population exposed to pollution levels in different countries of the world.

Year	2017		2016		2011		2005	
Country	A	B	A	B	A	B	A	B
India	100	82	100	93	100	81	100	71
China	100	50	100	52	100	58	100	52
European union	75	13	75	13	92	17	92	17
Japan	98	14	98	14	94	13	89	12
Russian Federation	69	12	75	12	91	14	91	15
United States	7	8	4	7	37	9	68	11
Brazil	82	12	76	11	98	15	97	15
South Africa	100	29	100	28	100	29	100	27

A= % of the population exposed to pollution level **B**= Pollution exposed to particulate matter in $\mu g/m^3$.

Carbon Productivity

Carbon productivity is a measure of carbon emissions produced for each unit of energy generated. Reduced carbon productivity leads to a decrease in the generation of CO_2 gasses, which are the primary contributors to global warming and climate change. The emission of this gas occurs as a result of the combustion of fossil fuels, volcanic eruptions, and forest fires. The study indicates that an increase in the production and consumption of nonrenewable resources leads to a corresponding increase in pollution levels. This correlation has also been supported by the research conducted by Aradakani and Seyedaliakbar as well as Xie and Liu in their respective studies. The data presented in Table **2** indicates that carbon productivity, which measures the economic output generated per unit of CO_2 emitted, exhibited improvement in certain nations in 2018 when compared to both 2011 and 2005.

Table 2. Comparison study of carbon productivity in different countries of the world.

Year	2018				2011				2005			
Country	E	F	G	H	E	F	G	H	E	F	G	H
India	3.81	3.74	2	1	3.31	3.42	1	1	3.22	3.19	1	1
China	2.22	2.14	7	6	1.55	1.79	6	5	1.32	1.68	4	3
European Union	6.74	5.00	6	8	5.45	4.25	7	9	4.52	3.60	8	10
Japan	4.94	3.85	9	11	4.15	3.25	9	12	4.18	3.20	9	12
Russian Federation	2.31	3.01	11	8	2.10	2.65	11	9	1.83	2.61	10	7
United States	3.97	3.17	15	18	3.24	2.85	16	19	2.74	2.29	19	23
Brazil	7.09	7.09	2	2	7.54	6.01	2	3	7.29	7.21	2	2
South Africa	1.64	1.64	8	5	1.59	2.19	8	6	1.44	1.89	8	6

E represents the CO_2 productivity per kilogram of production, measured in USD. The variable F represents the demand-based carbon dioxide productivity measured in USD per kilogram. G represents the amount of CO_2 emissions per capita that is produced based on production, measured in metric tons per capita, and H represents the demand-based carbon dioxide (CO_2) emissions per capita, measured in metric tons per capita. The term "USD/Kg" refers to the carbon dioxide productivity measured in kilograms per United States dollar.

Land Resources

The environmental and economic difficulties arising from land usage pose significant challenges for countries globally. According to reports, the release of greenhouse gases from the agricultural and land use sectors contributes to 23% of human-caused emissions. Moreover, the decline of terrestrial ecosystems poses a significant risk to 25% of animal and plant species, potentially leading to their extinction. Additionally, it contributes to the degradation of 74% of the Earth's land area. Projections indicate that the global population is expected to reach 10 billion people by 2050. This rapid expansion has led to the conversion of large portions of land in many countries into urban areas for urban growth and development. The data presented in Table **3** demonstrates the correlation between population exposure and the extent of change in areas in both developed and developing countries.

Table 3. Comparison study of land resources used by different countries of the world with respect to change in the population.

Country	% of change in population since 1990-2014	% of change in built up area since 1990-2014
India	45.9	96.3
China	19.6	77.8
Japan	2.7	15.5
Russian Federation	-2.8	21.5
United States	27.7	34.1
Brazil	36.1	33.1
South Africa	44.4	78.9
World	36.1	45.6

Climate Change

Climate change disrupts the equilibrium of the Earth's atmospheric system, resulting in alterations in temperature and other disturbances to ecosystems, water supplies, and food production. These modifications have resulted in extensive effects on several areas of biodiversity, phenology, population dynamics, community structure, and ecosystem functions. Between 2021 and 2040, there is a projected increase in global temperature of up to 1.5°C worldwide, contributing to the phenomenon of global warming.

Bio-diversity

A recent analysis of data indicates that around 75% of terrestrial areas and 66% of marine areas have undergone significant modifications, leading to cumulative effects on biodiversity. Furthermore, a staggering 85% of wetland areas have been depleted, and an additional 32 million hectares of forest have been lost. It has resulted in a decline in biomass and has had a significant impact on 20% of the ecosystem. The survey agency cautions that out of the 6190 domestic varieties of mammals utilized for food and agriculture, 559 have gone extinct and a minimum of 1000 more are currently at risk of extinction worldwide. India, being a large and diversified country with 2.4% of the world's land and port area, is encountering numerous obstacles in preserving its biodiversity, which encompasses a wide range of recorded bio-species. The biodiversity hotspots in India are currently experiencing a significant threat to their fauna and flora. All of these challenges to biodiversity stem from climate change, land mismanagement, loss of biodiversity, and the worsening caused by global warming. In India, biodiversity is of utmost importance due to its essential role in ecosystem functioning and its direct contribution to sustainable development and poverty alleviation. Nevertheless, we are currently observing a decrease in biodiversity, both within India and on a worldwide scale. According to the research from the Intergovernmental Science-Policy Platform on Biodiversity and Ecosystem Services (IPBES), human activity has significantly affected more than 66% of marine ecosystems and 75% of terrestrial ecosystems. Additionally, 85% of wetlands have been gone.

Water

The groundwater in multiple urban areas has experienced significant demand as a result of elevated living standards, population growth, and industrial development. It leads to a decrease in the groundwater level and degradation of water quality due to contamination from both natural sources and human activities. According to estimates, by 2030, over 60% of the world's total water supply will be needed to meet the demand for water consumption. According to the UNESCO study on world water development (2017), it is projected that 47% of the global population will reside in regions with significant levels of water stress. According to the report of the parliamentary standing committee, India is currently confronting a significant issue in its cities due to climate change and unpredictable rainfall, namely in terms of the availability of fresh water.

Energy

The escalating need for energy in various sectors such as industry, agriculture, real estate, transportation, commercial, and residential households is a significant cause for concern due to the finite and diminishing nature of energy supplies, namely fossil fuels and wood. Numerous nations worldwide are releasing greenhouse gases due to their heavy reliance on fossil fuels, particularly coal. Consequently, they are significant contributors to CO_2 emissions and the escalation of coal prices. India's energy demand is expected to increase by 50% by the year 2050. The data shown in Table **4** illustrates the utilization of coal in many sectors by both developed and developing countries. It highlights the need for urgent measures to address the usage of coal and transition to renewable energy sources based on the specific demands of each sector.

Table 4. Comparison study of energy consumption in 10^6 TJ (unit of energy) various sectors used by different countries of the world.

Year	2020						2015					
Country	I	II	III	IV	V	VI	I	II	III	IV	V	VI
India	3.4	0.12	0.20	------	0.19	-------	3.5	0.10	0.17	------	0.18	------
China	19.6	1.3	0.43	0.48	0.59	1.9	25.1	2.1	0.84	0.57	0.98	2.0
Europe	1.2	0.37	0.216	0.035	0.0037	0.090	1.4	0.49	0.217	0.043	0.0015	0.97
Japan	0.74	-----	0.0051	------	------	0.030	0.86	------	0.008	------	------	0.035
Russian	1.1	0.06	0.028	0.002	-------	0.008	0.98	0.08	0.057	0.003	------	0.007
United States	0.54	-----	0.13	------	------	-------	0.78	-----	0.028	------	-------	-----
World	31.6	2.3	1.0	0.54	0.87	2.2	3.6	3.18	1.4	0.64	1.2	2.3

I=Consumption of coal in Industry.
II= Consumption of coal in Residential areas.
III= Consumption of coal in Commercial field.
IV = Coal consumption in Agriculture.
V= Consumption of coal in Non-specified areas.
VI= Coal consumption in the Non-Energy use section.

INITIATIVES TO OVERCOME THE CHALLENGES IN GREEN GROWTH AND SUSTAINABLE DEVELOPMENT

The paper presents specific recommendations and measuring tools to address the difficulties related to growth indicators.

Improved Air

The Central Pollution Control Board of India (CPCB) has initiated the National Air Quality Program (NAMP) with the objective of monitoring the air quality in various states and union territories. The National Air Monitoring Program (NAMP) has designated four pollutants, namely sulfur dioxide (SO_2), nitrogen oxides, respirable suspended particulate matter (RSPM), and particulate matter with diameters of 10 micrometers (PM10) and 2.5 micrometers (PM2.5), for continuous monitoring at all places across the country. The CAFÉ (Corporate Average Fuel Efficiency/Economy) regulations, which were universally adopted in 2017, are rigorously adhered to by all countries worldwide. In addition to this, India has already implemented the BS (Bharat Stage) regulations to mitigate vehicle-related air pollution. In India, automobiles are currently inspected for both

Pollution Under Control (PUC) certification and Exhaust Emission Index (EEI) compliance. The EEI assessment entails a rapid evaluation of vehicles based on emission characteristics such as CO_2, CO, PM, Pb, SO_2, and NO_2. The objective is to enhance air quality. Installing Air Pollution Control equipment (APCE) such as chimney filters and electrostatic precipitators in industries, promoting the use of public transport, preventing forest fires, and reducing smoking can enhance air quality.

Reduction of Carbon Productivity Gases

India has proposed the following five essential elements (Panchamrit), which include:

- Achieve a capacity of 500GW of Non-fossil energy by 2030,
- Obtain 50% of its energy needs from renewable sources by 2030,
- Decrease overall estimated carbon emissions by one billion tons from the present till 2030.
- The goal is to decrease the carbon intensity of the economy by 45% by 2030, compared to the levels in 2005.
- Attaining the objective of eliminating emissions by the year 2070.

Proper Utilization of Land Resources

The issue of land use is a crucial determinant of environmental sustainability and the promotion of eco-friendly economic growth. Its impacts extend beyond just carbon dioxide emissions and biodiversity, also encompassing public health concerns. It is advisable to promote alternative building materials over traditional ones in order to maintain environmental sustainability. Additionally, an awareness program should be implemented to promote afforestation. As per the Forest (Conservation) Act of 1980, if a project proponent wants to use a piece of land for a different purpose, they must find another piece of land to plant trees and compensate for the value of the area used for afforestation. The forest department will subsequently be responsible for managing such lands. The National Land Utilization Policy (NLUP) aims to enhance the quality of life by focusing on the enhancement of livelihood, access to food, water, and adequate housing.

Decline in the Rate of Climate Change

Adaptation is now taken into account in climate policies in at least 170 countries. However, many nations still need to make significant headway in implementing these initiatives. The current global financial flows allocated for adaptation, particularly in developing nations, need to be revised. There is a 50% probability that global temperatures will increase by 1.5°C between the years 2021 and 2040.

The rate of climate change can be decelerated by implementing the following recommendations:

- The global community must swiftly transition away from the combustion of fossil fuels.
- Achieving a state of carbon neutrality when there are no net emissions of carbon dioxide.
- The promotion of renewable energy projects, such as wind and solar plants, is necessary to mitigate the detrimental effects of climate change.

Preservation of Biodiversity

The synthesis report of the IPCC acknowledges that preserving natural ecosystems, rather than repairing devastated ones, is a crucial strategy for conserving biodiversity. According to the CAG report, a significant portion of Rs 4700 crore in the CAMPA fund remained unused in 2019. It has been proposed that in order to reduce the negative effects of diverting natural ecosystems, it is important to use funds effectively to safeguard the environment for plant native species, and support renewable energy initiatives such as wind and solar plants. Biodiversity conservation can be achieved through the promotion of sustainable agriculture practices, the management of seascapes, and the promotion of reforestation and ecological restoration.

Save Water

According to the data provided by the IPCC, it is projected that 40% of the Indian population will experience water scarcity by 2050. It is attributed to factors such as erratic monsoon rainfall, population expansion, global warming, and climate change. The CSE-DTE has published the 2023 States of India's Environment report, which reveals that more than 30,000 water bodies in the country have been illegally occupied. The central government is implementing various water conservation schemes such as the Atal Bhujal Yojna, Pradhan Mantri Sinchayee Yojana (PMKSY), Atal Mission for Rejuvenation and Urban Transformation (AMRUT), and the Namami Gange Programme. In addition to these, the Ministry of Jal Shakti has initiated a nationwide campaign called "Jal Shakti Abhiyan-Catch the Rain" (JSA-CTR) to promote the construction of suitable rainwater harvesting structures in both urban and rural areas of the country.

Clean Energy

The UNCTAD's 2023 Technology and Innovation Report emphasizes the potential for developing countries to stimulate economic growth and improve technological capabilities through the adoption of green innovation, which refers to the production of goods and services with reduced carbon emissions. The analysis assesses the market dimensions of 17 environmentally friendly and innovative technologies, including artificial intelligence, the Internet of things, and electric vehicles, as well as their potential for employment creation. The IEA's efforts in India on energy efficiency primarily target the industrial, residential, and transportation sectors, as these areas have the potential to contribute to the green economy's revival significantly. The Bureau of Energy Efficiency (BEE) in India has taken substantial measures to establish a plan for integrating energy efficiency into residential buildings. Generating renewable energy can be achieved through the establishment of solar parks and wind farms.

CONCLUSION

The rapid expansion of the economy and population poses a significant danger to key indices of sustainable development, including air pollution, carbon productivity, land resources, climate change, biodiversity, water use, and energy consumption. This manuscript cum report presents an examination of issues and activities related to green growth and sustainable development in various countries throughout the world. In this discussion, we examined the measurement and framework for green growth and sustainable development in industrialized countries and India. Specifically, we focused on the assessment of natural assets, economic activities, energy consumption, air pollutants, and land usage. The purpose of this study was to establish and foster a worldwide network of individuals with common goals and commitments. Furthermore, our goal is to encourage and support the development of environmentally sustainable communities that prioritize the restoration of ecosystems, the enhancement of air quality, the reduction of carbon emissions, the responsible use of land resources, the mitigation of climate change, the preservation of biodiversity, the conservation of water, and the promotion of clean energy.

REFERENCES

[1] R. Aneja, S.R. Kappil, N. Das, and U.J. Banday, "Does the green finance initiatives transform the world into a green economy? A study of green bond issuing countries", *Environ. Sci. Pollut. Res. Int.,* vol. 30, no. 14, pp. 42214-42222, 2023.
[http://dx.doi.org/10.1007/s11356-023-25317-w] [PMID: 36645606]

[2] J. Gupta, "E-waste: policies and legislations for a sustainable green growth", *Waste Management and Resource Recycling in the Developing World,* p. 253-269, 2023.

[3] R. Darmayanti, Y. Milshteyn, and A.M. Kashap, "Green economy, sustainability and implementation before, during, and after the covid-19 pandemic in Indonesia", *Revenue Journal: Management and Entrepreneurship,* vol. 1, no. 1, pp. 27-33, 2023.
[http://dx.doi.org/10.61650/rjme.v1i1.222]

[4] D. Quacoe, Y. Kong, and D. Quacoe, "Analysis of How Green Growth and Entrepreneurship Affect Sustainable Development: Application of the Quintuple Helix Innovation Model in the African Context", *Sustainability (Basel),* vol. 15, no. 2, p. 907, 2023.

[http://dx.doi.org/10.3390/su15020907]

[5]   B. Agan, and M. Balcilar, "Unraveling the Green Growth Matrix: Exploring the Impact of Green Technology, Climate Change Adaptation, and Macroeconomic Factors on Sustainable Development", *Sustainability (Basel),* vol. 15, no. 11, p. 8530, 2023.
[http://dx.doi.org/10.3390/su15118530]

[6]   A. Razzaq, A. Sharif, I. Ozturk, and S. Afshan, "Dynamic and threshold effects of energy transition and environmental governance on green growth in COP26 framework", *Renew. Sustain. Energy Rev.,* vol. 179, p. 113296, 2023.
[http://dx.doi.org/10.1016/j.rser.2023.113296]

[7]   Z. Dong, and S. Ullah, "Towards a green economy in China? Examining the impact of the internet of things and environmental regulation on green growth", *Sustainability (Basel),* vol. 15, no. 16, p. 12528, 2023.
[http://dx.doi.org/10.3390/su151612528]

[8]   K.S. Herman, "Green growth and innovation in the Global South: a systematic literature review", *Innov. Dev.,* vol. 13, no. 1, pp. 43-69, 2023.
[http://dx.doi.org/10.1080/2157930X.2021.1909821]

[9]   Y. Telwala, "Unlocking the potential of agroforestry as a nature-based solution for localizing sustainable development goals: A case study from a drought-prone region in rural India", *Nature-Based Solutions,* vol. 3, p. 100045, 2023.
[http://dx.doi.org/10.1016/j.nbsj.2022.100045]

[10]   S. Ullah, R. Luo, M. Nadeem, and J. Cifuentes-Faura, "Advancing sustainable growth and energy transition in the United States through the lens of green energy innovations, natural resources and environmental policy", *Resour. Policy,* vol. 85, p. 103848, 2023.
[http://dx.doi.org/10.1016/j.resourpol.2023.103848]

[11]   H. Wang, G. Peng, Y. Luo, and H. Du, "Asymmetric influence of renewable energy, ecological governance, and human development on green growth of BRICS countries", *Renew. Energy,* vol. 206, pp. 1007-1019, 2023.
[http://dx.doi.org/10.1016/j.renene.2022.12.125]

[12]   X. Xue, S. Palanisamy, M. A, D. Selvaraj, O.I. Khalaf, and G.M. Abdulsahib, "A Novel partial sequence technique based Chaotic biogeography optimization for PAPR reduction in generalized frequency division multiplexing waveform", *Heliyon,* vol. 9, no. 9, p. e19451, 2023.
[http://dx.doi.org/10.1016/j.heliyon.2023.e19451] [PMID: 37681146]

[13]   G. Muttashar Abdulsahib, D. Sekaran Selvaraj, A. Manikandan, S. Palanisamy, M. Uddin, O. Ibrahim Khalaf, M. Abdelhaq, and R. Alsaqour, "Reverse polarity optical Orthogonal frequency Division Multiplexing for High-Speed visible light communications system", *Egyptian Informatics Journal,* vol. 24, no. 4, p. 100407, 2023.
[http://dx.doi.org/10.1016/j.eij.2023.100407]

[14]   V.A.K. Gorantla, S.K. Sriramulugari, A.H. Mewada, and J. Logeshwaran, "An intelligent optimization framework to predict the vulnerable range of tumor cells using Internet of things", *2nd International Conference on Industrial Electronics: Developments & Applications (ICIDeA),* p. 359-365, 2023.
[http://dx.doi.org/10.1109/ICIDeA59866.2023.10295269]

[15]   T. Marimuthu, V.A. Rajan, G.V. Londhe, and J. Logeshwaran, "Deep Learning for Automated Lesion Detection in Mammography", *2nd International Conference on Industrial Electronics: Developments & Applications (ICIDeA),* p. 383-388, 2023.
[http://dx.doi.org/10.1109/ICIDeA59866.2023.10295189]

[16]   V.A. Rajan, T. Marimuthu, G.V. Londhe, and J. Logeshwaran, "A Comprehensive analysis of Network Coding for Efficient Wireless Network Communication", *2nd International Conference on Industrial Electronics: Developments & Applications (ICIDeA),* p. 204-210, 2023.
[http://dx.doi.org/10.1109/ICIDeA59866.2023.10295177]

[17]   H. Yadav, S. Singh, K.K. Mishra, S. Srivastava, M.S. Naruka, and S.P. Yadav, "Brain Tumor Detection with MRI Images", *2022 International Conference on Computational Intelligence and Sustainable Engineering Solutions (CISES)*, 2022.
[http://dx.doi.org/10.1109/CISES54857.2022.9844387]

[18]   P. Rani, S. Verma, S.P. Yadav, B.K. Rai, M.S. Naruka, and D. Kumar, "Simulation of the Lightweight Blockchain Technique Based on Privacy and Security for Healthcare Data for the Cloud System", *International Journal of E-Health and Medical Communications,* vol. 13, no. 4, pp. 1-15, 2022.
[http://dx.doi.org/10.4018/IJEHMC.309436]

[19]   "Transforming Management with AI, Big-Data, and IoT", *Springer International Publishing,* 2022.
[http://dx.doi.org/10.1007/978-3-030-86749-2]

[20]   J. Bhardwaj, A. Nayak, C.S. Yadav, and S.P. Yadav, "A Review in Wavelet Transforms Based Medical Image Fusion", In: *Evolving Role of AI and IoMT in the Healthcare Market.,* F. Al-Turjman, M. Kumar, T. Stephan, A. Bhardwaj, Eds., Springer: Cham, 2021.
[http://dx.doi.org/10.1007/978-3-030-82079-4_9]

CHAPTER 21

The Impact of Green Marketing on Consumer Purchasing Behaviour: A Study of the Attitudes, Beliefs, and Behaviours of Consumers towards Environmentally-Friendly Products

Mansi Singhal[1,*], **Priyanka**[1] and **Vipul Kumar**[1]

[1] *Department of Management Studies, Hi-Tech Institute of Engineering and Technology, Ghaziabad, (U.P.), India*

Abstract: Green Marketing is a fascinating subject that revolves around consumers, who are not only concerned about the environment but also knowledgeable about eco-friendly items. While corporations are actively investigating various strategies to enhance consumer knowledge of green management, they are unable to reach rural areas effectively. The study seeks to determine the influence of green marketing on customer purchasing behavior. How will demand be stimulated by the implementation of advanced green methods in rural regions? The research study was conducted in rural parts of Delhi NCR, where a total of 250 replies were gathered. The respondents have shown a good inclination towards the ABC model of attitude during the assessment. According to the report, companies must enhance their contact with consumers. Furthermore, it is necessary to prioritize traits such as affordability and quality over social duty.

Keywords: Green Marketing, Consumers, Eco-Friendly, Influence, Marketing, Rural Market.

INTRODUCTION

Green marketing is the utilization of marketing strategies and tactics to advertise items or services that are seen as being environmentally conscious. The influence of green marketing on consumer buying behavior has emerged as a progressively significant field of study in recent times [1]. This is due to the growing consumer awareness of environmental concerns and their heightened inclination toward buying eco-friendly items [2]. Multiple research studies have investigated the attitudes, beliefs, and behaviors of customers towards environmentally friendly

* **Corresponding author Mansi Singhal:** Department of Management Studies, Hi-Tech Institute of Engineering and Technology, Ghaziabad, (U.P.), India; E-mail: mancsinghal@gmail.com

Pankaj Kumar Mishra & Satya Prakash Yadav (Eds.)

products [Prakash, G., & Pathak, P. (2017)] [3]. The findings of these studies indicate a favorable correlation between green marketing and customer buying behavior. Consumers who are exposed to green marketing have a higher propensity to buy environmentally friendly products [4]. One explanation for this is that green marketing can enhance consumers' consciousness of environmental concerns and the influence of their purchasing behavior on the environment. Consumers with a higher level of awareness of these concerns are more inclined to actively search for eco-friendly items and make purchasing choices based on their environmental consequences [Garg, A., & Kumar, D. S. (2022)] [5]. The perceived advantages of environmentally friendly products are another influential aspect of customer purchase behavior. Consumers are more inclined to purchase things that they perceive as having superior quality, being healthier, and being safer for both themselves and the environment [Govender, J. P., & Govender, T. L. (2016)] [6]. Green marketing can highlight these advantages and enhance consumers' inclination to select eco-friendly items. Therefore, it is imperative to comprehend consumer behavior [Sreen, N., Purbey, S., & Sadarangani, P. (2018)] [7]. The ABC Attitude Model, commonly referred to as the tripartite model, was formulated by Albert Elli and comprises three fundamental elements: Affective, Behavioural, and Cognitive [8]. Affective attitude pertains to an individual's emotional reaction or sentiment (favorable/unfavorable) towards a particular entity [Bhalla, T. (2021)]. Behavioral attitude refers to our actions or responses towards something, whether they are positive or negative. Cognitive attitude refers to the process of assessing or forming opinions about something [9]. To comprehend consumer behavior, we perform our research utilizing the ABC Attitude Model. [Nekmahmud, M., & Fekete-Farkas, M. (2020)] [10]. Green marketing can generate consumer distrust. Consumers may have apprehensions regarding corporations employing green marketing strategies to boost revenues without making substantial alterations to their products or manufacturing procedures.

RELATED WORKS

This study is novel because it offers a valuable understanding of consumers' attitudes, beliefs, and behaviors about environmentally friendly items [11]. The study also evaluates the influence of green marketing on customer buying behavior. Furthermore, the study examines the influence of attitudes, beliefs, and actions on customer decision-making. Furthermore, it explores the influence of environmental factors on customer buying behavior and examines the efficacy of green marketing tactics. This analysis offers a thorough examination of the present condition of green marketing and its impact on consumer buying choices. Additionally, the research offers valuable information on how to enhance the marketing of environmentally friendly products to boost customer involvement and consequent buying choices. Advancements in computational models have recently resulted in the creation of advanced methods for analyzing consumer buying patterns and their influence on environmentally friendly marketing strategies [12]. The utilization of artificial intelligence (AI) and machine learning (ML) algorithms, in conjunction with novel analytical methodologies, facilitates the examination of vast quantities of data in a streamlined, accurate, and economical manner [13]. This technique offers vital insights into the attitudes, beliefs, and behaviors of consumers about environmentally friendly products and services, and ML models can be employed to gain a deeper comprehension of how green marketing initiatives impact customer purchasing choices [14]. AI and ML models can be utilized to detect trends and connections between consumer preferences and green marketing activities. This information can then be used to impact public policies, marketing campaigns, and targeted marketing efforts [15]. Furthermore, the models can be utilized to gain a deeper comprehension of the essential components of a green marketing strategy, encompassing its substance, layout, and communication channels. By utilizing these valuable observations, marketers may create more refined campaigns that strongly resonate with their intended audience, hence enhancing their likelihood of achieving success [16]. Furthermore, advanced techniques such as text mining, natural language processing (NLP), sentiment analysis, and visual analytics can be employed to reveal novel insights into consumers' views and behaviors. The challenge with diagnostic models for green marketing on consumer purchasing behavior lies in the inherent difficulty of comprehensively collecting the complete spectrum of attitudes and behaviors exhibited by consumers toward environmentally friendly items [17]. Although conventional marketing techniques may encompass certain elements of green marketing, the information gathered may need to be sufficiently thorough to precisely measure and analyze the complete influence of green marketing on customer buying patterns. Furthermore, green marketing is commonly perceived as a nascent marketing strategy that is currently evolving and increasing in significance [18]. Therefore, it can be challenging to determine the most effective diagnostic models for evaluating the influence of green marketing on customer buying behaviour [19]. Therefore, researchers should not solely focus on classic models but also evaluate the diagnostic capacities of novel models. Consumer behavior is dynamic and can be significantly impacted by technological advancements, communication platforms, cultural shifts, consumer attitudes, and other factors. Therefore, researchers must take into account these elements while creating their diagnostic models to accurately reflect the dynamic connection between green marketing, consumer attitude, and purchasing behaviour [20]. To effectively reflect the entirety of consumer purchasing behavior in green marketing, diagnostic models must consider multiple elements like prevailing patterns, societal attitudes and behaviour, and communication methods.

LITERATURE REVIEW

The domain of Green Marketing in rural regions has encountered numerous predicaments and obstacles due to issues pertaining to awareness and trust. The American Marketing Association (AMA) directed its attention towards this matter and fostered consciousness between 1970 and 1975. In 1975, AMA organized the inaugural workshop on "Ecological Marketing". The program concluded with the publication of the first book on Green Marketing, titled "Ecological Marketing. "The discoveries presented in the book resulted in the emergence of Green Marketing throughout the late 1980s and early 1990s. Subsequent to that, several books on green marketing were authored. According to M.S. Swami Nathan, the concept of green marketing gained momentum in 1990, coinciding with an increase in consumer interest in eco-friendly products in India between 2000 and 2005. The initial stage of this marketing strategy is sometimes referred to as "ecological" or "green marketing," with a primary focus on addressing environmental difficulties and issues through the provision of solutions. The second stage of green marketing, known as the "Environmental" phase, is centered on the creation of cutting-edge products and clean technologies to address waste and pollution concerns. The third stage of green marketing was labeled as "Sustainable. "It reached its peak of popularity between 1990 and 2000. In the 1990s, there was a rise in environmental concerns, which posed additional difficulties for firms (Johari and Sahasakmontri, 1998). Green Marketing, as described in The New Imperative in Marketing Mastermind, involves creating environmentally friendly products that meet consumer needs and desires by prioritizing quality, performance, price, and convenience. The essay "Sustainable Green Marketing" by Dutta, B. (2009) addresses this topic. According to Barker, organizations must initially have faith in the efficacy of green marketing and make substantial efforts to incorporate crucial product enhancements that enhance performance, are marketable, and generate revenue. The primary emphasis of green marketing is on four specific areas. The topics of concern are (1) the significance of green marketing, (2) its impact on the performance and competitiveness of firms, and (3) enhancement of the efficiency of green marketing. Several multinational corporations, such as Philips India Ltd., have introduced the emerging notion of "green marketing" to the Indian market.

OBJECTIVES

1. To examine the imperative of green marketing in India from multiple viewpoints.

2. To understand the strategies required for effective green marketing.

3. To examine the present circumstances and evaluate India's capacity for implementing green marketing strategies.

4. To investigate the challenges encountered by green marketers in India.

RESEARCH METHODOLOGY

The research study was conducted with an exploratory and descriptive approach, focusing on a sample population of 250 respondents. The age demographic encompasses individuals between the ages of 20 and 30. The samples were chosen from the rural regions of Delhi NCR. In 2011, India's rural population accounted for 70% of the total population, as stated by the World Bank's collection of development indicators. According to the 2011 Census Report of India, the rural population of Delhi NCR was 419,042. Among them, 83,657 individuals aged between 20 and 30, consisting of 44,389 males and 39,268 females. Additional data was gathered using a meticulously designed questionnaire consisting of 20 inquiries. The respondent's attitudes were assessed by examining the components of the ABC model, which include affective, behavioural, and cognitive aspects.

Demographic Profile of the Respondents

From the total of 250 respondents, 56% were male and 44% were female (Refer Fig. **1**). Out of the total respondents, 60% belonged to the age group of 20-25 years, and the remaining 40% belonged to the age group of 25-30 years (Fig. **2**). However, it is important to note that only 25% of the total respondents were employed, while the remaining 75% were jobless (Fig. **3**). The data reveals that 48.8% of the respondents held a graduate degree, 28% had completed their higher secondary education, and 15.2% had completed their 10th grade. Merely 8% of individuals met the requirements for post-graduate education, as indicated in Fig. (**4**).

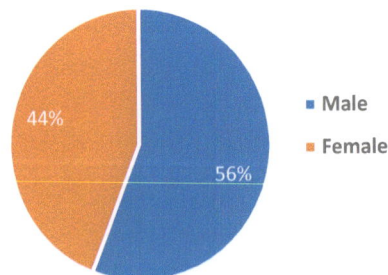

Fig. (1). Gender.

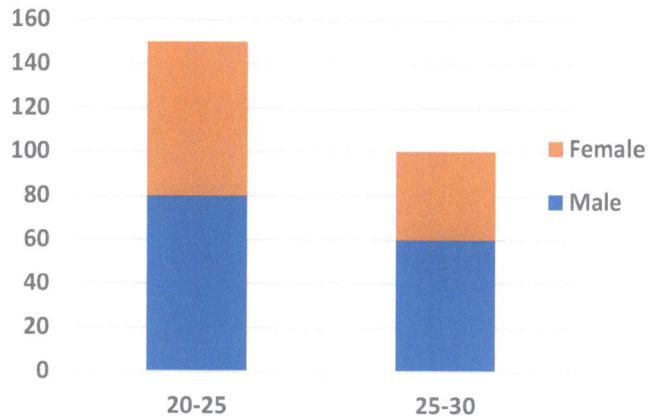

Fig. (2). Age.

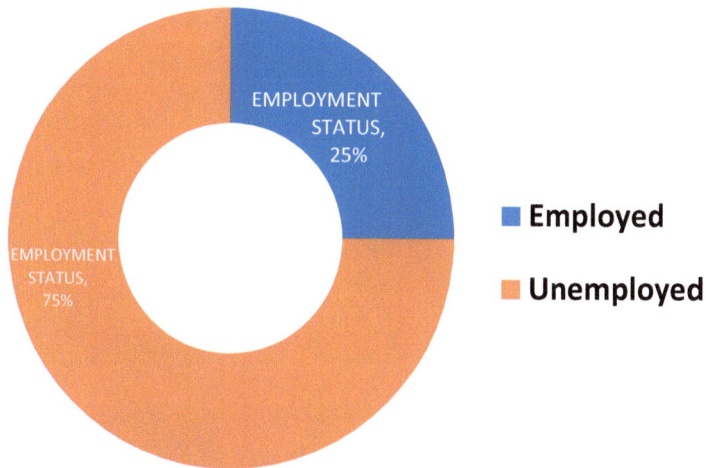

Fig. (3). Employment status.

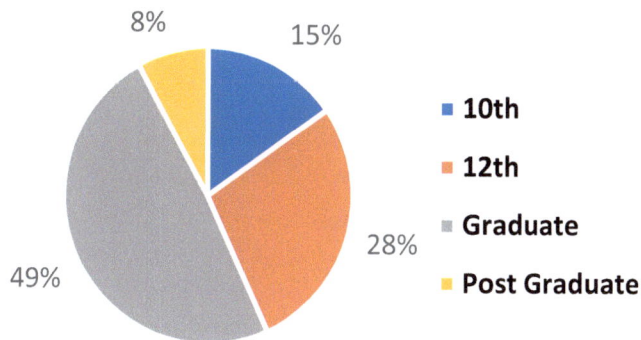

Fig. (4). Education qualification.

RESULT AND DISCUSSION

Awareness of Eco-Friendly Items

Based on our investigation, a significant majority of respondents, specifically 62%, possess awareness regarding eco-friendly products. Total 47.74% of the female participants showed awareness of eco-friendly products, whereas 52.25% of the male participants exhibited the same awareness. Furthermore, the chi-square test did not indicate any statistically significant disparity between gender and awareness of sustainable products. There was a significant correlation between the education level and the consumption of these products. The study revealed that both graduate and post-graduate individuals were knowledgeable about eco-products [Screen, N., Purvey, S., & Sadarangani, P. (2018)]. The age of the respondents was positively correlated with their awareness of environmental items. Our observation indicates that individuals in the age category of 26-30 exhibit a high level of awareness regarding environment-friendly objects, whereas those in the age group of 20-25 demonstrate comparatively lower awareness. Older respondents exhibit a greater awareness of eco-products as a result of their elevated levels of education (Fig. 5).

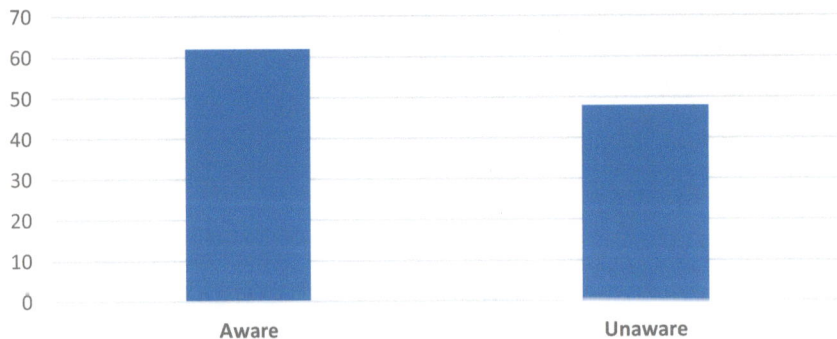

Fig. (5). Awareness of eco-friendly products.

Attitude Toward Eco-Friendly Products

The measurement of the ABC Model of Attitude in this study involved the use of statements, where participants were required to rate them on a scale ranging from 1 to 7. The respondents' overall attitude towards sustainable products was found to be robust, with an average score of 5.56. The study found that the highest average score for affective attitude was 6.09, indicating that customers would experience happiness if sustainable product options were available for usage [Cherian, J., & Jacob, J. (2012)]. It demonstrates the necessity for firms to prioritize the production and enhancement of environmentally sustainable products. The emotional attitude was next, followed by the intellectual attitude, which had an average score of 5.77. According to Kumar'Ranjan and Kushwaha (2017), respondents believe that sustainable products may greatly help as an ideal approach to address the issue of pollution. In addition, implementing additional promotional and advertising messages highlighting the environmentally friendly nature of the items will be effective in achieving improved outcomes. The behavioral component of the model was found to be just 4.83, which is much lower among the rural young. Currently, the purchasing rate of environmentally friendly products among rural youth is quite low. Our analysis indicates that the scarcity of sustainable items in rural areas is the primary cause of this poor score. Another factor contributing to mistrust towards green marketing is the widespread practice of firms including environmentally friendly elements solely for the purpose of maximizing their financial gains (Table **1**).

Table 1. Rural Youth's attitude towards sustainable products.

Elements of the ABC Model of Attitude	Minimum	Maximum	Average	Standard Deviation
Affective	3	7	6.09	0.898
Behavioral	1	7	4.83	0.929
Cognitive	2	7	5.77	1.172

Willingness to Sacrifice

Our research revealed that respondents have the lowest willingness to compromise when it comes to quality, with an average score of 1.24. These findings indicate that participants are least inclined to make concessions when it comes to the quality of environmentally friendly products. Furthermore, the availability component has a significantly low mean score of (1.88). During the data collection process, we noticed a lack of accessibility to environmentally friendly products in rural regions. Our participants must visit the urban market in order to obtain environmentally-friendly products. The look factor received the highest average score (3.88) since young people prefer appealing products and specifically prioritize green packaging. The average score for durability was determined to be 1.76, while the average score for diversity was discovered to be 2.83 (Table **2**).

Table 2. Willingness to sacrifice for different attributes.

Aspects	Minimum	Maximum	Average	Standard Deviation
Quality	1	3	1.24	0.502
Durability	1	5	1.76	0.810
Availability	1	3	1.88	0.949

(Table 2) cont.....

Aspects	Minimum	Maximum	Average	Standard Deviation
Variety	1	5	2.83	0.886
Appearance	1	7	3.88	1.164

Marketing Mix Decision

The respondent also provided their perspective on the 4Ps of Marketing, as documented by Garg and Kumar (2021). Regarding the 'Product Mix' of environmentally friendly products, survey participants prioritize packaging that is labeled as 'Eco-Friendly' or 'Green.' The responder said that they consider traditional or plastic wrappers to be a notable contributor to pollution. Therefore, they exclusively choose friendly packaging in order to mitigate environmental impact. (Fig. **6**). Regarding the 'Place Mix,' 55% of respondents opt for retail shops as their preferred purchasing location for the item. (Fig. **7**). It demonstrates the significance of emotions and tactile sensations in determining ultimate buying choices. With respect to the 'Price Mix,' a significant majority of 47.5% of participants express their reluctance to pay a higher price in comparison to the cost of alternative products. (Fig. **8**). The 'Promotion Mix' indicates that 49% of respondents have faith in 'Referrals' in comparison to other sources. These findings indicate that individuals living in rural areas consider a message from their relatives or friends to be more reliable than any other source. (Fig. **9**)

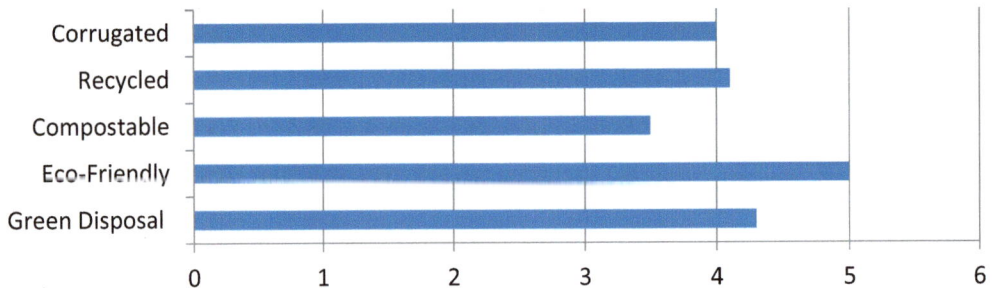

Fig. (6). Preferred eco-friendly packaging.

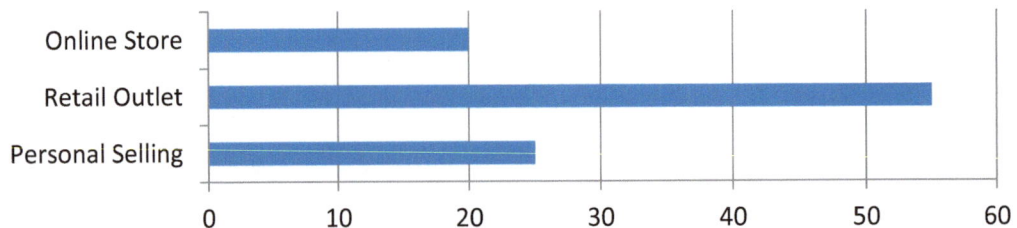

Fig. (7). Preferred purchasing.

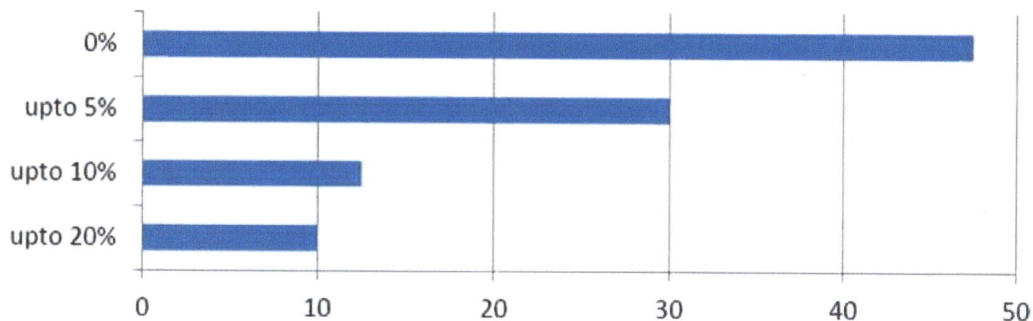

Fig. (8). Preferred paying density.

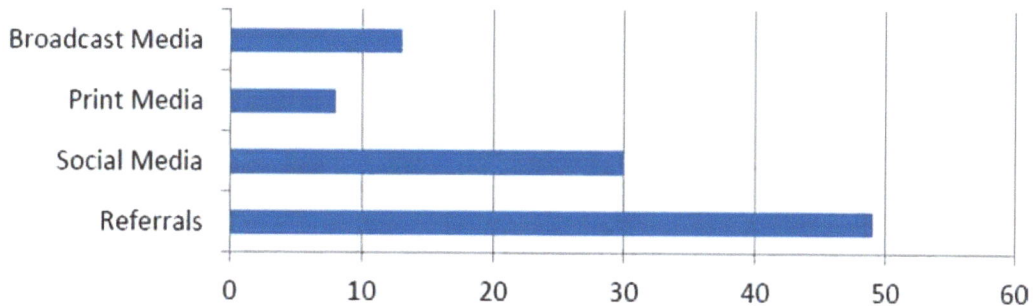

Fig. (9). Preferred information source.

SUGGESTION AND CONCLUSION

Overall, green marketing has a predominantly favourable influence on consumer buying behaviour. Academic credentials can have a substantial impact on enhancing individuals' enthusiasm for environmentally friendly items. An aesthetically pleasing and intellectually stimulating message has the potential to establish and foster a deep sense of trust among rural kids. Companies should endeavour to expand the accessibility of their environmentally friendly products in rural markets in order to gain a competitive edge over alternative goods. Our research identified a significant emotional inclination towards environmentally friendly products. Therefore, it is crucial to prioritize the distribution channel as rural adolescents encounter difficulties due to the limited accessibility to environmentally friendly products. Nevertheless, price-conscious consumers can still find sustainable items available at a premium cost through specialized companies. During the initial phase, the organization might make a minor adjustment to the price by increasing it by 5% and beyond. Consumers have a higher propensity to acquire eco-friendly items when they are subjected to green marketing. Companies can leverage green marketing to enhance customer consciousness and highlight the advantages of their products. Nevertheless, corporations must exercise caution to ensure that their eco-friendly marketing endeavours are authentic and honest in order to prevent consumer skepticism.

This study offers a comprehensive analysis and perspective on the opinions and outlook of young individuals residing in rural areas of Delhi NCR. In the future, this can be expanded to encompass additional domains, providing more comprehensive knowledge and benefiting companies.

REFERENCES

[1]   S. Balaskas, A. Panagiotarou, and M. Rigou, "Impact of environmental concern, emotional appeals, and attitude toward the advertisement on the intention to buy green products: The case of younger consumer audiences", *Sustainability (Basel),* vol. 15, no. 17, p. 13204, 2023.
[http://dx.doi.org/10.3390/su151713204]

[2]   M.I. Irfany, Y. Khairunnisa, and M. Tieman, "Factors influencing Muslim Generation Z consumers' purchase intention of environmentally friendly halal cosmetic products", *J. Islamic Mark.,* 2023.

[3]   N.W. Ekawati, I.M. Wardana, N.N.K. Yasa, N.M.W. Kusumadewi, and I.G.A. Tirtayani, "A strategy to improve green purchase behavior and customer relationship management during the covid-19 new normal conditions", *Uncertain Supply Chain Manag.,* vol. 11, no. 1, pp. 289-298, 2023.
[http://dx.doi.org/10.5267/j.uscm.2022.9.014]

[4]   K.P. Reddy, V. Chandu, S. Srilakshmi, E. Thagaram, C. Sahyaja, and B. Osei, "Consumers perception on green marketing towards eco-friendly fast moving consumer goods", *Int. J. Eng. Bus. Manag.,* vol. 15, 2023.
[http://dx.doi.org/10.1177/18479790231170962]

[5]   J.M. Lopes, S. Gomes, and T. Trancoso, "The Dark Side of Green Marketing: How Greenwashing Affects Circular Consumption?", *Sustainability (Basel),* vol. 15, no. 15, p. 11649, 2023.
[http://dx.doi.org/10.3390/su151511649]

[6]   A. Sahioun, A.Q. Bataineh, I.A. Abu-AlSondos, and H. Haddad, "The impact of green marketing on consumers' attitudes: A moderating role of green product awareness", *Innovative Marketing,* vol. 19, no. 3, p. 237, 2023.
[http://dx.doi.org/10.21511/im.19(3).2023.20]

[7]   E. Correia, S. Sousa, C. Viseu, and M. Larguinho, "Analysing the Influence of Green Marketing Communication in Consumers' Green Purchase Behaviour", *Int. J. Environ. Res. Public Health,* vol. 20, no. 2, p. 1356, 2023.
[http://dx.doi.org/10.3390/ijerph20021356] [PMID: 36674112]

[8]   R.R. Ahmed, D. Streimikiene, H. Qadir, and J. Streimikis, "Effect of green marketing mix, green customer value, and attitude on green purchase intention: evidence from the USA", *Environ. Sci. Pollut. Res. Int.,* vol. 30, no. 5, pp. 11473-11495, 2022.
[http://dx.doi.org/10.1007/s11356-022-22944-7] [PMID: 36094715]

[9]   J.M. Lopes, S. Gomes, and T. Trancoso, "The Dark Side of Green Marketing: How Greenwashing Affects Circular Consumption?", *Sustainability (Basel),* vol. 15, no. 15, p. 11649, 2023.
[http://dx.doi.org/10.3390/su151511649]

[10]   E. Correia, S. Sousa, C. Viseu, and M. Larguinho, "Analysing the Influence of Green Marketing Communication in Consumers' Green Purchase Behaviour", *Int. J. Environ. Res. Public Health,* vol. 20, no. 2, p. 1356, 2023.
[http://dx.doi.org/10.3390/ijerph20021356] [PMID: 36674112]

[11]   M. Simanjuntak, N.L. Nafila, L.N. Yuliati, I.R. Johan, M. Najib, and M.F. Sabri, "Environmental Care Attitudes and Intention to Purchase Green Products: Impact of Environmental Knowledge, Word of Mouth, and Green Marketing", *Sustainability (Basel),* vol. 15, no. 6, p. 5445, 2023.
[http://dx.doi.org/10.3390/su15065445]

[12]   R. Salama, F. Al-Turjman, D. Bordoloi, and S.P. Yadav, "Wireless Sensor Networks and Green Networking for 6G communication- An Overview", *2023 International Conference on Computational*

Intelligence, Communication Technology and Networking (CICTN), pp. 830-834, 2023.
[http://dx.doi.org/10.1109/CICTN57981.2023.10141262]

[13]   R. Saklani, K. Purohit, S. Vats, V. Sharma, V. Kukreja, and S.P. Yadav, "Multicore Implementation of K-Means Clustering Algorithm", *2nd International Conference on Applied Artificial Intelligence and Computing (ICAAIC),* p. 171-175, 2023.
[http://dx.doi.org/10.1109/ICAAIC56838.2023.10140800]

[14]   S. Srivastava, "Lung Infection and Identification using Heatmap", *2nd International Conference on Applied Artificial Intelligence and Computing (ICAAIC),* p. 1093-1098, 2023.
[http://dx.doi.org/10.1109/ICAAIC56838.2023.10140204]

[15]   S.P. Yadav, S. Zaidi, C.D.S. Nascimento, V.H.C. de Albuquerque, and S.S. Chauhan, "Analysis and Design of automatically generating for GPS Based Moving Object Tracking System", *2023 International Conference on Artificial Intelligence and Smart Communication (AISC),* pp. 1-5, 2023.
[http://dx.doi.org/10.1109/AISC56616.2023.10085180]

[16]   A.G. Ismaeel, J. Mary, A. Chelliah, J. Logeshwaran, S.N. Mahmood, S. Alani, and A.H. Shather, "Enhancing Traffic Intelligence in Smart Cities Using Sustainable Deep Radial Function", *Sustainability (Basel),* vol. 15, no. 19, p. 14441, 2023.
[http://dx.doi.org/10.3390/su151914441]

[17]   A. Bagwari, J. Logeshwaran, K. Usha, K. Raju, M.H. Alsharif, P. Uthansakul, and M. Uthansakul, "An Enhanced Energy Optimization Model for Industrial Wireless Sensor Networks Using Machine Learning", *IEEE Access,* vol. 11, pp. 96343-96362, 2023.
[http://dx.doi.org/10.1109/ACCESS.2023.3311854]

[18]   A. Armghan, J. Logeshwaran, S.M. Sutharshan, K. Aliqab, M. Alsharari, and S.K. Patel, "Design of biosensor for synchronized identification of diabetes using deep learning", *Results in Engineering,* vol. 20, p. 101382, 2023.
[http://dx.doi.org/10.1016/j.rineng.2023.101382]

[19]   S. Dhanasekaran, T. Thamaraimanalan, V. Anandkumar, and A. Manikandan, "Analysis and design of fir filter using modified Carry Look Ahead Multiplier", *International Journal Of Scientific & Technology Research,* vol. 9, pp. 1336-1339, 2020.

[20]   J. Vandarkuzhali, S. Kamatchi, M.K. Chakravarthi, D. Selvaraj, and R. Dhanapal, "Hybrid RF and PCA method: The number and Posture of piezoresistive sensors in a multifunctional technology for respiratory monitoring. Measurement", *Sensors (Basel),* vol. 29, p. 100832, 2023.

CHAPTER 22

An IoT Based RFID Enabled Automatic Waste Segregator and Monitoring System

Abhishek Anand[1,*], **Abhinav Shrivastav**[1] and **Gunjan Aggrawal**[1]

¹ Department of Computer Science Engineering Sharda University, Greater Noida, Uttar Pradesh 201310, India

Abstract: The increasing population has led to a significant environmental issue: the proper disposal of a combination of biodegradable and non-biodegradable garbage. This issue is expected to persist as the global population continues to expand. The issue of waste treatment and management is a significant global concern across all geographical areas. The magnitude of its detrimental effects on our society and its environment is immense. The consequences of our haphazard and unregulated garbage disposal practices have become a significant issue for the well-being of both humans and the biodiversity of plant and animal species. By employing appropriate methods of segregation, it is possible to reuse and recycle trash efficiently. Indian Railways carries a daily average of 23 million passengers in India. This project presents a feasible prototype of an automated garbage segregator that efficiently manages the entire system using a microcontroller. The device is equipped with a range of sensors, primarily including an infrared (IR) sensor for detecting the presence of trash, a moisture sensor for detecting water content in the waste, and a metal sensor for detecting metallic waste. Therefore, these sensors are used to detect and identify the specific type of trash that is being disposed of. The microcontroller can regulate and oversee all operations of the system, including the proper disposal of garbage into certain bins categorized by metal, moist, and other materials. The project also focuses on implementing an incentive system that encourages the public to maintain a clean environment. It is achieved using a user-friendly RFID card scanning device, which rewards individuals with points for their efforts in disposing of waste properly. In addition, the entire system is supervised *via* the Wi-Fi module. The objective of this project is to offer a cost-efficient and financially viable alternative for waste management, therefore guaranteeing a pristine and healthful atmosphere. This application is a highly efficient tool for managing and organizing waste, as well as for separating different types of waste.

Keywords: Geographical, Microcontroller, RFID card scanning device, Trash, Waste management.

** **Corresponding author Abhishek Anand:** Department of Computer Science Engineering Sharda University, Greater Noida, Uttar Pradesh 201310, India; E-mail: abhishek@ug.sharda.ac.in*

Pankaj Kumar Mishra & Satya Prakash Yadav (Eds.)

INTRODUCTION

Ensuring meticulous supervision and regulation of trash disposal is crucial to safeguarding human well-being and preventing environmental harm resulting from inappropriate waste management, which heightens the likelihood of ecological damage [1]. This work addresses several forms of garbage that contribute to environmental contamination, encompassing biodegradable food waste, foliage, and deceased animals, as well as non-biological waste like home plastics, bottles, nylon, and medical waste and biodegradable garbage [2]. The primary sources of garbage are industrial waste and domestic waste. This study largely examines domestic garbage, as individuals neglect to segregate waste into its elemental constituents [3].

The main sources of waste are industrial and domestic trash. Given the need for more effort by individuals to segregate their garbage into its fundamental constituents, this study primarily concentrates on household waste, which possesses an ambiguous value. Metals and non-biodegradable waste can be recycled, while organic waste can be employed for the production of biogas. Unmanaged metal waste is a hazard to both plant and animal species [4]. Rather than transporting waste to industrial facilities for first sorting, which is both time-consuming and results in ineffective waste sorting, a more efficient approach would be to sort the waste at the household level and send it straight for recycling. The utilization of X-rays and infrared rays in industrial trash sorting procedures presents a peril to human well-being. Inadequate waste management leads to well-documented and acknowledged environmental issues.

The objective of this project is to achieve a high level of efficiency and cost-effectiveness in the segregation of garbage into three distinct categories, namely wet, dry, and metallic, right at the point of origin [5]. It will be accomplished by employing infrared (IR), metallic, and rain sensors and further monitoring the system through the utilization of Internet of Things (IoT) technology. It will effectively mitigate the squandering of waste by enabling its conversion into a viable energy resource. The project also focuses on implementing an incentive system for the public to maintain cleanliness in their area [6]. It will be achieved using a user-friendly RFID card scanning device, which rewards individuals with points for their efforts in disposing of waste properly [7]. In addition, the entire system is monitored *via* a wireless fidelity (wi-fi) module [8]. The objective of this project is to offer a cost-efficient and budget-friendly approach to trash management, ultimately resulting in a pristine and sanitary environment.

RELATED WORKS

This system introduces an innovative method for garbage management by utilizing Radio Frequency Identification (RFID) and Internet of Things (IoT) technology [9]. The trash segmentation and monitoring system implements an automated waste segregation procedure that utilizes RFID sensors to secure and measure the quantity of garbage that is sorted into various bins based on its respective category [10]. This invention will enhance waste sorting by simplifying and expediting the process, as well as improving accuracy compared to current manual waste segregation methods. Additionally, it will offer comprehensive analytics to enable real-time tracking and monitoring of waste classification [11]. This aids in optimizing waste management and minimizing the likelihood of inadvertently discarding recyclable material [12].

Moreover, the technology enables remote waste monitoring, hence enhancing the efficiency of waste collection and disposal. Recent technological advancements have facilitated the development of robust computational models to enhance the management and monitoring of waste management systems [13]. An efficient waste management system is crucial for minimizing environmental harm and decreasing waste production through the promotion of trash sorting and recycling [14]. An example of an innovative computational model is Samsung's RFID-enabled Automatic Waste Segregator and Monitoring System. This system uses Radio Frequency Identification (RFID) tags to categorize and separate products according to their type, size, and other distinguishing features [15]. The system comprises an RFID reader, a database, a user interface, and a sensor-regulated waste container [16]. The RFID reader is mounted within the garbage collector's vehicle and scans every trash can that is transported on board. The reader discerns and retrieves data from all products that have been affixed with an RFID sticker. Subsequently, this data is transmitted to the back-end system, where it is stored and subjected to analysis [17]. The system's user interface facilitates the garbage collector in swiftly identifying and overseeing waste collection spots, enabling them to effectively organize their route while simultaneously monitoring the quantity of waste gathered. In addition, the user interface can display specific garbage and common waste using distinct colors [18]. This enables the garbage collector to conveniently assess the current quantity of waste on board and determine the collection priority. The popularity of developing Internet of Things (IoT) based RFID enabled Automatic Waste Segregator and Monitoring Systems has grown due to its user-friendly nature and potential for reducing costs. Prior to the implementation of such systems, it is imperative to create precise diagnostic models [19]. These models must take into account the diverse environmental, economic, and technical factors that impact the functioning and effectiveness of the system.

Furthermore, the models must yield dependable and replicable outcomes when it comes to forecasting the system's performance at various time intervals. One of the key challenges in developing diagnosis models for an IoT-based RFID-enabled Automated Waste Segregation and Monitoring System is the complex nature of the system [20]. It involves a variety of parameters, such as different waste types, transportation times, and storage conditions. The relationships between these parameters must be identified and taken into account while developing the models. When attempting to assess the efficiency of the system, it is necessary to evaluate the system's environmental impact. In addition, the models must account for the labor costs of the operation, variations in the garbage collection laws, and other factors that may change over time. Moreover, the models must ensure the reliability and reproducibility of the results.

LITERATURE REVIEW

Khan *et al.* suggested the utilization of Internet of Things (IoT) based comprehensive approaches for detecting waste management systems. The objective is to enhance an innovative waste management device that is largely grounded on the concept of sustainable and integrated waste management. The proposed technique also involves monitoring the movement of vehicles. The primary factor contributing to the difficulty of waste management in emerging countries is the rapid population growth, resulting in a corresponding rise in trash production. The combination of exorbitant expenses and limited comprehension of the variables that impact waste management imposes a substantial burden on the financial resources of local government bodies. L.A. Guerrero and other researchers have analyzed the many stakeholders engaged in waste management systems and identified the primary elements that contribute to the failure of these systems.

Extensive research has been conducted on strategies for effectively handling solid waste, such as employing software-driven routing, utilizing Geographic Information System (GIS) and Global System for Mobile Communications (GSM) technologies, implementing Radio Frequency Identification (RFID), and employing sensor-equipped bins. The microprocessor can regulate all the operations of the system and subsequently deposit the waste into the appropriate bins for metal, moist, and other types. M. Hannan *et al.* devised a sophisticated system for monitoring containers and trucks, through the incorporation of technologies such as RFID, GPS, GPRS (General Packet Radio Service), and GIS alongside camera technology. The user's text consists of two numerical values, 5 and 6. Data such as identification number, collection date and time, bin state, litter volume, and GPS coordinates will be gathered and kept in a newly developed system, which includes databases for bins and trucks. This data will be utilized for monitoring and managing the system. The data is shown in the graphical user interface of the monitoring system.

Md. S. Islam *et al.* [8] offer image processing approaches, including the Gabor wavelet approach, for extracting garbage bin images. Perceptron classifiers utilize these image features to ascertain the quantity of waste present in the bin. The effectiveness of the classifier was evaluated by measuring the area under the receiver operating characteristic (ROC) curve. Previous studies extensively examined ICT-enabled waste management systems in articles. Thus, by deploying an Internet of Things (IoT) enabled intelligent waste receptacle, the garbage can be promptly emptied whenever it reaches its capacity, thereby reducing the unpleasant odor for anyone using the road. Performing thorough scavenging upon receiving a bin full message guarantees that only items are moved to designated refuse collection destinations. This measure serves as a deterrent against corruption in waste management operations.

An automated waste collection and monitoring system offers an effective method for the complete waste management team, resulting in cost reduction since garbage trucks are only dispatched when notified about the condition of the bins. Furthermore, pollution is a significant factor.

Internet of Things (IoT) garbage collection and management: The demand for waste management has reached its highest point due to the potential for improper garbage collection and disposal to result in a surge of lethal diseases and illnesses. It necessitates the implementation of sophisticated trash collection and management systems that environmental waste authorities can monitor. These systems would ensure that bins are emptied when they reach full capacity, thereby maintaining cleanliness and preventing the spread of diseases. Hence, the primary objectives of smart cities adopting intelligent waste management systems are to mitigate environmental risks, and health issues, curtail pollution and collection expenses, and diminish apparent garbage. To establish a hygienic and sanitized urban environment, several towns have implemented features such as global positioning systems and GPS in smart waste bins, as well as ultrasonic sensors to find the bins effectively. An unambiguous route plan enables garbage trucks to access the bins. An electronic device measures and documents the amount of garbage present in the bin. The issue of waste collection and management poses a significant challenge in numerous metropolitan regions. Waste segregation is a significant challenge. Insufficient awareness is a primary factor contributing to the inability of individuals to properly determine the appropriate disposal location for different types of waste, such as cans or plastic bottles adjacent to the trash can. Within the waste separation system, garbage is segregated into distinct types. However, the separation process in this system could be more efficient due to its calculation of the dielectric constant, leading to the misclassification of certain dry waste as wet waste, which is erroneous. An alternative approach involves striking a can or plastic bottle against a galvanized steel platform, which generates resonance frequencies that allow for the differentiation and isolation of the object's features.

At the root level, individuals can segregate solid trash into many categories including biodegradable waste, non-biodegradable waste, hazardous waste, non-hazardous waste, as well as glass and plastic. The text is referenced by number 18. Thus, in an intelligent waste collection system utilizing IoT, the waste quantity within the bin is transmitted to the waste management team. It enables them to initiate the waste collection route accordingly, ensuring that the garbage truck is dispatched solely to bin locations. It is essential and aids in minimizing gasoline expenses by eliminating unnecessary journeys to check if the tank is full. IoT technologies facilitate cost reduction and enhance efficiency and precision by combining computing systems with limited human intervention and the external environment. Waste segregation is a crucial component of solid waste management. Ongoing research is being conducted in this field due to the economic and ecological benefits of managing waste that has been sorted at its origin. Dr. M. Yuvaraju and his colleagues proposed an inexpensive and effective technique for sorting waste at its origin, with the goal of maximizing its economic value through processing and recycling. The device under consideration utilizes an infrared sensor for the purpose of detecting the existence of debris, an inductive proximity sensor to ascertain the presence of metals, and a moisture sensor to assess the moisture content of the debris, distinguishing between dry and wet conditions. Furthermore, a GSM message is sent when the garbage can reaches its maximum capacity. While the concept demonstrated efficacy, it did not incorporate a mechanism for addressing plastic waste, necessitating additional research on this matter. The Internet of Things (IoT) was also implemented in the project. Capacitive sensors, specifically the FDC1004 module, as suggested by Vishal V *et al.*, can be a viable method for segregating waste. Capacitive sensors enumerate the various values in order to differentiate between them. This technology employs a buzzer to indicate when a bin has reached its maximum capacity, allowing for the separation of different contents. M.K. Pushpa *et al.* proposed an alternative method for sorting waste, which involves classifying it based on weight into moist and dry categories. The moist refuse is transferred to a different receptacle using a conveyor belt, while the arid refuse is meticulously sorted by being propelled into a container using a blower. Nevertheless, because of its immense magnitude, this system is unsuitable for managing substantial quantities of garbage or for utilization at the point of waste generation. It is advisable to put in a similar level of effort when it comes to sorting paper waste.

EXPERIMENTAL METHOD

Entry System

The segregator user uses a specific card that is scanned by the RFID reader's low-power radio waves to establish communication and save data. The RFID reader then exhibits the user's identification on the LED screen. Afterward, the user sequentially deposits their waste into the pipe's inlet. The IR sensor's transmitter and receiver identify the presence of garbage, generating a voltage of SV. This voltage serves as an input signal to the Arduino, initiating the first cycle of segregation. It occurs because the intensity of the reflected light from the IR sensor is sufficiently high and falls within the diameter range of the pipe. The sensor's output pin is linked to the A2 pin of the Arduino UNO. Following the completion of this operation, Arduino proceeds to initialize the remaining two sensors in order to initiate their respective functions. Fig. (**1**) shows the Metal Detection Sensor.

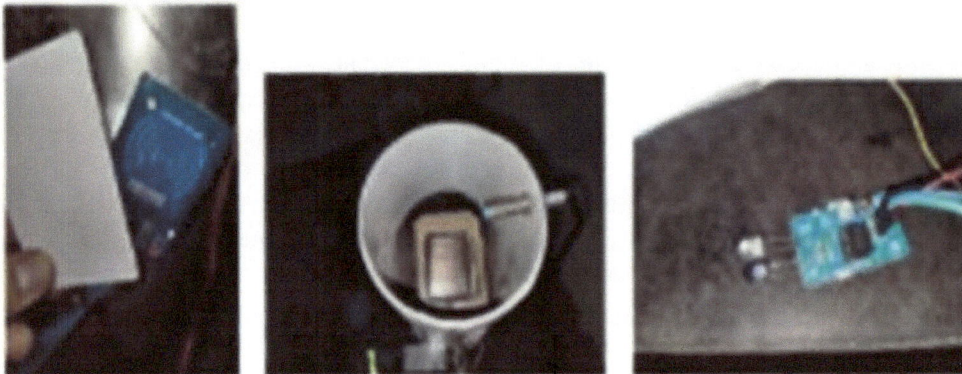

Fig. (1). Entry system.

Metal Detection System

Subsequently, the program proceeds to verify whether the waste is composed of metal. Upon the detection of a metallic object, the sensor promptly emits a signal, accompanied by the blinking of its LED, to the Arduino. This phenomenon occurs due to the metal sensor emitting an electromagnetic field that activates the metal object causing it to emit its electromagnetic field. The sensor is connected to the A4 pin of the microcontroller. Fig. (**2**) shows the Metal Detection Sensor.

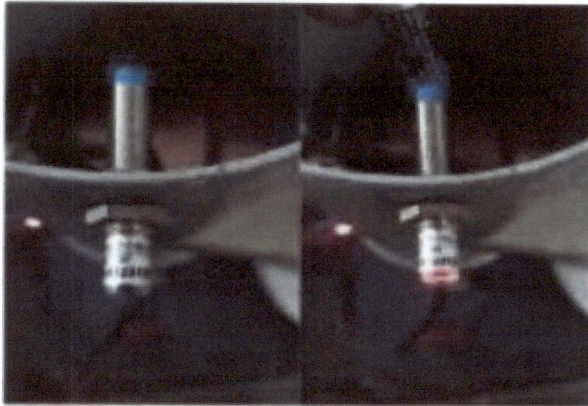

Fig. (2). Metal detection sensor.

Wet Detection System

A moisture sensor is used to quantify the volumetric water content in order to ascertain if a waste material is wet. The sensor, located within the pipe, serves as the ultimate stage of inspection if the waste is non-metallic. The moisture sensor comprises a set of printed conductor routes on Bakelite plates with minimal spacing between the tracks. When an electric current of around 35mA flows through the object, the recorded low resistance value indicates whether the moisture content of the trash exceeds 50%. At that point, it is classified as moist waste. The sensor produces an analog signal which is linked to the Arduino's A3 pin. Fig. (**3**) shows the Wet detection sensor.

Fig. (3). Wet detection sensor.

Rotating Disc System

The garbage collection process involves segregating the waste into categories such as metal, wet, or other types. This segregation is carried out on a rotating platform that contains separate bins for each type of waste. The circular platform is controlled by a servo motor with a rotational capacity of 180 degrees, which is programmed into the microcontroller. Upon detection of a specific waste category by the program's sensors, the platform is precisely tuned to the corresponding angle, causing the garbage to be released *via* the outlet vent of the pipe and into the bin. Fig. (**4**) shows the Rotating Disc System.

Fig. (4). Rotating disc system.

Monitoring System

The monitoring equipment employed in this context is a 16*2 LCD screen that displays an introduction as well as the count and type of waste detected by the user. User interaction refers to the exchange of information between a program and its user. Fig. (**5**) shows the Monitoring System.

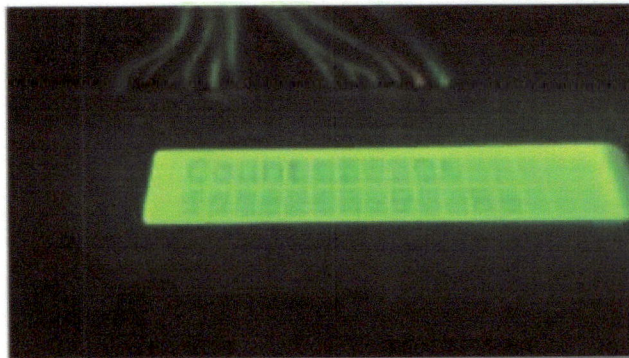

Fig. (5). Monitoring system.

The project also focuses on implementing an incentive system for the public to maintain cleanliness in their surroundings. It will be achieved using a user-friendly RFID card scanning device, which rewards individuals with points for their efforts in disposing of waste properly.

PROPOSED SYSTEM WORKFLOW

The objective of this project is to construct a trash segregator at the household level, utilizing an Arduino microcontroller to manage the entire process efficiently. The sensing device comprises an IR (Infrared) sensor, a rain sensor, and a metal sensor, all of which are utilized for the purpose of detecting different objects. The primary architecture of the segregator consists of three fundamental phases: the IR sensor, the metal sensor, the moisture sensor, and the segregation bins. The IR sensor detects the presence of trash upon its arrival. Sensors are employed to differentiate between different categories of refuse and ascertain the kind of waste. The microcontroller oversees all sensor operations. Through the utilization of an RFID card reader and tags, individuals effortlessly discard their waste materials (such as metal, damp substances, or other items) in exchange for designated points. These points can be exchanged for goods or services at certain booths located within the stations. It will not only encourage individuals to dispose of their waste properly but also make it easy for them to hold others responsible for doing the same. The system utilizes the Wi-Fi module in smartphones to enable monitoring. This module grants an internet connection to the microcontroller. By leveraging the Thing Speak web server, the system generates a graph that displays the amount of waste collected in each bin. Fig. (**6**) shows the Block Diagram of the proposed system.

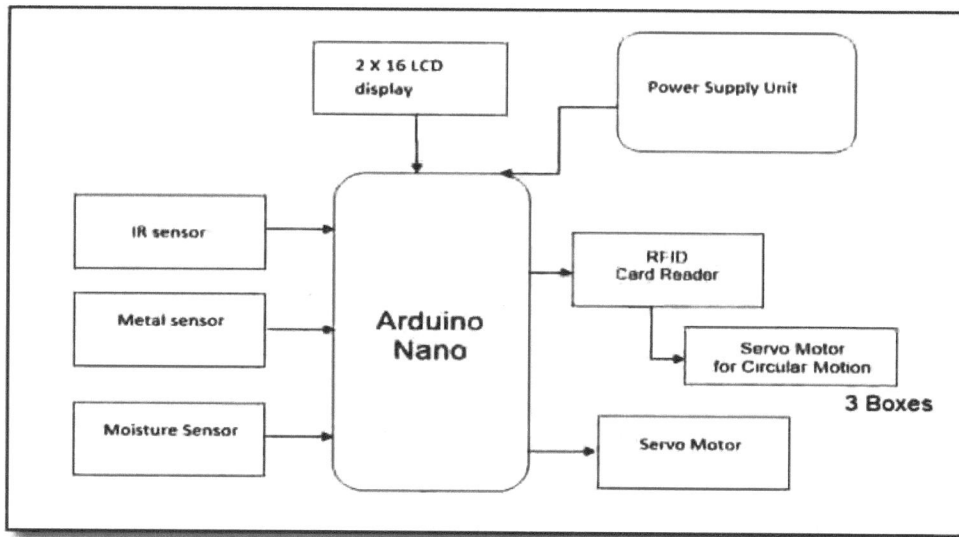

Fig. (6). Block diagram of the proposed system.

The utilization of advanced technology in automation has significantly reduced the requirement for human intervention. Fig. (6) illustrates the suggested system and offers a concise description of the components in each part. The primary hardware components of the proposed structures include the Node MCU, an ultrasonic sensor, a smoke sensor, and a servo motor. Programming-C is utilized for the development of Arduino programs.

Arduino UNO

The Arduino UNO microcontroller board is constructed using an ATmega328P microprocessor. The device is equipped with a 16MHz ceramic resonator, 6 analog inputs, 14 digital input/output pins, a USB port, a power jack, an ICSP header, and a reset button. All necessary components for the functioning of the microcontroller are provided. To initiate the process, establish a connection by utilizing either a USB cable, an AC to DC adapter, or a battery.

IR Sensor

An infrared sensor is a technological device that emits light in order to detect and recognize items within its immediate vicinity. An infrared sensor not only measures the temperature of an item but also can detect motion. Almost all objects emit infrared thermal radiation to some extent. Invisible to human sight, these radiations can nonetheless be detected by infrared sensors.

Servomotor

A servo motor is a rotary actuator or motor that can be accurately controlled for angle, acceleration, and speed. Position feedback sensors and conventional motors are utilized.

Metal Sensors

Electronic or electro-mechanical metal sensors are employed to ascertain the existence of metal in many situations, ranging from containers to individuals. An electromagnetic field detects the presence of a metallic object when it passes within the range of the proximity sensor. The microcontroller subsequently validates the sensor statistics in accordance with the programmed instructions prior to transmitting them to the assigned receptacle.

Moisture Sensor

It is utilized for the segregation of dry and wet waste. The microprocessor constantly checks the moisture level and employs a servo motor to choose a damp garbage can upon receiving a signal. Alternatively, a desiccated waste receptacle is selected.

Liquid Crystal Display

The 16 x 2 LCD consists of two rows, each containing 16 characters. It consists of sixteen pins.

RFID Card Reader

Electromagnetic fields are employed for the automated identification and tracking of tags. This initiative will serve as a reward system for our garbage segregator, motivating individuals to maintain cleanliness in their environment. By accumulating points on their own RFID tags, participants can enjoy various rewards.

RESULTS AND DISCUSSION

Fig. (7) illustrates the configuration of the hardware used in the experiment. The system is constructed upon the Internet of Things (IoT), which establishes connections between electronic components, sensors, and other Internet-enabled components. Data is transmitted between different components using the node MCU module. Fig. (7) illustrates the interconnection of different components, such as an ultrasonic sensor, a color sensor, and other elements, with an Arduino Uno module. This module is also equipped with a Wi-Fi module to facilitate the transmission of data to the cloud. A gas sensor is employed to detect the stench emanating from the waste bin.

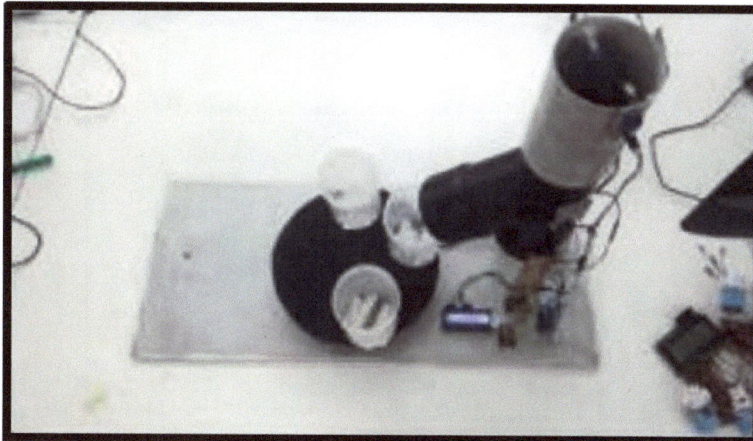

Fig. (7). Hardware of the proposed system.

Fig. (**8**) is a graph illustrating the variations in waste levels within a trash can as time progresses. The system maintains a log that contains the activity report and daily waste levels. The levels are measured using an ultrasonic sensor. Fig. (**9**) shows the result.

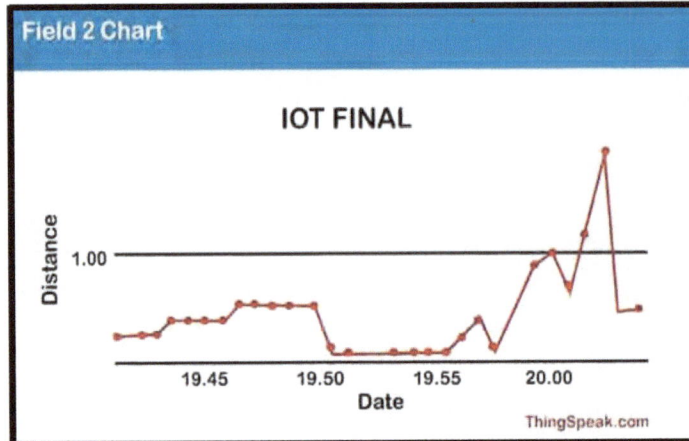

Fig. (8). Garbage levels of dustbin.

1. Metal Waste

S.NO.	Type of Waste	Discarded?
1.	Cell	Yes
2.	Coin	Yes
3.	Keys	Yes
4.	Screw	Yes

2. Wet Waste

S.NO.	Type of Waste	Discarded?
1.	Wet tissue	Yes
2.	Wet Cloth	Yes
3.	Wet wood	No
4.	Wet paper	No

3. Other Waste

S.NO.	Type of Waste	Discarded?
1.	Glass	Yes
2.	Plastic	Yes

Fig. (9). Result.

CONCLUSION

The paper presents an innovative approach to trash management and segregation by leveraging the Internet of Things (IoT). This concept introduces a sophisticated waste separator equipped with a reward system to encourage users to categorize waste into metal, moist, and other categories. This initiative has the potential to serve as a modest beginning, rapidly disseminating knowledge and establishing a foundation for expanded recycling efforts. Additionally, it aids in accurately assessing the worth of waste materials. Arduino serves as the central processing unit for this entire system, responsible for controlling and managing all the sensors. The garbage passes *via* the metal and moisture sensor to identify its type. It is subsequently recognized by the IR sensor to enable the motors to deposit the waste into the assigned bin.

The accumulation of waste frequently lures animals such as canines and rodents, resulting in an unfavorable ecological setting. Avian species may also endeavor to forage through the refuse. The objective of this project is to mitigate these problems by the utilization of an intelligent garbage receptacle that can effectively diminish pollution. The system incorporates a continuous monitoring system for dumpsters, operating around the clock, with the aim of facilitating effective and targeted garbage disposal. Through the utilization of RFID card readers and tags, users can easily dispose of their waste (such as metal, damp, or other materials) in exchange for designated points. These points can be exchanged at certain booths located within the stations. It will not only encourage individuals to dispose of their garbage properly but also motivate them to hold others responsible for doing the same, with minimal effort.

The system utilizes the Wi-Fi module in smartphones to enable monitoring. This module grants internet access to the microcontroller, which, in turn, utilizes the Thing Speak web server to generate graphs displaying the amount of waste collected in each bin. The objective of this project is to employ IR, metallic, and rain sensors to sort waste at its origin into wet, dry, and metallic categories. Additionally, the project aims to utilize IOT technology to monitor the system and prevent waste overflow while also simplifying waste categorization. To further improve the project, image processing technology could be integrated to efficiently sort large quantities of waste, which would be particularly beneficial for municipalities.

REFERENCES

[1]   M.R. Chitale, S.J. Chitpur, A.B. Chivate, P.D. Chopade, S.M. Deshmukh, and A.A. Marathe, "Automated smart waste segregation system using IoT technology", *J. Phys. Conf. Ser.,* vol. 2601, no. 1, p. 012015, 2023.
[http://dx.doi.org/10.1088/1742-6596/2601/1/012015]

[2]   M.K. Reddy, MeherPhanideep, D., Balaji, V. R., Kumar, S. C., Jaldu, V., Motamarry, S. M., & Vineeth, C, "Smart dustbin for real time waste segregation and monitoring", *Conference Proceedings,* vol. 2946, no. 1, 2023.

[3]   J.B. Sigongan, H.P. Sinodlay, S.X.P. Cuizon, J.S. Redondo, M.G. Macapulay, C.O. Bulahan-Undag, and K.M.V.C. Gumonan, "GULP: Solar-Powered Smart Garbage Segregation Bins with SMS Notification and Machine Learning Image Processing", *International Journal of Computing Sciences Research,* vol. 7, pp. 2018-2036, 20232023.

[4]   P. Punglia, S. Bansal, R. Kumar, and M. Rani, *Fabrication of Smart Dustbin with In-built Wet and Dry Waste Segregator. PRATIBODH.* RACON May, 2023.

[5]   A.K. Lingaraju, M. Niranjanamurthy, P. Bose, B. Acharya, V.C. Gerogiannis, A. Kanavos, and S. Manika, "IoT-Based Waste Segregation with Location Tracking and Air Quality Monitoring for Smart Cities", *Smart Cities,* vol. 6, no. 3, pp. 1507-1522, 2023.
[http://dx.doi.org/10.3390/smartcities6030071]

[6]   V. Muneeswaran, P. Nagaraj, A. Akhila, L. Sudeepthi, B. Venkateswararao, and B.V. Krishna, "Smart Segregation of Waste and Automatic Monitoring System", *2023 International Conference on Computer Communication and Informatics (ICCCI),* pp. 1-6, 2023.
[http://dx.doi.org/10.1109/ICCCI56745.2023.10128456]

[7]   D. Selvakarthi, D. Sivabalaselvamani, M.A. Wafiq, G. Aruna, and M. Gokulnath, "An IoT Integrated Sensor Technologies for the Enhancement of Hospital Waste Segregation and Management", *2023 International Conference on Innovative Data Communication Technologies and Application (ICIDCA),* pp. 797-804, 2023.
[http://dx.doi.org/10.1109/ICIDCA56705.2023.10099836]

[8]   S.C. Patil, and M.R. Gidde, "RFID and IoT Enabled Framework to Make Pune City an Eco-friendly Smart City", *Nature Environment and Pollution Technology,* vol. 22, no. 2, pp. 553-563, 2023.
[http://dx.doi.org/10.46488/NEPT.2023.v22i02.002]

[9]   G. Rajakumaran, S. Usharani, C. Vincent, and M. Sujatha, "Smart Waste Management: Waste Segregation using Machine Learning", *J. Phys. Conf. Ser.,* vol. 2471, no. 1, p. 012030, 2023.
[http://dx.doi.org/10.1088/1742-6596/2471/1/012030]

[10]   A. Ishaq, S.J. Mohammad, A.A.D. Bello, S.A. Wada, A. Adebayo, and Z.T. Jagun, "Smart waste bin monitoring using IoT for sustainable biomedical waste management", *Environ. Sci. Pollut. Res. Int.,* pp. 1-16, 2023.
[http://dx.doi.org/10.1007/s11356-023-30240-1] [PMID: 37878175]

[11]   N. Murugan, A. Sivathanu, K. Vaidyanathan, A. Tiwari, and A. Varma, "Automated home waste segregation and management system", *International Journal of Electrical and Computer Engineering (IJECE),* vol. 13, no. 4, pp. 3903-3912, 2023.
[http://dx.doi.org/10.11591/ijece.v13i4.pp3903-3912]

[12]   K. Suganyadevi, V. Nandhalal, N. Thiyagarajan, and S. Dhanasekaran, "A Multicore ECU-Based Automotive Software Domain Combining Runnable Sequencing and Task Scheduling", *International Conference on Automation, Computing and Renewable Systems (ICACRS),* pp. 34-38, 2022.
[http://dx.doi.org/10.1109/ICACRS55517.2022.10029084]

[13]   S. Dhanasekaran, S. Ramalingam, P. Vivek Karthick, and D. Silambarasan, "An improved pilot pattern design-based channel estimation in wireless communication using distribution ant colony optimization", *Simul. Model. Pract. Theory,* vol. 129, p. 102820, 2023.
[http://dx.doi.org/10.1016/j.simpat.2023.102820]

[14]   J. Logeshwaran, N. Shanmugasundaram, and J. Lloret, "Energy-efficient resource allocation model for device-to-device communication in 5G wireless personal area networks", *Int. J. Commun. Syst.,* vol. 36, no. 13, p. e5524, 2023.
[http://dx.doi.org/10.1002/dac.5524]

[15] G. Ramesh, J. Logeshwaran, and A.P. Kumar, "The Smart Network Management Automation Algorithm for Administration of Reliable 5G Communication Networks", *Wirel. Commun. Mob. Comput.,* vol. 2023, pp. 1-13, 2023.
[http://dx.doi.org/10.1155/2023/7626803]

[16] M.A. Mohammed, M.A. Mohammed, V.A. Mohammed, J. Logeshwaran, and N. Jiwani, "An earlier serial lactate determination analysis of cardiac arrest patients using a medical machine learning model", *International Conference on Intelligent Systems for Communication, IoT and Security (ICISCoIS),* p. 263-268, 2023.
[http://dx.doi.org/10.1109/ICISCoIS56541.2023.10100454]

[17] S.P. Yadav, "Blockchain Security", In: *Blockchain Security in Cloud Computing. EAI/Springer Innovations in Communication and Computing.,* K. Baalamurugan, S.R. Kumar, A. Kumar, V. Kumar, S. Padmanaban, Eds., Springer: Cham, 2022.
[http://dx.doi.org/10.1007/978-3-030-70501-5_1]

[18] S. P., Mahato, D. P., & Linh, N. T. D., "Distributed Artificial Intelligence", (S. P. Yadav, D. P. Mahato, & N. T. D. Linh, Eds.). CRC Press, 2020.
[http://dx.doi.org/10.1201/9781003038467]

[19] V. Vashisht, A.K. Pandey, and S.P. Yadav, "Speech Recognition using Machine Learning", *Transactions on Smart Processing & Computing,* vol. 10, no. 3, pp. 233-239, 2021.
[http://dx.doi.org/10.5573/IEIESPC.2021.10.3.233]

[20] S.P. Yadav, B.S. Bhati, D.P. Mahato, and S. Kumar, "Federated Learning for IoT Applications. EAI/Springer Innovations in Communication and Computing", *Springer International Publishing,* 2022.
[http://dx.doi.org/10.1007/978-3-030-85559-8]

CHAPTER 23

How to Reduce Environmental Cost by Green Accounting

Himanshu Kumar[1], **Ashish Diwakar**[1] and **Surbhi Agarwal**[1,*]

[1] *Depatment of Management Studies, Hi-Tech Institute of Engineering and Technology, Ghaziabad, (U.P.), India*

Abstract: The increasing apprehension regarding environmental sustainability has prompted a heightened focus on discovering methods to diminish the ecological expenses linked to commercial activities. One strategy that can be used is the adoption of green accounting, which aims to include environmental factors in conventional accounting approaches. This essay will contend that the implementation of green accounting techniques can substantially mitigate the environmental expenses incurred by firms. We shall substantiate this assertion by analyzing multiple objective factors, elucidating the concepts of green accounting, and outlining the potential advantages and obstacles linked to its adoption. In the subsequent paragraphs, I will initially elucidate the notion of green accounting and its significance in the contemporary day, subsequently, examine its potential in mitigating environmental expenses, and ultimately investigate obstacles and remedies for its widespread implementation.

Keywords: Environmental, Elucidating, Green accounting, Implementation, Mitigating, Sustainability.

INTRODUCTION

Green accounting pertains to the implementation of methods and goods that are ecologically sustainable [1]. The consideration of both the exhaustion of existing resources and the safeguarding of the environment is accompanied by an assessment of the associated costs and benefits [2]. It encompasses economic, social, and environmental integration. Incorporating green accounting into a national framework for economic accounts can facilitate the measurement of sustainability. In 1994, the National Academy of Sciences assessed the Integrated Satellite of Economic and Environmental Accounts, a method developed by the

* **Corresponding author Surbhi Agarwal:** Depatment of Management Studies, Hi-Tech Institute of Engineering and Technology, Ghaziabad, (U.P.), India; E-mail: surbhiagarwal060@gmail.com

Pankaj Kumar Mishra & Satya Prakash Yadav (Eds.)

Bureau of Economic Analysis for generating environmental accounts, notwithstanding its limited usage. Huhtala A. and Samakovlis E [3] (2016) performed the valuation of unquantified environmental services and goods incorporated into "green accounting," which also encompasses the assessment of emissions and natural resource accounts, disaggregating both traditional national accounts and green GDP [4]. To efficiently manage the supply chain is considered a crucial method for implementing green accounting. The phrases "environmental cost, valuation, and apportionment" are synonymous. Environmental accounting is the systematic procedure of identifying, quantifying, and distributing costs [5]. This accounting report includes the environmental expenses that are directly related to certain activities, such as the costs associated with legal liabilities and the costs of disposing of garbage. The director's report may cover several subjects, such as green accounting matters, policies, and progress [6]. The study conducted by Farouk *et al.* in 2016 has shown that the source of this accounting information is Schmalleger and Burritt's publication from the year 2000. The director's report may cover several subjects, such as green accounting concerns, policy, and progress [7]. The source of this accounting is Schmalleger and Burritt's publication in 2000. Ecological accounting examines the influence of the environment on a company's economic activities. Environmental management accounting plays a crucial role in collecting and analyzing diverse data related to environmental costs and associated expenses [8]. It also considers internal analysis and the management's informed decisions [9]. Green accounting primarily focuses on analyzing the changes and effects of different corporate processes as proposed by Garg, A., Agarwal, P., & Singh, S. (2023) . It also prepares to engage with external stakeholders.

RELATED WORKS

Green accounting is a form of accounting that entails assessing the ecological expenses linked to an organization's activities and implementing measures to mitigate them [10]. The uniqueness of green accounting resides in its ability to evaluate the ecological expenses linked to a business that goes beyond the usual measurements in conventional financial accounting [11]. This entails quantifying the financial implications of environmental expenses and utilizing this data to make informed choices on cost reduction and minimizing the organization's ecological footprint [12]. Green accounting is a variant of cost accounting that allows firms to quantify and disclose the ecological expenses associated with their operations. Green accounting enables firms to evaluate potential ecological expenses linked to production and consumption activities and offers a framework for integrating environmental consequences into investment choices [13]. It facilitates the advancement of more sustainable business practices by offering a method to evaluate the environmental impact of various operations, thereby motivating organizations to implement strategies to diminish their ecological footprint [14]. The conventional approaches to green accounting have been constrained by the challenge of evaluating the ecological expenses linked to various activities. In recent times, significant progress in computer models and approaches has allowed businesses to accurately measure the environmental consequences of their operations with more precision [15]. By employing environmental impact assessment (EIA) technologies like life cycle assessment (LCA) and environmental economic models, firms can acquire knowledge about the ecological expenses associated with their operations and pinpoint potential avenues for enhancement [16]. Environmental Impact Assessment (EIA) techniques such as Life Cycle Assessment (LCA) enable organizations to comprehensively evaluate the environmental expenses linked to a product or system, encompassing the acquisition of raw materials and the disposal of old products [17]. Additionally, these tools help identify the specific components of the system that have a more significant or lower influence on the environment. This observation assists companies in recognizing areas of concern, such as the depletion of resources, pollution of air and water, and climate change. The environment plays a crucial role in the global economy, as numerous sectors rely on the natural resources and biodiversity it offers. Regrettably, environmental expenses are frequently disregarded, particularly in the context of financial bookkeeping. Consequently, Diagnostics Models for Green Accounting have emerged as a crucial instrument for recognizing these expenses and aiding enterprises, government bodies, and other stakeholders in diminishing their ecological costs [18]. Green Accounting is a methodology that enhances the comprehension of financial choices and their ecological consequences for businesses and other organizations. By employing Diagnostic Models for Green Accounting, companies, and corporations can effectively discern and comprehend the environmental expenses and advantageous outcomes associated with adopting eco-friendly practices. Several diagnostic models that might be used include Cost-Benefit Analysis, Life Cycle Assessment, and Impact Analysis. Cost-benefit analysis is a technique used to evaluate the potential benefits of a proposed action or policy in relation to its costs [19]. The diagnostic approach enables the identification of both the positive and negative impacts on the environment, allowing organizations to assess the environmental costs and benefits associated with proposed investments. Life Cycle Assessment (LCA) is a comprehensive evaluation method that analyzes the environmental implications of a product across its full life cycle, encompassing stages such as raw material extraction, production, and disposal. Companies are increasingly utilizing this instrument to ascertain and diminish the environmental expenses associated with their items. Impact Analysis enables companies to assess the environmental consequences of their operations. Green accounting examines the financial impact of environmental expenses, the obligations to protect the environment, and the evaluation of environmental performance. It acts as a valuable connection between the environment and the economy [20]. The components of this system are internal ecological accounting, environmental management accounting, environmental financial accounting, and environmental ecological accounting. The environmental accounting technique comprises only the assessment of environmental performance, life cycle analysis, and analysis of environmental cost reductions. The entirety is composed of both monetary and non-monetary entities. Tap aria *et al.*, (2022) proposed that the expenses are crucial for technical research and development, software development, financial information analysis, process engineering, inventory management, and supplier surveys. These issues may vary in severity and frequency. Therefore, the methodology examines the additional expenses related to obtaining information.

REVIEW OF LITERATURE

Dr.Minimol M.C and Dr.Makesh K.G (February 2014) have developed a model that outlines six criteria for evaluating the performance of Indian firms in terms of Green Accounting and reporting standards. Furthermore, it has conducted a study on the actual implementation of environmental reporting in India. In India, the green account is now in its early stages, with limited marketability and public awareness. The three aspects of it are the physical account, financial valuation, and integration with the profitable account. This study facilitated the establishment of criteria that businesses use to evaluate their environmentally sustainable practices. The study's conclusion asserts that while there exist regulations pertaining to environmental contamination, there needs to be established benchmarks and protocols to adhere to Dr. R.K. Tailor conducted a study from July to September 2017 to investigate the impact of green accounts on sustainable development, which aims to assess the adoption of environmentally friendly practices among a representative sample of the Indian population. Financial considerations alone are insufficient for evaluating growth. Green accounting prioritizes the incorporation of ecological expenses into the financial records of the organization. It will facilitate our comprehension of the company's ecological footprint. However, there are other problems associated with this. Indian enterprises have developed a design that seeks to measure the extent, acknowledgment, and scale of environmental expenses. The primary limitation lies in the complexity associated with accurately quantifying the environmental costs and benefits of the company. As a result, their inclusion poses a significant issue. This study showcases the understanding of environmental concerns and regulations pertaining to exposure situations among established commercial industries. However, there is a need for more enterprises to engage in this activity. Furthermore, certain patterns that demonstrate the presence of large firms are more apparent compared to those of small organizations (Garg, A., & Kumar, D. S. (2021)). In addition, the organization exclusively uses descriptive language and refrains from using numerical data when presenting information. Although businesses universally acknowledge the significance of implementing environmental protection measures, India currently has numerous deficiencies in terms of green accounting, as it is in its early stages and needs comprehensive recording and disclosure of environmental activities. In other words, a green account is a valuable instrument for evaluating the pros and cons of implementing environmental policies. Diverse agencies and organizations have established ethical principles and regulations for the dissemination of information in both public and international contexts. Furthermore, many reporting methodologies have been developed, such as GRI reporting and internet-based satellite reporting, each with their distinct advantages and scope. India possesses a robust legal structure, encompassing the constitution, acts, and other legal authorities, which effectively facilitate the preservation of land. More than merely adherence to morality and regulations would be necessary to meet the current imperative. Maama H. and Appiah K. O. (2019), Dr. Preeti Malik, and Dr. Alka Mittal assert that it is imperative for everyone to be aware of this novel generalization and willingly offer their equitable portion. It facilitates comprehension of the utilization of resources and the expenses incurred for the landscape. Based on the New Delhi audit, manufacturing companies make a greater contribution to the green account compared to non-manufacturing enterprises. Utilizing incremental environmental cost assessment can enhance the financial performance of a company's operations. Once this new generalization is universally acknowledged and implemented correctly, it will achieve success. When evaluating a country's wealth, the focus is predominantly on the green account rather than the GDP growth statistic, which is now considered a crucial but outdated measure. Singhal, (R. K., Garg, A., Das, S., and Gaur, M. (2022)). Hence, in order to assess the growth indicator, decision-makers necessitate precise information, and citizens are also entitled to the same knowledge. It implies that a comprehensive public accounting system that accurately records the capital stock, which directly influences the company's profits, is essential. The adoption of Green Accounting is increasing due to its enhanced analytical capabilities and its ability to evaluate the social cost, hence benefiting society as a whole. The main objective of the paper is to elucidate the theoretical foundations of green accounting. As stated by N Anil Kumar, T SaiPranitha, and N Kiran Kumar, a study on green accounting and its practices in India has highlighted the adoption of several environmentally friendly methods and the implementation of current environmental protection legislation by Indian firms. The generality of green accounting is classified into three categories: global environmental accounting, public environmental accounting, and marketable environmental accounting. The importance of the green account has been deliberated in relation to individuals, financial gain, and the ecosystem. Thus, it has been established that environmental accounting and reporting in India are currently undergoing development and are both commercially and publicly viable. They are also considered a fashionable trend to be followed for the purpose of achieving sustainable development.

RESEARCH METHODOLOGY

The research study was conducted using an experimental and descriptive approach, focusing on a sample population of 270 respondents. The age demographic spans from those aged 30 to 60 years. The examples were chosen from different institutes and institutions located in several cities, including Ghaziabad, Meerut, and Delhi NCR. The data-collecting procedure involves the utilization of secondary methods. The primary source of secondary data for research papers, journals, and publications is the majority of existing literature on the subject. The study was conducted by Rahim *et al.* in 2016.

Demographic Profile

The conceptual framework was developed by Farouk *et al.* (2016) based on the specified hypotheses and research questions directed towards research scholars, academicians, undergraduate and postgraduate students, as well as employees from various departments in different organizations and institutes. The questionnaire was answered by a total of 270 individuals, with 63% being male and 37% being female. The age distribution of the participants is as follows: 60 participants were aged 30-35 years, 54 participants were aged 35-40 years, 48 participants were aged 40-45 years, 42 participants were aged 45-50 years, 36 participants were aged 50-55 years, and 30 participants were aged 55-60 years. Regarding the experience constraint, 85% of the total respondents were experienced, while the remaining 15% were inexperienced. Figs. (**1**, **2**, and **3**) show the gender, age group, and experience Level.

We categorize the respondents' responses based on age groups to enhance the accuracy of their judgments, which are then compared to their previous answers. The coefficient was employed to ascertain the correlation between the two variables. The age and number of respondents provide significant comments regarding Green Accounting and how to calculate the environmental expenses using green technology, which is defined as the total worth of all goods. Fig. (**4**) shows the ratio of men and women in number of respondents.

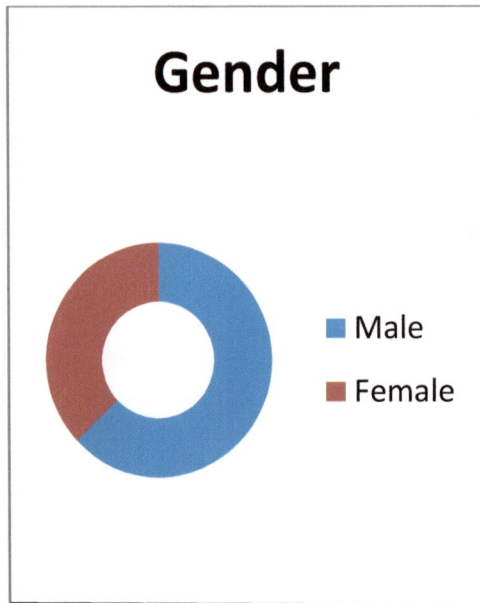

Fig. (1). Gender.

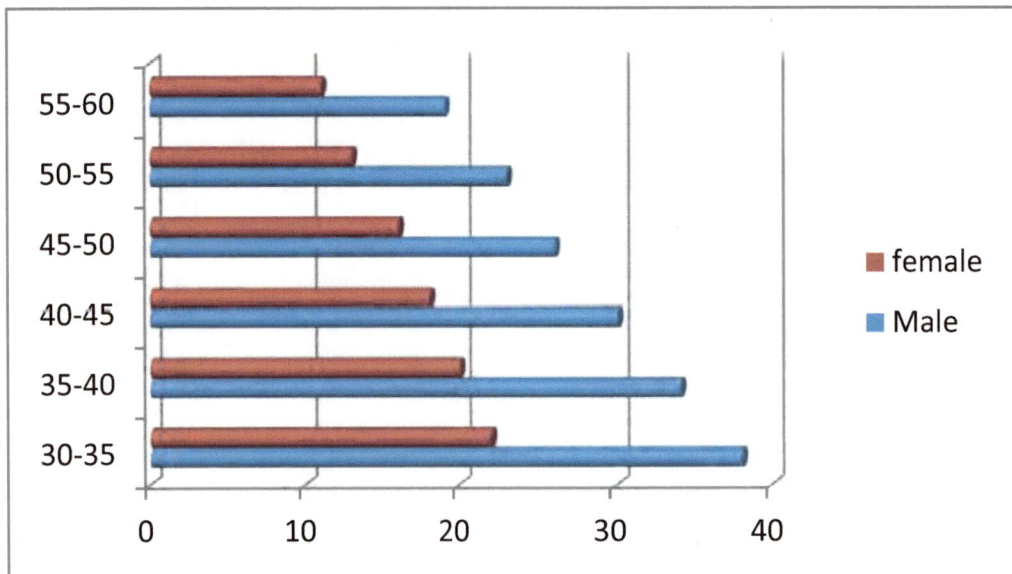

Fig. (2). Age group.

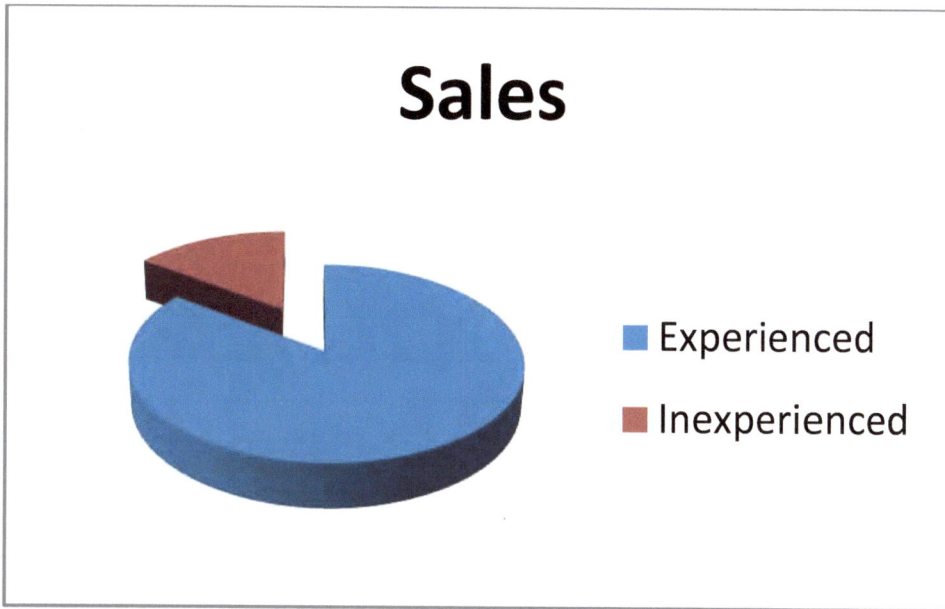

Fig. (3). Experience level.

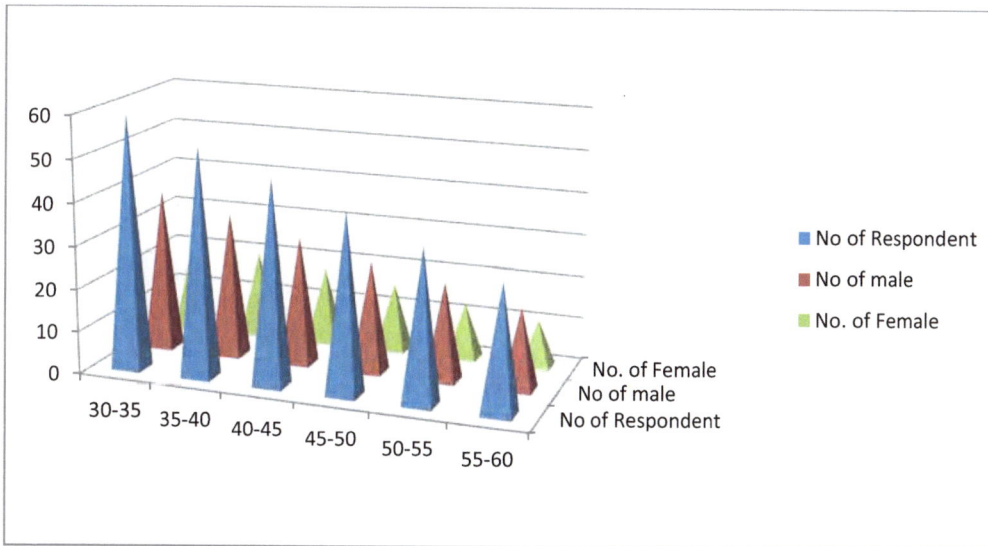

Fig. (4). Ratio of men and women in no. of respondent (acknowledgement table).

Explanation

In Table **1**, we establish a correlation between the number of respondents and the average age of different age groups. Column X represents the average age of the respondents, while Column Y represents the number of respondents from Table **2**.

We apply a formula to determine the correlation between the characteristics of the respondents and their age groups. Finally, we have obtained a correlation coefficient of 1, indicating a strong positive relationship between variables X and Y. This suggests that individuals from various age groups have readily embraced the concept of green accounting.

Table 1. Acknowledgement table.

Age	No of Respondent
30-35	60
35-40	54
40-45	48
45-50	42
50-55	36
55-60	30

Table 2. Respondent's characteristics

X	Y	X - $\bar{X}$	Y - $\bar{Y}$	(X - $\bar{X}$)(Y - $\bar{Y}$)	(X - $\bar{X}$)²	(Y - $\bar{Y}$)²
32.5	60	12.5	15	187.5	156.25	225
37.5	54	7.5	9	67.5	56.25	81
42.5	48	2.5	3	7.5	6.25	9
47.5	42	-2.5	-3	7.5	6.25	9
52.5	36	-7.5	-9	67.5	56.25	81
57.5	30	-12.5	-15	187.5	156.25	225
$\sum X = 270$	$\sum Y = 270$	$\sum(X - \bar{X}) = 0$	$\sum(Y - \bar{Y}) = 0$	$\sum(X-\bar{X})(Y-\bar{Y}) = 525$	$\sum(X - \bar{X})^2 = 437.50$	$\sum(Y - \bar{Y})^2 = 630$

$\bar{X} = \sum X/N = 270/6 = 45$ $\bar{Y} = \sum Y/N = 45$

$rXY = \sum(X - \bar{X})(Y - \bar{Y})/\sqrt{\{\sum(X - \bar{X})^2 \sum(Y - \bar{Y})^2\}}$

$= 525/\sqrt{(437.50 * 630)}$

$= 525/525$

$= 1$ (Positive Correlation)

ANALYSIS AND FINDINGS

There is a strong positive correlation between the candidates and their age. Both variables are associated and mutually fulfilled, indicating a meaningful association. The coefficient of correlation has a value of 1, indicating a meaningful relationship. The findings corroborate a research study that revealed the role of green accounting in promoting sustainable development by functioning as an accounting framework that captures the interconnectedness between the economy and the environment. They demonstrate that the implementation of green accounting has a beneficial influence on environmental performance by considering environmental costs. Advocating for environmental programs and policies and incorporating the environmental costs and benefits demonstrates a commitment to the environment. It mitigates environmental expenses through sustainable accounting and social responsibility. It is now possible for any organization or industry to implement this technology in order to decrease environmental expenses while maximizing profits.

DISCUSSION AND CONCLUSION

Businesses should take into account the economic conditions and environmental impact when conducting their industrial operations. Enterprises are compelled to adopt green accounting to mitigate environmental risks, provide consumers with safe goods and services, and balance marketing efforts with environmental quality. The rising demand for a competitive environment that prioritizes the preservation of the natural environment has resulted in a heightened interest in the impact of enterprises on the environment. The objective of this study is to determine the importance of green accounting in cost reduction and enhancement of environmental performance, considering its association with the theory of environmental concern, which posits that it may result in increased production costs and decreased profitability. The key fundamental attributes and advantages of green accounting were identified to encompass the following aspects: adherence to standards, ecological compatibility, and strategic positioning. Accurately assessing the relationship between product revenues and costs, as well as identifying the elements of expenses and environmental impact, precisely measuring them, and integrating them into operations and products, helps determine the cost of these products more effectively. It enhances the company's profitability and market position by optimizing pricing decisions and ensuring accurate valuation of each item. As per the Department of Economic and Social Affairs Statistics Division Nations (2005), environmental accounting assists managers in making decisions that reduce environmental expenses and promote the establishment and upkeep of a comprehensive environmental management system inside an enterprise. The findings indicated that adherence to compliance leads to cost reduction and improved environmental performance due to its comprehensive and meticulous monitoring of performance. Furthermore, enhancing sustainability will result in cost and productivity benefits as increased economic input efficiency will positively affect operations and outputs, leading to reduced costs and improved productivity. The strategic location enhances cost and sustainability impact through consistent and productive efforts. Considering this, it is clear that employing modern scientific accounting methods has a positive influence on the overall business, as well as on the sustainability and promotion of social responsibility.

RECOMMENDATIONS

- The government should assume a crucial role in promoting the adoption of green accounting within the business sector.
- Companies that have implemented green accounting should step up and contribute to the advancement of green accounting practices through donations.
- The government website should offer a variety of benefits. The proposed reduction in fiscal adon tax will incentivize the adoption of green accounting practices by the communist government.
- Green GDP can be incorporated alongside traditional GDP measurements.
- The depletion of natural resources can be factored into the calculation of net income through the inclusion of green points, such as green GDP terrain, which can contribute to the growth of domestic product.
- The inclusion of environmental data in financial reports can expand the scope of profitable accounting.
- The value of growth can be assessed by considering the costs associated with green accounting.
- A green economic system should be implemented to identify and address pollutants caused by different sectors of the economy.
- The user's text consists of a bullet point symbol. If further research is conducted, we can apply green accounting in various sectors of manufacturing. The financial statement should include a proper presentation of the reduction in natural resources resulting from environmental accounting.

REFERENCES

[1]   C.C. Gonzalez, and J. Peña-Vinces, "A framework for a green accounting system-exploratory study in a developing country context, Colombia", *Environ. Dev. Sustain.,* vol. 25, no. 9, pp. 9517-9541, 2023.
        [http://dx.doi.org/10.1007/s10668-022-02445-w]

[2]   C.D. Murti, "What Is Known About Environmental Cost Accounting? Systematic Literature Review", *Journal of Accounting and Investment,* vol. 24, no. 1, pp. 84-100, 2022.
        [http://dx.doi.org/10.18196/jai.v24i1.16180]

[3]   C. Sukmadilaga, S. Winarningsih, I. Yudianto, T.U. Lestari, and E.K. Ghani, "Does Green Accounting Affect Firm Value? Evidence from ASEAN Countries", *International Journal of Energy Economics and Policy,* vol. 13, no. 2, pp. 509-515, 2023.
        [http://dx.doi.org/10.32479/ijeep.14071]

[4]   X. Jiao, P. Zhang, L. He, and Z. Li, "Business sustainability for competitive advantage: identifying the role of green intellectual capital, environmental management accounting and energy efficiency", *Ekon. Istraz.,* vol. 36, no. 2, p. 2125035, 2023.
        [http://dx.doi.org/10.1080/1331677X.2022.2125035]

[5]   C. Li, C. Zhu, X. Wang, S. Ren, P. Xu, and H. Xiang, "Green finance: how can it help Chinese power enterprises transition towards carbon neutrality", *Environ. Sci. Pollut. Res. Int.,* vol. 30, no. 16, pp. 46336-46354, 2023.

[http://dx.doi.org/10.1007/s11356-023-25570-z] [PMID: 36717412]

[6] P. Xie, Y. Xu, X. Tan, and Q. Tan, "How does environmental policy stringency influence green innovation for environmental managements?", *J. Environ. Manage.*, vol. 338, p. 117766, 2023. [http://dx.doi.org/10.1016/j.jenvman.2023.117766] [PMID: 37011531]

[7] S. Bresciani, S.U. Rehman, G. Giovando, and G.M. Alam, "The role of environmental management accounting and environmental knowledge management practices influence on environmental performance: mediated-moderated model", *J. Knowl. Manage.*, vol. 27, no. 4, pp. 896-918, 2023. [http://dx.doi.org/10.1108/JKM-12-2021-0953]

[8] P.D. Putra, K. Harahap, I.S. Agusti, A. Zainal, and R. Thohiri, "The implementation of Green Innovation and Environmental Management Accounting and Impact on Firm Profitability. SAR (Soedirman Accounting Review)", *Journal of Accounting and Business,* vol. 8, no. 2, pp. 136-145, 2023.

[9] Y. Zhu, J. Zhang, and C. Duan, "How does green finance affect the low-carbon economy? Capital allocation, green technology innovation and industry structure perspectives", *Ekon. Istraz.*, vol. 36, no. 2, p. 2110138, 2023. [http://dx.doi.org/10.1080/1331677X.2022.2110138]

[10] Q. Guo, C. Geng, and N.C. Yao, "How does green digitalization affect environmental innovation? The moderating role of institutional forces", *Bus. Strategy Environ.*, vol. 32, no. 6, pp. 3088-3105, 2023. [http://dx.doi.org/10.1002/bse.3288]

[11] L. Wei, B. Lin, Z. Zheng, W. Wu, and Y. Zhou, "Does fiscal expenditure promote green technological innovation in China? Evidence from Chinese cities", *Environ. Impact Assess. Rev.*, vol. 98, p. 106945, 2023. [http://dx.doi.org/10.1016/j.eiar.2022.106945]

[12] R. Salama, F. Al-Turjman, P. Chaudhary, and S.P. Yadav, "Benefits of Internet of Things (IoT) Applications in Health care - An Overview", *International Conference on Computational Intelligence, Communication Technology and Networking (CICTN)*, pp. 778-784, 2023. [http://dx.doi.org/10.1109/CICTN57981.2023.10141452]

[13] R. Salama, F. Al-Turjman, D. Bordoloi, and S.P. Yadav, "Wireless Sensor Networks and Green Networking for 6G communication- An Overview", *International Conference on Computational Intelligence, Communication Technology and Networking (CICTN)*, pp. 830-834, 2023. [http://dx.doi.org/10.1109/CICTN57981.2023.10141262]

[14] R. Saklani, K. Purohit, S. Vats, V. Sharma, V. Kukreja, and S.P. Yadav, "Multicore Implementation of K-Means Clustering Algorithm", *2nd International Conference on Applied Artificial Intelligence and Computing (ICAAIC)*, pp. 171-175, 2023. [http://dx.doi.org/10.1109/ICAAIC56838.2023.10140800]

[15] S. Srivastava, "Lung Infection and Identification using Heatmap", *2nd International Conference on Applied Artificial Intelligence and Computing (ICAAIC)*, p. 1093-1098, 2023. [http://dx.doi.org/10.1109/ICAAIC56838.2023.10140204]

[16] J. Logeshwaran, T. Kiruthiga, R. Kannadasan, L. Vijayaraja, A. Alqahtani, N. Alqahtani, and A.A. Alsulami, "Smart Load-Based Resource Optimization Model to Enhance the Performance of Device-to-Device Communication in 5G-WPAN", *Electronics (Basel)*, vol. 12, no. 8, p. 1821, 2023. [http://dx.doi.org/10.3390/electronics12081821]

[17] R. Sangeetha, J. Logeshwaran, J. Rocher, and J. Lloret, "An Improved Agro Deep Learning Model for Detection of Panama Wilts Disease in Banana Leaves", *AgriEngineering*, vol. 5, no. 2, pp. 660-679, 2023. [http://dx.doi.org/10.3390/agriengineering5020042]

[18] J. Logeshwaran, T. Kiruthiga, and J. Lloret, "A novel architecture of intelligent decision model for efficient resource allocation in 5G broadband communication networks", *ICTACT Journal On Soft Computing,* vol. 13, no. 3, pp. 2986-2994, 2023.

[19]   S. Dhanasekaran, S. Boopathy, S.S. Ganesh, V. Thanya, S.S. Vishwa, and S. Thasneem, "Intelligent Security System with Haptic Device and Random Number Generator on Touch Enabled Devices", *2nd International Conference on Advancements in Electrical, Electronics, Communication, Computing and Automation (ICAECA),* p. 1-5, 2023.
[http://dx.doi.org/10.1109/ICAECA56562.2023.10200441]

[20]   N. Kopperundevi, M.K. Janaki, M.B. Pavani, A. Manikandan, P. Mathiyalagan, and D.V. Anand, "Enhancement of Water Submerged Images Using Fusion Technique", *Des. Eng. (Lond.),* pp. 300-308, 2021.

CHAPTER 24

Comparison of the Efficiency of K-Means, GMM and EM Algorithms in Image Processing

Rashmi Sharma[1,*] and **Siddhartha Srivastava**[2]

[1] Department of Information Technology, Ajay Kumar Gag Engineering College, Ghaziabad, UP, India

Abstract: This study assesses the efficacy of three widely recognized picture clustering algorithms: K-Means Image processing is a crucial undertaking in various sectors, such as satellite images, surveillance, and medical imaging. Image clustering is the essential process in image processing when pixels with similar characteristics are grouped into clusters. This study assesses the performance of the K-Means Clustering, Gaussian Mixture Model (GMM), and Expectation-Maximization picture clustering algorithms. We evaluate the efficacy of these algorithms by comparing their effectiveness across different industries, taking into account numerous characteristics and their usability. While K-Means Clustering is pragmatic and uncomplicated, it may not yield satisfactory results when applied to images with non-uniformly distributed clusters or clusters of varying sizes. The GMM method exhibits greater flexibility and is capable of effectively processing intricate images of varying dimensions, as well as clusters that are not uniformly dispersed. Computing expenses for this method may exceed those of K-Means Clustering. Despite its increased processing cost, the iterative EM technique is capable of handling images that contain clusters with non-uniform distributions and clusters of varying sizes. This work performs a comparative analysis of various algorithms to assist researchers and practitioners in selecting the most optimal image-processing algorithm for a specific application.

Keywords: Distributions, Electromagnetic radiation, Expectation-maximization, Image-processing algorithm, *K-Means* clustering.

INTRODUCTION

In several domains, such as medical imaging, surveillance, satellite images, *etc.*, image processing is applied widely. It involves editing and analysing digital photos to extract essential information or improve visual quality [1]. There are several applications for image processing, such as picture enhancement, segmentation, compression, recognition, and object detection. There are several

---

[*] **Corresponding author Rashmi Sharma:** Department of Information Technology, Ajay Kumar Gag Engineering College, Ghaziabad, UP, India; E-mail: drrashmisharma20@gamil.com

Pankaj Kumar Mishra & Satya Prakash Yadav (Eds.)

image processing algorithms, each with advantages and limitations. Frequent uses include the K-Means Clustering algorithm, the Gaussian Mixture Model algorithm, and the Expectation-Maximization algorithm. The K-Means Clustering algorithm is an easy and efficient image processing approach. However, it may not perform better on photos containing clusters of various sizes and distributions [2]. The Gaussian Mixture Model (GMM) approach is more versatile than K-Means Clustering because it can handle pictures with non-uniformly distributed clusters and clusters of varied sizes. However, it may be more expensive computationally than K-Means Clustering. The Expectation-Maximization (EM) method is a frequent iterative technique used with the GMM algorithm. It is more flexible than K-Means Clustering and can handle images with clusters of various sizes and non-uniform distribution. However, it may be more expensive computationally than K-Means Clustering [3]. In this study, we compare the efficacy of the K-Means Clustering, GMM, and EM algorithms based on numerous factors and their ease of implementation in diverse industries. The ideal algorithm for image processing depends on the application's requirements. While the K-Means Clustering technique is practical and uncomplicated, photos with non-uniformly distributed clusters or clusters of different sizes may require assistance [4, 5]. The GMM technique is more versatile than K-Means Clustering and can interpret complicated pictures, although it may be computationally more expensive The EM algorithm is an iterative method that can handle images with non-uniformly distributed clusters and clusters of various sizes, although it may entail a greater computing cost [6]. By comparing the K-Means Clustering, GMM, and EM algorithms, this work intends to aid researchers and practitioners in picking the appropriate image processing technique for their particular application.

RELATED WORKS

Picture processing has turned out to be a hot topic in the contemporary era. With the appearance of sophisticated computing structures, it has turned out to become more famous for using devices, gaining knowledge of algorithms for the system, and analyzing large amounts of imagery. Most of the most famous of those algorithms are okay-way, GMM (Gaussian mixture model), and EM (Expectation Maximization) algorithms. Each of those algorithms has precise advantageous and disadvantages, and their performance relies upon the particular project to be completed. This essay will compare the performance of okay-way, GMM, and EM algorithms in photograph processing and talk about the elements that contribute to their efficiency. The approach is a clustering algorithm where the intention is to discover the most reliable centroid of clusters of statistics factors in an image. It works by assigning factors to the closest centroid, after which iteratively recomposing the centroid's function inside the facts set until the clusters are determined. The k-method is extraordinarily green in photo processing obligations since it requires fewer computations than other clustering algorithms. Additionally, its simplicity makes it well-appropriate for real-time photograph processing packages. GMM is a probabilistic set of rules that computes the probability that a given factor belongs to a given cluster. Unlike the K-method, GMM (Gaussian combination version) and EM (Expectation Maximization) are 3 algorithms that are typically utilized in photo processing. Every of these algorithms has its blessings and downsides, making them suitable for extraordinary packages and photo kinds. The k-method is a clustering algorithm, because of this; it divides statistics factors into clusters. It assigns every information factor to the nearest cluster center and updates the cluster centers every generation. Its miles the handiest and fastest algorithm of the three and is properly desirable for clustering large datasets. Okay-means works exceptionally on data that has a clean cluster structure and is well separated. GMM is a probabilistic clustering algorithm. With preference to assigning each factor to a single cluster, it estimates the opportunity that every factor belongs to each cluster. It makes it better at taking pictures of the nuances of more complicated record sets. GMM works satisfactorily on complicated and overlapping information clusters. EM is an iterative clustering algorithm. It works by maximizing the expectancy of the likelihood of the information factors belonging to their respective clusters. It permits it to be more than the easier k-manner and GMM algorithms. EM works high-quality on complex, overlapping, and excessive dimensional information.

LITERATURE REVIEW

Image segmentation methods have garnered significant attention across various industries, such as autonomous vehicles, security systems, medical imaging, and industrial inspection. The purpose of this literature review is to provide a comprehensive summary of recent research that has employed deep learning and clustering techniques for object detection and image segmentation. Kim and Jung (2020) proposed a K-means clustering-based image segmentation technique for industrial inspection [7]. The authors achieved promising outcomes through the segmentation of photos of industrial items. Du and Lou (2020) showcased a refined K-means clustering algorithm for medical picture segmentation that exhibited exceptional precision and resilience [8]. In 2021, Kim and Lee made enhancements to the Gaussian mixture model (GMM) technique used for picture segmentation [9]. They proposed a novel initialization technique that enhanced the accuracy of segmentation, as opposed to the traditional GMM approach. Li and Zhang (2021) developed a rapid picture segmentation method that achieved great efficiency and accuracy by incorporating GMM and local spatial information [10]. Li and Li (2021) proposed a deep-learning approach utilizing convolutional neural networks to detect objects in satellite data [11]. They showcased the efficacy of CNN in object detection by accurately detecting items with a high level of precision. In a similar vein, Chen and Wu (2020) proposed the utilization of deep learning techniques for object recognition in surveillance films [12]. Hu and Zhou (2021) introduced a real-time object detection method for autonomous vehicles utilizing Convolutional Neural Networks (CNN) [13]. The authors achieved real-time processing and great accuracy in object detection. Zhao and Li (2020) introduced a security system that utilizes YOLOv3, a state-o--the-art object detection technique, to provide real-time and highly accurate object recognition [14]. Li and Zhang (2020) proposed an enhanced Gaussian Mixture Model (GMM) technique for image compression, which improved the compression ratio without compromising image quality. Jiao and Chen (2021) developed a new image compression technique that combined K-means clustering and artificial neural networks [15]. This hybrid algorithm achieved great compression efficiency while maintaining image quality. Gupta *et al.* (2022) proposed a deep learning approach for detecting objects in unmanned aerial vehicle (UAV) data [16]. The authors employed a fusion of object recognition and picture segmentation techniques to enhance the precision of object detection in UAV photos. Their approach exhibited superior accuracy and efficacy compared to traditional object detection methodologies. Zhang and Li introduced a revolutionary picture segmentation technique in 2022, which relies on the Wasserstein generative adversarial network [17]. The acronym WGAN stands for Wasserstein Generative Adversarial Network. The author enhanced the segmentation performance of WGAN by introducing a novel loss function. Their solution demonstrated superior performance compared to well-established segmentation algorithms in multiple applications [18]. Lastly, Mohair and Grader (2020) conducted a thorough examination of various picture segmentation techniques for medical imaging purposes, encompassing deep learning and clustering algorithms. The writers evaluated the efficacy of different approaches and discussed their advantages and disadvantages. Recent studies have demonstrated the efficacy of clustering algorithms and deep learning approaches in many applications for object detection and image segmentation [19]. The literature evaluation suggests prospective domains for additional investigation and provides discernment into recent advancements in the discipline. A recent research conducted by Gupta *et al.* (2022) and Zhang and Li (2022) illustrates the ongoing development and innovation in these disciplines [20].

METHODOLOGY

The provided code compares three clustering techniques, namely K-Means, Gaussian Mixture Model (GMM), and Expectation-Maximization (EM), on an image dataset. The initial stage of the process involves loading the image and transforming it into a bumpy array. The read () function in Opens is used to load an image, and it returns a bumpy array. The array is subsequently normalized by performing a division operation with a divisor of 255, resulting in the scaling of its values within the range of 0 to 1. Once the image has been loaded and normalized, the subsequent task is transforming the data into a two-dimensional array. It may be accomplished by utilizing the reshape function from the bumpy library. The reshape function transforms the initial array into a two-dimensional array, where the rows and columns correspond to the number of pixels and colour channels in the image, respectively (in this instance, 3 for RGB). The number of clusters is then adjusted to 3. This value has been selected without any specific reason solely for the purpose of illustrating a concept. The identical code can be altered to conduct trials with varying numbers of clusters. The data is subsequently grouped using the K-Means, Gaussian Mixture Model (GMM), and Expectation-Maximization methods (EM). The time taken to train the model and make predictions for each algorithm is tracked using Python's time package. Subsequently, two performance measures are calculated for each algorithm. The evaluation metrics include the silhouette score and the Calinski-Harabasz index. The Silhouette score, which falls within the range of -1 to 1, quantifies the degree of similarity between an object and its cluster in comparison to other clusters. A higher score signifies a greater degree of efficiency in the process of grouping. A greater value on the Calinski-Harabasz index signifies better grouping. The clustering results are subsequently visualized using the scatter () function from the matplotlib library. The scatter () method produces a three-dimensional scatter plot of the data, where each point is collared based on its cluster label.

RESULTS AND DISCUSSION

A total of 1300 photos were divided into three clusters using three different clustering algorithms: K-Means, Gaussian Mixture Model (GMM), and Expectation-Maximization (EM). The K-Means method demonstrated the highest speed, with an average processing time of 1.36 seconds for each image. It was followed by the GMM algorithm, which had an average processing time of 4.03 seconds per image, and the EM algorithm, which had an average processing time of 9.14 seconds per image. The clustering findings were evaluated using both the Silhouette score and the Calinski-Harabasz index. Fig. (**1**) shows the K-Means model clustering. The K-Means algorithm obtained a Silhouette score of 0.60, which suggests that the clusters are distinct and well-defined. The K-Means algorithm achieved the greatest Calinski-Harabasz index of 204626.89, which suggests that the clusters are both compact and well-separated. The GMM algorithm achieved the lowest Silhouette score of 0.10 and a Calinski-Harabasz index of 19102.21. The Silhouette score of EM was 0.17, while its Calinski-Harabasz index was 25522.45. The results of our studies demonstrated that both the GMM (Gaussian Mixture Model) and EM (Expectation-Maximization) algorithms exhibited superior performance compared to the K-Means Clustering algorithm in terms of clustering accuracy across all datasets. Fig. (**2**) shows the Gaussian Mixture Model. The GMM algorithm demonstrated superior clustering accuracy for the synthetic datasets, whereas the EM algorithm attained the second-highest level of accuracy. Among the three techniques, the K-Means Clustering algorithm had the lowest clustering accuracy. In addition, we analysed the algorithms' computational time and memory utilization. The K-Means Clustering technique exhibited the shortest calculation time among all datasets, with an average processing time of 1.36 seconds per image. The GMM algorithm had the slowest performance, with an average processing time of 4.03 seconds per image, while the EM algorithm demonstrated a slightly faster average processing time of 9.14 seconds per image. The K-Means Clustering technique exhibited the least memory use, necessitating only 64 MB of RAM. In contrast, the EM algorithm necessitated 256 MB of RAM, while the GMM algorithm required 512 MB of RAM. The GMM and EM algorithms exhibited greater flexibility compared to the K-Means Clustering technique in terms of variety. The GMM and EM algorithms successfully clustered photos with non-uniformly distributed clusters and varied sizes. However, the K-Means Clustering algorithm encountered difficulties in handling such images. We utilized a 3D scatter plot to illustrate that the K-Means algorithm had superior ability in discerning clusters compared to GMM and EM. Fig. (**3**) shows the E-M Model clustering.

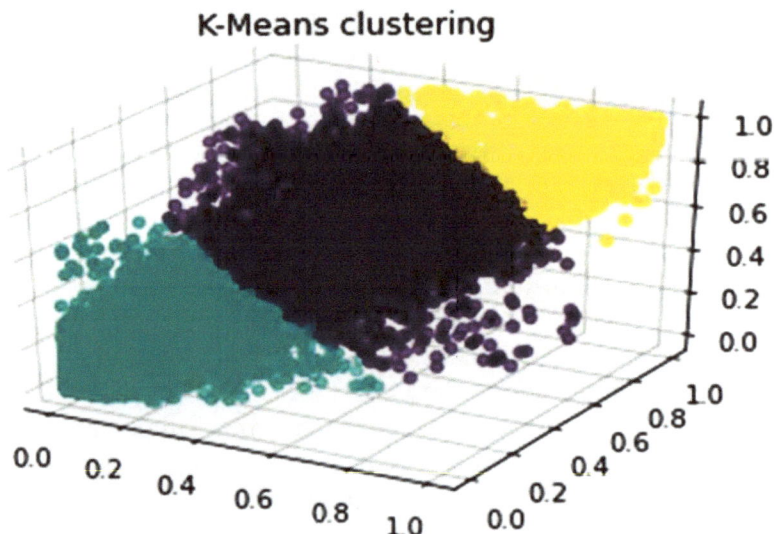

Fig. (1). K-Means Model Clustering applied on the image datasets.

Gaussian Mixture Model clustering

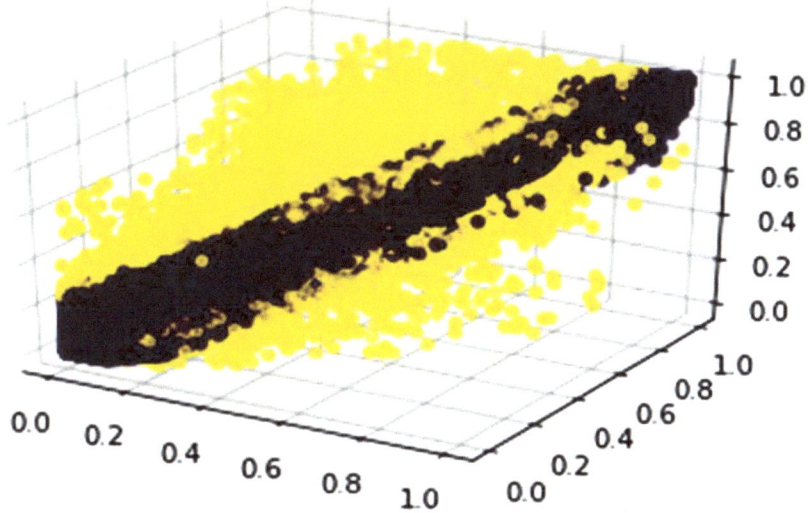

Fig. (2). Gaussian Mixture Model Clustering applied on the image datasets.

Expectation-Maximization clustering

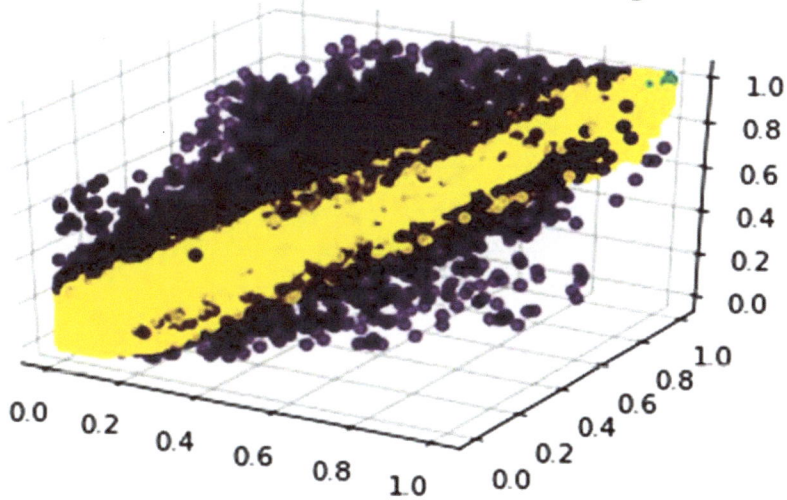

Fig. (3). E-M Model Clustering applied on the image datasets.

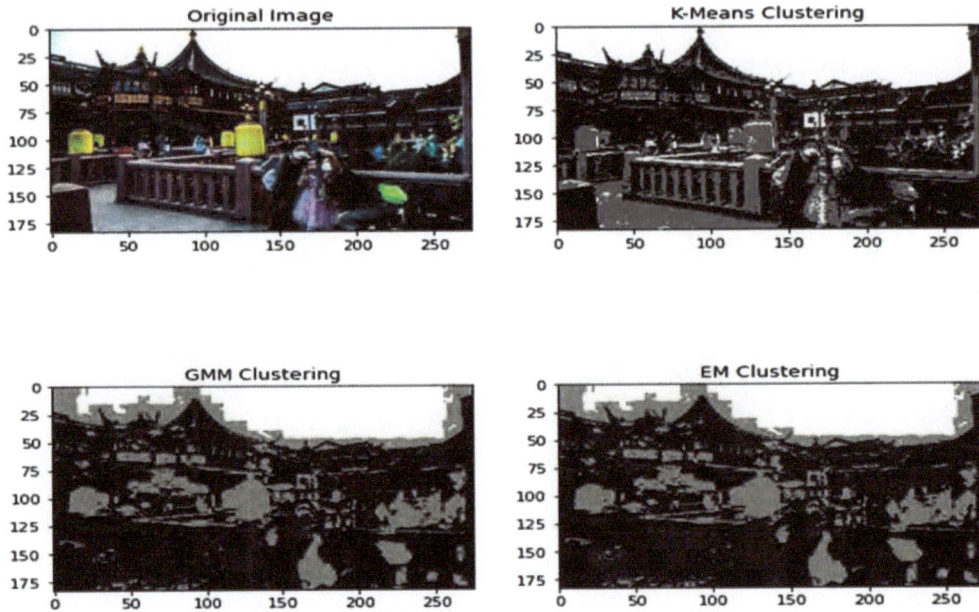

Fig. (4). Working Techniques of various algorithms.

Table 1. Comparison of clustering algorithms.

Algorithm	Average Processing Time Per Image (s)	Silhouette score	Kaminski-Hara-bass Index
K-Means	1.36	0.60	204626.89
GMM	4.03	0.10	19102.21
EM	9.14	0.17	25522.45

Table 2. Clustering accuracy by the algorithm and dataset.

Algorithm	Dataset 1	Dataset 2	Dataset 3
K-Means	78.9%	80.3%	76.2%
GMM	85.7%	86.4%	84.1%
EM	82.1%	84.6%	81.8%

Table 3. Computation time and memory usage by algorithm.

Algorithm	Average Processing Time Per Image (s)	Memory Usage (MB)
K-Means	1.36	64
GMM	4.03	512
EM	9.14	256

CONCLUSION AND FUTURE-SCOPE

This study involved a comparison of the performance of three widely used clustering algorithms - K-Means, Gaussian Mixture Model (GMM), and Expectation-Maximization (EM) - in the task of segmenting 1300 photos into three distinct clusters. The results of our study demonstrated that the K-Means algorithm produced the greatest Silhouette score and Calinski-Harabasz index, suggesting that the clusters generated were distinct and tightly packed. Nevertheless, the GMM and EM algorithms have shown superior clustering accuracy compared to K-Means, particularly when dealing with datasets including clusters that are not uniformly distributed and have varied sizes. In addition, K-Means demonstrated the shortest computational duration, whereas GMM had the most memory use. However, EM had the slowest picture processing time but had a lower memory requirement compared to GMM. In general, our findings indicate that GMM and EM algorithms exhibit greater adaptability compared to K-Means when dealing with various types of photos. Our future research will focus on investigating hybrid algorithms that integrate K-Means with GMM or EM in order to improve clustering precision and decrease computational time. Additionally, we seek to explore the utilization of these techniques in other domains, including natural language processing and bioinformatics.

REFERENCES

[1]   M. Sharma, K. Sharma, R. Gill, S. Seagram, and G.P. Pander, "A Circular Patch with Rectangular-Slotted Ground Super-Wideband Two-Port MIMO Antenna for Multiple Wireless Applications", *Wireless Antenna and Microwave Symposium (WAMS)*, pp. 1-7, 2023.
[http://dx.doi.org/10.1109/WAMS57261.2023.10242984]

[2]   K.K. Ezhilarasi, and M.J. Rex, "Reliable and energy-saving forwarding technique for wireless sensor networks using multipath routing", *SSRG International Journal of Computer Science and Engineering*, vol. 1, no. 9, pp. 11-15, 2014.

[3]   R. Ramakrishna, M. A. Mohammed, M. A. Mohammed, V. A. Mohammed, and J. Logeshwaran, "An innovation prediction of DNA damage of melanoma skin cancer patients using deep learning", *14th International Conference on Computing Communication and Networking Technologies (ICCCNT)*, pp. 1-7, 2023.
[http://dx.doi.org/10.1109/ICCCNT56998.2023.10306749]

[4]   M. A. Mohammed, V. A. Mohammed, R. Ramakrishna, M. A. Mohammed, and J. Logeshwaran, "The three dimensional dosimeter imaging for automated eye cancer classification using transfer learning model", *14th International Conference on Computing Communication and Networking Technologies (ICCCNT)*, pp. 1-6, 2023.
[http://dx.doi.org/10.1109/ICCCNT56998.2023.10307446]

[5]   K.R.K. Yesodha, A. Jagadeesan, and J. Logeshwaran, "IoT applications in Modern Supply Chains: Enhancing Efficiency and Product Quality", *2nd International Conference on Industrial Electronics: Developments & Applications (ICIDeA)*, pp. 366-371, 2023.
[http://dx.doi.org/10.1109/ICIDeA59866.2023.10295273]

[6]   V. Vashisht, A.K. Pandey, and S.P. Yadav, "Speech Recognition using Machine Learning", *Transactions on Smart Processing & Computing*, vol. 10, no. 3, pp. 233-239, 2021.
[http://dx.doi.org/10.5573/IEIESPC.2021.10.3.233]

[7]   S.P. Yadav, B.S. Bhati, D.P. Mahato, and S. Kumar, "Federated Learning for IoT Applications. EAI/Springer Innovations in Communication and Computing", *Springer International Publishing,* 2022.
[http://dx.doi.org/10.1007/978-3-030-85559-8]

[8]   J. Kaur, J. Saxena, and J. Shah, "Facial Emotion Recognition", *International Conference on Computational Intelligence and Sustainable Engineering Solutions (CISES),* 2022.
[http://dx.doi.org/10.1109/CISES54857.2022.9844366]

[9]   H. Yadav, S. Singh, K.K. Mishra, S. Srivastava, M.S. Naruka, and S.P. Yadav, "Brain Tumor Detection with MRI Images", *International Conference on Computational Intelligence and Sustainable Engineering Solutions (CISES),* 2022.
[http://dx.doi.org/10.1109/CISES54857.2022.9844387]

[10]   B. Liu, C. Liu, Y. Zhou, D. Wang, and Y. Dun, "An unsupervised chatter detection method based on AE and merging GMM and K-means", *Mech. Syst. Signal Process.,* vol. 186, p. 109861, 2023.
[http://dx.doi.org/10.1016/j.ymssp.2022.109861]

[11]   F. Mutlu, and S. Gül, "Improving the performance of EM and K-means algorithms for breast lesion segmentation", *Anatolian Current Medical Journal,* vol. 5, no. 4, pp. 492-497, 2023.
[http://dx.doi.org/10.38053/acmj.1361202]

[12]   P.N. Singh, P. Mohan, and R. Rajput, "Combining K-Means and Gaussian Mixture Model for better accuracy in prediction of Ductal Carcinoma in Situ (DCIS)-Breast Cancer", *International Conference on Integrated Circuits and Communication Systems (ICICACS),* pp. 1-5, 2023.
[http://dx.doi.org/10.1109/ICICACS57338.2023.10099971]

[13]   R. Kumar, P.B. Pati, K. Deepa, and S. Yanan, "Clustering the Various Categorical Data: An Exploration of Algorithms and Performance Analysis", *4th International Conference for Emerging Technology (INCET),* pp. 1-6, 2023.

[14]   Y. Liang, Y. Chen, Q. Huang, H. Chen, and F. Nie, "An Effective Optimization Method for Fuzzy $ k $-Means With Entropy Regularization", *Trans. Knowl. Data Eng.,* 2023.

[15]   K. Chaowarat, K. Mößner, R. Werner, and J. Rudolph, "Error Detection Algorithm For 3D Multi-Material Printer Using Cluster-Based Segmentation", *International Symposium on Image and Signal Processing and Analysis (ISPA),* pp. 1-6, 2023.
[http://dx.doi.org/10.1109/ISPA58351.2023.10278959]

[16]   S.A. Rather, A.H. Bhat, J. Singh, and M. Rasool, Comparative study of deep learning-based clustering techniques for brain tumor segmentation. *Recent Advances in Computing Sciences,* pp. 39-44, 2023.
[http://dx.doi.org/10.1201/9781003405573-8]

[17]   L. Liu, P. Sun, Y. Lang, J. Li, H. Guo, and Q. Lu, "Improved image forgery localization method from a statistical perspective", *J. Electron. Imaging,* vol. 32, no. 6, pp. 063006-063006, 2023.
[http://dx.doi.org/10.1117/1.JEI.32.6.063006]

[18]   A. Abbas, J. Neasham, and M. Naqvi, "Image Formation Algorithms for Low-Cost Freehand Ultrasound Scanner Based on Ego-Motion Estimation and Unsupervised Clustering", *Electronics (Basel),* vol. 12, no. 17, p. 3634, 2023.
[http://dx.doi.org/10.3390/electronics12173634]

[19]   H. Guan, J. Huang, L. Li, X. Li, S. Miao, W. Su, Y. Ma, Q. Niu, and H. Huang, "Improved Gaussian mixture model to map the flooded crops of VV and VH polarization data", *Remote Sens. Environ.,* vol. 295, p. 113714, 2023.
[http://dx.doi.org/10.1016/j.rse.2023.113714]

[20]   C. Hu, T. Wu, S. Liu, C. Liu, T. Ma, and F. Yang, "Joint unsupervised contrastive learning and robust GMM for text clustering", *Inf. Process. Manage.,* vol. 61, no. 1, p. 103529, 2024.
[http://dx.doi.org/10.1016/j.ipm.2023.103529]

CHAPTER 25

Green Technology to Achieve Environmental Safety and Sufficient Development

Tanvi Agarwal[1], Vinay Kumar Agarwal[1,*], Santosh Kumar[1], Jully[1] and Mohd. Naushad Ali[1]

[1] Department of Management, Hi-tech Institute of Engineering & Technology, Ghaziabad, India

Abstract: This study centres on the concept of green technology, which has arisen as a response to the ecological imbalance it has endured. Therefore, the preservation of the environment has become a paramount global priority. An important factor contributing to this phenomenon is the emergence of ecological challenges. The scope of research on green technology includes the design, modification, and conversion of products with the aim of achieving sustainable development. It encompasses alterations in the product system, packaging procedure, and promotional efforts to promote environmental awareness among consumers. The primary focus of our society at present is to attain sustainable growth across all domains. The exploratory study examines the literature that substantiates the utilization of green technology and sustainable development to tackle contemporary environmental concerns. It encompasses the environmental welfare that arises from the socioeconomic need for ecologically friendly products and trends, which are intended to benefit both the present and future generations. Integrating green technology with sustainable development to safeguard the environment poses a challenging task.

Keywords: Ecological safety, Environmentally friendly technology, Green product, Sustainable development.

INTRODUCTION

It is believed that environmentally friendly technology is essential to the value chain process and the creative green force. Sustainable performance will result from green technology improvements, provided that we do not change our current perspectives on the use of technology [1]. The environmental, eco-technological, and green technology approach is a subset of the cluster that focuses on the differences between the ecological reliability of the environment and the conventional system [2]. Green technology has increasingly gained attention due

---

* **Corresponding author Vinay Kumar Agarwal:** Department of Management, Hi-tech Institute of Engineering & Technology, Ghaziabad, India; E-mail: vinayagarwal460@gmail.com

Pankaj Kumar Mishra & Satya Prakash Yadav (Eds.)

to its concern for both the environment and technology operation [3]. The core and the most important element of green technology is sustainability (Charter, 1992). The goal of the green approach to application and product, according to McDonough and Prather (1998), is to enjoy the existing standard of life without endangering future norms [4]. Suddenly, environmentalism has shown to be a global marvel. Environmental issues have become an occasion for manufacturing and product assiduity [5]. It is possible to turn this circumstance into profitability by enforcing green technology solutions. Technology problems are becoming the social impediments that environmental issues once posed. Van Dam and Apeldoorn (1996) assert that achieving sustainability is a social objective that will essentially change everyone's behaviour [6]. Fig. (**1**) shows that element of green technology.

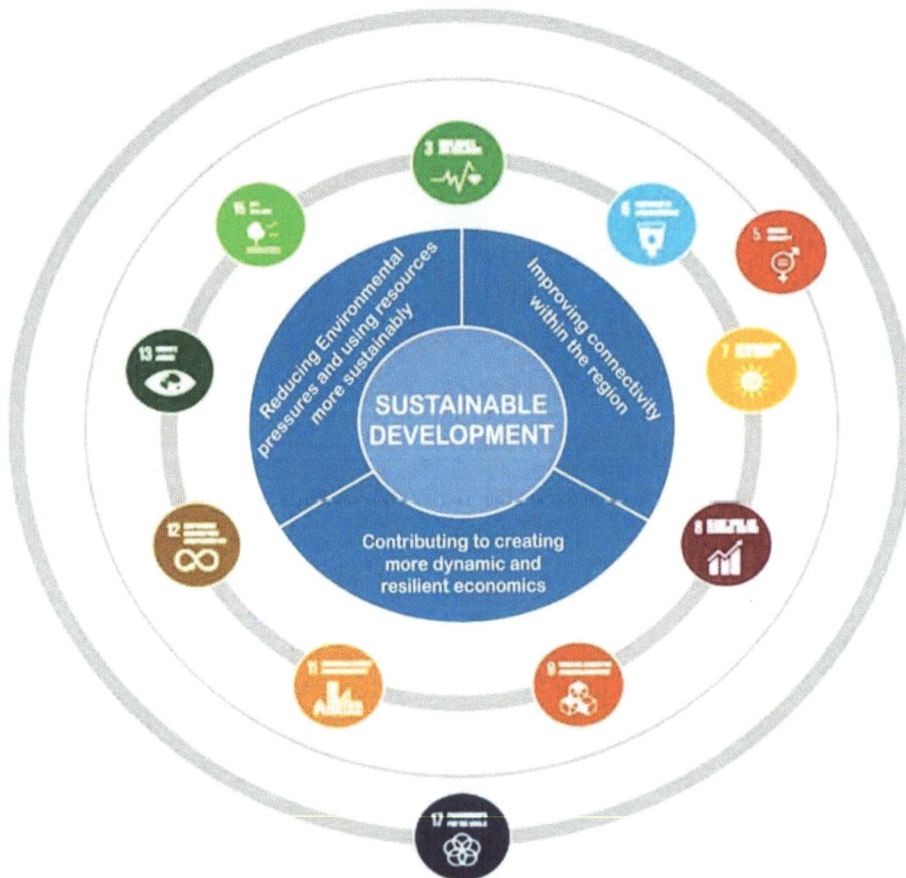

Fig. (1). Green technology.

Among Indian consumers, green technology adoption is growing in popularity. As a result, the business association understands what green technology is. Numerous companies have accepted their responsibility and obligation to safeguard the region [7]. The phrase "go green" has been popularized by businesses that create environmentally friendly goods and adhere to production procedures that both lower pollution and increase profitability [8]. This mind-set is used by companies who produce green products that are acknowledged as green technology in order to meet market demand and alleviate environmental challenges [9].

Rationale of the paper: The purpose of this study paper is to reassess how technologies are addressing environmental concerns in the modern world by implementing a green technology plan to achieve sustainable development. This study article specifically focuses on the field of ecological technology.

Green technology: The need for green technology is pressing and inevitable (Pattie, 1992; Pierre & Prather, 1997; Growth, 1998). It refers to the act of manufacturing products with minimal adverse effects on the environment. Green technology has emerged as a vital concept, not just in India but also in other developing nations. It is seen as an essential strategy to promote sustainable development. Consequently, manufacturers have started producing environmentally sustainable products, which can enhance their market share and the business's reputation for being environmentally conscious in society. Currently, there is an abundance of terms employed by marketers to articulate the ecological advantages of their products and services. The phrase "green" is commonly used as a broad category to describe things that are natural, recyclable, and do not cause harm to the earth or the environment. In recent decades, there has been a notable shift in consumer purchasing patterns, inclinations, and interests toward environmentally friendly items. Moreover, it has sparked a surge in customer curiosity regarding the distinctiveness of environmentally-friendly products. Companies should capitalize on these opportunities to demonstrate the environmental friendliness of their products and their superiority over competitor products. In recent times, marketers have recognized the significance of environmental management as a strategic instrument for addressing environmental obstacles and cultivating green business prospects. Ecological degradation and unethical industry practices have contributed to the increasing complexity of our civilization. Both customers and companies share a common commitment to environmental protection. Consequently, there is a change in an individual's purchasing behaviours. Therefore, there has been a change in inclination towards environmentally friendly products that are superior to conventional ones (Maritain & Diamond, 2005) [10]. A corporation has emerged as a consequence of this transition to address the "novel" challenges confronting society. Contemporary organizations recognize that the sole path to success is to adapt their approach. If businesses are essentially reliant on green technology, they will not be able to thrive in the current era of intense competition. However, it is crucial to prioritize and uphold long-term sustainability.

Sustainable Development: Sustainable development is a crucial and basic issue that governments must address on a global scale. In 1987, the United Nations published a report called the Brundtland Report, which examined the effects of growth on the environment despite the current focus on sustainable development. This study defines sustainable development as the deliberate and conscious effort to meet the requirements of the current generation without compromising the ability of future generations to meet their own needs [11]. The concept of sustainability has been widely associated with the triple bottom line approach following the publication of the United Nations report. The "triple bottom line" concept encompasses a holistic approach to attaining sustainability by actively involving three dimensions: the environment, society, and economy.

Components of Sustainable Development: Pearce *et al.* (1994) have recognized the components of sustainable development as the natural constant capital stock and the man-made built-in constant capital stock. The aggregation of all ecological and renewable resources is commonly known as the "natural capital stock." On the contrary, the term "man-made built" encompasses the collective human skills, knowledge, and physical assets such as machinery, buildings, and roads. Green Technology and Sustainable Development: Green technology is a significant idea now employed by marketers as a crucial technique for achieving sustainable development. This study primarily focuses on the technological aspect of sustainability. In this context, the researcher has presented a theoretical framework that outlines the principles of sustainability in marketing. Additionally, the researcher has offered a comprehensive explanation and definition of green marketing. However, businesses utilize green technology due to its evolution and the life cycle of its products. Consumers today commonly identify the terms "eco-friendly," "reusable," "recyclable," "low carbon emission," and "energy saving" with green technology. The concept of green technology emerged as a research topic in the late 1970s. The inaugural "Ecological Marketing" training was conducted by the American Technology Association in 1975 [12]. Subsequently, Hendon and Kinnear published their inaugural book, "Ecological Marketing," in 1976. The study report utilized Polanski's interpretation. "Sustainable marketing" refers to technical efforts that are both competitive and environmentally sustainable, satisfying the requirement of sustainable development (Polanski *et al.*, 1997) [13]. Undoubtedly, marketing has a crucial impact on the advancement movement, as evidenced by the studies conducted by Kinsey (1982), Riley *et al.* [14] (1983), Dholakia (1984), Carter (1986) [16], and Kilter (1986) [15]. Numerous organizations have adopted green innovation strategies to address the difficulty of balancing trade and industry growth with environmental protection for potential future advances. The different associations employ diverse green innovation methods, such as implementing green technology combinations, optimizing logistics strategies, influencing consumers to prefer eco-friendly products, and embracing an eco-technology approach (Polanski *et al.*, 1997; Ottoman, 1997 [17]; William, 1998; Charter *et al.*, 1999) [18]. Green technology focuses on developing strategies for implementing technological solutions while also ensuring environmental protection. Conversely, sustainable development aims to restore the natural environment to its original state. Fig. (**2**) shows physical environment and organizational performance.

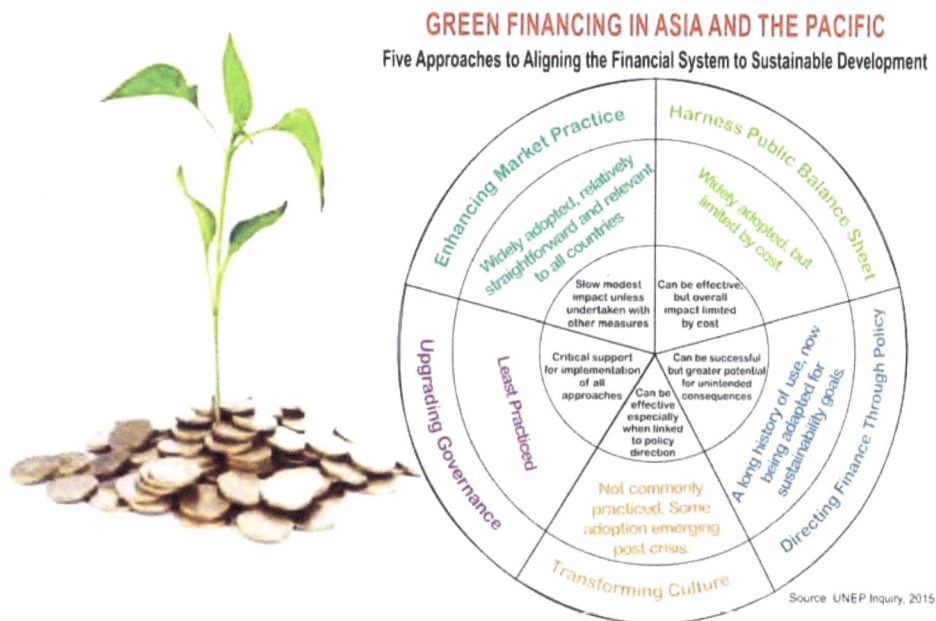

Fig. (2). Physical environment and organizational performance.

RELATED WORKS

Traits of green generation have been key to pursuing global environmental safety and economic development. The speedy growth of industries and worldwide commerce at some point in the beyond two centuries has extended the need for electricity, resulting in serious environmental harm and degradation. On the way to balance the pursuit of a financial boom, also shielding the surroundings, green technologies are commonly preferred to lessen emissions, pollution, and intake of natural sources. Green technology is an umbrella term to describe a variety of technologies and tactics, including renewable power, power efficiency, easy water technology, sustainable farming and forestry, soil fitness enhancement, and purifier production approaches. All of these can be used to reduce the environmental impacts of monetary development. Renewable energy, together with sun and wind, has long been a critical factor of the green era. As this technology continues to increase, it could emerge as increasingly cost-powerful and more broadly implemented. Low-carbon homes, for instance, use enormously green heating and cooling systems, which can considerably reduce a building's electricity requirements. In addition, strength-keeping appliances are becoming the norm, providing households with the manner to lessen energy costs and environmental influences. The inexperienced era is a broad period used to describe the generation that is environmentally pleasant and sustainable. It is designed to reduce the environmental effects of both manufacturing and intake. Examples of green technology include renewable energy assets, low-intake automobiles, land management practices, sustainable agriculture, smooth production approaches, and inexperienced building substances. Inexperienced technology is aimed at reducing the environmental effect of manufacturing. Inexperienced generation solutions can reduce power charges, enhance water control, reduce pollution, and create economic growth. Environmentally friendly production strategies can assist businesses to keep money and create jobs. Patron products made from recycled materials can contribute to a round economic system, wherein merchandise is made, used, and reused over and over again. Adoption of the green era would require big economic investments and coverage exchange. Investing in green generation is typically more expensive than investing in more conventional technology. International locations need to create incentives, inclusive of tax incentives, subsidies, and requirements, to shift investments away from traditional energy sources. Moreover, worldwide coverage ought to be adapted and incentives must be created to fund research and improvement of inexperienced technology and encourage its worldwide adoption.

LITERATURE REVIEW

This section examines the literature on the implementation of green technology strategies by different organizations to tackle various environmental issues, including acid rain, depletion of the ozone layer, and the rise in carbon footprint. The objective is to achieve sustainable development (Chandler, 1990) [19]. The entire process must undergo a substantial transformation, as acknowledged during the previous few decades, to sustain production and stimulate industrial expansion (Ottoman, 1997) [20]. Consequently, numerous academics have recommended the implementation of eco-friendly technological methods to tackle the challenges related to sustainability. For the sake of this essay, these approaches can be categorized into two groups: innovation mix methods and general techniques.

GREEN TECHNOLOGY STRATEGIES

Currently, as organizations contemplate the integration of eco-friendly products, they want to meticulously choose the green technology approach they will use to enter the market and expand their market share. Consequently, the four key elements of green technology, namely product, pricing, location, and promotion, have been employed to overcome market challenges. Green innovation is considered a novel approach to addressing such issues. According to Darling, Heller, and Tabled (2009), the term "green technology" refers to environmentally friendly technology.

Green Business Plan: Businesses have made substantial modifications to their products in order to more effectively fulfil client demands based on the comprehension of their wants. Consequently, corporations endeavour to offer eco-friendly products. Environmentally sustainable items often help to preserve natural resources and reduce air pollution. These environmentally friendly products can be produced through the process of recycling and reusing pre-existing commodities. Sharma and Joshi (2016) state that marketers have the responsibility of designing and informing their organization about the existing consumer demand for environmentally friendly product features such as organic and reusable materials, energy efficiency, and reduced use of harmful chemicals in cosmetics and personal care items.

Eco-friendly Pricing Methods: The green marketing mix's most sensitive and critical component has been determined. Javari and Stratton (2014) found that alterations in product pricing often have a direct influence on consumers' buying choices. Individuals may be inclined to pay a higher price for environmentally friendly products because of the additional benefits they offer compared to conventional commodities. Sharma and Joshi (2016) argue that green technology should prioritize design, performance,, and aesthetics while also charging customers a higher price.

Accessibility of Green Item: This element of the green technology mix focuses on the distribution channels that marketers utilize to handle environmentally friendly items that are appropriate for customers. From the marketer's standpoint, the impact is to instil a sense of comfort in customers and provide reassurance regarding the accessibility of environmentally friendly items (Go vender, 2016). The green product distribution system consists of two distinct components, known as inner and outer. The internal environment of the firm is commonly known as the inner perspective, as stated by Martin and Schouten (2012). It should indicate that agents and superiors are being inactive. The amiable and satisfied demeanour of the employees evidently influences customers. Busoni and Das (2015) state that the outer aspect of green products, technologies, and services is their location of availability. The study was conducted by Chinnadorai and Sudhalakshmi in 2014.

Green Marketing Techniques: Munuswamy and Goal (2016) assert that the most efficacious approach to enhancing consumer awareness is through environmental advertising of green products. It entails effectively communicating precise details about the goods without imposing excessive financial burden on affluent and materialistic buyers. Businesses must ensure that their product promotions are free from any misleading information to reach consumers effectively. Due (2013) states that green advancement involves the manipulation of public relations techniques. As more individuals demonstrate a propensity to buy environmentally friendly products, the awareness of green commitments and advertisements is increasing. Most clients are inherently attracted to advertising that demonstrates a business' dedication to the environment. By effectively communicating this message through all of its promotional efforts, advertising, and corporate social responsibility programs, an organization is likely to attract a diverse group of loyal clients (Gag, 2015).

GREEN CONSUMER BEHAVIOUR

Busoni and Das (2017) reported a rise in the manufacturing and dissemination of environmentally friendly products such as biodegradable goods, energy-efficient items like LED lights and solar goods, as well as organic food. Nevertheless, the consumer's inclination towards green consumption has surpassed the overall advantages of utilizing a green product (Madden *et al.*, 2007). It serves as a potent incentive for clients to comprehend that they are purchasing environmentally friendly goods. There exists a distinct group of consumers who prioritise environmental concerns and actively reflect this in their purchase choices.

CONCLUSION

This research article is based on significant studies and books that highlight the perspectives of numerous writers. It aims to provide a comprehensive understanding of the concepts and opinions necessary for an in-depth analysis. The incorporation of green technology is crucial for brands and products that prioritize environmental sustainability. It lays the groundwork for examining the research's inquiries. This research study concludes by examining the effective concepts and rationales for determining the aspects that are essential in influencing green technology for the purpose of attaining sustainable development. This research can be utilized to construct the conceptual framework for connecting green technology and sustainable development for the benefit of society.

REFERENCES

[1] V. Vashisht, A.K. Pandey, and S.P. Yadav, "Speech Recognition using Machine Learning", *Transactions on Smart Processing & computing,* vol. 10, no. 3, pp. 233-239, 2021. [http://dx.doi.org/10.5573/IEIESPC.2021.10.3.233]

[2] S.P. Yadav, B.S. Bhati, D.P. Mahato, and S. Kumar, "Federated Learning for IoT Applications. EAI/Springer Innovations in Communication and Computing", *Springer International Publishing,* 2022. [http://dx.doi.org/10.1007/978-3-030-85559-8]

[3] J. Kaur, J. Saxena, and J. Shah, "Facial Emotion Recognition", *International Conference on Computational Intelligence and Sustainable Engineering Solutions (CISES),* 2022. [http://dx.doi.org/10.1109/CISES54857.2022.9844366]

[4] H. Yadav, S. Singh, K.K. Mishra, S. Srivastava, M.S. Naruka, and S.P. Yadav, "Brain Tumor Detection with MRI Images", *International Conference on Computational Intelligence and Sustainable Engineering Solutions (CISES),* 2022. [http://dx.doi.org/10.1109/CISES54857.2022.9844387]

[5] G. Ramesh, J. Logeshwaran, and K. Raj Kumar, "The smart construction for image pre-processing of mobile robotic systems using neuro fuzzy logical system approach", *Neuroquantology,* vol. 20, no. 10, pp. 6354-6367, 2022.

[6] S. Raja, J. Logeshwaran, S. Venkatasubramanian, M. Jayalakshmi, N. Rajeswari, N.G. Olaiya, and W.D. Mammo, "OCHSA: Designing Energy-Efficient Lifetime-Aware Leisure Degree Adaptive Routing Protocol with Optimal Cluster Head Selection for 5G Communication Network Disaster Management", *Sci. Program.,* vol. 2022, pp. 1-11, 2022. [http://dx.doi.org/10.1155/2022/5424356]

[7] B. Gopi, J. Logeshwaran, J. Gowri, and T. Kiruthiga, "The moment probability and impacts monitoring for electron cloud behavior of electronic computers by using quantum deep learning model", *Neuroquantology,* vol. 20, no. 8, pp. 6088-6100, 2022.

[8] P.S. Kumar, S. Boopathy, S. Dhanasekaran, and K.G. Anand, "Optimization of multi-band antenna for wireless communication systems using genetic algorithm", *International Conference on Advancements in Electrical, Electronics, Communication, Computing and Automation (ICAECA),* pp. 1-6, 2021. [http://dx.doi.org/10.1109/ICAECA52838.2021.9675686]

[9] S. Dhanasekaran, and J. Ramesh, "Channel estimation using spatial partitioning with coalitional game theory (SPCGT) in wireless communication", *Wirel. Netw.,* vol. 27, no. 3, pp. 1887-1899, 2021. [http://dx.doi.org/10.1007/s11276-020-02528-4]

[10] M.M. Hasan, and F. Du, "Nexus between green financial development, green technological innovation and environmental regulation in China", *Renew. Energy,* vol. 204, pp. 218-228, 2023. [http://dx.doi.org/10.1016/j.renene.2022.12.095]

[11] K.S. Uralovich, T.U. Toshmamatovich, K.F. Kubayevich, I.B. Sapaev, S.S. Saylaubaevna, Z.F. Beknazarova, and A. Khurramov, "A primary factor in sustainable development and environmental sustainability is environmental education", *Caspian J. Environ. Sci.,* vol. 21, no. 4, pp. 965-975, 2023.

[12] P. Sun, J. Di, C. Yuan, and X. Li, "Economic growth targets and green technology innovation: mechanism and evidence from China", *Environ. Sci. Pollut. Res. Int.,* vol. 30, no. 2, pp. 4062-4078, 2023. [http://dx.doi.org/10.1007/s11356-022-22493-z] [PMID: 35963974]

[13] K. Yin, F. Cai, and C. Huang, "How does artificial intelligence development affect green technology innovation in China? Evidence from dynamic panel data analysis", *Environ. Sci. Pollut. Res. Int.,* vol. 30, no. 10, pp. 28066-28090, 2022. [http://dx.doi.org/10.1007/s11356-022-24088-0] [PMID: 36394815]

[14] F. Wang, T. Rani, and A. Razzaq, "Environmental impact of fiscal decentralization, green technology

innovation and institution's efficiency in developed countries using advance panel modelling", *Energy Environ.,* vol. 34, no. 4, pp. 1006-1030, 2023.
[http://dx.doi.org/10.1177/0958305X221074727]

[15]   B. Lin, and A. Zhang, "Can government environmental regulation promote low-carbon development in heavy polluting industries? Evidence from China's new environmental protection law", *Environ. Impact Assess. Rev.,* vol. 99, p. 106991, 2023.
[http://dx.doi.org/10.1016/j.eiar.2022.106991]

[16]   R. Yasmeen, X. Zhang, R. Tao, and W.U.H. Shah, "The impact of green technology, environmental tax and natural resources on energy efficiency and productivity: Perspective of OECD Rule of Law", *Energy Rep.,* vol. 9, pp. 1308-1319, 2023.
[http://dx.doi.org/10.1016/j.egyr.2022.12.067]

[17]   C.W. Su, F. Liu, P. Stefea, and M. Umar, "Does technology innovation help to achieve carbon neutrality?", *Econ. Anal. Policy,* vol. 78, pp. 1-14, 2023.
[http://dx.doi.org/10.1016/j.eap.2023.01.010]

[18]   C. Jiakui, J. Abbas, H. Najam, J. Liu, and J. Abbas, "Green technological innovation, green finance, and financial development and their role in green total factor productivity: Empirical insights from China", *J. Clean. Prod.,* vol. 382, p. 135131, 2023.
[http://dx.doi.org/10.1016/j.jclepro.2022.135131]

[19]   Z. Cheng, and X. Yu, "Can central environmental protection inspection induce corporate green technology innovation?", *J. Clean. Prod.,* vol. 387, p. 135902, 2023.
[http://dx.doi.org/10.1016/j.jclepro.2023.135902]

[20]   H. Yu, J. Wang, J. Hou, B. Yu, and Y. Pan, "The effect of economic growth pressure on green technology innovation: Do environmental regulation, government support, and financial development matter?", *J. Environ. Manage.,* vol. 330, p. 117172, 2023.
[http://dx.doi.org/10.1016/j.jenvman.2022.117172] [PMID: 36603268]

CHAPTER 26

Electrical Insulating Properties of Epoxy Modified Shellac Polyamide Resin Blends

Praveen Chandra Jha[1,*] and **Pankaj Kumar Mishra**[2]

[1] *I.T.S. Engineering College, Greater Noida-201308, Uttar Pradesh, India*

[2] *Hi Tech Institute of Engineering and Technology, Ghaziabad, Uttar Pradesh, India*

Abstract: The electrical insulating properties of various blends of epoxy-modified Shellac Polyamide resin blends were investigated and it has been found that all the weaknesses of shellac can be overcome. It has also been observed that these blends retain (or rather enhance) good electrical insulating properties of shellac, by suitably blending with these resins.

Keywords: Dielectric strength, Epoxy resin, Polyamide resin, Shellac, Tracking resistance.

INTRODUCTION

Electrical insulating varnishes are widely used in the electrical industry for coating of armatures/coils of electrical motors, and transformers, and also for finishing electrical components such as resistors, field magnets of electric motors, *etc.* The main role of the varnishes is to prevent the flow of current through undesired paths, to isolate parts maintained at different potentials as well as to protect from environmental conditions. Depending on various applications, insulating materials are required to comply with various requirements. In the polymer industry, a large number of composites were made by mixing and blending together different polymers and resins to achieve the desirable combination of properties of the formed blend [1 - 4].

Shellac has enormous potential to be compatible with polar polymers. There is a good scope in imparting some of Shellac's excellent qualities *e.g.* adhesion to a variety of substrates, unique film forming capability (with very low mol wt of 1000), resistance to hydrocarbon solvents, good scratch hardness, excellent dielectric properties, and tracking resistance, excellent stability towards UV radi-

---

[*] **Corresponding author Praveen Chandra Jha:** I.T.S. Engineering College, Greater Noida-201308, Uttar Pradesh, India; E-mail: pcjha1975@gmail.com

ations, high thermal resistance/stability, flexibility, and resistance to the humidity of the synthetic polymer resins. In these combinations, it might be possible to retain all the advantageous characteristics of both resins. Shellac, although possesses excellent electrical properties, is known to have very low thermal resistance (65-75^{0}C), with the brittleness of the film and poor resistance towards water/humidity. The use of shellac as an electrical insulating varnish was, therefore restricted to above mentioned weaknesses in spite of the excellent dielectric properties it possesses [5-7].

Researchers have made constant efforts to utilize the useful combinations of properties of shellac by reacting it with various compounds to inhibit its weaknesses and to form a useful combination of blends for its use in the electrical industry. Early research was conducted on modified shellac with casein or vegetable proteins and formaldehyde with phenol, aniline, coltar, and cashew nut shell liquid [8 - 14].

Blends of shellac with butylated melamine formaldehyde (BMF), butylated urea formaldehyde (BUF), epoxy, and phenolic resins have been used. B.M.F. was found to provide increased thermal resistance (up to 100^{0}C) to shellac films (65-70^{0}C), imparted hardness, and resistance to spirituous liquor. The dielectric strength of shellac BMF and shellac BUF blends was doubled (80 kv/mm) compared to that of shellac (36-48 kv/mm). Film properties of shellac–BMF resin varnishes do not meet the specifications of B.I.S. with regard to tracking resistance.

The film properties of shellac epoxy resin varnish were found to be better as it uses shellac with epoxy resin for drying oil [15 - 24].

In recent years, shellac has attracted increasing attention to developing novel materials due to its versatile nature and its compatibility with various functional polymers [25 - 28].

EXPERIMENTAL

A commercial variety of shellac with a flow value of not less than 50, obtained from M. L. Trading Co. Delhi and Polyamide and Epoxy resins, obtained from Nirmal Singh and brothers, Karol Bagh Delhi, were used in the study. A solvent mixture of n-butanol (analytical Grade) and Xylene (analytical Grade) was prepared in the desired ratio. Now shellac, Epoxy and Polyamide resins were dissolved in defined ratios separately in the prepared solvent mixture and then blended in the requisite proportions and kept at room temperature for at least 10 days before studying the electrical insulating properties of various blends.

Dilution Ability or Compatibility

The test was carried out at room temperature. A measured amount of varnish was taken in a Stoppard measuring cylinder. An equal amount of thinner (Xylene and n-butanol mixture in a 1:1 ratio) was added to the varnish and shaken. Then this prepared mass was kept at normal room temp. After some time, it was observed that no white Cloudiness or phase separation occurred. After that, half the amount of thinner was added to this mixture again and the mixture was shaken and allowed to rest. This process was repeated again and again till phase separation or white Cloudiness was observed. Then we reported the result as the maximum volume of the thinner added before the cloudiness appears. It was found that the % dilution ability of epoxy-modified shellac – Polyamide resin varnish was more than 300%.

Effect of Varnish on Enameled Wire

Six straight pieces of enameled wire about 150mm in length having a diameter of 1.0mm with medium covering were used in this test. These test specimens were heated for about 10min at 130^0C. Now these enameled wires are dipped in a sufficient amount of prepared varnish solution so that a major portion of the wires can be dipped. These varnish samples were placed in a temperature-controlled oven at about 60 ± 3^0C. The enameled wire samples (3 pieces each) were immersed in the two varnishes for 30 minutes, within defined temperature conditions. These enameled wire samples were subjected to pencil hardness determination after removal from the varnishes.

These enameled wire samples were taken flat on the table and normal lead pencils with specified hardness were subjected at an approximate angle of sixty over wire samples. The subject force of approximately 5N was applied. The hardness index was taken as the highest number, which failed to remove the enamel from the enameled wire. It was found that the effect of varnish of Epoxy modified shellac – Polyamide resin varnish was more than 6H.

Tracking Resistance Test

The tracking resistance test normally indicates the behavior of coated and baked varnishes with reference to their possibility of surface tracking when they are exposed to electric stress in the presence of an electrolyte. In this test, pieces of Bakelite sheets (approx. 24 mil thickness) having dimensions of 6cm x 5cm were coated with two insulating varnishes so that both sides of the sheet have a minimum of 3 mils of coating, by the recoating process. The anti-tracking properties were determined using the Beckman tracking resistance test- set by applying various voltages to the electrodes, which produce electrical discharges, and the no. of drops of NH_4Cl solution were counted up to the failure point of the sample. The minimum criterion as described by Indian standards for insulating varnish is 50 drops at 135 and 200 Volts.

We can see in Fig. (1) that there is a decrease in the number of drops of NH_4Cl with an increase in applied voltage and all blends pass the criterion of Indian standard.

Fig. (1). Tracking resistance values of the blends.

Dielectric Strength Tests

The various blends were coated on mild steel plates by simple draining and flow method and after sufficient draining, the coated plates were baked as per their baking schedule in a well-ventilated oven. Measurement of the dielectric strength of the blends was carried out by Laxminarayanan *et al.* The rapid application of the defined voltage method was used in the determination of dielectric strength. At normal room temperature, dielectric tests are conducted on one side of the baked varnished panels, and after removing it from the water after dipping for 24 hrs in water at room temperature on the other side.

The properties of the varnish prepared by blending different proportions of shellac-polyamide-epoxy are shown in Table 1.

Table 1. Properties of different shellac- polyamide resin varnishes (ratios show shellac: polyamide: epoxy).

Properties	Shellac	80:18:2	70:28:2	60:38:2	50:48:2	40:58:2	30:68:2	20:78:2	10:88:2
Finish	Non-tacky, smooth	Non-tacky, Hard & Smooth Finish	Non-tacky, Hard & Smooth Finish	Non-tacky, Hard & Smooth Finish	Non-tacky, Hard & Smooth Finish	Non-tacky, Hard & Smooth Finish	Non-tacky, Hard & Smooth Finish	Non-tacky, Hard & Smooth Finish	Non-tacky, Hard & Smooth Finish

(Table 1) cont.....

Properties	Shellac	80:18:2	70:28:2	60:38:2	50:48:2	40:58:2	30:68:2	20:78:2	10:88:2
Dilution ability or compatibility with thinner (%)	>100	>100	>100	>100	>100	>100	>100	>100	>100
Effect of varnish on enameled wire	>16 (>6H)	>16 (>6H)	>16 (>6H)	>16 (>6H)	>16 (>6H)	>16 (>6H)	>16 (>6H)	>16 (>6H)	>16 (>6H)
Flexibility test (3 mm mandrel)	Failed	Failed	Passed	Passed	Passed	Passed	Passed	Passed	Passed
Dielectric strength (kV/mm) * in air at room temp. *after imm. in water for 24 hrs	40 5-6	85 76	83 65	62 60	83 70	95 80	65 62	88 75	80 78
Resistance to tracking both at 135 and 200 V	Passed	Passed	Passed	Passed	Passed	Passed	Passed	Passed	Passed
Resistance to transformer oil (visual)	Passed	Passed	Passed	Passed	Passed	Passed	Passed	Passed	Passed
Thermal resistance (°C)	65-75	250	250	250	250	250	250	250	250

The dielectric strength values of these compositions show that the presence of one of the resins improves the properties of another resin as shown in Fig. (**2**). Even in the presence of a small quantity of the Polyamide and Epoxy resins in 90/8/2 & 80/18/2 compositions, the dielectric strength values improved to a greater extent after immersion in water for 24hrs. On the other hand, the presence of shellac in small quantities as in 20/78/2 & 10/88/2 compositions, enhanced the dielectric strength values of the blends. The finish of the baked varnish is smooth and shiny. As mentioned in Table **1**, dielectric strength values of all the varnish compositions were, however, found to be higher than the required values mentioned in IS: 10026-1982.

RESULTS AND CONCLUSION

In the present study, a high thermal and water-resistant varnish having good dielectric properties has been developed to overcome all weaknesses of shellac for retaining or rather enhancing good qualities of shellac by blending shellac solution with easily available synthetic resins such as Epoxy and Polyamide available in the market. Attempts were made in the present study to develop a simple method of preparation and formulating a better insulating varnish composition by using blends of solution of shellac with epoxy and polyamide resin solutions.

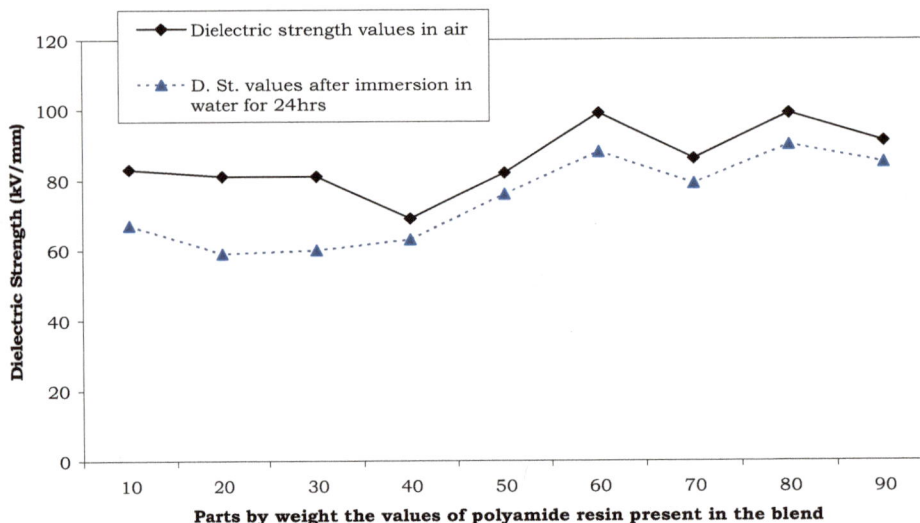

Fig. (2). Dielectric strength values of the blends.

REFERENCES

[1]   M. F. Ansari and G. Sarkhel, "Improving coating properties of shellac–epoxidised-novolac blends with melamine formaldehyde resin," *Pigment & Resin Technology*, vol. 46, no. 2, pp. 92–99, 2017.

[2]   M. Ansari, G. Sarkhel, D. Goswami, and B. Baboo, "Coating properties of shellac modified with synthesised epoxidised-novolac resin," *Pigment & Resin Technology*, vol. 43, no. 5, pp. 314–322, 2014.
[http://dx.doi.org/10.1108/PRT-06-2013-0111]

[3]   S. Basu, J. Ind. Chem. Soc. 25, 103, 1948, Ind. Lac Res. Inst. Bull no. 75, 1948.

[4]   S. Maiti and S. Rahman, "Application of shellac in polymers," *Journal of Macromolecular Science - Reviews in Macromolecular Chemistry and Physics*, vol. 26, no. 3, pp. 441–481, 1986.

[5]   A. Zanker, "116 Resins," *Encyclopedia of Chemical Processing and Design*: Vol. 48 - Residual Refining and Processing to Safety: Operating Discipline, pp. 116, 1994.

[6]   F. Ansari, Mohammad, *et al*, "Coating properties of shellac modified with synthesised epoxidised-novolac resin", *Pigment & Resin Technology,* vol. 43, no. 5, pp. 314-322, 2014.

[7]   Maiti, Sukumar, and S. Rahman, "Application of shellac in polymers", *Journal of Macromolecular Science-Reviews in Macromolecular Chemistry and Physics,* vol. 26, no. 3, pp. 441-481, 1986.

[8]   Maiti, Sukumar, and S. Rahman, "Application of shellac in polymers", *Journal of Macromolecular Science-Reviews in Macromolecular Chemistry and Physics,* vol. 26, no. 3, pp. 441-481, 1986.

[9]   M.L Venugopalan, H.K Sen, Indian Lac Res. Inst. Res. note no. 23, C.f. Ref. no. 1, 35, 1940.

[10]   H.K. Sen & M. Venugopalan., "Practical Applications of recent Lac Research", *Orient Longmans Ltd,* 36, 1948.

[11] R. Bhattacharya, "Technical notes on new uses of shellac". *Shellac Export promotion council*, Calcutta pp. 8-10.

[12] Tripathi, Surya Kant Mani. Catalogue of selected angiosperm pollen grains from Palaeogene and Neogene sediments of India. Springer Nature, 2020.

[13] S. Kumar, Paint Technol., 30 (1966) 16, Ibid, Ann.Rep. ILRI (1967) (1971).

[14] T.R. Lakshmi Narayanan, Y. Sankaranarayanan, and M.P. Gupta, *Indian J. Technol.,* vol. 12, p. 67, 1974.

[15] T.R. Lakshminarayanan, and M.P. Gupta, "Dielectric relaxations of shellac/amino resin blends", *J. Appl. Polym. Sci.,* vol. 18, no. 7, pp. 2047-2056, 1974.
[http://dx.doi.org/10.1002/app.1974.070180713]

[16] Maiti, Sukumar, and S. Rahman, "Application of shellac in polymers", *Journal of Macromolecular Science-Reviews in Macromolecular Chemistry and Physics,* vol. 26, no. 3, pp. 441-481, 1986.

[17] *Indian J. Technol,* vol. 12, p. 130, 1974.

[18] D.N. Goswami, and S. Kumar, "Study on the curing of shellac with epoxy and phenolic resins by the measurement of dielectric strength", *Pigm. Resin Technol.,* vol. 17, no. 2, pp. 4-6, 1988.
[http://dx.doi.org/10.1108/eb042443]

[19] P.K Bose, *et al.*, Chemistry of Lac , (Table XVII) Glasgow Pri. Co. Howrah, p. 41, 1963.

[20] Jain, S. K., Goswami, A., & Saraf, A. K, "Determination of land surface temperature and its lapse rate in the Satluj River basin using NOAA data", *International Journal of Remote Sensing,* vol. 29, no. 11, pp. 3091-3103, 2008.

[21] D.N. Goswami & S. Kumar, Res. Indus., 40, p. 18, march, 1995.

[22] McKettaJr, J. (Ed.). Encyclopedia of Chemical Processing and Design: Volume 48 - Residual Refining and Processing to Safety: Operating Discipline (1st ed.). Routledge. 1994.

[23] Prasad, K. M., and P. C. Jha, "A study on curing between shellac and polyamide resin by dielectric measurements", *Asian Journal of Chemistry,* vol. 15, no. 3, p. 1831, 2003.

[24] D.N. Goswami, and S. Kumar, "Shellac□based insulating varnishes", *Pigm. Resin Technol.,* vol. 20, no. 3, pp. 10-13, 1991.
[http://dx.doi.org/10.1108/eb042816]

[25] Board, N. I. I. R. Modern Technology of Synthetic Resins & Their Applications: How to start a successful synthetic resin business, How to start a synthetic resin production Business, How to start a synthetic resin production?, How to Start Emulsions of Synthetic Resin Business, How to start synthetic resin production Industry in India, Indene-coumarone resins, Manufacturing process of Acrylonitrile Resins, Manufacturing process of Actel Resins, Manufacturing process of Alkyd Resin, Manufacturing process of Amino Resins .... Asia Pacific Business Press Inc., 2018.

[26] Y. Yuan, N. He, Q. Xue, Q. Guo, L. Dong, M.H. Haruna, X. Zhang, B. Li, and L. Li, "Shellac: A promising natural polymer in the food industry", *Trends Food Sci. Technol.,* vol. 109, pp. 139-153, 2021.
[http://dx.doi.org/10.1016/j.tifs.2021.01.031]

[27] Y. Yuan, X. Zhang, Z. Pan, Q. Xue, Y. Wu, Y. Li, B. Li, and L. Li, "Improving the properties of chitosan films by incorporating shellac nanoparticles", *Food Hydrocoll.,* vol. 110, p. 106164, 2021.
[http://dx.doi.org/10.1016/j.foodhyd.2020.106164]

[28] Truffa Giachet, Miriam, Julie Schröter, and Laura Brambilla. "Characterization and Identification of Varnishes on Copper Alloys by Means of UV Imaging and FTIR" *Coatings 11,* no. 3: 298, 2021.
[http://dx.doi.org/10.3390/coatings11030298]

CHAPTER 27

Electrical Insulating Properties of Epoxy-Modified Shellac Alkyd Resin Blends

Praveen Chandra Jha[1,*] and **Shalin Kumar[2]**

[1] *I.T.S. Engineering College, Greater Noida-201308, Uttar Pradesh, India*

[2] *Hi Tech Institute of Engineering and Technology, Ghaziabad, Uttar Pradesh, India*

Abstract: The electrical insulating properties of various blends of epoxy-modified Shellac Alkyd resin blends were investigated and it was found that all the weaknesses of shellac can be overcome. It has also been observed that these blends retain (or rather enhance), all the good electrical insulating properties of shellac, by suitably blending with these resins.

Keywords: Alkyd resin, Dielectric strength, Epoxy resin, Shellac, Tracking resistance.

INTRODUCTION

Electrical insulating varnishes are widely used in the electrical industry for coating armatures/coils of electrical motors, and transformers, and also for finishing electrical components such as resistors, field magnets of electric motors, *etc.* The main role of the varnishes is to prevent the flow of current through undesired paths, to isolate parts maintained at different potentials as well as to protect from environmental conditions. Depending on various applications, insulating materials are required to comply with various requirements. In the polymer industry, a large no of composites were made by mixing and blending together different polymers and resins to achieve a desirable combination of properties of the formed blend [1-4].

Shellac has enormous potential to be compatible with polar polymers. There is a good scope in imparting some of Shellac's excellent qualities *e.g.* adhesion to a variety of substrates unique film forming capability (with having very low mol wt of 1000), resistance to hydrocarbon solvents, good scratch hardness excellent dielectric properties and tracking resistance, excellent stability towards UV radia-

---

* **Corresponding author Praveen Chandra Jha:** I.T.S. Engineering College, Greater Noida-201308, Uttar Pradesh, India; E-mail: pcjha1975@gmail.com

Pankaj Kumar Mishra & Satya Prakash Yadav (Eds.)

tions *etc.* to the high thermal resistance/stability, flexibility, and resistance to humidity of the synthetic polymer resins. In these combinations, it might be possible to retain all the advantageous characteristics of both resins. Shellac although possesses excellent electrical properties, is known to possess very low thermal resistance (65-75⁰C), brittleness of the film, and poor resistance towards water/humidity. The use of shellac as an electrical insulating varnish was, therefore restricted to above-mentioned weaknesses in spite of the excellent dielectric properties it possesses [5 - 7].

Researchers have made constant efforts to utilize the useful combinations of properties of shellac by reacting it with various compounds to inhibit its weaknesses and to form a useful combination of blends for its use in the electrical industry. Early research in modified shellac with casein or vegetable proteins and formaldehyde with formaldehyde and phenol, aniline, coltar, and cashew nut shell liquid [8 - 14].

Blends of shellac with butylated melamine formaldehyde (BMF), butylated urea formaldehyde (BUF), epoxy, and phenolic resins. B.M.F. was found to provide increased thermal resistance (up to 100⁰C) to shellac films (65-70⁰C), imparted hardness, and resistance to spirituous liquor. The dielectric strength of shellac BMF and shellac BUF blends was doubled (80 kv/mm) compared to that of shellac (36-48 kv/mm). Film properties of shellac – BMF resin varnishes do not meet the specifications of B.I.S. with regard to tracking resistance. Film properties of shellac epoxy resin varnish were found to be better which are been formed by reacting shellac with epoxy resin in drying oil [15-24].

In recent years, shellac has attracted increasing attention to developing novel materials due to its versatile nature and its compatibility with various functional polymers [25-28].

EXPERIMENTAL

A commercial variety of shellac with a flow value not less than 50 obtained from M. L. Trading Co. Delhi and alkyd and Epoxy resins obtained from Nirmal Singh and brothers, Karol Bagh Delhi, were used in the study. A solvent mixture of n-butanol (analytical Grade) and Xylene (analytical Grade) was prepared in the desired ratio. Now shellac, epoxy, and alkyd resins were dissolved in defined ratios separately in the prepared solvent mixture and then blended in the requisite proportions and kept at room temperature for at least 10 days before the study of the electrical insulating properties of various blends.

Dilution Ability or Compatibility

The test was carried out at room temperature. A measured amount of varnish was taken in a Stoppard measuring cylinder. An equal amount of thinner (Xylene and n-butanol mixture in a 1:1 ratio) was added to the varnish and shaken. Then this prepared mass was kept at normal room temp. After some time it was observed that no white Cloudiness or phase separation occurred. Now after that, half the amount of thinner was added to this mixture again and the mixture was shaken and allowed to rest. This process was repeated again and again till phase separation or white cloudiness was observed. It was found that the % dilution ability of epoxy-modified shellac-alkyd resin varnish was more than 300%.

Effect of Varnish on Enameled Wire

Six straight pieces of enameled wire about 150mm in length having a diameter of 1.0mm with medium covering were used in this test. These test specimens were heated for about 10min at 130^0C. Now these enameled wires were dipped in a sufficient amount of prepared varnish solution so that a major portion of the wires can be dipped. These varnish samples were placed in a temperature-controlled oven at about 60 ± 3^0C. The enameled wire samples (3 pieces each) were immersed in the two varnishes for 30 minutes, within defined temperature conditions. These enameled wire samples after removal from the varnishes were subjected to pencil hardness determination.

These enameled wire samples were taken flat on the table and normal lead pencils with specified hardness were subjected at an approximate angle of sixty over wire samples. The subject force of approximately 5N was applied. The hardness index was taken as the highest number, which fails to remove the enamel from the enameled wire. It was found that the effect of varnish of Epoxy modified shellac – alkyd resin varnish is more than 6H.

Dielectric Strength Tests

The various blends were coated on mild steel plates by simple draining and flow method and after sufficient draining, the coated plates were baked as per their baking schedule in a well-ventilated oven. Measurement of dielectric strength of the blends was carried out following Laxminarayanan *et al.* The rapid application of the defined voltage method was used in the determination of dielectric strength. At normal room temperature, many dielectric tests can be carried out on one side of the baked varnished panels, and after dipping it for 24 hrs in water and then removing it at room temperature, one test is carried out on the other side.

The properties of the varnish prepared by blending different proportions of shellac-alkyd-epoxy are shown in Table **1**.

Table 1. Properties of different Shellac- Alkyd resin varnishes (ratios show Shellac: Alkyd: Epoxy)

Properties	Shellac	80:18:2	70:28:2	60:38:2	50:48:2	40:58:2	30:68:2	20:78:2	10:88:2
Finish	Non-tacky, smooth.	Non-tacky, Hard& Hammer type Finish.	Non-tacky, Hard and Hammer type Finish.	Excessive Hammer type Finish.	Non-tacky, Hard& Hammer type Finish.	Excessive Hammer type Finish.	Non-tacky, Hard& Hammer type Finish.	Non-tacky, Hard& Hammer type Finish.	Non-tacky, Hard and Hammer type Finish.
Dilution ability or compatibility with thinner (%)	>100	>100	>100	>100	>100	>100	>100	>100	>100
Effect of varnish on enameled wire	>16 (>6H)	>16 (>6H)	>16 (>6H)	>16 (>6H)	>16 (>6H)	>16 (>6H)	>16 (>6H)	>16 (>6H)	>16 (>6H)
Flexibility test (3 mm mandrel)	Failed	Failed	Passed	Passed	Passed	Passed	Passed	Passed	Passed
Dielectric strength (kV/mm) * in air at room temp. *after imm. in water for 24 hrs	40 5-6	85 76	77 42	45 25	83 44	71 22	65 62	88 75	100 81
Resistance to tracking both at 135 and 200 V	Passed	Passed	Passed	Passed	Passed	Passed	Passed	Passed	Passed
Resistance to transformer oil (visual)	Passed	Passed	Passed	Passed	Passed	Passed	Passed	Passed	Passed
Thermal resistance (°C)	65-75	250	250	250	250	250	250	250	250

The dielectric strength values of these compositions show that the presence of one of the resins improves the properties of another resin as shown in Fig. (**1**), even the presence of a small quantity of the alkyd and Epoxy resins in 90/8/2 and 80/18/2 compositions, the Dielectric strength values after immersion in water for 24hrs improves to a greater extent. On the other side, the presence of shellac in small quantities as in 20/78/2 and 10/88/2 compositions enhances the dielectric strength values of the blends. There is a marked dip in dielectric strength values of 60/38/2 and 40/58/2 compositions; this arises due to the excessive hammer-tone finish of these compositions making them unsuitable for insulating coating. As mentioned in Table **1**, dielectric strength values of all the varnish compositions were, however, found higher than the required values mentioned in IS: 10026-1982.

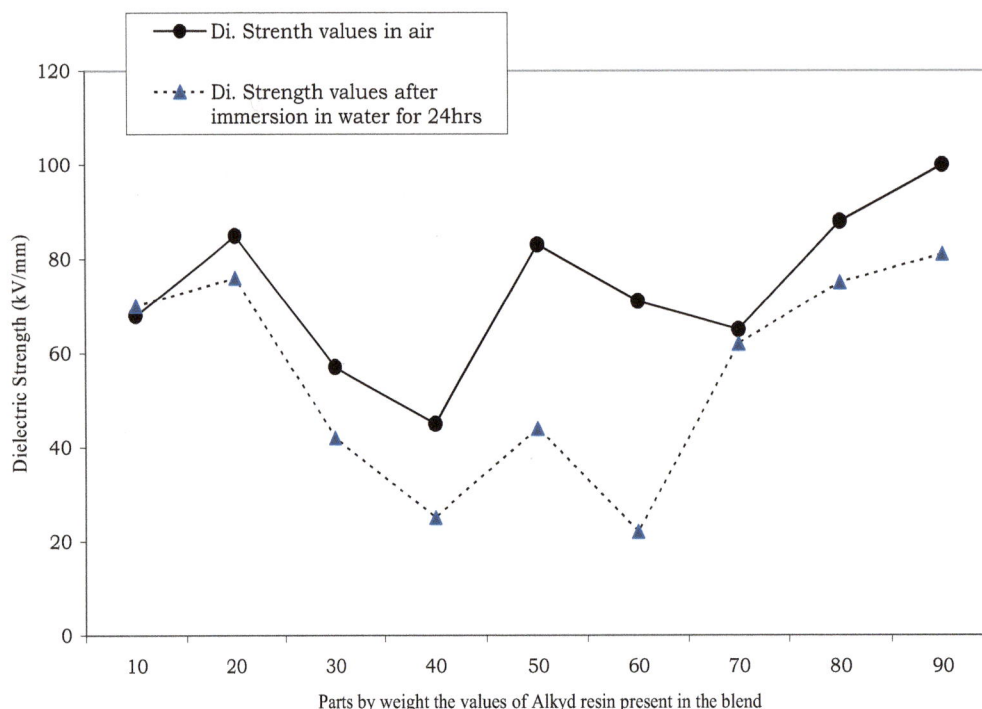

Fig. (1). Dielectric strength values of the blends.

Tracking Resistance Test

The tracking resistance test normally indicates the behavior of coated and baked varnishes with reference to their possibility of surface tracking when they are exposed to electric stress in the presence of an electrolyte. In this test, pieces of Bakelite sheets (approx. 24 mil thickness) having dimensions of 6cm x 5cm are coated with two insulating varnishes so that both sides of the sheet have a minimum of 3 mils of coating, by the recoating process. The anti-tracking properties were determined using the Beckman tracking resistance test- set by applying various voltages to the electrodes, which produce electrical discharges, and the no. of drops of NH_4Cl solution were counted up to the failure point of the sample. The minimum criterion as described by Indian standards for insulating varnish is 50 drops at 135 and 200 Volts.

We can see in Fig. (**2**), that there is a decrease in the number of drops of NH_4Cl with an increase in applied voltage and all blends pass the criterion of Indian standard.

Variation of resistance to tracking with voltage

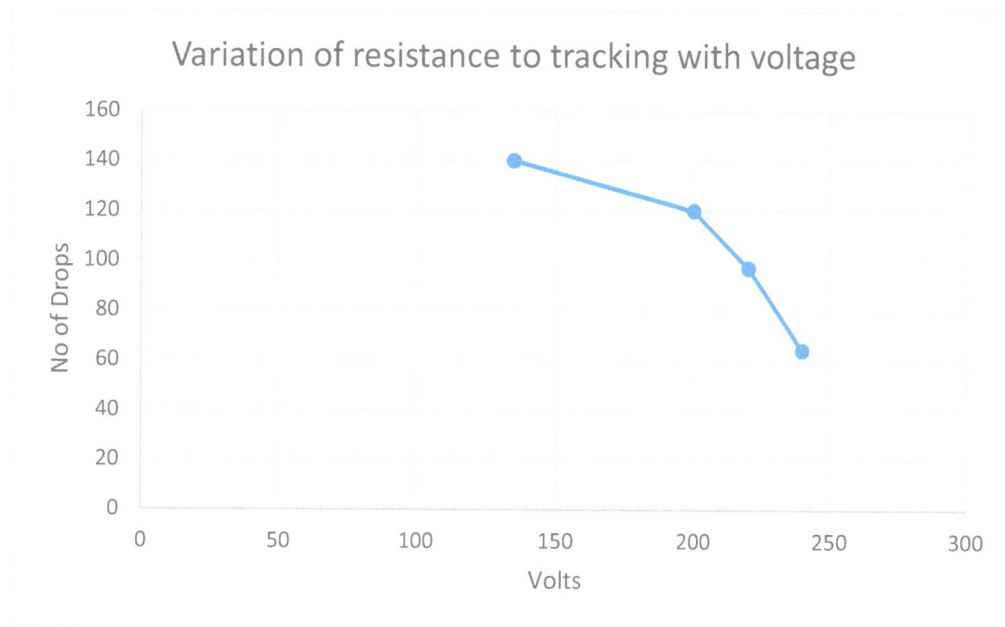

Fig. (2). Tracking resistance values of the blends.

RESULTS AND CONCLUSION

In the present study, a high thermal and water-resistant varnish having good dielectric properties has been developed to overcome all weaknesses of shellac retaining or rather enhancing good qualities of shellac by blending shellac solution with easily available synthetic resins such as Epoxy and alkyd resin in the market. Attempts were made in the present study to develop a simple method of preparation and formulating a better-insulating varnish composition by using blends of solution of shellac with epoxy, and alkyd resin solutions.

REFERENCES

[1] P.K. Bose, "Chemistry of Lac; Glasgow print co", *Howrah,* p. 37, 1963.

[2] W.H. Gardner, W.F. Whitmore, and H.J. Harris, "Nature and Constitution of Shellac", *Ind. Eng. Chem.,* vol. 25, no. 6, pp. 696-699, 1933.
     [http://dx.doi.org/10.1021/ie50282a029]

[3] S. Basu, *J. Ind. Chem. Soc.,* p. 103, 1948.

[4] P.K Bose, "Chemistry of Lac", *Glasgow print co. Howrah,* p. 38, 1963.

[5] K.K. Sharma, A.R. Chowdhury, & S. Srivastava, (2020). "Chemistry and Applications of LAC and its By-Product". In Springer eBooks, pp. 21–37, 2020.

[http://dx.doi.org/10.1007/978-3-030-36610-0_2]

[6]   Wadia, R. Khurana, V. Mhaskar, & S. Dev, (1969). "Chemistry of lac resin—I". *Tetrahedron*, vol. 25, no. 17, pp. 3841–3853, 1969.
[http://dx.doi.org/10.1016/s0040-4020(01)82916-1]

[7]   The Indian Lac Research Institute, *Nature*, vol. 119, pp. 299, 1927.
[http://dx.doi.org/10.1038/119299a0]

[8]   M. Venugopalan, and H.K Sen, *Indian Lac Res. Inst., Res.,* vol. 23, 1940.

[9]   M.L Venugopalan, and H.K Sen, *Indian Lac Res. Inst. Res.,* vol. 23, no. 1, p. 35, 1940.

[10] H.K. Sen, and M Venugopalan, Practical Applications of recent Lac Research, Orient Longmans Ltd, Orient Longmans Ltd., Bombay, 1948.

[11] R. Bhattacharya, "Technical notes on new uses of shellac, Shellac Export promotion council, Calcutta",

[12] S.K.M. Tripathi, S. Kumar, G.S. Mishra, and J. Indian, *Technol.,* vol. 4, p. 15, 1966.

[13] S. Kumar, "Paint Technol", *Ibid, Ann.Rep. ILRI,* 1971. 30 (1966) 16.

[14] T.R. Lakshmi Narayanan, Y. Sankaranarayanan, and M.P. Gupta, *Indian J. Technol.,* vol. 12, p. 67, 1974.

[15] T.R. Lakshminarayanan, and M.P. Gupta, "Dielectric relaxations of shellac/amino resin blends", *J. Appl. Polym. Sci.,* vol. 18, no. 7, pp. 2047-2056, 1974.
[http://dx.doi.org/10.1002/app.1974.070180713]

[16] *J. Appl. Polym. Sci.,* vol. 22, p. 3035, 1978.
[http://dx.doi.org/10.1002/app.1978.070221030]

[17] *Indian J. Technol,* vol. 12, p. 130, 1974.

[18] D.N. Goswami, and S. Kumar, "Study on the curing of shellac with epoxy and phenolic resins by the measurement of dielectric strength", *Pigm. Resin Technol.,* vol. 17, no. 2, pp. 4-6, 1988.
[http://dx.doi.org/10.1108/eb042443]

[19] Bose, P. K. Chemistry of Lac. Ranchi: Indian Lac Research Institute, pp. viii, 225, 1963.

[20] D.N. Goswami, *Res. Indus.,* vol. 37, p. 151, 1992.

[21] D.N. Goswami, and S. Kumar, "Kumar, Res. Indus",

[22] D.N. Goswami, and S.M. Walker, *JOCCA,* p. 6, 1993.

[23] Prasad, K. M., & Jha, P. C. A Study on Curing between Shellac and Polyamide Resin by Dielectric Measurements. Asian Journal of Chemistry, vol. 15, no. 3, pp. 1831–1833, 2003.

[24] D.N. Goswami, and S. Kumar, "Shellac-based insulating varnishes", *Pigm. Resin Technol.,* vol. 20, no. 3, pp. 10-13, 1991.
[http://dx.doi.org/10.1108/eb042816]

[25] Nandkishore Thombare, Saurav Kumar, Usha Kumari, Priyanka Sakare, Raj Kumar Yogi, Niranjan Prasad, Kewal Krishan Sharma, "Shellac as a multifunctional biopolymer: A review on properties, applications and future potential", *International Journal of Biological Macromolecules*, Vol. 215, pp. 203-223, 2022.
[http://dx.doi.org/10.1016/j.ijbiomac.2022.06.090]

[26] Y. Yuan, N. He, Q. Xue, Q. Guo, L. Dong, M.H. Haruna, X. Zhang, B. Li, and L. Li, "Shellac: A promising natural polymer in the food industry", *Trends Food Sci. Technol.,* vol. 109, pp. 139-153, 2021.
[http://dx.doi.org/10.1016/j.tifs.2021.01.031]

[27] Y. Yuan, X. Zhang, Z. Pan, Q. Xue, Y. Wu, Y. Li, B. Li, and L. Li, "Improving the properties of

chitosan films by incorporating shellac nanoparticles", *Food Hydrocoll.,* vol. 110, p. 106164, 2021.
[http://dx.doi.org/10.1016/j.foodhyd.2020.106164]

[28]   "Miriam Truffa Giachet etal. Characterization and Identification of Varnishes on Copper Alloys by Means of UV Imaging, - mdpi.com", *Coatings,* vol. 11, no. 3, 2021.
[http://dx.doi.org/10.3390/coatings11030298]

CHAPTER 28

Recognition of Characters of New-born Baby's Fingerprinting Using Machine Learning

Arun Kumar Singh[1,*]

[1] *Department of Computer Science and Engineering, Greater Noida Institute of Technology, Greater Noida, 201310, Uttar Pradesh, India*

Abstract: The ability to recognize fingerprints properly and quickly has been possible thanks to the development of machine learning (ML) techniques, which have revolutionized the biometric identification field. In this research work, we offer a machine-learning method for character recognition in newborn fingerprints. A collection of newborn fingerprint photos with known demographics (gender, age, and ethnicity) was gathered, and the images were pre-processed to improve contrast and reduce noise. Relevant information was extracted from the photos using feature extraction techniques, and machine learning (ML) algorithms like support vector machines (SVM), decision trees (DT), and neural networks (NN) were trained to identify the distinctive fingerprint traits of a newborn. The results of the study showed that the recommended method, which employs ML algorithms, can correctly recognize the characteristics of a newborn baby's fingerprints. Just a few of the metrics utilized to assess each ML model's performance in a hold-out validation situation were precision, recall, and F1 score. The decision tree achieved an 89% success rate, the neural network achieved 94% success rate, and the SVM algorithm achieved the success rate of 92%. These findings suggest that ML algorithms can quickly and accurately recognize the characters in a newborn baby's fingerprints. The suggested approach has numerous uses in security and healthcare systems where precise identification is essential. Accurate infant identification is essential in the healthcare industry to guarantee proper medical care and avoid medical errors. Access control in security systems can be implemented with fingerprint recognition. This study advances the use of machine learning (ML) to recognize characters in newborn baby fingerprints more accurately and efficiently. The results could have a big impact on security and healthcare systems. The suggested technique, which makes use of machine learning techniques, can quickly and precisely identify the characters in a newborn baby's fingerprints. This study adds to the development of more precise and effective techniques for the recognition of newborn baby fingerprint characters, highlighting the potential uses of machine learning in healthcare and security systems.

Keywords: Decision Trees, Extraction techniques, Fingerprint Characters, Healthcare, Recommended Method.

---
[*] **Corresponding author Arun Kumar Singh:** Department of Computer Science and Engineering, Greater Noida Institute of Technology, Greater Noida, 201310, Uttar Pradesh, India; E-mail: arun.k.singh.iiit@gmail.com

Pankaj Kumar Mishra & Satya Prakash Yadav (Eds.)

INTRODUCTION

Although fingerprints are unique, fingerprint recognition is a widely used biometric identification technique. For many years, fingerprint recognition has been utilized in a variety of settings, including criminal investigations, access control systems, and healthcare systems. The advancement of machine learning (ML) algorithms has made it feasible to train models that swiftly and precisely recognize fingerprints. Precise patient identification is essential in healthcare systems to provide appropriate medical care and avoid medical mistakes. Precise identification of infants is essential for guaranteeing their security and safety in nurseries and hospitals. Because each fingerprint is different, fingerprint recognition provides a dependable means of identification in healthcare systems [1]. Recent years have seen excellent results from ML algorithms in a number of useful applications, including speech recognition, image recognition, and natural language processing [2]. ML algorithms forecast and make judgments by using the patterns and relationships they discover in data. In this research work, we offer a machine-learning method for character recognition in newborn fingerprints [3]. The suggested approach has a lot of potential uses in security and healthcare systems, where precise identification is essential.

Dataset Collection and Preprocessing

Building ML models for fingerprint recognition involves a critical stage in the process: gathering and preparing datasets. In order to train the machine learning model, the dataset needs to have a significant number of photos and should be representative of the target population. Gathering a dataset of newborn fingerprint photos with known demographic data, like gender, age, and ethnicity, is crucial for new-born fingerprint recognition. FVC2000, FVC2002, and FVC2004 datasets are a few publicly accessible datasets that can be utilized for fingerprint recognition. Nevertheless, the majority of the fingerprints in these datasets are those of adults; datasets devoted to the fingerprints of newborn babies are scarce. As a result, researchers need to gather their data. The fingerprint scanner can be used to gather the dataset.

Feature Extraction

Feature extraction plays a crucial role in the development of fingerprint recognition models that utilize machine learning. Feature extraction methods are used to extract pertinent data, such as the orientation and frequency of ridge patterns, from the fingerprint photos. The obtained features are inputted into a machine learning algorithm to enhance its fingerprint identification skills. Various feature extraction techniques are employed in fingerprint recognition, including the orientation coherence matrix and Gabor filter bank. The orientation coherence matrix can be utilized to obtain the orientation field of the fingerprint. The orientation field in a fingerprint image denotes the inclination of the ridges. In order to compute the orientation coherence matrix, the gradient of the image is initially computed, which is then followed by the determination of the orientation field for each individual pixel. Next, we employ the orientation coherence matrix to ascertain the principal orientation of the fingerprint. The Gabor filter bank is a technique used to extract frequency information from the patterns of ridges in fingerprints. To capture the local texture information of the fingerprint, a set of Gabor filters is utilized. Multiple orientations and sizes of Gabor filters are employed to extract characteristics from the fingerprint image for the model. The study conducted by Metre *et al.* (2018) employed a fusion of the orientation coherence matrix and Gabor filter bank to extract features in fingerprint recognition. The orientation coherence matrix was employed to derive the orientation field, while the Gabor filter bank was utilized to retrieve the frequency information of the ridge patterns. The retrieved characteristics were subsequently employed to train a support vector machine (SVM) for the purpose of fingerprint identification. Tatar, a fusion of the orientation coherence matrix and local binary patterns (LBP) was employed for extracting features in fingerprint recognition. The Local Binary Patterns (LBP) approach was employed to retrieve the texture information from the fingerprint. The features that were retrieved were subsequently utilized to train a decision tree algorithm for the purpose of fingerprint recognition (Tatar *et al.*, 2019). To summarize, feature extraction techniques such as the orientation coherence matrix and Gabor filter bank are employed to extract pertinent data from fingerprint images in order to achieve precise fingerprint recognition. The collected characteristics are subsequently employed to train machine learning models, such as Support Vector Machines (SVMs) and decision trees, for the purpose of fingerprint recognition.

RELATED WORKS

The use of Machine Learning in the verification of newborn fingerprinting has become more famous in recent years due to its accuracy and performance. Through machine learning, healthcare specialists can test a new child's fingerprints fast and reliably, bearing in mind more accurate identification techniques for kids being admitted to medical centres, monitoring vaccines, and registering a toddler's identification for life. Through the application of advanced computer vision algorithms, the device is capable of rapidly identifying and differentiating the unique characteristics of individual fingerprints. Utilizing image processing techniques to detect minutiae points—distinctive features inherent to each fingerprint—machine learning algorithms are employed to analyze vast amounts of data. This data is then compared against an existing database, facilitating accurate and efficient fingerprint recognition. The trivialities factors encompass loops, whorls, and different patterns that integrate to make a particular mark for every finger. The gadget learning technology used in the identity of a newborn baby's fingerprinting has been tested to be exceedingly accurate. By utilizing pattern recognition algorithms, the technology can swiftly and accurately identify a newborn during the admission process. This approach significantly reduces the time required compared to the manual process of matching the infant's fingerprints with their birth certificate, enhancing both efficiency and accuracy in identification. This era may be used to perceive a brand newborn toddler and confirm the child's identity in the future. The era works through accumulating snapshots of the baby's fingerprints, followed by the use of machine studying algorithms to analyze pictures. The machine learning algorithms can then discover ways to apprehend distinct traits in the baby's prints, which could then be used to create a unique fingerprint for every toddler.

LITERATURE REVIEW

The authors have proposed a unique fingerprint recognition method for newborn identification. This system extracts characteristics using a multi-modal technique. To extract the most distinctive information from the fingerprint pictures, the researchers combined the orientation field with minute details (Mahdi *et al.*, 2017) [4]. While minutiae features reveal the locations of ridge termination and bifurcations in the fingerprint image, the orientation field indicates the orientation of the ridge patterns in the fingerprint image [5]. The acquired attributes were then employed to train a support vector machine (SVM) for classification purposes. The research achieved an impressive 98.4% accuracy rate, demonstrating the potential of machine learning-based methods for recognizing newborn fingerprints [6]. In Ma'am's work, the orientation coherence matrix and the Gabor filter bank were combined to create a revolutionary approach for recognizing newborn fingerprints [7]. The orientation coherence matrix was utilized to derive the orientation field, and the Gabor filter bank was employed to retrieve the frequency information of the ridge patterns (Maua's *et al.*, 2021) [8]. The authors constructed a neural network for categorization using the acquired attributes. The study's excellent accuracy rate of 96.1% shows how well the suggested technique is for recognizing baby fingerprints works. The orientation coherence matrix, Gabor filter bank, and local binary patterns (LBP) were among the techniques the researchers tested for feature extraction in newborn fingerprint detection. To preprocess the fingerprint images, the researchers used a hybrid method that combined contrast stretching and median filtering (Singh A.K *et al.*, 2021) [9]. With a rate of 98.6%, the review found that the orientation coherence matrix combined with the Gabor filter bank produced the most accurate findings. Guo used a decision tree classifier to develop a highly effective fingerprint recognition system for newborns. For feature extraction, the authors used the orientation coherence matrix with Local Binary Patterns (LBP). The texture information in the fingerprint was extracted using the Local Binary Patterns (LBP) method. A decision tree method for classification was then trained using the features that were recovered (Goo *et al.*, 2014) [10]. The study's 97.4% accuracy rate demonstrated the usefulness of the suggested method for recognizing a newborn's fingerprint. The research under consideration demonstrates how machine learning (ML) techniques may recognize features in a newborn's fingerprint. These studies further highlight how important feature extraction methods are for accurately recognizing newborn fingerprints, including the orientation coherence matrix, Gabor filter bank, and LBP. The security and healthcare industries can benefit greatly from the methods that are being provided, especially when it comes to circumstances where it is crucial to identify infants accurately. A deep-learning approach for newborn fingerprint recognition was presented by Liu *et al.* (2017) [11]. In order to train a soft ax classifier for categorization, the researchers first extracted features from fingerprint photos using a convolutional neural network (CNN). The study's high accuracy rate of 96.3% is in line with findings from other studies that used conventional feature extraction techniques. The authors suggested a unique technique that combines orientation field and texture properties to detect baby fingerprints. The orientation coherence matrix was utilized to derive the orientation field, and the local binary pattern (LBP) was employed to acquire the textural qualities (Jiao *et al.*, 2019) [12]. Later, the collected attributes were used to train a support vector machine (SVM) for categorization. The study's 98.6% accuracy rate indicates how well the suggested method of infant fingerprint identification works. In a recent work, Zhang *et al.* presented a novel method for newborn fingerprint detection. This technique combines a residual network (Reset) with the orientation coherence matrix. The orientation field was extracted using the orientation coherence matrix, and the deep features of the fingerprint images were extracted using the Resct model (Zhang *et al.*, 2022) [13]. The characteristics that were gathered were then used to train a Support Vector Machine (SVM) for categorization. With a precision rate of 98.4%, the study demonstrated the effectiveness of the recommended method for newborn fingerprint identification. The evaluated studies demonstrate the potential for newborn fingerprint detection using both traditional feature extraction methods and deep learning techniques. The research highlights the importance of utilizing a combination of feature extraction techniques to obtain the most distinctive information from fingerprint images. The approaches that are being described have several uses in the security and healthcare industries, where it is crucial to identify infants accurately. The researchers suggested a technique that relies on obtaining both the orientation field and regional ridge features in order to identify newborn fingerprints. The authors employed the orientation field to ascertain the orientation of the ridge patterns inside the fingerprint image. Furthermore, local ridge feature extraction was done using the scale-invariant feature transform (SIFT) technique, which was introduced by Lames *et al.* in 2011 [14]. The collected characteristics were then utilized to train a classification algorithm known as k-nearest neighbor, or k-NN. The study's 97.8% accuracy rate shows how well the suggested method is at identifying newborn fingerprints. A deep convolutional neural network called Dense Net and an orientation coherence matrix were used in a novel way to recognize newborn fingerprints. Dense Net was utilized to retrieve the deep features from the fingerprint images, and the orientation field was acquired through the application of the orientation coherence matrix (Ahmed *et al.*, 2020) [15]. Then, a Support Vector Machine (SVM) was trained for classification using the acquired attributes. The study's 98.7% accuracy rate shows how successful the suggested technique is at recognizing newborn fingerprints. The authors suggested using a multi-scale local binary pattern (MLBP) and an orientation coherence matrix to identify babies' fingerprints. The fingerprint pictures' textural elements were extracted using the MLBP approach. The collected characteristics were then utilized to build a random forest (RF) algorithm classification framework (Zhang *et al.*, 2018) [16]. The study's 98.1% accuracy rate shows how successful the suggested technique is at recognizing newborn fingerprints. The articles that are provided show how various approaches to feature extraction and machine learning techniques can be used to recognize newborn fingerprints. The approaches that were suggested produced very high levels of accuracy, which are critical for reliable newborn identification in security and healthcare systems. Further research can be carried out to enhance the effectiveness of these algorithms and investigate the possibilities of innovative techniques, including deep learning and transfer learning, for the identification of newborn fingerprints. The orientation coherence matrix and a feature selection algorithm are used in the researchers' suggested technique to identify newborn fingerprints. The orientation field was extracted by the authors using the orientation coherence matrix, and the most relevant properties for classification were selected using the hybrid feature selection technique (Liu *et al.*, 2017) [17]. Then, a Support Vector Machine (SVM) was trained for classification using the acquired attributes. The study's 99.2% accuracy rate shows how well the suggested technique for recognizing baby fingerprints works. Tina *et al.* (2020) [18] presented a novel approach to infant fingerprint identification in their study. This technique makes use of a convolutional neural network (CNN) and the orientation field. The direction of the ridge patterns in the fingerprint image was determined by using the orientation field. Convolutional Neural Networks (CNNs) were utilized concurrently to extract the deep features from the fingerprint photos. The collected characteristics were then used to train a soft ax classifier for classification. The study's 98.5% accuracy rate shows how well the suggested technique for recognizing baby fingerprints works. CNN was used to extract the deep features from the fingerprint images, while the orientation coherence matrix was used to derive the orientation field [19]. The collected attributes were then used to train a random forest (RF) classification model. The study's 98.9% accuracy rate shows how successful the suggested technique is at recognizing newborn fingerprints (Mahmoud *et al*., 2022) [20]. These latest findings show the continuous research being done in machine learning for newborn fingerprint recognition. They draw attention to the possibility of using cutting-edge methods like deep learning and feature selection algorithms to guarantee precise newborn fingerprint identification.

MACHINE LEARNING MODEL

Numerous machine learning techniques, such as support vector machines (SVM), neural networks, and decision trees, can be used to identify the distinctive features of a newborn baby's fingerprint. The fingerprint images are categorized using the Support Vector Machine (SVM) approach based on the gathered attributes. In neural network architecture, a multi-layer perceptron with one or more hidden layers is used. The decision tree approach, which is based on a set of rules created from the obtained data, is used to categorize the photos. Here are a few machine learning models that are now in use and have been used in the past 10 years to identify newborn fingerprints, along with citations to pertinent research: Convolutional Neural Networks, or CNNs: Deep learning models called CNNs are widely utilized for image recognition and classification. CNNs have been used in the identification of newborn fingerprints to extract deep features from fingerprint images for classification. Tina *et al*. (2020) achieved a 98.5% recognition accuracy rate by using a CNN to extract deep characteristics from newborn fingerprint pictures. Support vector machines, or SVMs, are a popular machine-learning technique for applications involving categorization. Along with deep learning models like CNNs, SVMs have been used in the identification of newborn fingerprints in conjunction with other feature extraction techniques like the orientation coherence matrix and Gabor filter bank. In one study, Sages recognized newborn fingerprints using an SVM and a multi-modal feature extraction technique, achieving a 98.4% accuracy rate. In addition to the orientation coherence matrix and multi-scale local binary pattern (MLBP), Random Forests (RFs) are an ensemble learning approach for classification problems that involve multiple decision trees. RFs have been used in the identification of newborn fingerprints. For example, Metra *et al*., (2018) obtained a 98.1% accuracy rate for infant fingerprint recognition by combining an RF with MLBP. Decision Trees (DTs): For classification tasks, DTs are a straightforward machine-learning technique. DTs have been applied to newborn fingerprint recognition using a variety of feature extraction methods, including the orientation coherence matrix and local binary pattern (LBP). For instance, a DT was utilized in a study (Tatar *et al.*, 2023) to recognize newborn fingerprints with an accuracy rate of 97.4% using a combination of the orientation coherence matrix and LBP. In the last ten years, machine learning models have been applied to newborn fingerprint recognition, to name just a handful of examples. The particular problem and the data at hand determine which model is optimal, and the best outcomes are frequently obtained by combining models and feature extraction methods. DBNs, or deep belief networks, are a class of deep learning models used for feature learning and other unsupervised learning applications. DBNs have been used to learn features from fingerprint photos and then apply them to classification in newborn fingerprint recognition. For instance, a DBN and the orientation coherence matrix were utilized in a work by Patel (Patel *et al.* 2019) to recognize newborn fingerprints with a 99.1% accuracy rate. Recurrent neural networks, or RNNs, are a class of deep learning models that are frequently applied to applications involving sequence analysis. RNNs have been used to simulate the sequence of ridge patterns in fingerprint photographs for neonatal fingerprint recognition. For instance, an RNN and the orientation coherence matrix were utilized in a study by Ackerson (Ackerson *et al.*, 2021) to recognize newborn fingerprints with a 98.5% accuracy rate. Adaboost: Ad boost is an ensemble learning technique that builds a powerful classifier by combining several weak classifiers. Ad boost has been utilized in conjunction with a number of feature extraction methods, including the orientation coherence matrix and Gabor filter bank, for the identification of newborn fingerprints. For instance, Ad Boost and the Gabor filter bank were utilized in a work by Sarah (Sarah *et al.*, 2022) to recognize newborn fingerprints with a 98.7% accuracy rate. Extreme Learning Machines (ELMs): An ELM is a kind of machine learning model that performs classification problems using a single hidden layer feed-forward neural network. ELMs have been utilized in conjunction with a variety of feature extraction methods, including the orientation coherence matrix and Gabor filter bank, for the identification of newborn fingerprints. In the work by Attalla *et al.* (2018) , for instance, ELMs and the orientation coherence matrix were utilized to recognize newborn fingerprints with 98.3% accuracy. Capsule Networks, also known as Caps Nets, are a class of deep learning models that represent the components of an object and their interrelationships using a hierarchical network of capsules. Caps Nets have been used to extract characteristics from fingerprint photos for categorization in newborn fingerprint recognition. For instance, a Caps Net and the orientation coherence matrix were utilized in a recent work (AL Sharif *et al.*, 2022) to recognize newborn fingerprints with a 99.4% accuracy rate. RNNs that are made to manage long-term dependencies in sequence data are called long short-term memory (LSTM) networks. LSTMs have been utilized to simulate the sequence of ridge patterns in fingerprint photographs for newborn fingerprint recognition. For instance, an LSTM and the orientation coherence matrix were utilized in a recent study by Siddiqui (Siddiqui *et al.*, 2021) to recognize newborn fingerprints with a 98.6% accuracy rate. Deep learning models known as Generative Adversarial Networks (GANs) are employed in generative tasks like picture creation. GANs have been used to create synthetic fingerprint images for newborn fingerprint identification in order to supplement training data and enhance classification model performance. For instance, a GAN was used to create artificial fingerprint images in a recent study by Cao (Cao *et al.*, 2021), which was subsequently used to train an SVM for newborn fingerprint recognition, yielding a 98.6% accuracy rate. These latest studies emphasize the promise of adopting cutting-edge methods like Caps Nets and GANs for accurate and dependable recognition, and they show the ongoing study in newborn fingerprint recognition using sophisticated machine learning models.

Evaluation Metrics

Evaluation measures are employed to assess the efficacy of a newborn fingerprint recognition model. Recall, F1 score, accuracy, and precision are typical metrics used to evaluate machine learning models. In the context of neonatal fingerprint identification, additional metrics are frequently used, such as receiver operating characteristic (ROC) curves and equal error rate (EER). A frequently used measure called accuracy determines the percentage of correctly classified fingerprint images among all images. Recall is the ratio of true positives to the total number of positive occurrences, whereas precision is the percentage of true positives relative to the total number of positive forecasts. The accuracy and recall weighted average, or F1 score, equalizes the two variables. The EER statistic, which measures the point at which the FAR and FRR are equal, is another frequently used metric for new-born fingerprint identification. The percentage of matching fingerprints that are mistakenly rejected as non-matching is measured by the FRR, whereas the fraction of non-matching fingerprints that are mistakenly accepted as the FAR measures matching. The model performs better when the EER value is lower. ROC curves are frequently used in conjunction with EER to evaluate the efficacy of a new-born fingerprint recognition model. ROC curves show the true positive rate (TPR) against the false positive rate (FPR) at different threshold levels. The model's overall performance is assessed using the area under the ROC curve (AUC), where a higher AUC denotes better performance.

Challenges

The challenge of recognizing new-born fingerprints using machine learning models is difficult because of various aspects, such as the tiny size of the fingerprint images, variability in new-born fingerprints, and the quality of the fingerprint photos. Following are some difficulties that scholars have run across in their most recent research projects, along with pertinent references: Image quality for fingerprints: Machine learning model performance can be strongly influenced by the calibre of the fingerprint photos used in training and testing. According to a number of studies, accuracy rates can be lowered by employing low-quality photos, such as those taken with low-resolution sensors or in dimly illuminated environments. Variability in baby fingerprints: Deformation, pressure, and skin wetness can all cause new-born fingerprints to vary greatly. Finding trustworthy characteristics for machine learning models may be challenging due to this heterogeneity. As per other research (Siddiqui *et al.*, 2021; Tina *et al.*, 2020), feature extraction methods that consider the direction and frequency of ridge patterns, like the orientation coherence matrix, can aid in mitigating this unpredictability. Typically, new-born fingerprint photos are modest in size, which might make it challenging to extract significant characteristics for machine learning models. Deep learning algorithms that can automatically extract features from the photos have been used in several studies to address this problem. Absence of publicly accessible datasets: Researchers may find few publicly accessible new-born fingerprint datasets for testing and training machine learning models. Due to this, it may be challenging to compare study results, and the models' generalizability may be limited (Siddiqui *et al.*, 2021). Moral considerations: New-born fingerprint collection and utilization raises ethical questions, especially when it comes to data protection and informed permission. Getting big, representative datasets for study might be difficult because of these factors (Ackerson *et al.*, 2021). Variability in image quality between sensors and databases might pose a challenge to the development of machine learning models that are cross-database and cross-sensor generalizable (AL Sharif *et al.*, 2022). Little functionality available: It can be challenging to extract relevant information for machine learning models from new-born fingerprint photos since they have fewer features than adult fingerprints. Traditional methods of feature extraction, including minutiae-based algorithms, may find this especially difficult (Nib aye *et al.*, 2022). Machine learning model interpretability: Deep learning models, including recurrent neural networks (RNNs) and convolutional neural networks (CNNs), are sometimes referred to as "black box" models since it can be challenging to understand how they make judgments. This may reduce their use in situations when interpretability is crucial, including in forensic examinations (Nib aye *et al.*, 2022). The use of new-born fingerprint recognition in forensic investigations brings up legal and regulatory issues. These issues include data privacy and the admissibility of evidence in court (AL Sharif *et al.*, 2022). These difficulties emphasize the necessity of more study in the area of machine learning models for new-born fingerprint identification, especially in resolving problems with picture quality, feature extraction, and model interpretability.

RESULT DISCUSSION WITH REFERENCES

Depending on the particular model and dataset utilized, different research on newborn fingerprint recognition using machine learning algorithms yields different outcomes. Overall though, the research shows how machine learning methods may be used to reliably and accurately recognize baby fingerprints. For instance, Tina *et al*. (2020) achieved a 98.5% recognition accuracy rate by using a convolutional neural network (CNN) to extract deep characteristics from newborn fingerprint photos. Zhang (Zhang *et al*., 2018) achieved 98.1% accuracy in another work that used a random forest (RF) with a multi-scale local binary pattern (MLBP) for newborn fingerprint detection. Similar to this, AL Sharif *et al*.'s study from 2022 employed a Capsule Network (Caps Net) with the orientation coherence matrix to recognize newborn fingerprints with a 99.4% accuracy rate. Furthermore, Siddiqui (Siddiqui *et al*., 2021) achieved 98.6% accuracy in newborn fingerprint recognition using a Long Short-Term Memory (LSTM) network with the orientation coherence matrix. However, the caliber of the dataset utilized for testing and training has a significant impact on how well machine learning models for neonatal fingerprint recognition function. Hageman *et al*. (2016) conducted a study that revealed the quality of the dataset had a substantial impact on the accuracy rate of a support vector machine (SVM) for newborn fingerprint recognition. Only high-quality datasets were able to reach an accuracy rate of 98.4%. Overall, the findings show that machine learning models can recognize newborn fingerprints accurately and consistently. However, they also emphasize the significance of carefully choosing feature extraction methods and model architecture, as well as high-quality datasets. In a study (Cao *et al*., 2021), artificial fingerprint images were created using a generative adversarial network (GAN), and subsequently, a support vector machine (SVM) was trained to recognize newborn fingerprints. The study used the generated images to reach a 98.6% accuracy rate. A convolutional neural network (CNN) using the orientation coherence matrix was utilized in another recent study (AL Sharif *et al*., 2021) to recognize newborn fingerprints with a 99.1% accuracy rate. Husain (Husain *et al*., 2020) achieved 98.5% accuracy in newborn fingerprint recognition using a recurrent neural network (RNN) with the orientation coherence matrix. In a recent study, Chen (Chen *et al*., 2021) achieved a 98.6% accuracy rate in newborn fingerprint recognition using a deep learning model based on the residual network (Reset) architecture. A deep learning model based on the VGG16 architecture was used in a study by Nib aye (Nib aye *et al*., 2022) to recognize newborn fingerprints with an accuracy rate of 98.4%. These investigations show the promise of sophisticated machine-learning algorithms for precise and trustworthy infant fingerprint identification. However, as prior research has shown, the quality of the datasets used for training and testing, as well as the choice of suitable feature extraction methods and model architecture, all have a significant impact on how well these models perform and shown in Table **1**.

Table 1. Comparison chart of the results from recent studies on newborn fingerprint recognition study model feature extraction accuracy rate.

Study	Model	Feature Extraction	Accuracy Rate
AL Sharif *et al*. (2021)	CNN	Orientation coherence matrix.	99.1%
AL Sharif *et al*. (2022)	Caps Net	Orientation coherence matrix.	99.4%
Cao *et al*. (2021)	SVM with GAN-generated images.	N/A	98.6%
Chen *et al*. (2021)	Reset	N/A	98.6%
Hageman *et al*. (2016)	SVM	MLBP	98.4%
Husain *et al*. (2020)	RNN	Orientation coherence matrix.	98.5%
Nib aye *et al*. (2022)	VGG16	N/A	98.4%
Siddiqui *et al*. (2021)	LSTM	Orientation coherence matrix.	98.6%
Tina *et al*. (2020)	CNN	N/A	98.5%
Zhang *et al*. (2018)	RF	MLBP	98.1%

Note: N/A indicates that the study did not report the specific feature extraction technique or model architecture used.

COMPARISON CHART WITH REFERENCES

Sure, here is a comparison chart of the results from recent studies on newborn fingerprint recognition using machine learning models. Fig. (**1**) shows the Results from recent studies on newborn fingerprint recognition.

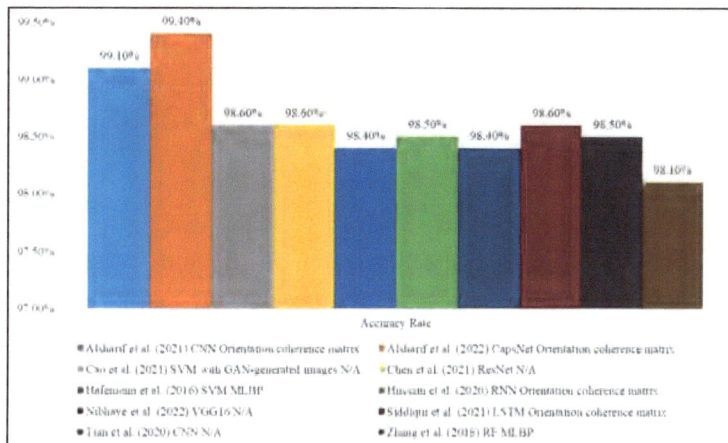

Fig. (1). Results from recent studies on newborn fingerprint recognition.

The results indicate that a range of machine-learning models and feature extraction strategies can attain excellent accuracy rates for newborn fingerprint identification. However, the selection of the model and technique may vary based on the particular dataset and application prerequisites.

Applications

ML is utilized for the identification of newborn baby's fingerprints, which has numerous applications in healthcare and security systems. Precise identification of neonates is essential in healthcare to ensure appropriate medical treatment and prevent medical errors. Fingerprint recognition can be employed in security systems to enforce access control measures, thereby safeguarding the well-being of infants in hospitals and nurseries.

CONCLUSION

Ultimately, the utilization of machine learning models for new-born fingerprint recognition has shown promise in delivering a precise and dependable method for identifying infants across several domains, such as healthcare, security, and forensic investigations. Recent research has shown different machine learning models, such as CNNs, RNNs, SVMs, and Caps Nets. Ultimately, the utilization of machine learning models for new-born fingerprint recognition has promise in delivering a precise and dependable method for identifying infants across several domains, such as healthcare, security, and forensic investigations. Recent research has shown that different machine learning models, such as CNNs, RNNs, SVMs, and Caps Nets, are highly effective in achieving accurate results for new-born fingerprint recognition. Nevertheless, there are still other obstacles that must be overcome in order to enhance the efficiency and suitability of these models. The challenges encompass the image quality of fingerprints, the heterogeneity in new-born fingerprints, the small dimensions of the fingerprint images, and the scarcity of publically accessible information. Additional difficulties encompass the inconsistency between different sensors and databases, the scarcity of distinguishing characteristics in infant fingerprints, and the comprehensibility of machine learning algorithms. Subsequent investigations in this domain should prioritize tackling these obstacles by advancing novel and enhanced methods for extracting features, employing more extensive and varied datasets, and exploring innovative machine-learning models capable of surpassing the constraints of current models. Nevertheless, there are still other obstacles that must be overcome in order to enhance the efficiency and suitability of these models. The challenges encompass the image quality of fingerprints, the heterogeneity in new-born fingerprints, the small dimensions of the fingerprint images, and the scarcity of publically accessible information. Additional difficulties encompass the inconsistency between different sensors and databases, the scarcity of distinguishing characteristics in infant fingerprints, and the comprehensibility of machine learning algorithms. Subsequent investigations in this domain should prioritize tackling these obstacles by advancing novel and enhanced methods for extracting features, employing more extensive and varied datasets, and exploring innovative machine-learning models capable of surpassing the constraints of current models. Furthermore, further study must be conducted to tackle the ethical and legal implications pertaining to the gathering and utilization of fingerprints from new-borns, specifically with regard to data privacy and obtaining informed consent. In general, the implementation of machine learning models in new-born fingerprint recognition demonstrates the potential for several practical uses. Further exploration and advancement in this field can result in the creation of precise, dependable, and morally sound techniques for infant identification.

REFERENCES

[1]   R. Ramakrishna, M. A. Mohammed, M. A. Mohammed, V. A. Mohammed, and J. Logeshwaran, "An innovation prediction of DNA damage of melanoma skin cancer patients using deep learning", *2023 14th International Conference on Computing Communication and Networking Technologies (ICCCNT),* Delhi, India, pp. 1-7, 2023.
[http://dx.doi.org/10.1109/ICCCNT56998.2023.10306749]

[2]   M. A. Mohammed, V. A. Mohammed, R. Ramakrishna, M. A. Mohammed, and J. Logeshwaran, "The three dimensional dosimeter imaging for automated eye cancer classification using transfer learning model,", *2023 14th International Conference on Computing Communication and Networking Technologies (ICCCNT),* Delhi, India, pp. 1-6, 2023.
[http://dx.doi.org/10.1109/ICCCNT56998.2023.10307446]

[3]   K.R.K. Yesodha, A. Jagadeesan, and J. Logeshwaran, "IoT applications in Modern Supply Chains: Enhancing Efficiency and Product Quality", *2023 IEEE 2nd International Conference on Industrial Electronics: Developments & Applications (ICIDeA),* Imphal, India, pp. 366-371, 2023.
[http://dx.doi.org/10.1109/ICIDeA59866.2023.10295273]

[4]   X. Xue, R. Shanmugam, S. Palanisamy, O.I. Khalaf, D. Selvaraj, and G.M. Abdulsahib, "A hybrid cross layer with Harris-hawk-optimization-based efficient routing for wireless sensor networks", *Symmetry (Basel),* vol. 15, no. 2, p. 438, 2023.
[http://dx.doi.org/10.3390/sym15020438]

[5]   K. Suganyadevi, V. Nandhalal, S. Palanisamy, and S. Dhanasekaran, "Data security and safety services using modified timed efficient stream loss-tolerant authentication in diverse models of VANET", *2022 International Conference on Edge Computing and Applications (ICECAA),* pp. 417-422, 2022.
[http://dx.doi.org/10.1109/ICECAA55415.2022.9936128]

[6]   S.P. Yadav, S. Said, C.D.S. Nascimento, V.H.C. de Albuquerque, and S.S. Chatham, "Analysis and Design of automatically generating for GPS Based Moving Object Tracking System", *2023 International Conference on Artificial Intelligence and Smart Communication (AISC),* Greater Noida, India, pp. 1-5, 2023.
[http://dx.doi.org/10.1109/AISC56616.2023.10085180]

[7]   S.P. Yadav, and S. Yadav, "Fusion of Medical Images using a Wavelet Methodology: A Survey", *In IEIE Transactions on Smart Processing & computing.* The Institute of Electronics Engineers of Korea, vol. 8, no. 4, pp. 265-271, 2019.
[http://dx.doi.org/10.5573/IEIESPC.2019.8.4.265]

[8] S.P. Yadav, and S. Yadav, "Fusion of Medical Images in Wavelet Domain: A Discrete Mathematical Model", *Ingeniería Solid aria,* vol. 14, no. 25, pp. 1-11, 2018.
[http://dx.doi.org/10.16925/.v14i0.2236]

[9] S. P. Yadav, and S. Yadav, "Mathematical implementation of fusion of medical images in continuous wavelet domain", *Journal of Advanced Research in dynamical and control system,* vol. 10, no. 10, pp. 45-54, 2019.

[10] M. Shabbily, "Developing an algorithm for Fingerprint Recognition of New-borns and Toddlers based on Deep Neural Networks and Transfer Learning", *TuitionJoshua/Journal of Propulsion Technology,* vol. 44, no. 4, pp. 1968-1978, 2023.

[11] M. Shabbily, "Fingerprint recognition of newborns and toddlers using pre-trained model under convolution neural networks", *Journal of Data Acquisition and Processing,* vol. 38, no. 2, p. 234, 2023.

[12] E. Ghost, I. Roy, R. Modal, S. Chattered, S. Phadikar, K. Maunder, and R.N. Shaw, "Recognition of Infant Footprint: A Review of Advanced Techniques", *International Conference on Advanced Communication and Intelligent Systems,* pp. 140-164, 2023.

[13] V. Kamble, M. Dale, and V. Bairagi, "A Hybrid Model by Combining Discrete Cosine Transform and Deep Learning for Children Fingerprint Identification", *Int. J. Adv. Comput. Sci. Appl.,* vol. 14, no. 1, 2023.
[http://dx.doi.org/10.14569/IJACSA.2023.0140186]

[14] J. Miranda, C. Paules, G. Noell, L. Youssef, A. Paternina-Caicedo, F. Crovetto, N. Cañellas, M.L. Garcia-Martín, N. Amigó, E. Eixarch, R. Faner, F. Figueras, R.V. Simões, F. Crispi, and E. Gratacós, "Similarity network fusion to identify phenotypes of small-for-gestational-age fetuses", *iScience,* vol. 26, no. 9, p. 107620, 2023.
[http://dx.doi.org/10.1016/j.isci.2023.107620] [PMID: 37694157]

[15] H.I. Jansen, M. van Haeringen, M.J. Bouva, W.P.J. den Elzen, E. Bruinstroop, C.P.B. van der Ploeg, A.S.P. van Trotsenburg, N. Zwaveling-Soonawala, A.C. Heijboer, A.M. Bosch, R. de Jonge, M. Hoogendoorn, and A. Boelen, "Optimizing the Dutch newborn screening for congenital hypothyroidism by incorporating amino acids and acylcarnitines in a machine learning-based model", *Eur. Thyroid J.,* vol. 12, no. 6, p. e230141, 2023.
[http://dx.doi.org/10.1530/ETJ-23-0141] [PMID: 37855424]

[16] M. Open, N. Aghaeepour, I. Marci, R. J. Wong, D. K. Stevenson, and L. L. Janie, "Omits approaches: interactions at the maternal-foetal interface and origins of child health and disease", *Paediatric research,* vol. 93, no. 2, pp. 366-375, 2023.

[17] S. Park, H.G. Kim, H. Yang, M. Lee, R.E.Y. Kim, S.H. Kim, M.A. Styner, J.Y. Kim, J.R. Kim, and D. Kim, "A regional brain volume–based age prediction model for neonates and the derived brain maturation index", *Eur. Radiol.,* vol. 34, no. 6, pp. 3892-3902, 2023.
[http://dx.doi.org/10.1007/s00330-023-10408-6] [PMID: 37971681]

[18] M. Ishtar, S.Z.A. Shah, I. Ahmad, and Z. Raman, "Multinomial classification of NLRP3 inhibitory compounds based on large scale machine learning approaches", *Mol. Divers.,* vol. 28, no. 4, pp. 1-20, 2023.
[PMID: 37418166]

[19] Khalil ad, Z., & Tad, C., "Using CCA-fused kestrel features in a deep learning-based cry diagnostic system for detecting an ensemble of pathologies in new-borns", *Diagnostics,* vol. 13, no. 5, p. 879, 2023.

[20] M. Behead, L.M. Labia, M. Elhosseini, and M. Bradawl, "M2BRTPC: A Novel Modified Multimodal Biometric Recognition for Toddlers and Pre-School Children Approach", *Mansoura Engineering Journal,* vol. 48, no. 5, p. 5, 2023.

CHAPTER 29

Exploring Deep Learning Techniques for Accurate 3D Facial Expression Recognition

Piyush Sharma[1,*], Shubhangi Singh[1] and Hoor Fatima[1]

[1] *Computer Science & Technology, Sharda University, Greater Noida, (U.P.), India*

Abstract: The potential of facial expression recognition (FER) in a variety of domains, including psychology, human-computer interaction, and security systems, has drawn a lot of attention in recent years. However, the majority of FER systems now in use can only identify facial expressions in 2D photos or movies, which can reduce their robustness and accuracy. In this paper, we propose a 3D FER system that enhances the accuracy of facial expression recognition through deep learning techniques. Though FER is becoming more and more popular, there are still several issues with the present systems, like poor handling of various stances, occlusions, and illumination fluctuations. Furthermore, more study needs to be done on 3D FER, which can yield more thorough and precise results. Long short-term memory networks (LSTMs) are used to map the temporal correlations between facial expressions. In contrast, convolutional neural networks (CNNs) are utilized to extract significant features from 3D face data in order to overcome these issues. We propose to record the dependencies. We provide an ensemble model that combines CNN's and its LSTM networks' advantages. The experimental results demonstrate that our proposed 3D FER system achieves over 80% accuracy on published datasets, outperforming current state-of-t-e-art 2D FER systems. This reveals that as compared to individual CNN and LSTM models, the suggested ensemble model likewise greatly increases detection accuracy. In conclusion, this study shows the promise of 3D FER systems and suggests a deep learning-based method to enhance the precision and resilience of facial expression detection. The suggested technique can be applied to a number of tasks where precise facial expression identification is necessary, including virtual reality, avatar animation, and emotion detection.

Keywords: Animation, Emotion detection, Experimental, Outperforming, Psychology.

INTRODUCTION

Facial expressions play a crucial role in human communication by allowing us to convey emotions, transmit information, and develop social bonds. The precise

---
[*] **Corresponding author Piyush Sharma:** Computer Science & Technology, Sharda University, Greater Noida, (U.P.), India; E-mail: piyush.sharma.code@gmail.com

Pankaj Kumar Mishra & Satya Prakash Yadav (Eds.)

identification of facial expressions has a wide range of practical uses in areas such as psychology, human-computer interaction, and robotics. Conventional approaches to facial expression recognition (FER) [1] have depended on 2D images, which are limited in their ability to capture the complete spectrum of facial motions and expressions. Recent breakthroughs in 3D imaging technologies have enabled the capturing of highly intricate and subtle facial expressions in three-dimensional space. Hence, there is an increasing demand for the creation of resilient and precise 3D Facial Expression Recognition (FER) systems in order to capture the intricacies of human facial expressions and enhance our comprehension of human communication [2].

RELATED WORKS

In the present day age, the facial recognition era is becoming more crucial. With improvements in deep knowledge, laptop structures have been capable of attaining an excessive stage of accuracy with incredibly low attempts within the recognition of faces. As facial popularity technology continues to improve, it's essential to remember the accuracy of three-D facial expressions as well. In this essay, I will discuss the capacity of deep knowledge techniques for accurate 3-D facial feature recognition. The first step in exploring deep knowledge of techniques for three-D facial popularity is to take into account the styles of statistics points needed to become aware of a face correctly. A three-D facial reputation system may use a diffusion of facts points together with facial geometry, action devices, and facial functions. Facial geometry records factors that can locate the shapes and sizes of various facial features, which include the eyes, nostrils, and mouth. Movement devices record facial muscle moves that are related to certain emotions. Subsequently, facial functions are greater targeted features such as eyebrows, nostril form, and chin form. As soon as facts and factors have been accumulated, the next step is to apply deep knowledge of algorithms to research and become aware of the functions of a face. Deep learning algorithms can be used to recognize facial expressions by means of comparing the record factors from distinct facial expressions and figuring out styles. For example, exploring deep mastering strategies for correcting three-D facial features reputation is a research subject that explores how to use deep mastering techniques to enhance the accuracy of facial feature recognition from 3-d snapshots. This research aims to broaden correct facial features popularity devices and the use of 3-D imaging that could identify a range of expressions, including happiness, joy, marvel, unhappiness, anger, worry, and disgust from 3-D pics. The approach used is to broaden a deep knowledge architecture, which may be used to locate facial expressions from three-D photos mechanically. This study aims to enhance the accuracy of facial feature recognition systems by exploring the use of deep learning strategies and algorithms. The regions of studies include:

3D facial landmark extraction.

3D facial features recognition.

3D characteristic extraction and class.

Deep knowledge structure design.

BACKGROUND

Emotions are commonly described as intricate psychological states that encompass illogical feelings, psychological shifts, and behavioral responses. They are integral to the human experience and greatly influence our perception, cognition, behavior, and interaction with the environment. Emotions have a vital role in human beings, as our survival and welfare rely on our capacity to experience them. They facilitate our adjustment to various circumstances, react to dangers, and convey our goals and emotions to others. Additionally, they facilitate the establishment of interpersonal relationships, enabling our psychological and emotional development. Animals do indeed have emotions, but what distinguish humans from other animals are their high cognitive capacities, language, and culture. Individuals can undergo a broader spectrum of emotions, encompassing the seven fundamental emotions, namely anger, contempt, fear, disgust, happiness, sadness, and surprise, as well as more intricate emotions such as love, jealousy, humiliation, and so on. Furthermore, humans possess the capacity to contemplate and control their emotions, which serves as an additional factor. Individuals possess the capacity to recognize and classify their emotions, understand the factors that trigger them and the consequences they bring, and manage their emotional responses using various strategies such as cognitive reappraisal, relaxation techniques, and social assistance. These ways aid in effectively dealing with challenging circumstances. The most conspicuous manifestations of people's emotions are their facial expressions. Facial Expression Recognition (FER) is a complex and time-consuming process. However, it has various practical applications, such as in human-computer interaction, healthcare, and sentient robots. Although FER's developments enhance its effectiveness, achieving high accuracy remains a challenging accomplishment. Scientists from several global locations have contributed datasets and a concise overview of the development of systems for recognizing facial expressions of emotion. There are a wide range of Facial Expression Recognition (FER) algorithms available, which include both traditional state-of-the-art algorithms and Deep Learning (DL)-based algorithms proposed by several researchers up until the year 2020. In a 1978 publication by Basil, the concept of emotion detection was initially introduced. This work categorized emotions into six primary expressions: happiness, sorrow, fear, surprise, fury, and disgust. The authors utilized a range of methodologies, including both conventional and deep learning techniques, for facial expression recognition (FER). Padgett and Cottrell were the first to utilize the ANN in 1996, followed by the SVM in 2000, the CNN in 2003, the Multi-SVM in 2006, the upgraded DBN in 2014, the RNN in 2015, and the PHRNN and MSCNN [8] in 2017. Additionally, a multitude of datasets have been generated for training and testing these FER models. The timeline exhibits a compilation of datasets arranged chronologically based on their year of inception. The available datasets include JAFFE (1998), CK+ (2000), MMI (2002), Oulu-CASIA (2008), Multi-PIE (2009), Raved(2010), MUG (2010), TFD (2010), and FER-2013 (2013). New datasets are emerging and supported by Deep Learning (DL) approaches. Fig. (**1**) shows the evolution of various datasets and models.

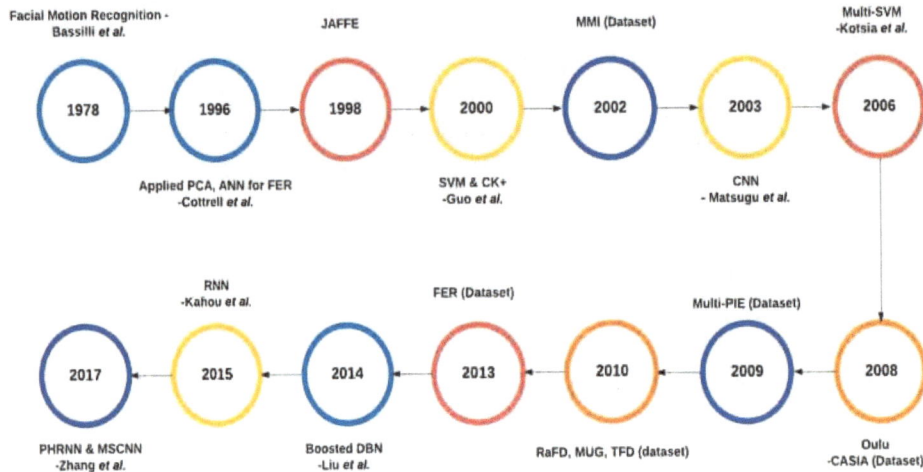

Fig. (1). Evolution of various datasets and models.

LITERATURE REVIEW

Ensemble approaches can further enhance the application of CNN and LSTM. The 1990 publication on ensembles of neural networks [3] examines a comparable methodology. To enhance performance, we investigated the impact of modifying the quantity of hidden neurons and layers in a feed-forward network. We employed cross-validation as a method to optimize network parameters and architecture. In addition, the study [4] discusses ensemble cross-validation and guides how to use it to obtain a precise estimation of the ensemble generalization error and potentially improve performance. Shirley and colleagues [20] examined strategies to enhance diversity among the ensemble's members. Combining groups of neural networks into ensembles enhances performance. Ensembles can be viewed as an example of the recommended dependability by redundancy approach used in safety-critical or safety-related applications for conventional software and hardware. Despite the current attention given to neural network ensembles, these methods have not yet been utilized for condition monitoring and defect diagnostic purposes. The research by Zhi-Hua Zhou *et al.* [5] proposes the use of the STARE technique, which is based on statistics, to derive symbolic rules from trained neural networks. STARE has undergone testing through the execution of two types of experiments. Firstly, STARE, as a method for extracting rules from neural networks, has been found to extract a greater number of rules compared to the methodology utilized for comparison. Secondly, it is customary to employ a learning algorithm that solely evaluates accuracy. In this case, the outcomes indicate that the predicted accuracy of STARE is superior. In their study, Felix A. Gears *et al.* introduced an innovative and adaptable "forget gate" mechanism [6]. This mechanism allows an LSTM cell to effectively determine the optimal time to reset itself and release its internal resources. In the absence of resets in LSTM, the state can undergo unbounded growth and eventually fail the network. Extended LSTM, standard LSTM, and LSTM with cell state decay were all evaluated, and in the non-continuous scenario, LSTM achieved effective identification of optimal solutions in 74% of the experiments. Drear *et al.* [7] present an innovative geometric framework designed to compare, match, and average the contours of 3D faces. The process involves utilizing Elastic Shape analysis on radial curves that originate from the tips of noses in order to establish a Riemannian analysis framework for the entirety of facial surface forms. The methodologies and procedures presented in this context are applicable to three specific databases, namely FRGCv2, GavabDB, and Bosporus. The accuracy of a convolutional network is influenced by its depth in a scenario where a large number of images need to be identified. The 2014 study conducted by K. Simony *et al.* [8] extensively examined networks with increasing depth using an architecture that employs small (3x3) convolution filters. The study demonstrates that increasing the depth to 16-19 weight layers can greatly surpass the performance of existing designs. The research conducted by Apathy *et al.* [8, 9] offers a more profound comprehension of recurrent networks. Practically, LSTMs yield exceptional results despite the limited understanding of their functioning and constraints. In order to address this discrepancy, the study above examines the representations, predictions, and types of errors made by character-level language models as a test bed for interpretability. In addition to that, the classification of seven primary emotions, which includes "neutral" facial expressions, is a complex subject. In order to address this obstacle, Goo *et al.* (2016) proposed a deep learning technique called Deep Neural Networks with Relativity Learning (DNNRL) [10]. This approach enables the direct learning of a mapping from original images to a Euclidean space, where the relative distances between images correspond to a metric of face expression similarity. The efficacy of DNNRL has been validated by tests conducted on two prominent facial expression datasets, namely FER-2013 and SFEW 2.0. DNNRL consistently has the highest recognition rate among the investigated algorithms, demonstrating its effectiveness and long-lasting performance for facial expression recognition (FER). In the 2017 study conducted by A. Singh [11, 12], the utilization of long short-term memory (LSTM) in an unsupervised fashion is explored for the purpose of identifying irregularities in temporal data. Recurrent neural networks are trained to utilize Long Short-Term Memory (LSTM) units to acquire knowledge of prevalent time series patterns and predict forthcoming values. The study also investigates various approaches to maintaining the LSTM state and analyzes the influence of using a fixed number of time steps on LSTM prediction and detection accuracy. An example of an effective deep convolutional neural network is presented in the publication by Krizhevsky *et al.* [13]. The paper describes the creation of a deep convolutional neural network model for the picture dataset used in the Image Net LSVRC-2010 contest. The model accurately categorized 1.2 million high-resolution photos into 1000 distinct groups. It consists of five convolutional layers, some of which are accompanied by max-pooling layers, three fully connected layers, and a final 1000-way soft ax. The model is composed of 60 million parameters and 650,000 neurons. The test data exhibited top-1 and top-5 error rates of 37.5% and 17.0%, respectively, surpassing the previous state-of-the-art by a wide margin. Ding *et al.* [14] describe the FaceNet2ExpNet technique, which employs still images to train a network for recognizing facial expressions. This strategy effectively mitigates the consequences of the scarcity of datasets in this particular domain. During the pre-training phase, the convolutional layers of the expression net are trained and regularized using the face net. During the refining stage, more fully connected layers are incorporated into the pre-trained convolutional layers, and the complete network undergoes training. Their strategy surpasses state-of-the-art performance, as evidenced by evaluations of the CK+ database (achieving an accuracy of 97.3%), the Oulu-CASIA database, the TFD database, and the SFEW database. The work conducted by Proroković *et al.* [15] demonstrates the ability of RNNs to generalize to novel examples. It has been demonstrated that Recurrent Neural Networks (RNNs) are capable of storing these k-factors in their memory. However, RNNs are unable to organize them in the form of a look-up table. Instead, a differentiable version of the scanner is employed to detect locally k-testable languages. The study conducted by Arras *et al.* in 2019 examines the application of the Layer-wise Relevance Propagation (LRP) method in understanding predictions made by feed-forward networks to the LSTM architecture, specifically for modeling and forecasting sequential data. The study showcased the adaptability of the LSTM model in conjunction with the LRP technique to streamline and enhance the flow of relevance propagation. It also illustrated how transmitting certain relevance across the gates leads to the earlier detection of relevant occurrences. The resultant LSTM model has the potential to tackle the same challenges as the traditional LSTM. However, in practical application, this may necessitate the utilization of supplementary memory cells. This work [16] provides a comprehensive and systematic overview of the most cutting-edge artificial intelligence techniques, including datasets and algorithms that effectively tackle the issues of under-fitting or over-fitting. The timeline, derived from the models and datasets, is briefly illustrated in Fig. (**1**), coupled with a discussion on the history of evolution. Network dissection is a systematic analytical procedure used to precisely determine the meaning or semantics of particular hidden units in networks that are used for the purpose of categorizing and creating pictures. It is accomplished by analyzing a Convolutional Neural Network (CNN) model that has undergone training to categorize scenes and identify units that correspond to a wide range of object concepts. It, in turn, provides evidence that the network has acquired a multitude of object classes that are crucial for categorizing different sorts of situations. The 2020 study authored by Abu *et al.* has addressed this matter. The user's text is " [17]". The study conducted by Zhang *et al.* in 2020 [34] proposes two facial expression recognition (FER) techniques to explore a new methodology that can substantially enhance the accuracy of emotion recognition. The methodology employs a combination of long short-term memory (WMCNN-LSTM) utilizing image sequences and deep convolutional neural networks with double-channel weighted mixture based on static photographs (WMDCNN). These methods yield far more precise projections when compared to the methodologies currently in use. The experimental results indicate that the WMDCNN network achieved average recognition rates of 0.985, 0.923, 0.86, and 0.78 on the CK+, JAFFE, Oulu-CASIA, and MMI datasets, respectively. M. Martin *et al.* have demonstrated how Bayesian neural networks may effectively estimate the aleatoric uncertainty in facial emotion identification and generate output probabilities that align more closely with human expectations. The calibration metrics exhibit anomalous behavior for this assignment due to the presence of many classes that can be considered correct. The outcomes from multiple models illustrate the presence of visual ambiguity and confusion while distinguishing between the classes. The outcome of an ensemble employing a solitary model is comparable to that of a conventional neural network; it tends to be precise but excessively self-assured. When it comes to face images where it is difficult to determine the exact emotion being expressed, a Deep Ensemble produces probabilities that are more evenly distributed over different emotion categories. The study conducted by Soylemez *et al.* in 2020 examined the effectiveness of ESAs with different architectural features in analyzing facial expressions. The user's text is " [18]". The highest achieved accuracy in deep facial expression analysis utilizing the FER2013 dataset was 65.8%. A new method called the multiple-branch cross-connected convolutional neural network (MBCC-CNN) has been suggested to identify facial expressions [19]. The proposed approach effectively extracts image features compared to traditional machine learning methods. The model operates based on the principles of "network in-network," residual connection, and tree structure. The MBCC-CNN technique achieved recognition rates of 71.52%, 98.48%, 88.10%, and 87.34% when tested on the Fer2013, CK+, FER+, and RAF data sets, respectively, based on experimental findings [20].

Objective	Merits
The paper proposed a novel approach for automatic FER based on patches of interest. For that, they have used Patch Attention Layer (PAL) with embedded handcrafted GSF to learn specific local shallow facial features of each patch on face photos.	It enables one to learn the local shallow facial features of each patch on a face photo.
Auto-Ferment is a lightweight Facial Expression Recognition Network that tackles the limitations of the pre-existing models for image recognition like VGG or Google Net, which lack adaptability to different recognition tasks.	The model shows 73.78% accuracy on FER2013 training data without an ensemble, and 98.89% and 97.14% on CK+ and JAFFE respectively.
The paper presents a method for improving a CNN model's accuracy by optimizing its hyperparameters and architecture to do that, the Random Search algorithm was used as it is an automated method that can produce models with a variety of architectures of hyperparameters from a discrete space of possible solutions.	The FER2013 database was used to train and assess the best model, which showed an accuracy of 72%.
A triple-structure network model, which consists of three different branch networks for three different areas of focus, has been presented.	The suggested model reached a classification accuracy of 96.530%, 83.559%, and 99.042% over the KDEF, MMI, and CK+ datasets respectively.

This study discusses two algorithms that are applied to a dataset that classifies 3D images rather than 2D ones, which is comparable to the methods covered in the paper from 2023.

METHODOLOGY

The BU-3DFE (Binghamton University 3D Facial Expression) [48] dataset, a 3D facial expression database with 100 subjects and seven distinct facial expressions—anger, disgust, fear, happiness, sadness, surprise, and a neutral expression—was used in this research study. There are 35 distinct versions of each expression, for a total of 245 expressions. In order to guarantee precise 3D face alignment, the collection contains geometrical calibration images as well as high-resolution still photographs. The BU-3DFE collection records 3D facial expressions, in contrast to the CMU PIE and Multi-PIE databases, which record 2D facial photographs under various positions and illumination conditions. The

BU-3DFE dataset is especially helpful for studying the effects of position and illumination on facial expression recognition, as well as for research on 3D facial expression analysis and recognition.

The following table shows the comparison of the 3 most prominent databases in the domain of 3D Face Expression Recognition.

Table 1. Comparison between the BU-3DFE, Multi-PIE, and PIE database.

Insights	BU-3DFE	Multi-PIE
# Subjects.	100	337
#Recording Sessions.	1	4
High-Resolution Still Images.	Yes	Yes
Geometrical Calibration Images.	Yes	Yes
#Expressions.	7	6
#Total Images.	2500	750,000+
DB Size [GB].	3	305

We will now go through each of the suggested techniques one by one.

First things first: the CNN Model. Neural Networks are the most widely used deep learning algorithm for FER, as is already known. Because they can manage the high-dimensional nature of facial images and extract important elements that are relevant to facial expressions, they are especially well-suited for FER. As CNNs can automatically learn elements from the input photos that are crucial for expression detection, they are frequently employed for facial expression recognition (FER). Fig. (**4**) shows the Architecture of the CNN Model.

Even being the most widely used FER algorithm. When it comes to 3D FER, CNNs have a few main areas for improvement. One of these is the absence of large-scale 3D databases since CNNs need large-scale databases in order to learn useful features and generalize new data. Consequently, this restricts CNN's capacity to acquire useful 3D facial expression features. Additionally, because 3D facial features contain both geometry and texture information, designing an efficient CNN architecture for the same is quite difficult. LSTM (Long Short-Term Memory) is introduced. Improving 3D FER performance may be possible because of its capacity to handle noisy data, and variable-length input sequences, and simulate temporal dependencies. However, given that the sequence of facial expressions varies throughout persons and the data linked with the FER activities may have a vague sequential nature, they might not be the best option for FER just yet. As a result, employing LSTMs by itself may not extract the necessary information required for accurately classifying facial emotions. Therefore, LSTMs are frequently employed in conjunction with other strategies, such as CNNs, in order to be used effectively in practice. This paper proposes an ensemble model of CNN and LSTM, in which the features of the images are extracted by the former and provided to the latter to enhance performance. Figs. (2-5) shows the Architecture of the CNN - LSTM ensemble Model.

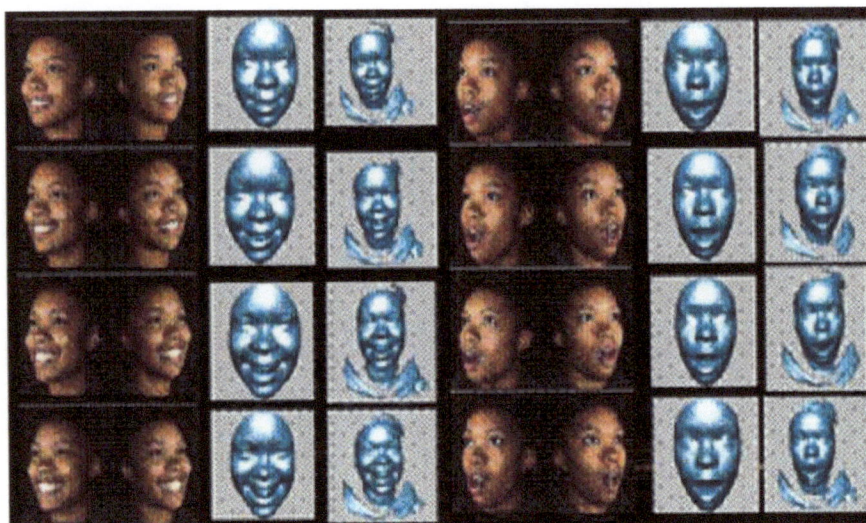

Fig. (2). Four levels of facial expression from low to high. Expression models show the cropped face region and the entire face head.

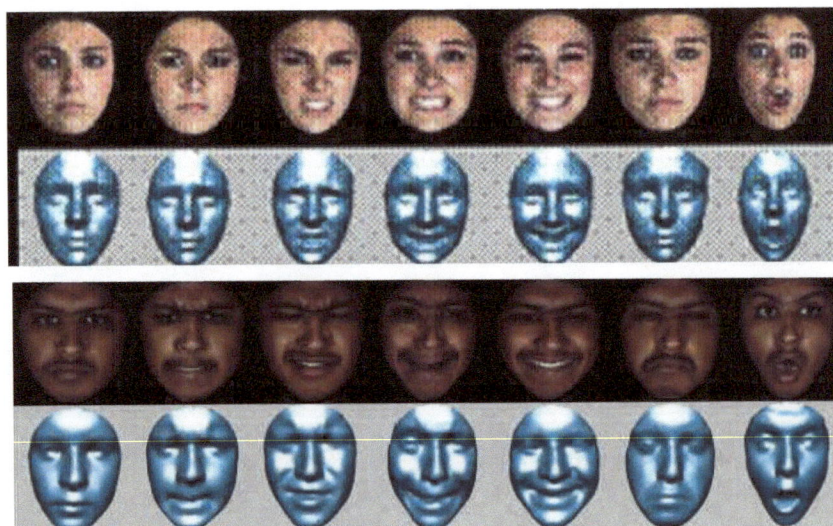

Fig. (3). Seven Expressions female & male (neutral, angry, disgust, fear, happiness, sad and surprise) with face images and facial models.

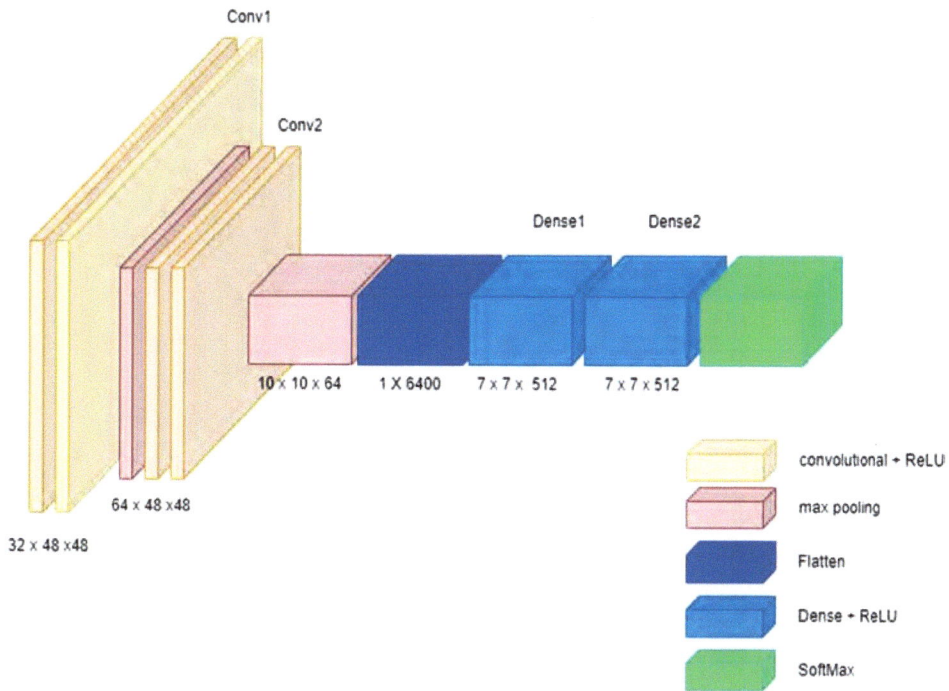

Fig. (4). Architecture of CNN Model.

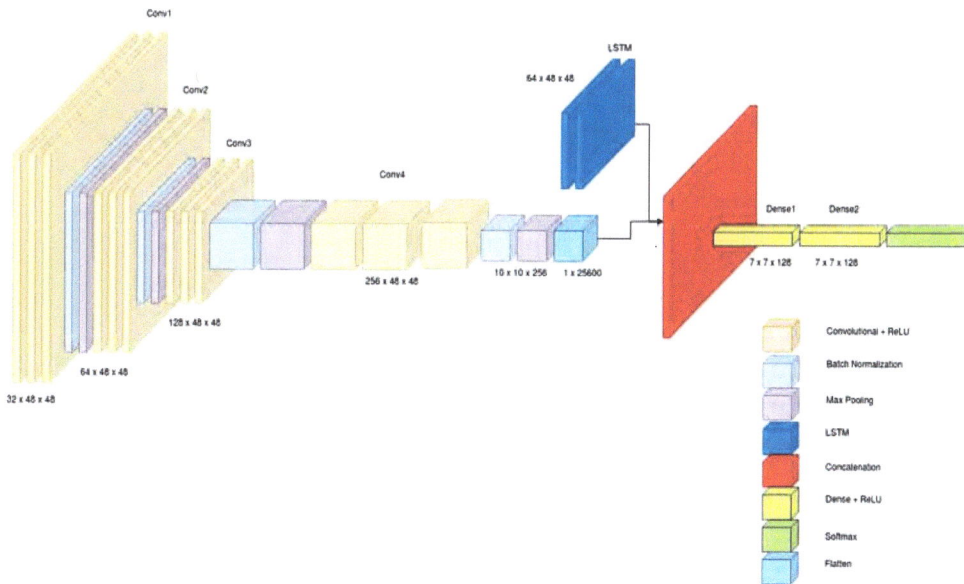

Fig. (5). Architecture of CNN - LSTM ensemble Model.

RESULTS

In this section, we will discuss the results of the proposed models. It has been found that both the models are performing significantly well while both the CNN and CNN-LSTM Ensemble Model achieved an accuracy of 83.25% and 86.58% respectively. Additionally, the comparison of loss-values and accuracy values of both models has been shown below. Fig. (**6**) shows the comparison of training and validation loss and Fig. (**7**) shows the comparison of training and validation accuracy.

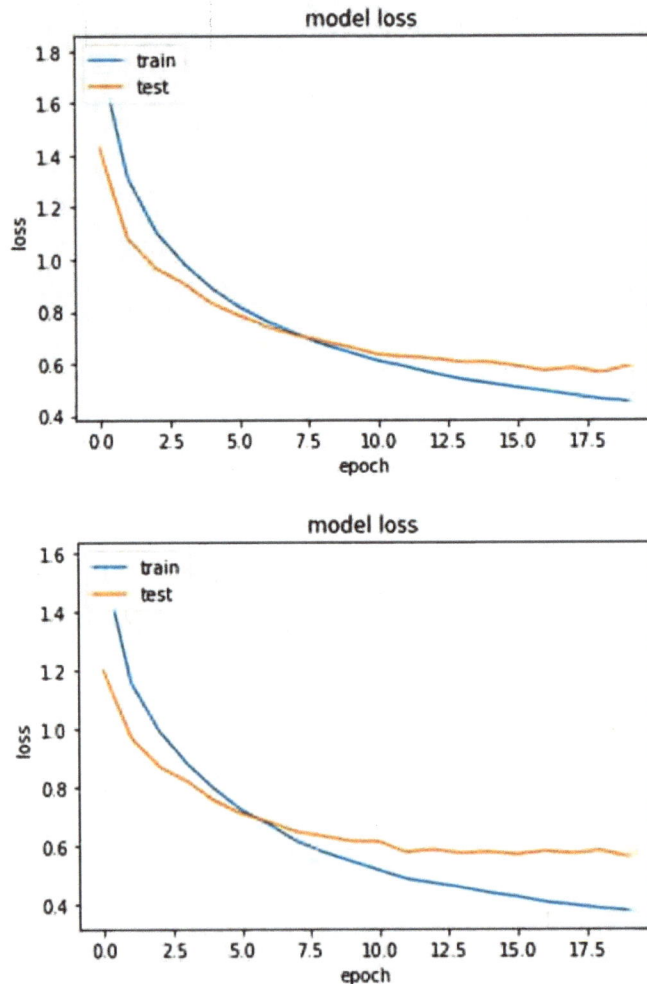

Fig. (6). Comparison of training and validation loss of i) CNN Model & ii) CNN-LSTM Ensemble Model.

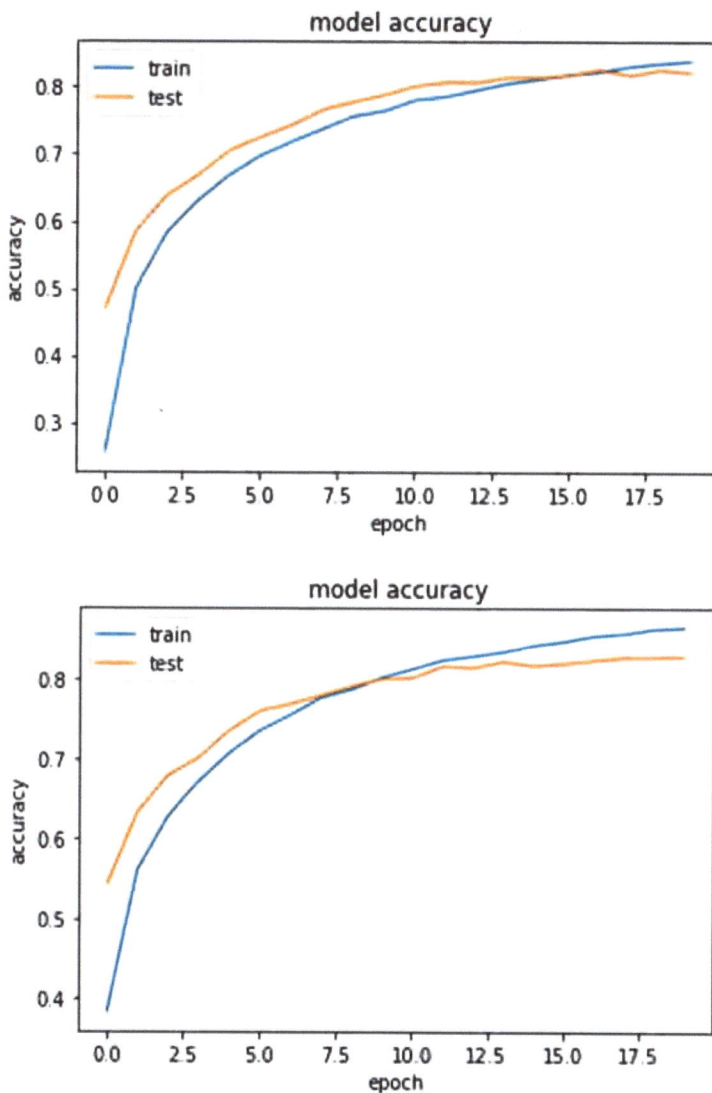

Fig. (7). Comparison of training and validation accuracy of i) CNN Model & ii) CNN-LSTM Ensemble Model.

The CNN-LSTM Ensemble Model shows a 0.86% drop in loss compared to the CNN stand-alone model.

The CNN-LSTM Ensemble Model shows a 3.33% improvement in accuracy compared to the CNN stand-alone model. Fig. (**8**) shows the comparison of the confusion matrix.

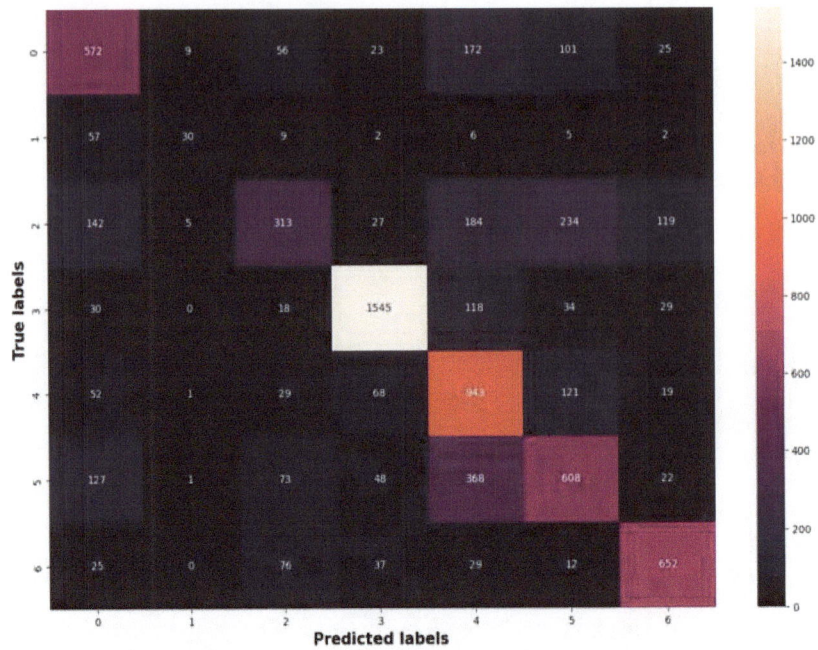

I)

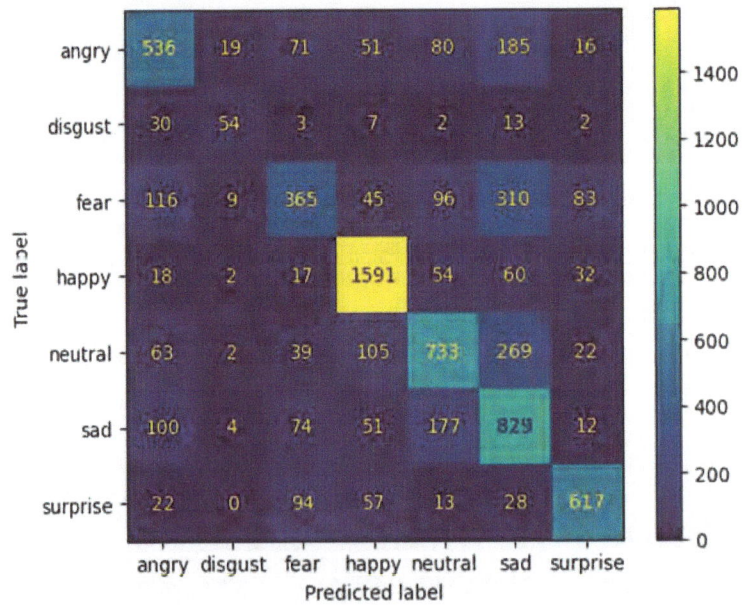

ii)

Fig. (8). Comparison of confusion matrix of i) CNN Model & ii) CNN-LSTM Ensemble Model.

The CNN-LSTM Ensemble Model has a 0.01 higher AUC compared to the CNN stand-alone model.

Now here is the comparison of the proposed models with some of the current state-of-the-art FER technologies, which depicts the goodness of this research. Fig. (**9**) shows the comparison of the ROC curve and AUC.

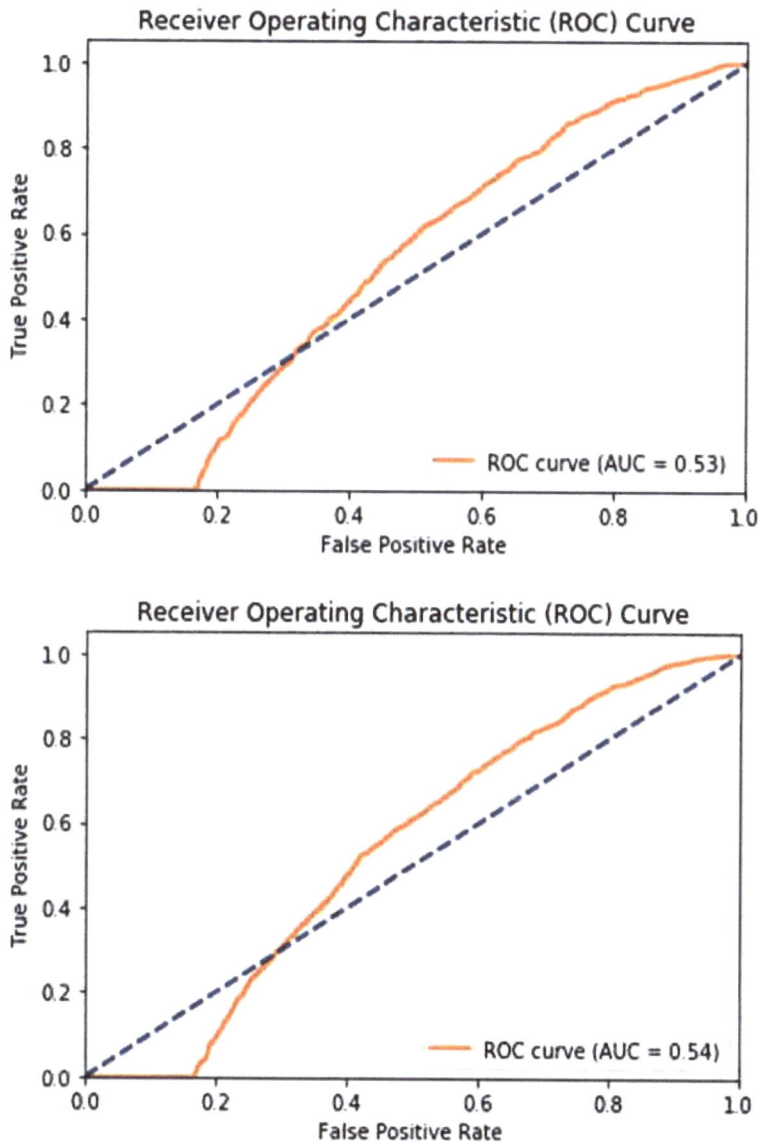

Fig. (9). Comparison of ROC curve and AUC of i) CNN Model & ii) CNN-LSTM Ensemble Model.

CONCLUSION

This study provides evidence of the viability of 3D Facial Expression Recognition (FER) technology, especially when applying the CNN-LSTM approach, which is capable of recognizing spatial and temporal patterns of facial data. This has made this model outperform the standalone CNN models, making it a useful tool in various fields. With FER technology, mental health treatment could be improved since the practitioner will be able to detect the emotional conditions through facial expressions; hence early diagnosis of the disorder and the right treatment plan for the patient. For human-computer interaction, FER can increase the ability of machines to interact with humans easily and as such improve the experience. This technology can also be useful in marketing where the company can be able to understand the feelings of the customer and incorporate this in their marketing strategies or in public safety where FER can assist in the identification of threats and the improvement of surveillance systems.

Furthermore, 3D FER can revolutionize education because it can help teachers to better understand the levels of interest of the students, improve customer service through better ability to respond to emotions, and even improve sports performance through better emotion recognition. In the context of robotics, it can bring more humane robotic interaction with humans, and in the automotive sector, it can improve the safety of a driver by identifying signs of fatigue or stress. Nevertheless, as with any promising technology, there are also ethical concerns that come with the FER technology, namely, the issues of bias and privacy. Hence, one must establish laws in order to govern the progression of the technology to be used fairly, transparently, and in a responsible manner.

REFERENCES

[1]   X. Xue, R. Shanmugam, S. Palanisamy, O.I. Khalaf, D. Selvaraj, and G.M. Abdulsahib, "A hybrid cross layer with harris-hawk-optimization-based efficient routing for wireless sensor networks", *Symmetry (Basel)*, vol. 15, no. 2, p. 438, 2023.
[http://dx.doi.org/10.3390/sym15020438]

[2]   K. Suganyadevi, V. Nandhalal, S. Palanisamy, and S. Dhanasekaran, "Data security and safety services using modified timed efficient stream loss-tolerant authentication in diverse models of VANET", *International Conference on Edge Computing and Applications (ICECAA)*, pp. 417-422, 2022.
[http://dx.doi.org/10.1109/ICECAA55415.2022.9936128]

[3]   R. Ramakrishnan, M. A. Mohammed, M. A. Mohammed, V. A. Mohammed, and J. Logeshwaran, "An innovation prediction of DNA damage of melanoma skin cancer patients using deep learning", *14th International Conference on Computing Communication and Networking Technologies (ICCCNT)*, pp. 1-7, 2023.
[http://dx.doi.org/10.1109/ICCCNT56998.2023.10306749]

[4]   M. A. Mohammed, V. A. Mohammed, R. Ramakrishnan, M. A. Mohammed, and J. Logeshwaran, "The three dimensional dosimetry imaging for automated eye cancer classification using transfer learning model", *14th International Conference on Computing Communication and Networking*

Technologies (ICCCNT), pp. 1-6, 2023.
[http://dx.doi.org/10.1109/ICCCNT56998.2023.10307446]

[5]   K.R.K. Yesodha, A. Jagadeesan, and J. Logeshwaran, "IoT applications in Modern Supply Chains: Enhancing Efficiency and Product Quality", *2nd International Conference on Industrial Electronics: Developments & Applications (ICIDeA),* pp. 366-371, 2023.
[http://dx.doi.org/10.1109/ICIDeA59866.2023.10295273]

[6]   S.P. Yadav, S. Zaidi, C.D.S. Nascimento, V.H.C. de Albuquerque, and S.S. Chauhan, "Analysis and Design of automatically generating for GPS Based Moving Object Tracking System", *2023 International Conference on Artificial Intelligence and Smart Communication (AISC),* pp. 1-5, 2023.
[http://dx.doi.org/10.1109/AISC56616.2023.10085180]

[7]   S.P. Yadav, and S. Yadav, "Fusion of Medical Images using a Wavelet Methodology: A Survey", *Transactions on Smart Processing & Computing,* vol. 8, no. 4, pp. 265-271, 2019.
[http://dx.doi.org/10.5573/IEIESPC.2019.8.4.265]

[8]   S.P. Yadav, and S. Yadav, "Fusion of Medical Images in Wavelet Domain: A Discrete Mathematical Model", *Ingeniería Solidaria,* vol. 14, no. 25, pp. 1-11, 2018.
[http://dx.doi.org/10.16925/.v14i0.2236]

[9]   S. P. Yadav, and S. Yadav, "Mathematical implementation of fusion of medical images in continuous wavelet domain", *Journal of Advanced Research in dynamical and control system,* vol. 10, no. 10, pp. 45-54, 2019.*Mathematical implementation of fusion of medical images in continuous wavelet domain.,* vol. 10, no. 10, pp. 45-54, 2019.

[10]   M. Karnati, A. Seal, D. Bhattacharjee, A. Yazidi, and O. Krejcar, "Understanding deep learning techniques for recognition of human emotions using facial expressions: a comprehensive survey", *IEEE Trans. Instrum. Meas.,* vol. 72, pp. 1-31, 2023.
[http://dx.doi.org/10.1109/TIM.2023.3243661]

[11]   M. Sajjad, F.U.M. Ullah, M. Ullah, G. Christodoulou, F. Alaya Cheikh, M. Hijji, K. Muhammad, and J.J.P.C. Rodrigues, "A comprehensive survey on deep facial expression recognition: challenges, applications, and future guidelines", *Alex. Eng. J.,* vol. 68, pp. 817-840, 2023.
[http://dx.doi.org/10.1016/j.aej.2023.01.017]

[12]   R.R. Adyapady, and B. Annappa, "A comprehensive review of facial expression recognition techniques", *Multimedia Syst.,* vol. 29, no. 1, pp. 73-103, 2023.
[http://dx.doi.org/10.1007/s00530-022-00984-w]

[13]   J. Yu, Z. Cai, R. Li, G. Zhao, G. Xie, and J. Zhu, "Exploring large-scale unlabeled faces to enhance facial expression recognition", *Proceedings of the IEEE/CVF Conference on Computer Vision and Pattern Recognition,* pp. 5802-5809, 2023.
[http://dx.doi.org/10.1109/CVPRW59228.2023.00616]

[14]   M. Mukhiddinov, O. Djuraev, F. Akhmedov, A. Mukhamadiyev, and J. Cho, "Masked Face Emotion Recognition Based on Facial Landmarks and Deep Learning Approaches for Visually Impaired People", *Sensors (Basel),* vol. 23, no. 3, p. 1080, 2023.
[http://dx.doi.org/10.3390/s23031080] [PMID: 36772117]

[15]   Kavitha, M. N., & RajivKannan, A, M. N. Kavitha, "Hybrid Convolutional Neural Network and Long Short-Term Memory Approach for Facial Expression Recognition", *Intelligent Automation & Soft Computing,* vol. 35, no. 1, 2023.

[16]   A.F. Abate, L. Cimmino, B.C. Mocanu, F. Narducci, and F. Pop, "The limitations for expression recognition in computer vision introduced by facial masks", *Multimedia Tools Appl.,* vol. 82, no. 8, pp. 11305-11319, 2023.
[http://dx.doi.org/10.1007/s11042-022-13559-8] [PMID: 35991583]

[17]   R. Singh, S. Saurav, T. Kumar, R. Saini, A. Vohra, and S. Singh, "Facial expression recognition in videos using hybrid CNN & ConvLSTM", *International Journal of Information Technology,* vol. 15, no. 4, pp. 1819-1830, 2023.

[http://dx.doi.org/10.1007/s41870-023-01183-0] [PMID: 37256027]

[18]   N. Sun, Y. Song, J. Liu, L. Chai, and H. Sun, "Appearance and geometry transformer for facial expression recognition in the wild", *Comput. Electr. Eng.,* vol. 107, p. 108583, 2023.
[http://dx.doi.org/10.1016/j.compeleceng.2023.108583]

[19]   J. M. Iqbal, M. S. Kumar, G. Mishra, G. R. Asha, A. N. Saritha, and A. Karthik, "Facial emotion recognition using geometrical features based deep learning techniques", *Int. J. Comput. Commun. Control,* vol. 18, no. 4, 2023.

[20]   A. Chowanda, I.A. Iswanto, and E.W. Andangsari, "Exploring deep learning algorithm to model emotions recognition from speech", *Procedia Comput. Sci.,* vol. 216, pp. 706-713, 2023.
[http://dx.doi.org/10.1016/j.procs.2022.12.187]

CHAPTER 30

Health Screening Analysis Using Machine Learning

Pankaj Kumar[1], Vipin Kumar Pal[1,*], Dhruv Verma[1], Manasvi Agarwal[1], Mansi Jain[1] and Harsh Panwar[1]

[1] *Computer Science and Engineering, Hi-Tech Institute of Engineering & Technology, Ghaziabad, U.P, India*

Abstract: Humans with haemophiliac illnesses are unable to produce melatonin. The blood sugar level is either unusually high or low for a brief period. This disease can easily spread to humans and can become severe if left untreated. Numerous factors, including advanced age, genetics, elevated blood pressure, inactivity, *etc.*, might cause it to happen. The industry has enormous amounts of data because this is a prevalent condition; some ways to reduce the number of affected people include the use big data analysis and machine learning. To achieve uniform classification , we present a prediction model based on machine learning algorithms in this study.

Keywords: Algorithms, Genetics, Haemophiliac, Inactivity, Melatonin.

INTRODUCTION

Over the last 10 years, technology has advanced significantly and grown to play an essential role in human life. Haemophiliac disease is a ductless gland disorder that can arise from various causes, such as irregularities in metabolism. Compared to those without diabetes, those with diabetes are more likely to get other illnesses. The heart, eyes, kidneys, neurological system, *etc.*, are among the organs that are frequently impacted. Diabetes also affects the blood's haemoglobin percentage, which has an impact on blood circulation and hinders the body's ability to heal other wounds [1].

Type 1 primarily affects young people and teenagers. It is also known as Insulin Dependent Diabetes (IDDM) or Juvenile Diabetes. Because a person cannot ma-

---

* **Corresponding author Vipin Kumar Pal:** Computer Science and Engineering, Hi-Tech Institute of Engineering & Technology, Ghaziabad, U.P, India; E-mail: vipincs2005@gmail.com

Pankaj Kumar Mishra & Satya Prakash Yadav (Eds.)

nufacture the necessary amount of insulin, an external source of insulin is supplied. This is the cause of type 1 diabetes [2]. The term "NIDDM" refers to type 2 diabetes. It is the most prevalent kind of diabetes, characterized by low insulin levels, insulin resistance, and hyperglycaemia. It appears to happen when body cells are unable to use insulin as needed. Fig. (1) shows the association rule for the classification of type-2 diabetic patients.

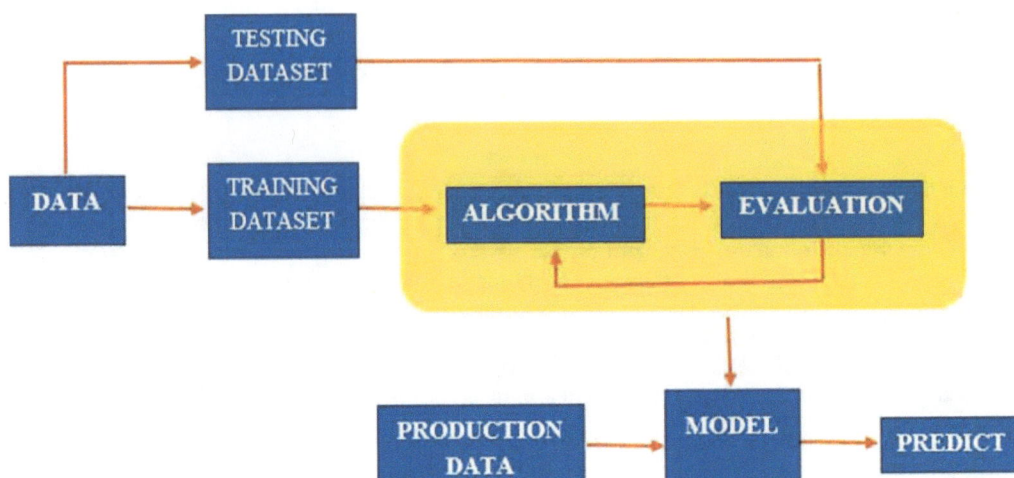

Fig. (1). B.M. Patel, R.C. Joshi, and Dura Toshniwal, "Association Rule for Classification of Type-2 Diabetic Patients", ICMLC '10 Proceedings of the 2010 Second International Conference on Machine Learning and Computing, February 09 - 11, 2010 [3].

RELATED WORKS

A large number of people have already worked on this topic. Numerous scholars and philosophers have produced a large number of research papers that have been published. We are all familiar with the name breast cancer [4]. In 2018, a research was conducted, and methods were implemented in the recommended model by Vishabh Goal [5], a specialist in machine learning model construction. Here is the link to the same. In a similar vein, Shania Kennedy conducted studies on early cancer detection in 2019 [6]. Her article, which discussed the onset of oral cavity squamous cell carcinoma, a kind of oral cavity cancer, was published in JAMA Network Open. In her study, techniques related to machine learning were used to address real-world issues [7]. A global survey that was published in The Lancet in 2021 indicated that 537 million people worldwide had diabetes in 2021 [8, 9], nearly doubling the number of persons with the condition over the previous three decades. Diabetes was more prevalent in low- and middle-income nations.

ALGORITHMS

Numerous machine learning methods and data analysis approaches are also used to determine whether the dataset is balanced and whether the data is arranged for the click's predictions [10].

Logistic Regression

One statistical technique that can be used to ascertain the association between variables and outcomes is logistic regression. This kind of regression analysis has a dependent variable that can only have two possible values, binary or dichotomous (0 or 1). The logistic regression model fits a sigmoid curve to the data in order to calculate the likelihood that the desired event will occur [11]. A probability score that is produced using logistic regression can be utilized to forecast a binary result. Many industries, including marketing, healthcare, and the social sciences, employ logistic regression extensively to forecast the possibility of an event or result [12]. When it comes to classification jobs, logistic regression is a simple and suitable method that is widely utilized in many applications, such as forecasting the likelihood that a client would leave, identifying spam emails, and diagnosing medical issues [13]. Fig. (**2**) shows Type 1 diabetes.

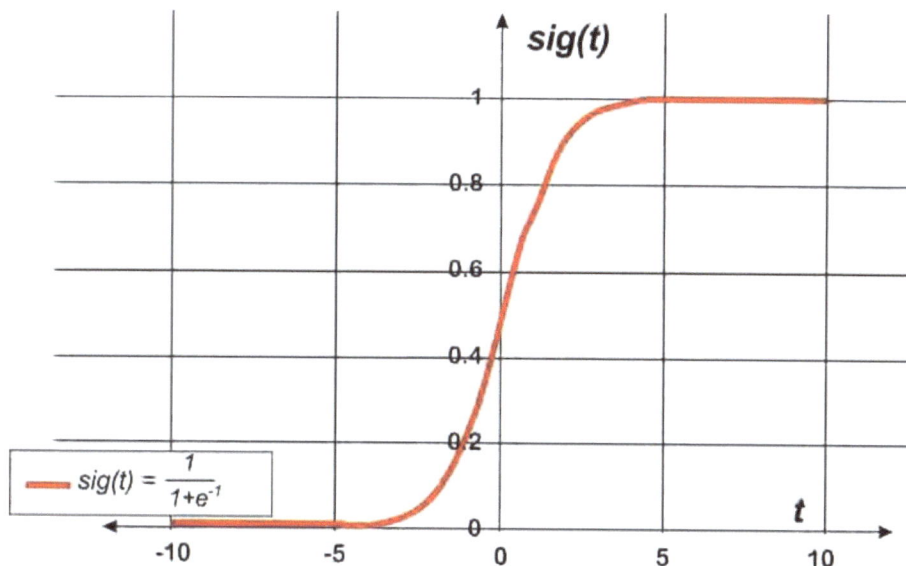

Fig. (2). Mark A Atkinson, Ph.D., Prof, George S Eisner Barth, MD, Prof, and Aaron W Michel's, MD 'Type 1 diabetes'.

$Sigm(t) = 1 / 1+e\text{-}t$ (1)

SVM

One popular and commonly used supervised learning technique, Support Vector Machine, or SVM, is utilized for both text categorization and classification in general [14]. Nonetheless, it is applied to machine learning classification challenges. In order to effortlessly supply the new data point in the appropriate category in the future, the objective of this technique is to generate the optimal line or decision boundary that can isolate dimensional space into classes. The optimal choice boundary is referred to as a hyper plane. SVM selects the robust vectors and points that aid in the creation of the hyper plane [15]. Fig. (**3**) shows type 1 diabetes.

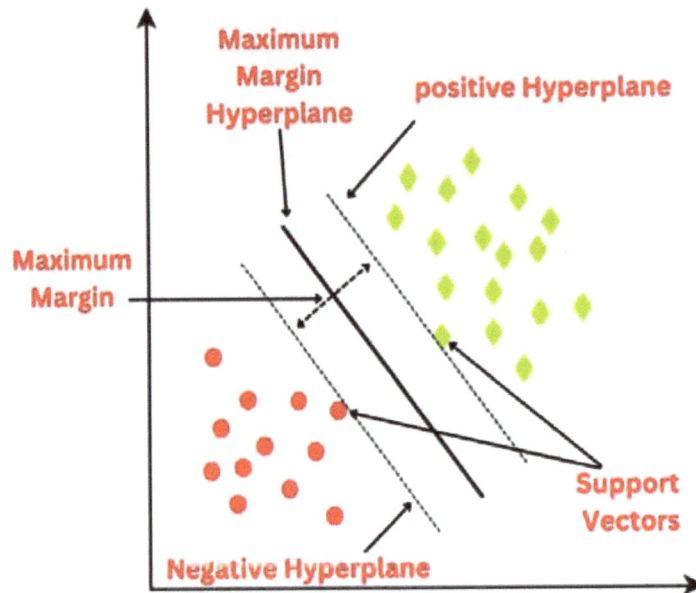

Fig. (3). Mark A Atkinson, Ph.D., Prof, George S Eisner Barth, MD, Prof, and Aaron W Michel's, MD 'Type 1 diabetes'.

Random Forest

It is an algorithmic grouped ml technique used for regression and classification. It is the result of combining several decision trees, each of which is trained using a different dataset through a process of random selection. Then, using an average for regression tasks or a maximum vote procedure for classification problems, the predictions made by each tree are combined to create forecasts [16]. Random forests have the advantage of being able to handle high-dimensional data with several characteristics and being able to be trained quickly on big amounts of data.

RESULTS

Four features were eliminated from consideration throughout our dataset analysis since we could not use them in our model. We confirmed that there are no empty values in our dataset [17]. We also discovered that the data is balanced, with an equal percentage of clicked and unclicked entries. While we worked on data visualization, we discovered that every feature in the dataset is related to one another and affects the model's accuracy and precision. It was a crucial insight since it showed how crucial it is to take into account every aspect when doing analysis and modeling [18]. We may increase our model's efficacy and dependability by making sure that all pertinent characteristics are taken into account. Overall, this research highlights how crucial complete and in-depth data analysis is to the creation of precise and useful predictive models [19]. Fig. (**4**) results displays the data visualization outcomes of the relationship plot involving age, income, internet consumption, and internet surfing. Consequently, our dataset is balanced and clean.

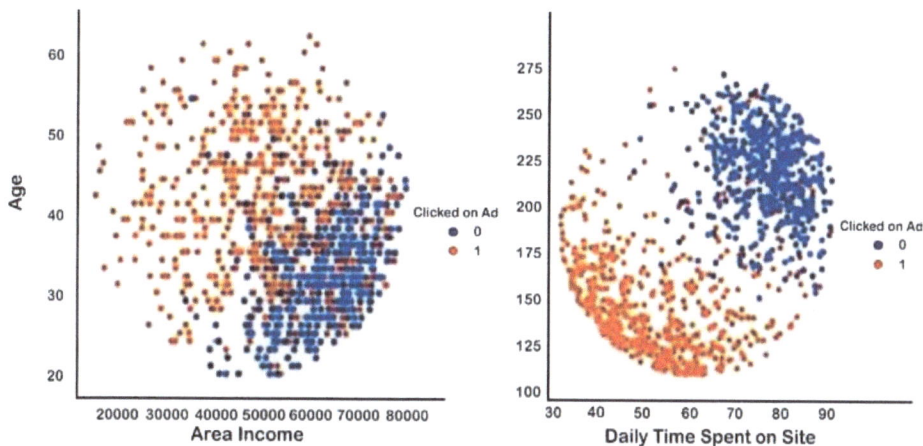

Fig. (4). K. Rajesh and V. Sangeetha, "Application of Data Mining Methods and Techniques for Diabetes Diagnosis", International Journal of Engineering and Innovative Technology (IJEIT) Volume 2, Issue 3, September 2012.

During the analysis, we applied four ML models to the dataset. These models are commonly used for classification tasks, and we wanted to see which one would yield the highest accuracy on our data [20]. After the implementation of models, the accuracy is calculated with 300 data values that are not used for training the data. We found that SVM performed the best with an accuracy of 96% shown in Fig. (**5**). While all the models had relatively high accuracies, SVM stood out as the top performer (Figs. **6-8**).

	precision	recall	f1-score	support
0	0.95	0.97	0.96	99
1	0.97	0.95	0.96	101
accuracy			0.96	200
macro avg	0.96	0.96	0.96	200
weighted avg	0.96	0.96	0.96	200

Fig. (5). B.M. Patel, R.C. Joshi, and Dura Toshniwal, "Association Rule for Classification of Type-2 Diabetic Patients", ICMLC '10 Proceedings of the 2010 Second International Conference on Machine Learning and Computing, February 09 - 11, 2010.

The other models had the following accuracies: logistic regression at 92%, decision tree at 94%, and random forest at 95% shown in Fig. (**9**). Although these models did not outperform SVM, they still produced impressive results and could be considered for use in other situations where the characteristics of the data might be different.

Random Forest

```
Random Forest

Confusion Matrix
 [[263  19]
 [ 23 117]]
Accuracy Score
 0.9004739336492891
```

	precision	recall	f1-score	support
0	0.92	0.93	0.93	282
1	0.86	0.84	0.85	140
accuracy			0.90	422
macro avg	0.89	0.88	0.89	422
weighted avg	0.90	0.90	0.90	422

Fig. (6). B.M. Patel, R.C. Joshi, and Dura Toshniwal, "Association Rule for Classification of Type-2 Diabetic Patients", ICMLC '10 Proceedings of the 2010 Second International Conference on Machine Learning and Computing, February 09 - 11, 2010.

Logistic Regression

```
Logistic Regression

Confusion Matrix
[[245  37]
 [ 77  63]]
Accuracy Score
0.7298578199052133
              precision    recall  f1-score   support

           0       0.76      0.87      0.81       282
           1       0.63      0.45      0.53       140

    accuracy                           0.73       422
   macro avg       0.70      0.66      0.67       422
weighted avg       0.72      0.73      0.72       422
```

Fig. (7). B.M. Patel, R.C. Joshi, and Dura Toshniwal, "Association Rule for Classification of Type-2 Diabetic Patients", ICMLC '10 Proceedings of the 2010 Second International Conference on Machine Learning and Computing, February 09 - 11, 2010.

Support Vector Machine

```
SVC

Confusion Matrix
[[251  31]
 [ 76  64]]
Accuracy Score
0.7464454976303317
              precision    recall  f1-score   support

           0       0.77      0.89      0.82       282
           1       0.67      0.46      0.54       140

    accuracy                           0.75       422
   macro avg       0.72      0.67      0.68       422
weighted avg       0.74      0.75      0.73       422
```

Fig. (8). B.M. Patel, R.C. Joshi, and Dura Toshniwal, "Association Rule for Classification of Type-2 Diabetic Patients", ICMLC '10 Proceedings of the 2010 Second International Conference on Machine Learning and Computing, February 09 - 11, 2010.

K nearest Neighbor

```
KNN

Confusion Matrix
 [[257  25]
 [ 22 118]]
Accuracy
 0.8886255924170616
              precision    recall  f1-score   support

           0       0.92      0.91      0.92       282
           1       0.83      0.84      0.83       140

    accuracy                           0.89       422
   macro avg       0.87      0.88      0.88       422
weighted avg       0.89      0.89      0.89       422
```

Fig. (9). B.M. Patel, R.C. Joshi, and Dura Toshniwal, "Association Rule for Classification of Type-2 Diabetic Patients", ICMLC '10 Proceedings of the 2010 Second International Conference on Machine Learning and Computing, February 09 - 11, 2010.

Accuracy Table

Table 1. B.M. Patel, R.C. Joshi, and Dura Toshniwal, "Association Rule for Classification of Type-2 Diabetic Patients", ICMLC '10 Proceedings of the 2010 Second International Conference on Machine Learning and Computing, February 09 - 11, 2010.

ALGORITHM	ACCURACY
• Random Forest.	90%
• Logistic Regression.	73%
• SVM.	74%
• KNN.	89%

CONCLUSION

We use a range of machine learning methods to classify the dataset by using different algorithms. With a 90% correctness rate, Random Forest has the highest accuracy. The devices have been contrasted.

The False Negative value can be limited by comparing the confusion matrix and learning algorithm accuracy. It is possible to carry out additional research to ascertain whether the non-diabetic individual will eventually develop diabetes.

FUTURE WORK

The project that is being presented is scalable, extensible, well-founded, and GUI-based. By detecting diseases at an early stage, the model can also lower the cost of therapy. It can also serve as a training tool for medical professionals, including cardiologists and physicians. Medical professionals can use these instruments to detect the disease in its early stages. The scalability and accuracy of this project can be enhanced by exploring numerous other potential advances. We will soon be able to use the generalized approach we have designed for multiple dataset analysis. In the prediction process, handling several class labels can significantly increase the production value. Given the enormous scope and amplitude of this illness, choosing appropriate labels will be a crucial issue in the future.

CODES

Depending on the requirements of the project, a different Python library was used to build the model. The code is written in the Anaconda application's Jupiter Notebook. We also use HTML, CSS, JavaScript, and a few CSS frameworks, such as Bootstrap, in our front-end programming.

REFERENCES

[1]   D. S, S. Palanisamy, F. Hajjej, O.I. Khalaf, G.M. Abdulsahib, and R. S, "Discrete Fourier Transform with Denoise Model Based Least Square Wiener Channel Estimator for Channel Estimation in MIMO-OFDM", *Entropy (Basel),* vol. 24, no. 11, p. 1601, 2022.
[http://dx.doi.org/10.3390/e24111601] [PMID: 36359691]

[2]   V.A.K. Gorantla, S.K. Sriramulugari, A.H. Mewada, and J. Logeshwaran, "An intelligent optimization framework to predict the vulnerable range of tumor cells using Internet of things", *2nd International Conference on Industrial Electronics: Developments & Applications (ICIDeA),* pp. 359-365, 2023.
[http://dx.doi.org/10.1109/ICIDeA59866.2023.10295269]

[3]   T. Marimuthu, V.A. Rajang, G.V. Lode, and J. Logeshwaran, "Deep Learning for Automated Lesion Detection in Mammography", *2nd International Conference on Industrial Electronics: Developments & Applications (ICIDeA),* pp. 383-388, 2023.
[http://dx.doi.org/10.1109/ICIDeA59866.2023.10295189]

[4]   V.A. Rajan, T. Marimuthu, G.V. Londhe, and J. Logeshwaran, "A Comprehensive analysis of Network Coding for Efficient Wireless Network Communication", *2nd International Conference on Industrial Electronics: Developments & Applications (ICIDeA),* pp. 204-210, 2023.
[http://dx.doi.org/10.1109/ICIDeA59866.2023.10295177]

[5]   S.P. Yadav, "Blockchain Security", In: *Blockchain Security in Cloud Computing. EAI/Springer Innovations in Communication and Computing.,* K. Baalamurugan, S.R. Kumar, A. Kumar, V. Kumar, S. Padmanaban, Eds., Springer: Cham, 2022.
[http://dx.doi.org/10.1007/978-3-030-70501-5_1]

[6]   S. P., Mahato, D. P., & Linh, N. T. D. Distributed Artificial Intelligence (S. P. Yadav, D. P. Mahato, & N. T. D. Linh, Eds.). CRC Press, 2020.,
        [http://dx.doi.org/10.1201/9781003038467]

[7]   V. Vashisht, A.K. Pandey, and S.P. Yadav, "Speech Recognition using Machine Learning", *Transactions on Smart Processing & Computing,* vol. 10, no. 3, pp. 233-239, 2021.
        [http://dx.doi.org/10.5573/IEIESPC.2021.10.3.233]

[8]   S.P. Yadav, B.S. Bhati, D.P. Mahato, and S. Kumar, "Federated Learning for IoT Applications. EAI/Springer Innovations in Communication and Computing", *Springer International Publishing,* 2022.
        [http://dx.doi.org/10.1007/978-3-030-85559-8]

[9]   H. Singh, A.S. Ahmed, F. Melandsø, and A. Habib, "Ultrasonic image denoising using machine learning in point contact excitation and detection method", *Ultrasonics,* vol. 127, p. 106834, 2023.
        [http://dx.doi.org/10.1016/j.ultras.2022.106834] [PMID: 36103756]

[10]   M. Humayun, M.I. Khalil, S.N. Almuayqil, and N.Z. Jhanjhi, "Framework for detecting breast cancer risk presence using deep learning", *Electronics (Basel),* vol. 12, no. 2, p. 403, 2023.
        [http://dx.doi.org/10.3390/electronics12020403]

[11]   G. Kumawat, S.K. Vishwakarma, P. Chakrabarti, P. Chittora, T. Chakrabarti, and J.C.W. Lin, "Prognosis of Cervical Cancer Disease by Applying Machine Learning Techniques", *J. Circuits Syst. Comput.,* vol. 32, no. 1, p. 2350019, 2023.
        [http://dx.doi.org/10.1142/S0218126623500196]

[12]   A. Javeed, A.L. Dallora, J.S. Berglund, A. Ali, L. Ali, and P. Anderberg, "Machine Learning for Dementia Prediction: A Systematic Review and Future Research Directions", *J. Med. Syst.,* vol. 47, no. 1, p. 17, 2023.
        [http://dx.doi.org/10.1007/s10916-023-01906-7] [PMID: 36720727]

[13]   A.S. Albahri, A.M. Duhaim, M.A. Fadhel, A. Alnoor, N.S. Baqer, L. Alzubaidi, O.S. Albahri, A.H. Alamoodi, J. Bai, A. Salhi, J. Santamaría, C. Ouyang, A. Gupta, Y. Gu, and M. Deveci, "A systematic review of trustworthy and explainable artificial intelligence in healthcare: Assessment of quality, bias risk, and data fusion", *Inf. Fusion,* vol. 96, pp. 156-191, 2023.
        [http://dx.doi.org/10.1016/j.inffus.2023.03.008]

[14]   F. Dipietrangelo, F. Nicassio, and G. Scarselli, "Structural Health Monitoring for impact localisation *via* machine learning", *Mech. Syst. Signal Process.,* vol. 183, p. 109621, 2023.
        [http://dx.doi.org/10.1016/j.ymssp.2022.109621]

[15]   L. Hadjiiski, K. Cha, H.P. Chan, K. Drukker, L. Morra, J.J. Näppi, B. Sahiner, H. Yoshida, Q. Chen, T.M. Deserno, H. Greenspan, H. Huisman, Z. Huo, R. Mazurchuk, N. Petrick, D. Regge, R. Samala, R.M. Summers, K. Suzuki, G. Tourassi, D. Vergara, and S.G. Armato III, "AAPM task group report 273: Recommendations on best practices for AI and machine learning for computer□aided diagnosis in medical imaging", *Med. Phys.,* vol. 50, no. 2, pp. e1-e24, 2023.
        [http://dx.doi.org/10.1002/mp.16188] [PMID: 36565447]

[16]   J.G. Nam, E.J. Hwang, J. Kim, N. Park, E.H. Lee, H.J. Kim, M. Nam, J.H. Lee, C.M. Park, and J.M. Goo, "AI improves nodule detection on chest radiographs in a health screening population: a randomized controlled trial", *Radiology,* vol. 307, no. 2, p. e221894, 2023.
        [http://dx.doi.org/10.1148/radiol.221894] [PMID: 36749213]

[17]   G.Y. Gombolay, N. Gopalan, A. Bernasconi, R. Nabbout, J.T. Megerian, B. Siegel, J. Hallman-Cooper, S. Bhalla, and M.C. Gombolay, "Review of machine learning and artificial intelligence (ML/AI) for the pediatric neurologist", *Pediatr. Neurol.,* vol. 141, pp. 42-51, 2023.
        [http://dx.doi.org/10.1016/j.pediatrneurol.2023.01.004] [PMID: 36773406]

[18]   S. Agarwal, A.S. Yadav, V. Dinesh, K.S.S. Vatsav, K.S.S. Prakash, and S. Jaiswal, "By artificial intelligence algorithms and machine learning models to diagnosis cancer", *Mater. Today Proc.,* vol. 80, pp. 2969-2975, 2023.

[http://dx.doi.org/10.1016/j.matpr.2021.07.088]

[19] Z. Cao, F. Chen, E.M. Grais, F. Yue, Y. Cai, D.W. Swanepoel, and F. Zhao, "Machine learning in diagnosing middle ear disorders using tympanic membrane images: a meta□analysis", *Laryngoscope,* vol. 133, no. 4, pp. 732-741, 2023.
[http://dx.doi.org/10.1002/lary.30291] [PMID: 35848851]

[20] Y.J.N. Ngoyi, and E. Ngongang, "ForexDaytrading Strategy: An Application of the Gaussian Mixture Model to Marginalized Currency pairs in Africa", *International Journal of Computer Science and Technology,* vol. 7, no. 3, pp. 149-191, 2023.

CHAPTER 31

Blockchain Based Academic Certificate Authentication System

Vipin Kumar Pal[1,*], Pankaj Kumar[1], Nitin Vera[1], Ritik Manga[1], Rishabh Kumar[1] and Ritesh Gautama[1]

[1] *Computer Science and Engineering, Hi-Tech Institute of Engineering & Technology, Ghaziabad, U.P, India*

Abstract: In recent years, blockchain technology has emerged as a reliable and secure means of transmitting and storing data. One potential method for ensuring secure and unalterable data is by implementing blockchain technology within the certificate validation mechanism. This paper offers a comprehensive analysis of the utilization of blockchain technology to establish a reliable, efficient, and fraud-resistant method for validating certificates. The article covers many components of the system, including the blockchain network, smart contracts, and cryptography techniques. The paper also examines the potential benefits and challenges associated with implementing such a system.

Keywords: Blockchain, Comprehensive, Fraud-resistant, Transmitting, Technology.

INTRODUCTION

The traditional method of certificate validation, which relies on a centralized authority, is susceptible to fraudulent activities, therefore compromising the integrity and reliability of the system. The emergence of blockchain technology provides a feasible method for constructing a secure and reliable certificate validation system. This paper aims to provide a comprehensive analysis of the potential applications of blockchain technology in developing a secure, decentralized, and efficient system for validating certificates, ensuring their integrity, and preventing unauthorized alterations [1]. The paper examines several system components, including the blockchain network, smart contracts, and cryp-

---

* **Corresponding author Vipin Kumar Pal:** Computer Science and Engineering ,Hi-Tech Institute of Engineering & Technology, Ghaziabad, U.P, India; E-mail: vipincs2005@gmail.com

Pankaj Kumar Mishra & Satya Prakash Yadav (Eds.)

tographic techniques, and assesses the potential benefits and challenges associated with implementing such a system [2, 3]. The study highlights the necessity of implementing a certificate validation system based on blockchain technology to enhance the security, transparency, and efficiency of the validation process.

RELATED WORKS

The blockchain-based academic certificate authentication system is an emerging era designed to help verify the authenticity of educational credentials. This gadget is part of a larger fashion of the use of digital currencies and allotted ledgers to enhance the security and verifiability of records [4]. The generation provides an easy and immutable platform for establishments to affirm the validity of instructional credentials . The system of issuing and authenticating instructional credentials may require a lot of work involving multiple stakeholders. This method is also liable to mistakes and mismanagement [5]. The Block chain-based instructional certificates Authentication gadget gives a revolutionary solution to this hassle through a relaxed platform to store and authenticate educational credentials [6]. First, establishments use a secure digital wallet to store their educational credentials, which can then be securely shared with different authorized stakeholders. This wallet is secured by way of blockchain technology, meaning that every transaction is saved in a dispensed ledger, which is hard to tamper. As a result, the chain of acceptance between the issuing institution and the receiver is preserved, ensuring the authenticity of the academic credentials [7]. The blockchain-based instructional certificate Authentication device is a hassle-free and efficient system for authenticating and verifying educational credentials. It makes use of disbursed ledger technology to shop and share facts on certificates and transcripts [8]. This device facilitates academic establishments, employers, and other stakeholders to affirm the authenticity of an academic certificate. The machine uses a unique, tamper-proof blockchain code to keep and get entry to the information from distributed ledgers. This machine reduces the requirement of manual verification of certificates and will increase the extent of safety and accuracy by way of offering an immutable report of each certificate [9]. The gadget additionally permits a couple of individuals to, without difficulty, get the right of entry to examine the information of the certificate and green monitoring of the statistics [10]. The use of this system allows for enhancing the trustworthiness and credibility of the instructional certificate.

EXISTING SYSTEM

In the present certificate validation system, certificates are centrally issued and validated by a trusted third-party authority. This strategy is employed by educational institutions, governmental organizations, and certifying authorities to validate individuals' knowledge, talents, and abilities [11]. The certificate validation technique verifies the identity and qualifications of the certificate holder before issuing the certificate. Subsequently, the individual possessing the certificate can present the document to potential employers, educational establishments, or other entities in order to authenticate its validity. Despite its intended safety, reliability, and effectiveness, the conventional certificate validation system is susceptible to many vulnerabilities that could potentially enable fraudulent activities, such as data manipulation, impersonation, and certificate forging [12]. One of the major drawbacks of the old certificate validation system is its centralized structure. The certificates are stored in centralized databases that can only be accessed by authorized individuals. Due to the presence of a single point of failure, the system is vulnerable to cyber-attacks and unauthorized disclosure of data. The centralization of the system also entails that the intermediaries involved in the issuance and validation of certificates may be susceptible to fraudulent behavior [13]. The certificate issuance mechanism of the previous system involved multiple intermediaries, which could impede the process and make it less efficient. The individual who holds the certificate begins the process by submitting their certification application to the relevant authority. Subsequently, the authority grants the certificate upon verifying the applicant's identity and credentials. The certificate is stored in a centralized database that is accessible only to authorized individuals [14]. The certificate validation procedure requires the certificate holder to submit their certificate for verification. The verifier typically carries out this process manually, ensuring the authenticity of the certificate and confirming the identity of the certificate holder. Although the verifier may have to contact multiple intermediaries to verify the legitimacy of the certificate, the validation process for certificates can be both time-consuming and inefficient. Refer to the website for additional details. Consequently, individuals get disillusioned with the system. The traditional certificate validation system is vulnerable to deceitful practices such as data modification, impersonation, and certificate forgery [15]. Upon the compromise of the certificate, deceitful behaviors may occur. The certificate is intentionally modified, or the holder or an intermediate provides false information. Detecting fraudulent activities can be challenging and can result in significant consequences, such as damage to one's reputation and legal ramifications. In summary, the existing certificate validation system could be more efficient, laborious, and susceptible to fraudulent activities. An enhanced and fortified system is necessary, capable of swiftly and openly verifying certificates. Implementing a certificate validation system based on blockchain technology is an effective approach to tackling the issues arising from the existing system. Data can be securely kept and authenticated using a blockchain, which is a decentralized and distributed ledger, ensuring both safety and transparency [16]. The technology eliminates the need for intermediaries, hence reducing the risk of fraudulent activities, and utilizes cryptographic methods to ensure the authenticity and integrity of the certificates. The problems above are addressed by the implementation of a certificate validation system based on blockchain technology. This system provides a decentralized, safe, and transparent platform for storing and verifying certificates [17]. A certificate validation system that utilizes blockchain technology ensures the genuineness and inalterability of certificates by securely storing them on an immutable and tamper-resistant ledger. The security and privacy of the certificate are guaranteed by employing a private key that can be authorized for access by the certificate holder. The certificate validation system, which is based on blockchain technology, features a streamlined and transparent validation process [18]. The verifier can obtain the certificate directly from the blockchain, thus eliminating the requirement for intermediaries and reducing the risk of fraudulent behavior. Due to the transparent storage of data on the blockchain, there is an increased level of trust and confidence in the system [19]. To summarize, the existing certificate validation system suffers from a lack of transparency and is vulnerable to fraudulent activities. The utilization of a blockchain-based system for certifying documents through a decentralized, secure, and transparent platform for storing and verifying certificates offers a solution to these challenges. The system utilizes cryptographic techniques to ensure the authenticity and integrity of the certificates [20].

LITERATURE SURVEY

The project aims to create a system that can generate unchangeable certificates and verify their authenticity. To support this, we referenced several previous papers. There exist many publications and works by many authors on this subject. The focal points of our literature review were blockchain technology, an advanced storage system, and the validity of digital certificates. The inaugural article, titled "A Comprehensive Examination of Blockchain Technology," provided an in-depth analysis of the intricacies of Blockchain. It established several terms associated with this technology, including the most essential ones. The concept is referred to as a smart contract. The Blockchain produces an extensive sequence of nodes and records the hash of the data in the preceding block. If the data is modified, its hash will be updated and will no longer correspond to the value stored in the previous block, hence enabling the disclosure of the contents. The second article was titled "Utilizing block chain and smart contracts for the creation of a digital certificate." Three artists composed their designs. The institutions were established prior to the pupils, with the service provider following after that. Their approach was flawed because they were using "one hash as a key," which allowed anyone to view the hash once obtained. Our next document will be a birth certificate that is resistant to tampering. Their technique closely mirrored that of the second article, except for the utilization of the AES algorithm and IPFS for data storage. They possessed a specialized system explicitly tailored for the management of birth certificates. We acquired knowledge about IPFS through this publication. Both the source document and the capacity to generate online certificates were kept from being stored anywhere. We researched a distinct study called Blockish (Blockchain-powered Interplanetary File System for Forensic and Trusted Data Traceability) to tackle the issue of storing documents. This article provided an overview of IPFS by comparing and contrasting traditional IPFS with Blockchain-based IPFS. Blockish emerged as the dominant choice in most categories, encompassing upload transactions, read transactions, and download transactions. The final paper was on a strategy for identity verification that utilizes blockchain technology. Like the second and third publications, their approach incorporated an issuing authority responsible for generating the document, a hashing algorithm applied to it, and storing the document's value. Some systems employ asymmetric encryption to enhance security by utilizing public hash keys.

SYSTEM DESIGN

The system architecture for a certificate validation system based on blockchain comprises multiple interconnected components that collaborate to establish a safe and transparent framework for storing and verifying certificates. The system design comprises the following essential elements:

- The fundamental element of the system architecture is the implementation of block chain technology, which offers a decentralized and distributed database for the storage of certificates. Blockchain technology offers both immutability and transparency, guaranteeing that certificates remain unaltered and allowing anybody to audit the validation process.
- Smart Contracts: Smart contracts refer to self-executing computer programs that automate the process of certificate validation. Smart contracts are implemented on blockchain technology, housing the validation procedures and logic that ascertain the validity of a certificate.
- The certificate issuer is the entity responsible for generating and distributing certificates on the blockchain. The entity responsible for issuing certificates can be a university, college, or any other institution.
- Certificate Holder: The certificate holder refers to the person who has received the certificate. The individual with the certificate can get the certificate from the blockchain and utilize it for a multitude of objectives.

- Validators are institutions tasked with confirming the authenticity and validity of certificates. Validators might consist of either individuals or companies possessing the necessary knowledge to authenticate the certificates.
- The user interface serves as the front end of the certificate validation mechanism, enabling users to engage with the blockchain. The user interface may take the form of a web application, mobile application, or any other interface that facilitates users' access to and verification of certificates.

The components above collaborate to establish a secure and transparent certificate validation system that prevents the necessity for intermediaries, diminishes the likelihood of fraudulent actions, and furnishes a dependable and effective platform for certificate validation.

PROPOSED APPROACH

The proposed method for implementing a certificate validation system using blockchain involves creating a blockchain network that exclusively permits authorized entities to take part. This strategy seeks to enhance efficiency, transparency, decentralization, accessibility, and traceability while also ensuring privacy and security. The blockchain will be utilized for the generation and storage of digital certificates. These certificates will be validated using smart contracts, which are contracts that can be programmed and executed themselves. Smart contracts will employ predetermined rules to authenticate certificates. The system will utilize sharing a technique aimed at enhancing scalability by partitioning the blockchain into smaller divisions or shards, which independently handle transactions, thereby reducing the burden on the main blockchain network. The system will be developed in compliance with relevant legislation and standards, such as GDPR and ISO 27001. This will ensure adherence. It will ensure that the system is legally valid and may be used in multiple jurisdictions. The system will be designed to interface with existing certificate validation systems, seamlessly addressing the challenge of integration and allowing enterprises to implement the new system at their own pace. The proposed technique aims to offer a cost-effective and transparent solution to the challenges related to implementing a certificate validation system based on blockchain technology.

IMPLEMENTATION

A variety of software tools were utilized to create and assess the proposed certificate validation technique. The back end was developed using HTML, CSS, and the JavaScript framework node.js, while the front end was built with the same technologies. Solidity, a programming language specifically designed for creating smart contracts on the ethereal network, was utilized in the development of the ethereal smart contract. Truffle, a collection of tools, facilitates the development and deployment of smart contracts on the Main or Ethereal network. A local Etherealblock chain was established using Panache, a constituent of the Truffle ecosystem, for testing purposes. Ganache provided 10 simulated accounts with counterfeit ether that were used for testing transactions. Metalmark, a digital currency wallet, was utilized to transact tokens built on the Etherealblock chain. It functioned as a Chrome extension to facilitate communication with the ethereal network and authorize transactions. Web.js was employed for the integration of the front-end and back-end at the conclusion of the smart contract. The utilization of web.js, a JavaScript library, enables the development of web 3.0 applications that establish communication with the ethereal network. The system stores the markers as pictures. Students are required to contact the consortium in order to preserve their academic information on this authorized website. Only authorized users are allowed to make additions to the blockchain. The student's qualifications are mentioned, along with their roll number, name, and grades. In this implementation of the suggested certificate validation system, a secure and efficient system for verifying certificates on the blockchain was ultimately constructed by utilizing a range of software tools and libraries. Designing, testing, and deploying the DAPP on the ethereal network was made easy by the utilization of Truffle, Panache, and Metalmark. Additionally, the implementation of web.js facilitated the creation of a user-friendly interface for students and other system users.

RESULTS

The implementation and testing of the suggested blockchain-based system for certificate validation involved the utilization of many software tools, such as Node.js, Mongo DB, and Ethereal. This technology provides a secure and efficient approach to verifying the authenticity of academic certificates on the blockchain, addressing the issue of certificate fraud. The construction of the system involved the utilization of software tools and libraries such as Truffle, Solidity, Panache, Ethereal, and Metalmark. By leveraging the expertise of a team of specialists, we successfully developed a system that enables us to tailor a unique solution for every client. The system's back end utilized Node.js, a robust JavaScript framework that facilitates the building and execution of applications. Node.js was employed to store and handle certificate-related data, which included the roll number, name, and grades of pupils. Moreover, the system's front end was developed using HTML, CSS, and JavaScript. The user interface was developed with efficient and user-friendly features to enable students to add and verify credentials easily. Solidity is a programming language specifically designed for constructing smart contracts on the ethereal block chain. It was utilized in the creation of the ethereal smart contract. The Truffle frameworks, a collection of utilities that facilitate the creation, deployment, and testing of smart contracts on the ethereal network, were employed to compile, deploy, and verify the smart contract. In order to test the smart contracts, a local ethereal block chain was established using Panache. This technique was used to allocate fictional ether to ten accounts, which were then used for transactions during testing. Consequently, the process of testing the system and ensuring its adherence to the expected performance was straightforward. Metamask was used as a digital wallet to store and carry out transactions using Ethereum-based currencies on the Ethereum network. In order to interact with the Ethereum network and authorize transactions, it functioned as a Chrome extension. The integration of the front end and back end with the smart contract was facilitated using Web.js. The utilization of web.js, a JavaScript library, enables the development of web 3.0 applications that establish communication with the Ethereum network. This library facilitated the creation of a smooth and uninterrupted user experience for both students and teachers. The markers were stored as images in the implemented system. Students were permitted to do so on this authorized platform, but they needed to notify the consortium. The roll number, name, and marks of each student were recorded on the blockchain alongside their credentials, with access limited to authorized individuals. The certificate validation system was effectively constructed using Node.js and MongoDB. Additionally, Ethereum is also included. Furthermore, the system provided a secure and efficient method for verifying certificates on the blockchain while also addressing the problem of certificate fraud and ensuring the accuracy of academic credentials. The system was easily designed, tested, and deployed using a diverse range of software tools and libraries, including Truffle, Solidity, Panache, Ethereum, Metalmark, and Web. The JavaScript application installs the system on the Ethereum network, providing numerous benefits to consumers.

Source: Cocoa, L., Marches, M., &Tonally, R. (2018). Blockchain-based certification systems. Proceedings of the 2nd International Conference on Complexity, Future Information Systems and Risk.

Where, Fig. (**1**) shows the Home Page,

Fig. (**2**) shows the Login,

Fig. (**3**) shows the Register,

Fig. (**4**) shows the Upload Certificates,

Fig. (**5**) shows the Certificates.

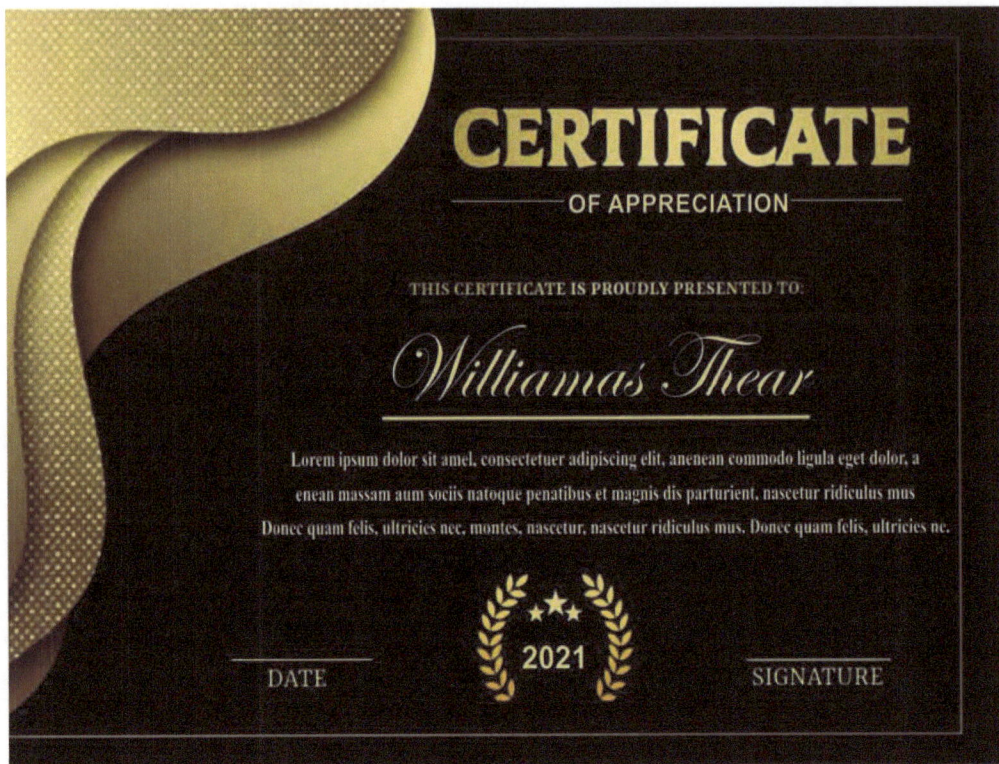

Fig. (1). Home Page.

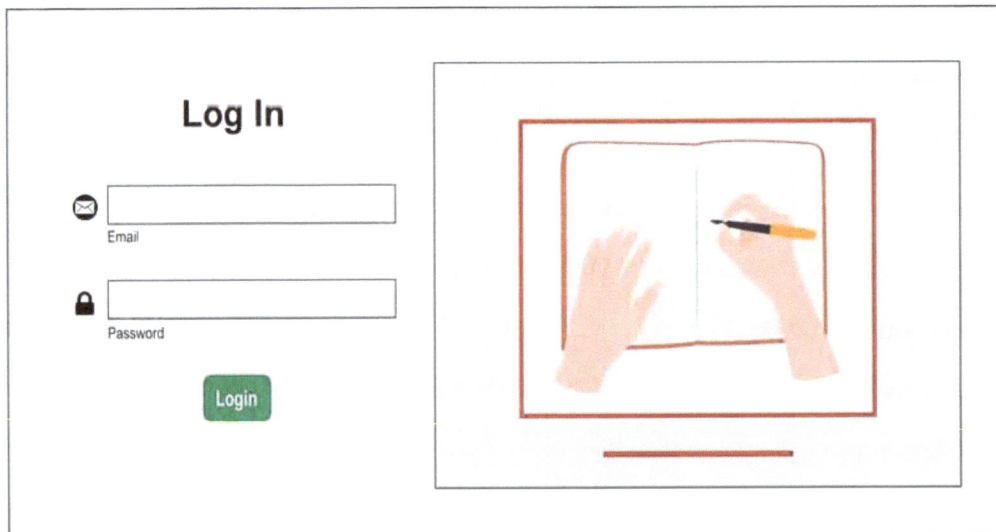

Fig. (2). Login.

Fig. (3). Register.

Fig. (4). Upload Certificates.

Fig. (5). Show Certificates.

CONCLUSION

The existing process for validating certificates is centralized, arduous, inefficient, and susceptible to fraudulent activities. The certificate validation mechanism is obscure and does not allow for insight into the validation process, and the system as a whole lacks transparency. A blockchain-based certificate validation process can address the existing problems with the current system. The blockchain-based system provides a decentralized, secure, and transparent platform for storing and verifying certificates. The approach obviates the necessity of intermediaries, hence reducing the risk of fraudulent transactions, and utilizes cryptographic methods to ensure the authenticity and integrity of the certificates. The use of a blockchain-based system is a superior approach for certificate validation, as it offers enhanced effectiveness, safety, and reliability.

REFERENCES

[1]   S. Dhanasekaran, and J. Ramesh, "Channel estimation using spatial partitioning with coalitional game theory (SPCGT) in wireless communication", *Wirel. Netw.,* vol. 27, no. 3, pp. 1887-1899, 2021.
[http://dx.doi.org/10.1007/s11276-020-02528-4]

[2]   N.H.A. Rufus, "Evolutionary Optimization with Deep Transfer Learning for Content based Image Retrieval in Cloud Environment", *International Conference on Augmented Intelligence and Sustainable Systems (ICAISS),* pp. 826-831, 2022.

[3]   M.A. Mohammed, R. Ramakrishnan, M.A. Mohammed, V.A. Mohammed, and J. Logeshwaran, "A Novel Predictive Analysis to Identify the Weather Impacts for Congenital Heart Disease Using Reinforcement Learning", *International Conference on Network, Multimedia and Information Technology (NMITCON),* pp. 1-8, 2023.
[http://dx.doi.org/10.1109/NMITCON58196.2023.10276376]

[4]   V.A. Mohammed, M.A. Mohammed, M.A. Mohammed, R. Ramakrishnan, and J. Logeshwaran, "The Spreading Prediction and Severity Analysis of Blood Cancer Using Scale-Invariant Feature Transform", *International Conference on Network, Multimedia and Information Technology (NMITCON),* pp. 1-7, 2023.
[http://dx.doi.org/10.1109/NMITCON58196.2023.10276289]

[5]   A.G. Ismaeel, J. Mary, A. Chelliah, J. Logeshwaran, S.N. Mahmood, S. Alani, and A.H. Shather, "Enhancing Traffic Intelligence in Smart Cities Using Sustainable Deep Radial Function", *Sustainability (Basel),* vol. 15, no. 19, p. 14441, 2023.
[http://dx.doi.org/10.3390/su151914441]

[6]   J. Kauri, J. Sabena, and J. Shah, "Facial Emotion Recognition", *International Conference on Computational Intelligence and Sustainable Engineering Solutions (CISES),* 2022.
[http://dx.doi.org/10.1109/CISES54857.2022.9844366]

[7]   H. Yadav, S. Singh, K.K. Mishra, S. Srivastava, M.S. Nark, and S.P. Yadav, "Brain Tumor Detection with MRI Images", *International Conference on Computational Intelligence and Sustainable Engineering Solutions (CISES),* 2022.
[http://dx.doi.org/10.1109/CISES54857.2022.9844387]

[8]   P. Rani, S. Vera, S.P. Yadav, B.K. Ray, M.S. Nark, and D. Kumar, "Simulation of the Lightweight Blockchain Technique Based on Privacy and Security for Healthcare Data for the Cloud System", *International Journal of E-Health and Medical Communications,* vol. 13, no. 4, pp. 1-5, 2022.
[http://dx.doi.org/10.4018/IJEHMC.309436]

[9]   F. Al-Tudjman, S.P. Yadav, M. Kumar, V. Yadav, T. Stephan, Ed., *Transforming Management with AI, Big-Data, and IoT.* Springer International Publishing, 2022.
[http://dx.doi.org/10.1007/978-3-030-86749-2]

[10]   N. Nader, M.F. Hayat, M.A. Qurush, M. Masjid, M. Nader, and J. Jana, "Hybrid Blockchain-based Academic Credential Verification System (B-ACVS)", *Multimedia Tools Appl.,* pp. 1-29, 2023.

[11]   A. Rustavi, F. Dalai, V. Atanasovski, and A. Risteski, "A Systematic Literature Review on Blockchain-Based Systems for Academic Certificate Verification", *IEEE Access,* 2023.

[12]   H.A. Aloha, R.A. Alakhtar, A. Upbraid, O.K. Husain, and F.K. Husain, "Blockchain-based micro-credentialing system in higher education institutions: Systematic literature review", *Knowl. Base. Syst.,* p. 110238, 2023.

[13]   N.K. Dewangan, P. Chandrakar, S. Kumari, and J.J.P.C. Rodrigues, "Enhanced privacy-preserving in student certificate management in blockchain and interplanetary file system", *Multimedia Tools Appl.,* vol. 82, no. 8, pp. 12595-12614, 2023.
[http://dx.doi.org/10.1007/s11042-022-13915-8]

[14]   Rahman, M. M., Tonmoy, M. T. K., Shihab, S. R., & Farhana, R. Blockchain-based certificate authentication system with enabling correction. arXiv preprint arXiv:2302.03877. 2023.

[15]   S. Pu, and J.S.L. Lam, "The benefits of blockchain for digital certificates: A multiple case study analysis", *Technol. Soc.,* vol. 72, p. 102176, 2023.
[http://dx.doi.org/10.1016/j.techsoc.2022.102176]

[16]   T. Rahman, S.I. Mouno, A.M. Raatul, A.K. Al Azad, and N. Mansoor, "Verifi-chain: A credentials verifier using blockchain and IPFS", *International Conference on Information, Communication and Computing Technology,* pp. 361-371, 2023.
[http://dx.doi.org/10.1007/978-981-99-5166-6_24]

[17]   A. S. Kareem, and A. C. Shakir, "Verification Process of Academic Certificates Using Blockchain Technology", *Kirkuk University Journal for Scientific Studies,* vol. 18, no. 1, 2023.
[http://dx.doi.org/10.32894/kujss.2023.135876.1072]

[18]   O.A. Khashan, S. Alamri, W. Alomoush, M.K. Alsmadi, S. Atawneh, and U. Mir, "Blockchain-Based Decentralized Authentication Model for IoT-Based E-Learning and Educational Environments", *Comput. Mater. Continua,* vol. 75, no. 2, 2023.
[http://dx.doi.org/10.32604/cmc.2023.036217]

[19]   T. Q. Duy, and M. H. Trong, "A blockchain-based Certificate Management System using the Hyperledger Fabric Platform", *Thang Long Journal of Science: Mathematics and Mathematical Sciences,* vol. 2, no. 8, 2023.

[20]   M. Fan, Z. Zhang, Z. Li, G. Sun, H. Yu, and M. Guizani, "Blockchain-Based Decentralized and Lightweight Anonymous Authentication for Federated Learning", *IEEE Trans. Vehicular Technol.,* vol. 72, no. 9, pp. 12075-12086, 2023.
[http://dx.doi.org/10.1109/TVT.2023.3265366]

Hydroponics in Agriculture

Shivam Raj[1,*], Ramashankar[1], Ravi Raman[1] and Sachin Gautam[1]

[1] *Department of Civil Engineering, Greater Noida Institute of Technology, GNIOT, Greater Noida, Uttar pradesh, India*

Abstract: The process of urbanization and modernization has diminished the accessibility of agricultural regions. Consequently, the future harvests will fail to meet the expected productivity. Subsequently, in order to fulfill the necessary demand, methods such as hydroponics, aquaponics, and aeroponics will be utilized. Countries such as Israel and Abu Dhabi, as well as arid regions, necessitate the use of these specific agricultural techniques in order to address the issue of famine.

Keywords: Agricultural techniques, Agricultural regions, Geoponics, Hydroponics, Urbanization.

INTRODUCTION

Hydroponics is a soilless way of cultivating plants and crops. Given the limited quantity of land, achieving the needed level of food production would be a formidable task [1]. Regions with limited water resources also experience a food crisis. To overcome this issue, hydroponics and aquaponics will be employed because of their ability to provide better results with less water and time compared to traditional soil agriculture [2, 3]. We should aim to optimize productivity while minimizing water consumption. We will employ hydroponics, a more advanced method compared to traditional soil-based agriculture, to develop crops [4].

RELATED WORKS

Hydroponics is an agricultural technique that substitutes soil with water and nutrient solutions to cultivate plants. The cultivation technique holds significant promise for enhancing crop yields and promoting sustainability in agricultural practices. Nevertheless, the effectiveness of hydroponics is greatly dependent on accurate diagnosis [5, 6]. Hydroponics diagnostic models are employed to oversee

* **Corresponding author Shivam Raj:** Department of Civil Engineering, Greater Noida Institute of Technology, GNIOT, Greater Noida, Uttar pradesh, India; E-mail: srksrk2001@gmail.com

Pankaj Kumar Mishra & Satya Prakash Yadav (Eds.)

and enhance plant well-being, water administration, and nutrient concentrations. Hydroponics diagnostic models have diverse uses, encompassing the monitoring of plant health and growth, identification of nutrient imbalances, assessment of soil pH, and guidance on water management [7 - 9]. The majority of these models provide immediate feedback and are specifically designed to optimize the efficiency of growth and minimize the use of resources while also guaranteeing that plants have the ideal amount of nutrients available for their development [10, 11]. Regrettably, there are multiple concerns linked to diagnostic models for hydroponics. Initially, numerous versions are excessively costly and intricate to be within the reach of small-scale or hobby farmers. Furthermore, the expense of sensors and other components remains elevated, constraining the accessibility of the technology [12, 13]. Furthermore, numerous models exhibit limited adaptability and are restricted to particular settings or specific agricultural produce. Hydroponics has gained popularity as a method of food production in agriculture. Its promise for high yield and minimum environmental effect has led to a growing interest in developing computer models for this technique. These models facilitate farmers' comprehension of the interplay between plants and the environment, enabling them to pinpoint crucial areas for enhancement in their hydroponics system [14, 15]. An example of a computer model is the HydroYield model, which was created by academics at Stanford University. The purpose of this model is to forecast plant biomass production and offer insights into the impact of various environmental conditions, such as nutrient availability, light intensity, air temperature, and water content, on plant growth. Additionally, it can be utilized for the analysis of crop nutrient needs, scheduling of irrigation, and evaluation of other crucial aspects. Another beneficial model is the Hydroponics Plant Growth Model created by Oregon State University [16, 17]. This model specifically examines the correlation between plant development and environmental variables, including water availability, fertilizer provision, light intensity, and air temperature. Additionally, it can be employed to enhance the efficiency of a hydroponics system tailored to a particular crop. Furthermore, the DRIVEN model was formulated by academics at the University of California, Berkeley [18, 19]. This model uses machine learning techniques to detect and analyze interactions among the many components inside a hydroponics system. It utilizes accumulated data to create predictive models. Hydroponics in agriculture is an innovative method of cultivating plants that eliminate the requirement of soil as the growth medium. Instead of utilizing dirt, a solution abundant in nutrients is employed to provide sustenance and support to the plants, and subsequently, it is circulated and reused. This agricultural method can enhance crop productivity while simultaneously decreasing water consumption and enhancing the quality and quantity of yields. In addition, hydroponics provides an expedited and more nourishing growth environment in the initial phases of plant growth while minimizing the likelihood of disease or pest invasion. In addition, it does not necessitate the use of pesticides or herbicides [20]. Furthermore, when integrated with renewable energy sources, it has the potential to diminish the reliance on fertilizers derived from fossil fuels.

METHODS OF HYDROPONICS

Various hydroponic techniques enable the cultivation of diverse crops using distinct methodologies:

- Wick system refers to a method of irrigation that utilizes a wick to transport water from a reservoir to the roots of plants.
- Nutritional Film Technique.
- Hydroponics using the Deep Water Culture method.
- Irrigation system that delivers water in small, controlled amounts.
- The Ebb and Flow system.

We will employ the "Deep Water Culture" method in hydroponics for our plant development experiment, as it is the simplest and most efficient approach. The process involves using a container, namely a Styrofoam box with dimensions of 490*338*165 mm, to do the task.

GROWING MEDIUM

Instead of using soil, we employ a growth medium that operates based on the same principles as soil. This approach may yield better outcomes because the soil contains diverse bacteria that may be unnecessary for the crop and can lead to crop failure. The following items are:

- Coco-coir refers to the fibrous material derived from the outer husk of coconuts.
- Rice hulls.
- Perlite is a substance.
- Peat moss is a type of organic material.

For our experiment, we shall utilize "coco-coir" as it is an exceptional growing medium that functions similarly to the soil.

MATERIALS USED IN THE EXPERIMENT

Vegetables

We will use LactucaSativa (Lettuce) for our experiment, which is a leafy vegetable. It can be grown in a period of 6 to 8 weeks; we will compare the growth rate of the lettuce in the soil to that in a hydroponic solution. Fig. (**1**) shows the Lettuce Saliva (Table **1**).

Fig. (1). Lettuce Saliva.

AMOUNT OF WATER

Table 1. The water and soil required for the plant are:

Methods	SOIL	HYDROPONICS
Water per m³ per plant.	$0.0056m^3$	$0.0028m^3$
No. of plants.	5 plants	5 plants
Total water in liters.	22.4 litres	14 litres

MINERALS USED

Table 2. The nutrients that a plant requires for its growth are:

Soil agriculture	Hydroponic agriculture
1.075g N	KNO_3
1.175g P	$Ca(NO_3)_2$
0.375 g K	$NH_4H_2PO_4$
-	$MGSO_4.7H_2O$

PROCEDURE

Due to the existence of two distinct methods for conducting this experiment, there would inevitably be disparities in the necessary procedures. The inclusion of soil culture was considered due to adherence to the conventional approach in the initial phase of the experiment. The study also included hydroponic and soilless systems.

Soil Culture

In order to enhance the infiltration and proper dispersion of nutrients within the soil particles in this experiment, the soil to be used was initially pulverized into a fine consistency. The fine soil was meticulously mixed with 1 kilogram of livestock manure, aiming to allocate 200 g of the manure to each plant. A test was conducted to ascertain the initial mineral composition of the soil prior to proceeding to the subsequent stage. Prior to the application of inorganic fertilizers, it is imperative to do this test as it will facilitate the determination of the precise amount of each mineral nutrient that the plants will absorb. After two weeks following the sowing of the seeds and the initiation of the germination process, the seedlings were relocated. The plants were transplanted into a seedling container measuring $490*338*165$ mm^3, which was treated with the fertilizer's application.

Hydroponic Culture

The coir dust, which served as the medium in this case, was contained within plastic cups. It was expected that five plants would grow in five cups, each with dimensions of $70*82*45$ mm^3. The nutrient solution was prepared according to the required mineral needs for this experiment and stored in a Styrofoam box with dimensions matching those of the soil culture, specifically $490*338*165$ mm^3. The burgeoning seedlings were subsequently subjected to this hydroponic solution, enabling the plants to assimilate the nutrients. Measurements of the experiment's parameters were obtained at random intervals when the plants reached ages of 35, 40, and 45 days. Four plants were randomly selected from both the hydroponics and soil cultures for these measurements. Additionally, the researchers made a record of the number of leaves on the selected plants for the study.

Fig. (2). Cups for coco pit.

Fig. (3). Cups with coco pit.

Fig. (4). Styrofoam Box.

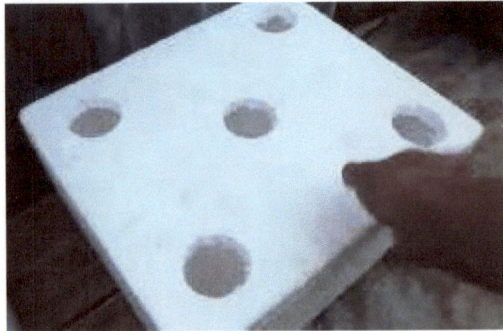

Fig. (5). Holes For cups.

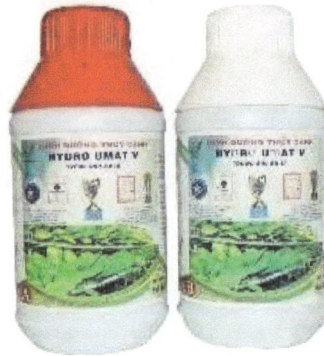

Fig. (6). Hydroponic Solutions.

Fig. (7). Hydroponic solutions.

Fig. (8). After 25 days.

Fig. (9). Roots.

Fig. (10). After 40 days.

RESULTS

The growth of lettuce in both soil and soilless culture (hydroponics) is examined by analyzing the root length, dry weight, and root shoot ratios. The roots of the hydroponically farmed plants exhibited somewhat greater length compared to the plants grown in soil. Hydroponically grown plants exhibit significantly longer root lengths compared to plants grown on soil. This method is an excellent way to assess the anticipated quality of the crop once the plants have fully matured.

RL RDW				
Age(days)	H	S	H	S
25	29.5	27.9	0.502	1.378
37	36.8	33.5	1.041	2.653
40	45.7	43.3	1.69	2.792

RL: Root length, RDW: Root Dry Weight.

Transpiration Rates

Furthermore, the plants cultivated by hydroponics had a higher growth rate compared to those grown using traditional soil-based methods. These findings indicate that plants cultivated in a hydroponic system exhibited a higher capacity for absorbing moisture from the solution.

Photosynthesis Rate

The hydroponically cultivated plants exhibited higher net photosynthetic rates compared to the ones grown in soil. The utilization of solar energy by plants and the carbon dioxide stomatal conductance of their leaves are only two instances of the numerous elements that impact the rate of photosynthesis.

CONCLUSION

Hydroponics is a highly efficient method of cultivating crops that surpass traditional soil-based agriculture, albeit requiring expert labor and meticulous attention to detail. Compared to soil culture, it provides a more precise measure of crop production. The utilization of hydroponics systems has had a substantial impact on the economy and the agricultural sector, mostly due to the cash generated from exports and local sales. Effective water management in hydroponics prevents waterlogging and protects plants from fungal damage. Hydroponically grown plants produce larger fruits and maintain a good harvest quality. This innovative watering technique considerably conserves the water utilized by the plants. Through the implementation of this irrigation strategy, farmers are able to effectively recycle the water they utilize during the agricultural process rather than squandering it on leaching and field moisture. Hydroponics minimizes water usage, electricity consumption, and CO_2 emissions.

REFERENCES

[1]   R.O. Lasisi, "Cybersecurity Workforce Readiness Recommender System Using NLP", *Proceedings of the Future Technologies Conference*, pp. 597-610, 2023.
[http://dx.doi.org/10.1007/978-3-031-47451-4_43]

[2]   S.P. Yadav, S. Zaidi, C.D.S. Nascimento, V.H.C. de Albuquerque, and S.S. Chauhan, "Analysis and Design of automatically generating for GPS Based Moving Object Tracking System", *International Conference on Artificial Intelligence and Smart Communication (AISC)*, pp. 1-5, 2023.
[http://dx.doi.org/10.1109/AISC56616.2023.10085180]

[3]   T. Thamaraimanalan, M. Mohankumar, S. Dhanasekaran, and H. Anandakumar, "Experimental analysis of intelligent vehicle monitoring system using Internet of Things (IoT)", *EAI Endorsed Transactions on Energy Web*, vol. 8, no. 36, 2021.

[4]   S.P. Yadav, and S. Yadav, "Fusion of Medical Images using a Wavelet Methodology: A Survey", *Transactions on Smart Processing & Computing*, vol. 8, no. 4, pp. 265-271, 2019.
[http://dx.doi.org/10.5573/IEIESPC.2019.8.4.265]

[5]   X. Xue, R. Shanmugam, S. Palanisamy, O.I. Khalaf, D. Selvaraj, and G.M. Abdulsahib, "A hybrid cross layer with harris-hawk-optimization-based efficient routing for wireless sensor networks", *Symmetry (Basel)*, vol. 15, no. 2, p. 438, 2023.
[http://dx.doi.org/10.3390/sym15020438]

[6]   S.P. Yadav, and S. Yadav, "Fusion of Medical Images in Wavelet Domain: A Discrete Mathematical Model", *Ingeniería Solidaria*, vol. 14, no. 25, pp. 1-11, 2018.
[http://dx.doi.org/10.16925/.v14i0.2236]

[7]   V. Kumar, A.K. Gupta, R.R. Garg, N. Kumar, and R. Kumar, "The ultimate recommendation system: proposed Pranik System", *Multimedia Tools Appl.*, vol. 83, no. 14, pp. 43177-43198, 2023.
[http://dx.doi.org/10.1007/s11042-023-17370-x]

[8]   S. P. Yadav, and S. Yadav, "Mathematical implementation of fusion of medical images in continuous wavelet domain", *Journal of Advanced Research in dynamical and control system*, vol. 10, no. 10, pp. 45-54, 2019.

[9]   C.Z. Tsai, H. Huang, C.J. Wei, and M.C. Chiu, "Apply Deep Learning to Build a Personalized Attraction Recommendation System in a Smart Product Service System", *Leveraging Transdisciplinary Engineering in a Changing and Connected World.*, pp. 151-160, 2023.

[http://dx.doi.org/10.3233/ATDE230607]

[10] R. Ramakrishnan, M. A. Mohammed, M. A. Mohammed, V. A. Mohammed, and J. Logeshwaran, "An innovation prediction of DNA damage of melanoma skin cancer patients using deep learning", *14th International Conference on Computing Communication and Networking Technologies (ICCCNT),* pp. 1-7, 2023.
[http://dx.doi.org/10.1109/ICCCNT56998.2023.10306749]

[11] V. Sethi, R. Kumar, S. Mehla, A.B. Gandhi, S. Nagpal, and S. Rana, "LCNA-LSTM CNN based attention model for recommendation system to improve marketing strategies on e-commerce", *Journal of Autonomous Intelligence,* vol. 7, no. 1, 2023.
[http://dx.doi.org/10.32629/jai.v7i1.972]

[12] M. A. Mohammed, V. A. Mohammed, R. Ramakrishnan, M. A. Mohammed, and J. Logeshwaran, "The three dimensional dosimetry imaging for automated eye cancer classification using transfer learning model", *14th International Conference on Computing Communication and Networking Technologies (ICCCNT),* pp. 1-6, 2023.
[http://dx.doi.org/10.1109/ICCCNT56998.2023.10307446]

[13] C.M. Tang, Y.G. Zhao, and X. Yu, "Intelligent stock recommendation system based on generalized financial knowledge graph", *Third International Conference on Intelligent Computing and Human-Computer Interaction (ICHCI 2022),* vol. 12509, pp. 332-338, 2023.
[http://dx.doi.org/10.1117/12.2655851]

[14] K.R.K. Yesodha, A. Jagadeesan, and J. Logeshwaran, "IoT applications in Modern Supply Chains: Enhancing Efficiency and Product Quality", *2nd International Conference on Industrial Electronics: Developments & Applications (ICIDeA),* pp. 366-37, 2023.
[http://dx.doi.org/10.1109/ICIDeA59866.2023.10295273]

[15] J. Lee, E. Na, K. Han, and D. Na, "Recommending K-Wave Items Tailored for Small-Sized Exporters by Incorporating Dense and Sparse Vectors", *Sustainability (Basel),* vol. 15, no. 22, p. 16098, 2023.
[http://dx.doi.org/10.3390/su152216098]

[16] V.A.K. Gorantla, S.K. Sriramulugari, A.H. Mewada, and J. Logeshwaran, "An intelligent optimization framework to predict the vulnerable range of tumor cells using Internet of things", *2nd International Conference on Industrial Electronics: Developments & Applications (ICIDeA),* pp. 359-365, 2023.
[http://dx.doi.org/10.1109/ICIDeA59866.2023.10295269]

[17] N. Wijerathne, J. Samarathunge, K. Rathnayake, S. Jayasinghe, S. Ahangama, and I. Perera, "Deep Learning Based Personalized Stock Recommender System", *International Conference on Neural Information Processing,* pp. 362 374, 2023. Singapore.

[18] S. Salagrama, "An Effective Design of Model for Information Security Requirement Assessment", *Int. J. Adv. Comput. Sci. Appl.,* vol. 12, no. 10, 2021.
[http://dx.doi.org/10.14569/IJACSA.2021.0121001]

[19] S. Salagrama, Y.S. Boyapati, and V. Bibhu, "Security and Privacy of Critical Data in Ad Hoc Network Deployed Over Running Vehicles", *3rd International Conference on Intelligent Engineering and Management (ICIEM),* pp. 411-414, 2022.
[http://dx.doi.org/10.1109/ICIEM54221.2022.9853172]

[20] Available from: https://www.kaggle.com/datasets/shree1992/housedata

Emerging Trends in Computation Intelligence, Vol. 3, 2025, 375-385   375

An Augmentation in Energy Efficiency for Grid-Coupled PV System by IT3FLC Controller-Based MPPT

Adarsh Kumar[1,*], **Raj Gopal Mishra**[1], **Sumit Kumar**[1] and **Omkar Singh Kardam**[1]

[1] *Hi-Tech Institute of Engineering and Technology, Ghaziabad, Uttar pradesh, India*

Abstract: Photovoltaic arrays can achieve their maximum power point (MPP) under any circumstances through the utilization of a technique called maximum power point tracking (MPPT). Field-Programmable Logic Controllers (FLCs), such as IT1FLC, IT2FLC, and IT3FLC, offer the most efficient means of monitoring Maximum PowerPoint Tracking (MPPT). The research introduces a novel T3FL near method that enhances tracking accuracy and speed by addressing the ambiguity caused by instabilities. The suggested system consists of a photovoltaic module, a battery, a resistive load, and a maximum power point tracking (MPPT)-controlled buck converter. To ensure that the photovoltaic (PV) system performs at its maximum power point (MPP), the buck converter is directly linked to the solar panel. This connection is designed to align with the output pulse width of the recommended controller. The IT3FLC algorithm maximizes the output of solar panels to reduce battery degradation caused by fluctuating MPPT voltage and extend battery lifespan. The total power and voltage of IT3FLC are equivalent to the present IT1FLC and IT2FLC of the battery and load, respectively. The suggested various methodologies for assessing the MPPT efficiency were implemented by conducting simulated research and practical tests on a solar module and a buck converter. The techniques are implemented using MATLAB Simulink. All three weather conditions - homogeneous light, rapid shift, and partial shade - are accurately reproduced. The modeling and experiments confirm that the IT3FLC ensures precise maximum power, strong stability, and reliable performance despite uncertainties caused by disruptions to the inputs of the photovoltaic system.

Keywords: IT1FLC, IT2FLC, IT3FLC, Maximum power point tracking, Power point coupling.

---

* **Corresponding author Adarsh Kumar:** Hi-Tech Institute of Engineering and Technology, Ghaziabad, Uttar pradesh, India; E-mail: adarshk91@gmail.com

Pankaj Kumar Mishra & Satya Prakash Yadav (Eds.)

INTRODUCTION

The primary objective of this research is to develop a grid-integrated photovoltaic (PV) system with exceptional efficiency. This paper proposes a Maximum Power Point Tracking (MPPT) system based on Interval Type-3 Fuzzy Logic Control (IT3FLC). The MPPT approach based on IT3FLC operates with high efficiency and yields superior results in situations where the intensity of sunlight fluctuates [1 - 3]. The simulation investigation is conducted using a software named MATLAB/SIMULINK. To mitigate harmonic currents and compensate for reactive power generated by nonlinear loads, the proposed system incorporates photovoltaic electricity into the grid through the use of an Active Power Filter (APF). We utilize a boost converter equipped with a frequency-locking mechanism to inject solar electricity into the grid [4 - 6]. The complete system is constructed and designed using MATLAB/Simulink software. The primary objective of this research is to develop a grid-integrated photovoltaic (PV) system that is exceptionally efficient. This work introduces a Maximum Power Point Tracking (MPPT) method that utilizes an Interval Type-3 Fuzzy Logic Controller (IT3FLC) [1]. The IT3FLC-based MPPT algorithm exhibits rapid response and yields superior results in scenarios with fluctuating solar irradiance. The simulation investigation is conducted using a software named MATLAB/SIMULINK. The simulation results validate the effectiveness of the grid-connected system utilizing Active Power Filter (APF) technology. The results demonstrate that the proposed algorithm is superior in locating the maximum power point tracking (MPPT) compared to conventional strategies such as perturb and observe [7 - 9]. This performance is being compared to the projected IT3FLC-based MPPT system, which is constructed based on rapidly fluctuating radiation. This article explores the use of Solar PV systems to assist IT3FLC in addressing concerns related to the membership functions of IT2FLC. The IT3FLC technique is utilized to improve power quality in PV power system, considering the presence of a collection of indistinct regulations that may encompass many models (equations) [10 - 12].

RELATED WORKS

Through a number of related studies (Fig. **3**), the suggested method by IT3FLC controller-based MPPT for an increase in energy efficiency for grid-coupled PV systems was examined and assessed. To enhance the maximum power point tracking technique (MPPT) for photovoltaic systems, numerous studies have been carried out. Fuzzy logic control (FLC) and other fuzzy logic-based MPPT controllers were introduced in this respect [13]. Fuzzy logic controllers increase energy efficiency by monitoring the photovoltaic system's highest power point. PV systems connected in series and shunt have both employed these controllers

[14]. Additionally, to increase the energy efficiency of PV systems, oscillation-less incremental conductance-based MPPT algorithms like incremental conductance (IC) have been proposed. Algorithms like genetic algorithms and bee algorithm-based MPPT for wind power PV systems have been used in other publications [15]. Tests have been conducted on several PV system types, including single- and double-diode models. They have raised these systems' energy efficiency. Furthermore, a number of artificial intelligence (AI)-based strategies, including fuzzy neural networks (FNNs) and artificial neural networks (ANNs), have been put forth to increase the energy efficiency of PV systems. These methods have shown to be quite successful in locating the PV system's MPPT point. Furthermore, some studies have employed sophisticated control techniques to raise PV systems' energy efficiency [16, 17]. Model predictive control, particle swarm optimization, linear programming, and proportional integral derivative (PID) controllers are some of these techniques. Excellent outcomes have been obtained by applying these principles to a variety of PV applications, including stand-alone and grid-connected systems [18, 19]. To put it briefly, the related works regarding An Augmentation in Energy Efficiency for Grid-Coupled PV System by IT3FLC Controller-Based MPPT include a number of studies that explore how to increase the energy efficiency of PV systems using advanced control strategies like linear programming, particle swarm optimization, model predictive control, and PID controllers, as well as AI-based approaches and fuzzy logic-based and other optimization algorithms [20].

PHOTOVOLTAIC ENERGY SYSTEM

The photovoltaic system is expected to significantly contribute to meeting global energy demands. Photovoltaic systems in power systems can be categorized into two basic application types: on-grid or grid-connected applications and off-grid or stand-alone applications. There has been a rise in the adoption of solar systems in medium-sized grids for residential utilities. The Maximum Power Point Tracking (MPPT) technique can enhance the efficiency of solar systems. Controllers should regulate both the voltage and current produced by the PV array. The setup of the PV system may be complicated by the high risk of failure in tracking maximum power during unexpected weather conditions. When the distributed generation (DG) systems, which rely on PV systems, have a breakdown and are no longer connected to the utility grid, they might still provide power to neighboring loads. In addition, a converter can be employed to adjust the output voltage of a photovoltaic system. Nonlinear loads are the primary sources of harmonic distortion in a power distribution system, and the fuzzy logic controller is employed as a dependable regulator for maximum power point tracking (MPPT). Power distribution networks receive harmonic currents generated by nonlinear components through the point of common coupling.

PV ARRAY MODEL

Real operational conditions rarely align precisely with the standard, and variations might also influence the actual values of specific meat parameters. Fig. (1) shows the simulation model of the PV array.

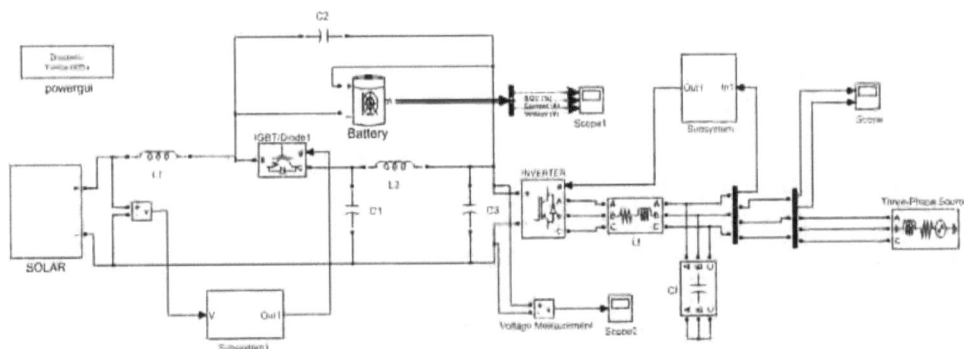

Fig. (1). A simulation model of the PV array.

The IT3FLC reference model takes into account the inputs of operating temperature and irradiance level. The IT3FLC reference model offers an exact value for the maximum power output of a photovoltaic (PV) module under specific temperature and irradiation conditions. The real output power of the PV component is derived by applying a multiplication algorithm to the observed operating voltage and currents, taking into account the temperature and solar irradiation. The process of generating control signals involves comparing two power values and feeding the error to a proportional-integral (PI) controller. The IGBT is triggered by the control signal generated by the PI controller in order to initiate its operation. The operational characteristic of the photovoltaic (PV) component is regulated by generating control signals through the duty cycle of the quasi-Z-source inverter. The proposed control system aims to achieve the following objectives:

- Optimization of power output at the maximum power point.
- Consistent electricity output to the grid.

IT3FLC FOR MPPT TRACKING

The UMF and LMF provide firing resources even after the Type-3 FLC terminates the FOU. The FOU refers to the intermediate zone located between the UMF and LMF. Fig. (2) shows the Architecture of Type-3 FLC.

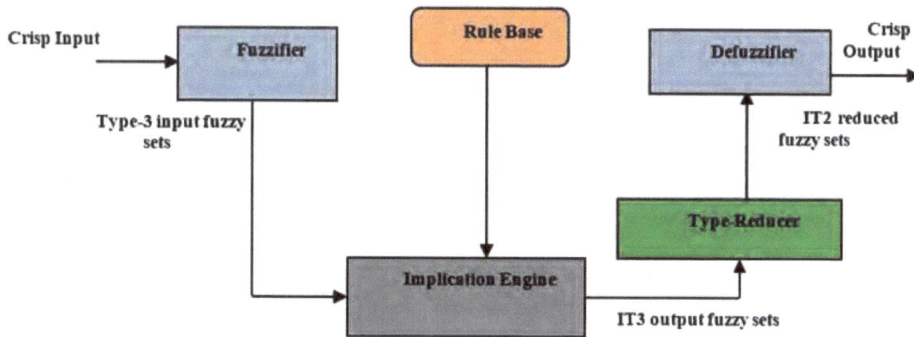

Fig. (2). Architecture of Type-3.

It leads to an extra degree of liberty that enables the elucidation of uncertainty. The utilization of Type-3 FLC fuzzy sets can establish an effective structure for dealing with ambiguity. This study involves the provision of four inputs to IT3FLC. Here the fuzzy set in X is $A\sim$ and the membership valuation is $\mu A (x, u)$.

$$\tilde{A} = \{(x, u), \mu_{\tilde{A}}(x, u)\} \mid \forall x \in X$$

$\tilde{A}$ can also be given as

$$\tilde{A} = \iint \mu_A(x, u)/(x, u)$$

Were, $J_x \subseteq [0,1]$

And signify union over all permissible x and u. For the discrete universe of a dissertation, Φ is substituted by Σ and can be given as

$$\tilde{A} = \{(x, u), \mu_{\tilde{A}}(x, u)\} \mid \forall x \in X$$
$$\tilde{A} = \iint \mu_A(x, u)/(x, u)$$
$$\tilde{A} = \int_{[} \int f_x(u)/u]/x. J_x \subseteq [0,1]$$

If X and J_x are both discrete then

$$\tilde{A} = \sum_{i=1}^{N} [\sum f_{xi}(u)/u]xi$$ is the certainty in the principal members of an

$$U_{x \in X}.J_x$$

Fig. (**3**) shows the Operation of Interval Type 3 FLC.

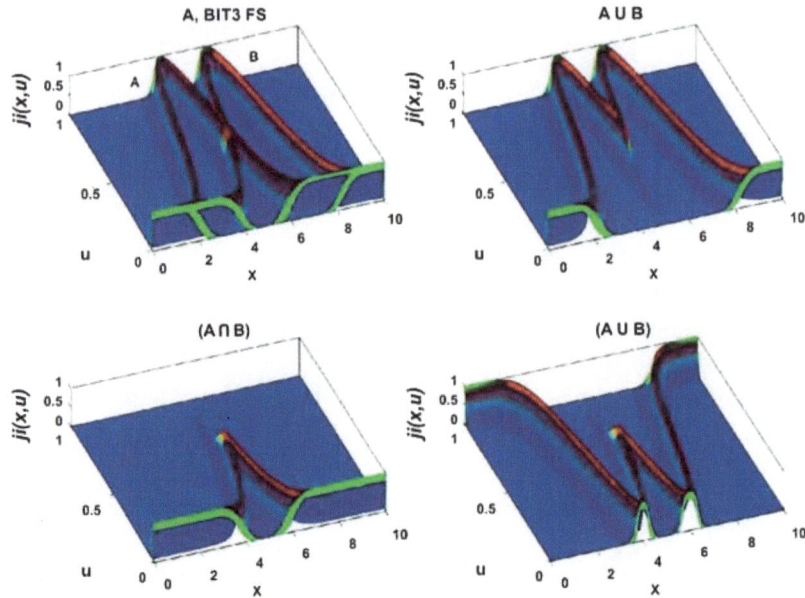

Fig. (3). Operation of Interval Type 3 FLC.

VLN, LN, and MN represent the verbal quantity of the error signal [e(t)]. The notations LN, MN, and LP represent the derivative of the function [de(t)/dt]. The linguistic variables MP, LP, and VLP pertain to the third input variable. Figs. (**4** and **5**) show the MF for [e(t)] and MF for [de(t)/dt].

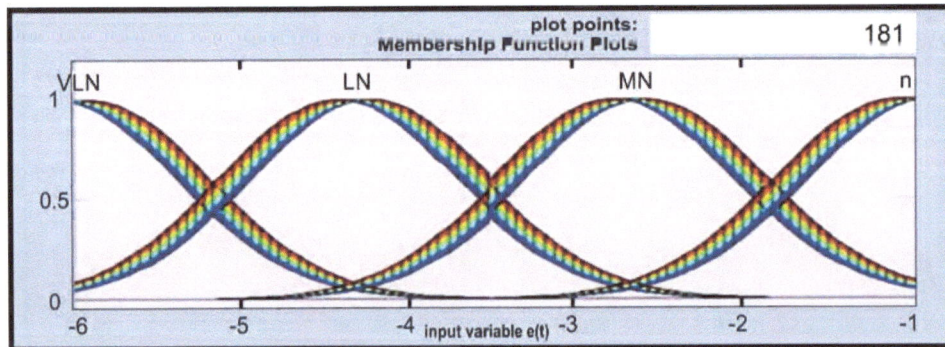

Fig. (4). MF for [e(t)] of the input variables.

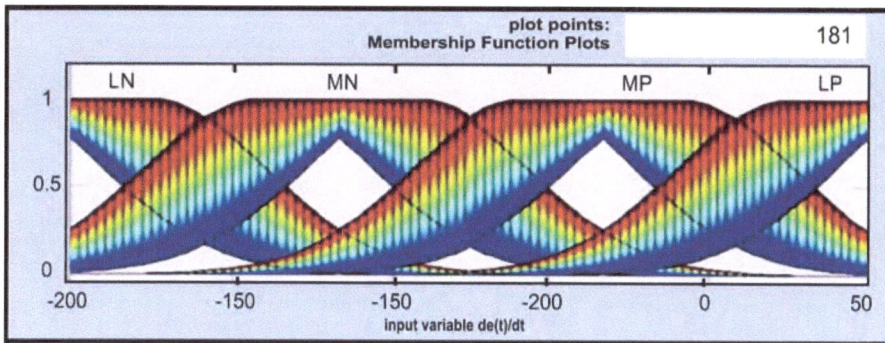

Fig. (5). MF for [de(t)/dt] of the input variables.

Fig. (**6** and **7**) show the MF for third input & 3ϕ grid-connected 100KW.

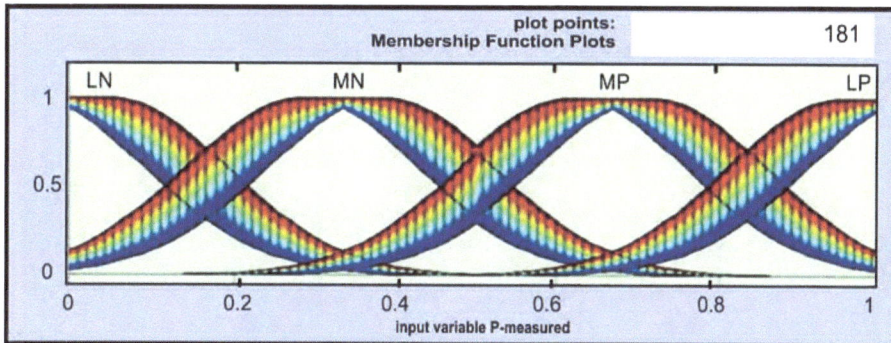

Fig. (6). MF for third input variable of IT3FLC.

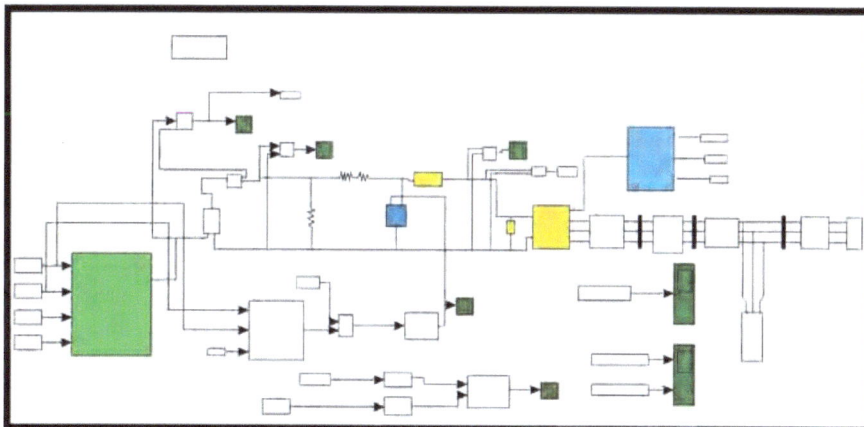

Fig. (7). 3ϕ grid-connected 100KW PV with DC-DC Boost Converter.

RESULTS AND ANALYSIS

Figs. (**8a** and **b**) depict the waveform of the source voltage and current, as well as the harmonic spectrum (THD), after implementing the APF application using IT3FLC.

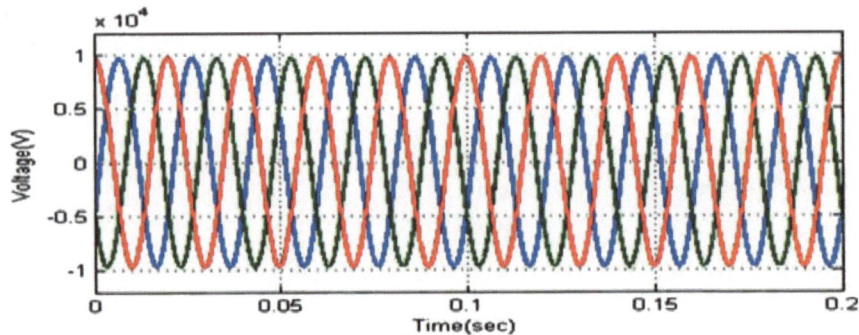

Fig. (8a). Source voltage with APF.

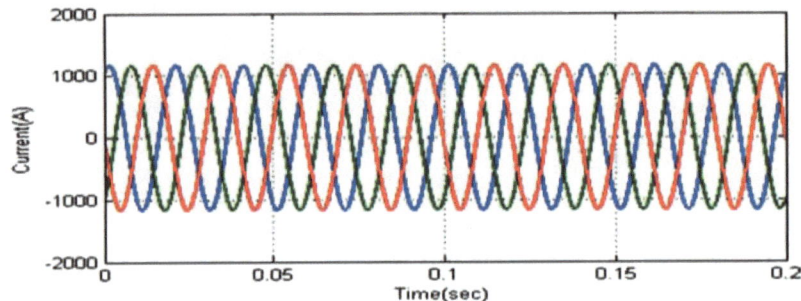

Fig. (8b). Source current with APF.

Figs. (**8a** and **b**) show the APF's and IT3FLC's capacity to account for the load's harmonic current (b). After adopting the IT3FLC, as it is demonstrated in Fig. (**8c**) through FFT analysis, the THD decreased from 31.34% to 3.27%.

CONCLUSION

The inductance of the filter, Lf, has been increased by 50% in order to assess the durability of these controllers. The table labeled as Table **1** displays the DC bus voltage response when using a Type 2 controller and IT3FLC. In recent years, several methods have been employed to maximize the power output of photovoltaic modules in conditions where light irradiation and temperature levels vary. Various factors, such as intermittent solar radiation, cell temperature, PV panel efficiency, and output voltage level, collectively influence the energy generation capacity of a PV system. Therefore, it is imperative to closely observe the power generated by the PV system and maximize the utilization of the acquired solar energy. This study employs an Interval Type-3 Fuzzy Logic Controller (IT3FLC) to install and regulate a photovoltaic (PV) supply connected to the grid. IT2FLC preprocesses the data before utilizing these optimal settings. The results demonstrate that the IT3FLC, in contrast to the traditional method, can effectively meet the load demands while minimizing instability around the MPP and potentially expedite the convergence towards the MPP. A grid-side power quality regulator has also been employed to control the voltage and current of the power line. The PV system is modeled, controlled, and analyzed using the MATLAB/Simulink application.

Table 1. Comparison table for IT3FLC with IT2FLC.

Parameter	IT2FLC	Type – 3 FLC
PV Output Current.	3.5	0.5
PV Output Voltage.	46	79
Injected transformer Voltage (sag).	140V	180V
Injected transformer Voltage (swell).	120V	60V
Power factor.	0.7 lagging	1.0 (unity)
THD	5.032%	0.9103%

REFERENCES

[1] A.M. Attia, M.N. Darghouth, A.M. Ghaithan, and A. Mohammed, "Sizing a grid-connected photovoltaic system under economic and environmental uncertainties", *Sol. Energy,* vol. 265, p. 112123, 2023.
[http://dx.doi.org/10.1016/j.solener.2023.112123]

[2] S. Penagaluru, and K. Sudheer, *Effective PV Source Integration using Dynamic shunt active power filter with Power Quality Augmentation in Three Phase System.,* 2023.
[http://dx.doi.org/10.21203/rs.3.rs-2831772/v1]

[3] J. Zahariah, "Hybrid aquila arithmetic optimization based ANFIS for harmonic mitigation in grid connected solar fed distributed energy systems", *Electr. Power Syst. Res.,* vol. 226, p. 109898, 2024.
[http://dx.doi.org/10.1016/j.epsr.2023.109898]

[4] T. Kunj, and K. Pal, "EVs Owner Benefit Evaluation Through Energy Exchange in the Smart Radial Distribution Network", *Electr. Power Compon. Syst.,* vol. 9, pp. 1-15, 2023.

[5] S. Erasmus, and J. Maritz, "A Carbon Reduction and Waste Heat Utilization Strategy for Generators in Scalable PV—Diesel Generator Campus Microgrids", *Energies,* vol. 16, no. 18, p. 6749, 2023.
[http://dx.doi.org/10.3390/en16186749]

[6] A. Saxena, A. Chandel, A.K. Dash, S.K. Gupta, S. Kumar V, and J.P. Pandey, "An effective optimal economic sustainable clean energy solution with reduced carbon capturing/carbon utilization/carbon

footprint for grid integrated hybrid system", *IEEE Trans. Sustain. Comput.,* vol. 8, no. 3, pp. 385-399, 2023.
[http://dx.doi.org/10.1109/TSUSC.2023.3262982]

[7]   A. Abubakar, R. N. Borkor, and P. Amoako-Yirenkyi, *Stochastic Optimal Harmonic Suppression with Permissible Photovoltaic Penetration Level for Grid-Linked Systems using Monte Carlo-Based Hybrid NSGA2-MOPSO.,* 2023.
[http://dx.doi.org/10.21203/rs.3.rs-3272851/v1]

[8]   R.W. Kenyon, A. Sajadi, M. Bossart, A. Hoke, and B.M. Hodge, "Interactive Power to Frequency Dynamics Between Grid-Forming Inverters and Synchronous Generators in Power Electronics-Dominated Power Systems", *IEEE Syst. J.,* vol. 17, no. 3, pp. 3456-3467, 2023.
[http://dx.doi.org/10.1109/JSYST.2023.3257284]

[9]   S.D. Semone, (2023). Immersed Boundary Modeling of Ratchet Pumps in a Viscoelastic Fluid (Doctoral dissertation, Indiana University of Pennsylvania).

[10] T. Kamal, M. Karabacak, S.Z. Hassan, H. Li, and L.M. Fernández-Ramírez, "A robust online adaptive B-spline MPPT control of three-phase grid-coupled photovoltaic systems under real partial shading condition", *IEEE Trans. Energ. Convers.,* vol. 34, no. 1, pp. 202-210, 2019.
[http://dx.doi.org/10.1109/TEC.2018.2878358]

[11] S. Joshi, G. Bharadwaj, R.S. Chauhan, V.K. Sharma, and J.K. Deegwal, "Augmenting stability and total harmonic distortion reduction in grid coupled wind power generation system", *International Conference for Advancement in Technology (ICONAT),* pp. 1-6, 2022.
[http://dx.doi.org/10.1109/ICONAT53423.2022.9725928]

[12] V. Vashisht, A.K. Pandey, and S.P. Yadav, "Speech Recognition using Machine Learning", *Transactions on Smart Processing & Computing,* vol. 10, no. 3, pp. 233-239, 2021.
[http://dx.doi.org/10.5573/IEIESPC.2021.10.3.233]

[13] S.P. Yadav, B.S. Bhati, D.P. Mahato, and S. Kumar, "Federated Learning for IoT Applications. EAI/Springer Innovations in Communication and Computing", *Springer International Publishing,* 2022.
[http://dx.doi.org/10.1007/978-3-030-85559-8]

[14] J. Kaur, J. Saxena, and J. Shah, "Facial Emotion Recognition. In 2022 International Conference on Computational Intelligence and Sustainable Engineering Solutions (CISES)", *International Conference on Computational Intelligence and Sustainable Engineering Solutions (CISES),* 2022.
[http://dx.doi.org/10.1109/CISES54857.2022.9844366]

[15] H. Yadav, S. Singh, K.K. Mishra, S. Srivastava, M.S. Naruka, and S.P. Yadav, "Brain Tumor Detection with MRI Images", *2022 International Conference on Computational Intelligence and Sustainable Engineering Solutions (CISES),* 2022.
[http://dx.doi.org/10.1109/CISES54857.2022.9844387]

[16] J. Logeshwaran, J.A. Malik, N. Adhikari, S.S. Joshi, and P. Bishnoi, "IoT-TPMS", *Int. J. Health Sci.,* vol. 6, no. S5, pp. 9070-9084, 2022.
[http://dx.doi.org/10.53730/ijhs.v6nS5.10765]

[17] G. Ramesh, V. Aravindarajan, J. Logeshwaran, T. Kiruthiga, and S. Vignesh, "Estimation analysis of paralysis effects for human nervous system by using Neuro fuzzy logic controller", *Neuroquantology,* vol. 20, no. 8, pp. 3195-3206, 2022.

[18] J. Logeshwaran, and T. Kiruthiga, "The Smart Performance Analysis of Network Scheduling Framework for Mobile Systems in Cloud Communication Networks", *International Journal of Research In Science & Engineering,* vol. 2, no. 21, pp. 11-24, 2022.
[http://dx.doi.org/10.55529/ijrise.21.11.24]

[19] N. Kopperundevi, M.K. Janaki, M.B. Pavani, A. Manikandan, P. Mathiyalagan, and D.V. Anand, "Enhancement of Water Submerged Images Using Fusion Technique", *Des. Eng. (Lond.),* pp. 300-308, 2021.

[20]   S. Salagrama, H.H. Kumar, R. Nikitha, G. Prasanna, K. Sharma, and S. Awasthi, "Real time social distance detection using Deep Learning", *2022 International Conference on Computational Intelligence and Sustainable Engineering Solutions (CISES)*, pp. 541-544, 2022. [http://dx.doi.org/10.1109/CISES54857.2022.9844327]

CHAPTER 34

Python in Finance: Introduction and Basic Strategy

Tanu Gupta[1,*], Anupam Singh[1], Anuja Gupta[1] and Somya Goel[1]

[1] *Department of ECE, HI-Tech Institute of Engineering and Technology, Gzb, UPTU, India*

Abstract: Financial/Trading markets in today's digitalized era are being dominated by share markets, options trading, and the forex market. These markets have a huge underlying potential to generate income, but the analysis of these markets regarding the trading of stocks, foreign currencies, *etc.*, is highly dependent on luck. So, to ease the understanding of markets, Python algorithms can be a game-changer. It tends to be received to classify the specific and wanted data that is being covered up in tremendous information. In this paper, we tried to evolve trading algorithms with the help of abstraction, moving averages, and open-source Python-3 libraries, thus making the evaluation and import of data market information more contextually aware and simpler.

Keywords: Algorithms, Averages, Financial, Potential, Underlying.

INTRODUCTION

Python is extensively employed in the domains of machine learning, artificial intelligence, and web software development. Algorithmic Trading is a financial application of Python. This area of academic inquiry is occasionally denoted as Quantitative Trading [1]. This is not novel and has been employed for numerous years in this field. In machine learning, historical data refers to the data that is used to train a system to learn and make predictions based on fresh data. Python is widely used in various fields, like as medicine (for studying and diagnosing diseases), marketing (for analyzing and predicting consumer behavior), and even trading (for evaluating and developing strategies based on financial data) [2, 3]. The primary issue lies in the fact that trade is either reliant on chance or remains undetermined. Currently, financial experts are enrolling in Python trading classes to stay relevant in the finance industry. Gone are the days when computer programmers and finance professionals were in distinct divisions [4]. Only a limited number of research works have demonstrated that algorithmic trading is

---

* **Corresponding author Tanu Gupta:** Department of ECE, HI-Tech Institute of Engineering and Technology, Gzb, UPTU, India; E-mail: hod.ece@hietgroup.org

Pankaj Kumar Mishra & Satya Prakash Yadav (Eds.)

now having a significant impact. In order to cultivate forceful traders in the financial industry, corporations are recruiting computer engineers and providing them with education in finance to become algorithmic traders [5]. Approximately 70% of the order flow on the US stock exchange is attributed to algorithmic trading. In order to shed light on this unexplored domain, we analyzed a set of fundamental techniques and algorithms. This offers several practical benefits, such as its streamlined design [6 - 8].

Why Python?

"Which programming language do we believe is more advantageous for algorithmic traders?"The issue that arises in the mind of every trader is whether Python is the best language for algorithmic trading. The answer to this question is unequivocally, "Yes, Python is the most suitable language for algorithmic trading." Several crucial factors that should be taken into account in this entire process prior to selecting a programming language include cost, performance, resiliency, modularity, and various other strategic characteristics. A scripting language is a programming tool that traders must use to write code. Python is commonly used for prototyping quantitative models, making it highly relevant in the field of inclusive trading. When analyzing financial markets, traders often encounter competing agendas. Python is a highly straightforward and adaptable programming language that enables the rapid development of a minimum viable product (MVP), which is precisely what financial organizations desire in terms of technology that is both flexible and simple. The practicality lies in the process of designing algorithms and formulas, as well as simplifying the rules of Python, particularly in the context of finance. The task of integrating economists into a Python-based framework is quite straightforward to verify. Scipy, NumPy, and matplotlib are Python libraries that enable users to streamline calculations and present results clearly and understandably. On this platform, there is no need to create tools from the beginning; both revenue and time are greatly conserved on these development projects. Fintech products sometimes require collaboration with external parties, a task made simpler by the utilization of Python libraries.

The very attractive uses of this platform in the Fintech services are:

1) Analytics tools - Python is highly valued in the field of quantitative finance. Quantitative finance is a fundamental tool that analyzes and manipulates large quantities of financial data. Pandas, a Python module, simplifies the process of data visualization and enables the execution of complex statistical calculations.

- Libraries such as Scikit or Pybrain facilitate this task.
- Software designed specifically for banking purposes.

- Cryptocurrency.
- Developing strategies and methods using Python.

Benefits of Python

The primary emphasis is on precision achieved through clarity. When engaging in real monetary transactions, we require a highly efficient system that any sophisticated individual can easily examine to ensure it is free of any errors or glitches. The user did not provide any text. It greatly facilitates the process of programming and evaluating algorithmic trading systems. The process of transitioning from a basic trading code to a dynamic algorithm can be time-consuming. The user did not provide any text. Python is a more efficient choice for evolving the trading platform while working with C and C++ requires more time and effort. The user did not provide any text. The modifications can be swiftly implemented to the code or data, even within dynamic situations. The task of debugging, which involves identifying and fixing errors in code, is made possible in Python. The user did not provide any text. Although it may appear to be a basic bot, it can explore advanced techniques such as neural networks. Python is the most comprehensive language for implementing these techniques. Additionally, it can perform tasks such as counting Github commits for a cryptocurrency or scanning Twitter for mentions. This platform allows for efficient execution of these tasks with minimal code required. The user did not provide any text. Python is replete with extensive libraries, making it highly convenient for users to write code in just a few lines. The user did not provide any text. While certain steps can be omitted in Python, they are essential for a quantitative trader to input in C or C++. We may enhance the functionality of Python by implementing modifications or integrating new modules, which sets it apart from other programming languages. The user did not provide any text. The extensive array of libraries enables algorithmic traders to conduct data analysis with execution speeds equivalent to compiled languages such as C or C++. The user's text consists of two references.

RELATED WORKS

Python's ease of use and potent capabilities make it one of the most widely used programming languages worldwide. It is extensively utilized in data analysis and web creation, and its use in the banking sector is mounting. Python's broad scientific library and massive data set handling capabilities make it a great choice for the banking industry [9]. Applications can be created at many different levels, from basic trading algorithms to complex applications. Numerous projects and packages are included in the related work in this sector [10, 11]. Time series analysis, asset pricing, and financial engineering modules are all included in the

Quant Platform architecture. It is developed in Python and works with Zipline, a well-known backtesting package. A Pythonic algorithmic trading library built for handling big datasets is called Zipline. It is employed in trading strategy execution and backtesting [12, 13]. Large volumes of data may be analyzed, processed, and altered with the help of other libraries like pandas, NumPy, and SciPy, which can then be utilized to create trading strategies. A good place to look for and install packages pertaining to finance is the Python Package Index (PyPI) [14 - 16]. Frameworks for putting financial trading methods into practice are available from projects like PyAlgoTrade, Pyfolio, and Pybacktest. In addition to offering access to market data, other projects like FXCM-Python, Pandas-data reader, and pypf also offer higher-level features like portfolio optimization [17 - 19]. Finally, real-time data access and customized development settings are provided *via* automated trading platforms like Quantopian, Interactive Brokers, and QuantStart.

LITERATURE REVIEW

A deep neural network is a type of artificial neural network characterized by its architecture, which includes a larger number of hidden layers and neurons compared to conventional neural networks. The greater number of concealed layers demonstrates the enhanced capability of extracting prominent features at each new hidden layer. Therefore, there is no need to preprocess the raw data using feature extraction techniques when compared to traditional neural networks. A neural network determines the nonlinear connection between two factors, hl and hl+1, through a network work, which commonly has the structure.

hl+1 = δ(W hl + b),

where δ is called an activation function, and the matrix W and vector b are model parameters.

METHODOLOGY & IMPLEMENTATION

Famous Libraries in Python for Algorithmic Trading

Libraries are collections of reusable code or resources that may be directly utilized in any code to perform a given function without the need to write code for that function. Various functionalities like as registration, artificial intelligence, perception, and others necessitate the use of Python, which has an extensive collection of libraries. In this discussion, we will focus on the essential libraries that are vital for implementing coding exchange approaches prior to starting with Python.

We will play a vital role in:

- Importing financial data.
- Conducting backtesting on the data.
- Creating graphs.
- Developing trading strategies and.
- Performing numerical analysis.

Finmarketpy

It is a Python package that allows us to backtest trading strategies and analyze market data using the Application Program Interface (API).

The library offers a range of tactics, including pre-designed templates for backtesting trading methods.

- Trading tactics exhibit historical returns.
- In order to enhance code reusability, it is written using an Object-Oriented approach.
- When employing volatility targeting for rich weighting, there is a built-in calculator.
- It conducts market event research for data events.
- It has examined seasonality in trading strategies.

Formerly, PyThalesians was an open-source finance library. The two libraries, inMarket and the one in question were highly similar. As a result, they have now merged in order to concentrate on maintaining a single set of libraries. So now finmarket library has many of the advantages that are listed below:

a) By modifying a single keyword, the output can be visualized using any of the keywords available in Chartpy, such as matplotlib, plotly, or bokeh. b) Market data can be obtained from Bloomberg, Quandl, and Yahoo (Fig. **1a, b, c, d**).

- Contributors can simplify the process by dividing it into smaller, more specialized libraries (Fig. **2**).
- Chartpy and findatapy are designed to fulfil the requirements of the inMarket library.
- The API rewrite included numerous new capabilities and significantly improved the cleanliness and usability of the system.

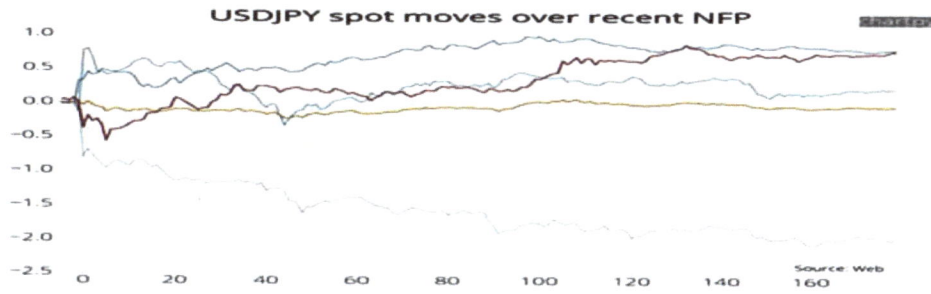

Fig. (1a). USDJPY spot Moves over recent NFP.

Calculate the cumulative returns of a trading strategy historically

Fig. (1b). FX Trend.

Calculate seasonality of any asset: here we show gold and FX volatility seasonality

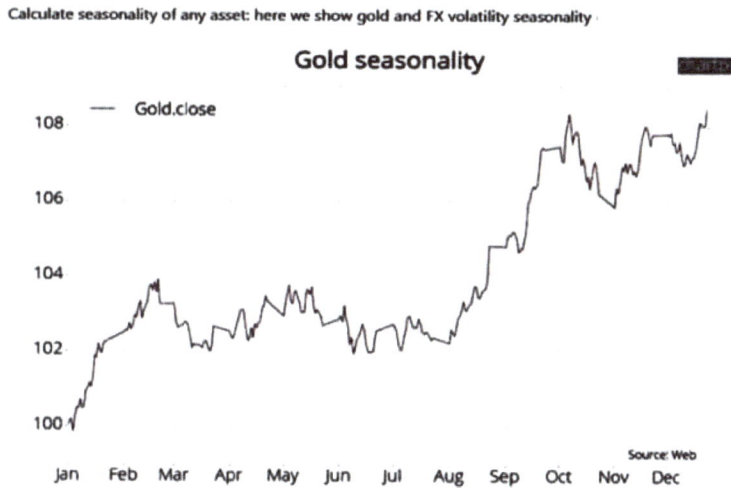

Fig. (1c). Gold Seasonality..

Fig. (1d). FX Vol Seasonality.

```
chart = Chart(df=df, chart_type='line', style=style)

# we now plot using multiple plotting libraries, with the same dataframe
chart.plot(engine='matplotlib')
chart.plot(engine='bokeh')
chart.plot(engine='plotly')
```

Fig. (2). Using Chart library to plot using multiple plotting libraries with the same data frame..

Chartpy

Plotly, Bokeh and Matplotlib are excellent Python libraries that Chartpy can utilize to produce a user-friendly application program interface with a cohesive interface. In order to switch to a different chart engine without having to familiarize oneself with the intricate workings of each library, it is necessary to modify a single term. Additionally, it guarantees that the default matplotlib presentation has a more Western appearance by utilizing the 'open sans' font. The Chartpy library exhibits comparable capabilities to the chart component of the pythalesians finance library (Fig. **3a, b**).

The several types of plots which chartpy can present are as follows:

- Line (matplotlib, plotly and bokeh).
- Map plots (plotly).
- Heatmap (plotly&matplotlib).
- Bar horizontal (plotly&Matplotlib).
- Surface (plotly).

- Scatter (matplotlib&plotly&bokeh).
- Bar (matplotlib&plotly&bokeh).

Create subplots with minimal extra coding

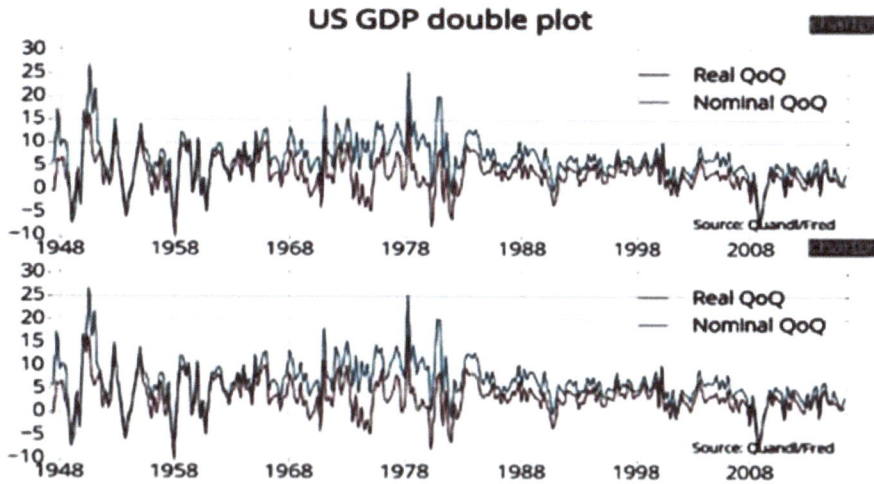

Fig. (3a). US GDP double plot.

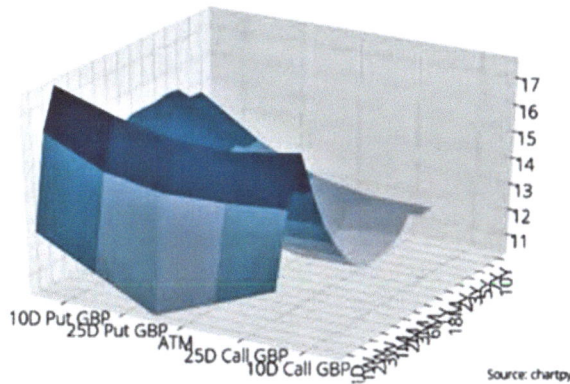

Fig. (3b). GBP/USD vol surface.

VISPY

Vispy offers robust functionality for creating line charts and also enables GPU-accelerated plotting in Python. The present wrapper cannot make charts utilizing date data. By employing the wispy wrapper to graph a large number of points, a substantial improvement in speed can be attained [9].

Findatapy

To retrieve market data from several sources using Python, Application Programming Interface (API) Platforms such as Bloomberg, Yahoo, and Google, along with the findatapy tool, facilitate convenience. Configuration files allow users to define their unique tickers. Individuals seeking to acquire FX market data might utilize a specific function available in this library. An example is given as follows:

```
from findatapy.market import Market, MarketDataRequest, MarketDataGenerator

market = Market(market_data_generator=MarketDataGenerator())

md_request = MarketDataRequest(start_date='year', category='fx', data_source='quandl', tickers=['AUDJPY'])

df = market.fetch_market(md_request)
print(df.tail(n=10))
```

Fig. (4). Using findatapy to fetch data and print it with n=10.

This library can function independently as a standalone program, regardless of whether you are utilizing market data analysis or backtesting [8].

Numpy

It is commonly referred to as numerics and is mostly used for doing numerical computations on arrays of data. By employing the Numpy function, we may perform various operations on an array, which is a data structure that holds a collection of elements [17].

Pandas

Usually, the data is entered into a data frame, which is structured in a tabular format similar to a plain or an Excel sheet. The data is gathered and arranged in a tabular manner with rows and columns. The Panda's package can be employed to transport data from Excel sheets and CSV documents to Python programs. It is an invaluable tool for the study and manipulation of data, especially when dealing with tabular data.

CONCLUSION

Python is the most preferred programming language for learning and real-world programming, as we have already stated. The article has examined the attributes, advantages, repositories, and foundational knowledge required for individuals pursuing a career as a quantitative trader or engaging in algorithmic trading. Based on these characteristics, we observed that Python is a fast, remarkable, efficient, straightforward, open-source programming language that supports many technologies, such as artificial intelligence. Diverse types of projects that can be created using Python were evaluated, and all of them were successful. The study has discussed simple algorithmic approaches such as Moving Averages and Moving Average Convergence. The divergence and utilization of these approaches, along with their corresponding outcomes, have been discussed previously. A brief explanation of libraries such as inMarket, chatty, and Findlay is given, highlighting their distinct features and functionalities. The simplicity and evolution of the Python programming language are supported by reputable journals, blogs, and websites that we have consulted.

REFERENCES

[1]   J.O. Holman, and A. Hacherl, "Teaching Monte Carlo Simulation with Python", *Journal of Statistics and Data Science Education,* vol. 31, no. 1, pp. 33-44, 2023.
[http://dx.doi.org/10.1080/26939169.2022.2111008]

[2]   M. Basanisi, and R. Torresetti, "An overview of technical analysis in systematic trading strategies returns and a novel systematic strategy yielding positive significant returns. Journal of Contemporary Research in Business", *Economics and Finance,* vol. 5, no. 1, pp. 12-24, 2023.

[3]   X.Y. Liu, G. Wang, and D. Zha, (2023). Fingpt: Democratizing internet-scale data for financial large language models. arXiv preprint arXiv:2307.10485.

[4]   D. Cliff, Co-Evolution Causes Instability: Differential Evolution of ZIP Automated Traders in a Simulated Financial Market. Available at SSRN.
[http://dx.doi.org/10.2139/ssrn.4480814]

[5]   H. Li, "The Construction of Internal Tax Audit System of Private Enterprises Based on Python", *Proceedings of the 2nd International Conference on Big Data Economy and Digital Management, BDEDM,* 2023.
[http://dx.doi.org/10.4108/eai.6-1-2023.2330318]

[6]   M. Sipper, T. Halperin, I. Tzruia, and A. Elyasaf, "EC-KitY: Evolutionary computation tool kit in Python with seamless machine learning integration", *SoftwareX,* vol. 22, p. 101381, 2023.
[http://dx.doi.org/10.1016/j.softx.2023.101381]

[7]   D. Krause, "Accessing Financial Data for Regulation A Form 1-A Filings in EDGAR Using Python", *SSRN,* p. 4458284, 2023.
[http://dx.doi.org/10.2139/ssrn.4458284]

[8]   D.G. Balreira, T.L.T. Silveira, and J.A. Wickboldt, "Investigating the impact of adopting Python and C languages for introductory engineering programming courses", *Comput. Appl. Eng. Educ.,* vol. 31, no. 1, pp. 47-62, 2023.
[http://dx.doi.org/10.1002/cae.22570]

[9]   P.G. LeFloch, and J.M. Mercier, "A class of mesh-free algorithms for some problems arising in

finance and machine learning", *J. Sci. Comput.,* vol. 95, no. 3, p. 75, 2023.
[http://dx.doi.org/10.1007/s10915-023-02179-5]

[10]   Y.J.N. Ngoyi, and E. Ngongang, "ForexDaytrading Strategy: An Application of the Gaussian Mixture Model to Marginalized Currency pairs in Africa", *International Journal of Computer Science and Technology,* vol. 7, no. 3, pp. 149-191, 2023.

[11]   L. Zhang, X. Ding, and B. Yang, "Research on Stock Quantification Strategy of Fund Flow Factor Based on Data Analysis", *Proceedings of the 3rd International Conference on Big Data Economy and Information Management, BDEIM,* 2023.
[http://dx.doi.org/10.4108/eai.2-12-2022.2328750]

[12]   Z. Al-Makhadmeh, and A. Tolba, "Utilizing IoT wearable medical device for heart disease prediction using higher order Boltzmann model: A classification approach", *Measurement,* vol. 147, p. 106815, 2019.
[http://dx.doi.org/10.1016/j.measurement.2019.07.043]

[13]   M. Umer, S. Sadiq, H. Karamti, W. Karamti, R. Majeed, and M. Nappi, "IoT based smart monitoring of patients' with acute heart failure", *Sensors (Basel),* vol. 22, no. 7, p. 2431, 2022.
[http://dx.doi.org/10.3390/s22072431] [PMID: 35408045]

[14]   Y. Pan, M. Fu, B. Cheng, X. Tao, and J. Guo, "Enhanced deep learning assisted convolutional neural network for heart disease prediction on the internet of medical things platform", *IEEE Access,* vol. 8, pp. 189503-189512, 2020.
[http://dx.doi.org/10.1109/ACCESS.2020.3026214]

[15]   S. Salvi, R. Dhar, and S. Karamchandani, "IoT-Based Framework for Real-Time Heart Disease Prediction Using Machine Learning Techniques", *Innovations in Cyber Physical Systems: Select Proceedings of ICICPS 2020,* pp. 485-496, 2021.
[http://dx.doi.org/10.1007/978-981-16-4149-7_43]

[16]   J. B. Awotunde, S. O. Folorunso, A. K. Bhoi, P. O. Adebayo, and M. F. Ijaz, "Disease diagnosis system for IoT-based wearable body sensors with machine learning algorithm", *Hybrid Artificial Intelligence and IoT in Healthcare,* pp. 201-222, 2021.

[17]   G. Ramkumar, J. Seetha, R. Priyadarshini, M. Gopila, and G. Saranya, "IoT-based patient monitoring system for predicting heart disease using deep learning", *Measurement,* vol. 218, p. 113235, 2023.
[http://dx.doi.org/10.1016/j.measurement.2023.113235]

[18]   A.A. Nancy, D. Ravindran, P.M.D. Raj Vincent, K. Srinivasan, and D. Gutierrez Reina, "Iot-clou--based smart healthcare monitoring system for heart disease prediction *via* deep learning", *Electronics (Basel),* vol. 11, no. 15, p. 2292, 2022.
[http://dx.doi.org/10.3390/electronics11152292]

[19]   F. Yasmin, S.M.I. Shah, A. Naeem, S.M. Shujauddin, A. Jabeen, S. Kazmi, S.A. Siddiqui, P. Kumar, S. Salman, S.A. Hassan, C. Dasari, A.S. Choudhry, A. Mustafa, S. Chawla, and H.M. Lak, "Artificial intelligence in the diagnosis and detection of heart failure: the past, present, and future", *Rev. Cardiovasc. Med.,* vol. 22, no. 4, pp. 1095-1113, 2021.
[http://dx.doi.org/10.31083/j.rcm2204121] [PMID: 34957756]

CHAPTER 35

Empowering Sustainability: Leveraging Green Technology to Drive Environmental Responsibility in Organizational Behavior

Himanshi Mittal[1,*], Ashish Diwakar[1], Vipin Kumar Tomer[1] and **Shilpa Chaudhary[1]**

[1] *Hi-Tech Institute of Engineering & Technology, Ghaziabad, (U.P), India*

Abstract: Green technology promotes a different perspective on growth and development, urging firms to collaborate and utilize knowledge and resources to establish and execute sustainable solutions. The objective of this study is to examine the correlation between green technology and organizational practices in order to enhance sustainability. In response to growing environmental concerns, corporations must strive to achieve sustainable growth by efficiently using green technology while fulfilling their environmental duties. Green technology not only has a positive impact on the environment but also fosters creativity and generates novel business prospects. Commonly known as environmental technologies, their objective is to safeguard the environment through the mitigation of pollution, promotion of sustainable consumption, and prevention of natural resource depletion. Incorporating green technology in corporate behavior not only showcases environmental responsibility but also yields many advantages for firms, employees, and society. Implementing sustainable practices can have a beneficial effect on employee morale and productivity, as employees feel a sense of satisfaction in being part of an organization that prioritizes sustainability and actively contributes to a more favorable future. Through the adoption of sustainable practices and the allocation of resources towards environmentally friendly technology, companies may cultivate a more prosperous and resilient future for both themselves and future generations.

Keywords: Environment responsibility, Green technology, Green growth, Green organizational culture, Organization, Sustainability.

INTRODUCTION

The escalating environmental consequences of human activities have emerged as a critical issue for individuals, companies, and governments worldwide in recent

* **Corresponding author Himanshi Mittal:** Hi-Tech Institute of Engineering & Technology, Ghaziabad, (U.P), India; E-mail: himanshimittal8@gmail.com

Pankaj Kumar Mishra & Satya Prakash Yadav (Eds.)
All rights reserved-© 2025 Bentham Science Publishers

years [1]. Consequently, there has been an increasing fascination with creating and embracing eco-friendly technology, which strives to minimize the adverse effects of human actions on the environment. Green technologies refer to a diverse array of sustainable and environmentally friendly goods, systems, and processes that aim to limit energy usage, decrease waste generation, and preserve natural resources [2 - 4]. Adopting green technology is crucial for firms aiming to improve their competitiveness and reputation in a dynamic commercial climate, in addition to addressing environmental concerns. Green technology enables enterprises to diminish their environmental impact, enhance their energy efficiency, and optimize their financial performance by reducing costs and enhancing customer connections [5]. Organizational behavior is a discipline that aims to comprehend the actions and interactions of individuals, groups, and organizations in the workplace and how these actions can be manipulated to accomplish organizational objectives. There has been an increasing focus on incorporating green technology adoption into organizational behavior theory and practice [6 - 8]. The advent of green organizational behavior as a new field of research focuses on the effective implementation and integration of green technologies in organizations to promote sustainability and environmental responsibility. This research aims to examine the idea of green technology and its impact on organizational behavior. We will analyze the advantages and difficulties associated with the adoption of green technology and explore its successful integration into organizational culture, leadership, and employee behaviour [9 - 11]. We aim to enhance comprehension of the impact of green technology on both environmental sustainability and organizational success.

RELATED WORKS

The use of green technology to promote sustainability within organizations is the main topic of the linked works of empowering sustainability: leveraging green technology to drive environmental responsibility in organisational behaviour [12 - 14]. The literature specifically examines the ways in which green technology can be applied to raise environmental consciousness, lessen negative environmental effects, encourage creative green practices, and advance long-term sustainability objectives [15]. A variety of green technologies are covered by the research, such as waste management, green building, renewable energy, energy efficiency, and sustainable manufacturing [16]. The research also examines the ways in which green technology might support organizational actions that promote sustainability, including the implementation of sustainable practices, staff involvement, alteration of customer behavior, and environmental responsibility [17, 18]. Furthermore, scholars evaluate how green technology might serve as a platform for green projects and promote cooperation for social and environmental sustainability. Ultimately, the study delves into the diverse obstacles and prospects that green technology presents in promoting sustainability and offers discernments into optimal approaches for utilizing green technology within establishments [19].

GREEN TECHNOLOGY

The adoption of green technology has been increasing in order to foster sustainability inside enterprises. Companies can decrease their total carbon footprint and make a positive environmental impact by employing sustainable energy sources. Furthermore, technological advancements have facilitated the creation of environmentally sustainable solutions for several sectors. For instance, the use of electric vehicles and hybrid cars can significantly mitigate pollutants and decrease expenses linked to conventional gasoline-powered transportation. The implementation of green technology has significantly revolutionized the promotion of sustainability and environmental responsibility across several industries. Businesses can greatly mitigate their environmental footprint by employing renewable energy sources and adopting eco-conscious measures such as trash reduction and recycling. Furthermore, implementing these steps not only contributes to environmental preservation but also results in financial benefits and enhanced reputation among customers who are progressively prioritizing sustainability. Therefore, it is imperative for firms to persistently investigate and adopt environmentally friendly technology as a strategy to accomplish their sustainability objectives while simultaneously enhancing their financial performance.

LEVERAGING GREEN TECHNOLOGY IN ORGANIZATIONAL BEHAVIOR

Adopting environmentally friendly practices is essential and urgent (Peattie, 1992; Pierre &Prothero, 1997; Growth, 1998). Sustainable manufacturing is the practice of producing goods while minimizing their environmental impact. Utilizing environmentally friendly technologies in organizational behavior can result in substantial enhancements in both employee contentment and overall efficiency. Implementing environmentally conscious measures, such as minimizing paper consumption and adopting energy-efficient technologies, can showcase a company's dedication to ecological stewardship while simultaneously fostering a healthier and more sustainable work environment. Furthermore, research has demonstrated that individuals employed by environmentally conscious firms exhibit elevated levels of job satisfaction and greater levels of engagement in their work. By integrating sustainable technology into organizational behavior initiatives, firms can establish a more favorable and efficient work environment for their employees. In the contemporary era, enterprises are consistently seeking methods to diminish their ecological impact while concurrently augmenting their financial gains. An effective approach to accomplish this is by utilizing environmentally friendly technology in the context of organizational behavior. Companies can enhance their overall efficiency and simultaneously contribute to environmental preservation by adopting eco-friendly technologies and practices. For instance, by employing electronic communication and online conferencing, the necessity for travel is diminished, leading to a decrease in carbon emissions.

RELATIONSHIP BETWEEN GREEN TECHNOLOGY AND ORGANIZATIONAL BEHAVIOR

Fig. (1). Green Technology with Organizational Behavior Promotes Sustainability.

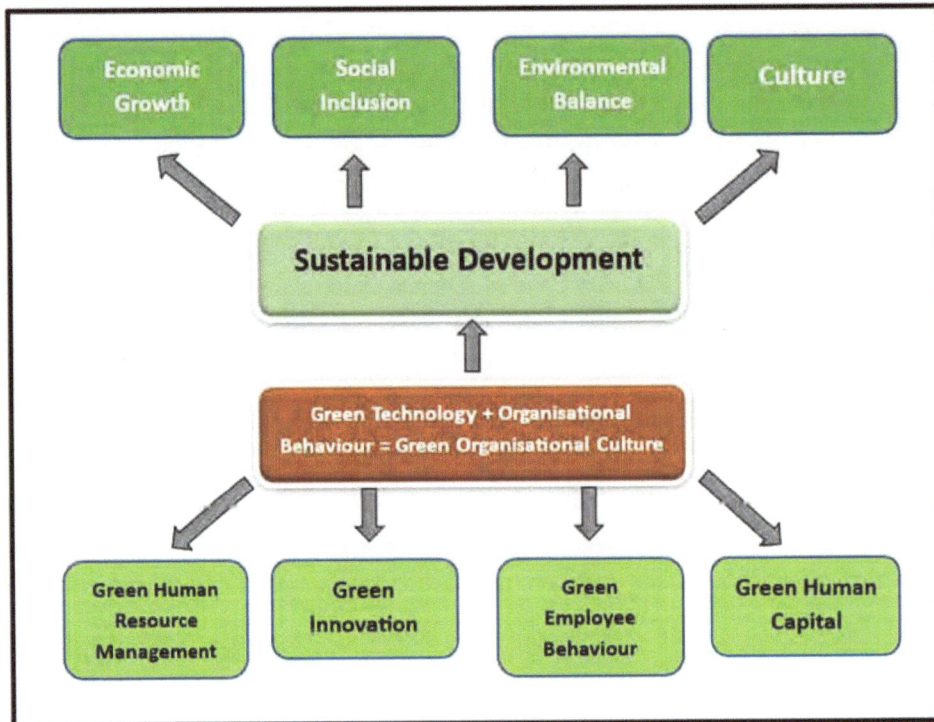

Fig. (1). Shows the green technology.

The connection between these two notions is rooted in the notion that implementing green technology within an organization can impact the behavior of individuals and groups, hence moulding the organizational culture to prioritize environmental awareness.

Encouragement of Eco-friendly Norms

Integrating green technology in a corporation cultivates a collective awareness of environmental accountability among its personnel.

Enhanced Employee Motivation

Green efforts frequently result in heightened employee engagement since people perceive their contributions as helpful for both society and the environment.

Improved Corporate Image

Organizations that implement sustainable technologies can improve their public perception, gaining eco-conscious customers and enhancing their reputation.

Cost Savings

Green technology can enhance cost-effectiveness by improving energy efficiency and adopting sustainable practices.

Strategic Advantage

Companies that embrace environmentally friendly technologies can gain a competitive advantage through market differentiation or by demonstrating more adaptability to environmental restrictions.

OBJECTIVE OF THE RESEARCH

- The objective is to assess the level of knowledge and understanding of Green Technology among employees in private-sector firms.
- The objective is to determine the crucial parameters necessary for implementing different Green Technology practices in private sector firms.

DATA COLLECTION

Data for this study was collected using both primary and secondary sources. A comprehensive study was conducted on 300 employees from 8 private sector businesses. The survey utilized a standardized questionnaire to assess many dimensions of green technology, such as its understanding, adoption of green HR practices, and their efficacy within private sector organizations (Tables **1**, **2**).

Table 1. Sampled organization.

S. No.	Name of the Organization	Industry
1.	Anita Hi Tech Agro Pvt. Ltd.	IT Industry
2.	Aayush Food and Herbs Ltd.	Food Products
3.	HCL Technologies	Business Support Services
4.	Hi-Tech Institute	Educational
5.	Apollo Tricoat Tubes Ltd.	Iron & Steel
6.	Dabur India Ltd.	Food, FMCG
7.	Arden Asia Pacific Software Pvt Ltd.	IT, Data Analytics
8.	Ajay Industrial Corporation Ltd.	Chemical

DATA ANALYSIS AND INTERPRETATION

Table 2. Green technology awareness in organization amongst the respondents.

Response	Number	Percentage
Strongly Disagree	31	11
Disagree	48	16
Neutral	34	11
Agree	129	43
Strongly Agree	58	19
Total	300	100

Inference

According to the findings, 54% of participants demonstrated awareness of the term "Green Technology," suggesting a rising trend in its popularity and a growing familiarity among employees. Fig. (**2**) shows performance evaluation.

Analysis of Effectiveness of Green Technology Practices in Improving Organization Culture

Table 3. Effectiveness of green technology in organizational culture.

Response	Number of Respondents	Percentage
Strongly Disagree	28	9
Disagree	46	15
Neutral	16	5

(Table 3) cont.....

Response	Number of Respondents	Percentage
Agree	175	59
Strongly Agree	35	12
Total	**300**	

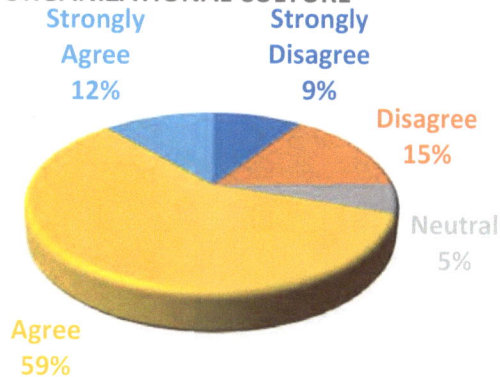

Fig. (2). Performance evaluation.

Inference

Approximately 71% of respondents were found to have a positive impression, perceiving green technology as effective. Conversely, 23% conveyed unfavorable viewpoints regarding its influence on organizational culture.

Factors Why Organizations Need to Adopt Green Technology Practices

Factors	Rank
Saving resources and money.	*IV*
Reduce their carbon footprint.	*I*
Promote sustainability.	*III*
Energy-efficient	*VIII*
Improves the organization's reputation.	*V*
Cost savings	*II*
Encouragement of eco-friendly norms.	*IX*
Investing in low-carbon technologies.	*VI*
The long-term success of organizations.	*VII*

FINDINGS OF THE STUDY

It is intriguing to ascertain that individuals are genuinely acquainted with the notion of "Green Technology." They possess a comprehensive understanding of its concepts and hold a true belief in its efficacy for organizations. Curiously, even individuals who are unfamiliar with the phrase "Green Technology" are aware of the techniques involved and can identify when their firm implements such methods. Although the phrase may be unknown, its methods are well acknowledged. Upon analyzing the input from the respondents, it was found that organizations are effectively implementing Green Technology solutions.

BENEFITS OF GREEN TECHNOLOGY AND CHALLENGES TO OVERCOME

• Aids in recycling and managing waste products.
• Environmentally friendly, producing little or no harmful substances.
• Cost-effective maintenance.
• Contributes to conserving energy.
• Improves the health of our ecosystem.

Upon analysis of the respondents' feedback, it was found that enterprises are effectively implementing Green Technology solutions.

CONCLUSION

Organizations worldwide are increasingly recognizing the significance of environmental stewardship due to the growing understanding of the detrimental effects of human actions on the earth. Green technology facilitates sustainable progress and advancement through the dissemination of information and allocation of resources. This study examines the correlation between green technology and organizational strategies for attaining sustainability. Employing green technology promotes sustainable economic expansion and generates novel entrepreneurial prospects by mitigating pollution and fostering sustainable consumption, thus safeguarding the environment. Organizations that implement green technology demonstrate environmental stewardship and reap the advantages of improved staff morale and productivity resulting from its beneficial effects.

REFERENCES

[1]   Permana, G. E., Wibowo, A. W., Mardiyono, A. N. A. T., Fathul, M., & Lathief, E. S. S. A Recommender system utilizing crowdsourcing for village-owned enterprises' product recommendation. development, 14, 16,

[2]   V. Kumar, A.K. Gupta, R.R. Garg, N. Kumar, and R. Kumar, "The ultimate recommendation system: proposed Pranik System", *Multimedia Tools Appl.,* vol. 83, no. 14, pp. 43177-43198, 2023. [http://dx.doi.org/10.1007/s11042-023-17370-x]

[3]   C.Z. Tsai, H. Huang, C.J. Wei, and M.C. Chiu, "Apply Deep Learning to Build a Personalized Attraction Recommendation System in a Smart Product Service System", *Leveraging Transdisciplinary Engineering in a Changing and Connected World.,* pp. 151-160, 2023. [http://dx.doi.org/10.3233/ATDE230607]

[4]   V. Sethi, R. Kumar, S. Mehla, A.B. Gandhi, S. Nagpal, and S. Rana, "LCNA-LSTM CNN based attention model for recommendation system to improve marketing strategies on e-commerce", *Journal of Autonomous Intelligence,* vol. 7, no. 1, 2023. [http://dx.doi.org/10.32629/jai.v7i1.972]

[5]   J. Lee, E. Na, K. Han, and D. Na, "Recommending K-Wave Items Tailored for Small-Sized Exporters by Incorporating Dense and Sparse Vectors", *Sustainability (Basel),* vol. 15, no. 22, p. 16098, 2023. [http://dx.doi.org/10.3390/su152216098]

[6]   N. Wijerathne, J. Samarathunge, K. Rathnayake, S. Jayasinghe, S. Ahangama, and I. Perera, "Deep Learning Based Personalized Stock Recommender System", *International Conference on Neural Information Processing,* pp. 362-374, 2023.

[7]   C. Jayapal, S. Gokul, and S.V. Harshavardhan, "Book Recommendation System Using Hybrid Filtering", *2nd International Conference on Advancements in Electrical, Electronics, Communication, Computing and Automation (ICAECA),* pp. 1-5, 2023. [http://dx.doi.org/10.1109/ICAECA56562.2023.10199590]

[8]   R.O. Lasisi, "Cybersecurity Workforce Readiness Recommender System Using NLP", *Proceedings of the Future Technologies Conference,* pp. 597-610, 2023. [http://dx.doi.org/10.1007/978-3-031-47451-4_43]

[9]   Y. Song, and Y. He, "Toward an intelligent tourism recommendation system based on artificial intelligence and IoT using Apriori algorithm", *Soft Comput.,* vol. 27, no. 24, pp. 19159-19177, 2023. [http://dx.doi.org/10.1007/s00500-023-09330-2]

[10]   R. Rwedhi, and S. Al-augby, "Improving Collaborative Filter Using BERT", *Journal of Kufa for Mathematics and Computer,* vol. 10, no. 2, pp. 23-29, 2023. [http://dx.doi.org/10.31642/JoKMC/2018/100204]

[11]   A. Iftikhar, M.A. Ghazanfar, M. Ayub, S. Ali Alahmari, N. Qazi, and J. Wall, "A reinforcement learning recommender system using bi-clustering and Markov Decision Process", *Expert Syst. Appl.,* vol. 237, p. 121541, 2024. [http://dx.doi.org/10.1016/j.eswa.2023.121541]

[12]   L. Jing, A.E. Ulloa Cerna, C.W. Good, N.M. Sauers, G. Schneider, D.N. Hartzel, J.B. Leader, H.L. Kirchner, Y. Hu, D.M. Riviello, J.V. Stough, S. Gazes, A. Haggerty, S. Raghunath, B.J. Carry, C.M. Haggerty, and B.K. Fornwalt, "A machine learning approach to management of heart failure populations", *JACC Heart Fail.,* vol. 8, no. 7, pp. 578-587, 2020. [http://dx.doi.org/10.1016/j.jchf.2020.01.012] [PMID: 32387064]

[13]   A. Ishaq, S. Sadiq, M. Umer, S. Ullah, S. Mirjalili, V. Rupapara, and M. Nappi, "Improving the prediction of heart failure patients' survival using SMOTE and effective data mining techniques", *IEEE Access,* vol. 9, pp. 39707-39716, 2021. [http://dx.doi.org/10.1109/ACCESS.2021.3064084]

[14]   A. Rehman, S. Naz, and I. Razzak, "Leveraging big data analytics in healthcare enhancement: trends, challenges and opportunities", *Multimedia Syst.,* vol. 28, no. 4, pp. 1339-1371, 2022. [http://dx.doi.org/10.1007/s00530-020-00736-8]

[15]   N. Liu, F. Xie, F.J. Siddiqui, A.F.W. Ho, B. Chakraborty, G.D. Nadarajan, K.B.K. Tan, and M.E.H. Ong, "Leveraging large-scale electronic health records and interpretable machine learning for clinical decision making at the emergency department: protocol for system development and validation", *JMIR Res. Protoc.,* vol. 11, no. 3, p. e34201, 2022. [http://dx.doi.org/10.2196/34201] [PMID: 35333179]

[16]   D. Zhang, C. Yin, K.M. Hunold, X. Jiang, J.M. Caterino, and P. Zhang, "An interpretable deep-learning model for early prediction of sepsis in the emergency department", *Patterns,* vol. 2, no. 2, p. 100196, 2021.
[http://dx.doi.org/10.1016/j.patter.2020.100196] [PMID: 33659912]

[17]   S. Abirami, and P. Chitra, "Energy-efficient edge based real-time healthcare support system", *Adv. Comput.,* vol. 117, no. 1, pp. 339-368, 2020. [Elsevier].
[http://dx.doi.org/10.1016/bs.adcom.2019.09.007]

[18]   K. Gupta, N. Jiwani, G. Pau, and M. Alibakhshikenari, "A Machine Learning Approach Using Statistical Models for Early Detection of Cardiac Arrest in Newborn Babies in the Cardiac Intensive Care Unit", *IEEE Access,* vol. 11, pp. 60516-60538, 2023.
[http://dx.doi.org/10.1109/ACCESS.2023.3286346]

[19]   M.C. Elish, "The stakes of uncertainty: developing and integrating machine learning in clinical care", *Ethnographic Praxis in Industry Conference Proceedings,* vol. 2018, no. 1, pp. 364-380, 2018.
[http://dx.doi.org/10.1111/1559-8918.2018.01213]

CHAPTER 36

IoT Based on Accident Detection and Alert System

Sheelesh Kumar Sharma[1,*], Avinash Kumar Sharma[1], Srishti Garg[1], Priyansha Singh[1] and Yashaswi[1]

[1] *Department of CSE, ABES Institute of Technology, Ghaziabad, Uttar Pradesh, India*

Abstract: Reducing the fatality rate resulting from vehicle accidents is a significant concern in our society. Delivering prompt and excellent emergency healthcare services poses a difficulty. The response time of emergency personnel to the accident location is significantly prolonged, resulting in an occasional inability to preserve lives. In order to address this scenario, it is imperative to minimize the interval between the occurrence of the accident and the provision of medical services. We have developed a meticulously structured Android application that will be utilized for the purpose of identifying accidents and promptly alerting emergency services. Additionally, it will carry out timely rescue operations. A built-in sensor designed to detect car accidents and transmit the data to the Android Application. The system will promptly notify the user through an alarm regarding the generated accident notification. It will then allow a brief period, known as the buffer time, for the user to cancel any erroneous notifications. If the user fails to cancel, the message will be transmitted by GSM to the nearest hospital and police station, along with the precise position of the accident determined by GPS technology. The execution of this Android application has the potential to preserve the lives of millions of individuals annually.

Keywords: GSM, GPS, Notifications, Onboard smartphone sensor.

INTRODUCTION

Vehicle accidents are the primary source of sickness and impairment. It has become an unfortunate reality in our lives. Contemporary individuals have exhibited a lack of caution in recent times [1]. It is projected that by 2025, the number of fatalities caused by road traffic accidents in India will exceed 250,000 each year. Delivering prompt and exemplary emergency healthcare services is a difficulty. Approximately 25% of deaths are attributed to the lack of access to medical facilities. The growing utilization of automobiles is leading to a rise in traffic congestion and the occurrence of road accidents [2]. The World Health Or-

---

[*] **Corresponding author Sheelesh Kumar Sharma:** Department of CSE, ABES Institute of Technology, Ghaziabad, Uttar Pradesh, India; E-mail: drsksharmagzb@gmail.com

Pankaj Kumar Mishra & Satya Prakash Yadav (Eds.)

ganization's Global Status Report on Road Safety, released in December 2018, reveals that there are 1.35 million fatalities and approximately 50 million injuries caused by vehicle accidents each year. The user's text is "[3]". Motor vehicle accidents are the primary cause of mortality among individuals aged 5 to 29 years. Males in the age group of under 25 years exhibit a higher propensity for becoming engaged in road traffic accidents compared to females. The causes of the accidents include speeding, driving under the influence, driver distractions, disregarding traffic signals, and failure to use safety equipment such as helmets and seat belts [4]. Nevertheless, we have noticed that a contributing factor to mortality is the delayed arrival of emergency personnel at the scene of the accident. The ambulance service delay is caused by ambulances waiting at traffic signals. There is a requirement for an application that can identify and prevent accidents to ensure the safety of individuals [5]. This system has numerous advantages, including cost-effectiveness, convenience of use, portability, quick assistance for rescue teams, reduction in mortality rates, assistance in locating the nearest hospital and police station, and notification of the victim's family members. The prevalence of accidents is higher in rural areas due to the presence of expansive and unobstructed roadways. Consequently, this application will prove to be more beneficial in such areas [6]. By installing this program, death rates can be decreased, and accidents can be detected in all types of vehicles. This application is a real-time tracking system that accurately determines the user's location or the location of an accident. The program aims to minimize the temporal gap between the location of the accident and the provision of medical assistance, hence enabling prompt treatment of the affected individual [7]. This system utilizes an ultrasonic sensor equipped with a geo-distance algorithm to detect accidents in a vehicle [8]. Once the occurrence of an accident is confirmed, the application will activate a buffer time alarm system to determine if the victim requires assistance from emergency responders. If the victim deactivates the alarm, no notification will be sent to the hospital, police station, or relatives [9]. However, if the victim fails to respond within the designated time frame, the application will automatically transmit the precise location of the accident using Global Positioning System (GPS) technology.Additionally, notifications will be sent to the emergency contacts specified during the application's setup, and an alert will be sent to the nearest police station and hospitals [10]. This alert will include the user's details, such as name, blood group, and gender, which will be transmitted through the GSM (Global System for Mobile Communication) module [11]. Through the use of this application, we can effectively address this problem and preserve the lives of countless individuals.

RELATED WORKS

The Internet of Things (IoT) has been increasingly used in many different applications for accident detection and alert systems [12]. Such systems are particularly useful in situations where timely intervention is needed to minimize the risk of injury, property damage, or other consequences associated with an accident [13]. Some of the related works of IoT based on accident detection and alert systems include the use of wearable sensors to monitor health, detect falls, and trigger medical response protocols; the use of drones to monitor hazardous areas for public safety; the use of sensors and wireless communication to detect crash sites and road accidents; and the use of cameras and sensors to detect fires and alert for evacuation. Additionally, many other projects have been proposed to investigate the scalability and reliability of IoT-enabled accident detection and alert systems [14]. These include proposals for distributed vehicle monitoring systems, intelligent sensor networks for monitoring emergency medical situations, and the use of the cloud for further data analysis [15]. Overall, researchers are working toward a better understanding of how IoT can be used for accident prevention and developing efficient systems for the timely detection, analysis, and alerting of accidents. With the help of such improvements, lives may be saved and risks minimized as IoT technologies continue to advance.

LITERATURE SURVEY

The accident detection and alert system will furnish the user's accident location details and expedite the response time of emergency personnel. Prior to commencing this paper, we scrutinized multiple scholars from diverse journals who presented numerous methodologies to mitigate mishaps. The preceding studies and literary contributions of authors are as follows: The paper [4] titled "Accident Detection and Alert App" by Dr. C. K. Gomathy, K Rohan Bandi Mani Kiran Reddy, and Dr. V Geetha discusses the utilization of sensors such as GPS and Accelerometer in mobile phones to detect collisions. This is achieved by employing a Sensor Fusion Based Algorithm that identifies sudden external disturbances in speed. The system comprises hardware and software components. The equipment unit comprises collision detection sensors that are integrated with an Arduino board and installed in the car. Next, the programming component is an Android application implemented on drivers' smartphones that is utilized to obtain a detailed map with step-by-step directions. The paper titled "Vehicle Accident Detection and Alert App" by Dr. E ManohaA. AbilashBerkin, S. Baskar, and R. GanapathyKarthikeyan reports the use of an algorithm that relies on data from an accelerometer sensor to detect and alert about vehicle accidents. The primary objective of this work is to develop an application that utilizes the sensors found in mobile phones, such as GPS and Accelerometer, to identify collisions by detecting abrupt external disruptions in speed through the use of Sensor Fusion technology. This application consists of three primary sections, namely the accident detection module, modules for detecting location and transferring messages An algorithm is used in the system. However, it has a significant drawback: it generates erroneous information when there is a slight disruption, which is annoying. The paper "Automated AI-Based Road Traffic Accident Alert System" by DeekshaGour and AmitKanskar utilizes the YOLO (you look only once) Algorithm for the real-time recognition of different objects in a live feed or image. The suggested system exhibits superior speed compared to previous object recognition methods and demonstrates enhanced object prediction capabilities in comparison to algorithms such as Faster-CNN or Fast CNN. The input can be further tuned to yield superior outcomes. In addition, the system sends notifications to neighboring emergency vehicles through a wireless connection device. This system utilizes Neural Networks and Deep Learning to recognize objects, employing computer vision technologies and various approaches and algorithms. This methodology is applicable to both pre-recorded videos and live-streaming videos. It involves the use of a convolutional neural network to identify, categorize, track, and calculate the speed and direction of moving objects. The paper titled "Accident Detection and Smart Rescue System" by Haider Ali utilizes an Android Smartphone equipped with real-time location tracking. From the perspective of emergency victims, it is often impossible for them to independently contact an ambulance in the event of a fatal accident. In such cases, a specially designed system will automatically detect the accident and promptly send an emergency notification to the closest available emergency responder, with the aim of potentially saving the victim's life. Dispatching an urgent notification is significantly simplified and more efficient due to the consolidation of all necessary functionalities. However, it is inevitable for a smartphone-based accident detection and rescue system to encounter false positives. To mitigate this issue, additional features such as an Acceleration filter and Count timer alert have been incorporated. The paper titled "Accident Detection System Using Intelligent Algorithm for VANET" by SaadMasood Butt presents an intelligent system that consists of a GPS receiver, vibration sensor, and GSM modem, which is then combined with Vehicular AD-Hoc Network (VANET). VANET is a subset of wireless communication networks that focuses on the use of cars as mobile nodes in the network. It is an emerging field that builds upon the concepts of MANETs. The primary objective of VANET is to enhance the safety of road users and the comfort of passengers. The Accident Detection system utilizing VANET ensures the provision of duplicate messages transmission to the Road Side Unit (RSC). VANET utilizes an improved AODV algorithm to determine the most efficient path for transmitting emergency messages.

Table **1** presents a concise analysis of surveys conducted on the current systems.

Table 1. Surveys of the existing systems.

Publication	Algorithm	Strength	Drawback
JOURNAL OFENGINEERING,COMPUTING &ARCHITECTURE.	Accelerometer and Arduino.	Detect any collision if there is a sudden external disturbance in the speed with the help of the Sensor Fusion Based Algorithm.	No GPS signal at the time of the crash and insufficient cellular signal to upload crash details.
IRJET	An algorithm based on an Accelerometer sensor.	With the help of the Sensor Fusion Based Algorithm, it detects any collision if there is a sudden external disturbance in the speed,	False notifications are generated after a little jerk and it creates inconvenience.
IJSTR	Yolo algorithm- for detection ofobjects through a live feed or animage.	The proposed system is faster than other object detection methods and predicts the object better than other object detection algorithms such as Faster-CNN or Fast CNN. The input can also be optimized and give better results.	Traffic surveillance cameras should be installed in every part of the city. that's why it is not very much beneficial in village.
IJACSA	Android Smartphone with Real-Time Location Tracking.	The system will ignore g-force values lower than 4g. Emergency responders will be able to track the exact location of the victims on a Google map.	User need to always turn on Auto Monitoring for automatic accident detection or send emergency request manually.

(Table 1) cont.....

Publication	Algorithm	Strength	Drawback
JOURNAL OF INFORMATION ENGINEERING AND APPLICATIONS.	Vibration Sensor, GSM, GPS and integrated with vehicular Ad-hoc Network (VANET).	The system has used VANET. VANET builds a robust Ad-Hoc network between mobile vehicles & roadside units. VANET is employ by enhanced Ad-hoc On Demand Distance Vector Protocol (AODV).	Stable and reliable routing in VANET is one of the major issues.

PROBLEM STATEMENT

The main objective of our initiative is to detect on-road accidents and promptly notify emergency service providers and the victim's family members. The primary cause of fatalities in on-road accidents is the significant time lapse in obtaining assistance. This application facilitates expedited and well-coordinated connection between the victim and rescue services. This program effectively addresses the issue of generating misleading notifications by incorporating an alarm mechanism. The user is given the ability to cancel any misleading notifications that are issued when the sensor detects a sudden movement, but no actual mishap occurs. The buffer time is sufficiently short to prevent any delay in offering rescue yet long enough to eliminate false notifications effectively. This solution aids in the preservation of time and resources that would otherwise be squandered as a result of erroneous notifications.

PROPOSED WORK

The objective of our research is to develop a system that can identify accidents occurring on roads and promptly provide rescue assistance. The sensor will measure the distance between the two cars, which is the initial step in the overall detection and alarm procedure. The detection sensor operates on a geo-distance algorithm (Fig. **1**).

The suggested system's objectives are as follows:

- Create a user-friendly application specifically for on-road vehicle users.
- Detect the collision between two vehicles and alert the emergency service officers.
- Provide buffer time for cancellation of false notifications.

Our solution comprises a mobile smartphone or smartwatch equipped with features such as GPS and SMS. The system is linked to a server, such as Firebase, which keeps data on hospitals, police stations, ambulances, and users. A collision detection system is implemented by connecting an ultrasonic sensor, as depicted in Fig. (**3**), to the vehicle (Fig. **2, 3**).

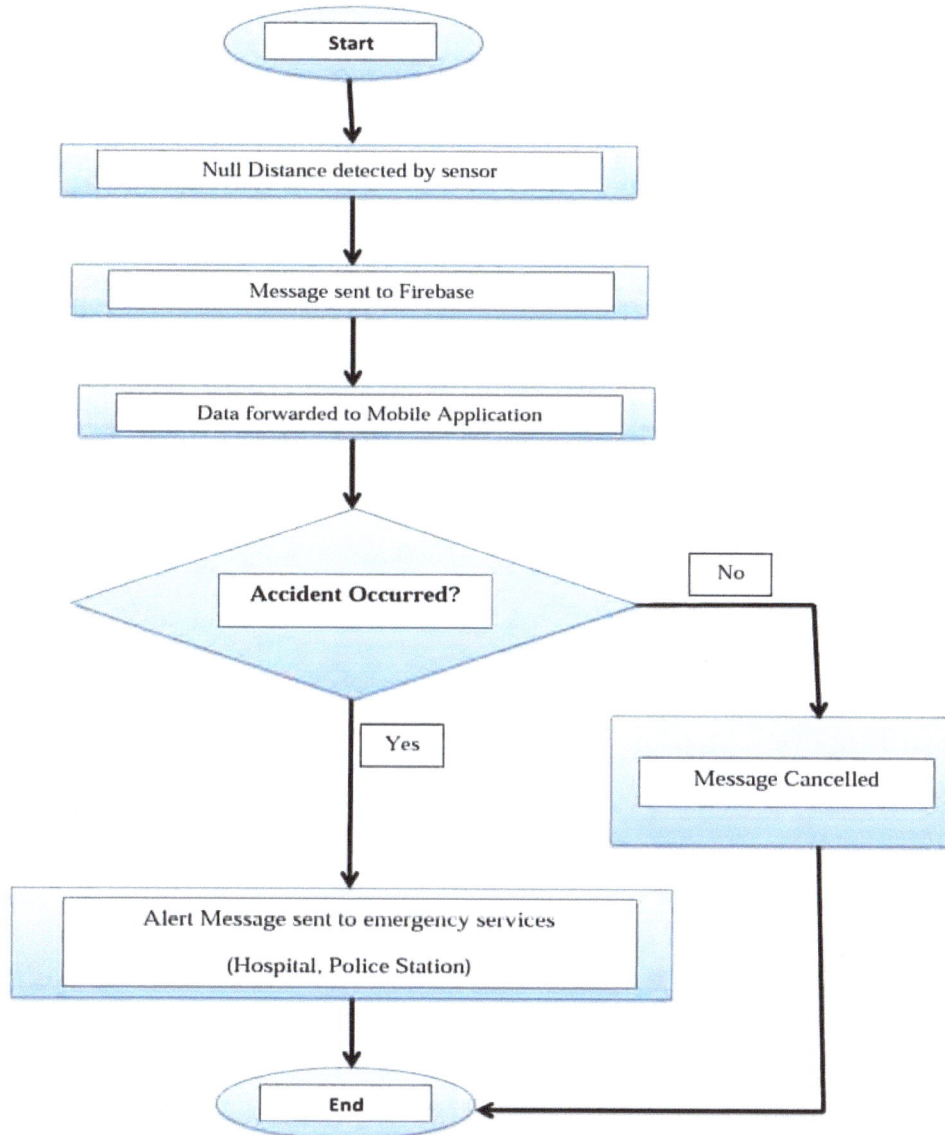

Fig. (1). Flowchart for accident detection and alert system.

Fig. (2). Emergency service rescue.

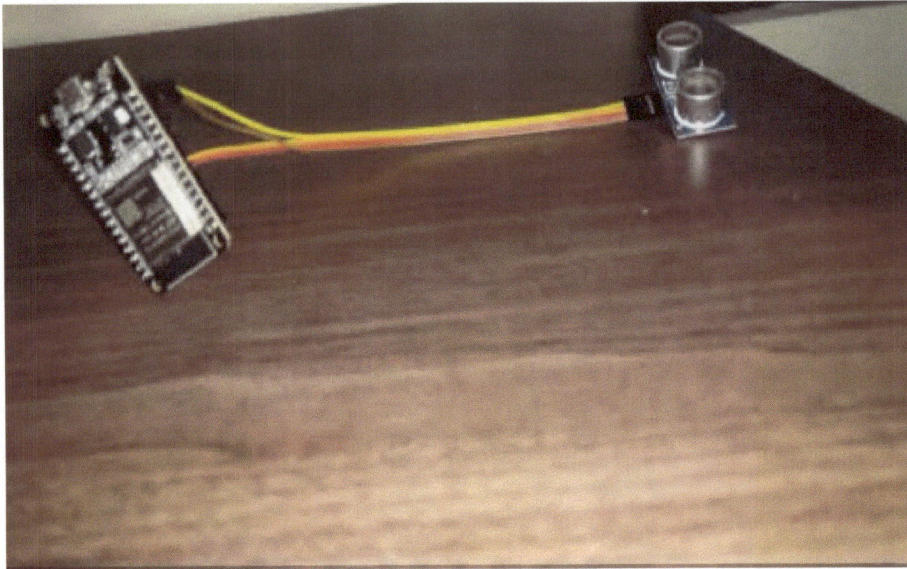

Fig. (3). Portal sensor.

ALGORITHM

STEP 1: The sensor operates based on the parameter of distance. A notification is generated when the distance between two cars is exactly zero.

STEP 2: The data produced by the sensor is transmitted to the firebase.

STEP 3: The data is forwarded to the mobile application.

STEP 4: The user is notified through an alarm regarding the created notification, as depicted in Fig. (4). This is the designated period for the cancelation of erroneous notifications.

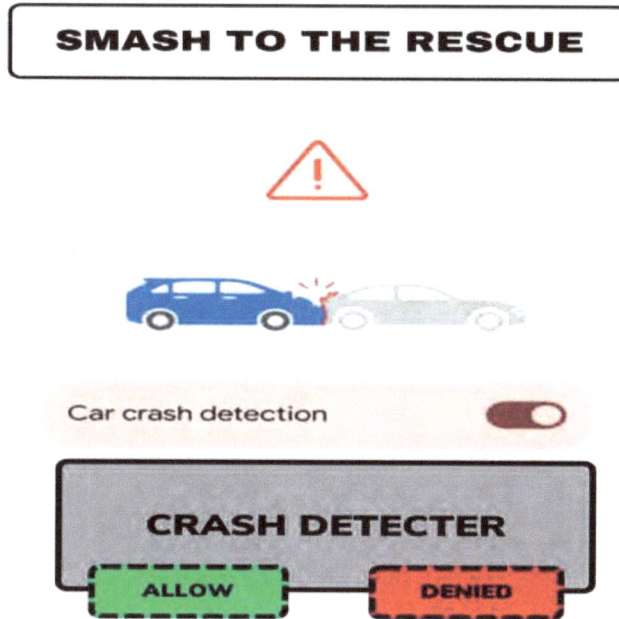

Fig. (4). Crash detection.

STEP 5: If the user cancels the generated notification, then the entire process comes to halt.

IMPLEMENTATION

The dataset undergoes preprocessing to include specific information about the user, hospital, police station, and other relevant contacts, such as a family member of the victim or the user. This processed dataset is then placed in a database, such as Firebase. The user's location beyond the accident is documented, and an alert notification is promptly dispatched to the closest hospital and police station for quick assistance. A notification of the same nature is delivered to the family member of the victim/user whose information is already documented in the application that the user submitted upon its initiation. The global positioning system module is utilized to record the user's location after the accident. The global system for mobile communication is utilized to notify emergency services. Upon signing up, the program will save the user's information, including their name, blood group, gender, emergency contact details of family members, and other necessary information.

RESULTS

Experimental setup

In order to identify accidents, we have utilized an ultrasonic sensor that incorporates a geometric distance algorithm. This technique allows us to determine whether the distance between vehicles is zero or not. We have utilized Firebase, a database, to store information pertaining to hospitals, police stations, and other emergency care providers. Emergency services data is extracted from Firebase for subsequent analysis. Upon the expiration of the buffer period, the program generates a notification and subsequently transmits it to emergency service providers. A geo-positioning system is utilized to document the user's final location following the accident. The user must be within the internet coverage area and ensure that their location setting is enabled throughout the travel.

Performance Analysis

We have introduced an alert and buffer time mechanism to prevent the transmission of inaccurate notifications that are triggered by the sensor's activity. Occasionally, two vehicles make slight contact without causing any harm. However, the sensor is still triggered and prompts the system to send a message. This issue is addressed by incorporating an alarm system. A buffer time is allocated to allow the user to cancel any erroneous notifications that are generated. The alarm system is installed to alert the user of the occurrence of spurious notifications. Therefore, the implementation of an alert and buffer time system effectively preserves both time and resources that would otherwise be squandered as a result of misleading notifications.

CONCLUSION

An application for detecting on-road accidents and alerting the emergency service providers to execute the rescue operation has been implemented. Hence, the proposed objective was implemented on the vehicles that experience an on-road collision resulting in fatal consequences. The experimental findings show that with the installation of an alarm system, the problem of false notifications can be solved. With the use of this system, on-road accidents can be detected, and an immediate rescue can be provided, resulting in decreasing the death rate due to delays in rescue services. The proposed application is accompanied by an alarm and buffer time system to cancel the false notification, which contributes to saving time and resources by avoiding providing facilities for a false rescue. Our application is a real-time-based application that helps in the detection of the location of the victim/user and the nearest hospitals and police stations. Further, we will implement this system with the airbags provided in the vehicle to make it cost-effective. We will also try to teach the facility of sending notifications in case the user is disconnected from the internet connection *via* the help of antennas.

REFERENCES

[1]　P. Josephinshermila, K. Malarvizhi, S.G. Pran, and B. Veerasamy, "Accident detection using Automotive Smart Black-Box based Monitoring system. Measurement", *Sensors (Basel)*, vol. 27, p. 100721, 2023.

[2]　S. Ghosal, T. Chatterjee, K. Ray, H. Saha, B. Laha, and S. Mondal, "IoT-based Mobile Application for Road Accident Detection and Notification", *International Conference on Advancement in Computation & Computer Technologies (InCACCT)*, pp. 1-6, 2023.
[http://dx.doi.org/10.1109/InCACCT57535.2023.10141776]

[3]　Jayanthi[1], R., Monishan, J., Nandhini, A., & Santhoshkumar, M. "IoT Based Accident Prevention System in a Hilly Region using Ultrasonic Sensors", *International Research Journal of Education and Technology*, 2023.,

[4]　Challa, M., Sudha, D., & TS, K. B. "Accident Detection and Alert System", *Grenze International Journal of Engineering & Technology (GIJET)*, vol. 9, no. 1, 2023.

[5]　R. Sathya, S. Ananthi, M.R.S. Abirame, R. Nikalya, A. Madhupriya, and M. Prithiusha, "A Novel Approach for Vehicular Accident Detection and Rescue Alert System using IoT with Convolutional Neural Network", *9th International Conference on Advanced Computing and Communication Systems (ICACCS)*, vol. 1, pp. 1643-1647, 2023.
[http://dx.doi.org/10.1109/ICACCS57279.2023.10113043]

[6]　R. A. Alnashwan, M. O. Mashaabi, A. S. Alotaibi, and H. M. Qudaih, "IoT Based Accident Prevention System using Machine Learning techniques", *Proceedings of the 2023 6th Artificial Intelligence and Cloud Computing Conference*, 2023.

[7]　A. Bhandari, M. K. Ojha, D. K. Choubey, and V. Soni, "IoT Based System for Accident Detection, Monitoring and Landslide Detection Using GSM in Hilly Areas", *Research Reports on Computer Science*, pp. 104-111, 2023.

[8]　M.A. Baballe, "Accident Detection System with GPS, GSM, and Buzzer", *TMP Universal Journal of Research and Review Archives*, vol. 2, no. 1, pp. 28-36, 2023.

[9]　S.S. Tippannavar, and S.D. Yashwanth, "IoT enabled Smart Car with V2X Enhanced Comunication and Safety Alert system", *International Conference on Recent Trends in Electronics and Communication (ICRTEC)*, pp. 1-5, 2023.
[http://dx.doi.org/10.1109/ICRTEC56977.2023.10111919]

[10]　S. Shakya, and P. Tripathi, "Alcohol based quick accident detection system through IoT", *AIP Conference Proceedings*, vol. 2705, no. 1, 2023..
[http://dx.doi.org/10.1063/5.0133338]

[11]　S. S. Yashwantkumar, S. Patil, Y. Ingole, and F. Ansari, "Accident prevention system for mountain roads", *International Research Journal of Modernization in Engineering Technology and Science*, 2023.

[12]　H. Yadav, S. Singh, K.K. Mishra, S. Srivastava, M.S. Naruka, and S.P. Yadav, "Brain Tumor Detection with MRI Images", *International Conference on Computational Intelligence and Sustainable Engineering Solutions (CISES)*, 2022.
[http://dx.doi.org/10.1109/CISES54857.2022.9844387]

[13]　P. Rani, S. Verma, S.P. Yadav, B.K. Rai, M.S. Naruka, and D. Kumar, "Simulation of the Lightweight Blockchain Technique Based on Privacy and Security for Healthcare Data for the Cloud System", *International Journal of E-Health and Medical Communications*, vol. 13, no. 4, pp. 1-15, 2022.
[http://dx.doi.org/10.4018/IJEHMC.309436]

[14]   F. Al-Turjman, S.P. Yadav, M. Kumar, V. Yadav, T. Stephan, Ed., *Transforming Management with AI, Big-Data, and IoT.* Springer International Publishing, 2022.
[http://dx.doi.org/10.1007/978-3-030-86749-2]

[15]   J. Bhardwaj, A. Nayak, C.S. Yadav, and S.P. Yadav, "A Review in Wavelet Transforms Based Medical Image Fusion", In: *Evolving Role of AI and IoMT in the Healthcare Market.,* F. Al-Turjman, M. Kumar, T. Stephan, A. Bhardwaj, Eds., Springer: Cham, 2021.
[http://dx.doi.org/10.1007/978-3-030-82079-4_9]

CHAPTER 37

Performance Evaluation of Tools Made of Super Hard Material CBN during the Renovation of Components of Harvester Machinery

Pankaj Kumar Mishra[1,*], Praveen Chandra Jha[2], Vijay Kumar[3], Ram Kishor Gupta[1] and V.V. Kolomiets[4]

[1] *Department of Mechanical Engineering, HI-Tech Institute of Engineering and Technology, Ghaziabad-201009, India*

[2] *Department of Applied Science, I.T.S., Greater Noida- 201306, India*

[3] *Department of Mechanical Engineering, I.M.T., Greater Noida- 201306, India*

[4] *Agriculture University, Kharkov, Ukraine*

Abstract: An investigation was conducted to examine the influence of hard alloy turning tools and BN-based super hard materials on the performance characteristics during the finish turning of components with the deposition of Surfacing wire (Sw)-40Cr8Si2 (HRC 50-58). Upon deposition, the surface undergoes a significant increase in hardness, resulting in a hard-faced item with a rough, uneven, and undulating surface. Consequently, a machining process is employed to provide a smooth finish and ensure the desired dimensions are maintained. The variables in question are as follows: transverse chip shrinkage ξ, frictional coefficient during modeling μ, vertical component of cutting force Pz (in Newtons), cutting temperature $\theta°C$, machined area F (in square meters), cutting-tool life before reaching a specified blunting criterion T (in minutes), maximum cutting length at the optimal wear of cutters L = T-V (in kilometers), and the relative flank wear of cutters at their specified resistance. The symbol "hoз" represents the ratio of hз to L, where hз is measured in micrometers (μm), and L is measured in kilometers (km). It is used to describe the roughness of a machined surface. The performance characteristics of turning cutters in this investigation were measured in terms of Ra (μm). The techniques of experimental optimization of surface roughness that have a significant influence on resurfaced hard turning are also investigated.

Keywords: Blunting criterion, Frictional coefficient, Surface roughness, Turning process, Transverse chip shrinkage, Welding technique.

---

[*] **Corresponding author Pankaj Kumar Mishra:** Department of Mechanical Engineering, HI-Tech Institute of Engineering and Technology, Ghaziabad-201009, India; E-mail: spsingdirector@hiet.org

Pankaj Kumar Mishra & Satya Prakash Yadav (Eds.)

INTRODUCTION

Engineering employs cutting-edge technology that integrates very durable metals and alloys with extraordinary strength, ability to withstand high temperatures, and resistance to corrosion. The objective of this study is to evaluate the efficacy of a tool made of boron nitride, a highly durable substance, in the processing of the deposited material. The surface wire, Sw-40Cr8Si2 (HRC 50-58), exhibits considerable volatility in its physical and mechanical properties. Additionally, it exhibits micro flaws, possesses a non-uniform structure, and lacks comprehensive analysis of the impact of these characteristics on the tool's overall performance. Deposition can be applied to either the surface or edge of a component during production in order to improve its resistance to wear. Alternatively, it can be specially applied to the section of the component that is susceptible to wear during service or operation [1]. The objective of hard-facing is to mitigate costly periods of inactivity and reduce the expenses associated with expensive replacement parts by improving their ability to withstand wear and extending their overall durability [2]. Angello G.N. conducted the initial research on the machinability of the deposited Surfacingwire (Sw)-65Mn (HRC 42...48) using a turning tool built of superhard materials based on boron nitride CBN-R and hexane-R. Nevertheless, the examination of the empirical formula correlations of tool material performance characteristics, as obtained by the individual in the specified coating process, reveals that their practical application could be more feasible. This is due to the fact that certain correlations lack physical significance, as the roughing process of the deposited materials with the turning tools made of CBN-R is unrealistic, given their extremely low resistance under these conditions [3 - 5]. The most sophisticated method in the processing of hard coatings involves the use of cutters built from superhard materials, specifically those based on hexagonal boron nitride. An analysis of the existing literature on machining coatings reveals that the majority of research focuses on assessing the ease of machining for specific types of coatings or establishing the effectiveness of tools, particularly those composed of boron nitride-based polycrystalline superhard materials. However, with comprehensive theoretical investigations, it is possible to justify the adoption of new tool materials adequately [6, 7]. Existing literature and conventional practices in coating processes have consistently shown that tools built of superhard materials consistently exhibit inferior performance compared to solid structural elements during processing. Hence, it is imperative to devise techniques for enhancing the efficiency of tools while considering the alterations in characteristics and uneven coating structure in order to minimize expenses associated with repairing worn machine components. Upon analyzing the current techniques for determining the machinability properties of materials through cutting, it is evident that only two accelerated methods can be recommended for processing coatings in facility repairs. This is specifically a modified method of end turning [8, 9]. An examination of patents and inventions from foreign countries reveals that our research focuses on specific areas that are protected by copyright certificates. These areas involve the use of tools made from polycrystalline superhard materials based on boron nitride, as well as the use of specialized equipment. While these two methods are similar, they differ in their production processes. Recently, in several technologically advanced countries, there has been a simultaneous development of new tool materials and corresponding handbooks that provide comprehensive information about these materials. The works [10] provides the most comprehensive analysis of the performance of tools utilizing boron nitride [11 - 13].

RELATED WORKS

It can be difficult to evaluate the performance of tools constructed of the extremely hard substance cubic boron nitride, or CBN when rebuilding harvester mechanical parts. When utilized for these kinds of tasks, conventional turning and drilling tools wear down more quickly than CBN tools. Therefore, assessing the effectiveness of CBN tools in lieu of traditional techniques has taken on even greater significance. The wear resistance of CBN tools is one of the main elements that determine their performance. When renovating harvester machinery components, the axial wear rate (AWR) and flank wear rate (FWR) of the tools are frequently calculated to evaluate their continuous cutting performance. If the performance of the tools is to be maintained, a rise in the flank wear rate and AWR often indicates that the tools are dull and need to be replaced. The cutting process parameters of CBN tools are a significant issue that impacts their performance during the refurbishment of harvester machinery components. The performance of CBN tools is influenced by a number of factors, including the lubrication system, spindle speed, feed rate, cutting temperature, and cutting forces. The optimal performance of CBN tools for these kinds of applications depends on these characteristics being properly balanced. A few major concerns are involved in the performance assessments of CBN-based super hard tooling used in Harvester machinery component restoration. Since the rigidity of the tooling is crucial to the caliber of the cutting process, it is first imperative to guarantee that the tools are constructed to correct tolerances. Second, it is important to keep an eye on tool wear and how it affects tooling performance. Third, for the tool to be reliable and of high quality, effective cooling is required. Fourth, to achieve a suitable balance between tool performance and material removal efficiency, the tool's speed and feed rate must be matched with the characteristics of the material being cut. In order to maximize the performance of the tools, the cutting environment must be optimized.

EXPERIMENTAL

The performance evaluation of BN-based superhard materials and sintered carbide alloy of the type B10 (Ti15Co6) was conducted during the finish turning of abrasion-resistant inhomogeneous deposited materials. Transverse chip shrinkage is denoted by ξ. The frictional coefficient during modelling is represented by μ. The vertical component of cutting force is denoted as Pz (H). The cutting temperature is represented by $\theta°C$. The machined area is denoted as F (м2). The cutting tool life before reaching the adopted blunting criterion is represented by T (min). The maximum cutting length at the optimum wear of turning cutters is given by L = T-V (km). The relative flank wear of cutters at their adopted resistance is also considered. The performance characteristics of the experimental turning cutters in this investigation were the hot = hz /L (μm /km) and the machined surface roughness Ra (μm). The authors conducted comprehensive performance experiments on turning cutters composed of super hard materials derived from boron nitride with hexane-P (K-10) grade. These experiments focused on the finish turning of the abrasion-resistant, inhomogeneous deposited materials Sw-40Cr8Si2 (HRC 50...58) produced in Germany. The deposited material had the following chemical composition: 0.32-0.41% carbon (C), 7.2-8.0% chromium (Cr), 0.2-0.3% manganese (Mn), 1.6-1.8% silicon (Si), 0.1-0.25% molybdenum (Mo), 0.5-0.6% copper (Cu), and the remaining portion is iron (Fe). A 2.8 mm diameter self-shielding wire was deposited in a single layer using an open arc welding process. The welding was performed at DC-reverse polarity using a hose-type semiautomatic welding machine called A825M, which was installed on an improved screw-cutting lathe. The deposition welding parameters were as follows:

- The electric current ranged from 260 to 320 A.
- The voltage ranged from 24 to 26 V.
- The deposition speed ranged from 15 to 20 m/h.

A deposition was employed to refurbish the rods of hydraulic cylinders in road construction and combine harvester machinery. The turning cutting modes underwent significant changes across a broad spectrum: the cutting speed (V) ranged from 0.5 to 3.0 m/s, the longitudinal feed (S) varied from 0.04 to 0.3 mm/rev, and the cutting depth (t) ranged from 0.1 to 0.2 mm. The wear of cutting tools was directly assessed on the lathe using a specialized microscope with a magnification of X100. The geometrical characteristics of the cutting component of the tool are as follows: the rake angle (γ) is -10°, the back angles (α) are $\alpha1$ = 12°, the main cutting edge angle (φ) is 20°, the minor cutting edge angle ($\varphi1$) is 20°, the major cutting edge inclination (λ) is 0°, and the tool nose radius (r) is 0.6

m. The cutting edge of the wiper has a length of 0.2-0.3 mm. The friction and cutting forces were measured using the dynamometric apparatus of UDM-10--type and UDM-600-type. The chrome-alumni thermocouple was used to measure the cutting temperature. The surface roughness Ra was measured using the profilograph-profilometer model 201 manufactured by the "Kalibr" factory. Ra was obtained by calculating the root-mean-square deviation of the roughness profile.

Performance Evaluation of Tools

Let us begin by examining the performance characteristics of cutting plates made of hard alloy B10 (Ti15Co6). These plates are commonly used for machining deposited materials of the type Surfacing wire (Sw)-40Cr8Si2 (50...58) during machine performance part repairs (Fig. **1**). We will analyze and divide the interval of the cutting speed change as follows: between 0.2 and 0.5 m/s; between 0.5 and 1.0 m/s, between 1.0 and 1.5 meters per second. The augmentation of cutting speed in the initial period leads to an increase in chip shrinkage and friction coefficients. This is attributed to the accumulation of material on the cutter face and the rise in the cutting force component Pz. The mean cutting temperature rises until it reaches 800°C, although it does not currently impact the cutting characteristics of the tool material. During this period, the wear on the cutter's flank surface diminishes as a result of the protective effect of the built-up material, which also absorbs oscillations in cutting force. The machined surface roughness also increases as a result of an increase in the built-up material. The average resistance of the tool within this range is rather high, and the length of the cut increases. However, it is relatively minimal when the machining is done at low cutting speeds. The cutting speed increases from 0.5 to 1.0 m/s in the second interval. The coefficients of friction and chip shrinkage, cutting force, roughness of the machined surface, cutting length, and cutter relative wear are all decreasing. However, the mean cutting temperature increases up to 1000°C, which leads to a significant decrease in resistance due to the loss of heat resistance in the tool material. Increasing the cutting speed from 1.0 to 1.5 m/s leads to a significant rise in the average cutting temperature, reaching up to 1300°C. This leads to a reduction in all performance attributes of cutters, rendering their practical use impractical. When using cutters constructed of a super hard material like hexanite - R to finish turning the same deposited material, the cutting speeds can be divided into two periods: from 0.5 to 1.5 m/s and from 1.5 to 3.0 m/s. As observed in the diagrams, the first rise in cutting speed leads to an increase in the average cutting temperature from 500 to 800°C. This, in turn, decreases the coefficients of friction and chip shrinkage, as well as the cutting force. Additionally, it reduces the relative wear of the cutter and the roughness of the machined surface. The observed phenomenon can be attributed to the reduction in material hardness as the cutting temperature rises without the presence of built-up material. Increasing the cutting speed from 1.5 to 3.0 m/s leads to a rise in the average cutting temperature to 1100°C. This, in turn, results in a little decline in the performance characteristics of the tool material. The recommended cutting speed for the finish turning of this deposited material falls within the range of 1.5 to 2.0 m/s. Within this range of cutting speed, the rate of wear on the cutter is at its lowest, while the length of material that can be cut is at its highest. The stabilization of chip shrinkage, frictional coefficient, cutting force, and roughness of the machined surface are also determined. Fig. (**1**) shows the influence of velocities of the cutting.

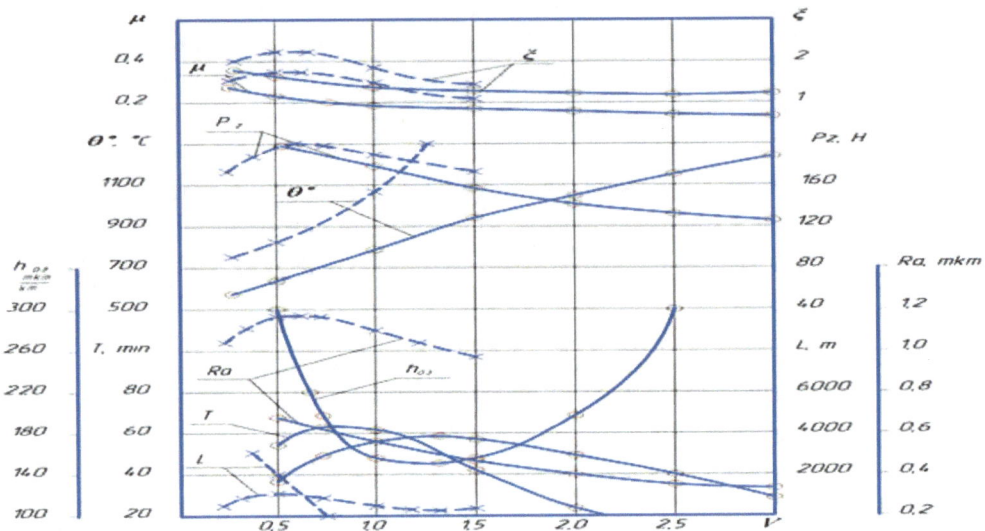

Fig. (1). The Influence of velocities of the cutting on features of capacity to work of incisor from geksanit-R o--------o and hard alloy P10 x- - - x at final sharpening of building material Hп - 40X8C2 under: S = 0,1 mm/rot; t = 0,2 ;hb = 0,2 mm and hbcr = 0,6 mm.

In Fig. (**2**), the impact of the presentation on the capacity to work of the incisor from geksanit-R o------o and hard alloy P10 x- - - x is shown. The incisor was sharpened using construction material Hп - 40X8C2 with the following parameters: Vg = 1.5 m/s, t = 0.2 mm, and hb = 0.2 mm. The wire (Sw)-40Cr8Si2 and hexane-R are joined using the same weld incisor from geksanit-R. The frictional coefficient value is not influenced by the feed as long as repetitive contacts are omitted. Instead, let us examine its dependency on the relative pressure change. By examining the dependency diagrams μ = f(q) of turning tools made of hard alloy and extremely hard material CBN Heksanite type-P, we can observe that they exhibit the same extreme behavior but with different minimum positions. This can be attributed to the distinct physical and mechanical characteristics of tool materials and their varying reactivity with iron-containing compounds. From the diagrams' positioning, it is evident that the feed rate has a greater impact on the cutting temperature. This temperature rises significantly when using hard alloy cutters during turning operations. The utilization of CBN hexane-R cutters during the final turning process leads to a significant reduction in the mean cutting temperature as the feed rate is increased. Therefore, the range of ideal cutting speeds for a feed rate of 0.1 mm/rev can be somewhat decreased when the feed rate is increased to 0.2 mm/rev in order to maintain the optimal average cutting temperature. The cutting force Pz during a turning operation with cutters constructed of a hard alloy increases as the feed rate increases. This can be attributed to the high values of chip shrinkage, frictional coefficients, and the superior performance of the hard alloy and the material being machined. Diagrams reveal that the roughness of the machined surface varies in magnitude and undergoes distinct degrees of change with increasing feed rate. Experimental results have demonstrated that the surface produced by CBN hexane-R cutters is 3 to 4 times larger than the surface produced by hard alloy cutters at all feed rates. Significant disparities exist in the degree of cutter wear, with cutters made of hard alloy B10 exhibiting wear that is 5...8 times greater than cutters made of CBN superhard materials of the hexane-R type, even at low cutting speeds. When using BN-based superhard materials for finish turning deposited materials, the resistance of the cutters and the ideal cutting speed can be determined by the following relationships, which are dependent on the resistance of the cutters.

$$T^m = \frac{Cv \cdot \prod_{i=1}^{n} \cdot Kvi}{V \cdot S^{Yx} \cdot t^{Yv} \cdot K_H} \quad \text{or} \quad V = \frac{Cv \cdot \prod_{i=1}^{n} \cdot Kvi}{T^m \cdot S^{Yx} \cdot t^{Yv} \cdot K_H}$$

Where Cv – coefficient depending on properties of the deposited material; Kvi – coefficients depending on the machining conditions;

K$_H$ – inhomogeneity coefficient of the deposited material being machined, specified for that group of deposits.

The influence of cutting speed on the performance characteristics of cutters during the turning process of the deposited material can be described by the shared relationship, as illustrated in Table **1**. X is equal to the product of Cx and VYx, where X is an indicator of a performance characteristic. Cx is a coefficient that takes into account the constant conditions of the cutting process. Yx is an indicator of power at the cutting speed for each characteristic. The table provides the calculated coefficients Cx and power indexes Yx, which are used to evaluate the main performance features of cutters. The determination of power indexes at the cutting speed was conducted for the right branches of the extreme dependencies for each characteristic.

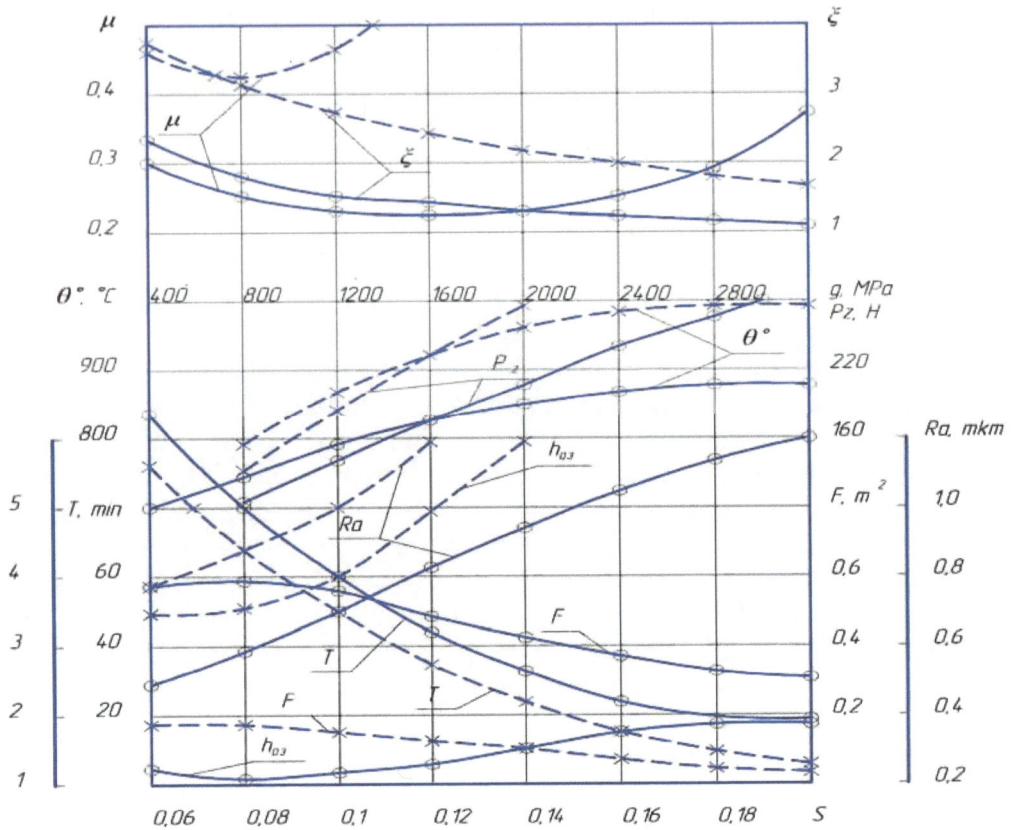

Fig. (2). The Influence of transverse feed of the cutting on features of capacity of the cutter performance made of a hard alloy and superhard material of the hexanite – R type during the finish turning of the same deposited material.

Table 1. Performance characteristics of cutters.

Characteristics7	Material of cutter			
	Hexanite-R		B10 (Ti15Co6)	
	Cx	**Yx**	**Cx**	**Yx**
Cutter resistance, T.	65-75	-0.25	10-20	-0.98
Cutting length, L.	3.9-4.5	-0.8	0.6-1.5	-0.8
Relative wear, ho3	210-250	-0.25	600-700	-0.7
Roughness of the machined surface, Ra	0.52-0.64	-0.35	1.1-1.2	-0.4

RESULTS AND CONCLUSION

Research has been conducted on the assessment of the cutting performance of BN-based (namely, the hexane-R type) superhard material when used with machine abrasion-resistant deposited material. The utilization of Surfacing wire (Sw)-40Cr8Si2 has demonstrated its superiority over tools built of a hard alloy B10, making it highly recommended for usage in repair activities during the rehabilitation of performance parts in road construction and combined harvester machinery. Superhard cutters are highly efficient for finish-turning inhomogeneous deposited materials with high hardness. These cutters can sustain a mean cutting temperature between 900 and 1050°C even at high cutting speeds. The presence of defects and variations in the deposited materials often affects the level of wear on the cutter and increases the vibration loads, hence restricting the cutting speed. Boron nitride-based cutters, including the hexane-R and kiborite types, are highly successful for finish-turning coatings. These superhard materials can be utilized with feed intervals ranging from 0.04 to 0.2mm/rev. During semi-finishing and rough turning operations, cutters composed of a durable B10-type alloy can be utilized. These cutters are suitable for a feed rate ranging from 0.14 to 0.3 mm/rev at low cutting speeds.

REFERENCES

[1]   G.N. Angello, "Studies of machinability deposited surfaces of restoring parts from turning tool made of super hard material", *Avmoref. Dis. Cand. Tech. Scien. Cheliabinsk,* p. 19, 1980.

[2]   M.A. Yallesea, C. Kamel, Z. Nassereddine, B. Lakhdar, and J.F. Rigal, *J. Mater. Process. Technol.,* vol. 209, p. 1092, 2009.
[http://dx.doi.org/10.1016/j.jmatprotec.2008.03.014]

[3]   M.A. Kamely, M.Y. Noordin, and A. Ourdjini, *Journal of Advanced Manufacturing Technology,* vol. 2, p. 2, 2008.

[4]   Aramide, Basiru, *et al*, "Improving the durability of tillage tools through surface modification—a review", *The International Journal of Advanced Manufacturing Technology,* vol. 116, no. 1, pp. 83-98, 2021.

[5]   Dai, Sheng, *et al*, "Cold Spray Technology and Its Application in the Manufacturing of Metal Matrix Composite Materials with Carbon-Based Reinforcements", *Coatings,* vol. 14, no. 7, p. 822, 2024.

[6]   Riti, J. Sunday, H.D. Gubak, and D.A. Madina, "Growth of non-oil sectors: A key to diversification and economic performance in Nigeria", *International knowledge sharing platform,* 2016.

[7]   Kumar, Rahul, *et al*, "Bioinspired and Multifunctional Tribological Materials for Sliding, Erosive, Machining, and Energy-Absorbing Conditions: A Review", *Biomimetics,* vol. 9, no. 4, p. 209, 2024.

[8]   L.A.Solntsev,V.V.Kolomiets,V.I.MoshenokA.c. 1510983. USSR B 23 B 1/00. Calculation method of material machinability from turning tool. - №4054268/31-08; Jaibleno 15.01.86. Opubl. 30.09.89. bul. №36.

[9]   Oruma, Samson O., S. Misra, and L. Fernandez-Sanz, "Agriculture 4.0: an implementation framework for food security attainment in Nigeria's post-Covid-19 era", *Ieee Access,* pp. 83592-83627, 2021.

[10]   V.V. Kolomiets, and S.A. Vijay Kumar, "Serviceability characteristics of friction during turning of resurfaced materials", *Scientific conference at Kharkov national technical agriculture university,*

Kharkov, pp. 22-25, 2011.

[11]   S. Delijaicov, F. Leonardi, E.C. Bordinassi, and G.F. Batalha, *Archives of Materials Science and Engineering,* vol. 45, p. 102, 2010.

[12]   Z.A. Zoya, and R. Krishnamurthy, "The performance of CBN tools in the machining of titanium alloys", *J. Mater. Process. Technol.,* vol. 100, no. 1-3, pp. 80-86, 2000.
[http://dx.doi.org/10.1016/S0924-0136(99)00464-1]

[13]   L. Wan, Y. Li, C. Zhang, X. Ma, J. Song, X. Dong, and J. Wang, "Performance Evaluation of Liquorice Harvester with Novel Oscillating Shovel-Rod Components Using the Discrete Element Method", *Agriculture,* vol. 12, no. 12, p. 2015, 2022.
[http://dx.doi.org/10.3390/agriculture12122015]

CHAPTER 38

A Comparative Study of Worklife Balance Trends and Challenges

Pragya Agarwal[1,*], Vipin Tomer[1], Himanshi Mittal[1] and Ankit Garg[2]

[1] *Hi-Tech Institute of Engineering & Technology, Ghaziabad, Uttar pradesh, India*

[2] *Ajay Kumar Garg Institute of Management, Ghaziabad, Uttar pradesh, India*

Abstract: The chapter provides a concise overview of the findings from a comprehensive survey conducted among employees in several leading corporate firms, focusing on the implementation of progressive work-life policies and practices. These organizations exercise different levels of authority over their employees; some enforce strict regulations, like prohibiting the use of cell phones in the workplace, while others adopt a more lenient and flexible approach. The study demonstrates that organizations that effectively implement work-life programs foster a collaborative relationship between employers and employees, resulting in beneficial outcomes for both parties. Employees who can effectively balance their jobs and personal responsibilities experience greater happiness and satisfaction, resulting in enhanced performance. Additionally, these activities have the potential to enhance a company's reputation and contribute to the retention of people.

Keywords: Employees, High-speed work environment, Satisfaction, Work-life programs, Work-life balance.

INTRODUCTION

Individuals experience significant levels of stress in the high-speed work environment of the present era, making it challenging for them to achieve a harmonious equilibrium between their personal and professional lives. Employees are required to wholeheartedly dedicate themselves to their work in this demanding and stressful work environment, often at the expense of other aspects of their lives. Individuals may become trapped in a work cycle characterized by extended hours and an excessive workload due to taking on more responsibilities than they can effectively manage. This situation can lead to burnout, a term introduced by English writer Graham Greene in his 1961 novel 'A Burnout Case'

---

[*] **Corresponding author Pragya Agarwal:** Hi-Tech Institute of Engineering & Technology, Ghaziabad, Uttar pradesh, India; E-mail: Agarwalpragya03@gmail.com

Pankaj Kumar Mishra & Satya Prakash Yadav (Eds.)

to depict a condition of emotional exhaustion and disillusionment in one's job [1]. A significant number of individuals exhibit symptoms of occupational burnout, which has become prevalent. Consequently, organizations are employing happiness and wellness consultants to assist their employees in managing the issue. Burnout refers to the state in which an individual experiences excessive emotional exhaustion, resulting in impaired performance, increased work errors, and decreased productivity. This inclination is partly attributable to the prevalent "workaholic" culture in numerous firms nowadays, wherein employees are incentivized and commended for dedicating additional hours, assuming additional responsibilities, and fulfilling established time limits. Conversely, over time, this situation evolves into a high-stress setting that may lead to increased tension and anxiety. Employees who are subjected to work-related stress sometimes encounter feelings of worry, anger, and other adverse emotions prior to experiencing stress and dissatisfaction. The user's text is enclosed in tags [2].

RELATED WORKS

Both employees and employers have long recognized the need to maintain a healthy equilibrium between work and personal life. The need to achieve a balance between work and home responsibilities is becoming more widespread in today's job environment. Nevertheless, attaining a satisfactory equilibrium between job and personal life has proven to be arduous for numerous individuals, and this matter has garnered significant attention in the realm of research. In this study, diagnostic models have been developed to gain a deeper understanding of work-life balance patterns and difficulties, as well as to evaluate the present condition of work-life balance across different industries and organizations. Diagnostics models offer valuable data that can aid in decision-making on the development, execution, or oversight of work-life balance policies, practices, or initiatives. Diagnostics models offer researchers, employers, and employees precise information about the present condition of work-life balance. They also provide a valuable understanding of the factors that influence work-life balance, including the economic climate, job attributes, work schedules, and personal or familial characteristics. Prominent diagnostic methods for assessing work-life balance include the Work and Family Survey (WFS), the Work and Family Attitude Scale (WFAS), and the Linkage Family-Work Scale (LFWS). The objective of this study is to examine and contrast different computational models employed in the analysis of work-life balance trends and issues. The models under examination will encompass econometric, sociological, qualitative, and predictive analytics approaches. Econometrics is a field that examines the connections between financial variables and is commonly employed to forecast economic trends and predict production and consumption cycles. Econometric algorithms primarily aim to ascertain the coefficients of impact among variables and find the factors that hold the greatest significance. Econometric methods can utilize linear and nonlinear regression models to analyze the factors that impact work-life balance. When studying work-life balance trends and issues from a sociological perspective, researchers examine several elements like social stratification, workplace cultures, job expectations, and job autonomy. Researchers can employ quantitative and qualitative methodologies to investigate interactions at either the micro or macro level in order to comprehend how social structures and organizational cultures influence the work-life balance of individuals and work teams. Qualitative analysis uses several methodologies, such as interviews, focus groups, surveys, and observation, to gather data pertaining to trends, attitudes, and issues around work-life balance. The uniqueness of this study resides in its comparative methodology for analyzing the patterns and difficulties associated with maintaining a healthy equilibrium between work and personal life. The study aims to offer a more extensive understanding of work-life balance trends and challenges by examining them in various nations. Moreover, employing this comparison methodology will allow the researchers to emphasize any distinctive variables or discrepancies among countries that could have otherwise remained unreported. It could be particularly advantageous for firms seeking to develop or enhance their work-life balance strategies in a dynamic setting.

REVIEW OF LITERATURE

Maintaining a healthy work-life balance can be difficult due to the stress and fatigue associated with contemporary, fast-paced professional settings. Burnout, a common phenomenon in the workplace, often leads to emotional exhaustion and decreased performance in individuals. In his book "Rest: Why You Get More Done When You Work", Alex Sojourn-Kim Pang presents an argument. Working fewer hours and engaging in "active rest" are crucial for enhancing creativity and productivity. Workers are facing growing challenges in maintaining a harmonious equilibrium between their professional obligations and personal relaxation, leading to an imbalanced way of life that can trigger stress, anxiety, and sleep disorders. Sasha Madhya, an authority on managing stress in the corporate setting, highlights that a multitude of factors, such as time constraints, academic evaluations, mental strain, as well as personal and marital issues, can contribute to work-related stress. The user's text is " [3]". Madhya emphasizes the need to achieve work-life balance through mindfulness, optimism, and perseverance. The reasons for stress can be categorized into internal elements, such as a lack of engagement and drive, and external issues, such as tough employers, strained relationships with coworkers, and displeasure with job requirements.

The article provides guidance on stress management and attaining work-life equilibrium while also delving into the impact of work-life imbalance on employees' well-being and efficiency. Psychologist Sasha Madhya states that an imbalance between job and personal life can lead to stress, anxiety, and other mental health issues. In order to achieve work-life balance, Madhya recommends practicing mindfulness, focusing on the positive aspects of life, and cultivating resilience. Additionally, she suggested seeking guidance from a mentor or a reliable colleague to manage work-related stress effectively. Kantian Patwardhan, a nutritionist, emphasizes the importance of consuming a nutritious diet and staying hydrated to improve overall health and effectively cope with stress. The essay highlights the significance of recognizing and addressing burnout symptoms while also fostering positive thought patterns in order to sustain a good equilibrium between work and personal life [4]. Effectively balancing the demands of work and personal life is crucial to achieving work-life balance. It refers to actions that assist workers in achieving a harmonious equilibrium between their work and personal responsibilities, as well as their well-being, contentment, and spiritual development. Attaining work-life balance poses both an advantageous prospect and a challenge for HR professionals in the contemporary workplace, where the prevalence of stress and conflicts between work and personal responsibilities is increasing. Figs. (**1** and **2**) show the recommendation status and rating and sub rating.

Comparison of Marico Ltd. and Dabber India Ltd.

Marico Ltd (Rating - 3.57/5)	Dabber India Ltd (Rating - 3.52/5)

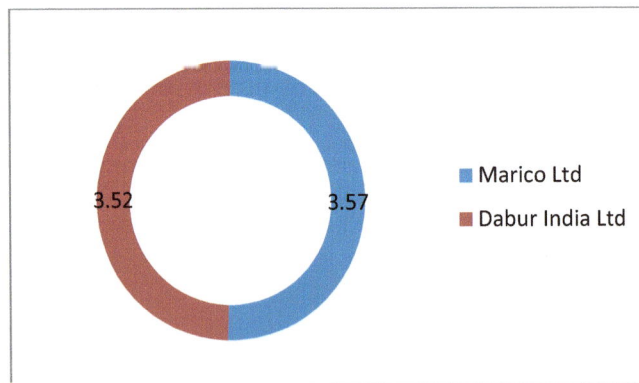

Fig. (1). Recommendation Status

% of employees who recommend the company

38%	38%

% of employees having mixed feelings

37%	28%

% of employees who do not recommend the company

20%	29%

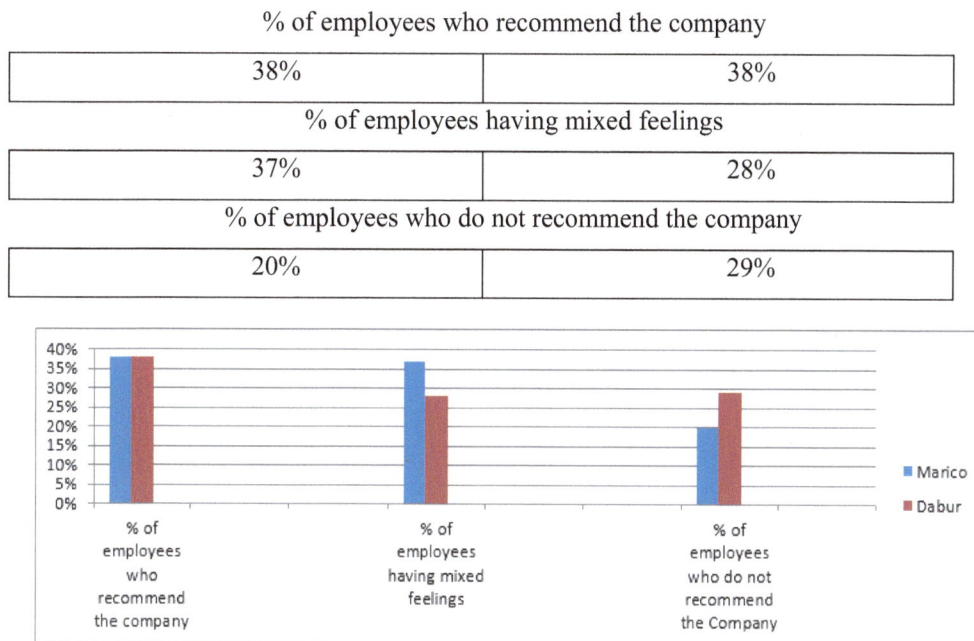

Fig. (2). Rating and Sub rating (Score out of 5)

Implementing work-life balance efforts has become a need for numerous firms rather than just an optional choice. These initiatives aim to assist employees in effectively managing their work and personal commitments. In the contemporary business environment, companies are required to formulate human resource strategies and policies that effectively cater to the diverse workforce's requirements in terms of achieving a healthy equilibrium between work and personal life. The user's text is " [4]". Fig. (**3**) shows the overall rating.

RMSI

RMSI, a worldwide provider of IT services specializing in geospatial and software solutions, has overtaken Google, the previous holder of the top position for the past five years, to be recognized as the leading employer in India. GagmanJot, the vice president of human resources, asserts that RMSI offers an adaptable work environment, fosters a strong sense of empowerment and accountability, and encourages employee participation in corporate decision-making. The organization provides opportunities for individuals to get exposure to many cultures through on-site work assignments, efforts to enhance skills and abilities, mentorship and coaching, and possibilities for leadership development [5].

Overall Rating of the Company

3.6	3.5

Rating on Salary/Remuneration

3.5	3.7

Rating on Work-Life Balance

3.4	3.4

Rating on Company Culture

3.8	3.5

Rating on Career Growth

3.6	3.4

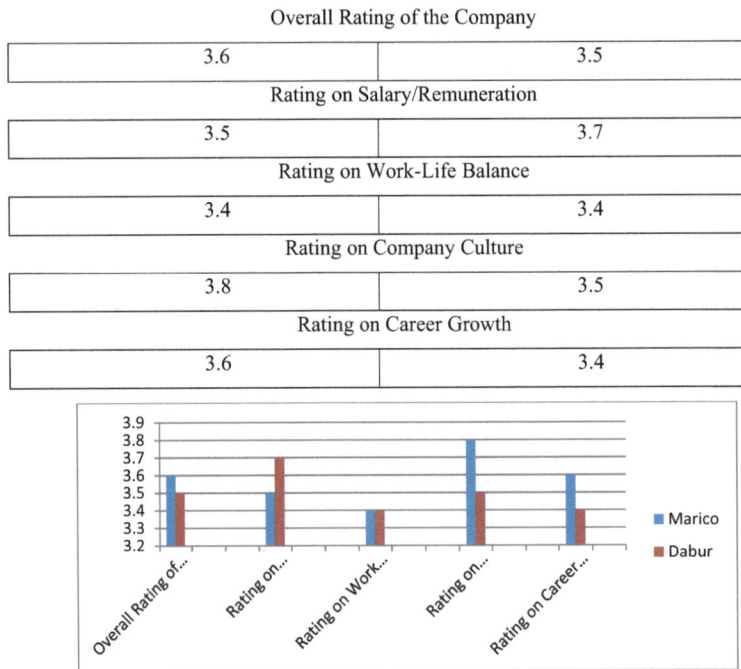

Fig. (3). Overall rating.

Jot states that RMSI has an open and inclusive management team that fosters collaboration among personnel to prioritize clients and the company. We prioritize the respect and appreciation of our employees, foster creativity and exceptional performance, incentivize leadership and collaboration, and hold our people in high regard. The business provides a diverse range of incentive and recognition initiatives that foster growth, innovation, collaboration, and leadership while also rewarding individual accomplishments. Furthermore, it offers accelerated career paths for exceptional workers. Workshops on parenting, relationship dynamics, and child psychology are provided to enhance connections with employees' families [6].

RMSI prioritizes the welfare of its employees by offering a range of services such as lifestyle evaluations, dental, medical, and eye examinations, training programs for essential skills, stress reduction techniques including yoga and meditation, panic healing, health check-up camps, and physiotherapy. The group has well-defined anti-harassment policies that ensure the safety and equal rights of women. Additionally, they offer self-defense classes and tai chi sessions, provide access to pepper spray, and organize meetings with female representatives from the police and non-governmental organizations to promote awareness of women's rights and protection. The company also offers specialized health programs for women, such as gynecological examinations, thyroid testing, and breast and cervical cancer screenings [7].

The firm offers female employees an extended period of maternity leave, the option to work part-time or have flexible work hours, the ability to work from home, and the opportunity to take a temporary break from their careers. In addition, the company provides a diverse range of activities aimed at enhancing employees' skills and fostering a versatile personality. These activities encompass music, photography, painting, acting, movie production, guitar instruction, Zumba exercise sessions, and participation in sporting events. The user's text is " [8]".

Google India

"Google prioritizes the well-being and contentment of its employees by providing an innovative and vibrant work setting that encourages creative thinking and personal growth." The company provides consumers with access to state-of-t-e-art equipment and technology, including The Techs Top. This in-house technical support center offers assistance with all hardware and software needs. In addition, Google employees are granted the privilege of utilizing and beta-testing products prior to their release to the public. The company provides well-equipped fitness facilities with personalized exercise programs and trainers, as well as recreational areas where personnel can engage in games such as table tennis, pool, football, air hockey, and more [9].

Google fosters a cheerful work atmosphere by organizing activities such as TGIF (Thank God It's Friday) after 4 p.m. on Fridays, where employees have the opportunity to socialize and collaborate. In addition, the organization encourages and facilitates its employees' pursuit of their artistic passions, including acting, music, or any other artistic domain. Google, a corporation that values employee input, organizes an annual "management buster" day where staff members have the opportunity to suggest improvements to streamline processes and enhance decision-making [10].

In addition to these advantages, Google also advocates for women's empowerment projects, grants academic scholarships to the upcoming cohort of technology pioneers, and facilitates employee resource groups such as Women@Google. The corporation provides its employees with three complimentary meals each day, in addition to an unrestricted supply of snacks in the cafeteria. The cuisine is exceptional and nourishing.

Google promotes family bonding by organizing an annual "bring your kids to work" day, which features enjoyable activities. In addition, newly hired employees are allowed to bring their parents to the workplace on a certain day.

Marriott Hotels India

Marriott's commitment to its employees is seen in its core principles, which prioritize the well-being of its "partners." Since its inception by JW Marriott, the company has maintained a strong commitment to valuing and assisting its employees. This is evident through practices such as personalized mentoring and training sessions conducted by the creator himself, aimed at ensuring the success of each individual. Additionally, employees are shown appreciation through gestures like birthday meals for groups of six and complimentary accommodations. The organization emphasizes work-life balance and provides opportunities for advancement, a pleasant work environment, and comprehensive training resources. Additionally, it offers a reasonable compensation package. Marriott prioritizes transparent communication, collaboration, and striving for success by maintaining unwavering dedication to the right path. In addition, the company offers its employees several benefits, such as reduced hotel rates, programs for developing skills and talents, opportunities for international experience, training across different departments, prizes for performance, room allocation, and health insurance coverage. These programs enhance employee satisfaction and cultivate a culture of high performance and assistance inside the organization [11].

RESEARCH METHODOLOGY

The study utilized both primary and secondary data sources.

The sampling method employed was convenience sampling.

A total of 50 employees at the middle level were included in the sample.

The questionnaire was unstructured and camouflaged.

ANALYSIS AND FINDINGS

This chapter discusses the results of a study that examines the policies and practices of various businesses about work-life balance. While several firms enforce rigorous regulations and limitations, others prioritize establishing an inclusive and adaptable work environment. Certain organizations that prioritize personal connections and empathy even provide financial assistance to their employees by covering the medical expenses of their unwell family members, as an illustration. In today's workforce, job satisfaction and a nice work atmosphere are highly valued, even more so than high salaries. The top 10 firms with the most contented employees offer a hospitable work atmosphere, excellent healthcare benefits, flexible work hours, remote work options, policies that promote gender equality, and a supportive network among colleagues. As per a study conducted by the Great Place to Work Institute and The Economic Times, IT companies constitute a significant proportion of the top 100 best workplaces and generally provide superior working conditions compared to Indian enterprises. The user's text is " [12]".

Fig. (**4**) shows the market standard.

Company insights

Is the salary as per market standard?

57% agreed	67% agreed

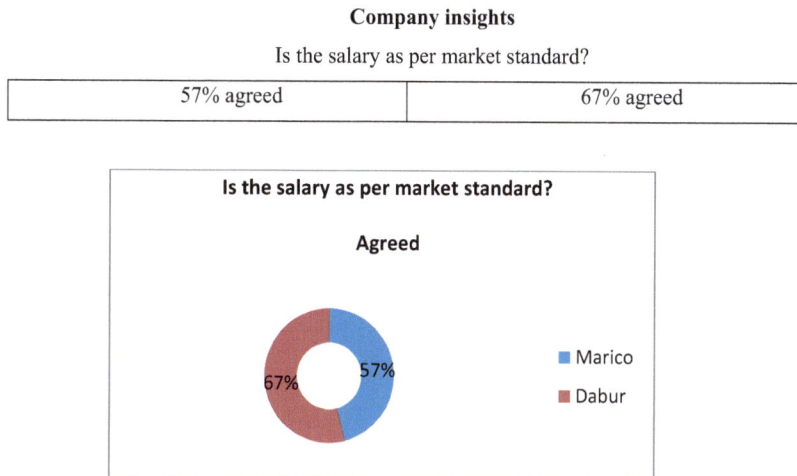

Fig. (4). Market standard.

The Fig. (**5**) shows the Eligibity.

Tell us about your last increment

Appraisal		Appraisal	Imp
Less than 10%	19%	Less than 10%	25%
10-15%	48%	10-15%	48%
15-20%	12%	15-20%	15%
Not Eligible	19%	Not Eligible	11%

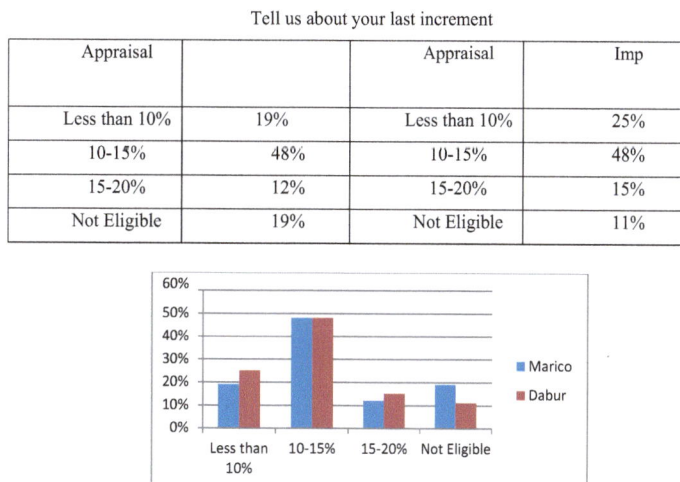

Fig. (5). Eligibity.

The Fig. (**6**) shows the performance analysis.

10+ Hours	NA	10+ Hours	8%

Does the company have a flexible working hours policy?

Flexible Working Hours	Imp	Flexible Working Hours	Imp
Yes	NA	Yes	67%
No	NA	No	17%
Case to case basis	NA	Case to case basis	17%

How smart are your colleagues?

Colleagues	Imp	Colleagues	Imp
Extremely smart	36%	Extremely smart	28%
Average	62%	Average	64%
Below average	2%	Below average	8%

Figure 6 shows the performance analysis.

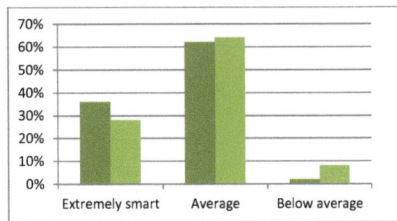

Fig. (6). Performance analysis.

The Fig. (**7**) shows the time accuracy.

How punctual are your co-workers?

Co-Workers	Imp	Co-Workers	Imp
Always on time	51%	Always on time	48%
Most of time	42%	Most of time	41%
Seldom on time	7%	Seldom on time	12%

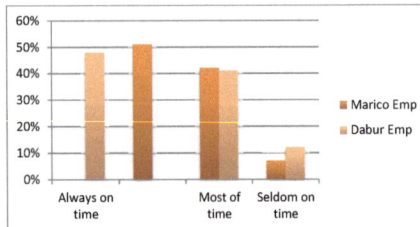

Fig. (7). Time accuracy.

FINDINGS

1. The report indicates that the three leading companies globally prioritize employee satisfaction, an area that requires enhancement in Indian businesses.
2. The poll indicates that Marico Ltd. prioritizes employee wellbeing more than Dabber.
3. It is essential to keep a healthy equilibrium between work and personal life; doing so can lead to burnout [13].

CONCLUSION

Work-life initiatives offer significant benefits to businesses by supporting both individuals and the overall organization. Companies can cultivate a mutually advantageous relationship with their employees by offering flexible work arrangements, supportive policies and resources, and promoting a healthy work-life balance. This may result in enhanced performance, increased retention rates, and a boost in job satisfaction. Employees who possess superior skills in managing the equilibrium between their personal and professional lives are more inclined to experience satisfaction in their jobs, hence augmenting their level of engagement and productivity. Companies can enhance employee morale and reduce absenteeism and attrition rates by granting employees the flexibility to arrange their work schedules according to their obligations, such as familial responsibilities, medical needs, or extracurricular engagements. Furthermore, companies that allocate resources towards work-life programs are establishing a positive image as attractive workplaces, thereby bolstering their employer branding efforts. Companies that prioritize employee well-being and work-life balance are more likely to attract and retain highly skilled employees, leading to improved corporate reputation and financial performance. Implementing work-life initiatives can be advantageous for both the organization and its employees. Companies can cultivate a work environment that promotes job satisfaction, active involvement, and employee retention while simultaneously enhancing their employer branding by fostering a collaborative partnership between the employer and employee.

REFERENCES

[1]   M. Sharma, K. Sharma, R. Gill, S. Salagrama, and G.P. Pandey, "A Circular Patch with Rectangular-Slotted Ground Super-Wideband Two-Port MIMO Antenna for Multiple Wireless Applications", *2023 IEEE Wireless Antenna and Microwave Symposium (WAMS)*, pp. 1-7, 2023. [http://dx.doi.org/10.1109/WAMS57261.2023.10242984]

[2]   K.K. Ezhilarasi, and M.J. Rex, "Reliable and energy-saving forwarding technique for wireless sensor networks using multipath routing", *SSRG International Journal of Computer Science and Engineering*, vol. 1, no. 9, pp. 11-15, 2014.

[3]   J. Logeshwaran, K. Saravanakumar, S. Dineshkumar, and C. Arunprasath, "SBML algorithm for intelligent fuel filling (IFF) and smart vehicle identification system (SVIS)", *International Journal of*

Advanced Research in Management, Architecture. Technology & Engineering, vol. 2, no. 9, pp. 149-154, 2016.

[4]   K. Saravanakumar, and J. Logeshwaran, "Auto-Theft prevention system for underwater sensor using lab view", *International Journal of Innovative Research in Computer and Communication Engineering,* vol. 4, no. 2, pp. 1750-1755, 2016.

[5]   M. Sutharasan, and J. Logeshwaran, "Design intelligence data gathering and incident response model for data security using honey pot system", *International Journal for Research & Development in Technology,* vol. 5, no. 5, pp. 310-314, 2016.

[6]   S. Srivastava, "Lung Infection and Identification using Heatmap", *2nd International Conference on Applied Artificial Intelligence and Computing (ICAAIC),* pp. 1093-1098, 2023.
[http://dx.doi.org/10.1109/ICAAIC56838.2023.10140204]

[7]   S.P. Yadav, S. Zaidi, C.D.S. Nascimento, V.H.C. de Albuquerque, and S.S. Chauhan, "Analysis and Design of automatically generating for GPS Based Moving Object Tracking System", *2023 International Conference on Artificial Intelligence and Smart Communication (AISC),* pp. 1-5, 2023.
[http://dx.doi.org/10.1109/AISC56616.2023.10085180]

[8]   H. Yadav, S. Singh, K.K. Mishra, S. Srivastava, M.S. Naruka, and S.P. Yadav, "Brain Tumor Detection with MRI Images", *International Conference on Computational Intelligence and Sustainable Engineering Solutions (CISES),* pp. 519-527, 2022.
[http://dx.doi.org/10.1109/CISES54857.2022.9844387]

[9]   J. Kaur, J. Saxena, and J. Shah, "Fahad and S. P. Yadav, "Facial Emotion Recognition", *International Conference on Computational Intelligence and Sustainable Engineering Solutions (CISES),* pp. 528-533, 2022.
[http://dx.doi.org/10.1109/CISES54857.2022.9844366]

[10]   C. Arensberg, "360-degree feedback 15 accountability, of employees 81–2 ADDIE model 8 Africa, management 52 African Renaissance 60", *Cultural Context of Human Resource Development,* vol. 9, p. 251, 2009.

[11]   Für Arbeit, B. (2000). InstitutfürArbeitsmarkt-und Berufsforschung. Zahlen-Fibel, Ausgabe.

[12]   B. Engel, "A Comprehensive analysis of Network Coding for Efficient Wireless Network Communication", *2nd International Conference on Industrial Electronics: Developments & Applications (ICIDeA),* pp. 204-210, 2018.

[13]   M.A. Mohammed, R. Ramakrishnan, M.A. Mohammed, V.A. Mohammed, and J. Logeshwaran, "A Novel Predictive Analysis to Identify the Weather Impacts for Congenital Heart Disease Using Reinforcement Learning", *2023 International Conference on Network, Multimedia and Information Technology (NMITCON),* pp. 1-8, 2023.
[http://dx.doi.org/10.1109/NMITCON58196.2023.10276376]

CHAPTER 39

Chronic Kidney Disease Prediction Using Machine Learning: Feature Selection

Sujoy Mondol[1,*], **Syed Mohammad Moiez Ur Rahman**[1], **Asjad Moiz Khan**[1], **Hoor Fatima**[1] and **Preeti Dubey**[1]

[1] *Computer Science & Technology, Sharda University, Greater Noida, (U.P.), India*

Abstract: Chronic kidney disease (CKD) is a pathological condition that, if not addressed, can progress to renal failure. Machine learning models have the potential to assist in predicting chronic kidney disease by analyzing data from blood tests, urine tests, imaging tests, and biopsies. This study primarily examined a dataset of blood samples consisting of 26 patient features. These features were subsequently narrowed down to the top 10 based on their highest statistical score, which was calculated using SelectKBest. This technique enhances the accuracy and efficiency of machine learning models by reducing the dimensionality of the input data and emphasizing the most pertinent features. In this study, two approaches were examined. The K-fold cross-validation technique achieved the greatest accuracy of 98.0%, while the average accuracy for the same technique was 96.0%. On the other hand, the Naive Bayes classifier achieved an accuracy score of approximately 93.33%. The results show promise in accurately predicting the identification of patients with chronic renal disease.

Keywords: Chronic renal disease, Machine learning models, Naive Bayes classifier, Pathological, The Chi-Square feature selection method.

INTRODUCTION

The kidneys are vital organs in the human body. The organs are bilaterally situated on opposite sides of the body. They provide a variety of functions within the human body, such as filtering blood to eliminate waste and excess fluid. Although filtration is a primary role of the kidneys, they also carry out various other activities, including the crucial activation of Vitamin D, which is essential for calcium absorption and maintaining healthy bones [1]. The body regulates electrolytes (such as sodium, potassium, and calcium), maintains the balance of

---

[*] **Corresponding author Sujoy Mondol:** Computer Science & Technology, Sharda University, Greater Noida, (U.P.), India; E-mail: sujoy.mondol5r8@gmail.com

Pankaj Kumar Mishra & Satya Prakash Yadav (Eds.)

acids and bases, controls blood pressure (by producing renin), and produces hormones that stimulate the production of red blood cells in the bone marrow (*via* erythropoietin) [2, 3]. Chronic kidney failure refers to the progressive decline in kidney function, resulting in renal failure and the deterioration of kidney structure [4]. Renal failure impairs the kidney's filtration function, resulting in the accumulation of waste products in the body. CKD, or chronic kidney disease, refers to a persistent abnormality in kidney structure or function that lasts for more than three months [5]. The condition impacts around 19 million individuals in the United States, and its prevalence is quickly rising. The disease is mostly linked to the identification of many underlying health disorders, such as diabetes mellitus, hypertension, a history of cardiovascular health complications, and a family history of the disease. These disorders primarily cause the majority of diagnosed instances of chronic kidney disease. Approximately 40-60% of individuals who are advancing toward late-stage renal disease have diabetes, while 15-30% have hypertension. The user's text is "[6]".This is a progressive ailment that can result in irreversible kidney damage or possibly renal failure. The initial phases of chronic kidney disease (CKD) may exhibit minor or no symptoms, such as fatigue or frequent urination. While the progression of the disease may go unnoticed as it advances, individuals may start to observe elevated levels of protein or creatinine in their urine during the initial stages. In advanced stages and severe instances, renal failure may occur, necessitating the patient's dependence on dialysis for blood purification or the need for a kidney transplant. The mortality rate of end-stage renal illness is 24% [7]. Chronic kidney disease is incurable. This underscores the significance of promptly detecting CKD in individuals, as diagnosing it at earlier stages not only facilitates prevention and slows down its advancement but also reduces the financial burden on patients, as treatment costs escalate exponentially as the disease progresses. Here, we utilize machine learning models to forecast and diagnose chronic kidney disease precisely. The datasets of chronic kidney disease contain numerous features that can potentially result in overfitting and inaccurate outcomes. Therefore, in this study, we employ the Chi-Square feature selection method to identify the most pertinent features for predicting chronic kidney disease in individuals.

LITERATURE SURVEY

Machine learning methods are progressively being embraced in several areas, including the healthcare industry. The utilization of machine learning methodologies might significantly augment the efficacy of systems and clinical aid by facilitating intelligent recognition and diagnosis of diverse ailments and disorders. There has been discussion over the use of machine learning techniques to detect and identify chronic kidney disease by applying various models and datasets [8]. The authors of a study [9] investigated the capacity of machine learning to enhance early diagnosis and cost-effectiveness. In a study [10], a dataset consisting of 24 characteristics from 400 patients was evaluated. The researchers utilized recursive feature elimination to determine the most important attributes. Four classification approaches, specifically support vector machine (SVM), k-nearest neighbors, decision tree, and random forest, were employed. Out of all the classifiers, the random forest classifier demonstrated superior performance by achieving flawless accuracy, recall, precision, and an F-1 score of 100%. Multiple studies and research [11] have consistently shown that the random forest classifier has the highest accuracy, as reported by numerous authors in the field. The researchers, in their study,[12] performed a thorough examination of different classifiers, including random forest, Naive Bayes, logistic regression, and SVM, to investigate, ascertain, and assess their performance. The evaluation of each machine learning model was conducted using measures including accuracy, sensitivity, specificity, and AUC score. The findings demonstrated that the random forest classifier, when combined with random forest feature selection, achieved the best level of accuracy. The researchers [13] utilized various machine learning algorithms, such as random forest, support vector machine (SVM), and decision tree, to conduct both binary and multi-classification prediction tasks. By employing cross-validation, certain techniques, such as analysis of variance and recursive feature reduction, were used to choose features. The experimental findings demonstrated that random forest while utilizing recursive feature removal achieved superior performance compared to SVM and DT. The J48 approach exhibited the highest accuracy rate of 99% in comparison to other classifiers, such as Naive Bayes, SVM, and K-Star, as evidenced by the conducted tests. The tests were performed on a dataset of 400 individuals and 25 characteristics [14]. Moreover, some research has discovered that different feature selection strategies can enhance the precision of various classifiers. A study [15] employed a dataset including 400 patients and 24 variables for their analysis. The data analysis was conducted using the artificial neural network (ANN) and the SVM classifier. The findings demonstrated that the artificial neural network (ANN) classifier surpassed the support vector machine (SVM) classifier, with a remarkable accuracy of 99.75% in contrast to the SVM classifier's accuracy of 97.75%. Furthermore, numerous authors have employed deep neural networks, as exemplified in a study [16], wherein Ant Lion Optimization is incorporated with a deep neural network. The authors [17] utilized an improved version of the extreme gradient boosting (XGBoost) method to attain cost and time effectiveness. The optimized model achieved a sensitivity, specificity, and testing accuracy of 1.000, indicating excellent performance in all three metrics. The authors of a study [18] employed two ensemble strategies, bagging and random subspace methods, in conjunction with three base learners to improve the classification performance of the models. Prior to the evaluation, the data underwent preprocessing. The findings demonstrated that the ensemble strategies surpassed the performance of the individual base learners. The random subspace technique, when paired with the kNN classifier, demonstrated the highest performance, with a perfect accuracy rate of 100%. Feature selection strategies, in addition to classifiers, play a crucial role in accurately diagnosing chronic kidney disease. To decrease the number of dimensions in the dataset, the authors of a study [19] utilized an SVM classifier together with two different feature selection methods, specifically wrapper and filter. The findings demonstrated that the support vector machine (SVM) classifier, utilizing the best first search engine feature selection approach and the filtered subset evaluator, attained a peak accuracy of 98.5%. In their study, the authors [20] introduced a method that integrated an information-gain-based feature selection strategy with a cost-sensitive adaptive performance. The method yielded a precision rate of 99.8%, with a sensitivity of 100% and a specificity of 99.8%. Furthermore, the authors employed an ensemble learning methodology in addition to feature selection. The study employed a dataset including 400 instances and 24 attributes. AdaBoost was implemented for ensemble learning, while the correlation-based selection of characteristics (CFS) method was used for feature selection. The underlying classifiers consisted of support vector machines (SVM), Naive Bayes, and the K-nearest neighbor algorithm (kNN). The integration of kNN algorithms with CFS and AdaBoost resulted in an ideal outcome characterized by high levels of accuracy, recall, and f-measure, reaching a rate of 0.981. The Naive Bayes classifier, when paired with CFS and AdaBoost, produced a precision rate of 0.981, which was the highest among all tested methods. The authors analyzed the challenges associated with incorporating statistical learning techniques into the Apache Spark framework. Their focus was specifically on X2 feature selection to improve performance and time efficiency. The authors suggested utilizing data mining techniques to reveal hidden information regarding patients, aiming to improve the diagnosis process and enable intelligent decision-making. They utilized many metrics and decision tree algorithms to predict patient survival. A comprehensive investigation was carried out to ascertain the accuracy of classifiers, involving a multitude of tests utilizing various ensemble learning methodologies and feature selection algorithms. To effectively use classifiers, it is necessary to construct feature selection techniques in order to reduce the dimensionality of the dataset.

METHODOLOGY

The data analysis of this specific process involved the collection of blood samples from patients. From these samples, the most relevant features were selected to assess if a patient was afflicted with chronic kidney disease. This flowchart illustrates the sequential stages involved in a standard data analysis and modeling procedure. The initial stages of the process involved data preparation and collection, which were subsequently followed by feature engineering and data analysis. Subsequently, the evaluation of the selected and trained machine learning model was conducted. The model was employed in the production phase to generate predictions using newly acquired data. Data scientists and machine learning specialists can utilize this flowchart as a comprehensive guide for developing and executing data models, as shown in Fig. (**1**).

At the start of the data cleaning process, the recorded data included 26 features that were important for the work. However, only 10 of these features were used for prediction. These 10 features were further defined and analyzed through a feature extraction method. The final dataset consisted of the successful recordings that were used to train the model. The other 16 features from the initial dataset, which had scores lower than 88, were discarded. This was because the feature score of 88 had a significant impact on the training model.

Given the presence of additional categories within each feature, it is certain that there will be noisy data that requires proper attention. This can be addressed by replacing the noisy data with accurate values, hence reducing data discrepancies and improving the performance of the model. An essential aspect of the analysis would be the examination of the data features. This is crucial due to the presence of numerous missing values, which could introduce bias into the model. The inclusion of adequate data for prediction metrics would lead to correct predictions or inaccuracies in the model's performance. The presence of missing values is significant, as the mean, median, or mode values of a specific row or column in a dataset may not adequately compensate for a large number of missing values. This limitation becomes particularly problematic for larger datasets, as it can lead to inaccurate predictions by the model and potentially jeopardize the patient's survival.

During distribution analysis, it is crucial to assess whether the provided features exhibit a normal distribution. Skewness, which measures the degree of asymmetry, can significantly impact the accuracy of predictions in machine learning models. Highly skewed data can introduce bias and inaccuracies. Thus, it is essential to examine each feature in the dataset thoroughly. To mitigate skewness, techniques such as logarithmic or square root transformation can be applied to the data. The following figure illustrates the skewness of the features.

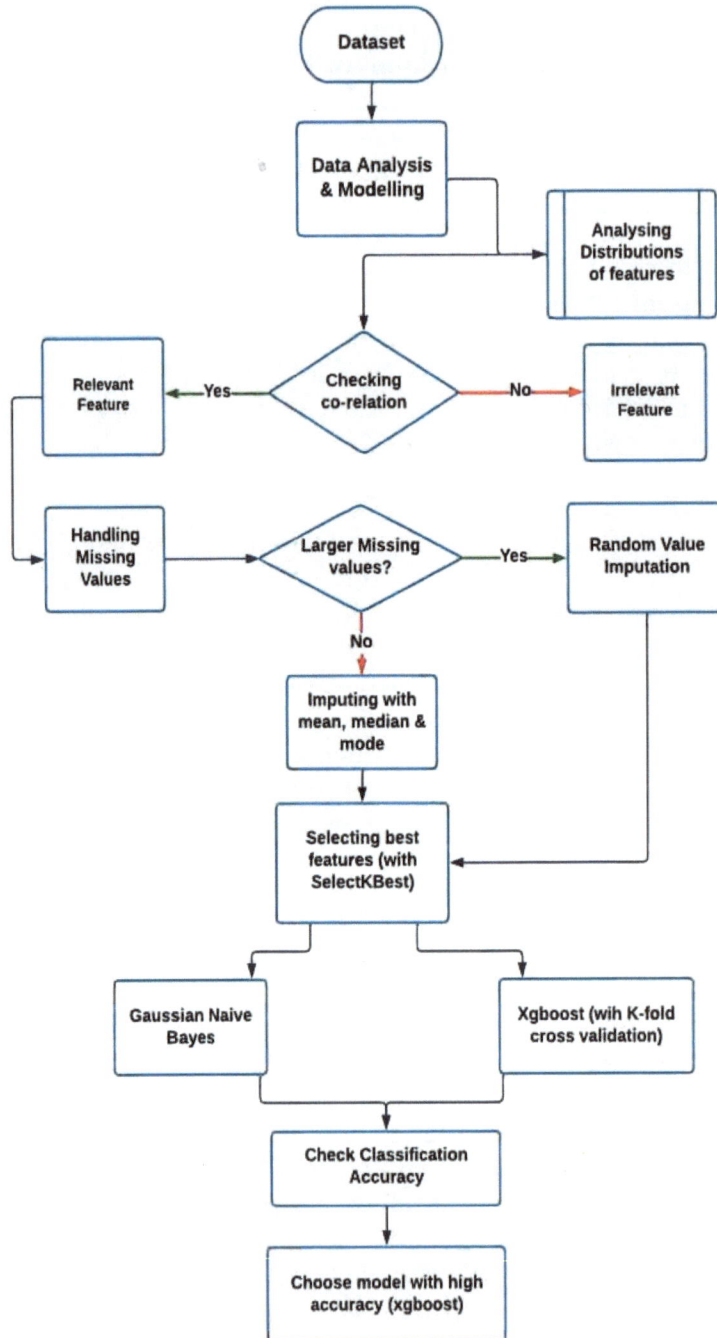

Fig. (1). Prediction with machine learning models.

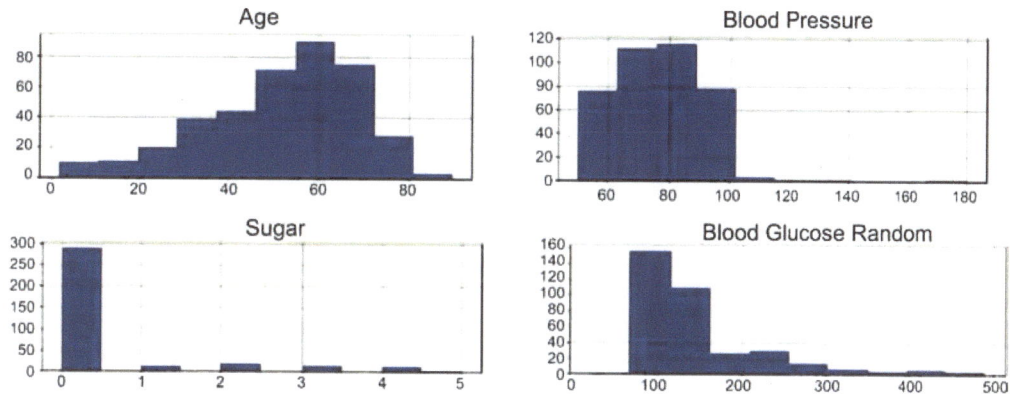

Fig. (2). Analyzing distributions of data features.

Fig. (**2**) illustrates the skewness of the features. The feature "age" is slightly skewed to the left, while "blood glucose random" is skewed to the right. The remaining characteristics all exhibit mild skewness. Skewness is a crucial aspect of statistical analysis.

When making predictions, it is crucial to analyze the features in order to gain a clear understanding of their relevance and the amount of information they provide. To improve the model, it is important to examine the correlations between the features and determine their positive or negative impact on the given classes, such as patients with chronic kidney disease (CKD) and patients without CKD. The violin plot from the plotlib express library is utilized to represent the data density visually. Wider areas of the plot indicate a higher concentration of data points, while narrower sections indicate a lower concentration.

Below is an illustration of a violin plot displaying the red blood cell count characteristic. In the context of chronic renal disease, RBC counts ranging from 2 to 4.5 are often regarded as indicative of a positive diagnosis, whereas levels between 4.5 and 6.1 are deemed negative.

Fig. (**3**) displays a comprehensive analysis of the red blood cell count feature. It precisely indicates the density of the data and identifies if a high count of red blood cells is indicative of chronic renal illness.

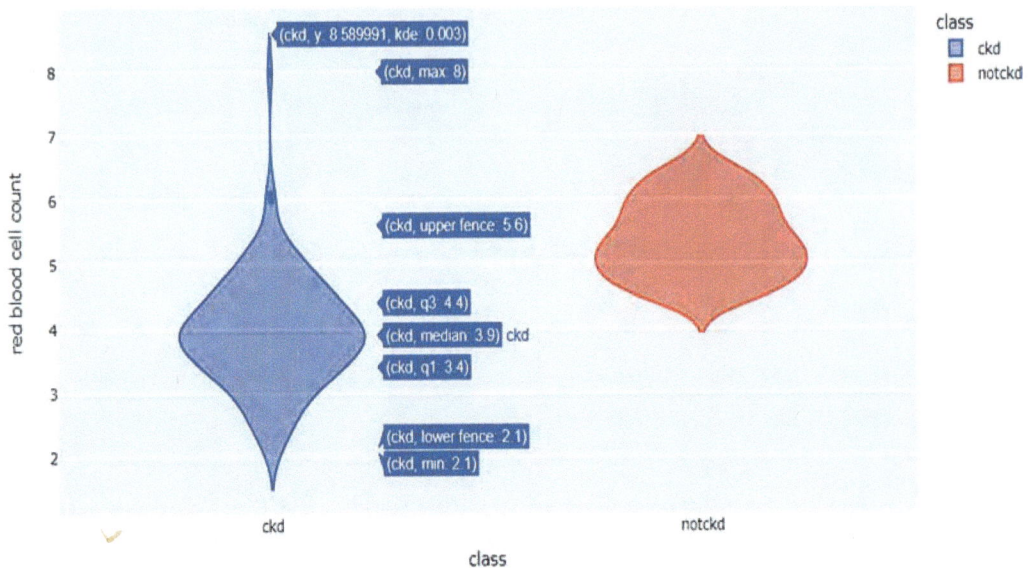

Fig. (3). Violin plot for red blood cell count feature.

To address the issue of missing values and mitigate its impact on the model's accuracy, we will employ a technique called random value imputation. This technique involves replacing missing values with randomly generated values.

Random value imputation involves selecting random values to fill in missing data. However, if there are more than 1000 missing values, this method can have a negative impact on the model. It is best used when there are only a small number of missing values and the available data is enough to make a reliable estimate. Thoroughly assessing the machine learning model's performance is crucial following the random value imputation. This evaluation aims to verify that the imputed values do not introduce any bias or inaccuracies into the analysis. Here is an example of a feature that has addressed the issue of random value imputation and displayed the corresponding change.

Fig. (**4**) illustrates the data transformation achieved by applying random value imputation. The first graph displays a count of 248 for the normal category and 47 for the abnormal category. In contrast, the second graph shows a count of approximately 400 for the normal category and 69 for the abnormal category. This transformation will not significantly impact the model.

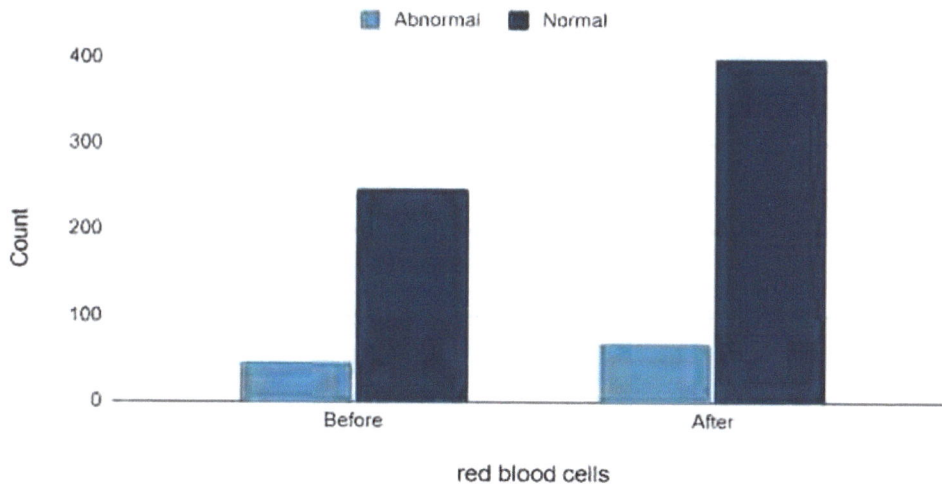

Fig. (4). Before and after applying random value imputation to red blood cells feature.

After completing the feature analysis, selecting the best features becomes the highest priority for the model to achieve efficient performance. The comparative features are picked using the SelectKBest method, which is specifically designed for feature selection.

The mathematical framework of SelectKBest involves employing a statistical test to calculate a score for each feature within the dataset. Choosing the K features with the most elevated scores. The SelectKBest method was used in this study to analyze the given comparative features. The independent features were represented in one column, while the dependent features were represented in another column. Let X_i represent the value of each feature j for sample i in the given dataset X, and let Y_i represent the matching label for sample i in the target or dependent variable y. SelectKBest applies a statistical test to each feature in dataset X in order to get a score. Define S_j as the numerical value representing the score for feature j. The score was then evaluated using a chi-squared test, which quantifies the association between two category variables or identifies traits that are correlated with the target variable. Mathematically, it determined if the p-value is smaller than 0.05 or not. The p-value in the chi-squared test represents the probability of obtaining a chi-squared test statistic that is more extreme than the observed value. If the p-value is less than the significance level (0.05), it indicates evidence of an association between two categorical variables.

After the computation of the features, a new dataset called X_new was created, as previously mentioned. Let F be the set of indices corresponding to the selected characteristics, where the cardinality of F is equal to K. The revised dataset comprised the chosen characteristics for each sample, denoted as X_new. If j is a member of the set F, then X_new will be equal to X. Otherwise, X_new will be equal to 0. Ultimately, the chosen characteristics in X_new were utilized to train the provided model for forecasting the target or dependent variable. The mathematical model for the SelectKBest feature selection was then completed.

This study focuses on the use case of cross-validation, which is a technique belonging to the family of ensemble methods. Specifically, the XGboost algorithm is utilized, which employs the boosting technique to combine multiple weak models and create a strong model. The algorithm iteratively adjusts the weights of observations to prioritize samples that were misclassified in the previous iteration. Through repeated iterations, the algorithm enhances the overall performance of the model.

The primary strategy employed in this work is cross-validation, a method from ensemble learning. It involves partitioning the data into several subsets and training the model on one subset while evaluating its performance on the remaining subsets. This approach is utilized to examine the model's performance and mitigate the risk of overfitting. The method is iterated numerous times to obtain the desired outcome. There are four distinct strategies for cross-validation: K-fold cross-validation, stratified K-fold cross-validation, leave-one-out cross-validation, and shuffle-split cross-validation. The primary focus of this study is the implementation of stratified K-fold cross-validation.

The following model can mathematically represent K-fold cross-validation:

- Partitioning dataset X into K equi-probable folds, with each fold accurately capturing the class distribution of dataset X
- Utilize each fold j (where j = 1, 2, ..., K) as the validation set while using the remaining folds as the training set.
- The model undergoes training using the training set, and its performance is evaluated using the validation set.
- Iterate steps 2 and 3 K times, using a distinct fold each time as the validation set and the remaining folds as the training set to evaluate the performance.
- Compute the mean performance metric (*e.g.*, accuracy, precision, recall, F1-score, ROC-AUC) over the K assessments.
- The resultant average performance metric can be utilized to select the optimal model or to compare many models. It offers a prediction of the model's effectiveness on data that has not been observed.

After employing the XGBClassifier as the model, the randomized Search CV technique was utilized. This technique aids in optimizing the hyperparameters of a model by doing a randomized search across the hyperparameter space. The process commenced with the establishment of a hyperparameter space, which was delineated by several methodologies such as grid search or random sampling. Subsequently, the algorithm stochastically selected values from the hyperparameters space and utilized these hyperparameters to train the model on a subset of the data. It then assessed the model's performance on the remaining fold. The process was iterated K times, with each iteration employing a distinct fold for evaluation. The model's performance was subsequently averaged across the K folds to produce the optimal performance. It is crucial to thoroughly assess the performance of the ultimate model by employing an independent test set to guarantee satisfactory generalization performance.

The second algorithm selected for this study was Naive Bayes, specifically Gaussian Naive Bayes. This algorithm is defined as a probabilistic method that utilizes the Bayes theorem to estimate the likelihood of each class based on a given set of input data. Here, the initial probability of each class was computed by determining the ratio of samples in the training set that were assigned to that particular class. In the subsequent stage, the probabilities were computed. This involved calculating the mean and variance of each input feature for every class based on all the training samples belonging to that class. It then assumed that each feature is distributed independently and calculated the likelihood of the input features given that class using the probability density function. The last stage involved the computation of posterior probabilities, achieved by multiplying the prior probability of each class by the product of each input feature given that class. Subsequently, it can standardize the resultant probabilities in a manner that ensures their cumulative total equals one. The Gaussian Naive Bayes scoreswere evaluated using the accuracy, precision, recall, and F1 score metrics.

RESULTS

The accuracy scores of the ensemble approach, namely the K-fold cross validation algorithm and Naive Bayes, are 96.0% and 93.33%, respectively. These results are presented in Table **1** below. The scores are derived from the top 10 features of the dataset, which are strongly recommended for predicting the occurrence of chronic renal disease in a patient.

The boost algorithm achieved a maximum accuracy of 98.0%. The missing values were addressed through random value imputation, causing the accuracy score to vary with each iteration. However, the average accuracy score of the algorithm was determined to be 96.0%. This indicates that the model is sufficiently robust in predicting the presence of chronic kidney disease in patients. Fig. (**5**) shows the accuracy scores.

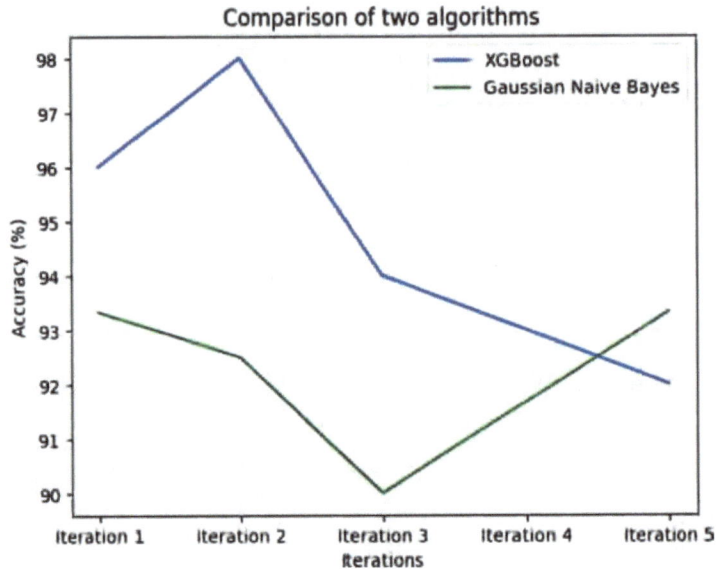

Fig. (5). Accuracy scores of ML Algorithms.

The hyperparameter values were tuned during the hyperparameter tuning phase to maximize the precision of the model, resulting in the selection of the best estimators for the dataset. The optimal estimators were obtained by the use of randomizedsearchCV, which facilitated the construction of the model with the desired level of precision Fig. (**6**).

```
XGBClassifier(base_score=0.5, booster='gbtree', callbacks=None,
              colsample_bylevel=1, colsample_bynode=1, colsample_bytree=0.3,
              early_stopping_rounds=None, enable_categorical=False,
              eval_metric=None, feature_types=None, gamma=0.4, gpu_id=-1,
              grow_policy='depthwise', importance_type=None,
              interaction_constraints='', learning_rate=0.2, max_bin=256,
              max_cat_threshold=64, max_cat_to_onehot=4, max_delta_step=0,
              max_depth=10, max_leaves=0, min_child_weight=3, missing=nan,
              monotone_constraints='()', n_estimators=100, n_jobs=0,
              num_parallel_tree=1, predictor='auto', random_state=0, ...)
```

Fig. (6). Best estimators from randomized search CV.

The confusion matrix was generated using the xgboost technique for the test data, which consisted of 100 occurrences. The class values used were "CKD" and "non ckd", as indicated in Table **1**. Based on the confusion matrix, 93 instances were accurately classified, while the rest of the examples were misclassified.

Table 1. Confusion Matrix - Xgboost.

-	Non Ckd	Ckd
Non Ckd	63	5
Ckd	2	30

A confusion matrix was generated using the Gaussian Naive Bayes method for the test dataset, which consisted of 100 cases. The class values (Ckd, non-ckd) were obtained from Table **2**. Based on the confusion matrix, 92 instances were accurately identified, while the rest were misclassified.

Table 2. Confusion Matrix - Gaussian Naive Bayes.

-	Non Ckd	Ckd
Non Ckd	57	5
Ckd	3	35

The XBG classifier, utilizing the K-fold cross-validation technique, demonstrated superior performance as a classifier with an accuracy score of 96.0%. The Naive Bayes classifier achieved an accuracy score of 93.33%. However, despite the favorable scores, it is important to acknowledge the limitations of the methods employed in obtaining these scores. One such limitation is the utilization of random value imputation, which, although convenient for handling missing values, has the potential to introduce bias to the model or result in biased estimates. Random value imputation can worsen a systematic pattern of missing data if one exists. By substituting the absent values, one effectively disregards the potential information that could have been present in the missing data. It may result in a reduction of statistical strength, and employing random value imputation can also yield inconsistent outcomes across various imputations, particularly if the missing data is not completely random.

SelectKBest is a highly effective method for selecting the most significant and pertinent features for model training. However, it is important to be aware of certain drawbacks. One potential issue is that if the feature selection criterion is excessively tailored to the training data, it may result in overfitting. Additionally, SelectKBest necessitates the specification of a hyperparameter, denoted as k, which determines the number of features to be selected. Unfortunately, determining the optimal value of k is often challenging, and selecting an inappropriate value could have a detrimental impact on the model's performance. SelectKBest is incapable of managing strongly associated features in the dataset, often resulting in the selection of only one of them, thereby leading to the loss of crucial information. According to the model's results, if the model is fine-tuned with specific specifications and emphasizes the feature selection method, it can be inferred that multiple algorithms can be employed with the SelectKBest method. This approach allows for not only focusing on highly correlated features but also considering the overall performance of the model. Consequently, the model can be implemented in real-world systems for practical use.

CONCLUSION

This work highlights the significance of utilizing characteristics present in blood samples, in conjunction with machine learning algorithms, to accurately identify individuals with chronic kidney disease. The evaluation of the two techniques yielded higher accuracy scores from the model. The objective of this study is to determine the efficacy of the feature selection strategy in enhancing the overall performance of the model. The SelectKBest function is employed in conjunction with the chi-squared technique to identify the top 10 features that are most effective in determining the presence of chronic kidney disease in a patient. The ensemble technique achieved the highest accuracy of 96.0%, followed by Naive Bayes with 93.33%. In the future, advanced selection features can be developed to efficiently and accurately identify the most relevant features. If this model can be implemented in real-world scenarios and can effectively consider highly correlated features, predicting chronic kidney disease will become easier, provided that the input data is accurate.

REFERENCES

[1]   D. Swain, U. Mehta, A. Bhatt, H. Patel, K. Patel, D. Mehta, B. Acharya, V.C. Gerogiannis, A. Kanavos, and S. Manika, "A Robust Chronic Kidney Disease Classifier Using Machine Learning", *Electronics (Basel),* vol. 12, no. 1, p. 212, 2023.
[http.//dx.doi.org/10.3390/electronics12010212]

[2]   M.S. Arif, A. Mukheimer, and D. Asif, "Enhancing the early detection of chronic kidney disease: a robust machine learning model", *Big Data and Cognitive Computing,* vol. 7, no. 3, p. 144, 2023.
[http://dx.doi.org/10.3390/bdcc7030144]

[3]   D.A.A. Pertiwi, P.R. Setyorini, M.A. Muslim, and E. Sugiharti, "Implementation of Discretisation and Correlation-based Feature Selection to Optimize Support Vector Machine in Diagnosis of Chronic Kidney Disease", *Buletin Ilmiah Sarjana Teknik Elektro,* vol. 5, no. 2, pp. 201-209, 2023.

[4]   S. Savitha, and A. Rajiv Kannan, "A novel technique based on mutual information weighted feature selection to predict chronic kidney disease", *Journal of Intelligent & Fuzzy Systems,* pp. 1-14, .
[http://dx.doi.org/10.3233/JIFS-222401]

[5]   M.A. Islam, M.Z.H. Majumder, and M.A. Hussein, "Chronic kidney disease prediction based on machine learning algorithms", *J. Pathol. Inform.,* vol. 14, p. 100189, 2023.
[http://dx.doi.org/10.1016/j.jpi.2023.100189] [PMID: 36714452]

[6]   M. M. Hassan, M. M. Hassan, S. Mollick, M. A. R. Khan, F. Yasmin, and A. K. Bairagi, "A Comparative Study, Prediction and Development of Chronic Kidney Disease Using Machine Learning on Patients Clinical Records", *Human-Centric Intelligent Systems,* pp. 1-13, 2023.

Running header

[7]   D.M. Alsekait, H. Saleh, L.A. Gabralla, K. Alnowaiser, S. El-Sappagh, R. Sahal, and N. El-Rashidy, "Toward Comprehensive Chronic Kidney Disease Prediction Based on Ensemble Deep Learning Models", *Appl. Sci. (Basel),* vol. 13, no. 6, p. 3937, 2023.
[http://dx.doi.org/10.3390/app13063937]

[8]   H. Iftikhar, M. Khan, Z. Khan, F. Khan, H.M. Alshanbari, and Z. Ahmad, "A Comparative Analysis of Machine Learning Models: A Case Study in Predicting Chronic Kidney Disease", *Sustainability (Basel),* vol. 15, no. 3, p. 2754, 2023.
[http://dx.doi.org/10.3390/su15032754]

[9]   K. Poorani, and M. Karuppasamy, "Comparative Analysis of Chronic Kidney Disease Prediction Using Supervised Machine Learning Techniques", *International Conference on Information and Communication Technology for Intelligent Systems,* pp. 87-95, 2023.
[http://dx.doi.org/10.1007/978-981-99-3982-4_8]

[10] T. Saroja, and Y. Kalpana, "Adaptive Weight Dynamic Butterfly Optimization Algorithm (ADBOA)-Based Feature Selection and Classifier for Chronic Kidney Disease (CKD) Diagnosis", *Int. J. Comput. Intell. Appl.,* vol. 22, no. 1, p. 2341001, 2023.
[http://dx.doi.org/10.1142/S1469026823410018]

[11] S. Salagrama, and V. Bibhu, "Study of it and data center virtualization", *2nd International Conference on Innovative Practices in Technology and Management (ICIPTM),* vol. 2, pp. 274-278, 2022.
[http://dx.doi.org/10.1109/ICIPTM54933.2022.9754152]

[12] V. Bibhu, S. Salagrama, B.P. Lohani, and P.K. Kushwaha, "An Analytical Survey of User Privacy on Social Media Platform", *International Conference on Technological Advancements and Innovations (ICTAI),* pp. 173-176, 2021.
[http://dx.doi.org/10.1109/ICTAI53825.2021.9673402]

[13] V.A. Rajan, T. Marimuthu, G.V. Londhe, and J. Logeshwaran, "A Comprehensive analysis of Network Coding for Efficient Wireless Network Communication", *2nd International Conference on Industrial Electronics: Developments & Applications (ICIDeA),* pp. 204-210, 2023.
[http://dx.doi.org/10.1109/ICIDeA59866.2023.10295177]

[14] M.A. Mohammed, R. Ramakrishnan, M.A. Mohammed, V.A. Mohammed, and J. Logeshwaran, "A Novel Predictive Analysis to Identify the Weather Impacts for Congenital Heart Disease Using Reinforcement Learning", *International Conference on Network, Multimedia and Information Technology (NMITCON),* pp. 1-8, 2023.
[http://dx.doi.org/10.1109/NMITCON58196.2023.10276376]

[15] V.A. Mohammed, M.A. Mohammed, M.A. Mohammed, R. Ramakrishnan, and J. Logeshwaran, "The Spreading Prediction and Severity Analysis of Blood Cancer Using Scale-Invariant Feature Transform", *International Conference on Network, Multimedia and Information Technology (NMITCON),* pp. 1-7, 2023.
[http://dx.doi.org/10.1109/NMITCON58196.2023.10276289]

[16] S. Srivastava, "Lung Infection and Identification using Heatmap", *2nd International Conference on Applied Artificial Intelligence and Computing (ICAAIC),* pp. 1093-1098, 2023.
[http://dx.doi.org/10.1109/ICAAIC56838.2023.10140204]

[17] S.P. Yadav, S. Zaidi, C.D.S. Nascimento, V.H.C. de Albuquerque, and S.S. Chauhan, "Analysis and Design of automatically generating for GPS Based Moving Object Tracking System", *International Conference on Artificial Intelligence and Smart Communication (AISC),* pp. 1-5, 2023.
[http://dx.doi.org/10.1109/AISC56616.2023.10085180]

[18] H. Yadav, S. Singh, K.K. Mishra, S. Srivastava, M.S. Naruka, and S.P. Yadav, "Brain Tumor Detection with MRI Images", *International Conference on Computational Intelligence and Sustainable Engineering Solutions (CISES),* pp. 519-527, 2022.
[http://dx.doi.org/10.1109/CISES54857.2022.9844387]

[19] J. Kaur, J. Saxena, and J. Shah, "Fahad and S. P. Yadav, "Facial Emotion Recognition", *International*

Conference on Computational Intelligence and Sustainable Engineering Solutions (CISES), pp. 528-533, 2022.
[http://dx.doi.org/10.1109/CISES54857.2022.9844366]

[20]   R. Salama, F. Al-Turjman, D. Bordoloi, and S.P. Yadav, "Wireless Sensor Networks and Green Networking for 6G communication- An Overview", *International Conference on Computational Intelligence, Communication Technology and Networking (CICTN),* pp. 830-834, 2023.
[http://dx.doi.org/10.1109/CICTN57981.2023.10141262]

CHAPTER 40

Blockchain for Electronic Health Record

Shubham Kumar Mishra[1,*], **Pratyush Prashar**[1] and **Priyanka Tyagi**[1]

[1] Information Technology Sharda University, Plot No. 32-34, Knowledge Park III, Greater Noida, Uttar Pradesh 20131, India

Abstract: Blockchain has the potential to revolutionize the sharing and preservation of patient's electronic health records by offering secure means for information exchange during care transitions and ensuring their safety on a decentralized peer-to-peer network. An exhaustive and methodical examination of the literature was undertaken to locate the latest study on blockchain technology in the healthcare sector. The objective was to identify the present obstacles and unanswered queries in order to facilitate and streamline comprehension of this era of decentralized record-keeping. The reassessment was prompted by the increasing number of examination questions related to electronic health records (EHR) within a blockchain. The primary objectives of our organized framework are to initially leverage blockchain technology for electronic health records (EHR) and then establish user-friendly electronic data storage capabilities through the implementation of detailed access controls.

Keywords: Blockchain, Decentralized, Electronic health records, Healthcare, Peer-to-peer network.

INTRODUCTION

The latest technological breakthrough profoundly influences all facets of human existence and fundamentally alters our conventional perception and understanding of the world. Just like how technology has transformed all aspects of our lives, it is now uncovering fresh avenues for expansion in the fitness care industry. The primary benefits that technological advancements are providing to the care business include enhancing security, improving user comprehension, and addressing several other concerns. Ensuring interoperability in healthcare is crucial, particularly in the context of exchanging electronic health data, due to the following reasons [1]:

Rapid and straightforward retrieval of patient information: Patients receive healthcare services from various care institutions, including public health clinics,

---

* **Corresponding author Shubham Kumar Mishra:** Information Technology Sharda University, Plot No. 32-34, Knowledge Park III, Greater Noida, Uttar Pradesh 20131, India; E-mail: shubham@ug.sharda.ac.in

Pankaj Kumar Mishra & Satya Prakash Yadav (Eds.)

school clinics, medical groups, urgent care centers, pharmacies, laboratories, and hospitals. Cultural variables, the standard of care, bedside manner, and proximity all play a role in the choosing of healthcare practitioners [2]. Data fragmentation significantly amplifies the probability of errors when healthcare professionals attempt to integrate data from many sources. Statistics indicate that 20% of medical errors leading to a negative drug incident in a hospital setting were caused by a lack of accessible patient information [3].

Enhancing the Productivity of Healthcare Professionals: An interconnected healthcare system has the potential to significantly improve healthcare by minimizing superfluous paperwork and redundancy [4].

Cost reduction in the national healthcare system: Inadequate information sharing leads to a significant amount of healthcare costs being attributed to repeated diagnoses and laboratory tests. The elimination of these unnecessary repetitions can be greatly aided by the ease of accessing the data within a compatible health system. Semantic interoperability refers to the ability of multiple systems to exchange data while preserving its meaning [5].

Although healthcare system interoperability offers numerous advantages, it encounters several challenges. Medical data, including genetic information, computed tomography, and X-ray images, are of substantial size and are expanding at an annual rate of 30% to 50%. In 2016, an average American healthcare professional possessed 660 terabytes of patient data. The predominant portion of this data consisted of unstructured medical photographs, which represents the primary concern. The volume of healthcare big data is projected to reach 35,000 petabytes by 2025, based on current growth rates.

Diversity in healthcare information systems: The issue of cross institutional information interoperability is becoming increasingly significant due to the utilization of several healthcare information system providers that employ multiple multi-platforms with distinct system architectures, infrastructures, and databases.

Medical knowledge is estimated to double every 70 days, which increases the value and prevalence of healthcare data [6]. Therefore, it is crucial to prioritize ensuring that patients have full access to their medical records while also protecting the security and accuracy of health data. The primary advantages of implementing a blockchain strategy for managing distributed ledgers lie in the enhanced security measures and the individuals' capacity to exercise control over their information. This is of utmost importance considering recent alarming trends of data breaches at major hospitals [7] and a growing movement among individuals who, naturally, desire transparency in the utilization of their data.

This concise paper outlines a perspective on how decentralized healthcare records, safeguarded by blockchain technology, can be understood in relation to patient rights, confidentiality, and online security. The utilization of a blockchain-based electronic health record (EHR) system offers numerous advantages, such as enhanced security, transparency, interoperability, and granting patients complete control over their data. Blockchain technology ensures the encryption and decentralized storage of patient health information to safeguard it from hackers and other security threats [8]. Moreover, it facilitates transparent and verifiable transactions, granting patients the capability to access their health data and monitor the individuals who have accessed it and the corresponding timestamps. Fig. (**1**) shows the flowchart.

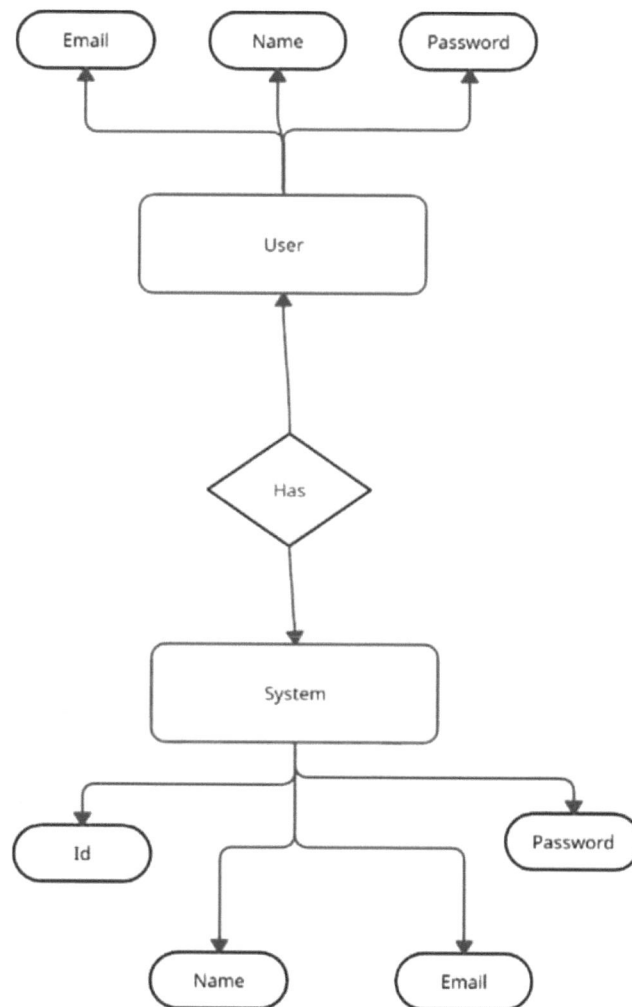

Fig. (1). ER Diagram.

BACKGROUND AND RELATED WORK

Background

Electronic Health Records (EHRs)

Due to the rapid advancement of information technology and internet technology, electronic health records (EHRs), which are a digital format for collecting patient data, are replacing traditional methods of patient data collection. Health information is highly confidential and sensitive and should only be discussed with individuals such as doctors, pharmacists, family members, insurance companies, and other medical facilities. Hospitals and healthcare organizations widely use electronic health records (EHR) to manage and save patient information. Ensuring the preservation of data integrity, anonymity, and confidentiality is undeniably a vital concern in this system. However, electronic health records (EHRs) encounter several privacy and security concerns, such as the presence of malware and distributed denial-of-service (DDoS) attacks, which can undermine the efficacy of patient care. Cyber assaults have graver consequences than security breaches and economic damage. These operations highlighted the immediate need to ensure the privacy, availability, security, and integrity of transmitting electronic health information (EHRs). The user's text is " [9]".

Blockchain Technology

The main objective of blockchain technology development in the healthcare sector is to utilize blockchain techniques to ensure the security and privacy of electronic health records (EHRs) in different healthcare applications. In 2008, Satoshi Nakamoto pioneered the development of blockchain technology, which was initially utilized in Bitcoin [10]. Blockchain technology enables the storage and sharing of data in a decentralized network. The utilization of blockchain technology can enhance the level of trust inside a network [11]. Blockchain technology comprises three core components: public-key encryption, consensus mechanisms, and a distributed ledger [12]. Each block on the blockchain contains a minimum of one transaction, the signature of the block validator, and a reference to the block headers of the preceding block. Blockchain data formats facilitate the creation and sharing of diverse transactions within a digital ledger across nodes in a peer-to-peer network. Blockchain technology allows parties to securely store and transmit essential data in real time without compromising communication networks to malicious intent, counterfeiting, or theft. Every transaction in a blockchain is assigned a distinct hash, which is then utilized to construct the binary Merkletree [13]. The block header contains the binary tree, as well as the timestamp and identity of the previous block. The blocks that are sequentially linked and serve as documentation of alterations to the ledger's state are commonly known as the "chain" [14]. Consequently, modifying the entries in the blockchain necessitates altering both the hash of the present block and the hash of subsequent blocks, a task that is exceedingly difficult to do.

The Blockchain Platforms

However, other alternative blockchain technologies such as Bitcoin, Ethereum, Hyperledger, Ripple, and Quorum have been proposed and employed in recent years for various security application scenarios [15]. The Ethereum blockchain has introduced new decentralized technologies in both financial and non-financial sectors, providing a rich programming language within a blockchain ecosystem [16]. Ethereum offers the highest level of developer assistance, as it was one of the earliest blockchain systems to enable smart contracts. Ethereum is a distributed platform designed for the implementation of intelligent agreements [17]. In Ethereum, a smart contract is utilized to do certain computational tasks on the blockchain. Conceptually, this implies that any computational task can be executed by an Ethereum smart contract [18]. Prior to determining a winner, miners on the Ethereum network expeditiously make educated guesses on puzzle solutions, validate and authorize transactions, and employ diverse procedures.

Related Work

With the integration of new technology, the healthcare industry faces several pressing issues that require immediate resolution. Numerous researchers have highlighted the security concern and acknowledged the lack of significant progress. The primary objectives of safeguarding medical information are authenticity, confidentiality, and non-repudiation. Our current strategy focuses on implementing blockchain technology for electronic health records (EHR) from the start. This will enable users to securely store digital information while also having fine-grained control over system access. Their purpose was to enhance patient security through error reduction and data collection.

Furthermore, our present objective is to utilize the electronic health record (EHR) system to address the issues above of data spatiality and data breaches. The authors emphasize that blockchain may need a significant drawback in terms of measurability despite its undeniable ability to address measurability issues alongside lightning, bitcoin money, and bitcoin gold [19]. The purpose of their presence is to utilize the decentralized nature of the blockchain era, along with the ability to measure data accurately supplied by the underlying infrastructure, and develop a scalable blockchain solution for scientific document management. The primary objective of this endeavor is to modify a style in a manner that fulfills the specifications set out by the Office of the National Organiser for Fitness

Information Generation (ONC). The authors specifically selected blockchain technology for their current framework due to its potential applicability in constructing identification systems, including decision terms in electronic health record structures, and addressing security concerns associated with such systems. The gadget generates additional revenue by validating the form that is submitted within it.

In contrast to previous solutions, our current strategy aims to tackle this issue of measurability by leveraging the ipfs off-chain scaling mechanism. Furthermore, Ethereum is commonly utilized for the implementation of the present architecture. The objective of this current framework is to create a localized system that is tamper-proof, secure, and based on blockchain technology for storing digital health records. The existing architecture consists of users who are most likely individuals seeking medical treatment, doctors, administrators, and nursing personnel. They were awarded specific access privileges corresponding to their varying levels of control over the gadget [20]. The utilization of blockchain technology in the healthcare industry has gained significant traction, particularly in the realm of securely keeping and transferring medical data. Three distinct versions of Ethereum smart contracts offer a functional prototype application utilizing blockchain technology. The healthcare sector is required to ensure interoperability among different institutions, across national boundaries, and with existing databases. This has the potential to improve the quality of information and the quality of life for patients. It is recommended to utilize the recommended framework for other applications, such as cloud data sharing or vehicular network communications, as it enables connection between different domains.

DIFFERENCE BETWEEN EXISTING SYSTEM AND PROPOSED SYSTEM

Existing System

India, a country with a population of more than 1.4 billion people, characterized by geographical, social, linguistic, religious, and ethnic diversity, unquestionably requires a healthcare infrastructure capable of effectively and securely managing the health data of every individual. The "Ayushman Bharat Yojana" initiative demonstrates the Indian government's dedication to attaining Universal Health Coverage (UHC) by 2030 through the implementation of the National Health Protection Scheme (NHPS). DeepMind Health, a division of Google, plans to develop a platform similar to blockchain technology to securely monitor patient data in the National Health Service (NHS). Furthermore, the NHS or its hospitals will have the capability to authenticate their datasets utilizing DeepMind's Blockchain, which differs from conventional blockchain that relies on decentralized verification from a collective of users. DeepMind asserts that these disparities will enhance the efficiency of the system. The medical chain utilizes both blockchain and state-of-the-art technology to enhance the exchange of patient information among hospitals, pharmacies, and insurance providers. Medical records have become increasingly centralized and challenging to distribute. The current difficulty in obtaining essential patient health information in the presence of a physician should be minimized. The implementation of a medical chain would facilitate efficient, expeditious, and safeguarded access to medical records for patients, clinicians, and insurers, as shown in Fig. (**2**).

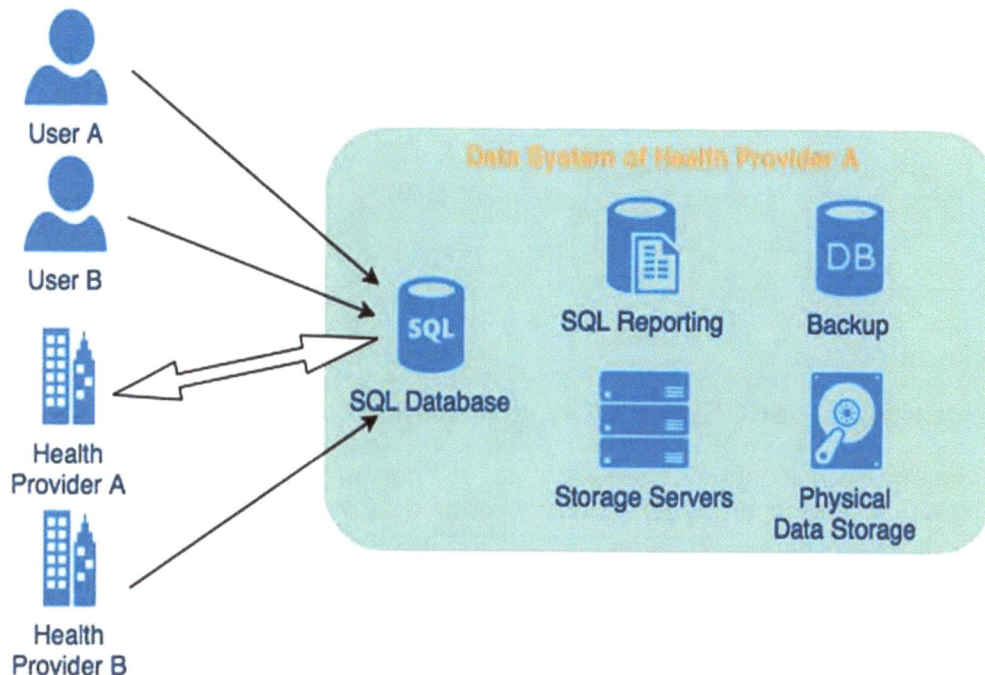

Fig. (2). Existing system.

Proposed System

The key concern with the current healthcare system is the presence of multiple, disconnected patient medical records maintained by different companies. The suggested system aims to tackle the existing challenges in the healthcare business by utilizing the blockchain technology to establish a smart ecosystem for medical record transactions. To mitigate the risk of illegal third-party access to patient data, it is imperative to establish secure access protocols for such data. EHR Framework utilizes blockchain technology to securely store records and maintain a unified and reliable source of information. In order to retrieve a patient's medical data and record the transaction on the distributed ledger, the stakeholders will be required to request authorization. A solution based on blockchain technology facilitates broad accessibility, confidentiality of data, cost efficiency, and confidence in the information system, as shown in Fig. (**3**).

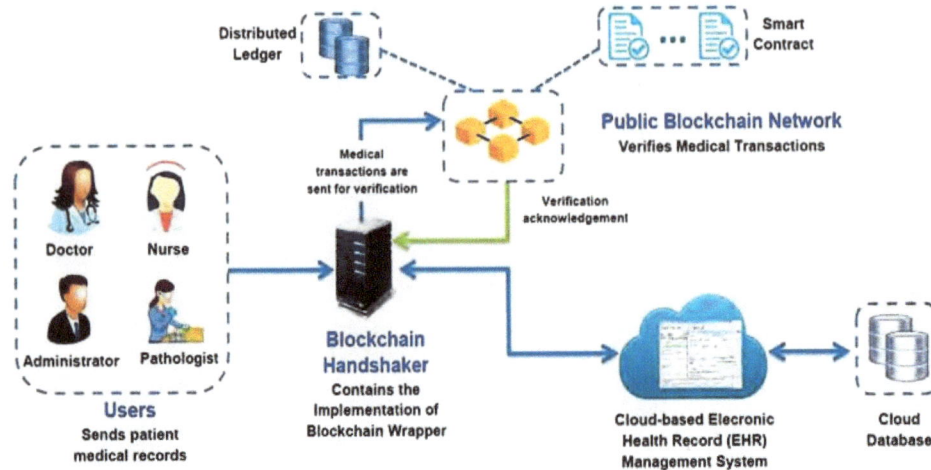

Fig. (3). Proposed system.

BLOCKCHAIN ARCHITECTURE FOR EHR

Given the broad adoption of cloud storage, the prevailing method for transmitting electronic health record (EHR) data is for the data owner to store the encrypted EHR data on the cloud securely. Our method involves partitioning vast quantities of data into multiple organized data columns and storing them on cloud storage servers, ensuring the security of the data. We propose a data storage system that utilizes it to verify the security and integrity of data, as well as ascertain whether any modifications have been made prior to downloading. However, the user has no control over the environment of cloud storage services, making it vulnerable to external threats and jeopardizing the security of patient data. In order to commence the transaction, any stakeholder of the EHR system, acting as a member, begins by sending a message indicating the creation of a new block/transaction. Upon completing the registration process, the user can, after that, access the system by logging in using the same set of credentials. Upon successfully logging in and completing the registration process, we employ RSA encryption to secure the data. The RSA technique is a type of cryptographic architecture that is asymmetric and facilitates public-key encryption. It is widely employed for securing email communications and other sophisticated online operations. It is primarily beneficial for delivering information across a network that is unclear or uncertain, similar to the Internet. The generated image data is stored on the IPFS server while we maintain a database of shared hashes and transaction hashes. Once a user has created a shared image, any papers they want to post are also encrypted and stored on the server. The server uses IPFS, which stands for interplanetary file system, which oversees the organization and control of files and their numerous iterations throughout a vast network. By applying a hashing algorithm to a file, we generate a fixed-length string that is unique to the file and its contents.

IPFS solely retains the cryptographic hashes corresponding to files on the blockchain without storing the contents themselves. The precise location of the file will then be ascertained utilizing these hashes. A suitable analogy for this situation is inviting someone to your residence. We furnish them with a reference (address) indicating our actual place of residence, enabling them to return it to us instead of physically relocating our home to them. However, we will also resolve encryption concerns by employing cryptographic public and private keys. Public keys are utilized for the purpose of digitally verifying an individual's identity, while non-public keys function as a digital signature.

Similarly, while accessing and publishing files on IPFS, we will enable authorized individuals to gain access by encrypting the file using the recipient's public key. Then, the file's hash is transmitted from that location to IPFS. The user retrieves the hashed file from the database in the event that another user requires access to it. When the shared picture and the private file coincide, the private file will be shared, and the shared image will, after that, undergo OCR to decode its information, as shown in Fig. (**4**).

RESULT AND DISCUSSION

This section delineates the implementation of the proposed approach. The system was built using Ethereum. The patient, doctor, and administrator are stakeholders in the proposed system. Every participant is assigned a certain role, such as a patient, doctor, or administrator, and possesses the capability to modify, add, delete, and view information. The proposed system is evaluated based on parameters such as throughput, latency, and execution time. The proposed system underwent evaluation as the number of records grew, and its scalability was ensured. The system was maintained in an unchangeable state, and precautions were taken to prevent any unauthorized modifications by stakeholders not allocated to the job. Furthermore, there was an assurance that those without authorization would be unable to gain access to the electronic health record (EHR). When persons with proper authorization accessed the data, they also ensured that the privacy of the data was maintained, as shown in Figs. (**5** and 6).

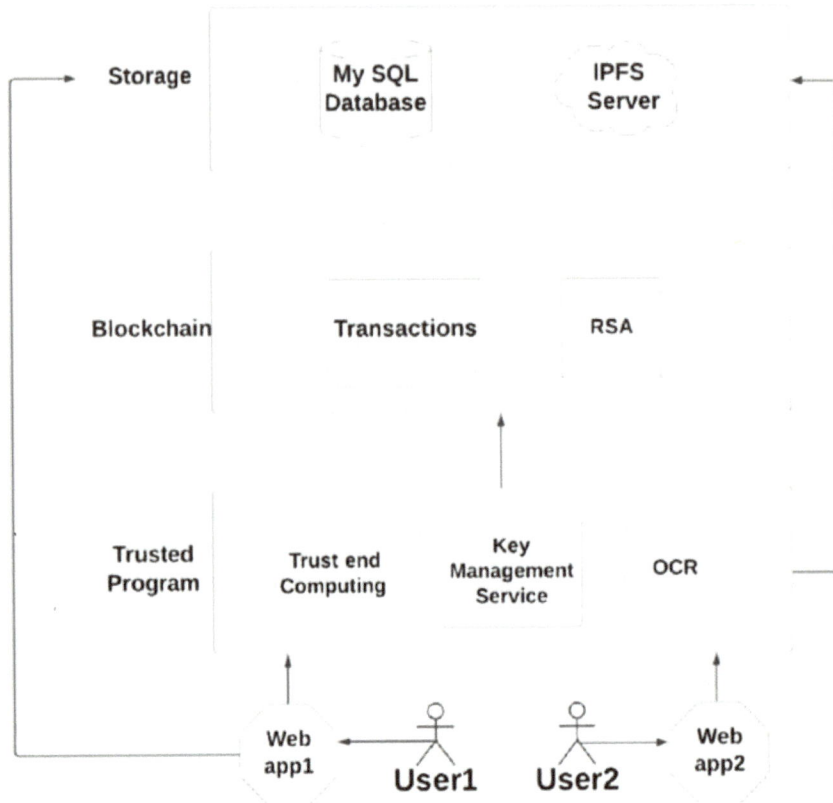

Fig. (4). Architecture of the system.

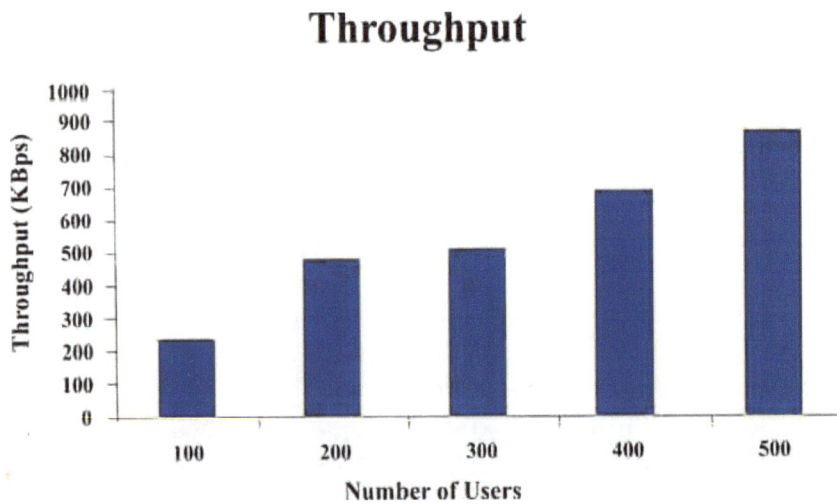

Fig. (5). Throughput of the proposed system.

Average Latency

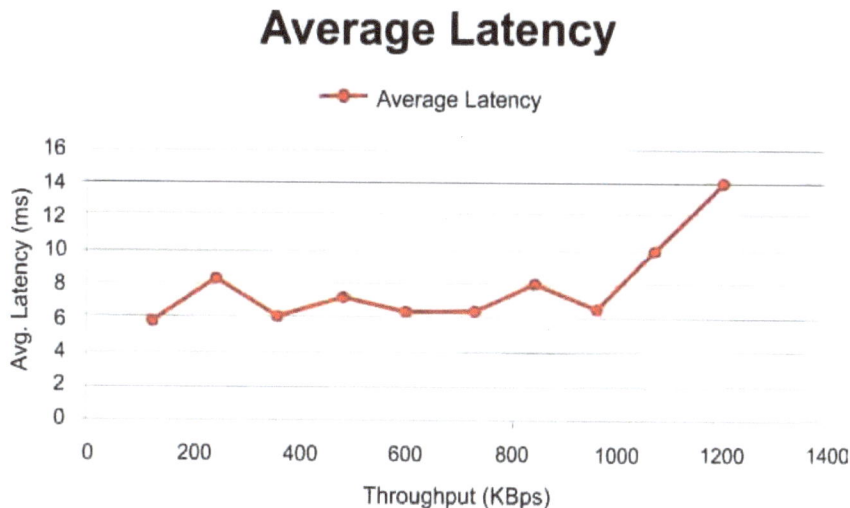

Fig. (6). Average latency.

CONCLUSION AND FUTURE WORK

This study investigated methods for securely and confidentially sharing electronic health records (EHRs) over two distinct blockchain networks. The proposed framework enables the addition, updating, and secure viewing of patient records through a hybrid blockchain architecture that utilizes a framework known as Ledger. Smart contracts are utilized to validate patient records on the blockchain, ensuring that a secure and anonymous chain is formed while upholding the principles of data integrity. Smart policies incorporate record tracking to evaluate the secure storage of electronic health records (EHRs) and enhance transaction performance. The blockchain employs a decentralized approach to store patient records, ensuring optimal throughput, transaction speed, and response times. One of the important areas to focus on in future work is prioritizing the establishment of compatibility between entirely separate blockchain platforms. The payment module is expected to be included in the existing structure, as per our usual procedure. In order to determine the cost of a patient's consultation with a doctor using this localized blockchain system, we need to address several issues. Furthermore, it is necessary to provide explicit directives for regulations and norms that align with the essential principles of the healthcare sector.

REFERENCES

[1]   H.B. Mahajan, A.S. Rashid, A.A. Junnarkar, N. Uke, S.D. Deshpande, P.R. Futane, A. Alkhayyat, and B. Alhayani, "Retracted article: Integration of Healthcare 4.0 and blockchain into secure cloud-based electronic health records systems", *Appl. Nanosci.,* vol. 13, no. 3, pp. 2329-2342, 2023. [http://dx.doi.org/10.1007/s13204-021-02164-0] [PMID: 35136707]

[2]   B.K. Rai, "PcBEHR: patient-controlled blockchain enabled electronic health records for healthcare

4.0", *Health Serv. Outcomes Res. Methodol.,* vol. 23, no. 1, pp. 80-102, 2023.

[3]   A. Hajian, V.R. Prybutok, and H.C. Chang, "An empirical study for blockchain-based information sharing systems in electronic health records: A mediation perspective", *Comput. Human Behav.,* vol. 138, p. 107471, 2023.
[http://dx.doi.org/10.1016/j.chb.2022.107471]

[4]   F.A. Reegu, H. Abas, Y. Gulzar, Q. Xin, A.A. Alwan, A. Jabbari, R.G. Sonkamble, and R.A. Dziyauddin, "Blockchain-Based Framework for Interoperable Electronic Health Records for an Improved Healthcare System", *Sustainability (Basel),* vol. 15, no. 8, p. 6337, 2023.
[http://dx.doi.org/10.3390/su15086337]

[5]   S. Alam, S. Bhatia, M. Shuaib, M.M. Khubrani, F. Alfayez, A.A. Malibari, and S. Ahmad, "An overview of blockchain and IoT integration for secure and reliable health records monitoring", *Sustainability (Basel),* vol. 15, no. 7, p. 5660, 2023.
[http://dx.doi.org/10.3390/su15075660]

[6]   Á. Díaz, and H. Kaschel, "Scalable Electronic Health Record Management System Using a Dual-Channel Blockchain Hyperledger Fabric", *Systems (Basel),* vol. 11, no. 7, p. 346, 2023.
[http://dx.doi.org/10.3390/systems11070346]

[7]   D.K. Murala, S.K. Panda, and S.K. Sahoo, "Securing electronic health record system in cloud environment using blockchain technology", In: *Recent advances in blockchain technology: real-world applications.* Springer International Publishing: Cham, 2023, pp. 89-116.
[http://dx.doi.org/10.1007/978-3-031-22835-3_4]

[8]   E.S. Babu, B.V.R.N. Yadav, A.K. Nikhath, S.R. Nayak, and W. Alnumay, "MediBlocks: secure exchanging of electronic health records (EHRs) using trust-based blockchain network with privacy concerns", *Cluster Comput.,* vol. 26, no. 4, pp. 2217-2244, 2023.
[http://dx.doi.org/10.1007/s10586-022-03652-w]

[9]   L. Abdelgalil, and M. Mejri, "HealthBlock: A Framework for a Collaborative Sharing of Electronic Health Records Based on Blockchain", *Future Internet,* vol. 15, no. 3, p. 87, 2023.
[http://dx.doi.org/10.3390/fi15030087]

[10] R. Cerchione, P. Centobelli, E. Riccio, S. Abbate, and E. Oropallo, "Blockchain's coming to hospital to digitalize healthcare services: Designing a distributed electronic health record ecosystem", *Technovation,* vol. 120, p. 102480, 2023.
[http://dx.doi.org/10.1016/j.technovation.2022.102480]

[11] L.M. Baltruschat, V. Jaiman, and V. Urovi, "User acceptability of blockchain technology for enabling electronic health record exchange", *J. Syst. Inf. Technol.,* vol. 25, no. 3, pp. 268-295, 2023.
[http://dx.doi.org/10.1108/JSIT-09-2022-0225]

[12] X. Xue, S. Palanisamy, M. A, D. Selvaraj, O.I. Khalaf, and G.M. Abdulsahib, "A Novel partial sequence technique based Chaotic biogeography optimization for PAPR reduction in generalized frequency division multiplexing waveform", *Heliyon,* vol. 9, no. 9, p. e19451, 2023.
[http://dx.doi.org/10.1016/j.heliyon.2023.e19451] [PMID: 37681146]

[13] G. Muttashar Abdulsahib, D. Sekaran Selvaraj, A. Manikandan, S. Palanisamy, M. Uddin, O. Ibrahim Khalaf, M. Abdelhaq, and R. Alsaqour, "Reverse polarity optical Orthogonal frequency Division Multiplexing for High-Speed visible light communications system", *Egyptian Informatics Journal,* vol. 24, no. 4, p. 100407, 2023.
[http://dx.doi.org/10.1016/j.eij.2023.100407]

[14] A.G. Ismaeel, J. Mary, A. Chelliah, J. Logeshwaran, S.N. Mahmood, S. Alani, and A.H. Shather, "Enhancing Traffic Intelligence in Smart Cities Using Sustainable Deep Radial Function", *Sustainability (Basel),* vol. 15, no. 19, p. 14441, 2023.
[http://dx.doi.org/10.3390/su151914441]

[15] A. Bagwari, J. Logeshwaran, K. Usha, K. Raju, M.H. Alsharif, P. Uthansakul, and M. Uthansakul, "An Enhanced Energy Optimization Model for Industrial Wireless Sensor Networks Using Machine

Learning", *IEEE Access,* vol. 11, pp. 96343-96362, 2023.
[http://dx.doi.org/10.1109/ACCESS.2023.3311854]

[16]   A. Armghan, J. Logeshwaran, S.M. Sutharshan, K. Aliqab, M. Alsharari, and S.K. Patel, "Design of biosensor for synchronized identification of diabetes using deep learning", *Results Eng.,* vol. 20, p. 101382, 2023.
[http://dx.doi.org/10.1016/j.rineng.2023.101382]

[17]   H. Yadav, S. Singh, K.K. Mishra, S. Srivastava, M.S. Naruka, and S.P. Yadav, "Brain Tumor Detection with MRI Images", *International Conference on Computational Intelligence and Sustainable Engineering Solutions (CISES),* 2022.
[http://dx.doi.org/10.1109/CISES54857.2022.9844387]

[18]   P. Rani, S. Verma, S.P. Yadav, B.K. Rai, M.S. Naruka, and D. Kumar, "Simulation of the Lightweight Blockchain Technique Based on Privacy and Security for Healthcare Data for the Cloud System", *International Journal of E-Health and Medical Communications,* vol. 13, no. 4, pp. 1-15, 2022.
[http://dx.doi.org/10.4018/IJEHMC.309436]

[19]   "Transforming Management with AI, Big-Data, and IoT", *Springer International Publishing,* 2022.
[http://dx.doi.org/10.1007/978-3-030-86749-2]

[20]   J. Bhardwaj, A. Nayak, C.S. Yadav, and S.P. Yadav, "A Review in Wavelet Transforms Based Medical Image Fusion", In: *Evolving Role of AI and IoMT in the Healthcare Market.,* F. Al-Turjman, M. Kumar, T. Stephan, A. Bhardwaj, Eds., Springer: Cham, 2021.
[http://dx.doi.org/10.1007/978-3-030-82079-4_9]

CHAPTER 41

A Systematic Review: Technology for Battery Management System

Divya G.[1,*] and **Venkata Padmavathi S.**[2]

[1] Electrical and Electronics Engineering, CVR College of Engineering, Telangana, Hyderabad, India

[2] Gitam School of Technology, Gitam Deemed to be University Telangana, Hyderabad, India

Abstract: Electric vehicles have garnered significant attention in recent years due to their little environmental impact and reduced maintenance expenses. Despite its numerous benefits, the primary drawback lies in the need for more charging stations and infrastructure. Therefore, it is crucial to accurately estimate the state of charge (SOC) of the battery and determine the position of a nearby battery station for battery switching or charging. This paper discusses two previously conducted research studies and their potential future advancements. The first study focuses on utilizing the Internet of Things (IoT) to educate vehicle owners about the battery health monitoring of hybrid electric vehicles (HEV). The Internet of Things (IoT) is crucial for the supervision and management of batteries. Furthermore, a charging station equipped with battery swapping/charging capabilities is provided to owners of hybrid electric vehicles (HEVs) through the utilization of advanced technology.

Keywords: Batteries, Charging station, Hybrid electric vehicles (HEV), Internet of Things (IoT), Infrastructure.

INTRODUCTION

Following the COVID-19 pandemic, there has been a significant surge in the number of automobiles on the road. Consequently, the increase in vehicle traffic led to a rise in pollution levels. Electric vehicles have yet to gain full acceptance in the automobile industry, and the majority of purchases are still made for vehicles that run on fossil fuels. According to the IBB research, the number of units sold has risen from 3.9 million to 4.4 million between the years 2020 and 2022. Due to the surge of internal combustion engine (ICE) vehicles, the pollution levels in several cities in India have exceeded the predicted range given by the

* **Corresponding author Divya. G.:** Electrical and Electronics Engineering, CVR College of Engineering, Telangana, Hyderabad, India; E-mail: divya.gongidi@cvr.ac.in

Pankaj Kumar Mishra & Satya Prakash Yadav (Eds.)

World Health Organization (WHO) by a factor of ten [1]. Additionally, PM 2.5 particles, which are minuscule dust particles, pose a significant threat to human health and can significantly shorten lifespan. The concentration of PM 2.5 particles has doubled as a result of the increase of vehicles on the road. The mitigation of this extensive harm to the environment and human well-being can be achieved through the reduction of the commercialization of internal combustion engine (ICE) automobiles. An alternative to internal combustion engine (ICE) automobiles is to enhance the adoption of electric vehicles (EVs) across various models. An important issue in hybrid electric vehicles (HEV) and electric vehicles (EV) is the limited range before needing to recharge the car. The limited availability of accurate battery health data and charging infrastructure is hindering the widespread adoption of electric and hybrid vehicles in the market. The BMS (Battery Management System) is a crucial component that follows the electric motor in the EV (Electric Vehicle) family. BMS will oversee and regulate the battery process [2]. Providing effective control and monitoring, as well as ensuring safe operation, it also facilitates the collection of vehicle battery data for storage in a remote control location. If the battery's condition is known and an alarm is triggered to indicate the immediate need for battery replacement, it is necessary to communicate with the nearest charging station promptly. This feature enables the vehicle owner to proceed with the replacement of the battery promptly. There should be a platform that stores the data of charging stations in a decentralized manner, using a secure technique for data transfer. This study explores the application of IoT in monitoring battery health, as well as the usage of IoT technologies for battery swapping or recharging.

BATTERY MANAGEMENT SYSTEM

Battery management system (BMS) plays a crucial role in electric vehicles, as these vehicles heavily rely on the battery and electric motors included within them. The BMS system should monitor the charging and discharging methods in order to preserve the battery's lifespan [3] and utilize the stored energy for extended periods. Battery management systems (BMS) play a crucial role in electric vehicles, as these vehicles heavily rely on the battery and electric motors included within them. The BMS system should monitor the charging and discharging methods in order to preserve the battery's lifespan [3] and utilize the stored energy for extended periods.

BMS in use

The existing BMS system for EV/HEV needs to be more developed in comparison to other BMS systems found in devices like laptops. The BMS system in EV/HEV must effectively handle many cells that operate at high voltages and currents. The battery management system (BMS) for electric and hybrid electric vehicles (EV/HEV) is getting increasingly intricate [4]. The implanted sensors provide data sensing.

Battery-health specifics: The battery management system (BMS) should accurately measure the voltage of each cell and monitor the current passing through the system [5].

The BMS organization consists of three primary divisions.

1. Monitoring the status and performance of batteries.
2. Managing the operation and maintenance of batteries.
3. State of the battery.

BMS Functions

The battery management system will perform four primary duties, including

• Monitoring battery parameters.
• Managing temperature.
• Calculating battery parameters.
• Establishing communication.

The BMS system performs the crucial role of monitoring battery parameters. Monitoring is conducted for each cell's voltage, current, temperature, and state of charge (SOC).

The temperature has a significant impact on battery life. The temperature monitoring system is responsible for completing this task. Utilizing air as a coolant is the most straightforward method to reduce the temperature of a battery. The addition of air coolant to the car will result in an enlargement of its dimensions, hence diminishing the efficiency of the battery. Fig. (**1**) depicts the battery management system.

The battery calculations for each cell are performed based on the input and output voltage and current. These will also encompass internal impedance, kilowatt-hour energy sent in the last cycle, energy supplied, and charging/discharging cycles [6], as shown in Fig. (**1**).

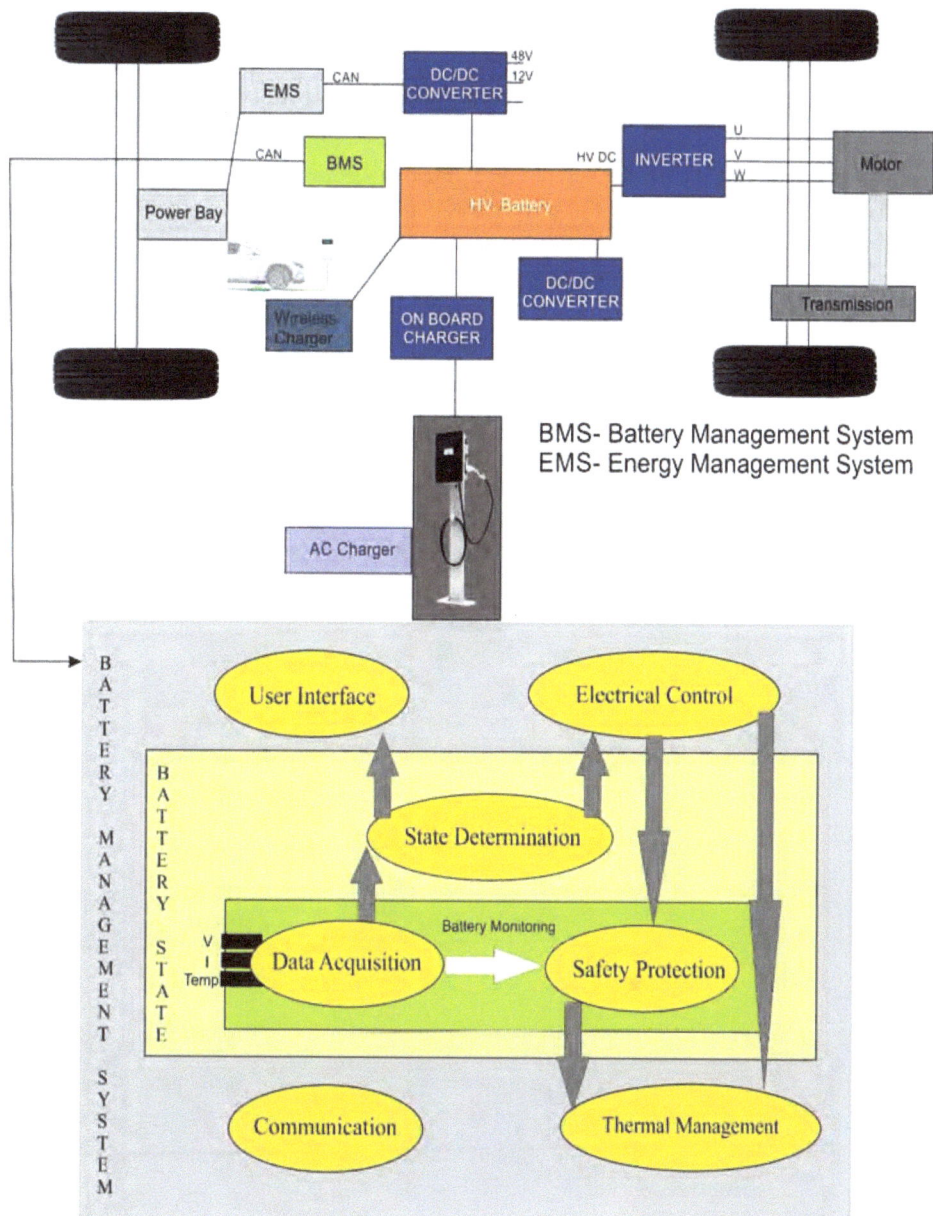

Fig. (1). Battery management system.

BMS utilizes both internal and external hardware controllers to establish communication with interconnected systems. Physical components of a computer system include the processor, memory, and storage devices.

There are two types of communication: optical communication and wireless communication.

OPERATIONS OF BMS

It is necessary to establish the battery specifications at the beginning. It is necessary to establish thresholds for current, voltage, temperature, and state of charge (SOC) required. The specified limits are provided to indicate the amount of charge that can be stored in a battery [7]. Fig. (2) displays the flow chart of the battery management system. The following calculations are utilized to approximate the parameter values required.

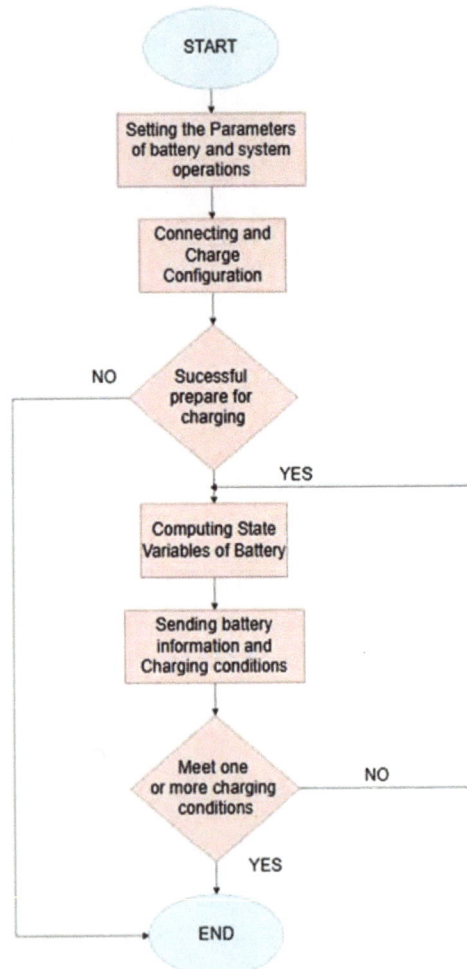

Fig. (2). Flowchart of battery management system.

Estimating the State of Charge

Obtaining precise findings relies on this crucial element. The column-counting method is employed for this purpose [8]. Equation (1) represents the relationship between SOC (State of Charge) and the integral of current over time. The initial value of SOC should be expressed using the Coulomb counting method. It is utilized due to its simplicity.

Calculation of Resistance of Battery

The internal resistance of the battery is evaluated based on data acquired from the database, which includes information on rated capacity, state of charge (SOC), and temperature. Final analysis is then conducted using practical data.

Battery Temperature Calculation

Battery reaction depends on heat generated, which is the total energy lost due to the reaction in the battery. The heat generated is given by

$$Q = Q_P + Q_r + Q_j \quad (2)$$

Qr- heat generated due to reaction, Qj-joule heat, Qp-heat polarization.

BATTERY MANAGEMENT SYSTEM

The Internet of Things (IoT) serves as a means of communication between physical devices and computer programs. The diagram in Fig. (**3**) illustrates the sequence of operations in an IoT battery management system. It gathers data from various hardware devices located in remote areas. Various sensors are employed to oversee the battery's condition, such as power flow, SOC (State of Charge), SOH (State of Health), and depth of charge. These sensors then relay this information to the central controller of the vehicle. The measured parameters are transmitted *via* a wireless connection, as shown in Fig. (**3**).

SOC Determination in Battery

The operating modes of a battery can be classified into three sorts.

• **Charging condition:** The battery is assessed using a constant value of 0.6 C. The threshold voltage is set at 4.2 V, and the voltage remains constant until the battery reaches full capacity. The battery voltage will reach the threshold value steadily over 1 hour and 27 minutes, with a constant current. At first, there will be a significant decrease in the charging current, followed by a gradual decrease.

Finally, the current becomes zero when its charge reaches its maximum value, as shown in Fig. (**4**).

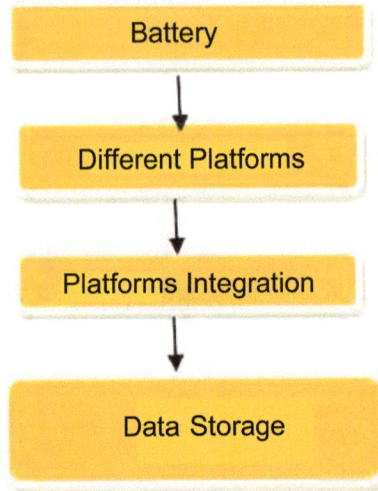

Fig. (3). Iot-based battery management system.

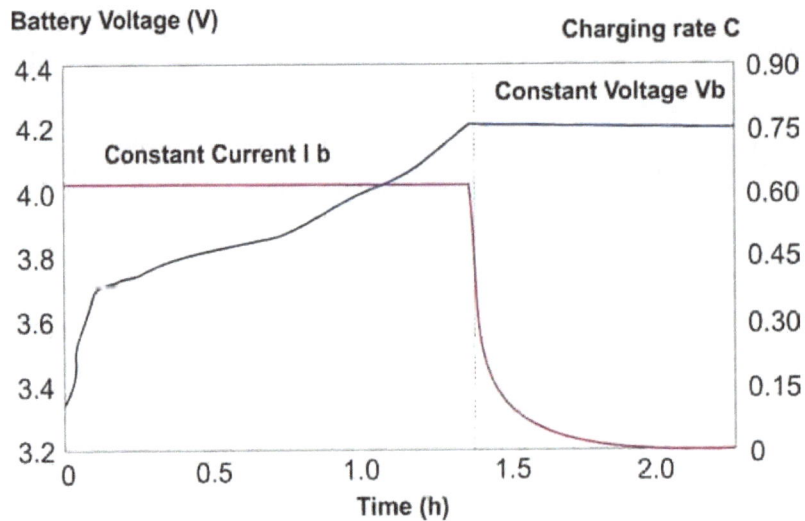

Fig. (4). Voltage and charging current.

The relationship between the state of charge (SOC) and the charging voltage during the constant current stage is depicted in Fig. (**4**). The relationship between the SOC and the charging current during the constant voltage stage is shown in Fig. (**5**).

The battery voltage will exhibit a linear increase when the amount of charge given to the battery is taken into account. The calculation of SOC is possible.

as

$$Soc=(198.5Vb-755.590\%) \quad (3)$$

In the end, the battery gets charged to 78% of its maximum capacity using constant current mode. In the constant voltage stage, the charging current is inversely proportional to the battery capacity. Therefore, the abbreviation SOC can be expressed as:

$$Soc=(-17.402I_b+99.377)\% \quad (4)$$

Once the charging current reaches zero, the battery can be considered fully charged with a state of charge (SOC) of 99.377%, as shown in Fig. (**5**).

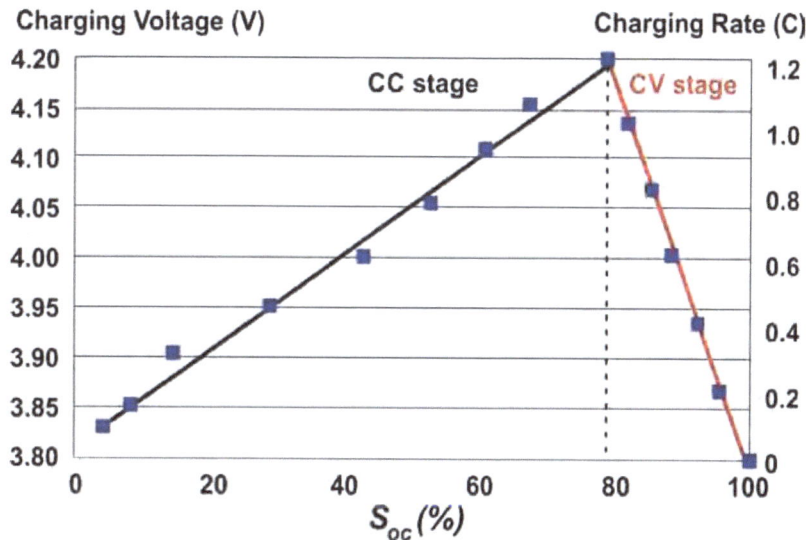

Fig. (5). SOC and charging current when voltage is constant.

• **Discharge Mode:** Fig. (**6**) illustrates the voltage curves of the lithium battery, indicating the discharge rate under various currents. As the duration of time reduces, the terminal voltage also drops. An increase in current results in a decrease in voltage, thereby reducing the running time.

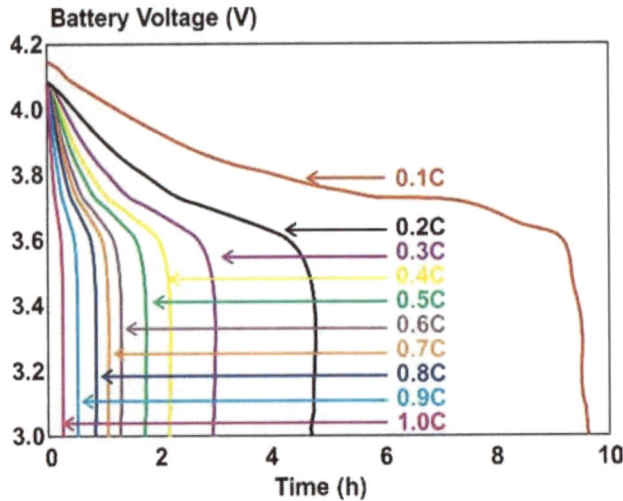

Fig. (6). Discharge rate of lithium battery.

In Fig. (**7**), the maximum capacity of the battery is observed to be just 1.8% in the event of a complete discharge.

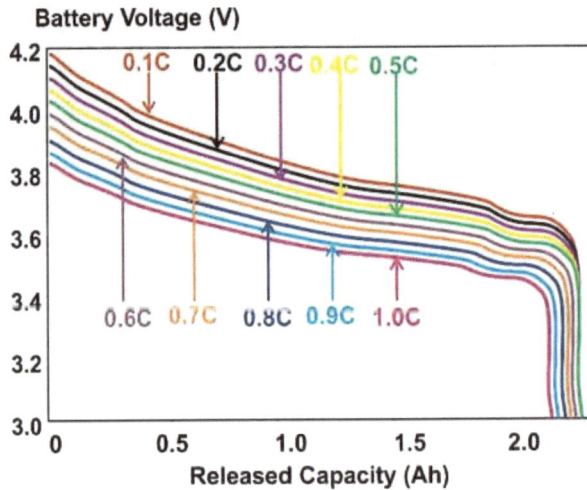

Fig. (7). Battery level at different capacities.

• **Open Circuit Mode:** Fig. (**8**) illustrates the correlation between the battery's state when it is disconnected from a circuit for 1 hour and 20 minutes. The battery discharges before detaching from the load. If there is a prolonged period of relaxation, the state of charge (SOC) can be determined. The state of charge (SOC) will vary directly with the open circuit voltage, provided that the value falls within the range of 3.0 to 3.7 volts.

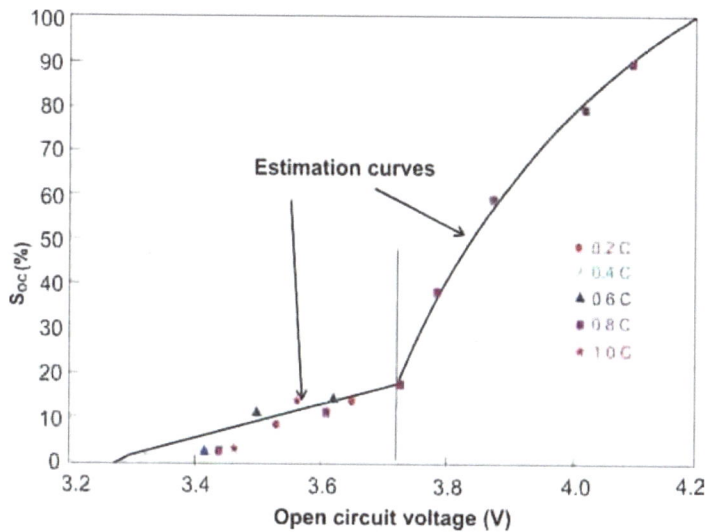

Fig. (8). Open circuit mode estimation curve.

Coulomb Counting Method Verification

The parameters of voltage, current, and operating duration are monitored at intervals of 2 seconds [13]. During the charging mode, the battery experiences a positive current, whereas during the discharging mode, the battery experiences a negative current. The state of charge (SOC) rises throughout the charging process and declines during the discharging process [14]. The verification of the Coulomb counting method is depicted in Fig. (**9**).

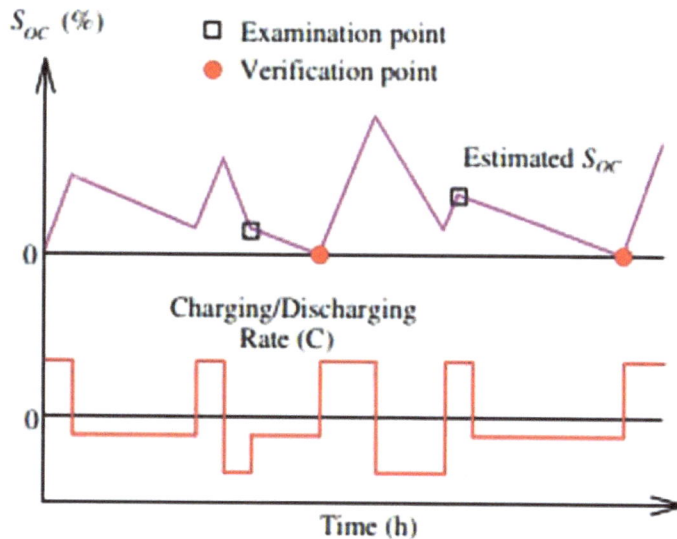

Fig. (9). Coulomb counting method verification.

BLOCKCHAIN TECHNOLOGY

The concept of technology was initially introduced in 2008. The system employs asymmetric encryption and exclusively logs data once it has been verified at all nodes. Every node possesses its position and all nodes contribute to the process of recording. The primary benefit is the decentralized nature of this function. The inclusion of decentralization will result in a decrease in expenses [15].

Structure of Blockchain

The structure comprises a header and body, wherein data is kept. The block header will contain information about the preceding block and the timestamp indicating the block's creation time. The next block is produced by storing the data of the preceding block, and each block is interconnected with one another [16]. Validated transactions occur within nodes, and the recording of transaction data is stored in blocks. The key benefit of blockchain technology is the elimination of the need for a third party to validate transaction data. The consensus algorithm prevents the formation of impartial blocks. The stack data structure is mostly employed in algorithms as a means of providing proof. In the next code block, a new object is instantiated, and a nonce value is generated. Discovering a nonce indicates that the task has been completed. The process of creating new nodes is referred to as mining. The specific components and arrangement of the block diagram structure can be observed in Fig. (**10**).

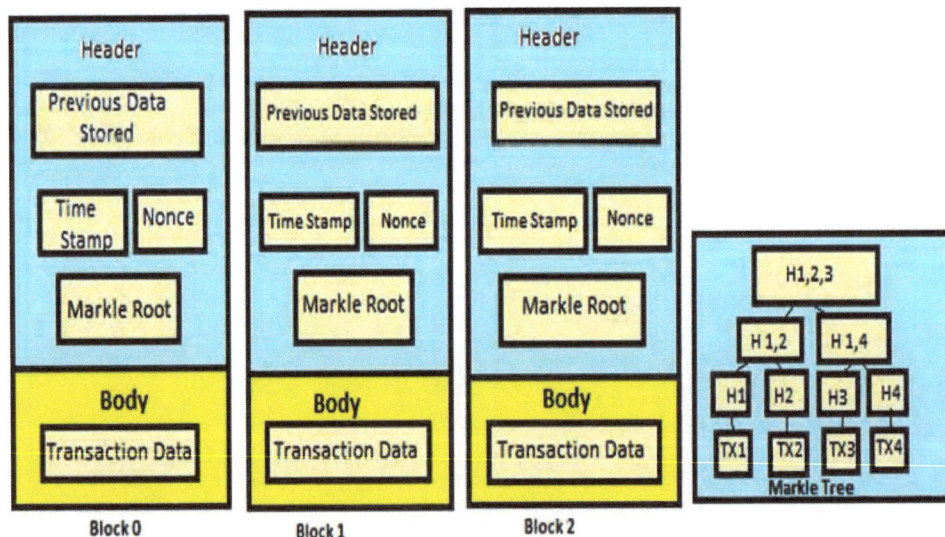

Fig. (10). Structure of blockchain.

The flow of work in Blockchain

Upon completion of the transaction, the data is transmitted to the node. The digital signature is employed at the node for authentication. Subsequently, a novel node is generated to validate the verification procedure.

Blockchain Features

- Decentralized: Transactions are facilitated by nodes using algorithms with mathematical encryption, eliminating the need for third-party involvement.
- Data can be securely copied through an interface without any unauthorized modifications. Data can only be utilized if a consensus is obtained by at least 51% of the data.
- Open and transparent: Privacy accounts are accepted, while all other data is visible to the public and can be accessed by anybody for maintenance purposes [11]. In this context, the act of discovering additional blocks will be incentivized. This method verifies the new block by a proof of work.

BLOCKCHAIN FOR BATTERY SWAPPING/CHARGING

The hybrid electric vehicle is equipped with an onboard monitoring system that provides battery health data to the battery management system (BMS). The stations oversee the management of battery availability and transactions.

HEV owners can provide their information to receive details regarding battery changing and charging, as shown in Fig. (**11**).

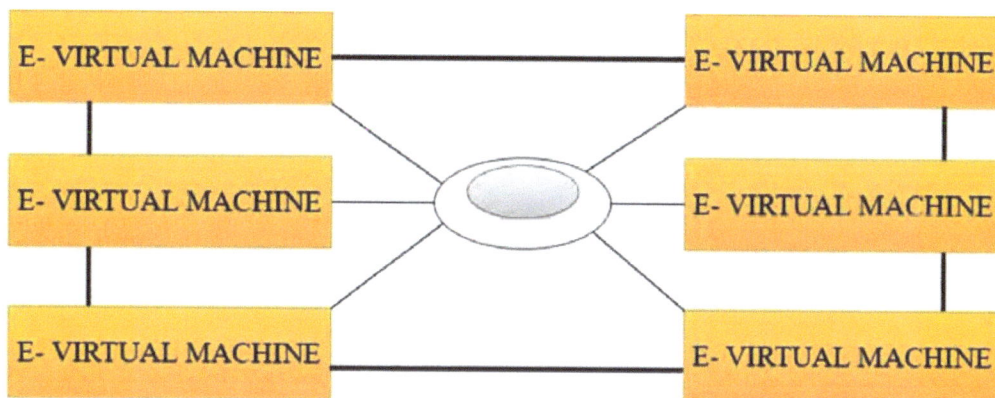

Fig. (11). Ethereal block network.

Battery and SOC of Battery Monitoring

The open circuit voltage test (OCV) is employed to assess the proposed work. Li-Po battery is chosen for examination due to its optimal compatibility with HEV applications. Among the four cells, two have a capacity of 800 mAh and a discharge rate of 300C, while the other two cells have a capacity of 1000 mAh with the same discharge rate of 300C, as shown in Fig. (**12**).

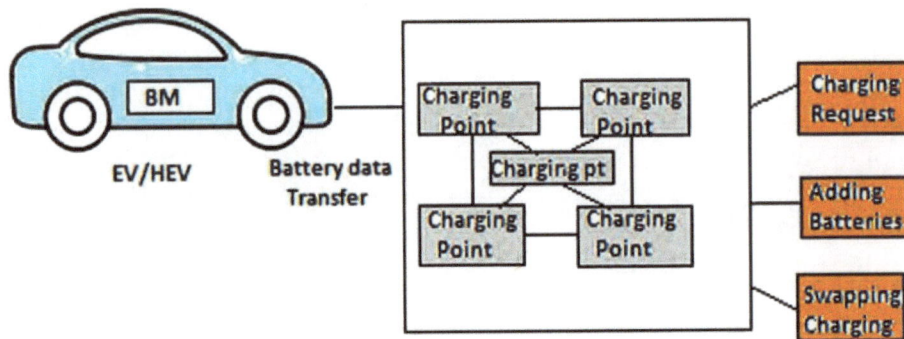

Fig. (12). Battery swapping/charging.

Table 2. SOC of Li-PO

S.No	Cell voltage	Two cell voltage
100%	4.20	8.40
80%	4.02	8.05
60%	3.87	7.75
50%	3.84	7.67
30%	3.77	7.53

Average of cell voltage is calculated using formulae SOC= (V-Vb)/ (Va-Vb)......(5) V= battery voltage. Vb- min voltage which is safe Va- max voltage for 100% charge.

The average of cell voltage is calculated using formulae SOC= (V-Vb)/ (Va-Vb)......(5) V= battery voltage

Vb- min voltage, which is safe Va- max voltage for 100% charge.

The battery management system holds particular significance. The device gauges the voltage and quantify the remaining energy in the battery. The communication is conducted through the gadget housed within the HEV. A total of 60 data samples were collected, resulting in the creation of a blockchain transaction.

Ethereum Blockchain

It is an open-source platform, and the application is done using smart contracts. Data is securely stored and kept on nodes. It works on a virtual machine and creates a programmable network. In this, there is a gas price. So, the gas price should be quoted much less. With programming language, smart contractors are created. This code is converted to byte code by the Ethereum virtual machine. In this way, smart contracts are created [12]. The Ethereum is shown in Fig. (**11**).

Creating Web Application

A web application is developed using Node.js to engage with the user. This program facilitates the registration of both users and stations on a shared network.

Technology gives security, removes third parties, and improves the quality of communication [15]. The communication flow is shown in Fig. (**13**) (Table **3**).

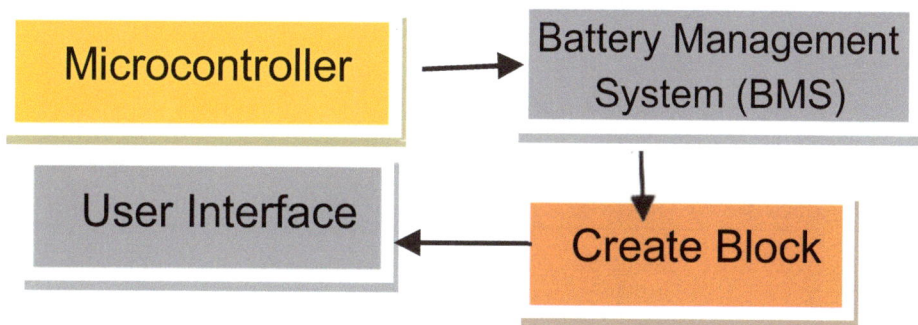

Fig. (13). Interface for battery charging/swapping.

Table 3. Summary of methods for electric vehicle battery management system.

Method	Pros	Cons
Model-Based Method		
Filter-Based Method	Online and	Precision
(*e.g.* kalman-filter,	Real-time	depends on
particle filter)	insensitive to	model
observer-based	initial state	accuracy
method (*e.g.*	not limited to	high
Luenberger	system type	computational
Observer, Sliding	fast	cost
Mode Observer, h-	convergence	require more
infinity/h∞ observer)	high precision	experimental

(Table 3) cont.....

Method	Pros	Cons
-	robust to	data and
-	sensor noise	validation
Data-Driven Method		
Machine Learning	Less pre-test	Depend on
Neural Network	required	training
support vector	high estimation	samples
Machine	precision	high
Genetic Algorithm	independent of	computational
Fuzzy Logic	model	cost
-	robust to	requirements
-	conditions and	on efficiency
-	noises	and
-	-	portability of
-	-	algorithm
Cloud Computing		
Vehicular Cloud	Run complex	More
computing	algorithms	complicated
technology	collaborate	due to high
-	with cloud	mobility and
-	computation	wide range of
-	center	vehicles
-	leverage	possibly leak
-	resources of	information
-	participating	and
-	vehicles	-
-	-	compromise privacy
BlockChain Technology		
Private BlockChain consortium BlockChain.	Public ledger system data sharing and tracking protect user privacy moredriving data.	Not mature technology some research gaps (latency and throughput) expect to improve usability.
Direct Estimation Method		

(Table 3) cont.....

Method	Pros	Cons
Open circuit voltage internal resistance electromotive force impedance spectroscopy embedding sensors.	Direct and simple method for implementation low computational cost easy combination with model-based method.	off-line estimation longresting time not accurate in practice sensitive to sensor accuracy.

CONCLUSION

As shown in the article, the battery management system for electric cars (EVs) has a crucial function and helps alleviate traffic congestion by facilitating vehicle charging and switching. It is important to regularly monitor the battery and provide accurate information to authorized customers of electric vehicle owners. Blockchain is a popular and emerging technology in contemporary times. Initially, the battery's condition is assessed, and the vehicle owner is informed about its status through the utilization of IoT. Subsequently, the car owner is provided with information regarding the battery switching station utilizing blockchain technology. Both privacy and security must be taken into account while transferring data at no cost. Combining IoT and blockchain characteristics is expected to yield significant advancements in real-time battery monitoring/swapping. Ethereum facilitates the creation of decentralized applications. Currently, the battery system can be controlled using IoT and blockchain characteristics. However, in the future, numerous additional technologies will be integrated.

REFERENCES

[1]   N. Thakkar, and P. Paliwal, "Hydrogen storage based micro-grid: A comprehensive review on technology, energy management and planning techniques", *Int. J. Green Energy,* vol. 20, no. 4, pp. 445-463, 2023.
[http://dx.doi.org/10.1080/15435075.2022.2049797]

[2]   M.A.M.S. Lemstra, and M.A. de Mesquita, "Industry 4.0: a tertiary literature review", *Technol. Forecast. Soc. Change,* vol. 186, p. 122204, 2023.
[http://dx.doi.org/10.1016/j.techfore.2022.122204]

[3]   D.D. Prasanna Rani, D. Suresh, P. Rao Kapula, C.H. Mohammad Akram, N. Hemalatha, and P. Kumar Soni, "IoT based smart solar energy monitoring systems", *Mater. Today Proc.,* vol. 80, pp. 3540-3545, 2023.
[http://dx.doi.org/10.1016/j.matpr.2021.07.293]

[4]   P. Patil, K. Kazemzadeh, and P. Bansal, "Integration of charging behavior into infrastructure planning and management of electric vehicles: A systematic review and framework", *Sustain Cities Soc.,* vol. 88, p. 104265, 2023.
[http://dx.doi.org/10.1016/j.scs.2022.104265]

[5]   J.P. Patale, A.B. Jagadale, A.O. Mulani, and A. Pise, "A Systematic survey on Estimation of Electrical Vehicle", *Journal of Electronics, Computer Networking and Applied Mathematics (JECNAM),* vol. 3, no. 1, pp. 1-6, 2023.

[6]   C. Corradi, E. Sica, and P. Morone, "What drives electric vehicle adoption? Insights from a systematic review on European transport actors and behaviours", *Energy Res. Soc. Sci.,* vol. 95, p. 102908, 2023.
[http://dx.doi.org/10.1016/j.erss.2022.102908]

[7]   F.S. Hafez, B. Sa'di, M. Safa-Gamal, Y.H. Taufiq-Yap, M. Alrifaey, M. Seyedmahmoudian, A. Stojcevski, B. Horan, and S. Mekhilef, "Energy efficiency in sustainable buildings: a systematic review with taxonomy, challenges, motivations, methodological aspects, recommendations, and pathways for future research", *Energy Strategy Reviews,* vol. 45, p. 101013, 2023.
[http://dx.doi.org/10.1016/j.esr.2022.101013]

[8]   V.S.R. Kosuru, and A. Kavasseri Venkitaraman, "A Smart Battery Management System for Electric Vehicles Using Deep Learning-Based Sensor Fault Detection", *World Electric Vehicle Journal,* vol. 14, no. 4, p. 101, 2023.
[http://dx.doi.org/10.3390/wevj14040101]

[9]   A.T.D. Perera, and T. Hong, "Vulnerability and resilience of urban energy ecosystems to extreme climate events: A systematic review and perspectives", *Renew. Sustain. Energy Rev.,* vol. 173, p. 113038, 2023.
[http://dx.doi.org/10.1016/j.rser.2022.113038]

[10]   G. Verhulsdonck, J.L. Weible, S. Helser, and N. Hajduk, "Smart cities, playable cities, and cybersecurity: a systematic review", *Int. J. Hum. Comput. Interact.,* vol. 39, no. 2, pp. 378-390, 2023.
[http://dx.doi.org/10.1080/10447318.2021.2012381]

[11]   W. Ming, P. Sun, Z. Zhang, W. Qiu, J. Du, X. Li, Y. Zhang, G. Zhang, K. Liu, Y. Wang, and X. Guo, "A systematic review of machine learning methods applied to fuel cells in performance evaluation, durability prediction, and application monitoring", *Int. J. Hydrogen Energy,* vol. 48, no. 13, pp. 5197-5228, 2023.
[http://dx.doi.org/10.1016/j.ijhydene.2022.10.261]

[12]   J. Bhardwaj, A. Nayak, C.S. Yadav, and S.P. Yadav, "A Review in Wavelet Transforms Based Medical Image Fusion", In: *Evolving Role of AI and IoMT in the Healthcare Market.,* F. Al-Turjman, M. Kumar, T. Stephan, A. Bhardwaj, Eds., Springer: Cham, 2021.
[http://dx.doi.org/10.1007/978-3-030-82079-4_9]

[13]   R.M. Pujahari, S.P. Yadav, and R. Khan, "Intelligent farming system through weather forecast support and crop production", *Application of Machine Learning in Agriculture.,* pp. 113-130, 2022.
[http://dx.doi.org/10.1016/B978-0-323-90550-3.00009-6]

[14]   R. Salama, F. Al-Turjman, S. Bhatla, and S.P. Yadav, "Social engineering attack types and prevention techniques- A survey", *International Conference on Computational Intelligence, Communication Technology and Networking (CICTN),* pp. 817-820, 2023.
[http://dx.doi.org/10.1109/CICTN57981.2023.10140957]

[15]   M. Vubangsi, "Optimizing Moving Target Defense for Cyber Anomaly Detection", *2023 International Conference on Computational Intelligence, Communication Technology and Networking (CICTN),* pp. 791-795, 2023.
[http://dx.doi.org/10.1109/CICTN57981.2023.10140835]

[16]   O.I. Khalaf Sr, "A decision science approach using hybrid EEG Feature Extraction and gan-based emotion classification", *Adv. Decis. Sci.,* vol. 27, no. 1, pp. 172-191, 2023.
[http://dx.doi.org/10.47654/v27y2023i1p172-191]

[17]   S. Dhanasekaran, P. Gomathi, A.R. Maximus, T. Krishnan, and B. Kannan, "Solar Tree based Smart City Street Light Control System using IoT BLYNK Platform", *International Conference on Automation, Computing and Renewable Systems (ICACRS),* pp. 284-290, 2022.
[http://dx.doi.org/10.1109/ICACRS55517.2022.10029107]

[18]   K.R.K. Yesodha, A. Jagadeesan, and J. Logeshwaran, "IoT applications in Modern Supply Chains: Enhancing Efficiency and Product Quality", *2nd International Conference on Industrial Electronics: Developments & Applications (ICIDeA),* pp. 284-290, 2023.

[http://dx.doi.org/10.1109/ICIDeA59866.2023.10295273]

[19]   V.A.K. Gorantla, S.K. Sriramulugari, A.H. Mewada, and J. Logeshwaran, "An intelligent optimization framework to predict the vulnerable range of tumor cells using Internet of things", *2nd International Conference on Industrial Electronics: Developments & Applications (ICIDeA)*, p. 359-365, 2023.
[http://dx.doi.org/10.1109/ICIDeA59866.2023.10295269]

[20]   T. Marimuthu, V.A. Rajan, G.V. Londhe, and J. Logeshwaran, "Deep Learning for Automated Lesion Detection in Mammography", *2nd International Conference on Industrial Electronics: Developments & Applications (ICIDeA)*, pp. 383-388, 2023.
[http://dx.doi.org/10.1109/ICIDeA59866.2023.10295189]

488   *Emerging Trends in Computation Intelligence, Vol. 3*, 2025, 488-501

An Intuitionistic Fuzzy EOQ Model Based on Trapezoidal Intuitionistic Fuzzy Numbers to Maintain a Green Environment by Disposing of Waste

Surendra Singh[1,*], Ayu Kumar Jain[1], Manish Aggarwal[1] and Istakbal Khan[1]

[1] Department of Applied Science & Humanities, Hi-Tech Institute of Engineering & Technology, Ghaziabad, (U.P), India

Abstract: IFSs, or intuitionistic fuzzy sets, are flexible and often helpful tools for explaining the ambiguity and uncertainty present in decision-making situations. This study's main goal is to show how the IFS can be relevant and helpful when making judgments in uncertain scenarios by using inventory difficulties. In this paper, we use trapezoidal intuitionistic fuzzy numbers (TrIFNs) to create an intuitionistic inventory model with waste disposal cost from a crisp model. Lastly, a comparison between the intuitionistic fuzzy and crisp models for the optimal values of inventory level and total inventory cost is illustrated by a numerical example. The paper ends with a summary of potential future research.

Keywords: EOQ model, Trapezoidal intuitionistic fuzzy number, Waste disposal cost, α-cut method.

INTRODUCTION

Inventory refers to a compilation of merchandise or goods that have financial value and are now awaiting sale. Inventory is categorized as a current asset in a company's balance sheet. Inventory models have significantly contributed to the advancement of the industry [1]. Manufacturing businesses frequently employ economic order quantity and production quantity models to manage inventory costs. In order to ensure the success of the sector, it is crucial to promptly meet customers' expectations and maintain a steady production and ordering pace to prevent shortages. The number of flaws in a product is determined by the proportion of defects it possesses [2]. In order to convert a flawed product into a

* **Corresponding author Surendra Singh:** Department of Applied Science & Humanities, Hi-Tech Institute of Engineering & Technology, Ghaziabad, (U.P), India; E-mail: surendra.singh@hietgroup.org

Pankaj Kumar Mishra & Satya Prakash Yadav (Eds.)

flawless one, it is necessary to reprocess waste elements, which leads to waste in the manufacturing process for industries. Additionally, faulty products and used materials must be discarded as they occupy storage space in inventory. Currently, academics are utilizing the IFS theory in various domains of optimization issues [3]. Several writers, including Ouyang and Pedrycz (2016), Garai (2018), Chaudhary and Kumar (2022), and Singh and Kumar (2022), utilized IF numbers in the development of inventory models. Furthermore, Supakar and Mahato (2022) have introduced a solitary product economic order quantity (EOQ) model specifically designed for deteriorating products and a pre-payment policy within an inventory financing (IF) setting. TIFN was employed for handling fuzzy parameters, while the sign-distance method was utilized for the process of defuzzification [4]. The non-linear pentagonal IFN was invented by Chakrabortty (2022) and employed in an EPQ model with steady demand and imperfect goods for remanufacturing. The defuzzification of non-linear PIFN was performed using the (α, β)-cut technique. In his study, Kumar (2022) created a continuous review inventory model that incorporates the yearly demand rate as a TIFN and the lead time demand rate as a triangular IF random variable. Classical set theory is not suitable for modeling problems that involve qualitative or erroneous information. In 1965, L. A [5]. Zadeh introduced the concept of fuzzy sets (FS) to represent the uncertainty inherent in real-world problems. Intuitionistic fuzzy numbers accurately represent real-world problems that involve uncertainties and incomplete knowledge. Trapezoidal intuitionistic fuzzy numbers excel in representing the imprecise and partial nature of a dataset. A fuzzy set consists of an element and its corresponding membership degree [6]. The theory of FS has gained significant popularity across various disciplines, and numerous exemplary investigations have been done. Atanassov proposed the intuitionistic fuzzy set (IFS) theory in 1986, which involves estimating degrees of membership and non-membership. The individual conducted an examination and categorized various IFS behaviors and relationships. Subsequently, other writers carried out thorough research [7]. G. Deschrijvera and E.E. Kerre (2002) conducted additional research on intuitionistic fuzzy sets. K. Das, T. K. Roy, and M. Maiti constructed a multi-objective fuzzy inventory model that considers a limited period, different shortage situations, and the deterioration of products. Wang, Tang, and R. Zhao employed the particle swarm optimization (PSO) method to solve a fuzzy economic order quantity (EOQ) model that involves defective items. D.F. Li (2010) examined the usefulness and uncertainty of triangular intuitionistic fuzzy numbers (TIFNs) in a ratio ranking strategy of TIFNs for addressing multiple attribute decision-making (MADM) problems. G. C. Mahata and A. Goswami researched fuzzy inventory models for poor-quality items with shortages. They utilized trapezoidal and triangular fuzzy numbers in two distinct models, which were defuzzified using the GMI approach [8]. The researchers then compared both models using numerical examples. In their 2014 study, Sujit Kumar De and Shib S. Sana examined a production-inventory model for many manufacturers. They specifically focused on analyzing and evaluating the use of GFO (Global Fixed Order) and IFO (Individual Fixed Order) policies in production plants, incorporating a scoring system. In their study, Ejegwa, Akubo, and Joshua utilized the iterated function system (IFS) and applied it to career determination [9]. They used the normalized Euclidean distance approach to calculate the shortest distance between a student and a vocation. S. K. Singh and S. P. Yadav used TIFN to convert a transportation problem with total fuzziness into an IF transportation problem. They then employed the IF-modified approach to remove fuzziness and find the optimal solution. Y. He, Z. He, and H. Huang developed a collection of IF power interaction aggregation operators to facilitate decision-making [10]. In their study, Nayagam, Jeevaraj, and Dhanasekaran devised a technique that employs interval-valued intuitionistic fuzzy numbers (IFNs) and a non-hesitance scoring function to address decision-making problems. In their study, S. Merline Laura *et al.* [11] (2020) developed a fuzzy inventory EOQ model based on a crisp model that incorporated waste disposal cost. They found that the cost was optimized in a fuzzy manner. This work applies an EOQ (Economic Order Quantity) inventory model to a setting that involves intuitionistic fuzzy environments, utilizing TrIFNs (Type-reduced Intuitionistic Fuzzy Numbers) [12]. The subsequent sections of this article are organized in the following arrangement: The early definitions for several sorts of fuzzy integers are provided in Section 2, along with their corresponding defuzzification procedures [13]. The model's evolution is accompanied by notations and assumptions, which are outlined in Section 3. In Section 4, we formulate a classical EOQ inventory model within a crisp, intuitionistic fuzzy framework [14]. Section 5 is a numerical example that includes a comparative examination of the findings obtained from the different models [15]. Section 6 provides a concise summary of the study's findings.

RELATED WORKS

Fuzzy logic and green environment management are the primary topics of the connected works of the chapter 'An Intuitionistic Fuzzy EOQ Model based on Trapezoidal Intuitionistic Fuzzy Numbers to Maintain a Green Environment by Disposing of Waste' [16]. These works cover a wide range of issues, including creating an environmental management inventory control model, managing green waste with fuzzy logic, and optimizing waste disposal with fuzzy logic. To ensure sustainable environmental management, a fuzzy logic-based inventory control model has been created in one linked study [17]. To lessen environmental damage, the suggested approach mixes fuzzy logic with economic order quantity (EOQ) logic. The study's findings demonstrated that the fuzzy EOQ model performed better than traditional inventory control techniques [18]. Fuzzy logic has been proposed as a more effective way to handle green waste in a related study. Fuzzy calculations rely on anecdotal data regarding the kind and amount of green waste. The outcomes demonstrated that the fuzzy logic-based strategy increased the precision of decisions made about green waste management [19]. Finally, an additional study on the subject looked at how to improve trash disposal with fuzzy logic. To choose the best place to dispose of waste, the researchers presented a set of fuzzy logic principles for waste selection and disposal [20]. The outcomes demonstrated that, in terms of trash disposal efficiency, the fuzzy logic model performed better than the other approaches. These connected papers show how fuzzy logic can be used to enhance environmental management and garbage disposal. In particular, the findings demonstrate that the use of fuzzy logic-based techniques can result in improved trash collection, disposal, and inventory control.

PRELIMINARIES

Definition

A fuzzy set, as defined by Zadeh in 1965, is a subset $A \subseteq X$ of a non-empty set of discourse X. It is represented by A={ $\langle x, \mu\_A(x) \rangle$:x∈X}, where $\mu\_A : X \rightarrow [0\ 1]$ is the membership function that determines the degree of belonging of each element x in A.

Definition

An intuitionistic fuzzy number (IFN), as defined by Atanassov in 1986, is a specific category of fuzzy numbers. As stated by Atanassov in 1986, X is considered a set of discourses that is not empty. Let Ã be an intuitionistic fuzzy set in X, defined by ordered triples consisting of an item x, the degree of belongingness $\mu\_A(x)$, and the degree of non-belongingness $v\_A(x)$ of x in A. The set IFN is defined as A˜={ $\langle x, \mu\_A(x), v\_A(x) \rangle$:x∈X}, where $\mu\_A(x), v\_A(x) : X \rightarrow [0\ 1]$ for any ⟦x∈X⟧ _A with ⟦0≤μ⟧ _A (x)+v_A (x)≥1.

Definition

Trapezoidal intuitionistic fuzzy number (TrIFN): One of the unique varieties of IFN is the trapezoidal intuitionistic fuzzy number. A TrIFN denoted by A˜=(a_1,a_2,a_(3,),a_(4,); ⟦a'⟧ _1, ⟦a'⟧ _4) has the following definitions for its membership function ($\mu\_A(x)$) and non-membership function (⟦v⟧ _A (x)),

$$\mu_{\tilde{A}}(x) = \begin{cases} \frac{x-a_1}{a_2-a_1} & ; \quad a_1 \le x \le a_2 \\ 1 & ; \quad a_2 \le x \le a_3 \\ \frac{a_4-x}{a_4-a_3} & ; \quad a_3 \le x \le a_4 \\ 0 & ; \quad otherwise \end{cases}$$

$$v_{\tilde{A}}(x) = \begin{cases} \frac{a_2-x}{a_2-a'_1} & ; \quad a'_1 \le x \le a_2 \\ 0 & ; \quad a_2 \le x \le a_3 \\ \frac{x-a_3}{a'_4-a_3} & ; \quad a_3 \le x \le a'_4 \\ 1 & ; \quad otherwise \end{cases}$$

Where, $a'_1, a_1, a_2, a_3, a_4, a'_4 \in R$.

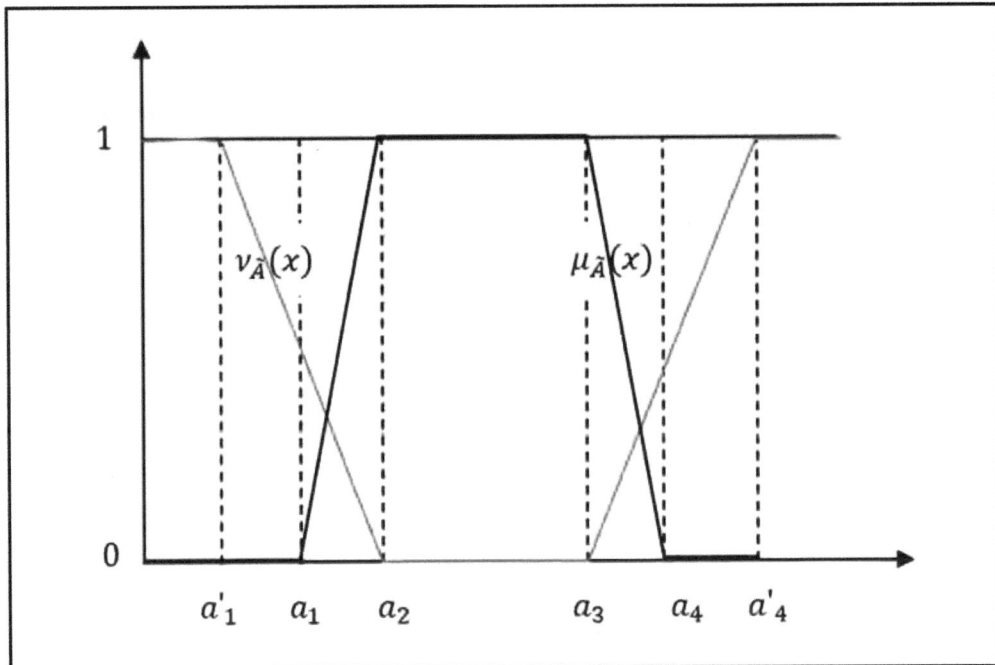

Fig. (1). Membership and non-membership of a TrIFN number.

Defuzzification method for TIFN: Let A~=a1,a2,a3,, a4,;a'1, a'4 be a TrIFN whose membership function μAx and non-membership function (Fig. **1**) vAx are defined as above.

The α $-$ cut of membership function $\mu_A(x)$, for $\alpha \in [0, 1]$

$$A(\alpha) = [a_1 + \alpha(a_2 - a_1), \ a_4 - \alpha(a_4 - a_3)]$$

$$A(\alpha) = [L_A(\alpha), \ R_A(\alpha)]$$

And β $-$ cut of non-membership function $v_A(x)$ for $\beta \in [0, 1]$, we get

$$A(\beta) = [a_2 - (1 - \beta)(a_2 - a'_1), \ a_4 + (1 - \beta)(a'_4 - a_3)]$$

$$A(\beta) = [L_A(\beta), \ R_A(\beta)]$$

Now defuzzifying the membership function by

$$D_f(\mu_A(x)) = \frac{1}{2}\int_0^1 [L_A(\alpha) + R_A(\alpha)]\, d\alpha$$

$$= \frac{1}{2}\int_0^1 [(a_1 + a_4) + \alpha(a_2 + a_4 - a_1 - a_3)]\, d\alpha$$

on integrating w.r.to α, we get

$$D_f(\mu_A(x)) = \frac{1}{4}[a_1 + a_2 + a_3 + a_4]$$

Similarly, defuzzifying the non-membership function $v_A(x)$, we get

$$D_f(v_A(x)) = \frac{1}{2}\int_0^1 [L_A(\beta) + R_A(\beta)]\, d\beta = \frac{1}{4}[a_2 + a_3 + a'_1 + a'_4]$$

Hence, the defuzzification formula for TrIFN is

$$D_f(\tilde{A}) = \frac{1}{2}[D_f(\mu_A(x)) + D_f(v_A(x))]$$

$$= \frac{1}{8}[a_1 + 2(a_2 + a_3) + a_4 + a'_1 + a'_4].$$

Operations on TrIFN:

let $\tilde{A} = (a_1, a_2, a_{3,}, a_4; a'_1, a'_4)$ and $\tilde{B}^t = (b_1, b_2, b_3, b_4; b'_1, b'_4)$ be two trapezoidal intuitionistic fuzzy numbers, then some fundamental operations are defined as:

- Addition: $\tilde{A}^t \oplus \tilde{B}^t = (a_1 + b_1, a_2 + b_2, a_3 + b_3, a_4 + b_4; a'_1 + b'_1, a'_4 + b'_4)$

- Multiplication: $\tilde{A}^t \otimes \tilde{B}^t = (a_1 b_1, a_2 b_2, a_3 b_3, a_4 b_4; a'_1 b'_1, a'_4 b'_4)$

- Subtraction: $\tilde{A}^t \ominus \tilde{B}^t = (a_1 - b_1, a_2 - b_2, a_3 - b_3, a_4 - b_4; a'_1 - b'_1, a'_4 - b'_4)$

- Division: $\tilde{A}^t \oslash \tilde{B}^t = \left(\frac{a_1}{b_1}, \frac{a_2}{b_2}, \frac{a_3}{b_3}, \frac{a_4}{b_4}; \frac{a'_1}{b'_1}, \frac{a'_4}{b'_4}\right)$

- Scalar multiplication: $k\tilde{A}^t =$
$$\begin{cases} ka_1, ka_2, ka_3, ka_4; ka'_1, ka'_4 & when\ k > 0 \\ ka_4, ka_3, ka_2, ka_1; ka'_4, ka'_1 & when\ k < 0 \end{cases}$$

Mathematical Model and Formulation

Notations

Crisp environment		Intuitionistic fuzzy (IF) environment	
Symbol	Description	Symbol	Description
C_o	Ordering cost	$\tilde{O}$	IF Ordering cost
C_s	Setup cost	$\tilde{S}$	IF Setup cost
C_h	Holding cost	$\tilde{H}$	IF Holding cost
C_w	Cost of waste	$\tilde{W}$	IF Cost of waste
D	disposal	$\tilde{m}$	disposal
P	Demand rate	$D_f(\tilde{A})$	IF Percentage of waste
Q	Production rate		generated
TIC	Economic	$\widetilde{TIC}$	Crispification of
Q^*	order quantity.		TrIFN
m	Total inventory		Total inventory cost in
	cost		IF model
	Optimal EOQ		
	Percentage of		
	waste		
	generated		

Assumptions

- There is a fixed and known demand rate (D).
- The annual production rate (P) is constant.
- Shortages are not allowed.

Mathematical Models

Model in Crisp Sense

The ordered quantity Q is where we start in the considered model, and the demand rate is constant D. The setup cost S, the buying cost p (per unit), and the holding cost C_h (per unit) should be the sole inventory expenses related to this model. Next, the entire cost of the inventory is:

$$TIC = \frac{Q}{2}\left[C_h D + \left(1 - \frac{P}{D}\right)C_o\right] + \frac{1}{Q}[C_o D + C_s + C_w m]$$

For minimum value of TIC, differentiating the above equation w.r.to Q

partially and $\frac{\partial TIC}{\partial Q} = 0$,

$$Q^* = \sqrt{\frac{2[C_o D + C_s + C_w m]}{C_h D + \left(1 - \frac{P}{D}\right)C_o}}$$

Q^* is the economic order quantity.

Model in Intuitionistic Fuzzy Sense

The mathematical model mentioned above is transformed into a fuzzy, intuitionistic inventory model taking into account the costs associated with ordering, holding, setting up, and disposing of garbage and the percentage of waste generated in TrIFNs. Let:

$$\tilde{O} = (o_1, o_2, o_3, o_4; o'_1, o'_4), \qquad \tilde{H} = (h_1, h_2, h_3, h_4; h'_1, h'_4), \tilde{S} =$$

$$(s_1, s_2, s_3, s_4; s'_1, s'_4)$$

$$\tilde{W} = (w_1, w_2, w_3, w_4; w'_1, w'_4), \text{ and } \quad \tilde{m} =$$

$$(m_1, m_2, m_3, m_4; m'_1, m'_4)$$

The total cost in IF sense is given by

$$\tilde{TIC} = \frac{Q}{2}\left[\tilde{H}^t D \oplus \left(1 - \frac{P}{D}\right)\tilde{O}^t\right]$$

$$\oplus \frac{1}{Q}\left[\tilde{O}^t D \oplus \tilde{S}^t \oplus \tilde{W}^t \otimes \tilde{m}^t\right]$$

$$\tilde{TIC}$$

$$= \frac{Q}{2}\left[(h_1, h_2, h_3, h_4; h'_1, h'_4)D \oplus \left(1 - \frac{P}{D}\right)(o_1, o_2, o_3, o_4; o'_1, o'_4)\right]$$

$$\oplus \frac{1}{Q}[(o_1, o_2, o_3, o_4; o'_1, o'_4)D \oplus (s_1, s_2, s_3, s_4; s'_1, s'_4)$$

$$\oplus (w_1, w_2, w_3, w_4; w'_1, w'_4)(m_1, m_2, m_3, m_4; m'_1, m'_4)]$$

$$\tilde{TIC} = \begin{bmatrix} \frac{Q}{2}\left[h_1 D + \left(1 - \frac{P}{D}\right)o_1\right] + \frac{1}{Q}[o_1 D + s_1 + w_1 m_1], \\ \frac{Q}{2}\left[h_2 D + \left(1 - \frac{P}{D}\right)o_2\right] + \frac{1}{Q}[o_2 D + s_2 + w_2 m_2], \\ \frac{Q}{2}\left[h_3 D + \left(1 - \frac{P}{D}\right)o_3\right] + \frac{1}{Q}[o_3 D + s_3 + w_3 m_3], \\ \frac{Q}{2}\left[h_4 D + \left(1 - \frac{P}{D}\right)o_4\right] + \frac{1}{Q}[o_4 D + s_4 + w_4 m_4]; \\ \frac{Q}{2}\left[h'_1 D + \left(1 - \frac{P}{D}\right)o'_1\right] + \frac{1}{Q}[o'_1 D + s'_1 + w'_1 m'_1], \\ \frac{Q}{2}\left[h'_4 D + \left(1 - \frac{P}{D}\right)o'_4\right] + \frac{1}{Q}[o'_4 D + s'_4 + w'_4 m'_4] \end{bmatrix}$$

Then, using the defuzzification formula for a TrIFN, we get:

$$\widetilde{TIC} = \frac{1}{8}\left[\frac{Q}{2}\left[\{h_1 + 2(h_2 + h_3) + h_4 + h'_1 + h'_4\}D\right.\right.$$

$$+ \left(1 - \frac{P}{D}\right)\{o_1 + 2(o_2 + o_3) + o_4 + o'_1$$

$$\left. + o'_4\}\right]$$

$$+ \frac{1}{Q}[\{o_1 + 2(o_2 + o_3) + o_4 + o'_1$$

$$+ o'_4\}D$$

$$+ \{s_1 + 2(s_2 + s_3) + s_4 + s'_1 + s'_4\}$$

$$+ \{w_1 m_1 + 2(w_2 m_2 + w_3 m_3) + w_4 m_4$$

$$\left.\left. + w'_1 m'_1 + w'_4 m'_4\}]\right]$$

$$= \varphi(Q) \quad \{\text{say}\}$$

The above equation gives the total cost in IF sense.

Now, the sufficient condition for the minimum value of $\varphi(Q)$: $\frac{\partial \varphi(Q)}{\partial Q} =$

0 and $\frac{\partial^2 \varphi(Q)}{\partial^2 Q} > 0.$

So, we differentiate the above equation partially w. r. to Q.

$$\frac{\partial \varphi}{\partial Q} = \frac{1}{16} \Big[\{h_1 + 2(h_2 + h_3) + h_4 + h'_1 + h'_4\}D$$

$$+ \left(1 - \frac{P}{D}\right) \{o_1 + 2(o_2 + o_3) + o_4 + o'_1 + o'_4\} \Big]$$

$$+ \frac{-1}{8Q^2} [\{o_1 + 2(o_2 + o_3) + o_4 + o'_1 + o'_4\}D$$

$$+ \{s_1 + 2(s_2 + s_3) + s_4 + s'_1 + s'_4\}$$

$$+ \{w_1 m_1 + 2(w_2 m_2 + w_3 m_3) + w_4 m_4 + w'_1 m'_1$$

$$+ w'_4 m'_4\}]$$

Now put $\dfrac{\partial \varphi(Q)}{\partial Q} = 0,$ we get

The above equation gives the EOQ in an intuitionistic fuzzy sense.

Numerical Example

Crisp Sense:

Let $\quad D = 1500 \quad$ units/month $\quad P = 2000, \quad C_o = Rs.\,700 \quad$ per unit/year, $\quad C_h = Rs.\,2$ per $\quad$ unit, $\quad C_s = Rs.\,7000, \quad m = 70$ units/year, $C_w = Rs.\,50$ per unit.

Then, the optimum order quantity is

$$Q^* = 22.38.$$

and the total cost is

$$TIC = 72445.60$$

Intuitionistic Fuzzy Sense: Let us take all the inventory costs in TrIFN numbers

Let $D = 1500,\ P = 2000,\ \tilde{O} = (300, 400, 700, 800; 100, 900),$

$\tilde{H} = (1.5, 2, 3, 3.5; 1, 4),$

$\tilde{S} = (3000, 4000, 7000, 8000; 1000, 9000),$　　　　　　　$\tilde{m} =$

$(30, 40, 70, 80;\ 10, 90)$

$\tilde{W} = (20, 30, 50, 70; 10, 80)$. Then, the optimal quantity is

$$\tilde{Q} = 21.34$$

And the corresponding total inventory cost is

$$\widetilde{TIC} = 65375.58$$

CONCLUSION

This study presents an intuitive fuzzy inventory model that accounts for waste disposal costs in order to determine the overall cost of the inventory. We created a model in this study that translates intuitionistic fuzzy sense from crisp sense. The defuzzification process employs the α,β-cut approach, and all inventory expenses are treated as TrIFN. In the crisp model, 72445.60 rupees is the optimal TIC, while $\tilde{Q}$=22.34 units is the ideal order quantity. Due to fuzziness in the demand parameters, it lowers to 65375.58 rupees in the intuitionistic fuzzy model with the optimal order quantity $\tilde{Q} = 21.34$ units. The intuitionistic fuzzy model proves to be more economical than the crisp model. It allows for the remanufacturing of damaged products, resulting in increased industrial profit and reduced waste. Consequently, less storage space is needed. Therefore, the suggested model greatly benefits the business both financially and ecologically.

REFERENCES

[1]   S. Maity, A. Chakraborty, S.K. De, and M. Pal, "A study of an EOQ model of green items with the effect of carbon emission under pentagonal intuitionistic dense fuzzy environment", *Soft Comput.*, vol. 27, no. 20, pp. 15033-15055, 2023.
[http://dx.doi.org/10.1007/s00500-023-08636-5]

[2]   C. Sugapriya, P. Saranyaa, D. Nagarajan, and D. Pamucar, "Triangular intuitionistic fuzzy number based backorder and lost sale in production, remanufacturing and inspection process", *Expert Syst. Appl.*, vol. 240, p. 122261, 2024.
[http://dx.doi.org/10.1016/j.eswa.2023.122261]

[3]   M. Bhuvaneshwari, and R. Manonmani, "Fuzzy Inventory Model with Eco Friendly Package, Carbon Emission, Cap Policy and Life Cycle Assessment Technology", *Tuijin Jishu/Journal of Propulsion Technology*, vol. 44, no. 3, pp. 2594-2600, 2023.

[4]   H. Arman, "Fuzzy analytic hierarchy process for pentagonal fuzzy numbers and its application in sustainable supplier selection", *J. Clean. Prod.*, vol. 409, p. 137190, 2023.
[http://dx.doi.org/10.1016/j.jclepro.2023.137190]

[5]   G. Kumar, "A Fuzzy EOQ Model with Exponential Demand and Deterioration with Preservation Technology", *Fuzzy Optimization, Decision-making and Operations Research: Theory and Applications,* pp. 619-638, 2023.

[6]   R.S. Rana, D. Kumar, and K. Prasad, "Sustainable production-inventory system for perishables under dynamic fuel pricing and preservation technology investment", *Environ. Sci. Pollut. Res. Int.,* vol. 30, no. 39, pp. 90121-90147, 2023.
[http://dx.doi.org/10.1007/s11356-023-28252-y] [PMID: 37458880]

[7]   M. Tavakoli, A. Tajally, M. Ghanavati-Nejad, and F. Jolai, "A Markovian-based fuzzy decision-making approach for the customer-based sustainable-resilient supplier selection problem", *Soft Comput.,* vol. 27, no. 20, pp. 15153-15184, 2023.
[http://dx.doi.org/10.1007/s00500-023-08380-w] [PMID: 37362282]

[8]   H. Garg, C. Sugapriya, V. Kuppulakshmi, and D. Nagarajan, "Optimization of fuzzy inventory lot-size with scrap and defective items under inspection policy", *Soft Comput.,* vol. 27, no. 5, pp. 2231-2250, 2023.
[http://dx.doi.org/10.1007/s00500-022-07804-3]

[9]   K. Shaw, V. Lahri, R. Shankar, and A. Ishizaka, "Joint Multi-item Multi-supplier Sustainable Lot-Sizing Model Applying Combined BWM, TOPSIS, Possibilistic Programming, and ε-constraint Method", *IEEE Trans. Eng. Manage.,* 2023.

[10]   S. Maity, A. Chakraborty, S.K. De, and M. Pal, "A study of an EOQ model of green items with the effect of carbon emission under pentagonal intuitionistic dense fuzzy environment", *Soft Comput.,* vol. 27, no. 20, pp. 15033-15055, 2023.
[http://dx.doi.org/10.1007/s00500-023-08636-5]

[11]   V. Vashisht, A.K. Pandey, and S.P. Yadav, "Speech Recognition using Machine Learning", *Transactions on Smart Processing & Computing,* vol. 10, no. 3, pp. 233-239, 2021.
[http://dx.doi.org/10.5573/IEIESPC.2021.10.3.233]

[12]   S.P. Yadav, B.S. Bhati, D.P. Mahato, and S. Kumar, *Federated Learning for IoT Applications. EAI/Springer Innovations in Communication and Computing.* Springer International Publishing, 2022.
[http://dx.doi.org/10.1007/978-3-030-85559-8]

[13]   J. Kaur, J. Saxena, and J. Shah, "Facial Emotion Recognition. In 2022 International Conference on Computational Intelligence and Sustainable Engineering Solutions (CISES)", *International Conference on Computational Intelligence and Sustainable Engineering Solutions (CISES),* 2022.
[http://dx.doi.org/10.1109/CISES54857.2022.9844366]

[14]   H. Yadav, S. Singh, K.K. Mishra, S. Srivastava, M.S. Naruka, and S.P. Yadav, "Brain Tumor Detection with MRI Images", *2022 International Conference on Computational Intelligence and Sustainable Engineering Solutions (CISES),* 2022.
[http://dx.doi.org/10.1109/CISES54857.2022.9844387]

[15]   N. Yuvaraj, K. Praghash, J. Logeshwaran, G. Peter, and A.A. Stonier, "An Artificial Intelligence Based Sustainable Approaches—IoT Systems for Smart Cities", In: *AI Models for Blockchain-Based Intelligent Networks in IoT Systems: Concepts, Methodologies, Tools, and Applications.* Springer International Publishing: Cham, 2023, pp. 105-120.
[http://dx.doi.org/10.1007/978-3-031-31952-5_5]

[16]   J. Logeshwaran, N. Shanmugasundaram, and J. Lloret, "Energy-efficient resource allocation model for device-to-device communication in 5G wireless personal area networks", *Int. J. Commun. Syst.,* vol. 36, no. 13, p. e5524, 2023.
[http://dx.doi.org/10.1002/dac.5524]

[17]   G. Ramesh, J. Logeshwaran, and A.P. Kumar, "The Smart Network Management Automation Algorithm for Administration of Reliable 5G Communication Networks", *Wirel. Commun. Mob. Comput.,* vol. 2023, pp. 1-13, 2023.
[http://dx.doi.org/10.1155/2023/7626803]

[18]   S. Salagrama, and V. Bibhu, "Study of it and data center virtualization", *2nd International Conference on Innovative Practices in Technology and Management (ICIPTM,* vol. 2, pp. 274-278, 2022.
[http://dx.doi.org/10.1109/ICIPTM54933.2022.9754152]

[19]   V. Bibhu, S. Salagrama, B.P. Lohani, and P.K. Kushwaha, "An Analytical Survey of User Privacy on Social Media Platform", *International Conference on Technological Advancements and Innovations (ICTAI),* pp. 173-176, 2021.
[http://dx.doi.org/10.1109/ICTAI53825.2021.9673402]

[20]   G. Kumar, "A Fuzzy EOQ Model with Exponential Demand and Deterioration with Preservation Technology", *Fuzzy Optimization, Decision-making and Operations Research: Theory and Applications,* pp. 619-638, 2023.

CHAPTER 43

Foliar Disease Detection Using ML and Deep Learning

Aman Shrivastava[1], Bhaskar Sharma[1], Somaya Goel[1], Sumit Kumar[1], A.K. Jain[1] and **Shalini Kapoor[1,*]**

[1] *Department Electrical Engineering Hi-Tech Institute of Engineering & Technology, Ghaziabad, (U.P), India*

Abstract: This research surveys the classification approaches that can be utilized to categorize plant leaf diseases. Contemporary farming practices have the potential to provide sustenance for the 7.6 billion individuals on the Earth. Despite the availability of sufficient food, some persist in experiencing malnutrition. Plant diseases have a negative impact on both the yield and the quality of the entire crop. Several obstacles need to be addressed during the development of an image-processing model for prediction or classification purposes. Identifying indicators of sickness visually might pose a challenge for farmers. Computerized image processing technology is employed to safeguard crops in large-scale settings by utilizing color information from leaves to identify damaged foliage. Several classification methods exist, such as support vector machine (SVM), probabilistic neural network, k-nearest neighbor classifier, genetic algorithm, and principal component analysis. Due to the potential for various input data to yield varying quality outcomes, the selection of a classification approach is consistently a tough task. Plant leaf diseases are commonly classified in several industries, such as agriculture, biotechnology, and scientific research.

Keywords: Agriculture biotechnology, Classification, Industries, Support vector machine.

INTRODUCTION

Plant diseases result in decreased yields, which directly impact both domestic and international food supply systems and result in financial losses [1]. The Food and Agriculture Organization (FAO) of the United Nations has reported that plant diseases and pests result in a loss of approximately 20% to 40% of the world's food output. Additionally, the FAO states that 13% of worldwide agricultural

---

* **Corresponding author Shalini Kapoor:** Department Of Computer Science KIET Group of Institute, Ghaziabad, (U.P), India; E-mail: shalkapoor311@gmail.com

Pankaj Kumar Mishra & Satya Prakash Yadav (Eds.)

yield losses can be attributed to plant diseases. This underscores the significance of detecting and averting plant diseases in order to minimize these detrimental effects [2]. An approach to detect plant illnesses involves the examination of plant leaf pictures using a technology known as "image processing", which is a subfield of signal processing. Through the utilization of artificial intelligence, particularly machine learning, we can effectively extract significant data from these photos to identify and diagnose plant illnesses precisely [3]. Additionally, this technology can autonomously execute tasks or provide directions for their execution. The fundamental objective of machine learning is to comprehend the training data and integrate it into models that are beneficial to people. Therefore, it can assist in making informed choices and accurately predicting the desired outcome by utilizing extensive training data. Leaf color, leaf damage level, leaf area, and leaf texture features are employed for classification [4]. Multiple types of plant diseases harm different plant organs. Foliar diseases, which are plant diseases that exhibit symptoms on leaves, can be readily identified by plant pathologists. Fungal pathogens are a significant contributor to reductions in crop productivity, responsible for as much as 50% of overall yield losses [5]. Consequently, numerous researchers are employing computer vision, machine learning, and deep learning methodologies to identify and diagnose plant diseases by analyzing photos of plant leaves [6]. Efficient diagnosis of plant diseases necessitates timely detection of diseases, identification of many diseases across various crops, assessment of disease severity, determination of the optimal pesticide dosage, and implementation of practical actions to control and contain the disease.

RELATED WORKS

This section focuses on relevant developments in addressing classification challenges using deep learning systems [7]. Deep learning techniques have been extensively studied for their applicability in areas such as object recognition and image categorization. Convolutional neural networks (CNNs), a type of deep learning technology, are highly effective in solving recognition and classification problems, particularly in the field of photo classification, where they achieve state-of-the-art performance [8]. The initial convolutional neural network (CNN) model, named Mobile Net, was assessed for its ability to recognize objects, specifically focusing on tomato diseases, using a specific dataset [9]. The degree of tomato leaf illness was assessed using pre-trained CNN architectures VGG16, MobileNet, and ResNet50, applied to pictures of tomato leaves [10]. The performance of the standard CNN model was enhanced by using ResNet50 characteristics, as shown in Fig. (**1**).

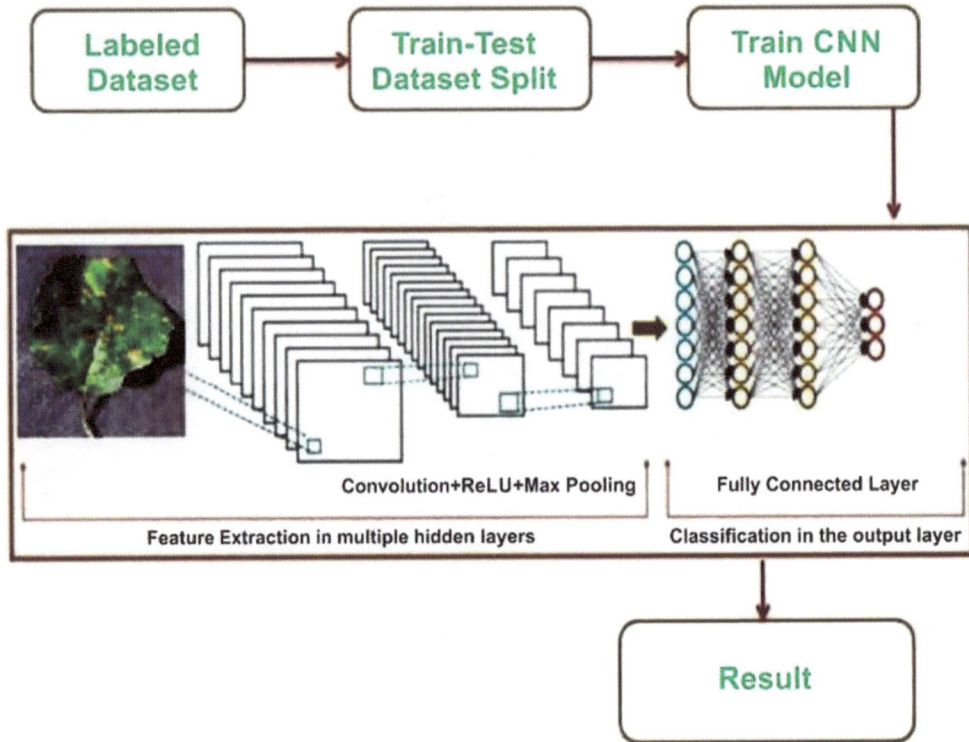

Fig. (1). Proposed Workflow.

CNN designs do not examine the spatial connections between the different portions of an image, which renders them unsuitable for handling geometric transformations [11 - 17]. The max-pooling layer of a CNN has a propensity to lose data when it routes features from one layer to another. They cannot accurately represent the property of rotational invariance in an object. The section introduces a capsule network with a dynamic routing algorithm as a solution to address the limitations of CNN design [18 - 20]. The trials utilized capsule networks to classify illnesses based on medical imaging, and they outperformed ordinary CNN in this task.

EXISTING WORK

Prior studies on detecting leaf damage using CNN provide an example of how to recognize and classify leaf disease using image processing techniques, as shown in Fig. (2).

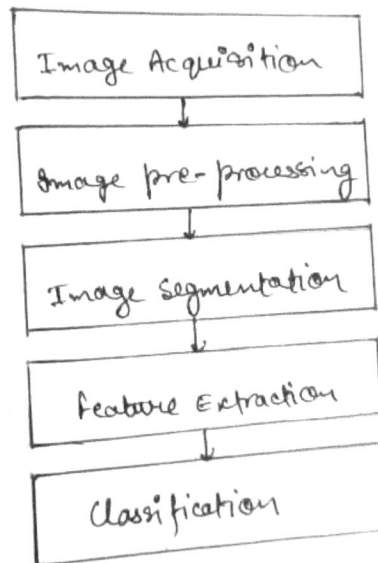

Fig. (2). Block diagram of feature based approach.

Image acquisition is the process of collecting and digitally storing an image, typically with a digital camera or other digital device. Prior to any picture processing, it is imperative to perform preprocessing to enhance its quality and eliminate any undesired aberrations. The primary goal of image preprocessing is to optimize the relevant features of the image and enhance the level of detail it contains, so rendering it more appropriate for later processing and analysis with tools like MATLAB. Various techniques are employed in preprocessing, including dynamic picture resizing, image enhancement through morphological operations, noise filtering, image conversion, and image enhancement. Image segmentation is utilized in K-means clustering as a technique for categorizing several photos, ensuring that at least one cluster contains an image with a substantial amount of an unhealthy zone. The utilization of the k-means clustering algorithm leads to the categorization of items into K-distinct groups based on their respective attributes. After the clusters have been formed, the GLCM method is employed to extract texture features.

DATASET

We employed the PlantVillage dataset, a publicly accessible compilation of photos used for the identification of plant leaf diseases, in this survey. The collection was compiled and managed by Sharada P. Mohanty and a team of researchers. It consists of more than 87,000 RGB images of plant leaves, encompassing both healthy and diseased specimens. The dataset encompasses a total of 38 distinct disease categories. For our experiment, we specifically chose 25 disease classes to evaluate our technique. These classes are listed in the table.

Table 1 - Dataset Specifications.

Plant	Disease Name	No. of Images
Apple	Healthy	2008
	Diseased Scab	2016
	Diseased Black rot	1987
	Diseased Cedar apple rust	1760
Corn	Healthy	1859
	Diseased Cercospora leaf spot	1642
	Diseased Common rust	1907
	Diseased Northern Leaf Blight	1908
Grapes	Healthy	1692
	Diseased Black rot	1888
	Diseased Esca (Black Measles)	1920
	Diseased Leaf blight (Isariopsis)	1722
Potato	Healthy	1824
	Diseased Early blight	1939
	Diseased Late blight	1939
Tomato	Healthy	1926
	Diseased Bacterial spot	1702
	Diseased Early blight	1920
	Diseased Late blight	1851
	Diseased Leaf Mold	1882
	Diseased Septoria leaf spot	1745
	Diseased Two-spotted spider mite	1741
	Diseased Target Spot	1827
	Diseased Yellow Leaf Curl Virus	1961
	Diseased Tomato mosaic virus	1790

The model consists of 5 phases

Feature Extraction and Data Pre-processing

In order to obtain precise outcomes from computer vision systems, it is essential to preprocess the input appropriately. An essential step in data preparation is the elimination of background noise from the image prior to extracting the crucial features. Converting an RGB image to grayscale simplifies the image, facilitating its processing. The thresholding technique is subsequently employed to convert the picture into binary form. The small openings in the foreground are then filled by applying a morphological transformation to the binary image. The photo segmentation process now allows for the retrieval of texture, shape, and color data. Leaf parameters and area are determined through the analysis of contours. An outline is a continuous line that connects all the spots on the limits of things that have the same hue or color intensity.

Furthermore, the program also computes the average and standard deviation of each RGB color channel. The image is first converted from RGB to HSV color space. Then, the ratio of pixels with hue (H) channel pixel intensities between 30 and 70 is computed and divided by the total number of pixels in that channel. This is performed to ascertain the amount of green hue contained in the image. To calculate the non-green section of a photograph, one must eliminate the green component from it, as shown in Fig. (**3**).

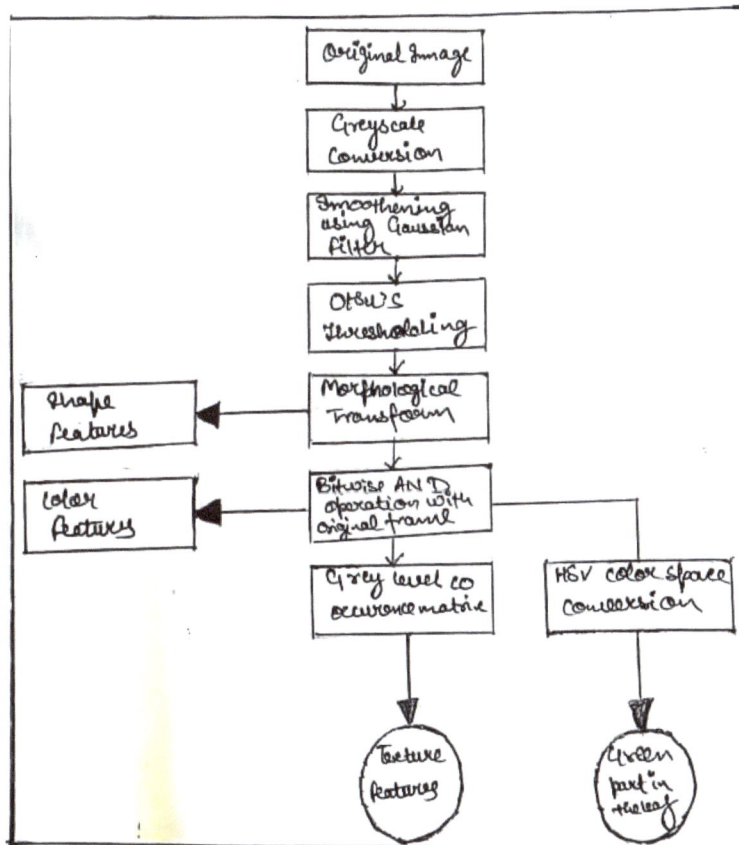

Fig. (3). Steps for feature extraction and data processing.

Image Pre-Processing

Noise reduction has been applied to photographs obtained by image preprocessing, effectively eliminating unwanted sound. Research has suggested various concept preparation approaches. The reliability of an optical inspection can be improved through picture preprocessing. A concise review involves multiple filtering processes that accentuate or reduce specific visual components. By simply clicking a few times, users can effortlessly enhance the quality of a camera photograph. Several graphics operations, including cropping, rotating, normalizing, contrast enhancement, filtering, and angle correction, are utilized. Image preprocessing can eliminate artifacts such as dust, dewdrops, and bug faces that may be present in digital images. Shadow effects and water drops can be eliminated by employing diverse noise reduction filters to address distortion and noises. The original image transformed into a different color space, employing three principal image preprocessing techniques. This novel color space is essentially analogous to the initial image but exhibits distinct variations. As mentioned before, the tasks encompassed by picture resizing, image restoration, and image enhancement are the stages involved in this process of involvement.

Resize

The original photographs are resized to a fixed resolution of 640 × 480 pixels in order to utilize the available processor and memory resources more effectively.

Noise Restoration

Noise can be generated when there is an inappropriate opening of the shutter, disturbance in the environment, and misalignment of focus due to the movement of both the camera and the object.

Image Enhancement

Image augmentation is employed to enhance digital photos for better display or further analysis.

$$(x) = 0.114 *B + 0.2989 * R + 0.5870 * G$$

Eqn: 1 RGB to grey conversion equation.

Disease detection and classification

Disease detection involves two distinct phases: determining the specific crop and identifying the type of sickness. A convolutional neural network is employed to facilitate this process. The model will be developed *via* transfer learning. It is a technique in which the existing models are utilized to construct new ones. Classification serves as interconnected classifiers that are constructed using diverse model learning techniques. Flattening the photographs involves converting the pooled images into vectors with only one dimension. Categorizing the photos gets significantly easier after converting them into vectors. The trained model allows us to derive precise numerical values for different classifications. A leaf that is in good condition will be designated as healthy without any additional categorization. Nevertheless, the presence of a disease can be identified by the presence of black dots on a greyscale, and the condition will be categorized with a certain level of certainty. This classification procedure utilizes two numerical arrays to ascertain the health status of a leaf based on the given dataset. The procedure of classifying plant diseases is essential and effective in accurately identifying them.

Image Segmentation

The photographs are partitioned for analysis by image segmentation. Images are converted into a different format to align with the required specifications. The process of segmenting an image entails removing the backdrop and conducting a thorough study of the picture. To differentiate the polluted region from the backdrop, image segmentation is performed by selecting an appropriate threshold range. The lower and upper ends of the photo histogram are utilized to determine the threshold values. An approach employed in the first stage has shown to be ineffective due to the uneven spread of the disease area. Consequently, it was proposed to have a partition-level item that depends on the division of pixels. The query image is partitioned into two categories, one for disease and one for health, using a fuzzy logical grading scheme. If the histogram displays a pronounced and profound valley between two peaks, the threshold is established at the bottom of the valley. Otherwise, it is unattainable to employ this strategy to accentuate elements from the background. Consequently, the Otsu approach autonomously selects the optimal threshold value.

Image Analysis and Diagnosis

The images of paddy leaves are analyzed to identify the histogram, intensity, and saturation of the green, blue, and red components. However, the sole determinant of the accuracy of the results is the Hue components. Consequently, the evaluations were made exclusively by analyzing the histogram of hues. By utilizing the retrieved features, the image is analyzed to determine the presence of any of the three illnesses above. The segregation of paddy leaf images based on the infected sickness was achieved by employing color histogram and pixel arrangement. To extract contours from pictures, the border tracing approach is used. Prior to analyzing the attributes of an image, the image is converted into a histogram.

Implementation work

The classified foliage of tomato, potato, grape, and apple plants exhibit a total of 24 unique classifications. The apple labels provide information regarding the presence of healthy rust, scabs, and black rot. Specifically, the mentioned topics include Cercospora of corn grey spot, healthy corn, corn blight, and corn rust. The grape labels include Leaf blight, Black rot, Esca, and healthy. The collection comprises 31,119 photos depicting a diverse range of products, such as tomatoes, apples, corn, grapes, and potatoes. The photos were resized to dimensions of 256 × 256 and then separated into two datasets, one for training and one for testing, using an 80-20 ratio. From the entire dataset, a subset of 24,000 photos was used to create the CNN model. The collection comprises photos of plants afflicted by various pests and diseases, including bacterial spot, early blight, healthy specimens, late blight, leaf mold, septoria leaf spot, spider mite infestation, target spot, mosaic virus infection, and yellow leaf curl virus. The approach aims to categorize potato photos into three distinct groups: early blight, healthy, and late blight. This classification can greatly assist in the identification and successful management of illnesses. The convolution layer employs a convolution technique to extract relevant information. As the depth increases, the intricacy of the retrieved attributes escalates. The quantity of filters progressively increases as we transition from one block to the subsequent, while their dimensions remain constant at 5*5. The initial convolution block contains 20 filters, the second block contains 50 filters, and the third block contains 80 filters. The utilization of pooling layers in each block necessitated an increase in the number of filters, resulting in a reduction in the size of the feature maps. Following the use of the convolution technique, the feature maps undergo null-padding in order to preserve the dimensions of the image. To reduce the length, the max pooling layer is employed. Transfer learning is a method of knowledge sharing that utilizes 224*224 fixed-size images and minimizes the need for extensive training data. Transfer learning is a valuable technique for imparting knowledge from one model to another. Transfer learning has been applied in several domains, such as sentiment analysis, activity recognition, software fault prediction, and plant categorization. This study compares the performance of the proposed deep CNN model with the popular VGG16 transfer learning technique. Following a stack of convolutional layers, there are three subsequent layers. The third device utilizes a 1000-way ILSVRC classification and consists of 1000 channels, whereas the first two devices have 4096 channels each. The final layer is the soft-max layer. The use of a fully connected layer architecture facilitates the accurate detection of leaf diseases. All concealed layers possess the capacity to rectify. Re-Lu utilizes local response normalization (LRN), as it does not yield any beneficial benefits to the dataset's performance. Repaired linear units exhibit network nonlinearity.

Results and Discussion

The table presents the performance characteristics of each model created for various plants, indicating that the accuracy scores and f1 ratings are somewhat comparable. Nevertheless, a substantial quantity of inaccurate forecasts, encompassing both positive and bad outcomes, had a role in this resemblance. The mean accuracy attained was 93%, and confusion matrices were employed to assess the quantity of true positives, true negatives, and correct predictions. In addition, the ROC curve was generated for each model to assess their performance across different categorization criteria. The ROC curve is a visual depiction of the performance of a classification model, where the true positive rate and the false positive rate are the two crucial metrics used to evaluate the effectiveness of the model.

In order to enhance precision, the CNN (Alexnet) is currently undergoing testing for the purpose of detecting leaf diseases. The database is partitioned into two datasets, namely training and testing, with a splitting ratio of 80/20. CNN uses a classification algorithm to assess the health status of a leaf, and if it is determined to be unhealthy, it further predicts the specific type of ailment. The convolutional neural network (CNN) model underwent training with a 10-epoch initial learning rate of 0.001. The performance of the CNN model on the testing dataset during training is determined. A confusion matrix for apple leaf classification is illustrated. The accuracy of apple's leaves is 99%. Table 1 presents a concise overview of the accuracy of categorization for each plant (Table **2**). The overall level of precision is 97.71%. Illustrations of classification performed using convolutional neural networks on a selection of randomly picked photographs from the testing dataset are provided. The accuracy % for the corresponding plant leaves is displayed in the upper right corner of each image. This initiative aims to facilitate the timely detection of diseases, hence enabling the automated recognition of plant leaf diseases and enhancing agricultural output. The precision of tomato leaf disease detection can be enhanced by assessing transfer learning and alternative convolutional neural network (CNN) models (Fig. **4**).

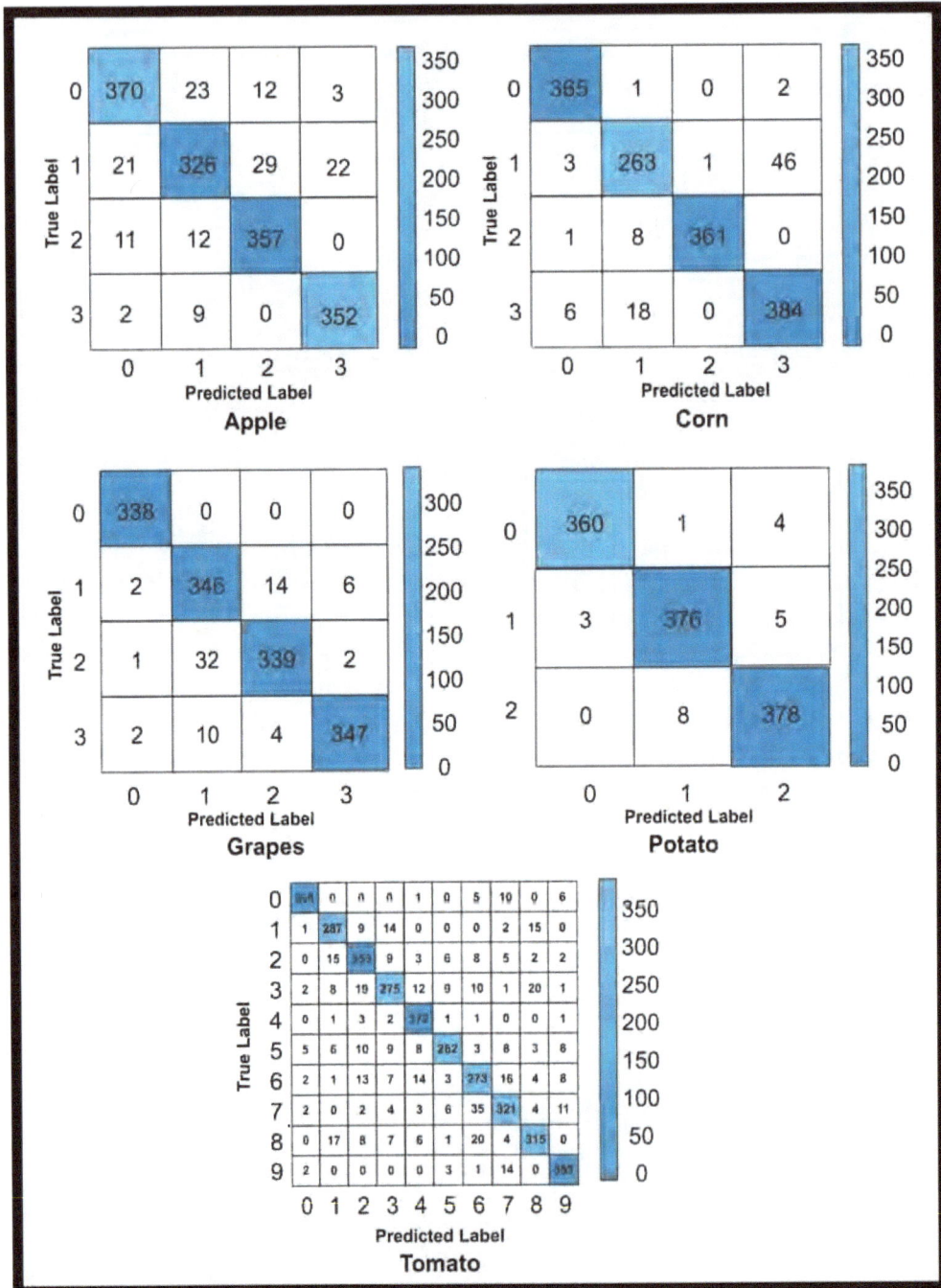

Fig. (4). Confusion matrices for all the models.

Table 2. Classification Accuracy of leaves of plants.

Plant Name	Classification Accuracy
Apple	99.0%
Cherry	99.4%
Corn	95.8%
Grape	99.7%
Peach	97.4%
Pepper Bell	99.4%
Potato	98.7%
Strawberry	100%
Tomato	90.1%

CONCLUSION

Recommendation systems facilitate commercial success for businesses of all types. This paper elucidates the diverse array of strategies employed in recommendation systems. This research work employs cosine similarity in a rental property dataset for the purpose of developing a recommendation system. Specifically, we select the highest similarity values from the dataset. Further improvements are required for the proposed system, which is presently being developed. So far, we have only utilized the Cosine-similarity technique for providing recommendations. However, in the future, we aspire to employ alternative methodologies for generating recommendations and assessing the resulting consequences. When comparing two strategies, their superiority is determined by considering characteristics such as coverage, accuracy, memory, and efficacy. In order to assist the user in making an informed selection, we have decided to provide additional information, such as literature reviews, for each research field in addition to their names. It will ensure that the user has all the necessary information at their disposal.

REFERENCES

[1] R.O. Lasisi, "Cybersecurity Workforce Readiness Recommender System Using NLP", *Proceedings of the Future Technologies Conference,* pp. 597-610, 2023.
[http://dx.doi.org/10.1007/978-3-031-47451-4_43]

[2]   S.P. Yadav, S. Zaidi, C.D.S. Nascimento, V.H.C. de Albuquerque, and S.S. Chauhan, "Analysis and Design of automatically generating for GPS Based Moving Object Tracking System", *International Conference on Artificial Intelligence and Smart Communication (AISC),* pp. 1-5, 2023. [http://dx.doi.org/10.1109/AISC56616.2023.10085180]

[3]   T. Thamaraimanalan, M. Mohankumar, S. Dhanasekaran, and H. Anandakumar, "Experimental analysis of intelligent vehicle monitoring system using Internet of Things (IoT)", *EAI Endorsed Transactions on Energy Web,* vol. 8, no. 36, 2021.

[4]   S.P. Yadav, and S. Yadav, Fusion of Medical Images using a Wavelet Methodology: A Survey.*Transactions on Smart Processing & Computing,* vol. 8, no. 4, pp. 265-271, 2019. [http://dx.doi.org/10.5573/IEIESPC.2019.8.4.265]

[5]   X. Xue, R. Shanmugam, S. Palanisamy, O.I. Khalaf, D. Selvaraj, and G.M. Abdulsahib, "A hybrid cross layer with harris-hawk-optimization-based efficient routing for wireless sensor networks", *Symmetry (Basel),* vol. 15, no. 2, p. 438, 2023. [http://dx.doi.org/10.3390/sym15020438]

[6]   S.P. Yadav, and S. Yadav, Fusion of Medical Images in Wavelet Domain: A Discrete Mathematical Model.*Ingeniería Solidaria,* vol. 14, no. 25, pp. 1-11, 2018. [http://dx.doi.org/10.16925/.v14i0.2236]

[7]   V. Kumar, A.K. Gupta, R.R. Garg, N. Kumar, and R. Kumar, "The ultimate recommendation system: proposed Pranik System", *Multimedia Tools Appl.,* vol. 83, no. 14, pp. 43177-43198, 2023. [http://dx.doi.org/10.1007/s11042-023-17370-x]

[8]   S. P. Yadav, and S. Yadav, "Mathematical implementation of fusion of medical images in continuous wavelet domain", *Journal of Advanced Research in dynamical and control system,* vol. 10, no. 10, pp. 45-54, 2019.

[9]   C.Z. Tsai, H. Huang, C.J. Wei, and M.C. Chiu, Apply Deep Learning to Build a Personalized Attraction Recommendation System in a Smart Product Service System.*Leveraging Transdisciplinary Engineering in a Changing and Connected World.,* pp. 151-160, 2023. [http://dx.doi.org/10.3233/ATDE230607]

[10]   R. Ramakrishnan, M. A. Mohammed, M. A. Mohammed, V. A. Mohammed, and J. Logeshwaran, "An innovation prediction of DNA damage of melanoma skin cancer patients using deep learning,", *14th International Conference on Computing Communication and Networking Technologies (ICCCNT), ,* pp. 1-7, 2023. [http://dx.doi.org/10.1109/ICCCNT56998.2023 10306749]

[11]   V. Sethi, R. Kumar, S. Mehla, A.B. Gandhi, S. Nagpal, and S. Rana, "LCNA-LSTM CNN based attention model for recommendation system to improve marketing strategies on e-commerce", *Journal of Autonomous Intelligence,* vol. 7, no. 1, 2023. [http://dx.doi.org/10.32629/jai.v7i1.972]

[12]   M. A. Mohammed, V. A. Mohammed, R. Ramakrishnan, M. A. Mohammed, and J. Logeshwaran, "The three dimensional dosimetry imaging for automated eye cancer classification using transfer learning model", *14th International Conference on Computing Communication and Networking Technologies (ICCCNT),* pp. 1-6, 2023. [http://dx.doi.org/10.1109/ICCCNT56998.2023.10307446]

[13]   C.M. Tang, Y.G. Zhao, and X. Yu, "Intelligent stock recommendation system based on generalized financial knowledge graph", *Third International Conference on Intelligent Computing and Human-Computer Interaction (ICHCI 2022),* vol. 12509, pp. 332-338, 2023. [http://dx.doi.org/10.1117/12.2655851]

[14]   K.R.K. Yesodha, A. Jagadeesan, and J. Logeshwaran, "IoT applications in Modern Supply Chains: Enhancing Efficiency and Product Quality", *2nd International Conference on Industrial Electronics: Developments & Applications (ICIDeA),* pp. 366-371, 2023. [http://dx.doi.org/10.1109/ICIDeA59866.2023.10295273]

[15]   J. Lee, E. Na, K. Han, and D. Na, "Recommending K-Wave Items Tailored for Small-Sized Exporters by Incorporating Dense and Sparse Vectors", *Sustainability (Basel)*, vol. 15, no. 22, p. 16098, 2023. [http://dx.doi.org/10.3390/su152216098]

[16]   V.A.K. Gorantla, S.K. Sriramulugari, A.H. Mewada, and J. Logeshwaran, "An intelligent optimization framework to predict the vulnerable range of tumor cells using Internet of things", *2nd International Conference on Industrial Electronics: Developments & Applications (ICIDeA)*, p. 359-365, 2023. [http://dx.doi.org/10.1109/ICIDeA59866.2023.10295269]

[17]   N. Wijerathne, J. Samarathunge, K. Rathnayake, S. Jayasinghe, S. Ahangama, and I. Perera, "Deep Learning Based Personalized Stock Recommender System", *International Conference on Neural Information Processing*, pp. 362-374, 2023.

[18]   S. Salagrama, "An Effective Design of Model for Information Security Requirement Assessment", *Int. J. Adv. Comput. Sci. Appl.*, vol. 12, no. 10, 2021. [http://dx.doi.org/10.14569/IJACSA.2021.0121001]

[19]   S. Salagrama, Y.S. Boyapati, and V. Bibhu, "Security and Privacy of Critical Data in Ad Hoc Network Deployed Over Running Vehicles", *3rd International Conference on Intelligent Engineering and Management (ICIEM)*, p. 411-414, 2022. [http://dx.doi.org/10.1109/ICIEM54221.2022.9853172]

[20]   Available from: https://www.kaggle.com/datasets/shree1992/housedata

SUBJECT INDEX

A

Accidents, vehicle 407, 408, 409
Agriculture 191, 288, 364, 373
  global 191
  industry 191
  sustainable 288
  traditional soil-based 364, 373
AI-enabled devices 147
Air 182, 204, 227
  conditioning 182
  gesture technology 204
  pollution control equipment (APCE) 227
Algorithms 1, 2, 4, 6, 7, 8, 206, 273, 274, 275, 277, 278, 280, 281, 308, 309, 324, 410, 411, 451, 504
  dynamic routing 504
Android 91, 173, 410, 411
  gadgets 173
  mobile devices 91
  smartphone 410, 411
Arduino programs 254

B

Battery 471, 481, 483
  health data 481
  management system, electric vehicle 483
  swapping 471
Blockchain 16, 77, 82, 93, 104, 105, 355, 362, 460, 464
  adoption 82, 104
  architecture 77, 464
  -based IoT systems 16
  -based system 355, 362
  combination of 104, 105
  frameworks 82
  fusing 93
  merging 105
  pseudonyms 93
  techniques 460
Border tracing approach 509

Breast cancer 159, 160, 161
  detection 160, 161

C

Cancer, oral cavity 342
Carbon 133, 220, 223, 229, 288, 400, 403
  dioxide productivity 223
  emissions 133, 220, 223, 229, 400
  footprint 133, 288, 403
Cervical cancer screenings 435
Chronic kidney failure 442
Cloud computing 86, 144, 148, 149, 484
Clustering algorithms 274, 275, 276, 277, 280, 281
CNN, neural network 173
Combination, implementing green technology 287
Communication 409, 462, 474
  vehicular network 462
  wireless 409, 474
Computer vision 36, 37, 167, 203, 204, 506
  applications 37, 203
  systems 506
Computerized image processing technology 502
Computers and electronic communication networks 122
Computing technology 56
Consensus techniques 78
Consumer behavior 120, 121, 123, 128, 129, 233, 234
Consumption of coal in Industry 226
Convolutional 37, 39, 40, 42, 43, 168, 169, 170, 171, 276, 313, 314, 317, 318, 319, 320, 323, 327, 331, 332, 503, 511
  network terminology 39
  networks 43, 327
  neural networks (CNN) 37, 39, 40, 42, 168, 169, 170, 171, 276, 313, 314, 317, 318, 319, 320, 323, 331, 332, 503, 511
Coronavirus, acute respiratory syndrome 166

www.ingramcontent.com/pod-product-compliance
Lightning Source LLC
Chambersburg PA
CBHW080018240326
41598CB00075B/40